NEW TESTAMENT INTRODUCTION

NEW TESTAMENT
INTRODUCTION

ALFRED WIKENHAUSER

HERDER AND HERDER

1963

HERDER AND HERDER NEW YORK

232 Madison Avenue, New York 16, N. Y.

Original edition ,,Einleitung in das Neue Testament''
Herder, Freiburg im Breisgau. Translated by Joseph Cunningham.

First edition 1958
Second impression 1958
Third impression 1960
Fourth impression 1963

Nihil Obstat· Garron Tower, 7th May 1958.
Imprimatur: Garron Tower, 9th May 1958.
Daniel Mageean, Bishop of Down and Connor.

Library of Congress Catalog Card Number: 58 — 5870
First published in West Germany © 1958 Herder KG
Printed in West Germany by Herder

CONTENTS

INTRODUCTION

PART I

THE CANON OF THE NEW TESTAMENT

CONTENTS

PART II

THE TEXT OF THE NEW TESTAMENT

CONTENTS

PART III

THE ORIGIN OF THE NEW TESTAMENT WRITINGS

Section I. The Gospels and Acts of the Apostles

CONTENTS

Section II. The Epistles of the New Testament

A. The Pauline Epistles

CONTENTS

ix

CONTENTS

CONTENTS

LIST OF ABBREVIATIONS

1. Biblical books

OT	= Old Testament
NT	= New Testament
LXX	= Septuagint

2. Journals, serial works, frequently cited general works

AGG	= Abhandlungen der Gesellschaft der Wissenschaften zu Goettingen, phil.-hist. Klasse
Ang	= Angelicum, Rome
AThR	= The Anglican Theological Review, Evanston, Illinois
Bb	= Biblica, Rome
BBC	= Bulletin of the Bezan Club
BFchTh	= Beitraege zur Foederung christlicher Theologie, Guetersloh
BJRL	= Bulletin of John Rylands Library, Manchester
Bonnard	= Commentaire du NT publié sous la direction de P. Bonnard et autres, Neuchâtel and Paris
BonnerNT	= Die Hl. Schrift des NT, ed. F. Tillmann, Bonn
BSt	= Biblische Studien, Freiburg i. Breisgau
BZ	= Biblische Zeitschrift, Freiburg i. Br. (1–18); Paderborn (19–24)
BZfr	= Biblische Zeitfragen, Muenster
CBQ	= The Catholic Biblical Quarterly, Washington
ChQR	= The Church Quarterly Review, London
CILSuppl	= Corpus Inscriptionum Latinarum: voluminis tertii Supplementum, Berlin 1902
CM	= Classica et Mediaevalia, Aarhus
CNT	= Coniectanea Neotestamentica, Lund
CSS	= Cursus Scripturae Sacrae, Paris
DB Suppl	= Dictionnaire de la Bible, Supplément, Paris
DivThomP	= Divus Thomas, Piacenza
DLZ	= Deutsche Literaturzeitung, Berlin
DThC	= Dictionnaire de Théologie Catholique, Paris
EB	= Estudios Bíblicos, Madrid
EphThL	= Ephemerides Theologicae Lovanienses, Louvain

LIST OF ABBREVIATIONS

EvTh	=	Evangelische Theologie, Munich
Exp	=	The Expositor, London
ExpT	=	Expository Times, Edinburgh
FF	=	Forschungen und Fortschritte, Berlin
GGA	=	Goettingische Gelehrte Anzeigen
GoettNT	=	Die Schriften des NT, ed. Joh.Weiss, Goettingen
HarvThR	=	Harvard Theological Review, Cambridge, Mass.
HarvThSt	=	Harvard Theological Studies
HistJB	=	Historisches Jahrbuch der Goerres-Gesellschaft
HistZ	=	Historische Zeitschrift, Munich
HThK	=	Herders Theologischer Kommentar zum NT, Freiburg i. Br.
ICC	=	The International Critical Commentary, Edinburgh
IKZ	=	Internationale kirchliche Zeitschrift, Berne
JBL	=	Journal of Biblical Literature, Philadelphia
JR	=	Journal of Religion, Chicago
JThSt	=	Journal of Theological Studies, Oxford
Lietzmann	=	Handbuch zum NT, ed. Hans Lietzmann, Tuebingen
LThK	=	Lexikon fuer Theologie und Kirche, Freiburg i. Br.
Meyer	=	Meyers kritisch-exegetischer Kommentar ueber das NT Goettingen
Moffatt	=	The Moffatt NT Commentary, London
MThZ	=	Muenchener Theologische Zeitschrift, Munich
Mus	=	Le Muséon, Louvain
NGGW	=	Nachrichten der Goettingischen Gelehrten Gesellschaft der Wissenschaften
NIC	=	The New International Commentary on the NT, London
NkZ	=	Neue kirchliche Zeitschrift, Leipzig
NRTh	=	Nouvelle Revue Théologique, Louvain
NtA	=	Neutestamentliche Abhandlungen, Muenster
NTDeutsch	=	Das NT Deutsch, Goettingen
NTSt	=	NT Studies, Cambridge
OCh	=	Oriens Christianus, Leipzig
OLZ	=	Orientalische Literaturzeitung, Leipzig
Or	=	Orientalia, Rome
RB	=	Revue Biblique, Paris
RBén	=	Revue Bénédictine, Maredsous, Belgium
RBPhH	=	Revue belge de philologie et d'histoire, Brussels
RegNT	=	Das NT uebersetzt und erklaert, Regensburg

RevSR	=	Revue des sciences religieuses, Strasbourg
RHPhR	=	Revue d'histoire et de philosophie religieuses, Strasbourg
RHR	=	Revue de l'histoire des Religions, Paris
RQ	=	Roemische Quartalschrift
RSR	=	Recherches de science religieuse, Paris
RStOr	=	Rivista degli studi orientali, Rome
SBBerlin	=	Sitzungsberichte der Berliner Akademie der Wissenschaften, phil.-hist. Klasse
SBHeidelberg	=	Sitzungsberichte der Heidelberger Akademie der Wissenschaften, phil.-hist. Klasse
SBU	=	Symbolae Biblicae Upsalienses, Upsala
SBWien	=	Sitzungsberichte der Akademie der Wissenschaften, phil.-hist. Klasse, Vienna
SO	=	Symbolae Osloenses, Oslo
StD	=	Studies and Documents
StTh	=	Studia Theologica, Lund
ThBl	=	Theologische Blaetter, Leipzig
ThHK	=	Theologischer Handkommentar, Leipzig
ThLZ	=	Theologische Literaturzeitung, Leipzig
ThQ	=	Theologische Quartalschrift, Tuebingen
ThR	=	Theologische Revue, Muenster
ThRdsch	=	Theologische Rundschau, Tuebingen
ThSt	=	Theological Studies, Baltimore
ThStK	=	Theologische Studien und Kritiken
ThWB	=	Theologisches Woerterbuch zum NT v. G. Kittel, Stuttgart
ThZ	=	Theologische Zeitschrift, Basle
TSt	=	Texts and Studies
TU	=	Texte und Untersuchungen zur altchristlichen Literatur
VCh	=	Vigiliae christianae, Amsterdam
VS	=	Verbum Salutis, Paris
Zahn	=	Kommentar zum NT, Th. Zahn, Leipzig
ZDMG	=	Zeitschrift der Deutschen Morgenlaendischen Gesellschaft
ZKG	=	Zeitschrift fuer Kirchengeschichte, Stuttgart
ZkTh	=	Zeitschrift fuer katholische Theologie, Innsbruck-Vienna
ZntW	=	Zeitschrift fuer die neutestamentliche Wissenschaft, Berlin
ZRGG	=	Zeitschrift fuer Religions- und Geistesgeschichte
ZsyTh	=	Zeitschrift fuer systematische Theologie, Berlin
ZThK	=	Zeitschrift fuer Theologie und Kirche, Tuebingen

3. Other abbreviations

MS., MSS.   = Manuscript, manuscripts
par   = synoptic parallel passages
§ with num. = reference to the paragraphs of this book

The raised figure after the book title (*Bibelatlas*[3]) or before the year ([2]1955) indicates the edition.

PREFACE TO THE FIRST GERMAN EDITION

THE present book is an entirely new work and is designed to cover in much greater detail the ground which was covered by the numerous impressions of the late Joseph Sickenberger's *Einleitung in das Neue Testament*. As Pope Pius XII has emphasized in his encyclical *Divino Afflante Spiritu* of 30th September 1943, where he deals with the promotion of Biblical studies, at the present day theological students require a more thorough grounding in Biblical science than was considered adequate at the beginning of the present century; and in fact theological schools in the last forty years have devoted more time to Biblical studies.

This work has grown from the author's lectures. The aim throughout the entire work has been to acquaint theological students, teachers of religion and the pastoral clergy with all the most important problems of Introduction, and so special attention has been paid to the present day state of the problems. The author has taken care to defend the solutions which he puts forward, while giving adequate notice to other views and the arguments which support them. It not infrequently happens that only a greater or lesser degree of probability can be attained, for the books themselves often give no clear information about their composition, and reliable ancient testimony is often wanting; moreover, it is not always easy to reconcile the testimony of early writers with the internal evidence. Hence there are cases where, in spite of the energy and acumen of scholars, it is not possible to make a categorical statement about certain problems of Introduction—where indeed such a statement will perhaps never be possible. In such cases the author has taken care to enumerate the *pros* and *cons,* so that the reader may have a faithful picture of the state of scholarship on the particular point.

Particular attention was given to producing a simple and clear-cut analysis of the content and literary structure of each book. Such an analysis is indispensible for an understanding of the problems of Introduction. Moreover, this feature should enhance the reader's grasp of and reverence for the message of the Sacred Books—and without such devotional reading all study of Scripture is vain.

The history of the text has been treated at length, for the finds of papyri and modern textual studies have led to great advances in this field in recent years. This is a difficult branch of Biblical study, in which students encounter difficulties; yet a knowledge of the fundamentals of textual criticism is indispensible if the *Apparatus criticus* of a modern text is to be used with profit.

The bibliography is not intended to be exhaustive, but it does mention the most important books and articles of the last half century, with particular reference to the last fifteen years. In this the author has received invaluable assistance from his friend and colleague Professor Josef Schmid of Munich, who also read the first proofs. To him the author's most sincere thanks are due.

Freiburg i. Br., November 1952

THE AUTHOR

TRANSLATOR'S PREFACE
TO THE ENGLISH EDITION

THIS English version is based upon the second, revised and enlarged German edition, which appeared in 1956.

In the bibliography a short summary of important modern studies has been added in square brackets. The commentaries on individual books of the New Testament are arranged in two groups: (a) Catholic and (b) non-Catholic.

TRANSLATOR'S NOTE

FOR the citations from Scripture I have used the Challoner revision of the Douay version, except in one place where I quoted from Monsignor Knox's version of the New Testament.

The bibliography has been brought up to the spring of 1957 by Professor Wikenhauser.

I would like to record here my thanks to those who assisted me in this work, particularly to my colleague Rev. J. Maguire, M.A., B.D., who helped me to read the proofs and who made many valuable suggestions.

Prosit lectori opus.

April 1957

St. Malachy's College,
Belfast

INTRODUCTION

§ 1. CONCEPT AND OBJECT OF INTRODUCTION

THE expression "New Covenant" or "New Testament" (καινὴ διαθήκη, Novum Testamentum) in the earliest Christian literature denotes the new economy of salvation established by Jesus Christ, which replaced the Old Covenant (cf. 2 Cor. 3, 6; Gal. 4, 24; Heb. 8, 6; 9, 15; 12, 24). The name goes back to Christ himself, who at the Last Supper referred to his Blood (that is, to his death on the Cross) as the foundation of a new covenant with men (Mt. 26, 28; Mk. 14, 24: "This is my Blood of the new Testament." Lk. 22, 20; 1 Cor. 11, 25: "This chalice is the new Testament in my Blood").

From the end of the second century the Christian Church also applied this name to the collection of its own early sacred writings while it applied the name Old Testament (παλαιὰ διαθήκη) to the sacred writings taken over from the Synagogue. Those early Christian writings were composed in the second half of the first century, but only in the course of the second century were they ranked as a second collection of sacred books having equal authority with the writings taken over from Judaism (cf. § 5,2). In the beginning their number was not fixed. Only in the fifth century was universal recognition given in the Greek and Latin Church to all the twenty seven books which to-day make up the Canon of the New Testament, namely the Gospels according to SS. Matthew, Mark, Luke, and John; Acts of the Apostles, by St. Luke; fourteen Pauline Epistles; seven Catholic Epistles, and the Apocalypse of St. John.

The name "Introduction" does not give a clear description of the nature and purpose of our subject. The name could be applied to the ensemble of sciences which are necessary or useful for a scientific understanding of the Bible (Hermeneutics, History of Biblical times, Geography, Archaeology, Philology etc.). But as a technical term in Biblical science "Introduction" has fairly generally become confined to the following topics:

1. The circumstances in which each book was composed (author, destination, time and place of composition, occasion and purpose, literary form, sources, integrity), that is, the questions which conventionally are dealt with in literary history.

2. How these books came to be collected, i. e., History of the Canon (strictly speaking a part of History of Dogma).

3. The transmission of the text of these books both in the original texts and in versions, i. e., History of the Text.

The name "General Introduction" is applied to 2 and 3; 1 is called "Special Introduction".

So we may define Introduction as that branch of Biblical science which investigates scientifically the circumstances in which each book of the New Testament was composed, the formation of the Canon, and the transmission of the text.

Introduction belongs to the historical (critico-historical) branches of Theology like Church History, Patrology, History of Dogma, History of Liturgy, Christian Archaeology and History of Christian Art.[1] In recent times this concept has been almost universally accepted even by Catholics, but some decades ago Introduction was usually grouped with Apologetics and Fundamental Theology (see F. Kaulen, F. S. Gutjahr). The method of Introduction is critico-historical, not dogmatic or speculative. It investigates the circumstances in which the New Testament books were written and the history of the Canon and the transmission of the text, in the light of

[1] Cf. J. Sickenberger, *Kirchengeschichte und ntl Exegese,* in Festgabe für Alois Knoepfler, Freiburg i. Br. 1917, pp. 317—324.

2

their own statements and the evidence of ancient tradition. Introduction does not accept this evidence blindly, but examines its reliability according to the principles of historical criticism as developed by historians and philologists. The use of such methods, however, does not compel the scholar to deny or ignore the supernatural factors in the origin of the New Testament books. The trustworthiness of the New Testament will be impugned only by those whose philosophy denies the possibility of a supernatural revelation and of miracles and prophecies. The method as such does not postulate such an attitude. So one must distinguish negative and positive criticism; only the former is to be avoided.

Catholic Biblical scholarship recognizes the possibility and the fact of divine revelation and the reality of supernatural factors in the writing of Holy Scripture. In accordance with the Church's teaching it firmly believes in Inspiration. Inspiration cannot be demonstrated by merely scientific means, for it does not belong to the natural sphere; it is guaranteed by the Church which has accepted only inspired books into the Canon.

The problems of Introduction are rather to be investigated and answered by historical methods in so far as the source material permits. The history of Theology shows that conflicts have arisen in the Church between the results of Catholic Biblical scholarship and traditional interpretations. Naturally there can be no conflict between the teaching of the Church and definite results of research. But not all traditional interpretations within the Church are an expression of the Church's teaching; closer examination shows in a number of cases that on many questions there was no uniformity in the early Church, or that some commonly accepted views are not based on reliable ancient tradition. The Catholic scholar must have unqualified respect for such tradition, but it is sometimes difficult to determine whether, in certain cases, such a tradition exists. So conflicts are possible either because traditional interpretations cannot be upheld, or because some scholars are too hasty in abandoning well-founded traditional opinions.

§ 2. HISTORY OF INTRODUCTION

NEITHER Christian antiquity nor the Middle Ages knew Introduction in the present day sense of the word. It began with the eighteenth century "Enlightenment", and an Oratorian, Richard Simon, was its founder. But since the circumstances in which the New Testament books were written became very early a matter of interest, the beginnings of Introduction lie far back in time.

The oldest documents of New Testament Introduction come from the second half of the second century. They are 1. the Marcionite prologues to the ten Epistles of St. Paul which Marcion accepted; they give information about the content, occasion and place of composition—2. the prologues to the four canonical Gospels which were composed against Marcion in Rome between 160 and 180 A.D.; only three of them (to Mk., Lk., John) survive—3. the ancient prologues to the pastoral Epistles (cf. § 5, 3) which were probably also composed there.

The oldest "Introduction to the New Testament", though of a primitive nature, is the catalogue of the Canon which Muratori discovered. Composed about 200 A.D., this catalogue not only enumerates the canonical books (together with some which are not in the Canon), but also gives information about the author, content, authenticity, occasion and purpose of each book.

At a later date numerous Biblical MSS. have prologues like those mentioned above, but their value is generally very slight (cf. § 11, 2). Particular questions of Introduction are discussed by many ecclesiastical writers on various occasions, thus by Papias, Irenacus, Tertullian, Clement of Alexandria, Origen, Eusebius, Jerome, Augustine, Rufinus, and others.

The name "Introduction" for a branch of Biblical science first occurs in Adrianos, an otherwise unknown Greek, who belonged to the Antioch school of exegetes. His *Introduction* (Εἰσαγωγή) *to the divine Scriptures* is a small work, composed about 450 A.D., and in reality it deals with Biblical Hermeneutics. Cassiodorus († c. 570 A.D.), the famous statesman who later became a monk, in his *Institutio divinarum lectionum* lists Adrianos among the *introductores divinae scripturae,* together with Tyconius the Donatist (c. 380 A.D.), St. Augustine († 430 A.D.), Eucherius of Lyons (c. 450), and Junilius Africanus (c. 550 A.D.). Their works mainly give hermeneutic rules for the interpretation of Holy Scripture or give elucidations of difficult passages. Only to a small extent do they deal with problems of Introduction in our sense of the word. The nearest approach to a work on Introduction in our sense is the *Instituta regularia divinae legis,* in two books, by Junilius, a high state functionary of Justinian, of African origin. His work is a free Latin version of a compendium of Biblical Introduction which a Nestorian of Persia, Paulus, who taught at the Nisibis theological school, composed in Greek and allowed Junilius to copy. In addition to the *Institutio* of Cassiodorus, mention may also be made of Isidore of Seville († 636 A.D.) with a number of relevant writings (*Prooemia,* etc.).

The Middle Ages drew upon these sources, (ecclesiastical writers and prologues). A concise summary of what had come down from antiquity was given by Hugh of St. Victor († 1141) in his little book *De Scripturis et Scriptoribus Sacris Praenotiunculae* (Migne PL 175, 9–28).

Since the beginning of the Reformation more attention has been focussed on the problems of Introduction, for the Protestant view of the Bible as the sole rule of faith brought to the fore the question of the reliability of the text and particularly of the extent of the Canon. Now we meet again the name "Introduction", but no longer in Cassiodorus' sense. Thus Santes Pagnino (Sanctes Pagninus),

O.P. (1470—1541), the orientalist and exegete, composed a work called *Isagoges seu introductionis ad sacras litteras liber* (Lyons 1528), and the Protestant Andreas Rivetus († 1651) entitled his work *Isagoge sive introductio generalis ad Sacram Scripturam V. et N. Testamenti* (Leyden 1627). The most important scriptural work of the sixteenth century was *Bibliotheca Sancta* of Sixtus of Sienna (1520–1569), a converted Jew who joined the Franciscans and later became a Dominican; his gigantic work runs to eight volumes (Venice 1566), and for a long time it was surpassed neither by Catholics nor by Protestants.

The real founder of strictly scientific "Introduction" to Scripture was Richard Simon, an Oratorian († 1712). He separated the Old Testament from the New, and besides a number of works on the Old Testament, broke new ground in textual criticism by his *Histoire critique du texte* (3 vols., Rotterdam 1689), *des versions* (1690), and *des principaux commentateurs du Nouveau Testament* (1693), and particularly in his work *Nouvelles observations sur le texte et les versions du Nouveau Testament* (1695); furthermore he led the way in literary-historical treatment of the New Testament, and to a large extent was the founder of historico-literary criticism of it. His ideas evoked violent censure from both Catholics and Protestants; ten of his works were put on the Index.

In Protestant circles great services were rendered to the science of Introduction by Johann David Michaelis († 1791), who was comparatively conservative, and by Johann Salomo Semler († 1791), a rationalist, who claimed to be the herald of the ideas of Richard Simon, thereby rendering them for a long time suspect. He ushers in the age of rationalist New Testament criticism. This tendency was followed especially by Johann Gottfried Eichhorn of Goettingen († 1827) and W. M. L. de Wette († 1849 in Basle). Of the Catholics, Johann Leonard Hug of Freiburg († 1846) opposed the prevailing rationalist tendency with great learning and skill and to good effect; his *Einleitung in die Schriften des Neuen*

Testaments, first published in 1808, reached its fourth edition in 1847.

The work of the so-called Tuebingen school had a particularly strong influence on Protestant treatment of the problems of Introduction. The leader of this school was Ferdinand Christian Baur, a Professor at Tuebingen († 1860). The representatives of this school are usually called "tendency critics" (Tendenzkritiker), because in regard to each book they inquired what tendency it was supposed to favour. Baur laid down the principle of taking the New Testament books in close connection with the history of the Christian religion and of regarding them as necessary products of a particular phase of development. He believed that he had found the key to understanding their origin in the struggle which divided primitive Christianity between the narrow-minded Judaeo-Christianity of the original Apostles and St. Paul's universal Christianity which was free from the Law. For Baur the New Testament writings mirror the great struggle between judaizing Christianity (Peter) and the Gentile-Christian Church (Paul), as well as the gradual assimilation and unification of these two streams in Catholicism. In his view only the four major Epistles of St. Paul (Romans, 1 and 2 Corinthians, Galatians) and the strongly judaizing Apocalypse belong to the apostolic age; the remaining books bear traces of the compromise and so belong to the second century, for example the Acts of the Apostles; at the end of the process are John and 2 Peter.

Baur is quite correct in his view that the New Testament writings are to be regarded as witnesses of the external and internal development of primitive Christianity, but he is quite wrong when he interprets the course of this history as a series of antagonisms and compromises according to the Hegelian pattern of thesis, antithesis and synthesis. It is recognized to-day that Baur's interpretation was erroneous. Yet with considerable modifications it was able to maintain itself for a long time. Indeed it was outdone by radical currents (David Friedrich Strauss † 1874, Bruno Bauer † 1882, Ernest Renan † 1892; the Dutch radicals who even denied the authenticity of the four major Pauline Epistles and attributed them to the second century); some of the radicals even went so far as to deny the historicity of Jesus (for example Arthur Drews † 1935, and Paul-Louis Couchoud in France).

Towards the end of the nineteenth century rationalist criticism became more moderate (Karl Heinrich Weizsaecker † 1899, Heinrich Julius Holtzmann † 1910, Adolf Juelicher † 1938). It was taken up and developed by the so-called "Comparative Religion School," which finds parallels to the facts and ideas of the New Testament in all areas of the East, and regards these parallels as direct or indirect sources of the New Testament (Johannes Weis † 1914, Wilhelm Bousset † 1920, Hermann Gunkel † 1932, Richard Reitzenstein † 1932). Side by side with this school, conservative Protestant scholarship continued, its most important representative being Theodor Zahn († 1933 in Erlangen).

On all important points Catholic Biblical scholars held fast to the tradition of the early Church and concentrated almost all their forces on defending it. They knew that in matters of Biblical scholarship they were bound by the solemn definitions of the Church and also by other utterances of the magisterium. The Council of Trent declared in its decree on the publication and use of Holy Scripture (cf. § 4): *ut nemo . . . in rebus fidei et morum ad aedificationem doctrinae christianae pertinentium Sacram Scripturam . . . contra eum sensum, quem tenuit et tenet sancta mater ecclesia, cuius est iudicare de vero sensu et interpretatione Scripturarum Sacrarum, aut etiam contra unanimem consensum Patrum ipsam Scripturam Sacram interpretari audeat* (repeated by the Vatican Council of 1870, sess. 3, cap. 2 "On Revelation").

In his encyclical *Providentissimus Deus* of 18th Nov. 1893 Pope Leo XIII gave a lengthy exposition of the fundamental principles of Catholic Biblical scholarship, particularly with reference to a current theological controversy within the Church between a strictly conservative school and a freer "progressive" school. The same Pope in 1902 created a Biblical Commission (Commissio Pontificia de re Biblica) for the promotion and supervision of Biblical studies.[1]

This commission has issued a large number of decrees, some of which refer to questions of New Testament Introduction (concerning the authorship, time of composition, credibility, canonicity of a New Testament book etc.). In so far as they are not applications of dogmas (for example, inspiration, canonicity, credibility) its decrees[2] have not the character of infallible and irreformable decisions (for example, those referring to the time of composition and the literary relations of particular writings). For that reason Pius X declared that there is an obligation in conscience to submit to the decisions of the Biblical Commission, so that those who in word or writing impugn *(impugnare)* them are guilty of disobedience or temerity *(Motu Proprio* of 18th Nov. 1907).

[1] Cf. art. *Commission Biblique* by L. Pirot in DB Suppl 2 (1934) 103—113.

[2] Collected in *Enchiridium Biblicum. Documenta ecclesiastica Sacram Scripturam spectantia auctoritate Pontificiae Commissionis de Re Biblica edita, ed. secunda aucta et recognita,* Rome 1954. When this second edition appeared, A. Miller, secretary of the Biblical Commission *(Benediktinische Monatschrift* 31, 1955, 49 sq.), and A. Kleinhans, the assistant secretary *(Antonianum* 30, 1955, 63—65), laid down fundamental principles concerning the obligation which ecclesiastical decisions on Biblical questions impose upon Catholic exegetes. According to them, the decrees of the Biblical Commission must be strictly distinguished into those which are connected with the truths of faith and morals, and those which are not. In the former case the decrees retain their binding force. "But in so far as these decrees deal with views which have neither direct nor indirect connection with the truths of faith and morals, scholars are, of course, quite free to pursue their investigations and to draw their own conclusions, with due respect for the magisterium of the Church" (Miller). Questions of authenticity (genuineness) and dating belong to this latter group. The approach to these problems at the present day is quite different from what it was 50 years ago. See also J. Dupont: RB 62 (1955) 414—419, E. Vogt: Bb 36 (1955) 564 sq., E. F. Siegman: CBQ 18 (1956) 23—29, and A. M. Dubarle: ZatW 66 (1954) 149—151.

In his encyclical in honour of St. Jerome, *Spiritus Paraclitus*, on 15th Sept. 1920, Benedict XV commended the hermeneutic and exegetical principles of this *doctor maximus in exponendis Sacris Scripturis*, especially in regard to the total inerrancy of Holy Scripture.

Finally Pope Pius XII on 30th Sept. 1943, on the occasion of the fiftieth anniversary of *Providentissimus Deus*, issued a lengthy encyclical on the promotion of Biblical studies: *Divino Afflante Spiritu*. In it he reviews the exertions of Leo XIII and his successors for the promotion of Biblical studies, and then expounds in detail the principles which should guide Biblical scholars in our time.[3]

§ 3. THE MOST IMPORTANT AIDS TO THE STUDY OF THE NEW TESTAMENT

1. General introduction (modern works):

Catholic: Joh. Ev. Belser, *Einleitung in das NT*[2], Freiburg i. Br. 1905. Frz. S. Gutjahr, *Einleitung zu den Hl. Schriften des NT*[7], Graz-Vienna 1923. H. Jos. Vogels, *Grundriß der Einleitung in das NT*, Muenster i. W. 1925. K. Th. Schaefer, *Grundriß der Einleitung in das NT*[2], Bonn 1952. Jos. Sickenberger, *Kurzgefaßte Einleitung in das NT*[6], Freiburg i. Br. 1938. M. Meinertz, *Einleitung in das NT*[5], Paderborn 1950. P. Gaechter S. J., *Summa introductionis in NT*, Innsbruck-Leipzig 1938. P. Morant O. Cap., *Introductio specialis in libros NTi*[2], Rome 1950. S. Rosadini S. J., *Institutiones introductoriae in libros NTi*, 3 vols., Rome 1938/39. Aug. Merk S. J. *Introductionis in Sacrae Scripturae libros compendium*[12], Paris 1940. H. Hoepfl O.S.B., *Introductionis in Sacros utriusque Testamenti libros compendium*, 3 vols. (I[5]: *Introductio generalis*, cura B. Gut O. S. B., Naples-Rome 1950; III[5]: *Introductio specialis in NT*, cura A. Metzinger O. S. B., ibid. 1949). E. Jacquier, *Histoire des livres du NT*, I[11] II[9] III[6] IV[6], Paris 1928—35.

Protestant: Th. Zahn, *Einleitung in das NT*[3], 2 vols., Leipzig 1906/07 (Reprint [4]1924). H. Appel, *Einleitung in das NT*, Leipzig-Erlangen 1921. F. Barth, *Einleitung in das NT*[5], Guetersloh 1921. M. Dibelius, *Geschichte der urchristlichen Literatur*, 2 vols. (Sammlung Goeschen), Berlin 1926. A. Juelicher, *Einleitung in das NT*[7], revised in collaboration with E. Fascher, Tuebingen 1931. W. Michaelis, *Einleitung in das NT*[2], Berne 1954. R. Knopf, H. Lietzmann, H. Weinel, *Einfuehrung in das NT; Bibelkunde des NT; Geschichte und Religion des Urchristentums*[5], Berlin 1949 (=[4]1934). Fr. Hauck, *Die Entstehung des NT*, Guetersloh 1949 (popular).

[3] G. Courtade, *Lettres encycliques concernant la Bible et les études bibliques:* DB Suppl 5 (1952) 375—387. Cf. also H. Hoepfl, *Critique biblique:* ibid. 2 (1934) 175—240.

P. Feine, *Einleitung in das NT*[9], revised by J. Behm, Leipzig 1950, [10]1954 (unchanged). M. Goguel, *Introduction au NT*, 4 vols., Paris 1922—1926. J. Moffat, *An Introduction to the NT*[3], Edinburgh 1918. A. H. McNeile, *An Introduction to the Study of the NT*[2], Oxford 1953, revised by C. S. C. Williams. E. J. Goodspeed, *An Introduction to the NT*, Chicago 1937. Kirsopp and Silva Lake, *An Introduction to the NT*, New York/London 1938. C. T. Craig, *The Study of the NT*, New York 1939. J. de Zwaan, *Inleiding tot het NT*, Haarlem 1941/42. H. Mosbech, *Nytestamentlig Isagogik*, Copenhagen 1949. R. Heard, *An Introduction to the NT*, London 1951. Th. Henshaw, *NT Literature in the Light of Modern Scholarship*, London 1952. M. Alberz, *Die Botschaft des NT* I: Die Entstehung der Botschaft. 1: Die Entstehung des Ev, Zollikon-Zürich 1947; 2: Die Entstehung des apostolischen Schriftkanons, 1952 (see also § 3, 14). D. T. Rowlingson, *Introduction to NT Study*, 1956. M. Albertz, *Die Botschaft des NT* II, 2: Der Inhalt der Botschaft — Die Gnade unseres Herrn Jesus Christus, Zollikon-Zurich 1957.

2. Grammars:

F. Blass-A. Debrunner, *Grammatik des ntl Griechisch*[8], Goettingen 1949. L. Radermacher, *Ntl Grammatik*[2], Tuebingen 1925 (Lietzmann 1). J. H. Moulton, *Einleitung in die Sprache des NT*, Heidelberg 1911. A. T. Robertson, *A Grammar of the Greek NT in the Light of Historical Research*[4], London 1923. F.-M. Abel O. P., *Grammaire du grec biblique*, Paris 1927. J. H. Moulton and F. W. Howard, *A Grammar of NT Greek*. I[3] (Prolegomena), Edinburgh 1949, II (Accidence and word formation) 1929, III (Syntax: in preparation). B. Botte O. S. B., *Grammaire grec du NT*, Paris 1933. C. F. D. Moule, *An Idiom Book of NT Greek*, Cambridge 1953. M. Zerwick, *Graecitas biblica exemplis illustratur*[3], Rome 1955. Idem, *Analysis philologica NiTi*, Rome 1953. J. H. Moulton and H. G. Mecham, *An Introduction to the Study of NT Greek*, New ed. 1955. E. D. Burton, *Syntax of Moods and Tenses of NT Greek*, 1956. H. E. Dana and J. Mantey, *A Manual Grammar of the Greek NT*, 1957.

3. Dictionaries:

W. Bauer, *Griechisch-deutsches Woerterbuch zu den Schriften des NT und der uebrigen urchristlichen Literatur*[4], Berlin 1950 ff. W. F. Arndt and F. W. Gingrich, *A Greek-English Lexicon of the NT and Other Early Christian Literature*, 1956 (An English edition of W. Bauer's Dictionary). W. Bauer, *Zur Einfuehrung in das Woerterbuch zum NT*, Lund 1955. G. Kittel, *Theologisches Woerterbuch zum NT*, Stuttgart 1952; already appeared: I (1933), II (1935), III (1938), IV (1944), V (1948 ff.). F. Zorell, *Novi Testamenti Lexicon graecum*[2], Paris 1931 (CSS). F. Rienecker, *Sprachlicher Schluessel zum griechischen NT nach der Ausgabe von E. Nestle*[8], Giessen-Basle 1952. J. H. Moulton-G. Milligan, *The Vocabulary of the NT, illustrated from the Papyri*[2], London 1949. E. Osterloh-H. Engelland, *Biblisch-Theologisches Handwoerterbuch zur Lutherbibel und neueren Uebersetzungen*, Goettingen 1954. R. C. Trench, *Synonyma des NT, ausgewaehlt und uebersetzt von H. Werner*, 1907.

4. Concordances:

C. H. Bruder, *Tamieion sive Concordantiae omnium vocum NT graeci*[7], Goettingen 1913. A. Schmoller, *Handkonkordanz zum griechischen NT*[8], Stuttgart 1949. W. F.

Moulton-A. S. Geden, *A Concordance to the Greek NT*[3], Edinburgh 1950. J. B. Smith, *Greek-English Concordance to the NT;* intr. by B. M. Metzger, 1956.

5. Encyclopedias:

Catholic: F. Vigouroux, *Dictionnaire de la Bible,* 5 vols., Paris 1895—1912; since 1926 a Supplement to it has appeared, ed. by L. Pirot, continued by A. Robert, to date 28 numbers (to Midrash). M. Hagen S. J., *Lexicon Biblicum,* 3 vols., Paris 1905—1911 (CSS). E. Kalt, *Biblisches Reallexikon*[2], 2 vols., Paderborn 1937—1938. H. Haag, *Bibellexikon,* Einsiedeln 1952—1956. J. E. Steinmueller and K. Sullivan, *Catholic Biblical Encyclopedia,* New York 1956.
Protestant: J. Hastings, *A Dictionary of the Bible,* 5 vols., Edinburgh 1898—1904. Idem, *Dictionary of the Christ and the Gospels,* 2 vols., Edinburgh 1906—1908. Idem, *Dictionary of the Apostolic Church,* 2 vols., Edinburgh 1915—1918. T. K. Cheyne and J. S. Black, *Encyclopaedia biblica,* 4 vols., London 1899—1903. K. Galling, *Biblisches Reallexikon,* Tuebingen 1937.

6. Hermeneutics:

E. v. Dobschuetz, *Vom Auslegen des NT,* Goettingen 1927. E. Fascher, *Vom Verstehen des NT,* Giessen 1930. F. Torm, *Hermeneutik des NT,* Goettingen 1930. J. Schildenberger, *Das Geheimnis des Gotteswortes. Einfuerung in das Verstaendnis der Heiligen Schrift,* Heidelberg 1950. E. Fuchs, *Hermeneutik,* Bad Cannstatt 1954.

7. History of NT times:

W. Staerk, *Ntl Zeitgeschichte*[2] (Sammlung Goeschen), Leipzig 1920. J. Felten, *Ntl Zeitgeschichte*[2], 2 vols., Regensburg 1925. C. Schneider, *Einfuehrung in die ntl Zeitgeschichte,* Leipzig 1934. H. Preisker, *Ntl Zeitgeschichte* (Sammlung Toepelmann), Berlin 1937. W. Foerster, *Ntl Zeitgeschichte,* I *Das Judentum Palaestinas zur Zeit Jesu und der Apostel*[2], Hamburg 1955, II 1956. U. Holzmeister, *Historia aetatis NTi*[2], Rome 1938. *The Beginnings of Christianity,* Part I: *The Acts of the Apostles,* vol. I, ed. by F. J. Jackson and Kirsopp Lake. Prolegomena I: *The Jewish, Gentile and Christian Backgrounds* London 1920. R. H. Pfeiffer, *History of NT Times with an Introduction to the Apocrypha,* New York 1949. E. Schuerer, *Geschichte des juedischen Volkes im Zeitalter Jesu Christi*[4], 3 vols., and index, Leipzig 1901—1911. A. Schlatter, *Geschichte Israels von Alexander bis Hadrian*[2], Stuttgart 1925. W. Bousset-H. Gressmann, *Die Religion des Judentums im ntl Zeitalter*[3], Tuebingen 1926. G. F. Moore, *Judaism in the first Centuries of the Christian Era. The Age of the Tannaim,* 3 vols., 1927—1930. J. Bonsirven S. J., *Le Judaïsme palestinien aux temps de Jésus-Christ, sa théologie,* 2 vols., Paris 1934—1935. M.-J. Lagrange, *Le Judaïsme avant Jésus-Christ,* Paris 1931. J. Juster, *Les juifs dans l'empire romain. Leur condition juridique, économique et sociale,* 2 vols., Paris 1914. J. Jeremias, *Jerusalem zur Zeit Jesu. Kulturgeschichtliche Untersuchung zur ntl Zeitgeschichte,* Leipzig 1923—1937. P. Volz, *Die Eschatologie der juedischen Gemeinde im ntl Zeitalter*[2], Tuebingen 1934. H. L. Strack and P. Billerbeck, *Kommentar zum NT aus Talmud und Midrasch,* 4 vols., Munich 1922—1928, [2]1955/56 (new edition with vol. 5: *Rabbinischer Index,* ed. Joach. Jeremias, revised by K. Adolph, 1956). C. G. Montefiore, *Rabbinic Literature and Gospel Teachings,* 1930. J. Abrahams, *Studies in the Pharisaism and the Gospels,* 2 vols., 1917—1924. P. Wendland, *Die hellenistisch-roemische Kultur in ihren Beziehungen zu Judentum und Christentum*[2], Tuebingen 1912. A. Deissmann, *Licht vom Osten. Das NT und die neuentdeckten Texte der hellenistisch-roemischen Welt*[4], Tuebingen 1923. J. Leipoldt, *Die Religionen in der Umwelt des Urchristentums* (in: H. Haas, *Bilderatlas zur Religionsgeschichte,* 9—10), Leipzig 1926. A.-J. Festugière O. P., *L'idéal religieux des Grecs et l'évangile,* Paris 1932. C. Clemen, *Religionsgeschichtliche Erklaerung des NT. Die Abhaengigkeit des aeltesten Christentums von nichtjuedischen Religionen und philosophischen Systemen*[2], Giessen 1924. R. Reitzenstein, *Die hellenistischen Mysterienreligionen in ihren Grundgedanken und Wirkungen*[3], Leipzig 1927. G. Kittel, *Die Religionsgeschichte und das Urchristentum,* Guetersloh 1932. K. Pruemm, *Religionsgeschichtliches Handbuch fuer den Raum der altchristlichen Umwelt,* Freiburg i. Br. 1943 (new impression Rome 1954). S. Angus, *The Religious Quests in the Graeco-roman World. A Study in the historical Background of early Christianity,* London 1929. Idem, *The Mystery Religions and Christianity,* London 1925. A.-J. Festugière and P. Fabre, *Le monde gréco-romain au temps de N. S.,* 2 vols., Paris 1936. S. Liebermann, *Greek in Jewish Palestine,* New York 1942. F.-M. Abel, *Histoire de la Palestine depuis la conquête d'Alexandre jusqu'à l'invasion arabe,* 2 vols., Paris 1951—1952. J. Bonsirven, *Textes rabbiniques des deux premiers siècles chrétiens,* Rome 1955. K. Schubert, *Die Religion des nachbiblischen Judentums,* Vienna 1955. D. Daube, *The NT and Rabbinic Judaism,* Oxford 1956. C. F. Grant, *Hellenistic Religions. The Age of Syncretism,* 1953. S. Liebermann, *Hellenism in the Jewish Palestine. Studies in Literary Transmission, Beliefs and Manners in the I. Century B. C. E.—IV. Century C. E.,* New York 1950. F. V. Filson, *The New Testament against its Environment,* 1952. C. K. Barret, *The New Testament Background,* 1956.

8. Biblical Geography and Archaeology:

M. Hagen, *Atlas biblicus,* Paris 1907. R. v. Riess, *Atlas Scripturae Sacrae*[3], Freiburg i. Br. 1924. H. Guthe, *Bibelatlas*[2], Leipzig 1926. E. G. Wright, F. V. Filson and W. F. Albright, *The Westminster Historical Atlas to the Bible,* Philadelphia 1946. L. H. Grollenberg, *Atlas of the Bible,* Nelson, N. Y. 1956. R. Koeppel, *Palaestina,* Tuebingen 1930. H. Guthe, *Palaestina*[2], Leipzig 1927. F. M. Abel, *Géographie de la Palestine,* 2 vols., Paris 1933, 1938. G. Dalman, *Sacred Sites and Ways,* S. P. C. K. 1935. Idem, *Jerusalem und sein Gelaende,* Guetersloh 1930. Idem, *Arbeit und Sitte in Palaestina,* 7 vols. to date, Guetersloh 1928 ff.

C. Watzinger, *Denkmaeler Palaestinas. Eine Einfuehrung in die Archaeologie des Heiligen Landes,* 2 vols., Leipzig 1933—1935. A.-G. Barrois, *Manuel d'archéologie biblique* I, Paris 1939; II, 1953. F. Noetscher, *Biblische Altertumskunde,* Bonn 1940. W. F. Albright, *The Archaeology of Palestine,* 1949 (Pelican Books). H. Vincent O. P. and F. M. Abel, *Jérusalem. Recherches de topographie, d'archéologie et d'histoire,* II: *Jérusalem nouvelle,* Paris 1914—1922. I. Press, *Topographical-historical Encyclopaedia of Palestine,* 4 vols., 1948—1954 (Jewish).

9. Modern commentaries on the entire NT:

Catholic: *Die Hl. Schrift des NT uebersetzt und erklaert,* in Verbindung mit Fachgelehrten hrsg. von Fr. Tillmann[3], 10 vols., Bonn 1931 ff. (= Bonner NT). —*Das NT uebersetzt und kurz erklaert,* hrsg. von A. Wikenhauser und O. Kuss, 9 vols. (and index), Regensburg 1938 ff. (= Regensburger NT).—*Die Hl. Schrift in deutscher Uebersetzung* (=Echter Bibel); das NT hrsg. von K. Staab, Wuerzburg 1951–1956 (6 vols).—*Herders Theologischer Kommentar zum NT* (14 vols.), hrsg. v. A. Wikenhauser, Freiburg i. Br. 1953 ff. (= HThK). *Die Hl. Schrift fuer das Leben erklaert,* 16 vols. (O and NT), hrsg. von E. Kalt und W. Lauck, Freiburg i. Br. 1935 ff.— *Cursus Scripturae Sacrae, Commentarii in NT,* ed. by German Jesuits, Paris 1890 ff. (= CSS).—In Études bibliques, by the École Biblique of the French Dominicans in Jerusalem, there are lengthy scholary commentaries on O and NT (Paris 1907 ff.). On the NT there are: Mt., Mk., Lk., John, Acts, Rom., 1 and 2 Cor., Gal., 1 and 2 Thess., Past. Epistles, Heb., Cath. Epistles (except 1 Pet.), Apc.—*Verbum salutis. Commentaire du NT,* ed. by French Jesuits, Paris 1924 ff. (= VS).—*La Sainte Bible, texte latin de la Vulgate, traduction d'après les textes originaux, commentaire exégétique et théologique,* ed. by L. Pirot and A. Clamer, 12 vols., Paris 1935 ff.— *La Sacra Bibbia, Volgata latina e traduzione italiana,* ed. by S. Garofalo, Turin 1947 ff.—*La Sainte Bible traduit en français sous la direction de l'École Biblique de Jérusalem,* Paris 1948 ff. (with lengthy Introduction and Commentary).

Protestant: *Kritisch-exegetischer Kommentar ueber das NT,* founded by H. A. W. Meyer, Goettingen 1832 ff., 16 vols.: the individual vols. have been repeatedly revised up to the present day (critical).—*Kommentar zum NT,* hrsg. von Th. Zahn, Leipzig 1903 ff., 18 vols. (only the Johannine Epistles are missing; strictly conservative).—*Die Schriften des NT, neu uebersetzt und fuer die Gegenwart erklaert,* 3rd ed. by W. Bousset and W. Heitmueller, Goettingen 1917–1919, 4 vols. (strongly influenced by Comparative Religion).—A. Schlatter, *Erlaeuterungen zum NT*[4], 10 Parts, Stuttgart 1948–1950 (conservative).—*Handbuch zum NT,* ed. by H. Lietzmann (now by G. Bornkamm), Tuebingen 1906 ff., 22 sections (short; critical-philological; copious material from Comparative Religion).— *Theologischer Handkommentar zum NT,* Leipzig 1928 ff. (= ThHK) (fairly conservative; Mk., Lk., Acts, Gal., Phil., 1-3 John, Apc. have appeared).—*Das NT Deutsch. Neues Goettinger Bibelwerk,* ed. by P. Althaus and J. Behm, Goettingen 1912 ff., [5]1949–1950, 12 vols. (fairly conservative).—*Commentaire du NT,* publié sous la direction de P. Bonnard, O. Cullmann etc., 14 vols., Neuchâtel et Paris 1949 ff.—*The International Critical Commentary on the Holy Scriptures of the Old and New T.,* Edinburgh 1895 ff. (=ICC).—The *Moffatt NT Commentary,* ed. by J. Moffatt, London 1928 ff. (17 vols., complete).—*Kommentaar op het NT,* ed. by S. Greijdanus, F. W. Grosheide and J. A. C. van Leeuwen, Amsterdam 1922 ff. (Dutch: lengthy, strictly Calvinist-conservative).—*The New International Commentary on the NT,* London 1950 ff. (= NIC).

9a. Modern commentaries on the Gospels:

Catholic: F. X. Poelzl, *Kurzgefasster Kommentar zu den vier heiligen Evangelien,* in 5 vols.; neue Bearbeitung (4. ed.) von Th. Innitzer and G. Stettinger, Graz 1928 ff. Vol 5. contains the "Passion and Glorification").

Protestant: A. Merx, *Die vier kanonischen Evv. nach ihrem aeltesten bekannten Text,* 3 vols., Berlin 1902–1911. A. Loisy, *Les évangiles synoptiques,* Ceffonds 1907 f.

Jewish: C. G. Montefiore, *The Synoptic Gospels*[2], 2 vols., London 1927.

§ 3. THE MOST IMPORTANT AIDS

10. Exegetical journals:

Catholic: *Revue biblique,* publiée par l'École pratique d'études bibliques établie au Couvent Dominicain St-Étienne de Jérusalem, Paris 1892 ff. (= RB).—*Biblische Zeitschrift,* ed. by J. Goettsberger and J. Sickenberger, Freiburg i. Br. 1903–1929 (Vol. 1–18); from 1931 ed. by B. Walde and J. Freundorfer, Paderborn 1931–1939 (Vol 19–24); from 1937 ed. by V. Hamp and R. Schnackenburg (= BZ).—*Biblica. Commentarii editi a Pontificio Instituto Biblico,* Rome 1920 ff. (= Bb).—*Verbum Domini, Commentarii menstrui de re Biblica omnibus sacerdotibus accommodati,* Rome 1921 ff.—*The Catholic Biblical Quarterly,* ed. by the Catholic Biblical Association of America, Washington 1939 ff.—*Estudios Bíblicos,* Madrid 1941 ff.

Protestant: *Zeitschrift fuer die ntl Wissenschaft und die Kunde der aelteren Kirche,* founded by E. Preuschen, Giessen 1900 ff., Berlin 1934 ff.; continued by H. Lietzmann (from 1921), ed. by W. Eltester (from 1943), with Supplements (= ZntW). —*Angelos, Archiv fuer ntl. Zeitgeschichte und Kulturkunde,* ed. by J. Leipoldt, Leipzig 1925–32 (4 vols.).—*The Expositor,* London 1875–1925 (Ser. I–IX).— *The Expository Times,* Edinburgh 1889 ff.—*Journal of Biblical Literature,* published by the Society of Biblical Literature and Exegesis, Philadelphia 1881 ff. (= JBL).—*Svensk Exegetisk Arsbok* (Swedish Exegetical Annual), ed. by A. Fridrichsen 1936–1948, by G. Lindeskog 1949 ff.

International and interconfessional: *NT Studies.* An international Journal published quarterly under the auspices of *Studiorum NiTi Societas,* Cambridge 1945 ff. (= NTSt).—*Novum Testamentum.* An international Quarterly for New Testament and related Studies based on international Co-operation, ed. by J. de Zwaan and J. W. Doeve, Leyden 1956 ff.

Internationale Zeitschriftenschau fuer Bibelwissenschaft und Grenzgebiete, Stuttgart 1952 ff.

11. Serial works:

Biblische Studien, founded by O. Bardenhewer, ed. by J. Goettsberger and J. Sickenberger, Freiburg i. Br. 1896 ff. (= BSt).—*Neutestamentliche Abhandlungen,* founded by A. Bludau, ed. by M. Meinertz, Muenster i. W. 1908 ff. (= NtA).— *Scripta Pontificii Instituti Biblici,* Rome 1913 ff.—*Forschungen zur Religion und Literatur des A und NT,* founded by W. Bousset and H. Gunkel, ed. by R. Bultmann, Goettingen 1903 ff.—*Untersuchungen zum NT,* founded by H. Windisch, 1912, from 1938 ed. by E. Klostermann.—*Neutestamentliche Forschungen,* ed. by O. Schmitz, Guetersloh 1923 ff.—*Beitraege zur Wissenschaft vom A und NT,* founded by R. Kittel, ed. by A. Alt and G. Kittel, Stuttgart 1926 ff.—*Wissenschaftliche Untersuchungen zum NT,* ed. by J. Jeremias and O. Michel, Tuebingen 1950 ff. —*Symbolae biblicae Upsalienses,* ed. by A. Fridrichsen, Lund 1936 ff.—*Coniectanea neotestamentica,* ed. by A. Fridrichsen, Lund 1943 ff.—*Abhandlungen zur Theologie des A und NT,* ed. by W. Eichrodt and O. Cullmann, Basle-Zurich 1942 ff.—*Acta Seminarii Neotestamentici Upsaliensis,* Uppsala 1935 ff.—*Beitraege zur Geschichte der ntl Exegese,* ed. by O. Cullmann and others, Tuebingen 1955 ff.—*Bonner biblische Beitraege,* ed. by F. Noetscher and K. Th. Schaefer, Bonn 1950 ff.

12. Life and teaching of Jesus:

Catholic: A. Reatz, *Jesus Christus, sein Leben, seine Lehre und sein Werk*[2], Freiburg i. Br. 1925. K. Adam, *Jesus Christus*, Augsburg 1933 and often. L. de Grandmaison S.J., *Jésus-Christ*, 2 vols., Paris 1928 and often. M.-J. Lagrange, *L'évangile de Jésus-Christ. Sa vie, sa doctrine, son oeuvre*, 2 vols., Paris 1933 and often). H. Felder, *Jesus von Nazareth*[2], Paderborn 1949. J. Lebreton, *La vie et l'enseignement de Jésus-Christ Notre Seigneur*, 2 vols., Paris 1930 and often. G. Ricciotti, *Vita di Gesù Cristo*, Milano 1941 and often.

Protestant: P. Wernle, *Jesus*[2], Tuebingen 1916. R. Bultmann, *Jesus*, Berlin 1925, Tuebingen 1951. P. Feine, *Jesus*, Guetersloh 1930. M. Dibelius, *Jesus*, Berlin 1939 (Sammlung Goeschen). M. Goguel, *Jésus*[2], Paris 1955. F. Buechsel, *Jesus*, Guetersloh 1947. V. Taylor, *The Life and Ministry of Jesus*, London 1954. G. Bornkamm, *Jesus von Nazareth*, Stuttgart 1956. A. Schweitzer, *Geschichte der Leben-Jesu-Forschung*, Tuebingen 1913; 6., photomechanical edition 1951. G. Bornkamm, *Jesus von Nazareth*, Stuttgart 1956. E. Stauffer, *Jesus, Gestalt und Geschichte*, Bern 1957. W. Grundmann, *Die Gesçhiçhte Jesu Christi*, Berlin 1957.

Jewish: J. Klausner, *Jesus von Nazareth. Seine Zeit, sein Leben und seine Lehre*, 3., erweiterte Auflage, Jerusalem 1952.

13. Primitive Christianity:

Joh. Weiss, *Das Urchristentum*, Goettingen 1917. E. Meyer, *Ursprung und Anfang des Christentums*, 3 vols., Stuttgart 1921–1923. A. Schlatter, *Die Geschichte der ersten Christenheit*, Guetersloh 1926. R. Bultmann, *Das Urchristentum im Rahmen der antiken Religionen*[2], Zurich 1954. M. Goguel, *La naissance du christianisme*[2], Paris 1955. Idem, *L'église primitive*, Paris 1947. J. Klausner, *From Jesus to Paul*, London 1943 (Jewish); reviewed by W. G. Kuemmel, Judaica 4 (1948) 1–35. Ph.-H. Menoud, *L'église naissante et le judaïsme*, Montpellier 1952. H. J. Schoeps, *Theologie und Geschichte des Judenchristentums*, Tuebingen 1949. Idem, *Urgemeinde, Judenchristentum, Gnosis*, Tuebingen 1955. L. Goppelt, *Christentum und Judentum im 1. u. 2. Jh. Ein Aufriss der Urgeschichte der Kirche*, Guetersloh 1954. C. Schneider, *Geistesgeschichte des antiken Christentums*, 2 vols., Munich 1954. On Paul, see § 31.

14. Theology of the NT:

Catholic: A. Lemonnyer, *Théologie du NT*, Paris 1928 (popular). O. Kuss, *Die Theologie des NT*[2], Regensburg 1937 (for wider circles). M. Meinertz, *Theologie des NT*, 2 vols., Bonn 1950. F. Prat, *La théologie de St. Paul*, 2 vols., Paris (numerous impressions). J. Bonsirven, *Les enseignements de Jésus-Christ*, Paris 1946. Idem, *L'évangile de St. Paul*, Paris 1948 (VS). Idem, *Théologie du NT*, Paris 1951. R. Schnackenburg, *Die sittliche Botschaft des NT*, Munich 1954.

Protestant: H. J. Holtzmann, *Lehrbuch der ntl Theologie*[2], 2 vols., Tuebingen 1911. H. Weinel, *Biblische Theologie des NT*[4], Tuebingen 1928. A. Schlatter, *Theologie des NT*, 2 vols., Stuttgart 1909; revised: *Geschichte des Christus*, [2]1923; *Theologie der Apostel*, 1922. P. Feine, *Theologie des NT*[8], Berlin 1950f. F. Buechsel, *Theologie des NT*[2], Stuttgart 1949. F. C. Grant, *An Introduction to the NT Thought*, New York (1950). M. Albertz, *Die Botschaft des NT* II: *Die Entfaltung der Bot-*

schaft, 1: *Die Voraussetzung der Botschaft. Der Inhalt der Botschaft. Die Gnade unseres Herrn Jesus Christus*, 1954 (see § 3, 1). R. Bultmann, *Theologie des NT²*, Tuebingen 1954. Cf. the critical reviews by H. Langenbeck (Gnomon 23, 1951, 1-15), P. Benoit (RB 1951, 252-257; 1952, 93-100; 1954, 432-435), N. A. Dahl (ThRdsch 22, 1954 21–46), and M. Barth (ThZ 11, 1955, 1–27).

15. Apocrypha

E. Hennecke, *Ntl Apokryphen²*, Tuebingen 1924. M. R. James, *The Apocryphal NT, being the apocryphal Gospels, Acts, Epistles and Apocalypses⁴*, Oxford 1950 C. C. Torrey, *The Apocryphal Literature. A brief Introduction*, New Haven 1946. W. Michaelis, *Die apokryphen Schriften vom NT* (in translation), 1956. — Cf. also the survey in B. Altaner, *Patrologie⁵*, Freiburg i. Br. 1958, 51–73, and especially E. Amann, Art. *Apocryphes du NT:* DBSuppl 1 (1928) 400–533.

W. Michaelis, *Die apokryphen Schriften zum NT,* translated and annotated, Bremen 1956 (Sammlung Dieterich, Vol. 129). E. Hennecke, *Neutestamentliche Apokryphen,* 3rd, completely revised edition edited by W. Schneemelcher, Tuebingen 1958.

PART I

THE CANON OF THE NEW TESTAMENT

The sources for the history of the Canon are the old catalogues of the Canon, various synodal decrees, MSS. of the Bible, and the writings of the Fathers; of particular importance is the *Ecclesiastical History* of Eusebius who (III 3) explicitly says that he will note specially which writings are recognized in all the individual churches, and which are disputed, cf. M. Mueller, *Die Ueberlieferung des Eusebius in seiner KG ueber die Schriften des NT und deren Verfasser*, ThStK 105 (1933) 425–455; E. Preuschen, *Analecta. Kuerzere Texte zur Geschichte der alten Kirche und des Kanons, II: Zur Kanongeschichte²*, Tuebingen 1910.
History of the NT Canon: Th. Zahn, *Geschichte des ntl Kanons*, vol. I (Erlangen 1888–1889): before Origen; vol. II (1890-1892): Urkunden und Belege zu Bd. III (vol. III never appeared). Idem, *Grundriss der Geschichte des ntl Kanons²*, Leipzig 1904. Joh. Leipoldt, *Geschichte des ntl Kanons* I (Die Entstehung), Leipzig 1907, II (Mittelalter und Neuzeit) 1908. E. Jacquier, *Le NT dans l'église chrétienne* I (Préparation, formation et définition du Canon du NT), Paris 1911. A. v. Harnack, *Die Entstehung des NT und die wichtigsten Folgen der neuen Schoepfung*, in: Beitraege zur Einleitung in das *NT* VI, Leipzig 1914. M.-J. Lagrange, *Histoire ancienne du canon du NT*, Paris 1933. S. Zarb, II *canone biblico*, Rome 1937. A. Souter, *Text and Canon of the NT*, rev. by C. S. C. Williams, London 1954. Th. Zahn, *Forschungen zur Geschichte des ntl Kanons und der altchristlichen Literatur* I–X (Leipzig 1881–1929). W. S. Reilly, *Le canon du NT et le critère de canonicité*: RB 30 (1921) 195–205. D. W. Riddle, *Factors in the Formation of the NT Canon*[9] JR 19 (1939) 330–345. G. de Rosa, *De apostolatu qua canonicitatis et inspirationis criterio animadversiones*: DivThomP 44 (1941) 53-64. Dewailly, *Canon du NT et histoire des dogmes*: RB 50 (1941) 78–93. H. Strathmann, *Die Krisis des Kanons der Kirche. Joh. Gerhards und Joh. Sal. Semlers Erbe*: ThBl 20 (1941) 295–310. E. W. Kamp, *Canonization and Authority in the Western Church*, London 1948. W. G. Kuemmel, *Notwendigkeit und Grenze des ntl Kanons*: ZThK 74 (1950) 277–313. W. C. van Unnik, *De la règle* μήτε προσθεῖναι μήτε ἀφελεῖν (Eusebius, H. E. V 16, 3): VCh 3 (1949) 1–36. J. Brinktrine, *Nach welchen Gesichtspunkten wurden die einzelnen Gruppen des ntl Kanons geordnet?*: BZ 24 (1938–1939) 125–135. H. Diem, *Das Problem des Schriftkanons*, Zurich 1952.

§ 4. DECREES OF THE COUNCILS OF TRENT AND THE VATICAN ON THE CANON

ON 8th April 1546 the council of Trent issued a decree *De canonicis Scripturis* in which it listed by name the books of both Testaments which the Catholic Church recognizes as canonical —27 books in the New Testament—and immediately solemnly decreed: *si quis autem libros ipsos integros cum omnibus suis partibus, prout in ecclesia catholica legi consueverunt et in veteri vulgata Latina editione habentur, pro sacris et canonicis non susceperit* . . ., *A. S.* According to the evidence of its minutes the council was merely repeating the catalogue of canonical books contained in the *Decretum pro Jacobitis* (i. e., Monophysites of Alexandria and Jerusalem) of the council of Florence, and in the bull of Eugene IV *Cantate Domino* of 4th Feb. 1442. The Vatican Council in its *Constitutio dogmatica de fide catholica* (3rd session on 24th April 1870) refers to the decree of Trent, repeats it, and adds the reason why the Church regards these writings as holy and canonical: *Eos vero Ecclesia pro sacris et canonicis habet, non ideo, quod sola humana industria concinnati, sua deinde auctoritate sint approbati; nec ideo dumtaxat, quod revelationem sine errore contineant; sed propterea, quod Spiritu Sancto inspirante conscripti Deum habent auctorem atque ut tales ipsi Ecclesiae traditae sunt.*

These decrees of the councils of Trent and the Vatican are infallible and irreformable decisions of the magisterium. On the other hand the decisions of different synods of antiquity on the extent of the Canon[1] have a merely disciplinary character, for they were not issued by general councils (cf. RB 1928, 276 n. 4). So for Catholics the decree of Trent is the end of the history of the Canon.

---

[1] The Greek word *canon* (ὁ κανών) means cane, or better rod, in a transferred sense a surveyor's staff, a measuring rule; then with reference to spiritual matters it meant a norm, an unerring measure for the discrimination of right and wrong, a rule of conduct in Ethics (cf. 2 Cor. 10, 13-15 sq., Gal. 6, 16). The word had also the meaning list or index in mathematics, astronomy, or historical writing.

In the Christian Church *canon* was used very early for ecclesiastical regulations. Thus 1 Clem. 7, 2 wishes that the Christians should live "according to the excellent and elevated rule of our tradition". Since the fourth century κανών or κανονικός has also referred to certain concrete things, e. g., the Scriptures, decrees of councils (canon law!), the unchanging part of the Liturgy of the Mass.

The use of the words *canon* and *canonical* in reference to the Scriptures is attested, for example, by Athanasius in his 39th Paschal letter of 367 A.D. (cf. § 7), where the divine writings entrusted to the Church are described as βιβλία κανονιζόμενα;

§ 5. THE EARLY HISTORY OF THE CANON

1. K. Benz, *Jesu Stellung zum atl Gesetz* (BSt XIX, 1 : 1914). J. Haenel, *Der Schrift-begriff Jesu,* Guetersloh 1919. B. H. Branscomb, *Jesus and the Law of Moses,* New York 1930. W. G. Kuemmel, *Jesus und der juedische Traditionsgedanke:* ZntW 33 (1934) 105 ff. A. Oepke, *Jesus und das AT,* Leipzig 1938. H. D. Wendland, *Geschichtsanschauung und Geschichtsbewusstsein im NT,* Goettingen 1938, 71–81. J. Hempel, *Der synoptische Jesus und das AT:* ZatW 15 (1938) 1–34. K. Pieper, *Die Stellung Jesu zu den religioesen Urkunden seines Volkes: Ntl Untersuchungen* (Paderborn 1939) 1–45. O. Michel, *Paulus und seine Bibel,* Guetersloh 1929. H. Windisch, *Paulus und das Judentum,* Stuttgart 1935. A. v. Harnack, *Das AT in den pl Briefen und Gemeinden:* SB Berlin 1928, XII, 124–141. W. Bauer, *Rechtglaeubigkeit und Ketzerei im aeltesten Christentum,* Tuebingen 1934 (pp. 198–230: Das AT, der Herr und die Apostel).
2. A. v. Harnack, *Ueber das Alter der Bezeichnung "die Buecher" fuer die heiligen Schriften der Christen:* ZB 45 (1928) 337–342. Idem, *Die Briefsammlung des Apostels Paulus* etc., Leipzig 1926 (against this: W. Bauer, *Rechtglaeubigkeit* etc. pp. 215 to 230). O. Cullmann, *Die Pluralitaet der Evv als theologisches Problem im Altertum:* ThZ 1 (1945) 25–42. C. H. Buck, *The Early Order of the Pauline Corpus:* JBL 68 (1949) 351–357. A. E. Barnett, *Paul becomes a literary Influence,* Chicago 1941 (before Irenaeus). R. M. Grant, *The Bible of Theophilus of Antioch:* JBL 66 (1947) 173–196. Ch. Maurer, *Ignatius v. A. und das Joh-Ev,* Zurich 1949. E. Massaux, *Influence de l'Évangile de St. Matthieu sur la littérature chrétienne avant St. Irénée,* Louvain 1950. C. L. Mitton, *The Formation of the Pauline Corpus Letters,* London 1955. K. L. Caroll, *The Expansion of the Pauline Corpus:* JBL 72 (1953) 230–237. [About 95 A.D. there was a collection of seven epistles; it was expanded by the addition of

---

concerning the *Pastor* of Hermas he says "it does not belong to the Canon" (*De decretis Nicaenae synodi* 18, 3). Amphilochius of Iconium at the end of the fourth century concludes his enumeration of the holy Scriptures with the words οὗτος ἀψευδέστατος κανὼν ἂν εἴη τῶν θεοπνεύστων γραφῶν. The Latins simply took over the word from Greek and spoke of *canon* (Jerome, Ep. 71, 5) and of *scripturae canonicae* (synod of Carthage of 397).

The word *canon* as used by the Greeks therefore primarily meant a catalogue or index, just as it did in profane Greek, though they were also conscious that it referred to normative writings, namely the authoritative documents of the Christian truth. The Latins on the other hand applied the word *canon* to something authoritative on matters of faith, so that for them *canon* and *canonical* in reference to the Bible denoted a finally established official collection of sacred (inspired) writings with absolutely binding authority.

H. W. Beyer, Art. κανών: ThWB III (1938) 600–608. H. Oppel, ΚΑΝΩΝ, *Zur Bedeutungsgeschichte des Wortes und seiner lateinischen Entsprechungen (regula–norma)* (Philologus, Suppl. XXX, 4) Leipzig 1937. L. Wenger, *Canon in den roemischen Rechtsquellen und den Papyri,* 1942 (SB Wien, vol. 200, pt. 2).

the Pastoral Epistles which are part of the anti-Marcionite movement; 1 and 2 Cor. and 1 and 2 Thess. were separated. Tatian is responsible for this expansion.] Idem, *The earliest NT:* BJRL 38 (1955) 45–57. [The deliberate creation of the Canon took place between 170 and 180, for the purpose of excluding the numerous Apocrypha which were appearing then.]

H. Radke, *Die Benutzung der Paulusbriefe durch Ignatius v. Antiochien,* Diss. Rostock 1956 (ThLZ 1957, 310–312). J. Finegan, *The Original Form of the Pauline Collection:* HarvThR 49 (1956) 85–103.

3. A. v. Harnack, *Marcion: Das Evangelium vom fremden Gott*[2], Leipzig 1924 D. de Bruyne, *Les plus anciens prologues latins des Évangiles:* RBén 40 (1928) 193 to 214. A. v. Harnack, *Die aeltesten Evv-Prologe und die Bildung des NT:* SB Berlin 1928, 322–341. R. M. Grant, *The oldest Gospel Prologues:* AThR 23 (1941) 231–245. E. Gutwenger, *The anti-Marcionite prologues:* ThSt 7 (1946) 393–409. A. v. Harnack, *Der marcionitische Ursprung der aeltesten Vulgata-Prologe zu den Paulusbriefen:* ZntW 24 (1925) 204–218. J. Knox, *Marcion and the NT. An Essay in the early History of the Canon,* Chicago 1942 (JThSt 44, 1943, 220–224). M. S. Enslin, *The Pontic Mouse:* AThR 27 (1945) 1–16. E. C. Blackmann, *Marcion and his Influence,* London 1948. R. G. Heard, *The old Gospel Prologues:* JThSt NS 6 (1955) 1–16. [Originally the four prologues were not joined together, and they were not all written at the same time. Probably the prologues to Mk., Lk., and John were composed in Greek.] G. Bardy, *Marcion:* DB Suppl. 5, fasc. 27 (1954), 862–877. Idem, *Marcionites* (prologues), ibid. 877–881. [There is no Marcionite element in the prologues to the Pastoral Epistles. It is probable, but not certain, that the prologues to the other Pauline Epistles are of Marcionite origin. The three oldest Latin prologues, to the Gospels of Mk., Lk., and John, were probably written in Rome at an early date, but they do not appear to be connected with one another, though they are anti-Marcionite.] H. J. Vogels, *Der Einfluss Marcions auf Text und Kanon des NT:* Synoptische Studien, Festschrift f. A. Wikenhauser, Munich 1953, 278–289.

1. Sources of Revelation in Primitive Christianity

FROM the first day of its existence the Christian Church possessed a Canon of sacred inspired writings—the Old Testament. Like every pious Jew, Jesus accepted the Old Testament as the word of God and appealed to it. He proves the indissolubility of marriage from Gen. 1, 27; 2, 24 (Mk. 10, 6 sq. par); the resurrection of the dead from Ex. 3, 26 (Mk. 12, 26 sq. par); the superiority of the Messias to David from Ps. 110, 1 (Mk. 12, 36 par). Yet he also takes an independent critical attitude to the Old Testament. As the eschatological Fulfiller he shows himself equipped with complete authority in regard to the Old Testament to decide what is really God's word and therefore eternal and unchangeable, and what has merely a temporary character; this is clearly shown, for example, by his position on the question of divorce (Mk. 10, 2 sq. par) and by the so-called antitheses of the Sermon on the Mount (Mt. 5, 21–48: "of old it was said to you... but I say to you"). He explains that he has come not to destroy but to fulfil the Law and the Prophets, that is, to bring them to completion (Mt. 5, 17); this statement, as well as demonstrating his deep respect for the Old Testament, shows at the same time that he is conscious of his vocation and duty as Messias to explain the true and most profound meaning of the Law, in other words that in a definite sense he stands above the Law. When he repeals certain of its prescriptions, for example those dealing with cleanliness, he regards that not as an attack on the Law, but as a setting aside of its imperfect and transient element. In the writings of the Old Testament he finds his coming, his work and his death foretold (cf. Lk. 4, 16 sqq.; 24, 24–27 44–46; John 5, 39).

As for Jesus, so for the primitive Church, the Old Testament had absolute authority. Just as he had argued from the Old Testament Scriptures, so the Apostles and early Christian preachers appealed to them to demonstrate the correctness of the Christian faith. The primitive Christian writings are full of such scriptural proofs (see especially Rom., Gal., Heb., and the discourses of St. Peter in Acts). Although St. Paul unvaryingly emphasizes that Christ is the end of the Law (i. e., of the way to salvation) (Rom. 10, 4), he has no thought of denying the authority of the Old Testament as Holy Scripture; but he takes a critical attitude to it in so far as he is convinced that only the Christians understand its true meaning correctly (cf. 2 Cor. 3, 6; 15–17; 1 Cor. 10, 11).

For primitive Christianity the Old Testament is essentially a foretelling of Christ and this prophecy has obtained its fulfilment in Jesus of Nazareth (cf. John 5, 39; Acts 17, 2 sq.; 2 Tim. 3, 15; Heb. 10, 1 etc.). It followed that it could be rightly interpreted only with reference to this fulfilment. This high regard of the primitive Church for the Old Testament is fundamentally due to the conviction that it is inspired and therefore is the word of God, as is explicitly said in 2 Pet. 1, 20 sq.: "Understanding this first: That no prophecy of scripture is made by private interpretation. For prophecy came not by the will of man at any time: but the holy men of God spoke inspired by the Holy Ghost." (Cf. 2 Tim. 3, 16, "all Scripture inspired of God".)

For the Apostolic Fathers also the Old Testament is authoritative in matters of religion, though there are notable variations in their use of it. Ignatius of Antioch treats it as Holy Scripture, but his letters contain only two explicit quotations from the book of Proverbs (*Eph.* 5, 2; *Magn.* 12) and a couple of allusions. In his eyes the Gospel, which is the flesh (the Incarnation) of Jesus Christ, is dominant, though he recommends "love of the Prophets because they foretold the Gospel and hoped for it, and awaited it" (*Philad.* 5, 2). The *Pastor* of Hermas shows absolutely no acquaintance with the Old Testament. On the other hand the first epistle of Clement, which was also composed in Rome forty years earlier, gives over one hundred long or short citations from the Old Testament and only two from the Gospels. For Clement God speaks to the Christians through the Old Testament. He continually reinforces his instructions, exhortations and orders by citations from Scripture, to which he gives an unquestionably Christian reinterpretation. The first and longer part of the epistle of Barnabas uses an allegorical and typical interpretation of the Old Testament to prove that the Jews have entirely misunderstood God's will and the Law of Moses, and that there never was an Old Covenant; the Christians were the first to understand the Old Testament correctly. If it had no authority in the eyes of the author and his readers, there would have been no need to reinterpret its content.

But the very fact that a Christian interpretation was given to it, and that it was retained only in this sense, shows that the really supreme authority was not this book (the Old Testament), but Christ, whose form, work and word they saw shining through it. The Apostles and their helpers and successors did not preach the Old Testament; they bore witness to Christ—the true Master and the risen heavenly Lord. They depicted before their hearers' eyes his work of redemption and Christ crucified (Gal. 3, 1), and they set his example and his words before them as a norm for their whole spiritual life. Even Paul, who had never known Jesus on earth, refers to his word as a norm which decides matters without further discussion (1 Cor. 7, 10; 9, 14; Acts 20, 35). So even at a relatively early date they began to record the words and deeds of Jesus (Lk. 1, 1–4). The need for such writings and their use in the Liturgy shows that the authority of the Lord had first place in the Christian communities, even though his words are not often quoted in the New Testament Epistles and the Apostolic Fathers. Thus, for example, Ignatius writes to the community at Smyrna (7, 2) that they beware of false teachers and "hold fast to the prophets and especially to the Gospels", and 1 Clem. 13, 1 urges the Christians "to be obedient to the words of the Lord Jesus which he spoke, teaching meekness and patience", whereupon he quotes further.

Next to the Lord comes the authority of the Apostles whom he called; they are authorized and equipped with the power of the Holy Ghost for preaching the Gospel and for establishing and directing the Christian community (Lk. 24, 49; Acts, 1, 4 sqq.). St. Paul explicitly declares that he has the Spirit of God (1 Cor. 7, 40; 14, 37 sq.) and has received revelations (Gal. 1, 15 sqq.; Rom. 11, 25; Eph. 3, 3 sq.). In the case of the original Apostles there is the additional factor that they were first-hand witnesses of the works of Jesus (Lk. 1, 2; Acts 1, 21 sq.; 10, 39). In the struggle against false teachers Jude 17 sq. and 2 Peter 3, 2 make express reference to the Apostles.

In the sub-apostolic age their authority became even greater. Ignatius exhorts the Magnesians to hold fast to the precepts of the Lord and of the Apostles (13, 1), and Polycarp sets before the Philippians the example of "Paul and the other Apostles" (9, 1; cf. 3, 2; 11, 2 sq.). Nevertheless the authority of the Apostles is not yet equated to the Lord's authority, and so they are invoked much less often. But as early as 200 A.D. Serapion of Antioch could explain: "We accept Peter and the other Apostles as we accept Christ" (Eusebius, H. E. VI 12, 3).

Thus the primitive Church possesses three authoritative sources of revelation—the Old Testament, the Lord, and the Apostles— but the finally decisive authority is Christ the Lord, who speaks directly through his word and work and indirectly through the testimony of his chosen witnesses. This situation was bound inevitably to lead to the establishment of a second Canon in addition to the Old Testament. At first, of course, the words of the Lord were preached and spread orally, but at a very early date they began to be committed to writing. With the steady expansion of the mission territory the Apostles found themselves compelled to substitute for oral preaching by sending letters to the individual Churches in order to instruct them on the important questions of Christian faith, to warn them against errors, and to give all sorts of directions. Naturally, these writings were regarded not as private letters but as official declarations, though a considerable time elapsed before they were accorded the same authority as the Old Testament.

In the mid second century the second epistle of Clement puts "the Apostles" on the same level as "the Books of the Prophets" (14, 2). But the more distant the apostolic age became and the weaker oral tradition became, the more frequent became appeals to these writings, in which the word of the Lord and of his Apostles was to be found. Yet when we recall that these writings of the apostolic age were mainly written to meet particular situations and were addressed to particular churches or limited areas, it is understandable that a considerable time had to elapse before they became a second canon of incontestable authority alongside the Old Testament. If, for example, the letters of Paul had been regarded as canonical from the beginning, it would be impossible to explain the loss of some of them (cf. 1 Cor. 5, 9 and § 36, 3). A Gospel of St. Mark which was considered canonical in the full sense would hardly have been copiously incorporated by Luke and the Greek redactor of Matthew, both of whom certainly intended to expand and improve on St. Mark. Even around 200 A.D. the composer of the Muratorian fragment (cf. § 6, 2) thought it necessary to point out that the Epistles of Paul and those of Apc. 2–3 were addressed to seven churches, and, therefore, were intended for the entire Church.

2. *The growth of the substance of the New Testament Canon*

The beginnings of the growth of the New Testament Canon are shrouded in deep darkness. But at least it is clear that there were at first two collections which provided the basis for the formation of the full Canon of 27 books—namely the collection of four Gospels and the *Corpus paulinum* of thirteen writings.

The four Gospels were written in the second half of the first century and were primarily intended for particular areas—Mt. for the Jewish-Christian communities in Syria and Palestine, Mk. for Rome (and Italy), and Lk. for Italy also (or perhaps for Achaea, cf. § 25, 6). But at an early date they circulated even outside their country of origin. Luke and the unknown redactor of Greek Matthew knew and used Mk. (cf. § 25, 4; 26, 6); the unknown composer of the longer conclusion of Mk. knew Mt., Lk. and John; John was published in Middle Egypt shortly after 100 A.D. as $\mathfrak{P}^{52}$ shows (cf. § 12, 3). Our four canonical Gospels were known to the author of an apocryphal Gospel which was published in Egypt not later than 150 A.D., papyrus fragments of which have recently been discovered.[1] Papias, bishop of Hierapolis in Phrygia (c. 130 A.D.) knew Mt. and Mk., and gives us the earliest account of their composition (cf. § 23, 2; 24, 2); and he also knew John (cf. § 28, 2). It is impossible to say with certainty when and where the four Gospels were united into a collection; Harnack thought that the collection and arrangement of four books of Gospels took place in Asia Minor in the reign of Hadrian (117–138). Justin Martyr (c. 165 A.D.) knew all four Gospels, though he does not mention them by their authors' names.

Before the mid second century, however, the four Gospels did not possess the full canonical authority of the Old Testament books. In the writings of the Apostolic Fathers there are only three cases of a saying of Our Lord being introduced by the formula which is used for citations from the Old Testament: Epistle of Barnabas 4, 14 ("as is written: Many are called, but few are chosen": Mt. 22, 14); 2 Clem. 2, 4 ("Another Scripture says: I am not come to call the just but sinners": Mt. 9, 13); 14, 1 ("If we do not the will of the Lord we are of that Scripture which says [i.e., of those of whom the Scripture says]: My house is become a den of thieves": Mk. 11, 17).[2] The words of Our Lord, precisely those which

[1] Pap. Egerton 2, published by H. J. Bell and T. C. Skeat, *Fragments of an unknown Gospel*, London 1935. On this see Schmidt and Jeremias ThBl 15 (1936) 34–45; Lagrange RB 44 (1935) 327–343; Lietzmann ZntW 34 (1935) 285–291; M. Goguel RHR 1936, 42–87; G. Mayeda, *Das Leben-Jesu-Fragment Pap. Eg. 2 und seine Stellung in der urchristlichen Literaturgeschichte*, Berne 1946 (on it H. J. Bell: HarvThR 42, 1949, 53–63).

[2] G. Kittel (*Der Jak. und die Apostolischen Vaeter*: ZntW 43, 1950–1951, 54 to 112) considers it practically certain that "as is written" in Barn. 4, 14 is intended to introduce a Biblical passage which the author thinks is from the OT (p. 99). On the other hand 2 Clem. (composed towards 150 A.D.) begins the "inclusion under a common Scripture citation" of the citation of Our Lord's words (p. 103). See also: *The NT in the Apostolic Fathers*, by a Committee of the Oxford Society of Historical Theology, Oxford 1905.

are in our four Gospels, are usually cited with the formula "the Lord says (has said)"; in other words it is not a scripture, a Gospel book, which is invoked as authority, but Our Lord himself. Furthermore in the *Didache* (8, 3; cf. 11, 3; 15, 3 4) and in the second Epistle of Clement (8, 5) we find the expression "the Lord says (has commanded) in His Gospel," which refers to an established written account of Jesus' life and work, but does not denote a definite written scripture (in 2 Clem. 8, 5 an apocryphal saying of Our Lord is quoted). This is consistent with the fact that, when words of Our Lord are quoted, the citation as a rule agrees in content but not in wording with the form in the Gospels. There are good examples of this in 1 Clem. 13, 1–2; 46, 7; Ep. of Polycarp 2, 3. Moreover, the Apostolic Fathers contain sayings of Our Lord which are not in our four Gospels, and so must derive either from oral Tradition or from apocrypha (Ignatius, Smyrn. 3, 2; 2 Clem. 4, 5; 5, 2–4; 8, 5; 12, 2). But since such sayings are relatively few, it cannot be doubted that only our four canonical Gospels were accepted in the Church from the beginning. Justin Martyr and the *Diatessaron* of Tatian (composed about 170 A.D.) also know and use Gospel traditions which are not in our four canonical Gospels (*Apol.* I 35, 6; Dial. 47. 49. 51. 78. 88, 3 8. 101). But Justin never cites them with the formula "the Scripture says".

No satisfactory answer has yet been given to the problem of the source of these sayings of Our Lord which Justin quotes, but which are missing from the Synoptics or appear there in much different wording. E. Lippelt (*Quae fuerint Justini M.* ἀπομνημο- νεύματα, Halle 1901), J. M. Heer (RQ 28, 1914, 97–186) and others uphold the thesis that Justin knew a liturgical book of Lessons which was composed from Mt., Mk. and an apocryphal source. On the other hand E. R. Buckley recently (JThS 1935, 173–176) attempted to show that he had a non-canonical Gospel from which he usually quoted the words of Our Lord because he had studied this instead of the Synoptics. A. Baumstark (Bb 16, 1935, 292 sq.) maintained the view that Justin had the Gospel of the Hebrews as well as the canonical Gospels.

Justin is the first witness to tell us that the Gospels were read in the Liturgy, and he attests this as a firmly established custom.

According to Apology I (67, 3)—composed about 155 A.D.—at liturgical assemblies they first read the "recollections" (ἀπομνημονεύματα) of the Apostles ("which are called Gospels," 66, 3) or the writings of the Old Testament Prophets, and this was followed by a sermon. He is aware that these recollections were written partly by Apostles and partly by their associates (*Dial.* 103, 8). St. John's Gospel does not figure prominently in Justin's work, he quotes from it only once (John 3, 35; Apol. I 61, 4 sq.). He speaks once of the Recollections of Peter, meaning the Gospel of St. Mark (*Dial.* 106, 3; cf. Mk. 3, 16 sq.). It is significant that he speaks of the Gospels in the plural—though in *Dial.* 100, 1 the old formula appears: "as is written in the Gospel", and in *Dial.* 10, 2 he says: "in the work called the Gospel"—unlike the Apostolic Fathers who spoke only of the Gospel in the singular. This shows that the books of the Gospels were assuming greater importance in the consciousness of the Church. Yet when Our Lord's words are quoted they are introduced not by the formula used for Old Testament citations: "the Scripture says", but by an expression like: "Our Lord says"; this shows that the authority of the written Gospels is not yet equal to that of the Person of Our Lord.

Tatian the Assyrian, a pupil of Justin's, according to Eusebius (H. E. IV 29, 6), composed a so-called Gospel Harmony about 170 A.D.; this was a continuous account of the works and teaching of Jesus composed from the Gospels which were available to him by omitting the parallel passages; in it he used our four canonical Gospels as well as some apocryphal material. Probably he composed the work in Rome before he left the Church. The name which he gave to his book: Τὸ διὰ τεσσάρων

(Diatessaron), was a musical term for harmony, but his Gospel Harmony presupposes the existence and authority of our four Gospels. St. Jerome tells us that Theophilus of Antioch († 186) composed a similar work[3]; but it is doubtful whether this work was a harmony of the Gospels, as Harnack and Lietzmann think, or simply a commentary on the four Gospels without a sharp division of the text of the individual Evangelists.

The collection of the Pauline Epistles took place earlier than the collection and arrangement of the four Gospels. It is highly probable that our *Corpus paulinum* with thirteen Epistles (omitting Hebrews) existed in the late first century or early second century in Greece, Asia Minor or Italy. When 2 Pet. 3, 15 sq. speaks of all the Epistles of the Apostle Paul, the reference is not to all the Epistles which we possess, but to all which were known to the writer and those to whom he wrote. So at the time when 2 Pet. was composed (cf. § 51, 6) a collection of Pauline Epistles was in existence, though we do not know its extent. Ignatius of Antioch certainly used 1 Cor., Rom., Eph., and Gal., and it is probable that he also used Col., 1 Tim., and 1 Thess.

The most important evidence concerning the time at which the Pauline Epistles were collected is Polycarp's letter to the community of Philippi. This letter is usually dated before the martyrdom of Ignatius (between 107 and 117 A.D.), but recently it has been split into two letters (I = cap. 13–14; II = cap. 1–12), and the second has been attributed to the fourth or fifth century. In the letter the author shows knowledge of all 13 Pauline Epistles except 1 Thess., Tit., and Philemon. He often incorporates passages from 1 Pet. and 1 Clem. into his own text, though he never treats them as authorities, but three times (chs. 3, 9, 11) he prefaces passages from Paul with the formula: "as Paul teaches", and more often (1, 4, 5, 9) he introduces him with the words: "you already

---

[3] Ep. 121 ad Hedibiam et Algasiam: *qui quattuor evangelistarum in unum opus dicta compingens ingenii sui nobis monumentum dimisit.*

know"; it follows from this that the Philippians also knew the collection of Epistles and acknowledged its doctrinal authority (Harnack). Probably the collection which Polycarp's epistle presupposes was made in Corinth; at any rate this would be the best explanation of the fact that the oldest discernible list of the Epistles began with 1 Cor., as we know from the Muratorian Canon (§ 6, 2), 1 Clem. 47, 2, and Tertullian.

Justin knows the following Epistles: Rom., 1 and 2 Cor., Gal., Eph., Phil., Col., 2 Thess., 1 Tim., Heb.; however, he never makes citations from them, but merely uses them without ever mentioning Paul's name.

The History of the Text throws light on the history of the Pauline collection. All the MSS. and text families go back to a single collection whose content was identical with our *Corpus paulinum*. In the earliest ages there were collections of the Pauline Epistles which varied considerably from one another in arrangement[4], but we have not the slightest reason to believe that in addition to the collection which we know there ever was another with a different number of Epistles. No one ever cites a word of Paul which is not in our collection of Epistles, though he wrote other Epistles which have not come down to us.

We have no evidence to suggest that any collection of other apostolic writings existed in the first half of the second century. Clement of Rome (36, 2) knows and uses Heb., Polycarp (7, 1; 10, 2) and Papias (Eusebius, H. E. III 39, 17) know and use 1 Pet. and 1 John; the latter also knew the Apocalypse of John (Frag. 5 Bihlmeyer).

It cannot be doubted that in the second century the Gospels, the Pauline Epistles and other writings from the apostolic age (Acts of the Apostles, Apocalypse, Epistles of other Apostles) were highly valued in the various churches, and were more

[4] Cf. Buck (supra) and Hatch (§ 46).

or less frequently read at divine worship. But the question remains at what point the primitive Church possessed, in addition to the Old Testament, a second corpus of holy inspired Scriptures to which it ascribed the same decisive authority, and which it cited in similar formal terms.

We can establish that the expression "Holy Scriptures of the Old and New Testament" was used around 170–180 A.D. Eusebius tells us (H. E. IV 26, 14) that Melito, bishop of Sardes, says in his work *Excerpts from the Law and the Prophets* that he had taken great care to determine exactly the books of the Old Testament (τὰ τῆς παλαιᾶς διαθήκης βιβλία); it follows that "books of the New Testament" must have been a familiar expression to him. The oldest evidence of the title "New Testament" being applied to the primitive Christian inspired writings appears in a book by an anonymous anti-Montanist in the year 192 A.D. (Eusebius, H. E. IV 16, 3). Yet some decades earlier 2 Clem. 14 juxtaposes "the Books and the Apostles", that is, the Old Testament and the authoritative Christian writings. So at that time both groups had not yet been included under a single name. Though not quite on a level with the Old Testament, the Apostolic writings are authoritative— but not precisely as writings, for he refers to "the Apostles".

The growth of the substance of the Canon, which was complete about 200 A.D., took place in two stages:

1. At first only the record of Our Lord's words, the Gospels, were equated to the Old Testament as a canonical authority in the full sense of the word. Justin cites only the Gospels as authoritative sources; in the *Dialogue with Tryphon* (48, 8) he explains: "Christ ordered us to follow not the doctrines of men, but the preaching of the blessed Apostles and of Christ himself." He introduces his numerous Gospel citations with the formula γέγραπται, and uses it also in one passage where he mentions not a saying of Our Lord but an observation of the Evangelist (*Dial.* 49, 5). About 180 A.D. Hegesippus, a Jewish Christian who travelled to

Rome by way of Corinth, writes: "In each city and succession the situation (in regard to the faith) is as the Law and the Prophets and the Lord command" (Eusebius, H. E. IV 22, 3). Since at this time the Apostle Paul had already an established position in Rome and Corinth beside the Old Testament and Our Lord, Hegesippus' statement may be understood in reference rather to the Jewish Christian communities of Palestine in his own time, or else he is describing the situation in Justin's time. The little community of Scillium in Numidia also lagged behind, for when their martyrs (in July 180 A.D.) were asked by the proconsul what they had in their satchel (capsa), they replied: "*libri et epistulae Pauli viri iusti*"; "books" referred to the Old Testament and the Gospels, for there were copies of the Gospels in every place which had the Pauline Epistles. Only the Old Testament and the Gospels were described as "the Books" (that is, the Holy Scripture, as in the prologue to Ecclus. and 2 Tim. 4, 13), and so they alone had the standing of decisive authorities of equal rank; the Pauline Epistles on the other hand had not yet this standing, although they were honoured as books read in the Liturgy.

It now becomes more frequent to preface Gospel citations with the formula which is usual for Old Testament texts. Tatian introduces John 1, 5 with the solemn formula "and this is written" (*Or. ad Graec.* 13, 1) and Athenagoras of Athens uses φησίν (it is said) to refer to Mk. 5, 28 and Proverbs 8, 22 (Suppl. 32, 1 sq.; 10, 3).

2. In the course of the second half of the second century other writings also gained the same full canonical standing as the Gospels, namely the Pauline Epistles, Acts, Apocalypse and two Catholic Epistles (1 John and 1 Pet.). In some circles the authority of the Pauline Epistles was weakened by the special favour which the Gnostics (Marcion, Valentinus and others) had for Paul. The Severians (Encratites) according to Eusebius (H. E. IV. 29, 5 6) used the Law, the Prophets, and the Gospels, but deprecated the Apostle Paul and rejected his Epistles and even Acts of the Apostles. On

the other hand the apologist Athenagoras of Athens when dealing with the resurrection refers to 1 Cor. 15, 53 and 2 Cor. 5, 10 with the solemn formula: δεῖ κατὰ τὸν ἀπόστολον (*De resurr.* 18, 22 sq.). Theophilus of Antioch (about 190 A.D.) knows and uses the thirteen Pauline Epistles; in his work we find the sentence (*Ad Autolyc.* 3, 13): "The divine Logos commands us to be subject to our superiors and to pray for them that we may be able to lead a quiet and peaceful life" (Tit. 3, 1; Tim. 2, 1 sq.; Rom. 13, 7 sq.). In the letter of the communities of Vienne and Lyons about the persecution which they had suffered, Apc. 22, 11 is cited as "Scripture" (Eusebius, H. E. V 1, 58).

3. *Marcion and his significance for the establishment of the Church's Canon*

When Marcion, a wealthy ship owner of Sinope in Pontus, came into conflict with his bishop at home because of his Gnostic ideas, he travelled through Asia Minor and visited the Church authorities there—Papias of Hierapolis in Phrygia and Polycarp of Smyrna. When they did not recognize his orthodoxy, he went to Rome and about 139 was received into the Roman Church; but by 144 A.D. he was out of communion with it. Marcion rejected the Old Testament as being from the Jewish Creator God, the avenging God of Justice; Christianity, on the other hand, he regarded as proclaiming the Father of Mercy and the God of all consolation; therefore only those scriptures should be acknowledged which originated from this God, the God of Jesus Christ, and proclaimed him. For Marcion, Paul was the only genuine envoy and preacher of the mission of Christ. According to Marcion the original Apostles had immediately contaminated Christ's teaching with Jewish admixtures. Against the Old Testament, which he rejected, Marcion set up a collection of sacred writings of early Christianity which consisted of one Gospel—by St. Paul's pupil Luke—and ten Pauline Epistles (the Pastoral Epistles were not included): he called this collection *Euangelion* and *Apostolos*. Although Marcion's collection of sacred writings had apparently no comprehensive title, yet it must be regarded as a coherent Canon, for it took the place of the Old Testament and therefore had the character of a Canon of Scripture, and it comprised a fixed number of books.

Marcion's action undoubtedly accelerated the process of fixing the Church's Canon, a process which had already begun. There is much to be said for the view that Marcion's act was the occasion of the Church acknowledging the highly esteemed apostolic writings as having the same authority as the four Gospels, and of their establishment as a second group beside the four Gospels. Furthermore the Church found itself obliged to take a stand in favour of those writings which the heretics rejected and excluded from their canon though the Church had recognized their authority. If a hypothesis which D. de Bruyne O.S.B. produced and A. v. Harnack developed, is correct—and it is well founded—the Roman Church between 160 and 180 A.D. took the following measures against Marcion:

1. For each of the four Gospels which it recognized it produced a prologue which it prefixed to the particular Gospel—only the prologues to Mk., Lk., and John have survived.

2. It took over the prologues to the ten Pauline Epistles which Marcion or one of his followers had composed.

3. It produced prologues for the three Pastoral Epistles which it also recognized.

4. In the longest of the Gospel prologues, the prologue to Luke, it accepted explicitly Acts of the Apostles as a work of Luke, and Apocalypse as a work of John the Apostle. In regard to both these books we know that Marcion had explicitly rejected them.

§ 6. THE CANON OF THE WESTERN CHURCH AROUND 200 A.D.

1. J. Hoh, *Die Lehre des hl. Irenaeus ueber das NT* (NtA VII, 4/5: 1919). W. Sanday, C. H. Turner, A. Souter, *Novum Testamentum S. Irenaei Ep. Lugdunensis,* Oxford 1923 (Old-Latin Biblical Texts VII). W. L. Dulière, *Le canon néotestamentaire et les écrits chrétiens approuvés par Irénée:* Nouvelle Clio 6 (1954) 199–229.
2. Th. Zahn, *Hippolyt als Verfasser des Muratorischen Kanons:* Forschungen X (1929) 58–75 (= NkZ 33 [1922] 417 sqq.). A. v. Harnack, *Ueber den Verfasser und den literarischen Charakter des Murator. Fragments:* ZntW 24 (1925) 1–16 (against this H. Koch, ibid. 25, 1926, 154–160); 25 (1926) 160–163. A. A. T. Ehrhardt, *The Gospels in the Muratorian Fragment:* Ostkirchl. Studien (Wuerzburg 1953) 121–138. G. Bardy, *Muratori (Canon de):* DB Suppl V, 1399–1408.
3. Lagrange, *Le canon d'Hippolyte et le fragment de Muratori:* RB 42 (1933) 161–186.

1. *The evidence of Irenaeus for Southern Gaul*

IRENAEUS was born in Asia Minor and at the time of Marcus Aurelius' (161–180) persecution was a priest of the church of Lyons; in 177–178 he was sent to Rome with a letter from the clergy of Lyons and Vienne to Pope Eleutherus, and on his return was chosen bishop of Lyons. His principal work *Against Heresies* was composed between 180 and 190 A.D.

He acknowledges the following 21 (22) scriptures as canonical:

1. The four Gospels.
2. Acts of the Apostles by Luke.
3. The Epistles of Paul (except Philemon which he never cites), but he includes them among the *Scripturae* only in III 12, 12.
4. Of the Catholic Epistles 1 Pet. and 1 and 2 John; not Jas.: it is uncertain about the others.
5. The Apocalypse of John, the disciple of the Lord.

He knew Hebrews, but never formally quoted from it and, according to a later account, he did not admit its Pauline origin. The fact that he does not quote Philemon must be due to its slight content. He introduces the *Pastor* of Hermas with the formula "scripture says" (cf. Tertullian). He does not use the name New Testament for the Christian canonical writings, but describes them as "the evangelical and apostolic writings".

According to Irenaeus (III 11, 8) the number of the Gospels is four, not because of an accidental historical development, but because of the significance of the number *four* in the order of creation and salvation (four directions and four chief winds, four beasts in Ez. 1, 10 and Apc. 4, 7; four compacts of God with mankind). Since God does everything by measure and number, there can be neither more nor less than four Gospels; and therefore it is lawful neither to add another (the "Gospel of truth") nor to confine oneself to one of them like the Ebionites (Mt.), Marcion (Lk.), Cerinthus (Mk.), or the Valentinians (John).

2. The Canon of the Fragmentum Muratorianum (Rome)

This document, which is in a fragmentary condition, was discovered by the Italian historian L. A. Muratori in the Ambrosian Library at Milan, and was published by him in 1740. It is in a MS. of the 7th or 8th century from the monastery at Bobbio. Composed towards the end of the second century, it is the oldest ecclesiastical document about the New Testament Canon, if we except the anti-Marcionite prologues to the Gospels. The document probably began with the Old Testament Canon. It is written in barbarous Latin and is in bad condition. A number of scholars consider it a translation from Greek, but this cannot be proved.

The fragment not only contains a list or enumeration of the books which are recognized as canonical, as do the other lists of the Canon from Christian antiquity, but it also gives particulars about the author, destination, occasion and purpose of the works which it lists, and rejects certain writings as uncanonical or heretical. It could be described as a kind of Introduction to the New Testament, but evidently it is an authoritative document and not merely a private didactic work. Where there are doubts or uncertainties the fragment justifies at greater or lesser length the decision of the church or churches (in whose name the author writes) on the canonicity of the particular part in question. Thus concerning two spurious Pauline Epistles which were in circulation he says that they cannot be accepted (lines 63–66) by the "Catholic Church" *(ecclesia catholica);* and of the *Pastor* of Hermas he says that it may be read, but not publicly to the people in church. So the author speaks not as a private person, but in the name of a Church, and is conscious that he is upholding the doctrine of the Catholic Church, especially in opposition to the heretics.

Unfortunately the author, place and time of composition of this important document are unknown. But it may be said with fair certainty that it was composed towards the end of the second century either in Rome or else in a church closely connected with Rome, for the author says of the *Pastor* of Hermas that "it was composed shortly before our time in Rome by Hermas when bishop Pius, his brother, sat in the see of the city of Rome" (lines 74–77). Pope Pius reigned from 142 to 154 A.D.

The Muratorian Canon admits 22 (23) writings to the New Testament, viz.:

1. The four Gospels in the order Mt., Mk., Lk., John. The last is ascribed to the Apostle John *(discipulus* = one of the twelve Apostles).

2. Acts of the Apostles by Luke.

3. 13 Epistles by Paul. Like John (Apc. 2–3) he wrote to seven churches: Corinthians, Ephesians, Philippians, Colossians, Galatians, Thessalonians, and Romans; but in reality these Epistles are addressed to the Church throughout the entire world. He also wrote one Epistle to Philemon, one to Titus and two to Timothy.

4. Three Catholic Epistles, one of Jude and two of John (including 1 John, for its exordium is quoted in lines 29–31).

5. The Apocalypse of John and the Apocalypse of Peter, "which last, however, some of our people do not wish to be read in church".

Hebrews is missing; it was not included in the Canon of the Western Church until c. 370–380 A.D., although it was known and used (cf. § 46, 2). It is surprising however that 1 Pet. is missing, for it was acknowledged as canonical by Irenaeus, Tertullian, Clement of Alexandria and Hippolytus; we may surmise that its absence is due to the scribe's private opinion. The Apocalypse of Peter was also acknowledged as Holy Scripture in various other places of the West, for example, in the catalogue of the Canon in Codex Claromontanus (§ 7, 1). The lengthy argument against accepting the *Pastor* of Hermas (lines 73–80) presupposes that in the author's milieu this mid-second century work was seriously competing with the recognized canonical scriptures. This is not an isolated phenomenon, as is shown by the position which the *Pastor* occupies in Irenaeus, Tertullian and Clement of Alexandria.

The authorship and time and place of composition of the Muratorian Canon are still a subject of keen discussion. Many scholars regard it as a work of Hippolytus, the most important writer of the Roman Church around 200 A.D., who later became anti-pope against Callistus. Thus Th. Zahn tried to show that it is a youthful work of Hippolytus of about 190 A.D. and is one of the *Odes on all the scriptures* which are attributed to him on the well-known statue in the Lateran Museum in Rome; since the Roman priest Gaius attacked the Gospel and Apocalypse of John under Pope Zephyrinus (198–217) and the fragment makes no mention of this, Zahn argued that it must have been composed earlier. Against this it is pointed out that Zahn's reading of the doubtful words on the statue of Hippolytus does not tally with the fact that this document is no private work but has an authoritative character (Harnack), and the attack of Gaius on the Johannine writings does find an echo in it (Lagrange). For this reason Lagrange suggested that Hippolytus composed the document as anti-pope (after 217 A.D.). The close literary relation between the fragment and Hippolytus' writings would support this suggestion, although these unquestionable relationships do not amount to proof; the picture of the Canon which we get from the writings of Hippolytus does not entirely correspond to that of the fragment. One can only say that Hippolytus' authorship is a serious possibility, but that it has not been proved conclusively. Harnack favours Pope Victor (189–199) or Zephyrinus (199–217) as the author, and considers the fragment an official document for the direction and guidance of all Christendom.

3. Hippolytus of Rome († 235)

Hippolytus was a pupil of Irenaeus, and after 217 A.D., on his election as anti-pope against Callistus, was head of a schismatic sect. He was an exceptionally profilic writer; many of his works (he wrote in Greek) have perished, and some are preserved only in translations. Hippolytus knows that there are two testaments; he calls them "the breasts of Christ" and thereby puts the Old Testament under the lordship of Christ. When he mentions them separately he calls the Old Testament "the Prophets" and the New "the Apostles" (*In Dan.* IV 12, 1). His New Testament includes at least 21 writings, viz.:

1. the four Gospels, 2. Acts of the Apostles, 3. 12 Epistles of Paul (Philemon is missing probably only by accident), 4. 3 Catholic Epistles: 1 and 2 Pet. and 1 John, 5. Apocalypse of John.

He uses Hebrews without mentioning its name, but regards it as not Pauline and therefore uncanonical; according to Dionysius bar Salibi († 1171) he maintained that Clement of Rome wrote it. Lagrange and Meinertz think that he quoted from James, but this is disputed by Arnold Meyer (cf. § 47, 2). He also knows apocryphal writings (certainly the Acts of Paul and probably also the Apocalypse of Peter) and also the *Pastor* of Hermas and the epistle of Barnabas, but they have no importance in his writings.

4. Tertullian's evidence for Africa

Tertullian has a completely clear idea of the Canon. According to him the New Testament may be divided into the evangelical and apostolic "instrument" (*evangelicum et apostolicum instrumentum: Adv. Marc.* IV, 2 sqq.; *De pudic.* XII), as he likes to say instead of testament. The only canonical writings are those of the early Church which were composed by the Apostles or, under their authority, by their disciples (Mk., Lk.).

The New Testament of Tertullian, which is also that of the African Church, contains 22 writings. They are: 1. the four Gospels (like the Muratorian Canon he knows nothing of apocryphal Gospels), 2. Acts of the Apostles, 3. 13 Pauline Epistles, 4. the Catholic Epistles 1 Pet., 1 John, Jude, 5. Apocalypse of John.

He regards Hebrews as an epistle of Barnabas; while he does not include it in the Canon, he says (as a Montanist) that it is more widely received by the churches *(receptior apud ecclesias)* than the apocryphal *Pastor* of Hermas, and he cites 6, 4–8 (*De pudic.* XX). Yet in his Catholic period he attributed to the *Pastor* a certain authority in matters of discipline (*De orat.* XVI).

5. Synthesis of the results

The Western Church around 200 A.D. possessed a collection of sacred writings from the apostolic age which not only were read at divine worship, but also were recognized as authoritative and stood on the same footing as the Old Testament.

This collection was the foundation of our present Canon of 27 books and it contained the majority of the canonical books, that is, the four Gospels, Acts, 13 Epistles of Paul, at least two Catholic Epistles (1 Pet. and 1 John), and the Apocalypse of John—so, at a conservative reckoning, 21 writings.

There was no unanimity about the number of the so-called Catholic Epistles. 1 John and 1 Pet. were universally accepted;

41

Irenaeus and the Muratorian Canon know also a second Epistle of John; we have no information about 3 John. Jude is attested by Tertullian and the Muratorian Canon; Hippolytus quotes from 2 Pet. James was in circulation from 90 till 150 A.D.; thereafter we scarcely find a trace of it; yet it must have been known, for we have an Old-Latin version of it (Codex Corbeiensis), but it was not accepted as canonical in the west until 350 A.D.

The New Testament at this time is not a closed collection. The Church is still prepared to accept apostolic writings into her Canon if such are presented to her (Muratorian Canon, lines 77–80). Only the Gospel part of the Canon is closed.

In the West this remained the position until the mid-fourth century. Cyprian of Carthage († 258) never quotes from Hebrews and of the Catholic Epistles he cites only 1 Peter and 1 John. The Canon Mommsenianus, so called from its editor, is a North African catalogue of the books of both Testaments, written about 360 A.D.; in the New Testament it enumerates the four Gospels, 13 Epistles of Paul, Acts, Apocalypse, 3 Epistles of John and 2 of Peter; so Heb., Jas. and Jude are missing, and in one of the two MSS. which contain this Canon the comment *una sola* appears after the mention of the Epistles of John and Peter; so evidently the writer of this intended to describe only 1 John and 1 Peter as canonical.

After the mid-fourth century the West quickly drew level with the more advanced East (see § 8).

§ 7. THE CANON OF THE GREEK CHURCH FROM CLEMENT OF ALEXANDRIA († AFTER 217) TO THE FINAL ESTABLISHMENT OF THE CANON IN THE EAST

P. Dausch, *Der ntl Schriftcanon und Clemens von Alexandrien*, Freiburg i. Br. 1894. J. Ruwet, *Clément d'Alexandrie: Canon des Écritures et Apocryphes:* Bb 29 (1948) 77–99; 240–268; 391–408. Idem, *Les antilegomena dans les oeuvres d'Origène:* ibid. 23 (1942) 18–42. Idem, *Le canon Alexandrin des Écritures. S. Athanase:* ibid. 33 (1952) 1–29. M. Mueller, *Die Ueberlieferung des Eusebius etc.* (see bibliography at § 4). Chr. Baur, *Der Canon des hl. Chrysostomus:* ThQ 105 (1924) 258–271.

1. *Egypt and Palestine*

DEEP darkness surrounds the history of the Canon in the East before the time of Clement of Alexandria. The earliest writers of the Greek Church whose writings have come down to us in considerable volume and content are Clement and Origen. In their time the Egyptian Church had still no firmly defined Canon. It possessed and used all the 27 books of our Canon, but in addition to these it also used a large number of others to which it attributed a high degree of authority. Athanasius was the first to delimit the Canon strictly.

Clement knows and uses all our 27 New Testament books with the possible exception of 3 Catholic Epistles (Jas., 2 Pet., 3 John); the fact that he does not quote from the short Epistle to Philemon has no significance. The *Hypotyposes* of Clement was a short commentary on the whole Scripture, which has survived only in fragments. Eusebius (H. E. VI 14, 1) tells us that in it he commented on all the Catholic Epistles "without passing over in silence those books which are disputed, that is, Jude and the other Catholic Epistles, the epistle of Barnabas, and the book which is called the Apocalypse of Peter". A number of scholars consider that Eusebius expressed himself loosely or that he is mistaken (cf. Ruwet), for in the extensive writings of Clement which have survived only 1 Pet., 1 and 2 John, and Jude are used, and Cassiodorus in his *Adumbrationes Clementis Al. in epistolas canonicas* translated into Latin only the commentary on 1 Pet., Jude and 1 and 2 John (cf. his *Institutio div. litter.* c. VIII). Clement thought that Heb. was composed by Paul in Hebrew, and translated into Greek by Luke (cf. § 46, 2).

But in addition to these books Clement also quoted from a number of primitive and early Christian writings, some of which he regarded as inspired. In the *Hypotyposes* he commented on the epistle of Barnabas, whose author he identified with Barnabas, the companion of St. Paul, and on the Apocalypse of Peter. In his eyes the *Didache, Pastor* of Hermas, *Kerygma of Peter,* and probably the first epistle of Clement are inspired writings, but that does not apply to the Gospel of the Egyptians, the Gospel of the Hebrews, and the Traditions of Matthias. So he does not yet recognize a strict distinction between canonical and uncanonical. Nevertheless he says explicitly that the Church accepts only four Gospels. Referring to a citation from the Gospel of the Egyptians he says: "We have this word not in the four Gospels which are handed down to us, but in the Gospel of the Egyptians." (*Strom.* III 93, 1).

Origen (185–255), who followed Clement as head of the catechetical school at Alexandria, enumerates the New Testament writers in his seventh homily on the Book of Josue. He recognizes the following books as canonical: the four Gospels of Mt., Mk., Lk. and John; 2 Epistles of Peter; James, Jude; Epistles of John (no number mentioned); Acts of the Apostles by Luke, and 14 Epistles of Paul. The absence of the Apocalypse of John from this list is perhaps due to textual corruption or to the fact that this homily was delivered in Caesarea in Palestine; at any rate he accepts it in his commentary on John.

Since Origen is certainly repeating the view of the Egyptian Church and not merely his own personal opinion, it follows that the Egyptian Church at that time recognized the whole 27 New Testament writings as canonical, though its Canon was certainly not yet firmly marked out. Like Clement, he acknowledges a certain authority and inspiration in some other writings. He did not regard the Gospel of the Hebrews as canonical, but equally he did not reject it; he occasionally cites from it an (alleged) saying of Our Lord with the comment: "if one will accept it" (*Com. in Joh.* II 6). Furthermore he regards the *Pastor* of Hermas, the epistle of Barnabas and the *Didache* as inspired. He quotes on a few occasions from the first epistle of Clement, the Acts of Paul, and Doctrina Petri, but he did not regard them as inspired.

This great scholar and much-travelled man was aware of the difference between writings which were universally accepted as canonical and those which were still a subject of controversy. He knows that not all churches accept Hebrews as Pauline (apud Euseb. H. E. VI 25, 13, quotation from a homily on Hebrews): "Peter left only one universally accepted Epistle (μίαν ἐπιστολὴν ὁμολογουμένην); it may be that he left a second; it is specially disputed (ἀμφιβάλλεται)". In addition to the Gospel and Apocalypse, John, the beloved disciple left "also an Epistle of very few lines, and perhaps a second and third Epistle; these two are not universally recognized as authentic" (apud Euseb. H. E. VI 25, 10, quotation from Book V of the *Commentary on John*). He speaks of Jude with the reservation, "if one accepts the Epistle of Jude" (*Commentary on Mt.* XVII n. 30). He also lets us see that Jas. is not universally accepted.

In the Greek-Latin sixth century Codex D (Claromontanus) of the Pauline Epistles, between the text of Philemon and Hebrews, is a catalogue of the books of the Old and New Testaments with information about the number of *stichoi;* this is called Canon Claromontanus, and it contains all seven Catholic Epistles as well as the epistle of Barnabas, Apocalypse of John, Acts of the Apostles, *Pastor* of Hermas, Acts of Paul and Apocalypse of Peter. The four uncanonical books are marked with a horizontal stroke, which must indicate that these books are not accepted as Holy Scriptures by the writer of the MS. or in the ecclesiastical practice of his district. The catalogue was probably drawn up in Egypt in the third century.

When a certain Nepos, bishop of the Arsinoe district in the Fayum, appealed to the Apocalypse of John in support of his chiliast doctrines, expounded them in a book and found many followers, Dionysius of Alexandria († 264) composed against him a book *Concerning the promises* (at some time between 253 and 257) in which he explained that he did not wish to reject the Apocalypse since many brethren valued it highly; he would admit that it is the work of a holy and divinely inspired man, but could not agree that it was composed by the Apostle John (apud Euseb. H. E. VII 24–25). His vigorous denial of the apostolic origin of the book did the Apocalypse hardly any harm in Egypt, but it did have effect in the Church of Palestine, Syria, and Asia Minor.

Eusebius, bishop of Caesarea in Palestine († c. 340 A.D.), is of importance, not so much for his evidence about the Canon of the Palestinian Church, as because of the copious information which his Church History contains about the state of the Canon in each province of the Church. In III 25 he gives a comprehensive survey of all the writings which call for notice in the History of the New Testament Canon. He divides them into the following groups:

1. *Homologoumena* (those about whose canonicity there is unanimity) namely "the holy fourfold number of the Gospels", Acts of the Apostles, the Epistles of Paul, first Epistle of John (cf. also III 3, 4) and the first Epistle of Peter (also cf. III 24, 17); "to these may be added, if one wishes, the Apocalypse of John, about which there are different opinions". Eusebius expresses himself more accurately in III 3, 5 about the Epistles of Paul: "Definitely and certainly the fourteen Epistles are by Paul; but it must be noted that some have opposed the Epistle to the Hebrews, appealing to the Roman Church which does not acknowledge it as Pauline."

2. *Antilegomena* (those whose canonicity is challenged). He subdivides these into two groups: a) the *antilegomena* which are acknowledged (γνώριμα) by the majority, "the so-called Epistle of James, the Epistle of Jude, the second Epistle of Peter, and the so-called second and third Epistles of John which were written either by the Evangelist or by another John"—making five Catholic Epistles; the spuriousness of this group is not maintained. Else-

where he remarks (II 23, 24 sq.) "The first of the so-called Catholic Epistles is supposed to have been composed by James the brother of the Lord. But it is to be noted that it should be considered spurious, for not many of the ancients mention it or the so-called Epistle of Jude, which is also one of the seven so-called Catholic Epistles. Yet we know that these have been publicly read in most churches just like the others." Cf. also III 3, 1–2 on 2 Pet. and the apocryphal Petrine writings.

b) In the second sub-division, which he describes as spurious (νόθα) writings, he enumerates the Acts of Paul (cf. also III 3, 5), the *Pastor* of Hermas (cf. also III 3, 6), the Apocalypse of Peter, the Epistle of Barnabas, the Doctrine of the Apostles (*Didache*), and also, according to some, the Apocalypse of John, which, as was mentioned, some reject and others include under the *homologoumena*. The Gospel of the Hebrews is also included here by many.

3. Heretical writings, which are not merely to be considered "spurious writings", but are to be utterly rejected. They are the apocryphal Gospels (of Peter, Thomas, Matthias and other Apostles) and Acts of Andrew, John and other Apostles. "No ecclesiastical writer who is recognized in tradition has deemed these writings worthy of the slightest notice."

Eusebius' classification is very interesting. The *homologoumena* coincide—except for Hebrews—with the writings which were universally recognized in the West around 200 A.D. They and the first group of *antilegomena* make up the collection of 27 writings of the complete Canon. Eusebius' personal inclination to include the Apocalypse with the spurious writings is due to the influence of Dionysius of Alexandria.

Cyril of Jerusalem (315–386) informs us about the extent of the Canon of the Palestinian Church. In the fourth of his catechetical instructions of the year 348 he says: "Of the New Testament (read) only the four Gospels; the others are spurious and harmful . . . Take also the Acts of the twelve Apostles, the seven Catholic Epistles of James and Peter and John and Jude, and finally . . . the 14 Epistles of Paul." Only the Apocalypse of John is missing from this list. Jerome testifies that even in his time it was not accepted as canonical in Palestine (*Tract. in Psalmos:* Anecd. Mareds. III 2, 5).

Egypt was the first province of the Church to have a fixed and definite Canon; it appeared in 367 A.D. in the 39th Paschal letter of the patriarch Athanasius of Alexandria. In this letter he enumerated in the canonical writings of both Testaments; in the New Testament they are the following and in this order: the four Gospels of Mt., Mk., Lk., John; Acts of the Apostles; the seven so-called Catholic Epistles of the Apostles: by James 1, by Peter 2, by John 3, and by Jude 1; in addition 14 Epistles of Paul in the following order: Romans, 1 and 2 Corinthians, Galatians, Ephesians, Philippians, Colossians, 1 and 2 Thessalonians, Hebrews, 1 and 2 Timothy, Titus and finally Philemon; also the Apocalypse of John. After this list Athanasius adds: "These are the sources of salvation, for here the thirsty may make rich use of the words to be found in them; in these alone is the doctrine of piety recorded. No one must add or take away anything from them." (Cf. Apc. 22, 18.) Athanasius is the first to list the 27 books of our New Testament as the only canonical ones. But in order not to break entirely with the tradition of the Alexandrian Church, he expressly permits the use of the *Didache* and *Pastor* of Hermas for the instruction of catechumens.

2. Syria (Antioch) and Asia Minor

In the fourth century, and even well into the fifth century, the Church of Antioch on the Orontes acknowledged as canonical only the three major Catholic Epistles (James, 1 Peter and 1 John), and also rejected the Apocalypse. This attitude to the New Testament Canon mirrors the work of the Antioch school of exegetes whose founder was Lucian of Antioch (martyred in 312). He was born in Samosata (north of Edessa), was educated in Edessa and then settled in Antioch. Unfortunately, Eusebius does not tell us which books Lucian recognized as canonical, but it cannot be doubted that he rejected both the Apocalypse and the four minor Catholic Epistles. John Chrysostom accepted only James, 1 Peter and 1 John, and never quotes from the Apocalypse. Severian of Gabala (near Laodicea in Syria, † after 408 A.D.) also rejected the four minor Epistles. Both they and the Apocalypse are missing from the Peshitta.

Other Antiochenes were Diodorus of Tarsus († before 394) and Polychronius (brother of Theodore of Mopsuestia), bishop of Apamea in Syria († between 428 and 431). Diodorus wrote a commentary on 1 John and treated 1 Peter as Holy Scripture. Polychronius used James, and Nestorius used 1 Peter as canonical scripture. Amphilochius of Iconium, the friend of the great Cappadocians, in his didactic poem *Iambi ad Seleucum,* puts the Canon with the three Epistles on the same footing as the Canon with seven, and testifies that the Apocalypse was generally but not universally rejected. From Jerome we learn that the Church in Phoenicia also admitted the Apocalypse to the Canon (*Tract. in Psalmos:* Anecd. Mareds. III 2, 5). The Apostolic Constitutions, compiled in Syria by an unknown Apollinarist around the beginning of the fifth century, when listing (II 57, 7) the Sacred Scriptures to be read at divine worship, name only Acts of the Apostles, the Epistles of Paul and the four Gospels. On the other hand Apollinaris of Laodicea († before 392) accepts the three major Catholic Epistles.

In the course of the fifth century the Syrian theologians followed the example of other provinces of the Church and accepted all seven Catholic Epistles as canonical. The oldest evidence for this is in the Apostolic Canons, a later addition to the eighth book of the Apostolic Constitutions. The 85th Canon includes the seven

Catholic Epistles in the New Testament Canon, but not the Apocalypse. But these books were little used or cited, and even in the sixth century were in various ways regarded as second rank authorities.

Our information about the Church of Asia Minor is defective. Eusebius tells us (H. E. V 18, 14) that Apollonius of Asia Minor in his work against the Cataphrygian heresy, composed about 200 A.D., used the Apocalypse of John. Firmilian of Caesarea in Cappadocia refers to 1 Pet. 3, 2 in his letter to Cyprian of Carthage in 256 A.D. (apud Cyprian. Ep. 75, 6). Methodius of Olympus in Syria, who was martyred in 311 A.D., regarded all 27 books as canonical, and of the Catholic Epistles certainly used James, 1 Pet., 1 John and Jude. He attributed the Apocalypse to John.

In the fourth century the seven Catholic Epistles were fairly generally accepted. Canon 60 of the council of Laodicea in Phrygia, which is usually dated 363 A.D., enumerates the canonical books of the New Testament one by one; only the Apocalypse is missing; but this Canon is often regarded as a later interpolation. Of the great Cappadocians, Basil († 379) accepted the Apocalypse; we cannot establish the extent of his Canon. Gregory of Nazianzus († c. 390) has left a verse catalogue of the New Testament books, from which only the Apocalypse is missing. Gregory of Nyssa († after 394) also knows and uses the Apocalypse of John. Amphilochius of Iconium has already been mentioned. Epiphanius of Salamis († 403) includes both the Apocalypse of John and the seven Catholic Epistles in his Canon.

Only in the early sixth century did the Apocalypse of John regain its place in the Canon of the Church of Palestine and Antioch; but it did not succeed in obtaining the same authority as in the West. About 530 A.D. Leontius of Byzantium († c. 543) in his lectures, which he gave in a monastery near Jerusalem, described the Apocalypse as the last book of the New Testament Canon (*De sectis actio* II, 4); but it is probable that this work is not by him; its author may have been the priest monk Theodorus of Raithu in the Sinai peninsula, who lived in the first half of the sixth century (Altaner). About 580 A.D. Eustratius, a priest of Constantinople, treats the Apocalypse as a work of the Apostle John and as canonical Scripture. At this time the Greek Church also began to produce commentaries on the Apocalypse; they were composed by the Monophysite Oecumenius in the first half of the sixth century and by two archbishops of Caesarea in Cappadocia—Andrew (between 563 and 614), and Arethas (about 900 A.D.). Cf. also § 54, 3.

§ 8. THE FINAL FIXING OF THE CANON IN THE LATIN CHURCH (c. 400 A.D.)

L. Schade, *Die Inspirationslehre des hl. Hieronymus* (BSt XV, 4–5: 1910). E. v. Dobschuetz, *Das Decretum Gelasianum de libris recipiendis et non recipiendis im kritischen Text herausgegeben und untersucht* (TU 3. R. VIII, 4: 1912). E. Schwartz, *Zum Decretum Gelasianum:* ZntW 29, 1930, 161–168. G. Bardy, *Décret de Gélase:* DB Suppl III (138) 579–590. M. Stenzel, *Der Bibelkanon des Rufin von Aquileja:* Bb 23 (1942) 43–61.

IN the Western Church the mid fourth century is a landmark in the History of the Canon; it is the time when the West drew level with the East. The Arian struggle which occupied almost the whole century, resulted in a closer contact and a more intensive exchange of ideas between East and West. The numerous synods which were held brought eastern and western bishops together; various spokesmen in the dogmatic struggles remained for longish periods in foreign lands, either voluntarily or of necessity—as examples we may recall Athanasius who lived in Treves (336–337), Rome (340–343) and other cities of the West, and Hilary of Poitiers who lived in Asia Minor from 356 till 360. Pilgrimages to the Holy Places of Palestine began at this time; this was also the period when the fashion of translating Greek Fathers into Latin began; Jerome and Rufinus in particular devoted themselves to making the Latin Church familiar with the greater riches of Greek theological literature. No one was better qualified for this task than Jerome, who lived for various periods in the leading cities of Ròme, Constantinople, Alexandria and Antioch, and spent the last decades of his life continually in Palestine, had a thorough grasp of the Greek language and could use Latin in a masterly fashion. The Vulgate, his revision of the Latin version of the New Testament, which contains all 27 books (§ 14, 2), exercised a far-reaching influence on the History of the Canon.

The formulation of the Canon by the Synod of Rome

The so-called *Decretum Gelasii Papae de recipiendis et non recipiendis libris* consists of five chapters, of which the first three go together and, in four MSS., have the heading: *Concilium urbis Romae sub Damaso Papa de explanatione fidei*. Fron. other sources we know that Damasus (366–384) did hold a synod in Rome in 382 A.D., and that this synod was attended not only by many western bishops but also by bishops of the Greek Church, including Paulinus of Antioch and Epiphanius of Salamis, who were accompanied by Jerome. The second chapter of the decree contains a catalogue of the canonical books of both Testaments; at this point it reads: *Item ordo scripturarum Novi Testamenti, quem sancta et catholica Romana suscipit et veneratur ecclesia*. All 27 books are listed (4 Gospels, Acts, 14 Epistles of the Apostle Paul, the Apocalypse of John, 7 Catholic Epistles); the list of Catholic Epistles reads: *Petri Apostoli epistulae duae, Jacobi Apostoli epistula una, Johannis Apostoli epistula una, alterius Johannis presbyteri epistulae duae, Judae Zelotis Apostoli una*.

If the first three chapters of the work really do go back to the synod of 382, we have here a decision of the Roman Church on the extent of the Canon of the New Testament; but its authenticity is disputed even to-day. While von Dobschuetz has vigorously denied that it goes back to Damasus, E. Schwarz regards this as "probable at least". In favour of its authenticity it is emphasized that Jerome, who certainly exercised a strong influence at the synod of Rome, was the first to describe the authors of James and Jude as Apostles, and that he distinguished between John the Apostle as author of 1 John and John the Presbyter as author of 2 and 3 John. Lagrange, however, would say that the list was drawn up at some other time under the influence of Jerome, and was ascribed to Pope Damasus, his patron.

We are on firmer ground with the letter of Pope Innocent I to Exuperius, bishop of Toulouse, in 405 A.D., where at Exuperius' request Innocent gives him the list of canonical books; for the New Testament it reads: 4 Gospels, 14 Epistles of the Apostle Paul, 3 Epistles of John, 2 of Peter, 1 of Jude, 1 of James, Acts of the Apostles, Apocalypse of John.

Hebrews was known in the West from the time of the first epistle of Clement, but until the mid fourth century it was not considered Pauline or canonical (§ 46, 2). It was first treated as Pauline and canonical by Hilary of Poitiers († 367) and Lucifer of Cagliari in Sardinia († 370), both of whom lived in exile in the East for some years during the reign of Constantinus. Priscillian the Spaniard († 385) did the same. But the great Latin Fathers, Ambrose, Jerome, and Augustine, were the first to give it a secure position in the West. The commentary which goes under the name *Ambrosiaster* and was composed about 370, deals with only 13 Epistles of Paul; the author does not regard Hebrews as Pauline, though he admits its canonicity. Pelagius also in his brief commentary on Paul, composed about 405 A.D., comments on 13 Epistles only, though he almost certainly accepted Hebrews as Pauline and canonical. Philaster of Brescia, who wrote his *Liber de haeresibus* about 383 A.D., personally accepted Hebrews as Pauline and canonical, but he acknowledges that it is not everywhere read in church, and he does not include it in his catalogue of the Canon (c. 88). In Latin MSS. of the Bible, Hebrews almost always stands last of the Epistles of Paul, after the private Epistles, a sign that it is a later addition to the collection. Cf. also §46,2.

In the period before 380 A.D. there are only traces of the circulation of the following five Catholic Epistles: James, 2 Peter, 2 and 3 John, and Jude. Philaster speaks in his canon of "13 Epistles of Paul and 7 others". The influence of the Greek Church, especially of Athanasius' Canon, brought about the recognition of all the Catholic Epistles by 400 A.D. James and Jude are freely described as Apostles, though they did not use this title in the exordium of their Epistles.

The three African synods of Hippo Regius (393) and Carthage (397 and 419). In these three synods the African Church accepted all 27 books as canonical, but the first two place Hebrews *extra numerum* (Jerome, Ep. 53, 9) by decreeing *Pauli Apostoli epistulae tredecim, eiusdem ad Hebraeos una,* whereas the last synod joins them all as *Pauli Apostoli epistulae quattuordecim.* This last synod decided to send the Canon for endorsement to the ecclesia transmarina; the decision of 419 A.D. reads: *Hoc etiam fratri et consacerdoti nostro Bonifatio* (Pope 418–422) *vel aliis earum partium episcopis pro confirmando isto canone innotescat, quia a patribus ista accepimus in ecclesia legenda.* This last African Canon agrees with the list of St. Augustine, *De doctr. christ.* II 8, 13 (composed before 397 A.D.). Augustine was aware that Heb. was not everywhere accepted as Pauline (*De civ. Dei* XVI, 22), and that it had not previously been in the Canon of the Latin Church (*De peccat. merit.* I 72). After 409 he no longer cited it as a work of the Apostle Paul, but he did not deny that it belonged to the Canon.

§ 9. THE CANON OF THE NATIONAL SYRIAN CHURCH

W. Bauer, *Der Apostolos der Syrer,* Giessen 1903. Idem, *Rechtglaeubigkeit und Ketzerei im aeltesten Christentum,* Tuebingen 1934, 6–48. P. Kahle, *The Cairo Geniza,* London 1947.

1. To the introduction of the Peshitta

THE national Syrian Church embraces the Adiabene, that is, the territory around Mosul (on the upper Tigris), and Osrhoëne, the territory around Edessa (in Syriac Orhai, is present-day Urfa), a little east of the upper Euphrates, and Nisibis (Nusaybin).

The Canon of the Syrian Church before the introduction of the Peshitta (see § 16, 3), comprised the Gospels, Acts of the Apostles and the Pauline Epistles (see also § 18). *Doctrina Addaei,* a work composed about 400 A.D., tells us that the legendary founder of the Church of Edessa, the Apostle Addaeus (Thaddaeus), when dying advised his disciples: "The Law, the Prophets, the Gospel and the Epistles of Paul and the Acts of the Apostles, these are the writings which you must read in the Church of Christ, but beyond them you must read nothing, for there is nothing else in which the truth is written" (p. 46 of Phillips' German translation). From another passage we may infer that by the Gospel he means the *Diatessaron* of Tatian. Since Ephraem († 373) wrote a commentary on it, and Aphrahat in his homilies (in 337 and 344 A.D.) cites its wording (see § 16, 1), the Gospels in liturgical use must have been in the form of Tatian's *Gospel Harmony*. There was also a Syriac version of the four separate Gospels, which is preserved in two MSS.: Syr[sin] and Syr[cur] (see § 16, 2); however, the date of their composition is hotly disputed; most scholars date them to the third or early fourth century, but some (for example P. Kahle) consider them earlier than Tatian's *Harmony*. In liturgical use, however, this *Gospel of the Separated* (Evangelion da-Mephareshe), as the Syrians call it after 350 A.D., was unable to supplant the *Gospel of the Harmonized* (E. da-Mehallete) until the fifth century. At that time Theodoretus of Cyrrhus (west of the Euphrates) († 457) removed more than 200 copies of the *Diatessaron* from the Syrian churches of his diocese (*Haer. fab. comp.* 1, 20) and Rabbula, bishop of Edessa (412–435) expected his clergy to have on hand and to read in all churches the *Gospel of the Separated*. The *Diatessaron* is not mentioned in a Syrian catalogue of the Canon which A. S. Lewis discovered in the monastery of St. Catherine on Mt. Sinai; this catalogue, which was composed about 400 A.D., mentions separately the four Gospels Mt., Mk., Lk., John. The *Apostolos* of the Syrians contains, in addition to the Acts of the Apostles, only the 14 Epistles of Paul, including (in fifth place) Hebrews. Philemon is missing, and Ephraem did not deal with it in his commentary on the Pauline Epistles. On the other hand there is in the Syrian Canon a third (apocryphal) epistle to the Corinthians, or, to be precise, a correspondence between the Corinthian community and St. Paul imprisoned in Philippi; it is based on the Acts of Paul, a work composed about 180–190. Ephraem wrote a commentary on it, and censured the followers of Bardesanes for not accepting it as canonical scripture. It does not appear in the catalogue discovered at Sinai, which, however, does contain Philemon; the Sinai catalogue, however, recognizes no canonical scriptures except the four Gospels, Acts of the Apostles, and the Pauline Epistles, for it ends with a note that the enumerated books are all which the Church accepts as Holy Scripture.

2. *Since the introduction of the Peshitta*

With the introduction of the Peshitta the Syrian Church accepted the three major Catholic Epistles (Jas., 1 Pet., 1 John), which were acknowledged about 400 A.D. by the Antioch school of exegetes (e. g., Chrysostom and Theodoret). The eastern half of the Syrian Church, which fell into schism through loyalty to the Patriarch Nestorius despite his condemnation by the Council of Ephesus in 431, has continued to hold to these 22 books of the Peshitta. For a long time they retained the *Diatessaron* of Tatian as well as the four separate Gospels, but for private rather than liturgical use. The Nestorian Ishodad of Merw (c. 850) wrote a commentary on Jas., 1 Pet. and 1 John.

After the condemnation of Monophysitism by the Council of Chalcedon in 451 A.D. the western half of the Syrian Church, which held this doctrine, broke away; they are also known as Jacobites after Jacob Bar Adai, bishop of Edessa († 578), the effective organizer of the Syrian Monophysite Church. Since the mid fifth century they have been cut off from the Universal Church, but have maintained close relations with the Greek and Coptic Monophysites. The four minor Catholic Epistles and the Apocalypse were accepted in the version of the New Testament which the chorepiscopus Polycarp made (§ 16, 4) with the encouragement of Philoxenus, bishop of Mabbug (Hierapolis). Another Monophysite, Dionysius bar Salibi († 1171) wrote a commentary on all 27 New Testament writings. But so far as is known, these five writings are not used in their liturgy. "The *Peshitta* remained the Bible of the Syrian Church, although it was split into sects" (Th. Zahn).

§ 10. THE CANON IN MEDIEVAL AND EARLY MODERN TIMES

J. Leipoldt, *Geschichte des ntl Kanons II: Mittelalter und Neuzeit,* Leipzig 1908. A. Maichle, *Der Kanon der biblischen Buecher und das Konzil von Trient,* Freiburg i. Br. 1929. P. G. Duncker, *De singulis S. Scripturae libris controversis in Concilio Tridentino:* Miscellanea A. Miller (Rome 1951) 66–93.

THE New Testament Canon of 27 books which had been universally accepted in the fifth century by the Greek and Latin Church, was taken over by the Middle Ages and maintained without further discussion. Yet the fact that certain books (Heb., Apc., and 5 Catholic Epistles) were long the subject of controversy and that they did not receive canonical authority everywhere until relatively late, was never entirely forgotten. Thus Isidore of Seville points out that the apostolic authorship of Heb., Jas., 2 Pet., and 2 and 3 John had been a subject of dispute, but he considers them unquestionably inspired and canonical. Only the authorship of Heb. seems to have been seriously disputed in the Middle Ages. In the prefaces to their commentaries on Heb. Thomas Aquinas († 1274) and Nicholas of Lyra († 1340) go to trouble to prove St. Paul's authorship. It is noteworthy that the apocryphal epistle of Paul to the Laodiceans (cf. Col. 4, 16) had many partisans in the medieval Latin Church, but it was never admitted to the Canon; yet many considered it genuinely Pauline, and it appears in more than a hundred Latin Biblical MSS. In the Codex Fuldensis (see § 14, 2) of the Vulgate it stands between Col. and 1 Tim. It also appeared in the pre-Luther German version of the Bible. Like Priscillian († 385 A.D.) and Pope Gregory the Great (590–604) before him, John of Salisbury (c. 1165) among others considered it authentic but not canonical. The *Pastor* of Hermas and the third epistle to the Corinthians are also found in some medieval Latin Biblical MSS., but this does not imply that they were considered canonical; it is a survival of an Old Christian practice of regarding certain writings as useful for the edification of the faithful and the instruction of catechumens, without accepting them into the Canon (cf. Muratorian Canon § 6, 2 and Athanasius § 7, 1).

With the spread of Humanism and the more intensive study of Christian antiquity which it fostered, there arose on the part of many theologians a somewhat different attitude to the traditional Canon. Thus Erasmus of Rotterdam († 1536) in particular, by studying the writings of St. Jerome, cast doubt on the apostolic authorship of seven books (Heb., Jas., 2 Pet., Jude, 2 and 3 John, Apc.); he did not, however, impugn their canonicity, since the original Author of a canonical book is the Holy Ghost. Cardinal Cajetan (Thomas de Vio of Gaeta † 1534) was bolder; in regard to five of the above-mentioned books (Heb., Jas., Jude, 2 and 3 John), he not merely doubted whether they were composed by the writers whose names they bear, but he asserts that for this reason they have less authority; so a question of faith could not be settled only with reference to Heb., for example. Cajetan was vigorously attacked by various theologians because of his bold Biblical criticism, but he also found defenders even at the Council of Trent, though they did not prevail.

Martin Luther was much bolder, indeed he was downright radical in his criticism of the traditional Canon; the basis of his criticism was, however, not historical but dogmatic or religious. He set up his interpretation of Paul as the criterion for testing everything which is alleged to be divine and holy. Of the "really certain important books" of the New Testament he reckons in the first place Romans, Galatians, and the Gospel of John, "the one tender correct chief Gospel". He places the others in a secondary position, as, for example, the Synoptics, because they have so few words of Jesus. In addition he also establishes a third group on which he pronounces severe censure "because they do not emphasize Christ"; these are Heb., which, he says, gives false teaching about penance, Jude, which with 2 Pet. is "an unprofitable epistle", Jas., which he calls "an epistle of straw", because "in direct contradiction to St. Paul and to all other Scripture, it attributes justification to works", and the Apc., of which he "could not see that it was 'produced' by the Holy Ghost".

In the sixteenth century such criticism of the traditional Canon was to be heard both inside and outside the Church; in the face of this criticism the great reforming Council of Trent fixed the attitude of the Church precisely in its decree of 8th April 1564 *De canonicis scripturis* (cf. § 4). In the preliminary discussions which began on 8th February there were violent differences of opinion amongst the Fathers of the council. A conservative group maintained that they should dispense with critical examination of the question, and should simply accept and sanction authoritatively the traditional Canon which had been proclaimed by the Council of Florence. Seripando, General of the Hermits, and Bertano, bishop of Fano, led a critical group which advised the adoption of St. Jerome's distinction between books with a canonical character in the proper sense of the word, and those which could be called canonical only in a loose sense: the former alone were to be the legitimate sources of the faith, while the latter could serve only purposes of religious edification (cf. Jerome's preface to the Books of Solomon: *ad aedificationem plebis, non ad auctoritatem ecclesiasticorum dogmatum confirmandam*). A third group was inclined to compromise by simply taking over the Canon of the Council of Florence, but not excluding a critico-historical discussion. After lengthy discussions they agreed to adopt the Canon of the Council of Florence; by a majority vote it was decided not to include in the decree a scientific defence of the Canon. The conservatives prevailed also on the question of grading the various books. But a large majority voted against their proposal to name explicitly and declare canonical the New Testament passages which were often rejected as spurious (Mk. 16, 9–20; Lk. 22, 23 sq.; John 7, 53 to 8, 11); yet in the final version of the passage they inserted *cum omnibus suis partibus* . . .

In the enumeration of the 27 books of the New Testament mention is made of 14 Epistles of the Apostle Paul, and therefore Heb. (which is placed last) is ascribed to Paul; furthermore all three Johannine Epistles and the Apc. are attributed to John the Apostle, and the authors of Jas. and Jude are declared to be Apostles. Yet theological scholars are unanimous that the Council intended to declare as an article of faith only that the enumerated books with all their parts belong to the Canon; it had no intention of settling merely historical questions about the authorship of the books and the authenticity of the disputed passages. It pronounces anathema only on those who do not recognize these books with all their parts as holy and canonical. Authenticity and canonicity are therefore quite distinct concepts. So the decree of the Council imposes only acknowledgement of the canonicity of these passages; it does not touch on the authenticity of the *pericopa de adultera* (John 7, 53 to 8, 11), nor of the longer conclusion of Mk. (16, 9–20); likewise it does not involve the identification of the author of Jas. with James "the brother of the Lord", (James the Less), nor of the author of Jude with the Apostle Jude Thaddaeus.

PART II

THE TEXT OF THE NEW TESTAMENT

C. R. Gregory, *Textkritik des NT,* Leipzig 1900–1909. Herm. von Soden, *Die Schriften des NT in ihrer aeltesten erreichbaren Textgestalt hergestellt auf Grund ihrer Textgeschichte,* Berlin and Goettingen 1902–1913 (see § 20). E. Nestle, *Einfuehrung in das griechische NT⁴,* völlig umgearbeitet von E. v. Dobschuetz, Goettingen 1923. E. Jacquier, *Le NT dans l'église chrétienne II: Le texte du NT,* Paris 1913. H. J. Vogels, *Handbuch der ntl Textkritik²,* Bonn 1954. F. G. Kenyon, *Handbook to the Textual Criticism of the NT³,* London 1926. Idem, *Recent Developments in the Textual Criticism of the Greek Bible,* London 1933. Idem, *The Text of the Greek Bible. A Student's Handbook,* London 1937. A. T. Robertson, *An Introduction to the Textual Criticism of the NT,* London 1925. K. Lake, *The Text of the NT¹⁰,* London 1943. L. Vaganay, *Initiation à la critique textuelle néotestamentaire,* Paris 1934. M.-J. Lagrange, *Introduction à l'étude du NT. Deuxième partie (Critique textuelle) II: La critique rationelle,* Paris 1935. H. J. Vogels, *Codicum Novi Testamenti Specimina,* Bonn 1929 (54 reproductions of MSS. and early printing). F. G. Kenyon, *Our Bible and the ancient MSS., being a History of the Text and its Translations³,* London 1939 (with 32 plates). O. Paret, *Die Bibel. Ihre Ueberlieferung in Druck und Schrift,* Stuttgart 1949 (with 61 plates). E. C. Colwell, *What is the best NT?* Chicago 1951 (History of the NT Text since Erasmus; popular).

B. M. Metzger, *Annotated Bibliography of the Textual Criticism of the NT 1914 to 1939,* Copenhagen 1955 (Studies and Documents 16; more than 1200 entries). M. Karnetzki, *Textgeschichte als Ueberlieferungsgeschichte:* ZntW 47 (1956) 170–180.

§ 11. THE MANUSCRIPTS OF THE NEW TESTAMENT IN GENERAL

W. Schubart, *Einfuehrung in die Papyruskunde,* Berlin 1918. Idem, *Das Buch bei den Griechen und Roemern²,* Berlin 1921. Idem, *Das antike Buch:* Die Antike XIV (1928) 171–195. F. G. Kenyon, *Books and Readers in Ancient Greece and Rome,* Oxford 1932. K. Preisendanz, *Papyruskunde und Papyrusforschung,* Leipzig 1933. H. Ibscher, *Der Kodex: Jahrbuch fuer Einbandkunst,* ed. by E. Klette IV (1937) 3–15. H. A. Sanders, *The Beginning of the modern Book:* The University of Michigan Quarterly Review 44 (1938) 95–111. O. Roller (see § 30). C. C. McCown, *Codex and Roll in the NT:* HarvThR 34 (1941) 219–250. G. Bardy, *Simples remarques sur les ouvrages et les manuscrits bilingues:* RB 52 (1944) 242–267. C. H. Roberts, *The Christian and the Greek Papyri:* JThSt 50 (1949) 155–168 (cf. ThLZ 1950, 55–58). A. Dain, *Les Manuscrits,* Paris 1949 (cf. Gnomon 23, 1951, 233–242). *NT MS-Studies. The Materials and the Making of a Critical Apparatus,* ed. by M. M. Parvis and A. P. Wikgren, Chicago 1950. F. F. Bruce, *The Books and the Parchments,* London 1950. A. Harnack, *Ueber den privaten Gebrauch der Heiligen Schriften in der alten Kirche,* Leipzig 1912 (Beitraege zur Einleitung in das NT V). R. Devreesse, *Introduction à l'étude des manuscrits grecs,* Paris 1954. L. Koep, Buch I: Real-lexikon f. Antike u. Christentum II 664–688. H. J. Vogels, *Handbuch²,* Bonn 1954. K. Preisendanz, *Papyruskunde :* F. Milkau, *Handbuch der Bibliothekswissenschaft,* 2nd ed. by G. Leyh, vol. I (1950 f.) 163–248. C. H. Roberts, *The Codex: Proceedings of the British Academy* 40 (1953) 169–204.

1. *Originals and copies; writing materials and styles of script; volumen and codex*

THE originals (αὐτόγραφα) of the New Testament books were lost at an early age. Tertullian, it is true, writes (*De praescr. haer.* 36) that the authentic writings (ipsae authenticae litterae) of the Apostles were still read at Corinth, Philippi, Thessalonica, Ephesus and Rome, but this merely means that these places were in possession of apostolic letters addressed to them. Even in the second century when the heretic Marcion engaged in forgeries (cf. § 5, 3), no one appealed to the original texts although such an appeal would have put an immediate end to the controversy about the genuine wording.

The early disappearance of the originals was mainly due to the perishable nature of papyrus, on which books and letters were then generally written. The soft porous pith from the stem of the papyrus plant, which in antiquity grew freely in the Nile Delta and elsewhere, was cut into the thinnest and widest strips possible; these were then laid crosswise in pairs over each other, glued, pressed, dried, and smoothed on one side. This is how a writing page (ὁ χάρτης, 2 John 12) was made.

A number of such sheets were laid end to end with their narrow ends touching, in such a way that the fibres always ran in the same direction. The resultant strips—19–33 feet long and $8\frac{1}{2}$–$10\frac{1}{2}$ inches wide (6–10 metres by 22–27 cm.)—were rolled together in such a way that the fibres running horizontally lay on the inside. (τὸ εἰλητόν, *volumen*). In the case of written rolls which were intended for frequent use they fixed on the right end of the strip a handle whose points projected above and below (cf. Hebr. 10, 7:

κεφαλὶς βιβλίου). As a rule only the inner surface of the roll was written upon. They wrote on papyrus with a sort of ink (τὸ μέλαν, 2 Cor. 3, 3; 2 John 12) which was made from lamp-black and gum; they used a writing reed (κάλαμος γράφιχος, 3 Mac. 4, 20; κάλαμος, 3 John 13) which was cut from a reed found particularly in Egypt.

Another writing material from early times was leather-(skin) prepared by tanning with lime, the skin being from sheep, goats, calves, asses or other animals (μεμβράνη, διφθέρα, δέρμα, cf. 2 Tim. 4, 13). In the second century B.C. a special process for this was discovered at Pergamum, and thereafter this material, which was called *charta pergamena* (parchment), began to compete seriously with papyrus. The earliest sheets of parchment which have been found do not date beyond the second (or probably the first) century of our era. Parchment would hardly have been used by the authors of the New Testament books, for it was much dearer than papyrus. The parchments which Paul left behind him in Troas (2 Tim. 4, 13) were probably copies of Old Testament books. None of the surviving parchment MSS. of the New Testament books was written before the fourth century.

All the Greek MSS. of the pre-Christian era of which fragments have survived are in the roll form. At first parchment was also arranged in rolls (cf. the Thora rolls—rolls of the Law—of the Jews). But since it was not so suitable for rolling as papyrus, the practice arose in pre-Christian times of folding single leaves of parchment in the middle and putting inside one another as many leaves as were estimated to be necessary for the work which was to be copied; this made a book of the kind which we use nowadays.

Since this could not be done in the case of more extensive works, the practice soon arose of putting together only a small number—generally three or four—of folded sheets in each unit, or "quaternion"; a series of such quires or signatures was then stitched and bound together into one tome (τεῦχος, codex), like our book. This is how the codex came to be made, and as well as the parchment codex there was soon a papyrus codex.

The papyrus discoveries of recent decades have shown that the age of the codex begins shortly after the birth of Christ; it is certain that by the second century the Christian communities of Egypt were using the codex form for the Sacred Scriptures; this was an economical practice, since both sides of the papyrus could be used. The oldest papyrus fragment of a New Testament book, the Gospel of Saint John, is from a codex of about 130 A.D. (§ 12, 3). On the other hand the roll form continued in general use for profane literature until the end of the second century, and even in the third century it was predominant. The majority of pre-third-century papyrus codices with Greek and Coptic text which have survived consist of a single form containing fifty—or slightly more—double sheets. So, for example, the celebrated codex of the Pauline Epistles in the Chester Beatty collection (𝔓 46) originally consisted of 52 double sheets which were in a single forme (§ 12, 3). On the other hand the Bodmer Papyrus (see § 12, 3), as we have it, consists of 5 unequal formes (with 4, 5 and 8 double sheets), while 𝔓 45 (Gospels) consists of double sheets which are simply placed side by side.

In the fourth century the more durable, though dearer, parchment book replaced the papyrus book, except in Egypt where the papyrus book continued for a longer time. According to St. Jerome (ep. 34), Acacius of Caesarea (Palestine) and his successor Euzoius, between 340 and 380 A.D., went to great expense to have Origen's library copied upon parchment, and thereby preserved it from perishing. About 331 A.D. the emperor Constantine commissioned Eusebius, bishop of Caesarea, to have fifty parchment copies of the text of the entire Greek Bible made for him; they were for the churches of his new capital on the Bosporus (Eusebius, *Vita Const.* IV 36 sq.).

Because of the cost of parchment, the practice soon arose of treating superfluous codices so that other texts of which copies were not available, could be written on them; they were prepared for this purpose by erasing the original writing with sponge, knife, or pumice stone. Such MSS. are called *codices rescripti* or palimpsests (from ψάω, I rub). Generally the erased text is of greater value to us, and more or less successful efforts have been made to render such texts legible again. The chemical means which were formerly employed for this purpose damaged the parchment seriously, but nowadays palimpsest photography, which is free from this drawback, gives much better results. It is based on the observation that parchment glows when subjected to ultra violet rays, while the erased writing remains fairly dark;[1] the reason for this is that iron gallnut ink was used for writing the MSS. and the particles of iron, which have been driven into the parchment, block or lessen the illumination; this was the case with almost all parchment palimpsest MSS.

Finally paper, which is cheap, entirely superseded parchment, which remained expensive. Paper, which is made from cloth (rags) was in use for a long time in China and Central Asia; it was known in Syria and Egypt from the 8th century, but only in the 13th century was it used for Biblical and liturgical purposes. The last parchment MSS. were made in the fifteenth century.

The oldest MSS. of the Greek New Testament were written in what was then the usual script for books—uncial (from *uncia* = inch, the original size of the letters); the script is also called majuscule, and the MSS. are described as Uncial MSS. or Majuscule MSS. This script consists of clear capital letters which are not joined and are written without punc-

---

[1] Cf. A. Dold, *Ueber Palimpsestforschung und das Beuroner Palimpsest-Institut:* Jahresbericht der Goerres-Gesellschaft, 1924/25, 87–108. Idem, *Palimpsest-Hss, ihre Erschliessung einst und jetzt, ihre Bedeutung:* Gutenberg-Jahrbuch 1950, 16–24. S. Stenger reviews the work of the Beuron P. Institute on the Latin Bible in: St. Wiborada, Jahrb. f. Buecherfreunde, 7 (1940) 1–12.

tuation or spaces between the words *(scriptio continua)*. The abbreviations are confined to a limited number of words, the so-called nomina sacra like $\overline{\Theta C}$, $\overline{\Pi TP}$, $\overline{YC}$, $\overline{\Pi NA}$, $\overline{IC}$, $\overline{XC}$, $\overline{KC}$ and some others. This script is attractive and easily legible, but it requires much time and material.

It is unlikely that the original texts of the New Testament books were written in cursive script, though it was then fully developed; in it most of the letters were formed without lifting the pen, and abbreviations were freely used. The originals were probably written in an uncial script with cursive elements (majuscule cursive), for the rough surface of papyrus made it difficult to use cursive. (Roller.)

In the ninth century minuscule script developed from majuscule with borrowings from cursive. Its letters are more flowing so that they can each be formed by one or at most two strokes of the pen. It uses linkings and abbreviations (especially in the first and last syllables) very freely. Separation of words, punctuation, accents and breathings now become the rule, though they were used occasionally in uncial codices of the eighth century. Minuscule script is quicker and takes up less paper, but it is harder to read. By the eleventh century it was universal.

2. Size and layout of the Manuscripts; stichometry and colometry; scholarly additions

From an early age there was great variety in the size of the MSS., but it may be said that smaller sizes were preferred for private use because of their convenience, while larger sizes were chosen for use in the churches. As examples of such Church MSS., which were produced with great attention to calligraphy also, we may mention the codices ℵ (43 × 38 cm.: 17 × 15 in., in four columns), and B (28 × 28 cm.: 11 × 11 in., but it was originally larger, for the edges have been clipped; it is in three columns). The fifty codices which the emperor Constantine commissioned for the Churches of Constantinople (see above n. 1) would also have been of this kind. A huge MS. of the Middle Ages is the Codex Gigas, which is now in Stockholm, containing the whole Latin Bible and other writings as well (cf. § 14, 1).

The division of the page into two columns is the rule in the old parchment MSS.; later this practice was abandoned. In the Minuscules it is noticeable that the Byzantine copyists almost always have one column, while in the West two columns are the rule, even in the Greek MSS. from southern Italy (cf. § 12, 4).

From the fourth century a profuse luxuriousness in the production of Biblical MSS. became widespread (e. g., gold and silver lettering on purple dyed parchment); this lavishness evoked complaints from Chrysostom (*In Joh. Hom.* 32, 2) and Jerome (*Ep.* 18; 22, 32; 107, 12; *Praef. in Job*). A number of such luxury Bibles have survived, such as the Codex Purpureus Petropolitanus (N^ev), whose leaves are now divided among many libraries, the Codex Rossanensis (Σ) written in silver letters on purple parchment, in Rossano (Calabria), the Codex Sinopensis (O), now in Paris, which is closely related to it in layout, especially in the miniatures, and the Codex Beratensis (Φ) in Berat in Albania—all of the sixth century. It is clear that they are from the same scriptorium, probably from Constantinople. At a later date the accessory decoration of the book became more highly valued than the magnificence of the material and ink. The copying and painting shop of the Palace of Blachernae at Constantinople produced, among others Min. 38 (Coisl. gr. 200, Paris), 280 (Paris), 1505 (Athos), and also the Gospels of Karahissar (Leningrad, Public Bibl. Graec. 105); [cf. *The four Gospels of Karahissar*, ed. by E. C. Colwell and H. R. Willoughby, Chicago, 1936, 2 vols.].

Codices b e i j f (with Old-Latin text) are Latin illuminated MSS. from antiquity.

The Gothic codex argenteus (§ 15) also calls for mention here.

In the MSS. we find repeated at the end of each book information about the number of stichoi (στίχος, a row); this practice is as early as the oldest Pauline MS. ($\mathfrak{P}^{46}$). As a rule, however, this information does not tally with the actual number of stichoi, so evidently it has been copied from a preceding MS. Stichometry was used by the ancients for reckoning the size of a book and its price, and it was the basis on which the copyist was paid. A stichos was the length of a line, for which the sixteen syllable hexameter served as a standard. So the information that a book contains 1000 stichoi means not that it is exactly 1000 lines long, but that it has 16000 syllables.

Stichometry must not be confused with colometry, writing the lines as intelligible units. This method was first introduced for poetry, but was later adopted for oratorical prose as an aid to intelligent reading. Eusebius (H. E. VI 16, 4) tells us that Origen had the poetical books of the Old Testament copied colometrically (πρὸς κῶλον). St. Jerome claims that he was the first to extend this method of writing to the non-poetical books of the Bible (*Praef. i. Is.*). None of the surviving MSS. in which colometry is used (D^{pl}, E^{act}, H^{pl}) is older than the sixth century. The name of the mysterious Euthalius (see below) is attached to a colometric recension of Acts, Catholic and Pauline Epistles. At a later date space was saved by using red points to break the text into units.

Ammonius of Alexandria (c. 220) wrote on the margin of the text of Mt. the parallel passages from the other Gospels; this inspired Eusebius of Caesarea to divide the individual Gospels into passages or sections with consecutive numbers which he marked on the margin (355 in Mt., 233 in Mk., 342 in Lk., 232 in John). He arranged these numbers together in ten *canones* (lists) in which the passages occurring in all 4 Gospels, or in 3, 2, or only 1 of them, are set together. The number of the appropriate canon was marked in red beside the black marginal number, so that it was possible with a minimum of trouble to determine in regard to each passage (section) of a Gospel whether it occurs in other Gospels and what number it bears there. Eusebius explained his system at length in a letter to Carpianus (which Nestle prints in his edition of the New Testament). This letter and the list of canons are usually found copied at the beginning of the Gospel MSS.[2]

This division of the text into sections serves purposes of comparison; in addition to it, almost all the Greek MSS. of the Gospels contain another division which aims exclusively at making the text easy to understand. The individual sections are described in the MSS. as *Kephalaia (capitula)*,[3] and each of them has a heading (τίτλος) describing its content. Mt. has 68 such sections, Mk. has 48, Lk. 83, and John 18. This division first appears in Cod. A (Alexandrinus); Cod. B has a different division and no *titloi*. As a rule the Greek MSS. of the other New Testament books are laid out with a division into *Kephalaia* and with *titloi*.

Stephen Langton, Chancellor of Paris, († 1228 as Archbishop of Canterbury), is the author of the chapter division which prevailed generally in the Latin Church and is now universal. Robert Estienne, a Parisian printer, introduced the division into verses which today is general; it first appeared in his 4th edition of the New Testament (Geneva 1551).

All the New Testament books except the Apc. appear in the MSS. with longish introductory comments or prologues, which are usually called *hypothesis* (Latin *argumentum*).[4] These deal with the author, content, and circumstances of composition of the particular book. The oldest Gospel prologues were written probably between 160 and 180 A.D. (§ 5, 3). Towards the end of the third century a Latin version of these was incorporated into a

[2] Cf. C. Nordenfalk, *Die spaetantiken Kanontafeln,* Goeteborg 1938, and on this work H. Lietzmann, DLZ 1941, 193–196; A. Baumstark, OCh 36 (1941) 258–265; M. McGurk, JThSt NS 6 (1955) 192–198.

[3] Cf. B. Kraft, Art. *Kapitularien, biblische:* LThK V (1933) 804 sq.

[4] Cf. B. Kraft, Art. *Argument:* LThK I (1930) 632 sq.

newly revised edition of the African translation of the Gospels. These similar prologues were used in the fourth century by Instantius the Priscillianist for the ten oldest Pauline Epistles; these latter prologues were the work of Marcion himself or of one of his closest collaborators (§ 5, 3).

Many MSS. contain editions of the Pauline Epistles, Acts, and the Catholic Epistles, which are attributed to a (bishop or deacon) Euthalius; in these editions the text is divided into small units as an aid to easier and more intelligent reading, the division being based on the rules of the Greek rhetorical schools; also the Old Testament quotations are noted and collected at the beginning of each book, and there is a chapter division (with τίτλοι), which already existed in the case of the Pauline Epistles, but which Euthalius himself made for the Acts and Catholic Epistles. This Euthalius, who is otherwise quite unknown, is said by Zuntz to have been a Christian grammarian and to have edited the text about 360 A.D. at Caesarea in Palestine, using the autograph of the presbyter Pamphilus (i. e., the text which Pamphilus produced). Cf. § 12, 2 (Cod. H); 21, 3.[5]

The supplements to the text (prologues, capitula etc.) have been printed and examined for the Greek MSS. by H. von Soden, *Die Schriften des NT* I (1902) 293 sqq., and for the Latin MSS. by Wordsworth and White, *Novum Testamentum*, 1889 sqq. (in their Introductions).

3. The effects on the text of the multiplication of copies

For close on fifteen centuries these extensive writings were reproduced countless times. Since copies were multiplied not

---

[5] Cf. B. Kraft, Art. *Euthalius:* LThK III (1931) 867 sq.; G. Bardy: DB Suppl 2 (1934) 215–218; G. Zuntz, *The Ancestry of the Harklean NT,* London 1945, 77–121, RB 57 (1950) 553 sq.; ZDMG 101 (1951) 174–196; Euthalius=Euzoius?: Vigiliae Christianae 7 (1953) 16–22. [The pseudonyms Euzoius and Acacius belong to Euthalius and his presumed correspondent Athanasius.]

mechanically but by scribes, it was inevitable that considerable changes should creep into the text in the course of time. When we recall that each new copy had some fresh variants and that the variants established themselves and increased by addition, it is no wonder that our sources for the text of the New Testament coincide with one another in scarcely half the words. The experts agree that we have no MSS. which has preserved the original of all 27 books, or even of one of them, quite unchanged in every particular. The task which faces New Testament scholarship is therefore to restore as far as possible the texts of the originals. This difficult task calls for methodical examination of the history of the text. Biblical scholarship is still far from the goal, but important advances have been made in the last century (cf. § 21).

For a correct assessment of the countless variants (i. e., different readings in the sources for the text) it is important to know their nature and origin. They fall into two main groups: changes in the parent or original text which are inadvertent, and those which are deliberate; there are cases in which it is impossible to be certain to which of these groups a variant reading belongs.

a) Inadvertent changes may be due to various kinds of causes. Consideration must be given to:

Errors of the ear (when writing to dictation): Rom. 5, 1 εἰρήνην ἔχωμεν πρὸς τὸν θεὸν B* ℵ* D lat sy al.] ἔχομεν B³ ℵ¹ G al.—1 Cor. 12, 27 μέρους] μέλους D* lat (vos autem estis corpus Christi et membra de membro) Orig Euseb Aug Hier etc.

Itacism (i. e., at that time ει, η, ι, οι, υ were pronounced almost like i, and αι was pronounced like e): 1 Cor. 15, 54 νῖκος (victory); but νεῖκος (strife, contentio) 𝔓⁴⁶ B 088 Tert Cypr Hier—Heb. 13, 22 ἀνέχεσθε] ἀνέχεσθαι Ψ D* min vg (ut sufferatis)—Mt. 11, 16 ἑτέροις] ἑταίροις G S U V W Θ Φ vg (coaequalibus) sy al.—John 19, 34 ἔνυξεν (pierced)] ἤνοιξεν (opened) 56 68 Aug vg.—Apc. 2, 25 ἄχρι οὗ ἂν ἥξω] ἀνοίξω ℜ al.—Apc. 4, 3 ἶρις] ἱερεῖς ℵ A al.

Errors of the eye (of the copyist): Rom. 6, 5 ἀλλὰ καὶ τῆς ἀναστάσεως] ἅμα G lat (simul): the scribe read ΑΛΛΑ as AMA.

If two neighbouring lines of a MS. begin or end with the same group of letters or if two similar words stand near each other in the same line, it is easy for the eye of the copyist to jump from the first group of letters to the second, and so for a piece of the text to be omitted *(homoioarcton—homoioteleuton)*; conversely he may go back from the second to the first and a passage may be written twice (dittography). While dittography is relatively uncommon, errors due to *homoioteleuton* are very numerous; as an example: Apc. 20, 5a ends with χίλια ἔτη, and so does 20, 4; now 20, 5a is missing from ℵ al.

Errors where the sense is retained, though the wording is changed: 1 Cor. 5, 2 πράξας] ποιήσας 𝔓⁴⁶ BDG al.—Interchange of εὐθύς and εὐθέως, of ὅτι and διότι, of περί and ὑπέρ etc. The copyist expressed the thought correctly, but not in the original wording. This is the explanation of the frequent interchange or even cumulation of the names Ἰησοῦς, Χριστός, and Κύριος.

The infiltration of parallel readings when the copyist was thinking of the wording of the parallel passage: Mt. 6, 24 οὐδείς] + οἰκέτης L Λ Φ al. because of Lk. 16, 13—1 Tim. 1, 17 μόνῳ θεῷ] μόνῳ σοφῷ θεῷ K L P got. Greg. Naz. Chrys. because of Rom. 16, 27—Mk. 9, 29 προσευχῇ ℵ* B k Clem] + καὶ νηστείᾳ all other witnesses. Cf. Lk. 2, 37 (by fastings and prayers); Acts 14, 23 (prayed with fasting); 1 Tim. 5, 5 (in supplications and prayers); 1 Cor. 7, 5 τῇ προσευχῇ] τῇ νηστείᾳ καὶ προσευχῇ min sy Ephr; Acts 10, 30] + νηστεύων D.

b) The variants which must be regarded as deliberate corrections are much the more important. With few exceptions they can be traced to the 2nd and early 3rd centuries. At that time more attention was paid to the meaning than to the wording of the text, and quotations were freer than at a later date.[5a] The second century was also the age of Gospel harmonies (cf. § 22).

Elucidations, such as the replacement of an unusual word by a common one, are relatively harmless: Tit. 1, 5 ἀπέλιπον] κατέλιπον L P K al., Tit. 2, 11 ἡ σωτήριος] τοῦ σωτῆρος ἡμῶν G lat (vg Salvatoris nostri) al. The same applies to the replacement of a colloquial vulgarism by a literary word (particularly in the Koine Text; cf. § 21, 4); cf. Michaelis, Der Attizismus und das NT: ZntW 22, 1923, 91–121).

Explanatory additions: John 7, 39 οὔπω γὰρ ἦν πνεῦμα] + ἅγιον L X T Δ Λ; + ἅγιον ἐπ' αὐτοῖς D f; + δεδομένον B lat sy.—In Jas. 5, 7 πρόϊμον is sometimes explained by ὑετόν (A K L P), sometimes by καρπόν (ℵ bo).—John 9, 38 is missing from ℵ W b l copt and is probably an addition (RB 1950, 400 n. 2).

Elimination of grammatical and stylistic harshness (especially in the sources for the Koine Text form): 1 Cor. 11, 24 τὸ σῶμά μου τὸ ὑπὲρ ὑμῶν] + κλώμενον ℜ G it sy; + θρυπτόμενον D*; + διδόμενον sa bo arm f vg (quod ... tradetur) Cypr. In the Apc., which has many faults of Greek grammar, Aν and K, the more recent recensions, regularly correct the text in such passages.

Elimination of obscurities in the text: In 1 Tim. 2, 6b the apposition is transformed into a relative clause by the addition of οὗ — ἐδόθη: D* FG Ambrst. In John 13, 10 εἰ μὴ τοὺς πόδας is missing from ℵ c Orig Tert and numerous Fathers; these words were probably added by a scribe who did not appreciate the distinction between λούειν (to wash all over) and νίπτειν (to wash a part of the body). (RB 1950, 400 n. 2.)

The following cases are more serious: Alteration of the word order for reasons of style (particularly frequent in the Western Text: cf. § 21, 2): Lk. 5, 5 sq.: οὐ μὴ παρακούσομαι· καὶ εὐθὺς

[5a] C. S. C. Williams, *Alterations to the text of the Synoptic Gospels and Acts*, Oxford 1951.

χαλάσαντες τὰ δίκτυα D^e; similarly 5, 11 sq.—Acts 5, 22: καὶ ἀνοί-
ξαντες τὴν φυλακὴν οὐχ εὗρον αὐτοὺς ἔσω Dd vg.

Assimilation (harmonizing parallel passages in the Synoptics,
filling out passages): In many textual sources the shorter form of
the Pater Noster of Lk. 11, 2–4 has been filled out from the longer
form of Mt. 6, 9–13: (1) ἡμῶν ὁ ἐν τοῖς οὐρανοῖς; (2) γενηθήτω
τὸ θέλημά σου; (3) ἀλλὰ ῥῦσαι ἡμᾶς ἀπὸ τοῦ πονηροῦ.—Mt.
23, 14 in many sources has been taken from Mk. 12, 40 (= Lk.
20, 47); in the same way Mk. 11, 25 from Mt. 6 14; Mk. 15, 28
from Lk. 22, 37; Mt. 17, 21 from Mk. 9, 29; Mt. 27, 35 b from
John 19, 24; Acts 9, 5 is expanded from 26, 14; Gal. 6, 15 from
5, 6; Mt. 20, 16 b from Mt. 22, 14; Mt. 18, 11 from Lk. 19,10.

The Old Testament citations, which are often very free, are frequently assimilated to the familiar Septuagint Text, and sometimes
are completed: Rom. 4, 18] + ὡς οἱ ἀστέρες τοῦ οὐρανοῦ καὶ τὸ
ἄμμον τῆς θαλάσσης G (Ephr) from Gen. 15, 5; 22, 17.—Rom.
10, 16] + Καὶ ὁ βραχίων Κυρίου τίνι ἀπεκαλύφθη 104 547 bo
from Is. 53, 1 (the whole passage is quoted in John 12, 38).—
Eph. 5, 30] + ἐκ τῆς σαρκὸς αὐτοῦ καὶ ἐκ τῶν ὀστέων αὐτοῦ
𝔎 D G pl latt sy (from Gen. 2, 23).

The most important textual alterations are those which were
made to eliminate actual difficulties (frequently miscalled "dogmatic" corrections). We know that Marcion mutilated the
Gospel of St. Luke, and eliminated alleged Jewish forgeries both
from it and from the ten Pauline Epistles which he accepted.
Some of his tendentious emendations have penetrated even into
the MSS. of the Catholic Church, for example, the absence in
many sources of the Western Text of Lk. 5, 39; 24, 12; 24, 40
and of πρῶτον in Rom. 1, 16.[6] Tatian also in support of his En-
cratite doctrine and anti-Jewish bias made a number of extensive

[6] On this question see A. von Harnack, *Marcion*[1] 229; *Neue Studien zu Marcion*.
Leipzig 1923, 27, 32 sq.; H. J. Vogels, *Evangelium palatinum* (§ 14, 1) 98 sq.— Cf.
also A. Bludau, *Die Schriftfaelschungen der Haeretiker*. Ein Beitrag zur Textkritik
der Bibel (NtA XI, 5, 1925).

and significant "corrections"; these have found a place in a number of textual sources of the Gospel, for example, in John 2, 3 read e 1: factum est per multam turbam vocitorum vinum consummari—in Lk. 2, 34 ἐν τῷ Ἰσραήλ is missing from Tat Iren. But Tatian's influence on the New Testament seems principally to have been confined to Syria; at any rate the two MSS. of the old Syriac version (syr^cur and syr^sin; cf. § 16, 2) have been strongly influenced by him.[7]

Moreover ecclesiastical copyists or correctors sometimes made alterations in the text, because the wording which they had before them (or which was traditional) either gave offence or did not exactly correspond to the expression of the faith in their time. The following list contains a number of characteristic instances:

In Mt. 1, 25 there are two concurrent readings υἱόν and τὸν υἱὸν αὐτῆς τὸν πρωτότοκον; of these the second is original; in the first τ. πρωτότ. was eliminated in view of the perpetual virginity of Mary.—In Mt. 5, 22 εἰκῇ (= without reason) is missing from ℵ B Just Orig Tert vg; the word is probably an insertion since according to Scripture there is also a righteous wrath.—Lk. 2, 33 ὁ πατὴρ αὐτοῦ] Ἰωσήφ AEGHKMΘ al it syᵖ (similarly 2, 41 etc.).— In Lk. 3, 22 in place of σὺ εἶ ὁ υἱός μου ὁ ἀγαπητός, ἐν σοὶ εὐδόκησα (Is. 42, 1) the reading of D a b c ff² Ir Just Clem is: υἱός μου εἶ σύ· ἐγὼ σήμερον γεγέννηκά σε which probably is merely an assimilation to Ps. 2, 7.—Lk. 22, 19b–20 is missing in one branch of the Western Text (cf. *Benoit:* RB 48, 1939, 358–378; J. Jeremias, *Abendmahlsworte Jesu²*, 1949, 67–79; H. Schuermann: Bb 32, 1951, 364–392; 522–541, and K. Th. Schaefer ibid. 33, 1952, 237–239).

Lk. 22, 43 sq. (sweat of Our Lord in the garden) was eliminated from numerous MSS. for reasons of delicacy (cf. L. Braun: ZntW 32, 1933, 256–276).

Lk. 23, 34a ("forgive them") is missing from many sources

[7] On this matter cf. Burkitt, *Evangelion da-Mepharreshe II* (1904) 173–212.

because it was inconvenient in the polemic against the Jews.— In John 6, 15 many sources have ἀνεχώρησεν instead of φεύγει ℵ ff² l Chrysost. — In John 7, 8 very many sources read οὔπω instead of οὐ because according to 7, 14 Jesus did go up to the feast at Jerusalem.

In Acts 15, 20 29 (21, 25) the sources of the Western Text omit καὶ τοῦ πνικτοῦ and add the so-called "Golden Rule", thereby turning a regulation about food into a moral prescription. (cf. § 29, 4).—In 1 Cor. 15, 51 the original reading (B al) caused offence because it seemed to conflict with the universality of death (cf. Jerome, *Ep.* 119; Oppenheim: ThQ 112, 1931, 92 to 135; Vaccari: Bb 13 1932, 73–76; Brandhuber, ibid. 18, 1937, 303–333; 418–438).—In Gal. 2, 5 οὐδέ has been dropped from a number of sources of the Western Text, obviously with reference to Acts 16, 3.

The doxology at the end of the Pater Noster in Mt. 6, 13 ("for thine is the kingdom, the power and the glory for ever. Amen") is missing from the best sources, but appears in W Θ 𝔎 it sy al; it was introduced from the Liturgy (cf. *Didache* 8, 2; 1 Paralip. 29, 11–13).

In a relatively insignificant number of passages it must be assumed that no witness has transmitted the text correctly, e. g., Jas. 2, 18.

Even though the number of variants in the New Testament text is beyond surveying, yet it must be remembered that the vast majority of them are of absolutely no account. Westcott and Hort, the great English textual critics (§ 20), have computed that only one thousandth part of the text is critically not entirely certain. And only a few of these passages are of importance theologically; and since the truths of faith and morals are enunciated in the New Testament not merely in one place, but generally in numerous passages, the critically uncertain passages of the text cannot obscure or even modify its doctrinal content. So it may be said with the highest scientific certainty: The text of the New Testament is preserved, not critically but dogmatically unimpaired.

But since the text has variants in a whole series of important passages, the exegete must pay full attention to *Textual Criticism*. It is very much his concern that *Textual Criticism* should bring us closer to the text of the originals.

§ 12. THE GREEK MANUSCRIPTS

C. R. Gregory, *Die griechischen Hss des NT,* Leipzig 1908. W. H. P. Hatch, *The Principal Uncial MSS. of the NT,* Chicago 1939. K. W Clark, *A Descriptive Catalogue of Greek NT MSS. in America,* Chicago 1937. F. F. Bruce, *Recent Discoveries in Biblical MSS.:* Journal of transactions of the Victoria Institute 82 (1950) 131–149. F. G. Kenyon, *Der Text der griechischen Bibel,* German transl. by H. Bolewsky, Goettingen 1952 (from the 1936 edition with addenda and corrigenda from 1948). H. W. Huston, *A Critical Survey and Evaluation of the Earliest Greek Manuscripts of the NT,* Durham 1949. W. H. Hatch, *Facsimiles and Descriptions of Minuscule Manuscripts of the NT,* Cambridge Mass. 1951. [This important work, which contains 100 plates, deals with the most important Minucsule MSS. (e. g. 1, 13, 33, 565), minuscule script, and the supplements to the text, and gives a sketch of the history of the text (cf. RB 1953, 601–603).] K. Aland, *Zur Liste der griechischen ntl Hss:* ThLZ 78 (1953) 465–496. Idem, *Zur Liste der griechischen ntl Hss V:* ZntW 45 (1954) 179–217. B. Botte, *Manuscrits grecs du NT:* DB Suppl 5, fasc. 27 (1954) 819–835.

1. Number, content, age, and present day names of the Greek Manuscripts

THE number of Greek MSS. of the New Testament which are known at the present day is about 4500; there are 241 Majuscules, 2533 Minuscules, 1838 Lectionaries (i. e., books containing passages for liturgical use) and 68 Papyri, the majority of which contain only small fragments of New Testament books. Only about 50 of the MSS. contain the entire New Testament. Four Majuscule Codices (ℵ B A C) were probably complete Bibles originally, containing the entire Greek Old and New Testaments; but only ℵ has the complete New Testament; B contains the greater part of it. As a rule only particular parts of it are united in one codex: the Gospels or the Pauline Epistles, or the Catholic Epistles (with or without Apc.). The Gospels are commonest; then come the Pauline Epistles followed by Acts and the Catholic Epistles; MSS. of Apc. are fewest in number.

In almost all the Greek MSS. the parts of the New Testament are arranged in the following order: Gospels, Acts, Catholic Epistles, Pauline Epistles, Apocalypse, but sometimes other arrangements are found, for example, some MSS. including ℵ have the order: Gospels, Pauline Epistles, Acts, Catholic Epistles, Apocalypse, while the Muratorian Canon, Eusebius and others have: Gospels, Acts, Pauline Epistles, Catholic Epistles, Apocalypse.

The oldest parchment MS., Codex Vaticanus (B), is of the mid-fourth century, but a number of Papyri are older. The oldest papyrus fragment of a New Testament book (Gospel of John) which we have is dated to the first half of the second century, about 130 A.D. (cf. § 12, 3). The papyrus codex of the Pauline Epistles in the Chester Beatty Collection ($\mathfrak{P}^{46}$), the greater part of which is preserved, comes from the first half of the third century.

As long as the number of known and valuable MSS. was small, it was possible to name them after their place of origin (e. g., Cod. Alexandrinus), their (former) owner (e. g., Cod. Bezae, Cod. Laudianus), their location (Cod. Vaticanus), or an accidental peculiarity (e. g., Cod. Ephraemi rescriptus). But as their number kept increasing it became necessary to have a short and clear method of referring to them. To meet this need, Johann Jakob Wettstein († 1754), a Protestant theologian of Basle, in his critical edition of the New Testament, printed in 1751–1752 at Amsterdam, used Arabic numerals to denote the Minuscules and Latin capitals for the Majuscules—these were later supplemented by the Greek and Hebrew alphabets. Later editors adopted his system in spite of its serious shortcomings; for the division of MSS. according to the style of handwriting is purely extrinsic, while the capitals, even with the help of the Greek and Hebrew alphabets—the latter is quite unsuitable for typographical reasons—were insufficient; a very serious drawback is the independent use of the signs for each group of books (Gospels, Pauline Epistles, Acts, Catholic Epistles, and Apocalypse), so that the same letter may refer to quite different MSS.—thus D with reference to the Gospels is Cod. Bezae, but for the Pauline Epistles it means Cod. Claromontanus.

To avoid these drawbacks Hermann von Soden († 1914) produced an entirely new system for denoting the MSS. He abandoned the practice of dividing the MSS. according to their script, and grouped them according to content. So a prefixed δ (= διαθήκη) signifies that a particular MS. contains the whole New Testament (with or without Apc.), ε (= εὐαγγέλιον) that it contains the Gospels, and α (= ἀπόστολος) the remaining books (Acts, Pauline and Catholic Epistles, Apc.), in whole or in part. Each of the three groups has its own series of numbers (δ1, δ2, etc.) whose figures are selected to indicate as a rule the age of the MS. (thus ε 103 is 11th century, ε 203 is 12th century). Because of its complexity this system has not yet been generally accepted.

At present most scholars use a system closely related to Wettstein's, which was proposed by C. R. Gregory († 1917). This system denotes the Majuscules by Arabic numerals preceded by zero (e. g. 015), but permits the use of the customary naming with capitals (e. g., B or 03). If correctors have worked over a MS. after its completion, the original reading is denoted by an asterisk (B⋆), and the various emendations by small Latin letters or by Arabic numerals set high (Ba, Bb, B¹, B²); marginal corrections are denoted by mg (margo). The Minuscule MSS. are numbered consecutively by Arabic numerals without reference to their content; if necessary the content may be described by Latin letters after the number: e for the Gospels, a for Acts and Catholic

Epistles, p for Pauline Epistles, and r (revelatio) for Apc. The Papyri are numbered separately, the numeral following 𝔓 (in broken type). Correspondingly Lectionaries are denoted by l, Ostraka (potsherds) and talismans by a broken 𝔒 or 𝔗 respectively, with an Arabic numeral set high.[1]

The Lectionaries or ecclesiastical books of pericopae, of which a very great number has survived, have been little examined. There is a short survey of research on them in H. Greeven: ThLZ 76 (1951) 513–522. Since 1933 E. C. Colwell and D. W. Riddle have been issuing *Studies in the Lectionary Text of the Greek New Testament*, Chicago; up to the present there have appeared: I 1933; II, 1 1934; II, 2 1936; II, 3 1944; III, 1 1955. B. M. Metzger, *The Saturday and Sunday Lessons from Luke in the Greek Gospel Lectionaries,* Chicago 1944.

The Lectionaries contain passages from either the Gospels or the Apostolos (Epistles and Acts); the Greek Church has not accepted a single passage of the Apc. into a Lectionary. Their text is not a homogeneous unity, for the various passages belong to different textual forms. Obviously the Lectionary itself did not undergo a century long historical development, for once chosen the text of a lesson was clung to for centuries, so that even late MSS. may offer an old text. Sometimes in the Lectionaries only the beginning and end of the pericope is modified to give a more intelligible text. Sometimes also the text was filled out from the synoptic parallels, e. g., Lk. 23, 43 sq. (Our Lord's sweat in the garden) was added after Mt. 26, 39. It must also be borne in mind that MSS. with continuous text may have undergone the influence of Lectionaries, especially in harmonized readings; this would provide an explanation of the fact that in the so-called Ferrar-group (cf. § 12, 4) the *pericopa de adultera* John 7, 53 to 8, 11 stands after Lk. 21, 19; for in the Lectionaries this text often appears on

---

[1] A very useful guide is B. Kraft, *Die Zeichen fuer die wichtigeren Hss des griechischen NT,* Freiburg i. Br. 1955 (3rd edition expanded; cf. ThLZ 1955, 655 sq.).

the 8th October, while for the 7th October the Gospel pericope is Lk. 21, 12–19.

2. The most important Majuscule Manuscripts

B (03, δ1), Codex Vaticanus, in three columns; size of leaves 27.5 × 27.5 cm.; written in Eygpt about 350 A.D.; its 759 very beautifully written pages contain almost the entire Old Testament and the New Testament as far as Heb. 9, 14a (Past, Philem., Apc. are missing; there are 142 pages of New Testament). It is the oldest surviving parchment MS., and was in the Vatican Library by 1475.

Bibliorum ss. graecorum Codex Vaticanus 1209 (Cod. B) denuo phototypice expressus etc., P. II. Testamentum Novum, Milan 1904 (Codices e Vaticanis selecti IV). On it E. Tisserant, Ang 20 (1943) 237–248.

ℵ (also S; 01, δ2), Codex Sinaiticus (graecus), in four columns; size of leaves 43 × 37.8 cm.; 347 leaves surviving. Discovered by Konstantin von Tischendorf in the monastery of St. Catherine on Mount Sinai (1844 and 1859), it was presented by the monks to Czar Alexander II because of his generous gifts; it remained in St. Petersburg until 1933 when it was purchased at £ 100,000 for the British Museum in London. The New Testament has survived almost entirely. It also contains at the end the Epistle of Barnabas and part of the *Pastor* of Hermas. It was written to dictation by three hands about the mid-fourth century in Egypt or Caesarea Pal.; its foundation is an Egyptian MS.; the script is very beautiful, but textually it is careless.

Photographic reproduction: Kirsopp Lake, *Codex Sinaiticus Petropolitanus. The New Testament,* Oxford 1911. H. J. M. Milne and T. C. Skeat, *Scribes and correctors of the Codex Sinaiticus²,* British Museum, 1954. On the discovery and sale of the Codex cf. W. Hotzelt, ThLZ 74 (1949) 457–470.

A (02, δ4), Codex Alexandrinus, written in the middle or towards the end of the 5th century, probably in Egypt; in two columns; four volumes. The Codex, which from 1098 had been in the Patriarchate Library at Alexandria, was sent to Charles I of England in 1628 by Cyril Lucar, Patriarch of Constantinople (formerly of Alexandria). It has been in the British Museum since 1751. It consists of 773 pages, and contains the Old Testament, the New Testament (with some *lacunae*) and the two epistles of Clement. The missing parts are: Mt. 1, 1 to 25, 6; John 6, 50 to 8, 52; 2 Cor. 4, 13 to 12, 7. In the Gospels its text shows the oldest stage of the so-called Koine Text; for the remaining parts of the New Testament it is one of the best sources for the "neutral" text (cf. § 21, 1 and 3).

F. G. Kenyon, *The Codex Alexandrinus in Reduced Photographic Facsimile. NT and Clementine Epistles,* London 1909.

The MSS. B ℵ A are the most important textual sources for the Greek New Testament.

C (04, δ3), Codex Ephraemi rescriptus, in one column, in the National Library in Paris, the most important palimpsest of the New Testament; deciphered by Tischendorf. It was written (presumably in Egypt) as a full Bible in the 5th century; in the 12th century it was erased and a Greek version of Ephraem the Syrian's treatises was written over it. It contains only a small part of the Old Testament (on 64 leaves), but about $^5/_8$ of the New (on 145 leaves) with parts of almost all the books. Its text shows the same character as the text of B and ℵ, but it has been influenced by the Antiochene revision and also has some Western readings.

C. v. Tischendorf, *Codex Ephraemi Syri rescriptus sive fragmenta Novi Testamenti,* Leipzig 1843.

Dᵉᵛ ᵃᶜᵗ (05, δ5), Codex Bezae or Cantabrigiensis, the oldest surviving bilingual codex of the Bible. 406 leaves written colometrically; on the left side of the open book is Greek and on the right the Latin text of the four Gospels in the order Mt., John, Lk., Mk., together with a fragment of 3 John and Acts. The Gospels are almost entire, and a large part of Acts is preserved. The MS. was written in the 6th or perhaps the late 5th century. Its place of origin is quite uncertain; southern Gaul, Southern

Italy, Sicily, Egypt and Illyria (Dacia or Moesia) have all been suggested.

From the 9th century it was in Southern France (presumably in Lyons) and was seized from the monastery of St. Irenaeus at Lyons by the Huguenots in 1561; it came into the possession of Theodore of Beza, the scholar, who was Calvin's friend, and in 1581 he presented it to Cambridge University. It is the most remarkable of all the New Testament MSS. which we possess; its text substantially agrees with the Old Latin sources, and shows a close relationship to the Old Syriac version. The Latin side has influenced the Greek in many respects. There is a society for the study of this MS. in England which was founded by Rendall Harris, and which issues a special (private) review (Bulletin of the Bezan Club).

Photographic reproduction: *Codex Bezae Cantabrigiensis* . . . 2 vols., Cambridge 1899. The text of Acts in B and D is in Ropes, *The Text of the Acts* (cf. § 29). R. C. Stone, *The Language of the Latin Text of Cod. Bezae,* Urbana 1946.

W (032, ε 014), of the 5th century, containing one column to the page; in Washington; it was acquired in Egypt by C. L. Freer in 1906; 187 parchment sheets; it contains the four Gospels in the order Mt., John, Lk., Mk. Its text belongs to no single group (cf. *Botte:* DB Suppl III, 527–529; Lagrange, *Crit. text.* 147–149). The apocryphal continuation of Mk. 16, 14—the so-called Freer Logion (cf. § 23, 5)—which is also attested by Jerome, is of importance.

H. A. Sanders, *The Washington Manuscript of the Four Gospels,* New York 1912.

Θ (038, ε 050), Codex Coridethi, so called from the monastery in the Caucasus; a Gospel MS. with two columns to the page, of the 7th or 9th century; now in the State Museum at Tiflis. The text shows close affinity with fam 1 and 13 and with Minuscules 28, 565, 700 (cf. HarvThR 1923, 267–286).

G. Beermann and C. R. Gregory, *Die Koridethi-Evv.,* Leipzig 1913 (an edition of the Text). B. Botte: DB Suppl 5 (1950) 192–196.

E^a (08, α1001), Codex Laudianus (so called from its former owner, the Anglican Archbishop Laud of Canterbury, † 1645); a Latin-Greek (!) MS. of Acts, written probably in the 6th century, presumably in Sardinia. It is now in the Bodleian at Oxford.

For a long time this MS. was regarded as the second best source for the Greek form of the Western Text, but it has now been established that its basis is the Alexandrian Text, which then was widespread (cf. Lagrange, *Crit. text.* 401). For the history of the MS. see Ropes, HarvThR 16 (1923) 175–186, and Laistner, ibid. 30 (1937) 37–50.

D^{paul} (06, α1026), Codex Claromontanus, a Greek-Latin MS. contemporary with D$^{ev\ act}$, also written in cola; it was discovered in the monastery of Clermont near Beauvais by Theodore of Beza and is now in the National Library at Paris. It contains the 13 Pauline Epistles, then the Canon Claromontanus (cf. § 7, 1), and finally (from a different source) Hebrews. Its Latin text is closely related to the citations of Lucifer bishop of Cagliari in Sardinia (mid-fourth century); cf. § 13.

C. von Tischendorf, *Codex Claromontanus* . . . , Leipzig 1852. Cf. also H. J. Vogels, *Amicitiae Corolla Presented to J. R. Harris,* London 1933, 274–299.

G^{paul} (012, α1028), Codex Boernerianus (because it was formerly the property of Prof. C. F. Boerner of Leipzig, † 1753), written in St. Gallen in the 9th or 10th century; it is now in the Saxony Landesbibliothek at Dresden. It contains the Pauline Epistles (without Hebrews) with an interlinear Latin translation.

A. Reichardt, *Der Codex Boernerianus der Briefe des Apostels Paulus,* Leipzig 1909 (photographic). *Codex* Δ, a MS. of the Gospels from St. Gallen, with interlinear Latin translation, makes a unity with G.

F^{paul} (010, α1029), Codex Augiensis (because it came from Reichenau in Lake Constance), a Greek-Latin MS. of the 13 Pauline Epistles—Hebrews in Latin only—of the 9th century. The Greek text corresponds so closely to G that F and G must have a common origin, or else F is simply a copy of G (so Lagrange).

W. H. P. Hatch, *On the Relationship of Cod. Augiensis and Cod. Boernerianus:* Harv. St. in Class. Phil. 60 (1951) 187–199.

D and G have a common ancestry and are the principal sources for the Western Text of the Pauline Epistles (cf. § 14, 1 c; 21, 2).

H[paul] (015, α 1002), Codex Euthalianus, originally found at Mount Athos; 41 leaves survive, one column to a page; written in the 6th century; the leaves are scattered over various libraries; it contains fragments of 1 and 2 Cor., Gal., Col., 1 Thess., Heb., 1 and 2 Tim., Tit. A note at the end of the last page tells us that it was compared with a MS. of Pamphilus in the library at Caesarea Pal; it has Euthalius' division.

I[paul] (016, α 1041), fragments of a 6th century Egyptian MS. with parts of all the Pauline Epistles (except Rom.) and of Heb.; one column to a page; it belongs to the Freer Collection.

The NT Manuscripts in the Freer Collection, P. II: The Washington MS. of the Epistles of Paul, by H. A. Sanders, New York 1918.

H and I are important sources for the Alexandrian text of the Pauline Epistles (cf. Lagrange, *Crit. text.* 467 sqq.).

3. *The most important Papyri*

The New Testament Papyri which have been discovered in Egypt are significant for two main reasons: 1) some fragments are 100 to 150 years earlier than the oldest surviving parchment MSS. of the Greek Bible; and 2) they tell us authentically what textual forms were available and in use in Egypt from about 200 A.D. till the 7th century.

G. Maldfeld, *Die griechischen Hssbruchstuecke des NT auf Papyrus:* ZntW 42 (1949) 228–253 (the most recent and complete list, with 62 entries; cf. also ThLZ 75, 1950, 692–696, and ZntW 43, 1950/51, 260 sq.).

The oldest Papyrus fragment of a New Testament text, 𝔓[52] (John 18, 31–33 37 38: only partially preserved) is from a Papyrus codex which was written about 130 A.D. Its discoverer C. H. Roberts published it in 1935: *An unpublished Fragment of the Fourth Gospel in the John Rylands Library,* Manchester 1935 (cf. Benoit RB 45, 1936,

269–272; Jeremias, ThBl 15, 1936, 97 sqq.). Cf. also R. Collin, *An early Papyrus of the First Gospel:* HarvThR 46 (1953) 233–237 [three second-century fragments (of Mt. 26) from Magdalen College, Oxford].

𝔓¹: Mt. 1, 1–9 12–20 (3rd or 4th century).

𝔓⁴: fairly large fragments of Lk. 1–6 (4th century); re-edited by J. Merell in RB 47 (1938) 5–22.

𝔓⁵ (= P. Oxyrhynch. 208 + 1781): fragments of John 1 16 20 (3rd century).

𝔓¹³ (= P. Oxyrhynch. 657): Heb. 2, 14 to 5, 5; 10, 8 to 11, 13; 11, 28 to 12, 17 (the remnant of a roll written about 300).

𝔓³⁷: Mt. 26, 10–52 (3rd century): published HarvThR 1926, 215–226; cf. RB 38 (1929) 161–177.

𝔓³⁸: Acts 18, 27 to 19,6 12–16 (4th century). Reprinted by S. Lake in *Beginnings of Christianity* (cf. § 3, 7) V 262 sqq.

Between 1930 and 1936 A. Chester Beatty, the English collector, discovered in Egypt extensive remains of 12 papyrus codices, among which are three 3rd century New Testament MSS., viz.:

𝔓⁴⁵: 30 fragmentary pages of a codex which contained the four Gospels in the order Mt. John, Lk. Mk., and Acts.

𝔓⁴⁶: 86 leaves (44 × 26 cm. in size) of a 104 leaf codex of the Pauline Epistles (without Past). The surviving passages are Rom. 5, 17 to 6, 14; 8, 15 to 16, 27; Heb., 1 and 2 Cor., Eph., Gal., Phil., Col., 1 Thess. 1, 1 to 2, 3; 5, 5–28. The Chester Beatty Collection has 56 pages, 30 are at the University of Michigan, Ann Arbor, USA.

𝔓⁴⁷: 10 pages of a codex of the Apc. (9, 10 to 17, 2 with insignificant *lacunae*).

An edition with photographic reproductions by F. G. Kenyon: *The Chester Beatty Biblical Papyri, I: General Introduction; II: The Gospels and Acts; III: Pauline Epistles and Revelation.* London 1933–36; Supplement 1936/37. The numerous studies on them are listed by W. G. Kuemmel: ThRdsch NF 10 (1938) 292 sq.; F. W. Beare, *The Text of the Epistle to the Hebrews in* 𝔓⁴⁶: JBL 63 (1944) 379–396; R. V. G. Tasker, *The Chester Beatty Papyrus of the Apc. of John:* JThSt 50 (1949) 60–68.

𝔓⁴⁸: Acts 23, 11–17 23–29 (3rd century) published by G. Mercati in *Papyri della Società Italiana* X, 112–118 under No. 1165; printed ZntW 32 (1933) 187, and in Clark, *The Acts of the Apostles* (cf. § 29) 409–413. It attests the existence of the Greek form of the Western Text in Egypt in the third century.

𝔓⁵⁰: Acts 8, 26–32; 10, 26–31 (mid 4th century), published by Kraeling in *Quantulacumque* presented to K. Lake, London 1937, 163–172.

𝔓⁵³: Mt. 26, 29–40; Acts 9, 34 to 10, 1, published by Sanders, ibid. 151–162 (ThLZ 64, 1939, 341).

𝔓⁶⁶: John 1, 1 to 6, 11; 6, 25 to 14, 26 (first half of 3rd century, 16 × 14 cm., one column; published by V. Martin, *Papyrus Bodmer II* (1956).

K. Aland, *Papyrus Bodmer II* (= p⁶⁶). A first report. ThLZ 82 (1957) 161–184; id.: *Neue ntl Papyri*: NTSt 3 (1957) 261–286; id.: Zur Liste der ntl Hss VI: ZntW 48 (1957) 141–191. A. F. J. Klijn, *Papyrus Bodmer II (John I–XIV) and the Text of Egypt*: NTSt 3 (1957) 327–334. M.-E. Boismard, *Le Papyrus Bodmer II*: RB 64 (1957) 363 398.

Of the Papyri listed here, 𝔓 ¹ ⁴ ⁵ ¹³ ⁴⁵ (Acts), ⁴⁶ ⁴⁷ ⁵⁰ ⁵³ ⁶⁶ represent the Alexandrian Text, 𝔓³⁸ ⁴⁸ the Western Text and 𝔓³⁷ ⁴⁵ (Gospels) the Caesarean Text.

4. *The most important Minuscule Manuscripts*

The vast majority of Minuscule MSS. have little or no value for textual criticism, but an exception must be made for the few Minuscules which are copies of lost valuable Majuscules. Hermann von Soden's (cf. § 20) great service was to make more extensive use than before of the Minuscule MSS. for reconstructing the New Testament text. He and his collaborators were the first to discover many of them or to inspect them more accurately.

William Hugh Ferrar († 1871), the Irish scholar, had previously recognized the homogeneity of MSS. 13, 69, 124, 326, which go back to a common archetype and which attest the existence of a text whose individuality and diffusion has only recently been recognized (the so-called Caesarean Text, cf. § 21, 3): it is called Ferrar group (Nestle: φ) or fam 13. It is known to-day that this group has at least 10 members (543, 788, 826, 828, 983, 1689 also). They belong to the 11th century and come mainly from southern Italy, but the archetype seems to come from Palestine or Syria (Lake). As Soden had already recognized, they fall into 3 sub-groups: a (13, 346, 543, 826, 828), b (69, 124, 788), c (983, 1689).

B. Botte: *Ferrar,* in DB Suppl III (1938) 272–274; K. and S. Lake, *Family 13 (The Ferrar Group). The Text According to Mark with a Collation of Codex 28 of the Gospels,* London 1941 (cf. ThLZ 1947, 29 sq., RB 1946, 473; J. Geerlings: JBL 67, 1948, 347 sqq; Kenyon, JThSt 43, 1942, 94-98).

Kirsopp Lake († 1946), the textual critic, discovered a textual family related to the Ferrar group: 1, 118, 131, 209 belong to it; it is called Lake group (Nestle: λ) or fam 1. According to Tasker, at least 22, 1582 also belong to it.

The Minuscules 22, 28, 565, 700 are related to fam 1 and fam 13.

K. Lake, *Codex 1 of the Gospels and its allies* (ThSt VII, 2) Cambridge 1902.

Valuable sources for the so-called Alexandrian ("Neutral") Text are 33 (New Testament without Apc.; 9th century); 81 (Acts; written in 1044 A.D.); 579 (Gospels; 13th century).

A. Schmidke, *Die Evv. eines alten Unzialkodex* (B ℵ – Text) nach einer Abschrift des 13. Jh. (= 579), Leipzig 1903.

1739 (α 78), a 10th century MS. at mount Athos, which E. von der Goltz discovered in 1879, originally contained the whole New Testament (the Gospels and Apc. are lost). The original copyist, who wrote the ancestor of this MS. towards the end of the fourth century, informs us that the text of the Pauline Epistles agrees with the text on which Origen commented, while in the case of Romans he took it directly from Origen's commentary. For this reason 1739 is an authentic witness of the Alexandrian Text.

The MS. was freshly collated by K. Lake and S. New: *Six collations of NT MSS.,* HarvThSt 17 (1933) 141–219; cf. K. W. Kim, *Cod. 1582, 1793 and Origen:* JBL 69 (1950) 167–175.

614 (α 364) of the 13th century is of particular importance for the Western Text.

A. V. Valentine-Richards, *The Text of Acts in Codex 614 and its Allies,* Cambridge 1934. On this cf. JThSt 1935, 191–194; 1937, 195–399; Univ. of Missouri Studies, 1936, 141–189.

2053 in Messina, of the 13th century, contains the Apc. with Oecumenius' commentary; with AC and Min. 2344 it is the best source for the text of the Apc.

Published by H. C. Hoskier: Univ. of Michigan Studies, Humanistic Series XXIII, Ann Arbor 1928.

The great antiquity of a considerable number of Biblical MSS. can be appreciated by a glance at the sources for classical Greek and Latin authors. Our libraries possess practically no ancient MSS. of the classical Greek writers, whose MSS. tradition generally begins with the so-called Byzantine renaissance (9th–11th century). Oxford possesses the oldest MS. of Plato († 347 B.C.) which was written in 895 A.D. In the case of the Latin authors the situation is somewhat better; there is a small number of MSS. from late antiquity (of Cicero, Virgil, Livy, Plautus, Terence), but the majority are from the Carolingian era, having been copied from MSS. of the 4th–6th centuries (cf. H. Lietzmann, Die Antike 11, 1935, 139–148).

§ 13. THE CITATIONS AND COMMENTARIES OF THE FATHERS

BESIDES the Greek MSS. we have two other important groups of sources for the New Testament text, namely: 1) the citations of the ancient Christian writers from the New Testament and their commentaries on the individual books, and 2) the ancient version of the New Testament. It would be an error to regard these as merely subsidiary helps for establishing the original wording; they are in no way inferior to the Greek MSS. in value, for without them it would be impossible to elucidate the History of the Greek Text, and such a history is indispensible for a correct evaluation of the Greek MSS. and for the reconstruction of the oldest possible Greek Text.

The significance of the patristic citations lies in the fact that they enable us to establish the Biblical text of a particular time and place, a thing which generally is not the case with the Greek MSS.; they are also of importance because the text which the Fathers use is often older than most of our Greek MSS. So, for example, from Cyprian's († 258) writings we can form a picture of what kind of Bible text the African Church had in the first half of the third century.

The citations of patristic writers quite often differ from the text of our MSS., and it has frequently been thought that they cited freely from memory; more recent investigations have demonstrated that this is not the case, but that the Fathers—except the most ancient, who give allusions rather than citations—quote the Bible text much more accurately than is generally acknowledged. If they depart from the text of our MSS., this is because they are following a different text, and one which is older and nearer to the originals (cf. § 21, 1).

Particular importance attaches to the not uncommon occasions when the writer refers to a peculiarity of wording or collates various readings. Thus, for example, St. Jerome in Ep. 119 reviews the three forms of the text of 1 Cor. 15, 51 and says that one of them is found only in the Latin sources; Eusebius assures us that the so-called canonical Ending of Mk. is missing from the oldest and best MSS., and Jerome informs us that he also finds an apocryphal addition of a few lines in some MSS. (cf. § 23, 5).

Because of the great importance of these Biblical citations for the History of the Text there is need for a reconstruction of the text which each writer used, and a comparison of these texts with the Bible MSS.; this work has already been done to some extent, but it has not yet reached a satisfactory or complete conclusion.

For the Greek writers, in addition to the work *The NT in the Apostolic Fathers* (Oxford 1905), we possess investigations of the text of the Gospels of

Justin Martyr (by W. Bousset, Goettingen 1891, and E. Lippelt, Halle 1901); of Marcion's NT text (by A. Harnack, *Marcion*[2], Leipzig 1924); of Irenaeus of Lyons (Sanday, Turner, and Souter, *Novum Testamentum S. Irenaei,* Oxford 1923, and B. Kraft, *Die Evangelienzitate des hl. Irenaeus,* Freiburg i. Br. 1924); of Clement of Alexandria (P. M. Barnard, Cambridge 1899, on Gospels and Acts); of Origen's text of Romans (by O. Bauernfeind, Leipzig 1932); of Chrysostom's text of the Pauline Epistles (by K. Gifford, Halle 1902), and his text of Mark (by J. Geerlings and S. New: HarvThR 24, 1931, 121–142). In the Festschrift for M. Meinertz, (Muènster 1951) K. Th. Schaefer examines the citations in the Latin version of Irenaeus and reaches the conclusion that the translator kept substantially to his original even in Biblical citations, and was only to a limited degree influenced by the Latin Bible text (pp. 50–59). K. W. Kim demonstrates that the text of Mt. in Origen's *Contra Celsum* is more closely related to the Minuscules 1 and 1582 than to any other sources: JThSt NS 4 (1953) 4–29; he deals with the text of Mt. in Origen's commentary on Mt. in JThSt 68 (1949) 125–139. H. S. Murphy investigates the NT text of Eusebius: *Demonstratio evangelica* (JBL 73 (1954) 162–168, and C. H. Dicks deals with Chrysostom's text of Mt. (JBL 76, 1948, 365–376). Studies and Documents, vol. 17, gives an inquiry—with meagre results—by J. H. Greenlee, *The Gospel Text of Cyril of Jerusalem* (Copenhagen 1955).

For the Greek Fathers there is also important material in the *catenae*[1] of which only a few have been critically edited: K. Staab, *Pauluskommentare aus der griechischen Kirche aus Katenenhss,* Muenster 1933. J. Sickenberger collected the fragments of Titus of Bostra's sermons on Luke which are preserved in *catenae* (Leipzig 1901), and he investigated the Luke *catenae* of Nicetas of Heraclea (Leipzig 1902). J. Reuss plans to produce a critical edition of the ample fragments of patristic commentaries on Mt. and John, which are contained in the *catenae* (cf. his examination of the Mt. Mk., Lk. *catenae,* NtA XVIII, 4/5: 1941).

J. Reuss, *Matthaeuskommentare aus der griechischen Kirche*, collected from catena manuscripts and edited, Berlin 1957. J. N. Birdall, *The Text of the Gospels in Photius,* I: JThSt NS 7 (1956) 42–55. M. J. Suggs, *The Eusebian Text of Matthew,* NT I (1956) 233–245.

For the Latin Church we also possess some important studies: Hans von Soden undertook to reconstruct the *Latin NT in Africa in the time of Cyprian* on the basis of the oldest MSS. and patristic citations (cf. § 14, 1). G. D. J. Aalders dealt with Tertulllians' Gospel citations (*Zitate Tertullians aus den Evv. und die altlateinische Bibeluebersetzung,* Amsterdam 1932), and more recently with the citations from Lk. in particular (Mnemosyne, 1937, 241–282); after him A. J. B. Higgins published a longish study on the Latin text of Lk. in Marcion and Tertullian (VCH 5, 1951, 1–42). H. J. Vogels demonstrates that the Biblical citations in three pseudo-Ambrosian sermons on Lk. 12, 33 show a very strong affinity to Cyprian's Bible. (ZntW 46, 1955, 60–68). The same scholar published a comprehensive work, *Untersuchungen zur Geschichte der lateinischen Apk. Uebersetzung* (Duesseldorf 1920) where he assembled exhaustively the quotations of the Fathers, and the Apc. text of the commentaries (Victorinus of Pettau, Tyconius, Primasius) and of the Old-

---

[1] R. Devreesse, Art. *Chaînes (Catenae):* DB Suppl 1 (1928) 1084–1233.

Latin MSS. K. Th. Schaefer (1929; cf. § 46, 2) did the same work for Heb. The Bible text of Novatian and so of the Roman Church in his day, has been treated in rather short articles by A. d'Alès (Bb 4, 1923, 56–90) and A. Baumstark (OCh III 5, 1930, 1–14). F. J. Bonnassieux (Lyons 1906) deals with Hilary's text of the Synoptics; Lucifer of Cagliari's quotations from John are treated by H. J. Vogels (ThQ 1922, 23–37; 183–200), while his citations from Acts and the Pauline Epistles are studied by A. M. Coleman (Welwyn 1927; Oxford 1946, 1947). Ambrose's text of Lk. and John has been reconstructed respectively by G. Rolando and T. Caragliano (Bb 27, 1946). Studies on Augustine's Bible text have been published by S. H. Milne (Cambridge 1926, *The Gospels;* unsatisfactory, cf. Burkitt, JThSt 1927, 101–105) and D. de Bruyne (Collectanea Biblica Latina V, Rome 1921, and Miscellanea Agostiniana II, 1931, 521–606). The article of B. Botte mentioned in § 14 gives further references.

R. P. Casey deals at length with the significance of the patristic witnesses for the NT text in Parvis-Wikgren (cf. § 14).

§ 14. THE LATIN VERSION

Note: In Parvis-Wikgren (cf. § 11) pp. 25–68, B. Metzger gives a survey of research during the last fifty years on NT versions up to 1000 A.D. A. Vööbus, *Early versions of the NT MSS.*, Stockholm 1954 (Papers of the Estonian Theolog. Society in exile, vol. 6) [Tatian's Diatessaron (1–31), the Latin (33–65), Syriac (67–131), Armenian (133–171), Georgian (173–209), Coptic (211–241), Ethiopian (243–269), Arabic (271–297) and Gothic (299–309) versions]. B. M. Metzger, *A Survey of Recent Research on the Ancient Versions of the NT:* NTSt 2 (1955) 1–16 (covers the years 1950–1954).

F. Stummer, *Einfuehrung in die lateinische Bibel²*, Paderborn 1938, H. Rost, *Die Bibel im Mittelalter, Beitraege zur Geschichte und Bibliographie der Bibel,* Augsburg 1939. B. Bischoff, *Neue Materialien zum Bestand und zur Geschichte der altlateinischen Bibelueberetzungen:* Misc. Mercati 1 (1946) 407–436. G. Bardy, *La question des langues dans l'église ancienne* 1 (Paris 1948). A. Cordoliani, *Le texte de la Bible en Irlande du Ve au IXe siècle:* RB 57 (1950) 1–38. B. Botte, Art. *Latines (versions) antérieures à St. Jérôme:* DB Suppl 5 (1952) 334–347. W. G. Kuemmel, ThRdsch NF 10 (1938) 304 sqq. B. Fischer, *Der Vulgata-Text des NT:* ZntW 46 (1955) 178–196.

W. Thiele, *Untersuchungen zu den altlateinischen Texten der drei Johannes-Briefe,* Diss. Tuebingen 1956 (ThLZ 1957, 71 sq.).

1. *The Old-Latin version*

THE name Old-Latin version *(Vetus Latina,* sc. *versio)* is applied to the Latin text of the Bible which was available and in use before St. Jerome's Vulgate. In the past (and sometimes even yet) it was called *Itala* because of a passage of St. Augustine, *De doctrina christiana* II 15, 22 *(in ipsis autem interpretationibus itala ceteris praeferatur; nam est verborum tenacior cum perspicuitate sententiae)*. The meaning of this passage is disputed even to-day[1], but since Augustine himself says that there were not one but many Latin versions *(qui enim scripturas ex hebraea lingua in graecam verterunt, numerari possunt, latini autem interpretes nullo modo,* ibid. II 16), he can only intend the name Itala to refer to one of these versions, and it must mean the version in use in Italy. It is for this reason that present day scholars prefer to speak of the Old-Latin Bible or the pre-Vulgate, though to be strictly accurate they ought to speak of Old-Latin versions.

Our information about the Old-Latin translation of the New Testament is very defective, but it is certain that it was not one uniform work; the books were translated a number of times and no single translator did all 27 books. It is almost universally agreed to-day that there were at least two quite distinct Old-Latin versions: the *Versio Itala* (or perhaps better *Europaea*) and the *Versio Afra*.

From the writings of Cyprian of Carthage it is certain that the *Versio Afra* was in existence about 240 A.D.; but it is older than that, and must have been made before the year 200. It may be deduced from Tertullian that in Africa in his time there was not only a Latin version of Marcion's Bible, but also a Catholic translation of the New Testament which was used in the Liturgy, and that this Catholic version is identical with the one which Cyprian used.[2]

---

[1] B. Botte reviews this dispute Art. *Itala:* DB Suppl 4 (1949) 777–782. On the name *Itala* cf. also J. Schildenberger, *Die Itala des hl. Augustinus, Festschrift fuer A. Dold,* Beuron 1952, pp. 84–102.

[2] Cf. Hans von Soden, *Das lateinische NT in Afrika zur Zeit Cyprians* (TU 3, vol. III, 1909); Idem, *Der lateinische Paulustext bei Marcion und Tertullian* (Festgabe fuer Adolf Juelicher), Tuebingen 1927, 229–281. K. Th. Schaefer, *Die Ueberlieferung des altlateinischen Galaterbriefes 1* (Braunsberg 1940) 1–40. See also Aalders and Higgins (§ 13). Cf. also the report on the philological dissertation of M. C. Tenny, *The Quotations from Luke in Tertullian as Related to the Texts of the 2. and 3. Centuries* (HarvSt in Class. Phil. 56/57, 1947, 257–260).

Tertullian used this Catholic version, though he occasionally finds fault with it and corrects it in the light of the Greek MSS., as he himself admits; in general, however, he remains very faithful to it as may be seen by comparing his text with that of the MSS. (Vercellensis, Palatinus) or of the African Fathers (Victorinus, Augustine). (Thus Boismard, RB 1954, 275.) Being acquainted with Greek he was able to undertake such corrections.[3]

There are two reasons for considering the *Versio Afra* the older: 1) it does not follow the original as closely as the *Versio Itala* does; 2) around 200 A.D. Africa was much more thoroughly latinized than Rome: Tertullian wrote in Latin while Marcus Aurelius († 180) and Hippolytus wrote Greek.

It is difficult to say when Italy got a Latin New Testament. At all events the Roman Church used Greek in its Liturgy until well into the 3rd century[4]; the tomb inscription of the catacombs until the year 250 are predominantly in Greek, and until that time the Popes generally have Greek names. Yet even in the first half of the 3rd century there was a strong minority of Latin speaking Christians at Rome, and in the course of the century Latin became universal there. It would be reasonable therefore to fix a date before 250 for the beginnings of the Latin version of the New Testament, at least of the Gospels and Pauline Epistles. The first epistle of Clement and the *Pastor* of Hermas were also translated into Latin at an early date. It is probable that the European form of the Latin New Testament was not made without knowledge of and

---

[3] According to G. Quispel, *De bronnen van Tertullianus Adv. Marc.*, Utrecht 1943. T. translated the Marcionite Bible also from Greek. Higgins (VCh 5, 1951, 1–42) denies this; he holds that T. used two Latin versions, one Catholic and one Marcionite. The Latin Bible text which he used himself was an older form of the African version which Cyprian used.

[4] Cf. G. la Piana: HarvThR 18 (1925) 201–277; C. H. Turner, *The oldest MS. of the Vulgate Gospels,* Oxford 1931; Bardy, 1, 81–121; Th. Klauser, Miscell. Mercati 1 (1946) 467–482. C. Mohrmann, *Les origines de la latinité chrétienne à Rome:* VCh 3 (1949) 67–106; 163–183 (but cf. C. Charlier: RBén 61, 1951, 185–187).

reference to the older African version; yet it must be considered a separate version, not merely a recension of the *Versio Afra*.

The material for the Old-Latin Bible has come down in MSS. (or MS. fragments) and in the citations of the Latin ecclesiastical writers. The material which was then known was collected for both testaments by the Maurist Pierre Sabatier: *Bibliorum sacrorum latinae versiones antiquae seu vetus Italica*, 3 vols., Rheims 1739–1751 (vol. 3 contains the New Testament); even to-day this work is indispensible. Jos. Denk (1927) devoted many years to revising and completing Sabatier's work; his extensive collection is preserved in Beuron Abbey. As a continuation and completion of this work Herder has been publishing at Freiburg since 1950: *Vetus Latina. Die Reste der altlateinischen Bibel nach Petrus Sabatier neu gesammelt und herausgegeben von der Erzabtei Beuron*. The more important MSS. of the Old-Latin Bible are published in two works: *Old-Latin Biblical texts* (Oxford 1883 onwards), 7 vols., and *Collectanea biblica latina* (Rome 1912 onwards), 8 vols. so far. T. Ayuso Maranzuela plans to publish a comprehensive work on the Spanish Old-Latin Bible; of the eight projected folio vols. he has issued vol. 1 *(Prolegómenos, introducción general, estudio y análisis de los fuentes)*, Madrid 1953.

An edition of the Old-Latin Bible on the basis of the MSS. was begun by A. Juelicher, of which three vols. have appeared to date: *Itala. Das Neue Testament in altlateinischer Ueberlieferung nach den Hss herausgegeben*. I. Matthaeusevangelium (Berlin 1938); II. Markusevangelium (ibid. 1940); III. Lukasevangelium (ibid. 1954), seen through the press by W. Matzkow. (Reconstruction of the *Versio Itala* and *Afra*).

The MSS. of the Old-Latin Bible are denoted by the small letters of the Latin alphabet: a, b, c, etc.

Review of the most important sources

a) For the Gospels we have about 20 MSS. or fragments of MSS.

but only four of them (k e a j) are recognized by present day scholarship as uncontaminated texts of the pre-Vulgate. The others are more or less overlaid with the Vulgate text.

The text of the *Versio Afra* is represented by k and e and by Cyprian and Pseudo-Cyprian.

k (Bobbiensis) 5/6th century; only 96 pages survive (fairly large portions of Mk., smaller parts of Mt.). The codex was presumably made in Ireland, and credible tradition says that it was brought to Bobbio (Northern Italy) by St. Columban; it is now in the National Library at Turin.—Editions: *Old-Lat. Bibl. Texts* II (1886); C. Cipolla, Turin 1933 (photostatic). A. H. A. Bakker, *A Study of Cod. Evang. Bobbiensis* (k), Amsterdam 1933. P. W. Hoogterp, *Étude sur le latin du Cod.Bobb.,* Wageningen 1930.

e (Palatinus) 5th century, purple parchment with silver writing, defective, formerly in the Hofbibliothek at Vienna, since 1919 in Trent.—Edition: C. von Tischendorf, *Evangelium Palatinum,* Leipzig 1949. H. G. Vogels, *Evangelium Palatinum, Studien zur aeltesten Geschichte der lateinischen Evangelienuebersetzung* (NtA XII, 3: 1926). It contains the African text in a strongly europeanized form.

The most important sources for the *Versio Itala* are the codices a b j f ff² c.

a (Vercellensis) 4/5th century, in the Cathedral treasury at Vercelli, badly damaged. According to tradition it was written by Eusebius († 371), bishop of Vercelli; it is probably the oldest Latin Gospel MS.—Edition: A. Gasquet in *Collect. bibl. lat.* III (1914). Cf. Vogels: BZ 1920/21, 301–308.

j (Sarzanensis) 5/6th century, written in Italy, purple codex, in Sarezzano (Piedmont), fragments of John 1–11; 18–20. Edition: G. Godu, *Codex Sarzanensis,* Monte Cassino 1936 (*Spicilegium Casinense* II).

b (Veronensis), purple parchment with silver writing of the 5th century; in the possession of Verona Cathedral Chapter.—

Edition: E. S. Buchanan in *Old-Lat. Bibl. Texts* VI (1911). W. Telfer, *The Codex Verona* LX (58): HarvThR 36 (1943) 160–246 (History of studies of the MS.).

f (Brixianus), purple, parchment with silver writing of the 6th century, in Brescia; closely related to the famous *Codex argenteus* of Uppsala (cf. § 15). Both MSS. are copies of a bilingual Latin-Gothic original. Cf. also RB 1950, 467.—Edition: Wordsworth-White, *Novum Testamentum latine,* vol. I, 1889.

ff² (Corbeiensis II) 5/6th century, from the monstery at Corbey in France; now in the National Library in Paris.—Edition: E. S. Buchanan, *Old-Lat. Bibl. Texts V* (1907).

c (Colbertinus) written in the 12th century, probably in southern France, now in the National Library at Paris: a mixed MS. with African (Mk., Lk.), European (Mt.) and Vulgate Text. —Edition: H. J. Vogels, *Evangelium Colbertinum, hrsg. und untersucht* I (Text), II (Untersuchungen), Bonn 1953 (*Bonner Biblische Beitraege* 4 and 5). [The only MS. which gives the African text of the four Gospels completely, though not uncontaminated. Vogels dates the MS., which was probably written in the Languedoc, to the 2nd half of the 12th century, and regards it as a careful copy of an older original; cf. ThLZ 1955, 599–601.]

b) For Acts we have only about 6 MSS. The oldest Latin version of this book is in the Fleury palimpsest (Floriacensis, h) of the 7th century, but it contains only a quarter of Acts. Since its text form agrees with Cyprian's, this translation must be regarded as an African version. But it circulated almost everywhere, and still had its authority in Africa even in Augustine's time.

Codex Gigas (gig or g) contains another Old-Latin text form of Acts. This is an entire Latin Bible which was written in the 13th century in Bohemia; it is exceptionally large, and in 1648 it was taken to Stockholm by the Swedes as war booty. Only in Acts and Apc. does it contain an Old-Latin text. Since its text form for Acts agrees with the text of Acts of Lucifer of Cagliari in

Sardinia—who cites more than an eighth of Acts verbatim in his writings between 355 and 362 A.D.—gig therefore attests a translation of Acts which was made before 350 A.D. It was not independent of the African version although its author intended to make a completely new work.

An edition of h was produced by E. S. Buchanan in *Old-Lat. Bibl. Texts V* (1907) and better by Ropes, *The Text of Acts,* 1926 (cf. § 29); edition of gig.— J. Belsheim, *Apg. und Apk. in einer alten lateinischen Uebersetzung,* Christiania 1879. See also A. Juelicher, *Kritische Analyse der lateinischen Uebersetzungen der Apg.:* ZntW (1914) 163–188; Th. Zahn, *Die Urausgabe der Apg. des Lucas,* Leipzig 1916, 11–202; Ropes, loc. cit. pp. CVI—CXXVII.

c) For the Pauline Epistles we have the Latin columns of the four bilingual codices D[paul] (Claromontanus), G[paul] (Boernerianus), F[paul] (Augiensis), E[paul] (Leningrad)—only d and g are of real importance—and the MS. fragments gue (palimpsest leaves of the 6th century in Wolfenbuettel) and r (the Freising fragments, mostly in Munich, the remains of a corpus of the Pauline and Catholic Epistles, written in the 6th or 7th century). The paucity of MSS. is offset to some degree by a number of commentaries on the Pauline Epistles by Latin writers: Marius Victorinus (converted in 355 A.D.) on Gal., Eph., Phil.; Ambrosiaster and Pelagius on all 13 Pauline Epistles; Jerome on Philem., Gal., Tit.; Augustine on Rom., Gal.

Das Corpus Paulinum des Ambrosiaster ed. H. J. Vogels, Bonn 1957.

There is only one Old-Latin version of the Pauline Epistles which was probably made in Africa around 200 A.D. or even earlier, but it appears in a number of recensions (Lagrange).

D. de Bruyne, *Les fragments de Freising,* 1921 (Collect. bibl. lat. V); cf. DB Suppl 3 (1938) 530–532, and Lagrange, *Crit. text.* 491–498. K. Th. Schaefer deals with the four bilingual MSS. mentioned above in the Festgabe *Scientia Sacra,* for Cardinal Schulte, Duesseldorf 1935, 41–70.

d) Before Jerome there were (at least) two Latin versions of the Epistle to the Hebrews; one is represented by d (Claromontanus), the other by r (Freising fragments), Augustine and the Carthaginian bishop Capreolus.

K. Th. Schaefer, *Untersuchungen zur Geschichte der lateinischen Uebersetzung des Hebr.*, Freiburg i. Br. 1929. Bischoff, *loc. cit.*, publishes from a Munich MS. Heb. 7,8–20 and 10, 23–39.

e) For the Catholic Epistles the material is very scanty; indeed we have not a complete Old-Latin text of all 7 Epistles. The Codex Corbeiensis ff, a 10th century MS. which is now in Leningrad, gives the full text of Jas. in an Old-Latin form (it is printed by J. Belser in his commentary on Jas.). In the case of the Catholic Epistles also at least two versions may be distinguished: the African version, attested by h (Floriacensis), r^2 = q (Freising fragments), m (the so-called *Speculum* of Augustine, i. e., *Liber de divinis scripturis*), and the European version attested by ff.

f) The Old-Latin Apocalypse survives completely in only one MS.: gig; there are also some pages of it in the palimpsest of Fleury (h). But this scarcity is counterbalanced by numerous citations in the writings of the Latin Fathers and the commentaries on the Apocalypse by Victorinus of Pettau († 304), Tyconius the Donatist (a somewhat older contemporary of Augustine), and Primasius, bishop of Hadrumetum in Africa († before 567). Their Bible text is of great value for investigating the Old-Latin translation of this book which was much esteemed in the West. H. J. Vogels (1920) collected their texts in a new recension (cf. § 13).

It is virtually certain that there were two mutually independent versions of the Apc. also, an African and a European version. The African version survives at its purest in Cyprian's citations, and it is also found in h and in Primasius' commentary: it evidently had a kind of supremacy in Africa throughout three centuries. Tyconius has a textual form which can hardly be a new independent version; it is probably to be regarded as a recension of the older Catholic version which Tyconius himself made for the use of the Donatist Church.

The European version also exists in two forms. For one form the principal source is gig, while the other is contained in the text which Victorinus of Pettau used.

§ 14. THE LATIN VERSION

2. The Vulgate of St. Jerome

F. Kaulen, *Geschichte der Vulgata*, Mainz 1868. S. Berger, *Histoire de la Vulgate pendant les premiers siècles du moyen âge*, Paris 1893. H. Gluntz, *History of the Vulgate in England from Alcuin to Reger Bacon*, London 1933.—F. Kaulen, *Sprachliches Handbuch zur biblischen Vulgata*[2], Freiburg i. Br. 1904. W. E. Plater and H. J. White, *A Grammar of the Vulgate, being an Introduction to the Study of the Latinity of the Vulgate Bible*, Oxford 1926.—H. J. Vogels, *Vulgatastudien. Die Evv. der Vulgata, untersucht auf ihre lateinische und griechische Vorlage* (NtA XIV, 2–3: 1928). A. v. Harnack, *Studien zur Vulgata des Hebr.* (SB Berlin 1920). Idem, *Beitraege zur Einleitung in das NT VII: Die Bedeutung der Vulgata fuer den Text der kath. Briefe etc.*, Leipzig 1916.

The variety of forms of the Latin Bible and the influence of these forms on one another created an unfortunate situation; in time the text got so badly out of control that no two MSS. agreed. *Tot sunt paene quot codices,* said Jerome of the Latin texts. Pope Damasus (366–384) undertook to remedy this intolerable situation, and the scholar to whom he entrusted this arduous and thankless task—though a work which brought great blessings to the Church—was the great Biblical scholar of the ancient Latin Church: Eusebius Sophronius Hieronymus (St. Jerome). Born at Stridon in Dalmatia, he got a first-class training in grammar and rhetoric at Rome, and later acquired a solid theological education in the Greek east (Antioch 374–379; Constantinople 379–82). Here he also learned Greek thoroughly and studied Hebrew under a converted Jew in the desert of Chalcis—being probably the first Westerner to learn it. In the year 382 Pope Damasus summoned him to Rome as advisor at a synod. Having learned to value Jerome's extensive erudition he kept him there as his secretary.

In the following year, though Jerome was probably no more than thirty five years of age, Damasus commissioned him to produce a uniform and dependable text of the Latin Bible; he was not to make a new version, but to revise the texts which were in circulation. By 384 Jerome was able to present Damasus with the first fruits of his work—a dependable text of the four Gospels, where the variations had been extreme.

The principles which he followed in his work are expressed in a letter which he wrote to Damasus as a kind of foreword to his emended Gospel text (it is printed in Nestle's edition of the New Testament). He complains particularly of the numerous errors in the MSS. due to harmonizing the parallel accounts. In order to prevent similar textual corruptions in the future he adds Eusebius' sections and canons (cf. § 11, 2) to his edition, so that the parallels may be found without difficulty. The chief aim of his work must therefore have been to eliminate the harmonizing additions and assimilations of the Latin versions. For this purpose he used a relatively good Latin text as the basis for his revision, and compared it with old Greek MSS. He emphasizes that he treated the current Latin text as conservatively as possible, and improved it only when the meaning was distorted. Sweeping changes in the wording to which the people were accustomed would only have irritated them.

We do not know nor possess the Latin MSS. which Jerome used as the basis of his revision. In his *Vulgatastudien* (1928) Vogels attempted to reconstruct this text for the Gospels. He believes that it is possible substantially to restore Jerome's material from the MSS. a b ff[2] i q l, which show least influence of the Vulgate; this is the reconstruction which he proposes in his book. Assuming that it is substantially accurate, Jerome changed the text before him in about 3500 places in the four Gospels, either to correct evident mistranslations or to obtain stylistic improvements or to bring the text before him into harmony with the Greek text. Yet his work is not perfect, for he left a number of obvious errors uncorrected, for example, Mk. 1, 44 *principi sacerdotum* instead of *sacerdoti;* Lk. 9, 44 *cordibus* instead of *auribus;* John 7,25 *Hierosolymis* instead of *Hierosolymitis.*[5]

In Jerome's time there was a number of forms of the Greek text of the Gospels (cf. § 21), so it is of great importance to

---

[5] See the lists in Wordsworth-White, NT I (at the end of the Gospels), II (at the end of Romans).

determine to which of these forms the Greek MSS. which he used for his work belong. It is certain that they do not represent the so-called Western Text, for he was opposed to "harmonizing" readings, which are a special feature of the Western Text. Everything points to his having used the Alexandrian form, which is represented by B and ℵ, though he did not reject the Koine Text (represented for the Gospels by A) as uncompromisingly as he did the Western Text.

Pope Damasus died on 11th December 384. In August 385 Jerome left Rome, and the following year he settled for good in Bethlehem. Did he revise the other New Testament books also? De Bruyne, B. Fischer and Cavallera have denied this recently; but Jerome several times says explicitly that he revised the entire New Testament *(Vir. Ill.* 135: *Novum Testamentum graecae fidei reddidi)*. In these other books, however, he did not follow the Latin text as closely as in the Gospels, nor did he everywhere maintain the careful standard of his first work. For Acts Jerome used the gig text as his foundation, but in everything substantial he followed the text form which ℵ B C and A represent (Alexandrian Text). In general he eliminated western readings, though small traces of them remain in almost every chapter. For the Pauline Epistles he used as his basis a Latin text which has not survived, since generally we have only Greek-Latin MSS., which are not relevant. He based his revision of Heb. on the version contained in d (Claromontanus) but in many passages he also undertook independent corrections in the interest of clarity and stylistic improvement. For his revision of the Catholic Epistles he used an excellent Old-Latin text which goes back to a very old Greek text of the Alexandrian type; he also referred to the Greek text, using MSS. whose text is related to B, except in 1–3 John where the text is akin to A. In the Apocalypse, as in the Catholic Epistles, Jerome's work was of moderate extent; as his basis he used a text related to gig, which he assimilated to the Alexandrian Text, though he kept more closely to ℵ (B does not contain the Apc.) than to A, the best source for Apc.

In his letter to Pope Damasus Jerome expresses his fear that his work would meet with violent opposition, and he was not mistaken. His patron was long dead when his Latin Bible (both testaments) was ready in 405 A.D. It was never officially adopted for liturgical use—neither his revision of the whole New Testament, and of parts of the Old, nor his translation of the Old Testament direct from Hebrew—indeed for centuries it had a severe struggle to gain acceptance at all. Its text differed markedly from the familiar wording of the Old-Latin version, particularly in the Old Testament books which he translated from Hebrew. Even a learned and sensible man like Augustine was not enthusiastic about the translation from the Hebrew, though he thanked Jerome for his "version" of the Gospels from Greek *(Ep.* 104, 6 *ad Hier.).* Most of our MSS. of the Old-Latin Bible were written after 400 A.D.

Yet with time Jerome's Bible prevailed because of its intrinsic worth. Pope Gregory the Great († 604) used both forms of the Latin Bible side by side. Isidore of Seville († 636) asserts *Hieronymi editione generaliter omnes ecclesiae usque quaque utuntur. (De eccl. off.* I, 12). The Venerable Bede († 735) calls it *nostra editio* as opposed to *vetus translatio.* Yet even though Jerome's text had prevailed almost everywhere by the 8th or 9th century, occasional copies of Old-Latin Bible texts were still being made as late as the 13th century (cf. Colbertinus, c, in the 12th century and Acts and Apc. in Codex Gigas of the 13th century). By the end of the Middle Ages Jerome's text was universally accepted, and it was at this time that it acquired the name *Editio Vulgata*—which in any case is merely a translation and adaptation of κοινὴ ἔκδοσις, the description of the Septuagint.[6]

---

[6] On the name *Vulgata* cf. E. F. Sutcliffe: Bb 29 (1948) 345–352, and A. Allgeier: ibid. 353–390.

Yet the text of Jerome did not remain free from corruptions. The existence (and multiplication) side by side of the Old-Latin and Jerome's versions throughout centuries resulted in Vulgate readings creeping into the majority of Old-Latin texts which were copied after 400 A.D., and Old-Latin readings in turn penetrating the Vulgate. Attempts were made to remedy this confusion of textual forms by homogeneous revisions and so-called Bible Correctories. Such revisions were made by Cassiodorus († 570) (according to Burkitt and Turner), Alcuin († 804) and Theodulf, bishop of Orleans († 821).

However, all these efforts to produce a homogeneous text of the Latin Bible were fruitless; furthermore the Reformers of the 16th century in their struggle against the ancient Church kept harping on the variety of current Bible texts, and this made the call for a dependable edition of the Latin Bible ever more imperative. So the Council of Trent, which declared the *vetus et vulgata editio, quae longo tot saeculorum usu in ipsa ecclesia probata est,* to be authentic [7] (that is, standard for use in the Church), at the same time decreed that it should be published *quam emendatissime* (decree of 8th April 1546 mentioned in § 4).

Yet a long time elapsed before this decree was carried into effect. In 1590 an official edition was published at the command and with the collaboration of Sixtus V; it was introduced by the Bull *Aeternus ille* of 1st March 1590. But immediately after the Pope's death in 1590 this so-called Sixtine edition was withdrawn because of its faultiness, and in 1592 it was replaced by the so-called *Clementina,* an edition published by order of Clement VIII.

---

[7] Cf. A. Maichle, *Das Dekret "De editione et usu sacrorum librorum", seine Entstehung und Erklaerung,* Freiburg i. Br. 1914; W. Koch, *Der authentische Charakter der Vulgata im Lichte der Trienter Konzilsverhandlungen:* ThQ 96–98 (1914/1916); A. Allgeier, *"Authentisch" auf dem Konzil zu Trient:* HistJb 60 (1940) 142–158. On the meaning and bearing of the authenticity of the Vulgate cf. especially Pius XII's encyclical *Divino afflante Spiritu* of 30 Sept. 1943 II 1; J. Vosté, *La Volgata al Concilio di Trento:* Bb 27 (1946) 301–319.

The misprints of this edition were partly eliminated by a second (1593) and a third (1598) edition (the latter together with an *Index corrigendorum*).

This is the official Latin Bible text of the Catholic Church to the present day; the most dependable editions are by A. Grammatica (Milan 1914, ²1922) and M. Hetzenauer (Regensburg and Rome 1914).

To fulfil the mandate of Trent—for in fact it was not discharged satisfactorily even by the Clementine edition—and in view of the important advances which have been made since then by research on the history of the Bible text and its ancient versions, Pope Pius X in 1907 commissioned the Benedictine Order to undertake exhaustive MSS. enquiries and produce as pure a form as possible of Jerome's original text. This so-called Vulgate commission now has its quarters in the newly founded St. Jerome Abbey in Rome, which since 1953 has been on Monte Mario (Via di Torre rosso, no. 1). Only the revision of a number of Old Testament books has so far appeared.

Even before that time F. Wordsworth († 1911) and H. J. White († 1934), the Anglican scholars, had undertaken the production of a critical edition of the New Testament, which was finished in 1954: *Novum Testamentum Domini Nostri Jesu Christi latine secundum editionem S. Hieronymi ad codicum manuscriptorum fidem,* 3 vols. 1889–1954. In 1911 H. J. White published at Oxford a handy *editio minor* of the whole New Testament on the basis of the best MSS. B. Fischer (see above p. 93) gives a critical evaluation of the whole work.

Survey of the most important sources

The MS. material for the investigation of the Vulgate, from which Jerome's text can be almost completely restored, is even more extensive than the material for the Greek text of the New Testament. These MSS. are denoted by Latin (and Greek) capitals or by the first syllable of their names. Of the ancient and well-known Vulgate MSS., the following may be mentioned:

Sangallensis (Σ, san), the oldest MS. of the Vulgate Gospels, probably written in Verona towards the end of the fifth century. More than half of it survives in St. Gallen (MS. Collection 1935) and other libraries. Edition: C. H. Turner, *The Oldest Manuscript of the Vulgate Gospels,* Oxford 1931; Supplements by P. Lehmann in ZB 50 (1933) 50–76 and A. Dold, ibid. 709–717 and Bb 22 (1941) 105–147.

The Autun palimpsest, a Gospel MS. from the late 5th or early 6th century, formerly in Autun Cathedral Library, now in the City Library. 89 pages (= $^1/_3$) survive. Edited by A. Royet in RB 1922 and 1923. Idem: DB Suppl 1 (1928) 676–682.

Claromontanus (h), a sixth century Gospel MS.; Mt. is Old-Latin, Mk., Lk., and John are in the Vulgate text; it is now in the Vatican Library. Wordsworth and White do not mention it (in Merk it is: U).

Mediolanensis (M), a Gospel MS. of the early 6th century in the Ambrosian Library at Milan.

Fuldensis (F, fu), in Fulda (in the Landesbibliothek); it was written between 541 and 546 in Capua on the orders of Victor, the bishop of that see, and was corrected by him personally. It contains the whole New Testament, but the Gospels are in a harmony which derives from Tatian's *Diatessaron* (cf. § 16, 1).— Edited: E. Ranke, *Codex Fuldensis,* Marburg and Leipzig 1868.

Amiatinus (A, am), written on the orders of Ceolfrid, Abbot of Jarrow and Wearmouth, and sent by him as a gift to the Holy See in 716. It contains the whole Bible. For a long time this codex was in the abbey of Monte Amiato (Tuscany); it is now in the Laurentian Library at Florence.

Lindisfarnensis (Y), a Gospel MS. of 7/8th century in the British Museum, London.

Codex Lindisfarnensis ed. T. J. Brown, 2 vols., 1957

Harleianus (Z), a Gospel MS. of 6/7th century in the British Museum.

Cavensis (C), a 9th century New Testament in La Cava monastery near Salerno. It was written in Spain.

Toletanus (T), a Spanish complete Bible of the 8th century, in Madrid.

Gatianus (gat) a Gospel MS. of the 8th century in Paris: it came from S. Gatian in Tours. Edition: J. M. Heer, *Evangelium Gatianum*, Freiburg i. Br. 1910.

Fragmentum Pragense Evangelii S. Marci vulgo autographi. Edited: J. Dobrovsky, New edition: Prague 1953. [One of the oldest and best Vulgate MSS.; cf. RB 1954, 271.]

The best sources for Jerome's text are Codices AFMZΣ, the palimpsest of Autun, and to a certain extent also C and T. Of less value are the main sources for Alcuin's (V = Vallicellianus and K = Carolinus) and Theodulf's Bible (Θ, Paris, written under his personal direction).

§ 15. THE GOTHIC VERSION

Lagrange, *Crit. rat.* (cf. § 21) 325–341, 523–524. G. W. S. Friedrichsen, *The Gothic Version of the Gospels. A Study of its Style and Textual History*, Oxford 1926 (cf. on this Wilmart: RB 36, 1927, 46–61). Idem, *The Gothic Versions of the Epistles*, Oxford 1939. G. Bardy, *Ulfilas:* DThC 15 (1948) 2048–2057. F. Mossé, *Bibliographia gotica:* Mediaeval Studies, Toronto, 12 (1950) 237–324 (pp. 255–264 on the Gothic Version of the Bible) and 15 (1953) 169–183. H. Steubing, *Miscellen zur gotischen Bibeluebersetzung des Ulfilas:* ZKG 64 (1952/53) 137–169. [The original for the NT is substantially the text of Chrysostom, therefore the Antiochene Text.]

THE Gothic version of the Bible, the oldest monument of Germanic literature, was composed in the mid-fourth century, and was based on the Greek text. Unfortunately only scanty fragments of it remain. The most important MS. is the famous Codex argenteus, which was written in Northern Italy; it was taken to Sweden as war booty in 1648 and has been in Uppsala University library since 1662; in 1927 the library issued a facsimile edition of it. It is written in gold and silver on purple-dyed parchment and contains the Gospels in the order Mt., John, Lk., Mk. There were originally 320 pages of which 187 have survived. According to K. Kauffmann, the Germanic philologist, the Codex argenteus and Codex Brixianus (f) are in the same script, and were written in the same place in Northern Italy in the sixth century; probably both derive from a bilingual Gothic-Latin source. The existence of such bilingual MSS. is proved, among other reasons, by a Gothic-Latin parchment fragment with some parts of Lk. 22–23, which is in the University of Giessen.

There are also substantial remains of the Pauline Epistles (except Heb.), for example, in the two sixth century codices A and B in the Ambrosian Library in Milan, while there are 40 verses of Romans 11–15 in Gothic-Latin text on four leaves of the Codex Carolinus, a fifth century palimpsest (at Wolfenbuettel), which derives from the same archetype.

The Gothic version of the Bible was made by Wulfila ("Little Wolf") or Ulphilas, who was consecrated bishop by the Arian Eusebius of Nicomedia about 341, and who died about 383. His forefathers belonged to Cappadocia, and they were taken from there as captives by the Goths. Around the middle of the fourth century he translated the Bible (except the Books of Kings: Philostorgius II 5) from Greek into Gothic for his Goths who were settled in Moesia (the territory south of the Danube from Belgrade to the Black Sea); for the purpose of writing it he created the Gothic alphabet, 15 of whose 25 letters are certainly derived from the Greek alphabet.

So the Gothic Bible was made in the spiritual domain of Byzantium, though all the surviving MSS. are from Northern Italy which belonged to the Ostrogothic kingdom of Theodoric the Great. Since the indigenous population there spoke Latin,

Gothic-Latin Biblical MSS. were made. As the basis of his version Ulphilas used the Greek text which was current in Byzantium around 350 A.D. The "Western" readings, which are numerous in the Pauline Epistles, though negligible in the Gospels, come from the Old-Latin MSS., to which the Gothic text gradually became more and more assimilated.

Editions: W. Streitberg, *Die gotische Bibel I: Der gothische Text und seine griechische Vorlage,* ³1950; *II: Gotisch-griechisch-deutsches Woerterbuch,* ²1950 (Heidelberg). A. Jano de Vries, *Wulfilae Codices Ambrosiani Rescripti Epistularum Evangelicarum textum goticum exhibentes phototypice editi et prooemio instructi,* Turin 1936, 3 vols. G. Galbiati, *Die Ausgabe des Ulfila der Ambrosiana:* St. Wiborada, Jahrb. f. Buecherfreunde 4 (1937) 38–42.

§ 16. THE SYRIAC VERSION

Th. Zahn, *Die Urausgabe der Apg.,* 1916, 203–220. A. Baumstark, *Geschichte der syrischen Literatur,* Bonn 1922, 17 sqq., 73 sq., 144 sq., 188 sq. Lagrange, *Crit. rat.* (cf. § 21), 184 sqq., 442 sqq., 516 sqq., 571 sqq. P. Kahle, *The Cairo Geniza,* London 1947, 197–228. C. C. Torrey, *Documents of the Primitive Church,* New York 1941, 249 sqq. A. Vööbus, *Studies in the History of the Gospel Text in Syriac,* Louvain 1951 (*Corp. Script. Christ. Orient.,* vol. 128. Subsidia t. 3). A review of scholarship: W. G. Kuemmel, in ThRdsch NF 10 (1938) 318–322; 11 (1939) 84–86 (covering 1914–1937).

1. The Diatessaron of Tatian

Th. Zahn, *Tatians Diatessaron,* Erlangen 1881 (Forschungen z. Geschichte des ntl Kanons I). E. Preuschen, *Untersuchungen zum Diatessaron Tatians:* SB Heidelberg 1918/XV. D. Plooij, *A Primitive Text of the Diatessaron. The Liège Manuscript of a Medieval Dutch Translation,* Leyden 1923. Idem, *A Further Study of the Liège Diatessaron,* Leyden 1925. A. Juelicher, *Der echte Tatiantext:* JBL 43 (1924) 132–171. G. Bardy: DThC 15, 59 sqq.

Review of scholarship: Fr. Drexl on the years 1916–1925: Bursians Jahresb. ueber d. Fortschr. d. klass. Altertumswiss. 220 (1929) 176–184. D. Plooij, *Die heutige Lage des Tatianproblems:* OCh 1929, 201–222. C. Peters, *Das Diatessaron Tatians. Seine Ueberlieferung und sein Nachwirken im Morgen- und Abendland sowie der heutige Stand seiner Erforschung,* Rome 1939 (*Orientalia christiana Analecta* 123). Idem, *Neue Funde und Forschungen zum Diatessaron:* Bb 23 (1942) 68–77.

SINCE Tatian's Harmony of the Gospels has not survived, it must be reconstructed from later translations (or adaptations) and from the citations in the Syrian Fathers. This is an extremely difficult task which is still far from completion. The materials for such reconstruction are:

1. The commentary of Ephraem the Syrian on the Diatessaron, which consists of homilies. About two thirds of the original Syriac was discovered (1957) in the Chester Beatty collection in Dublin. The finding is to be published by Dom Leloir. It also survives in an Armenian version.

J. B. Aucher and G. Moesinger, *Evangelii concordantis expositio facta a. S. Ephraemo Doctore Syro in latinum translata.* Venice 1878. *Ephraem Syrus. Commentaire de l'évangile concordant. Version arménienne.* Ed. et trad. par L. Leloir, I Text (1953), II (literal) Latin translation (1954) (Corp. Script. Christian. Orient. 137, 145).

2. Citations in the homilies of Aphrahat the Wise (delivered 337–344) and other Syrian Fathers: the most valuable source for the form of the text.

The homilies of Aphrahat were published in Syriac by J. Parisot, Paris 1894 to 1907 (Patrol. Syr. I 1 and 2),

3. The Arabic version of the Syriac Diatessaron by the Nestorian Abul Faradj Abdallah ibn at-Tajib in Nisibis († 1043). His Syriac original was a MS. of the 9th century in which the original text was largely replaced by the Peshitta, the official Bible of the Church.

Edition by A. Ciasca, *Tatiani Evangeliorum Harmoniae arabice,* Rome 1888, according to two Roman MSS. H. W. Hogg, *The Diatessaron of Tatian,* Edinburgh 1897, is a careful English translation. A faulty German version is E. Preuschen, *Tatians Diatessaron, aus dem Arabischen uebersetzt,* hg. von A. Pott, Heidelberg 1926. A. Marmardji (Beyrouth 1936) made a new edition of the Arabic Diatessaron on the basis of the two above-mentioned MSS. and a further MS. from the library of the Coptic Patriarchate at Cairo. The Bodleian at Oxford possesses a further source for the Arabic Diatessaron in a recently acquired MS. (A. F. L. Beeston, *The Arabic Version of Tatian's Diatessaron:* Journal of the Royal Asiatic Soc. 1939, 608–610). Cf. also Higgins, *The Arabic Version of Tatian's Diatessaron:* JThSt 45 (1944) 187–199.

4. The witnesses for the existence of an Old-Latin Gospel Harmony, the most important of which are the Codex Fuldensis of the Vulgate (§ 14, 2) and the so-called "Munich Gospel Harmony" which survives in two MSS.

H. J. Vogels, *Beitraege zur Geschichte des Diatessarons im Abendland* (NtA VIII 1 : 1919). A. Vaccari: Bb 12 (1931) 326–354 (the Diat. in the West).

5. A medieval Dutch Life of Our Lord of the 13th century. It derives from an Old-Latin Diatessaron, and is itself a Gospel Harmony. The Dutch scholar D. Plooij († 1935) recognized its unique value; its principal witness is a MS. in Luettich (Liège).

Most recent edition: *The Liège Diatessaron Edited with a Textual Apparatus* by D. Plooij, C. A. Phillips, and A. H. A. Bakker, Amsterdam, sections 1–5 (1929 to 1938)—rather more than the half (= vol. XXXI Proc. of the Royal Acad. of Sciences of Amsterdam. Literary Section, New Series). Cf. also G. Baesecke, *Die Ueberlieferung des althochdeutschen Tatian,* Halle 1948 (Hallische Monographien Nr. 4).

6. Two Old-Italian Gospel harmonies, namely a Venetian Diatessaron in a 13th century MS., and a Tuscan Diatessaron which is contained in numerous MSS. Both must have been made in the 13th or 14th century, and are versions of the Old-Latin Diatessaron, of which the Codex Fuldensis is a witness.

Edition: V. Todesco, A. Vaccari, M. Vattasso, *Il Diatessaron in volgare italiano,* Vatican 1938 (Studi e testi 81). Cf. A. Merk, *Tatian im italienischen Gewande:* Bb 20 (1939) 294–305; A. Baumstark, *Zwei italienische Diatessarontexte:* OCh III 14 (1939/40) 225–242; C. Peters, *Die Bedeutung der altitalienischen Evv.-Harmonien:* Roman. Forschungen 56 (1942) 181–192.

7. A Persian translation of the Syriac Diatessaron. It was probably made between 1230 and 1300, and certainly from a Syriac original, though not the primitive form of the Diatessaron; its author was a certain Iwannis ʿIzz al-Din. It surpasses even the medieval Dutch life of Our Lord in importance.

Edition: G. Messina, *Il Diatessaron persiano. Introduzione, testo, traduzione.* Rome 1951 (Biblica et Orientalia 14). Cf. also Bb 44 (1943) and B. M. Metzger, *Tatian's Diatessaron and the Persian Harmony of the Gospels:* JBL 69 (1950) 261–286.

In modern times it has been much debated whether Tatian drew up his Diatessaron in Syriac only, or first in Greek and then in Syriac. Before Th. Zahn (1881) it was commonly accepted that the Syriac Diatessaron was a translation of a Greek harmony which Tatian himself made, and it was thought that this conclusion followed necessarily from the words of Eusebius H. E. V 13, 1. In spite of this, Zahn, in his reconstruction of the Diatessaron, tried to show that it was composed immediately in Syriac by Tatian himself; this hypothesis was accepted by scholars like Plooij (1923), A. Baumstark (1931), C. Peters (1939), P. Kahle (1947) and A. Vööbus (1948).

A new find in the ruins of Dura-Europos seems to have settled the question; this city, which is on the Euphrates, was destroyed about 256 A.D.; in 1933 a small fragment of a parchment was discovered there containing 14 lines of a Greek Gospel Harmony; there is no possible doubt that it is from Tatian's Gospel Harmony.[1] The text corresponds so very exactly with the Greek text of our Gospels that there can hardly be any question of it being a translation as Baumstark[2], Peters[3], and Kahle[4] maintain. Yet it is certain that the Greek Diatessaron cannot have circulated widely in Greek-speaking territory properly so called, for Origen, who was deeply interested in the text of the Bible, shows no acquaintance with the Diatessaron, while Eusebius knows of it but never saw it (H. E. IV 29, 6).

According to Burkitt's researches[5], the original arrangement of the Diatessaron is faithfully preserved by the Arabic version and by Ephraem in his commentary, while it is changed in the western forms.

The western forms of the Diatessaron derive ultimately from an Old-Latin Gospel Harmony, whose existence is explicitly

[1] C. H. Kraeling, *A Greek Fragment of Tatian's Diatessaron from Dura-Europos*, London 1935 (Studies and Documents III). Cf. on this Lagrange: RB 44 (1935) 321–345; Burkitt, JThSt 1935, 255–259; Plooij, ExpT 1935, 471–476; Merk, Bb 17 (1936) 234–241.

[2] OCh III 10 (1935) 244–252.

[3] Orientalia Christ. Periodica 8 (1942) 468–476.

[4] Tatian made his Diatessaron in Syriac probably for the Christians of his homeland Assyria (between the Tigris and Media), using a Syriac version which was already in existence. The Diat. was used in the Liturgy and pushed the Old-Syriac version of the Gospels into the background. The Dura-Europos fragment is from a Greek adaptation of the Syriac Diatessaron; such a version was needed because of the large number of Greek speakers in that district, but it had no influence. Vööbus now agrees with this (Studies in the Gospel Text, see above).

[5] *Tatian's Diatessaron and the Dutch Harmonies:* JThSt 25 (1924) 113–130.

attested by Victor of Capua in the preface to the Codex Fuldensis.[6]
It is not entirely clear what relation this Harmony has to Tatian.
Burkitt suggests that Tatian modelled his Diatessaron on the
Latin Harmony which had been made at Rome and which was
the oldest Gospel text of the Latin Church. Other scholars (Plooij,
Baumstark, C. Peters) maintain that Tatian composed his Harmony
at Rome in Syriac, while he was still in communion with the
Church, and that he intended it for a particular stratum of the
Roman population (domestic servants and artisans) among whom
there was a strong Syrian element; because of its popular character
this Life of Our Lord was soon translated into Vulgar Latin.
Since there was no Latin version of the four separate Gospels in
those early days, this Gospel Harmony in Latin circulated widely
and influenced the text of the Latin version of the four separate
Gospels which was made later. This is the explanation of the
harmonizing readings of the so-called Western Text; they are
really "Tatianisms". Even before these scholars, Hermann von
Soden (cf. § 20) and H. J. Vogels[7] had proposed a similar explanation of the problem of the Western Text.

Other scholars, however, reject this hypothesis. They say that
there was a "Western" text of the Gospels at Rome around 150
A.D., and that this is the basis both of Tatian's Harmony and of
the Old-Latin (and Old-Syriac) version of the four Gospels (cf.
§ 21, 2); they maintain that Tatian composed his Diatessaron in
Greek and that a Latin Gospel Harmony was made from it before
400 A.D.; this Latin Harmony used the language of the Latin
versions of the Gospels, which had been made about 200 A.D.

---

[6] Cf. D. de Bruyne: RBén 39 (1927) 5–11.

[7] *Die Harmonistik im Evangelientext des Codex Cantabrigiensis*, Leipzig 1910
(TU, 3. R. VI 1 a); *Die altsyrischen Evv in ihrem Verhaeltnis zu Tatians Diatessaron*
(BSt XVI 5: 1911).

2. The Old-Syriac version of the four Gospels, Acts, and Pauline Epistles

A. Vööbus, *Neuentdecktes Textmaterial zur Vetus Syra:* ThZ 7 (1951) 30–38. Idem *The Old-Syriac Version in a New Light, an Urgent Task in Textual Criticism of the NT.* Apophoreta Tartuensia (Stockholm 1949) 144 sqq. Idem, *A Critical Apparatus for the Vetus Syra:* JBL 70 (1951) 123–128. Idem, *Die Evangelienzitate in der Einleitung der persischen Maertyrerakte:* Bb 33 (1952) 222–234. Idem, *Neue Angaben über die textgeschichtlichen Zustaende in Edessa i. d. Jahren 326—340,* Stockholm 1951 (Papers of the Estonian Theol. Soc. in exile, vol. 3). [Aithalla bishop of Edessa (326–345) used a Tetraevangelium.] Idem, *Das Problem des altsyrischen Apostolos:* Orientalia Christiana Periodica 1955.

The Old-Syriac version of the four separate Gospels is preserved in two MSS., both of which have large gaps. They are 1) a parchment MS. which originated from the monastery of S. Maria Deipara in the Nitrian desert to the west of Cairo; it was discovered by William Cureton in 1842 and brought to the British Museum, London; it was published in 1858 (syr^{cur}); 2) a palimpsest MS. which Agnes Smith Lewis discovered in the monastery of St. Catherine on Mount Sinai in 1892; the older writing with the text of the Gospels is probably from the end of the fourth century (syr^{sin}).

Editions: *Remains of a Very Ancient Recension of the Four Gospels in Syriac . . .* ed. by William Cureton, London 1858.—*Evangelion da-Mepharreshe. The Curetonian Version of the Four Gospels with the Reading of the Sinai-Palimpsest and the Early Syriac Patristic Evidence,* ed. by F. C. Burkitt, 2 vols., Cambridge 1904. W. D. McHardy, *Disputed Readings in the Syriac Sinaitic Palimpsest:* JThSt 45 (1944) 170–174. [He examines various passages of this edition in the light of the MS.] *The Old-Syriac Gospels or Evangelion da-Mepharreshe, being the Text of the Sinai or Syro-Antiochene Palimpsest . . . with the Variants of the Curetonian Text . . . ,* ed. by Agnes Smith Lewis, London 1910.—A facsimile edition of the Syrus Sin. was produced by A. Hjelt in 1930 in Helsinki (with introduction in German).

Both MSS. represent one and the same Syriac version, but they differ so widely that they must be regarded as two separate recensions. The date and place of the translation are unknown. According to the discoverer of Syr^{sin} and other scholars (Hjelt, Kahle) it was made in the middle or second half of the second century and was used by Tatian in the composition of the Diatessaron.

Most scholars, however, maintain that it is more recent, and that it probably comes from the beginning of the fourth century. In any case Tatian's Diatessaron was used exclusively in the Liturgy of the Syrian Church until the beginning of the fifth century. The first mention of a Syriac version of the four separate Gospels occurs in the canon from Sinai (§ 9, 1). The Old-Syriac version which both MSS. contain was undoubtedly influenced by the' Diatessaron; its harmonizing readings, however, do not all derive from Tatian but to a large extent go back to a Greek text of Western type which the translator used.

The Old-Syriac version of Acts and the Pauline Epistles has not survived in MSS.; we know it only from citations by the Syrian writers. Ephraem also composed a commentary on Acts and the Pauline Epistles, but both these works have survived only in an Armenian version. In the case of Acts F. C. Coneybeare has reconstructed Ephraem's commentary from Armenian sources; it is printed in a Latin version in the appendix to Ropes' edition of Acts (cf. § 29). This version also is of the Western Text form; it is probably much older than the translation of the separate Gospels. Ephraem's text of St. Paul has been reconstructed by J. Molitor (Rome 1938).

3. The Peshitta ("The Syriac Vulgate")

F. C. Burkitt, *Evangelion da–Mepharreshe*, Cambridge 1904, II 100–160. Idem, *Urchristentum im Orient*. German version by E. Preuschen, Tuebingen 1907, 25–48. H. B. Downs, *The Peshitto as a Revision: its Background in Syriac and Greek Texts of Mark:* JBL 63 (1944) 141–159. A. Vööbus, *Investigations into the Text of the NT used by Rabbula of Edessa,* Pinneberg 1947. Idem, *Researches on the Circulation of the Peshitta in the Middle of the Fifth Century,* ibid. 1948. Idem, *Neue Ergebnisse in der Erforschung der Geschichte der Evv-Texte im Syrischen* (kurze Mitteilung), ibid. 1948 (Contributions of Baltic University N. 59, 64, 65). Idem, *The Oldest Extant Traces of the Syriac Peshitta:* Mus 63 (1950) 191–204. M. Black, *Rabbula of Edessa and the Peshitta:* BJRL 33 (1950/51) 203–210. Idem, *The Gospel Text of Jacob of Serug:* JThSt 1951, 57–63. Idem, *Zur Geschichte des altsyrischen Evv-Textes:* ThLZ 77 (1952) 705–710. A. Vööbus, *Das Alter der Peschitta:* OChr 38

(1954) 1–10. M. Black, *The NT Peshitta and its Predecessors: Bull. of Studiorum NiTi Societas* 1950 pp. 51–62. Cf. also Benoit, RB 1953, 441–443. M. Black, *The Text of the Peshitta Tetraevangelium:* Studia Paulina f. J. de Zwaan (1953) pp. 20–27.

The name *Peshitta (the Single)* is applied by the Syrians to the version of the Bible which has been used in their Liturgy since the tenth century. The Peshitta New Testament contains only 22 books, not the whole 27; the four minor Catholic Epistles and Apc. are missing (cf. § 9, 2).

We have no ancient tradition about the maker of the New Testament Peshitta. Burkitt, the English textual critic, suggested in 1904 that it was made by Rabbula, bishop of Edessa (411–431). A biography of Rabbula which was written shortly after his death by an enthusiastic pupil, tells us that at the beginning of his episcopate "through the wisdom of God which was in him, he translated the New Testament exactly as it was from Greek into Syriac, in order to supersede the variety of texts which were current." This version, which is not described more accurately, is almost certainly to be identified with the Peshitta, according to Burkitt. He adds that in view of Rabbula's great energy and his familiarity with the Greek language and culture, it is easy to believe that he himself made the New Testament Peshitta; the basis for his work was the text form which was in use in the Patriarchal Church of Antioch, and he took over the Antiochene Canon also. The personal influence of Rabbula and his official position as Metropolitan of the Syrians would easily explain the striking success of his work, which soon became the official Bible of the Syrians. In his *Praecepta et monita ad sacerdotes et regulares* we read: "The priests and deacons should see to it that the Gospel of the Separated is available and that it is read in every church." If the Peshitta was made in the early years of his episcopate, there was time enough for it to become established before 431 when the condemnation of Nestorius split the Syrian Church; this is particularly probable, since the Peshitta was officially prescribed in order to supersede the *Diatessaron,* as Theodoret of Cyrus explicitly says (cf. § 9, 2), and since the Old-Syriac version of the separate Gospels was never used in the Liturgy. Burkitt supports his theory by the observation that no citations from the Peshitta appear in the writings of the Syrian Fathers before 400 A.D., while from 450 onwards citations corresponding to the text of the Peshitta become common, and quotations in the textual form of the *Diatessaron* and the Old-Syriac separate Gospels very soon disappear (?).

This thesis of Burkitt is almost universally accepted, but according to the studies of Arthur Vööbus it has no historical foundation. It can be demonstrated that Rabbula used the Old-Syriac version until his death. Unquestionably the Peshitta was made in the last decades of the fourth century, while Syrian Christendom was still united. Both forms of the Syriac New Testament, the Old-Syriac version and the Peshitta, coexisted for a long time, and it was only after some centuries that the Peshitta prevailed. From the beginning the hierarchy (bishops, priests and other clergy) favoured the Peshitta, but the monasteries preferred the Old-Syriac version; indeed, in the East Syrian monasteries—unlike the West Syrians, they claimed independence from the hierarchy—the Peshitta could not get a foothold at all. And even among the clergy the Old-Syriac Gospels were still in use in the 8th and 9th centuries. The long coexistence of the two textual forms explains the existence of mixed MSS. which show a Peshitta text heavily interlarded with Old-Syriac readings.

Black checked Vööbus' researches and came to the following conclusions: Rabbula certainly knew the Peshitta, but he also used the Old-Syriac text. The confusion of Old-Syriac and Peshitta readings is due to the fact that he usually quotes his own revision of the Old-Syriac version, although this " Syriac Vulgate" is not yet identical with the Peshitta which has come down to us. His revision marked a stage between the Old-Syriac text and the final form of the Peshitta. The first revision of the Old-Syriac version is probably the text of syr^cur. Burkitt's thesis is not affected, for Rabbula was responsible for the standard revision of the Old-Syriac version; on the other hand, the view which hitherto was almost universally entertained must be abandoned, namely that Rabbula's revision of the Old-Syriac version has reached us uncorrupted. This difficult question calls for further elucidation.

The textual form of the Peshitta has not yet been satisfactorily investigated. But it may be taken as certain that—with the exception of the three major Catholic Epistles (Jas., 1 Pet., 1 John) which are not in the Old-Syriac version—the Peshitta is not an entirely new and completely independent translation of the Greek text. But it is not certain, though it is often asserted, that the Peshitta gives the Antiochene Text which is also to be found in Chrysostom. The maker of the Peshitta, like Jerome, eliminated Western readings to a large extent from the Gospels, but yet in Acts we find a great number of striking agreements with the Western Text form.

Black has demonstrated in a number of articles that the text which the 5th century Syrian writers—including Rabbula—used was a mixture of the Vetus Syra and the Peshitta. This text is an earlier stage of the Peshitta Text which later became standardized. Such a mixed text is preserved by the MS. Phillips 1388 and by other sources (cf. OCh III 7, p. 1–15). Two conclusions follow from this: 1) The Peshitta underwent an historical evolution, and Gwilliam's text (see below) can hardly be the original form of the Peshitta; 2) the majority of our MSS. were written when the text had already been established, and so most of the variants are simply slips of the pen.

Editions: *Tetraevangelium sanctum iuxta simplicem Syrorum versionem ad fidem codicum* etc., by Ph. E. Pusey and G. H. Gwilliam, Oxford 1901, reprinted 1950 (a full, critical edition founded on 42 Mss). *The NT in Syriac*, London 1905/20 (small edition without Apparatus criticus), British and Foreign Bible Society: I (Gospels) is a reprint of Gwilliam's text, II (Acts-Apc.) is by Gwilliam and J. Gwynn.

4. *The Philoxenian version*

J. Lebon, *La version Philox. de la Bible*: Rev. d'hist. eccl. 12 (1911) 413–436. S. New:
HarvThR 21 (1928) 376 sqq. Clark, *The Acts of the Apostles* (cf. § 29) 305 sqq. Hatch:
HarvThR 30 (1937) 141 sqq. Ropes, The Acts of the Apostles (cf. § 29) CXLIX-
CLXXX. G. Zuntz, *The Ancestry of the Harklean NT,* Oxford 1945 (British
Academy, Suppl. Papers VII); cf. RB 54 (1947) 127–131; Philologus 97 (1948)
203–204; Kilpatrick, JThSt 48 (1947) 92–95, and W. D. McHardy, JThSt 48 (1947)
95–99. Idem, *Études harcléennes*: RB 57 (1950) 550–582. Hatch, *To what Syrian
Version or Versions of the Gospels did Thomas of Harqel Refer in his Margin?*: JBL 65
(1946) 371–376. P. Kahle. *The Chester Beatty MS. of the Harklean Gospels*: Misc.
Mercati VI (1946) 208–233. G. Zuntz, *Die Subscriptionen der Syra Harclensis*:
ZDMG 101 (1951) 174–196. A. Vööbus, *New Data for the Solution of the Problem
Concerning the Philoxenian Version*: Spiritus et Veritas (Festschrift for K. Kundzins),
Entin 1953, 169–186. [The solution of the problem is to be found in Philoxenus'
commentary on John, which is in the British Museum and is still unpublished;
it contains fragments of the lost text of the Philox. version. Philoxenus undertook
a real revision of the Peshitta, keeping closer to the Greek original than it did
(= Philoxenian vers.). On the basis of this text Thomas made a new revision
(Harclensis), namely the text published by J. White.] E. Bergstraesser, *Philoxenus
von Mabbug*: Gedenkschrift f. W. Elert, Berlin 1955.

Both Nestorians and Monophysites retained the Peshitta when
they broke off from the Universal Church. But apparently the
Monophysites were not quite satisfied with it, for all later attempts
at revision were made by them. The Syrian writer Moses of Aghel
(between 550 and 570) tells us that on the instructions of Philoxenus, Monophysite bishop of Mabbug (Hierapolis) near the
Euphrates, his chorepiscopus Polycarp translated the New Testament from Greek into Syriac in 507/08, following the original more
closely than the Peshitta did.

It is keenly disputed how much of this version (syr^{ph}) has
survived. Some scholars (S. New, Lagrange, McHardy) say that the
version of the whole New Testament which is contained in some
MSS. and which differs textually from the Peshitta, is this so-
called Philoxenian version. Zuntz maintains that the Philoxenian
version was made from the Caesarean Text in its best form, that is,
the text made by Pamphilus ("the model of Pamphilus"), but that
it has survived only for the Apc. and the four minor Catholic

Epistles, where it was used to complete the Peshitta which has not these books.

There is only a very unsatisfactory edition by J. White, Oxford 1778 (*Gospels*), 1779 (*Acts and Catholic Epistles*), and 1803 (*Pauline Epistles*)—with a supplement by Bensly 1889: Heb. 11, 28 to 13, 25; McHardy is preparing a new edition. The four minor Catholic Epistles and Apc. in the Philoxenian version (ed. by J. Gwynn) are in the edition of the Peshitta, London 1905/20.

At the end of various MSS. of the Syriac version of the Gospels Acts and Catholic Epistles and Pauline Epistles, there is a *colophon* (postscript) by a certain Thomas; he tells us that this version was made in 508 A.D. under Philoxenus, bishop of Mabbug, and copied by him (Thomas) in 616 A.D. at the monastery of St. Anthony at the ninth milestone from Alexandria; he adds that it was compared with good Greek MSS., the Gospels with three MSS., the Pauline Epistles with two, and Acts and the Catholic Epistles with one. The writer is Thomas of Charquel (Harqel, Heraclea), Monophysite bishop of Mabbug, who found refuge in Egypt at the monastery of St. Anthony near Alexandria when he was expelled from his see by the Emperor Maurice.

The question arises whether Thomas was content to compare the Philoxenian text with some Greek MSS., and to incorporate the results of his work in the form of critical sigla (asterisks and obeloi) and marginal notes, or whether he also wove them into the text and made a real revision; his own evidence seems to favour the former, while the latter view seems supported by the fact that Syrian tradition calls the text in these MSS. Heraclean (and not Philoxenian). The problem has not yet been satisfactorily solved.

The marginal readings of the versio Harclensis (syh) of Acts are of particular importance; they are mainly Western readings, and often show an earlier form than D (cf. § 21, 2).

5. *The Syro-Palestinian version*

Lagrange: *L'origine de la version syro-palestinienne des évangiles:* RB 34 (1925) 481–504. M. Black, *The Palestinian Syriac Gospels and the Diatessaron:* OChr 35

(1939) 101–111. Idem, *A Christian Palestinian Syriac Horologion,* Cambridge 1954 (Texts and Studies II 1). [Contains the Magnificat and Benedictus.] See also RB 1953, 85, 526. [On fragments which were found in the vicinity of the Dead Sea.]

By the 4th and 5th centuries Palestine had become almost entirely Christian. The dominant ecclesiastical language was Greek, but in addition to the Greek speaking population there was a strong element of indigenous converts who knew little or no Greek. The pilgrim Aetheria (*Peregrinatio* 47, 3–4) and Eusebius in his book on the Palestinian martyrs (I 1, Procop. syr. text) tell us that for the benefit of these people the Lessons from Scripture and the sermon at liturgical assemblies were sometimes translated into Syriac. The Syriac dialect to which they refer was markedly different from the language spoken east of the Euphrates; it belongs to the Judaeo-Palestinian branch of Aramaic and was the language which Jesus spoke.

A version of the New Testament was made in this dialect, according to Lagrange in Northern Palestine in the fifth century; this is the Syro-Palestinian version (Syr^{pal}), which seems quite independent of the other Syriac versions. A. Baumstark, C. Peters and M. Black, on the other hand, have attempted to show that this version depends on the *Diatessaron*.[1]

Not a single complete book of the New Testament survives in this version. Its most important sources are 3 lectionaries of the 11th and 12th centuries; in addition fragments of the Gospels in a continuous text and some pieces of Acts and the Pauline Epistles have come down to us.

The most recent textual research regards the Syro-Palestinian version as a witness to the so-called Caesarean Text form.

The most important of the surviving texts are: 1) a lectionary of the Gospels (which has come down in 3 MSS.), published by A. S. Lewis and M. D. Gibson, *The Palestinian Syriac Lectionary of the Gospels,* London 1899; 2) a lectionary with passages from the OT, Acts, and the Pauline Epistles, published by A. S. Lewis, *A Palestinian Syriac Lectionary* (Studia Sinaitica VI), London 1897; 3) Frag-

[1] Baumstark, OCh 1936, 195; Peters, *Das Diatessaron Tatians* 121–125; cf. also HarvThR 1928, 314–320.

ments of the Gospels, Acts and the Pauline Epistles of the 6th century, published by A. S. Lewis, *Codex Climaci rescriptus* (Horae semiticae VIII), Cambridge 1909. Cf. also H. Duensing: ZntW 37 (1938) 42–46, and M. Black: BJRL 23 (1939) 201–214 (Fragments from Acts); P. Kahle, *Das zur Zeit Jesu in Palaestina gesprochene Aramaeisch*: ThRdsch NF 17 (1949) 201–216. L. Delekat, *Die syrisch-palaestinische Uebersetzung der Paulusbriefe und die Peschitta*: NTSt 3 (1957) 223–233.

§ 17. THE COPTIC VERSION

Lagrange, *Crit. rat.* 313–324, 450–453, 521 sq., 569 sq., 617–619. Kenyon, *Rec. Developments* (see above § 11) 35–37. J. M. Heer, *Neue griechisch-saïdische Evv-Fragmente*: OCh 1912, 1–47 (printed separately). J. L. Koole, *Studien zum Koptischen Bibeltext. Kollationen und Untersuchungen zum Text der Paulusbriefe in der unter- und oberaegyptischen Ueberlieferung*, Berlin 1936. Idem, *Die koptischen Uebersetzungen der Apg*: BBC 12 (1937) 65–73. G. Bardy, *Les premiers temps du christianisme de langue copte en Égypte: Mémorial Lagrange,* Paris 1940, 103–116.

THE Copts are the direct descendants of the ancient Egyptians and their language is a more modern form of ancient Egyptian. From shortly after the beginning of the Christian era it was written in the Greek alphabet, with six additional letters. In spite of the quick spread of Greek after Alexander the Great, and of Arabic after the Arab conquest in the seventh century, Coptic maintained itself for a long time among the indigenous population. This was the case particularly in the country districts, while Greek was spoken by the settlers and in the large cities. Coptic (and Greek) disappeared from the Nile Delta about the 10th century, but it was still spoken in Upper Egypt in the 15th century. At present there are about one and a half million (Monophysite) Copts in Egypt who use a certain amount of Coptic in their Liturgy.

It is usual to distinguish three or four Coptic dialects:
1. Upper Egyptian or Sahidic (from Saïd = highland, hinterland), i. e., the district around Thebes (Luxor).
2. Lower Egyptian or Bohairic, called from the province of Behêre or Boheira (= littoral), i. e., the Nile Delta.
3. Middle Egyptian with two subgroups, Fayumic (Oase el Fajjûm, formerly called Lake Moeris near the ancient Memphis [Sakkara]) and Achmimian, so called from the city of Achmim beyond Asiût.

Extensive remains of the New Testament survive only in the Sahidic and Bohairic dialects.

a) The Sahidic version (= sa) was made gradually from about 200 A.D. onwards. In general it agrees with the Alexandrian text form, but in the Gospels and especially in Acts it has many Western readings. The same phenomenon appears also in ℵ L C 33 and for Mk. in Δ Ψ, which are witnesses to the Alexandrian text form. The canonical ending of Mk. is missing (16, 9–10).

b) The Bohairic version (= bo) seems to be considerably later than the Sahidic version. Scholars date it to the 5th, 6th, or 7th centuries. We have numerous MSS. but they are very late.

At Deir el-Bala'izah, about 12 miles south of Asiût on the west bank of the Nile, numerous MS. fragments have been found; among them is one of the 4th or 5th century containing Phil. 3, 19 to 4, 9 in a semi-Bohairic dialect; it is closely related to the Bohairic version. From this it may be inferred that the Bohairic version is older than was generally admitted hitherto.

The Greek prototype of this version is closely related in all parts of the New Testament to the two MSS. B and ℵ, and to B even more than ℵ; so it is regarded as one of the most valuable representatives of the Alexandrian Text. All the MSS. contain the canonical ending of Mk., and two of them also have the shorter ending (like L). The old MSS. of this version have not the verses about the sweat of blood (Lk. 22, 43 sq.) nor the *pericopa de adultera*.

G. Horner, *The Coptic Version of the NT in the Northern Dialect otherwise called Memphitic, Bohairic etc.*, 4 vols., Oxford 1898/1905. Idem, *The Coptic Version of the NT in the Southern Dialect otherwise called Sahidic and Thebaic etc.*, 7 vols., Oxford 1911/24. H. Thompson, *The Coptic Version of the Acts of the Apostles and the Pauline Epistles in the Sahidic Dialect*, Cambridge 1932 (MS. of the early 7th century possessed by Chester Beatty). Idem. *The Gospel of St. John According to the Earliest Coptic MS.* London 1924 (of the last quarter of the fourth century in a dialect which stands between Achmimian and Sahidic).

A number of important fragments in the Sahidic dialect (4 Gospels, Paul, Cath. Ep. etc.) which were discovered in 1910 in Hamuli (Fayûm) have not yet been published (H. Hyvernat, *A Check List of Coptic Manuscripts in Pierpont Morgan Library*, New York 1910). See also the lists of published fragments: Le

Muséon 46 (1933), 53 (1940), 59 (1946). Also W. Till: ZntW 39 (1940) 1–57 (Vienna fragments); J. Simon, *Bibliographie copte*: Or 18 (1949) 100–120. Le Muséon 62 (1949) 199–205, 63 (1950) 147–157, 66 (1953) 1–30 (fragments of the Gospel of Lk.). W. Till, *Coptic Biblical Fragments in the John Rylands Library*: BJRL 34 (1952) 432–458. P. E. Kahle, *Bala'izah*. *Coptic Texts from Deir el-Bala'izah in Upper Egypt*, London 1954 (fragments of various books of the NT; contains a list of all pre-sixth century Coptic MSS. 162 in number). A. Vaschalde, *Ce qui a été publié des versions coptes de la Bible*, serially in RB 28 (1919)–31 (1922) (this part also separately, Geuthner, Paris 1922), and in Muséon 43 (1930) 45–6 (1932–3).W. Kammerer *et al.*, *A Coptic Bibliography*, Ann Arbor (Mich.) (1950) Nos. 754–1012.

§ 18. THE ARMENIAN VERSION

A. Merk, *Die arm. Evv und ihre Vorlage*: Bb 7 (1926). St. Lyonnet in Lagrange, *Crit. rat.* 342–375, 454–460, 525–528. Idem in various articles: RB 43 (1934) 69–87; Mél. Univ. S. Joseph, Beyrouth 19 (1935) 25–66; RSR 25 (1935) 170–187; Bb 19 (1938) 121–150; RB 47 (1938) 355–382; also: *Les versions arm. et géorg. du NT*, Paris 1935; *Les origines de la version arm. de la Bible et le Diatessaron*, Rome 1950 (cf. RB 59, 1952, 112–114). P. Essabalian, *Le Diatessaron de Tatian et la première traduction des Év. arm.*, Vienna 1937 (cf. Bb 1938, 214–218). Metzger in Parvis-Wikgren (cf. § 14) 38–41. A. Vööbus, *La première traduction arm. des Év.*: RSR 37 (1950) 581–586. There are surveys of research in E. C. Colwell, *Slandered or Ignored: The Arm. Gospels*: JR 17 (1937) 48–61. C. Peters, *Das Diatessaron Tatians* (cf. § 16, 1) 63–83.—F. C. Coneybeare, The *Armenian Version of Revelation*, London 1907. A. Vööbus, *Studies in the History of the Gospel Text* (cf. § 16) 144–151 [against Lyonnet]. B. Kraft, *Der Roemerbrieftext des arm. Irenaeus*: Festschrift Handes Amsorya (Monatsschrift f. arm. Philologie) 1927, 641–670 [proves that there was an Old-Arm. text of Paul, whose original belongs to the Western Text sources]. A. Wikgren, *Additional Armenian NT MSS. in the Kurdian collection*: JBL 72 (1953) 115–126. A. F. J. Klijn, *An Old Witness of the Armenian Text* (of the gospels): JThSt NS 2 (1951) 168–170. P. H. Oskian, *Two Armenian Gospel MSS. in Zahle*: Handes Amsorya 65 (1951) 65–69. A. Szekula, *The "short" Ending of Mark in the Armenian Version*: ibid. 64 (1950) 448–452.

THE origin of the Armenian version is still in dispute. Bishop Koriun († c. 450) and the historian Lazarus of Pharb (c. 500) say that St. Mesrop († 440) made it from the Greek text; Moses of Chorion on the other hand says that the Catholicus Sahak (Isaac the Great 390–439) made it from the Syriac Text. Both views, with various modifications, have found defenders among modern scholars. A close textual relationship with the so-called Caesarean Text is generally admitted. There are several hundred MSS. of fairly late date; the oldest of them, the Tetraevangelium of Moscow, is of the year 887.

The question remains, however, whether this is the oldest form of New Testament version in the Armenian Church.

The older view, which has been revived by A. Vööbus, appeals to the citations in the Armenian Fathers up to the eighth century and maintains that the old Armenian version of the Gospels depends on the text of the Old-Syriac separate Gospels, and that it comes from a time when the latter was recognized as the standard Church Text.

The more modern view (Essabalian, Lyonnet, Colwell and others) says that the Armenians first translated a Syriac *Diatessaron*, and that shortly afterwards they made a version of the separate Gospels, which probably goes back to the "translators" whom Sahak sent to Edessa and Constantinople, and who brought back from the latter city an "authentic" text of the Holy Scriptures together with the canons of Nicaea and Ephesus. The version of the Gospels was made from a Greek MS. which contained a so-called Caesarean Text. The *Diatessaron* was still cited throughout the fifth century and it was known as late as the seventh century.

According to Lyonnet, in addition to the translation of the Gospels there was also an Old-Armenian version of Acts and of the *Corpus Paulinum* (without Philemon, but including 3 Cor.); so this version had the same canon as the Old-Syrian Church (cf. § 9, 1).

There was also, probably as early as the 5th century, an Old-Armenian version of Apc.; in many MSS. it appears as part of the Acts of John, which the Armenians called "Prochorus" for short (ed. Fr. Murad, Jerusalem ² 1911). Apc. was first added to the Canon of the Armenian Church by Nerses, the learned archbishop of Lampron († 1198); he also produced a version of Apc. on the basis of the Av text form (cf. § 21 on this) which became the canonical text of the Armenians, and was received into Zohrab's edition.

The Mechitarist John Zohrab using the majority of the MSS. produced an edition of the Armenian Bible (Venice 1805); a photostatic edition of the Tetraevangelium E 229 of Etschmiadzin was produced by F. Macler (*L'Évangile arménien,* Paris 1914).

§ 19. THE GEORGIAN VERSION

K. Kekelidze, *Die Bekehrung Georgiens zum Christentum,* Leipzig 1928 (Morgenland, vol. 18). F. Zorell, *Grammatik der altgeorgischen Bibeluebersetzung,* Rome 1930. J. Karst, *La littérature géorgienne chrétienne,* Lyons 1934. St. Lyonnet in Lagrange, *Crit. rat.* 375–386, 460–463, 625 (with bibliogr. to 1934). A. Baumstark, *Zum georgischen Evv-Text:* OCh 3-4 (1930) 117–124. C. Peters, *Das Diatessaron Tatians* 83–88. Metzger in Parvis-Wikgren (cf. § 14) 41–45. St. Lyonnet, *Les origines de la version arménienne,* 144–165. J. Molitor, *Die georgische Bibeluebersetzung:* OCh 37 (1953) 23–29 [on Black and Lyonnet]. Idem, *Das Adysh-Tetraevangelium neu uebersetzt und mit altgeorgischen Paralleltexten verglichen,* ibid. 30–55; 38 (1954) 11–40. Idem, *Georgien und seine Bibel,* Trierer Th. Ztschr. 1953, 91–98. M. Tarchnisvili, *Kurzer Ueberblick ueber den Stand der georg. Literaturforschung:* OCh 37 (IV 1: 1953) 89–99. J. Molitor, *Zur Harmonistik des altgeorgischen Evangelientextes:* BZ NF 1 (1957) 289–296. Id., *Das Adysh-Tetraevangelium* (newly translated into Latin): OrCh 37 (1953) 33–55; 38 (1954) 11–40; 39 (1955) 1–32; 40 (1956) 1–15. G. Garitte, *L'ancienne version Géorgienne des Actes des Apôtres d'après deux manuscrits de Sinai,* Louvain 1956 (Bibl. du Muséon).

THE Georgian version was not made from a Greek text, but from the Armenian translation (Blake, Lyonnet), and must have appeared shortly after the completion of the Armenian version about the year 450 or even earlier. Like the Armenian version, it is an important witness of the so-called Caesarean Text (§ 21, 3).

The oldest Georgian Gospel MSS. are the MS. of Adysh (of 897 A.D.), of Opiza (913 A.D.), and of Tbet' (955 A.D.).

There is no edition of the Georgian Bible corresponding to J. Zohrab's Armenian Bible. Beneševic, *Quattuor Evangeliorum Versio Georgiana Vetus I* (Mt.) S. Petersburg 1909; II (Mk.) 1911 (according to the MSS. of Tbet' and Opiza). *Patrologia Orientalis* contains the four Gospels (Mk. 1929; Mt. 1933 by R. P. Blake; John 1950 by Blake and M. Brière; Lk. 1955 by M. Brière according to the Adysh MS. with the variants of the Opiza and Tbet' Gospels); the accompanying Latin translation by Blake is not reliable. A. Shanidze, *Two Old Recensions of the Georgian Gospels According to Three Shatberd MSS. (A.D. 897, 936, and 973),*

Tiflis 1945, Academy of Sciences (= Monuments of the Old-Georgian language 1). R. P. Blake and S. Der Nersessian, *The Gospels of Bert'ay. An Old-Georgian MS. of the tenth century:* Byzantion 16 (1942/43) 226–285.

Appendix: The ancient versions, which have not been mentioned here, have not yet been carefully studied and some of them are relatively late. There are surveys of the research on them in LThK 11 (1931) 296–325: *Bibeluebersetzungen,* and in the report by Metzger in Parvis-Wikgren (cf. § 14). On the Arabic version cf. C. Peters, *Grundsaetzliche Bemerkungen zur Frage der arabischen Bibeltexte:* RStOr 20 (1942) 129–134, and G. Graf, *Geschichte der christlichen arabischen Literatur 1* (Rome 1944) 138–185. M. Vööbus, *Spuren eines aelteren aethiopischen Evv-Textes im Lichte der literarischen Monumente,* Stockholm 1951. [The Ethiopian Text was made on the basis of the Old-Syriac Gospels.] Cf. RB 1953, 444, and ThZ 1953, 144 sq. G. Bonfante and B. M. Metzger, *The Old-Slavic Version of the Gospel According to Luke:* JBL 73 (1954) 217–237. J. Hofmann, *Vergleichende Untersuchungen zur aethiopischen Uebersetzung der Joh-Apk,* Diss. phil. Wuerzburg *1956.*

§ 20. EDITIONS OF THE TEXT AND TEXTUAL CRITICISM TO THE PRESENT DAY

E. Reuss, *Bibliotheca Novi Testamenti graeci cuius editiones ab initio typographiae ad nostram aetatem impressas quotquot reperiri potuerunt collegit, digessit, illustravit,* Brunswick 1872. H. Schneider, *Der Text der Gutenbergbibel,* Bonn 1954 (Bonner Biblische Beitraege vol. 7). [The MS. which the printer followed has not so far been found. The most closely related text form is in the "Georg-Orlandus-Bibel" in the Mainzer Stadtbibliothek, of the early 14th century.] A. Bludau, *Die beiden ersten Erasmus-Ausgaben des NT und ihre Gegner,* Freiburg i. Br. 1902 (BSt VII, 5). C. C. Tarelli, *Erasmus' MSS. of the Gospels:* JThSt 44 (1943) 155–163, 48 (1947) 207 sqq.

FOR a long time after the invention of printing only Latin Bibles were printed. One of the first books to be printed was a Latin Bible, the celebrated 42 line Gutenberg Bible (1452–1455). By the year 1500 there had been about 100 printings of Latin Bibles.

Francisco Ximenes de Cisneros, Cardinal Archbishop of Toledo (1437–1517), has the glory of having commissioned the first printed edition of the Greek New Testament text; it is the fifth volume of his *Complutensian Polyglot* (a six volume work of large folio size). The printing of this volume, which contained the Vulgate as well as the Greek text, came to an end on 10th January

1514; but Pope Leo X·did not give his approval for the sale of the collected work until 22nd March 1520, after the MSS. which had been borrowed from the Vatican Library had been returned. The Greek text of the New Testament is based on late, but carefully chosen MSS. and is relatively good. It is regrettable that the *Complutensian* had so little influence on subsequent printed editions.

Froben, the Basle printer, wished to anticipate the publication of Ximenes' edition, and on 15th March 1515 he commissioned the famous humanist, Erasmus of Rotterdam (1467–1536) to edit the Greek New Testament. It appeared in small folio on 1st March 1516 with a dedication to Pope Leo X. In two parallel columns it gives the Greek text and an elegant Latin translation by Erasmus. Erasmus himself later admitted that it was a hasty work; he gave the printer only three late MSS. from the Dominican friary at Basle (one for the Gospels, one for Acts and Epistles, and one for Apc.), and contented himself with occasional corrections of the text on the basis of other MSS. There were four editions of this up to 1535, but they marked no real improvements. Martin Luther based his New Testament translation on the second edition of 1519.[1] Because of vigorous criticisms Erasmus accepted the Johannine Comma into his third edition.

The fifth edition of Erasmus and the Complutensian (Alcalá) Polyglot were the principal sources for the text of Robert Estienne (Stephanus), the Parisian printer, which appeared in four editions in 1540, 1549, 1550, 1551. The best-known of them is the *Editio regia* of 1550 in two folio volumes with apparatus criticus on the inner margin. This afterwards became the standard text, and it remained so in England until 1880. It is denoted by ς (sigma) = Stephanus.

---

[1] On the question how far Luther's translation depended on the Greek text cf. H. Dibbelt: Archiv f. Reformationsgeschichte 38 (1941) 300–330 [he only occasionally referred to the Greek], and for the opposite view H. Bornkamm: ThLZ 72 (1947) 23–28 [Luther translated from a Greek-Latin combined text (Erasmus' edition) and from the Vulgate which he had in his head].

The nine editions (three in folio and six in octavo:1564–1605) of Theodore von Beza, Calvin's successor in Geneva, show no textual advance. The same applies to the seven editions which from 1624 onwards were produced by the Elzevier brothers who were printers in Leyden and later in Amsterdam. The preface to their second edition contains the sentence: *Textum ergo habes nunc ab omnibus receptum in quo nihil immutatum aut corruptum damus;* this is the origin of the name *textus receptus.*

The text of the Elzevier brothers had a huge circulation in the following period, especially on the Continent. In 1710 it was taken over by the Canstein Bible Foundation in Halle, and from there it passed to the British and Foreign Bible Society (from 1810 to 1904), and superseded the text of Stephanus, which until then had been current in England. A convenient edition of the *textus receptus* is: *Η ΚΑΙΝΗ ΔΙΑΘΗΚΗ, Novum Testamentum textus Stephanici* A.D. *1550 cum variis lectionibus editionum Bezae, Elzeviri, Lachmanni, Tischendorfii, Tregellesii, Westcott-Hortii, Versionis Anglicanae emendatorum curante F. H. A. Scrivener, editio quarta ab Eb. Nestle correcta,* London and Cambridge 1906.

As early as the 17th century efforts were made to produce a critically reliable text, but they had little success because they were confined to procuring material for textual criticism (MSS. citations of the Fathers, versions). Mention may be made of John Mill (1645–1707), R. Bentley (the philologist, † 1742)[2] J. A. Bengel (1687–1752)[3], J. J. Wettstein (1693–1754), J. S. Semler (1725–1791), J. J. Griesbach (1745–1812), and the Catholics J. M. A. Scholz in Bonn (1794–1852) and J. Leonard Hug in Freiburg (1765–1846).

Wettstein, the theologian of Basle who fled to Holland because

---

[2] A. Fox, *John Mill and Richard Bentley,* Oxford 1953.

[3] Cf. K. Hermann, *Johann Albrecht Bengel, der Klosterpraezeptor von Denkendorf,* Stuttgart 1937.

he was suspect of heresy, published his celebrated edition of the New Testament in Amsterdam in 1751/52; it is in two folio volumes, and was the first work to denote the Majuscules by capital letters and the Minuscules by Arabic numerals (cf. § 12). As well as the textual *apparatus criticus* the edition also gives a second more extensive *apparatus* containing a large number of parallels from Greek, Roman, Rabbinical and Christian literature; these give the work a permanent value.[4]

Semler was the first to recognize in the Greek MSS. evidence of recensions of the text; in the case of the Gospels he distinguished three recensions: the Alexandrian, Oriental, and Western. His pupil Griesbach developed this discovery by distinguishing more accurately the witnesses to the three recensions, which he called Alexandrian, Western, and Byzantine; he assigned the primacy to the ancient Majuscules; he also appreciated the great value of the Father's citations and of the ancient versions. But in his editions he held mainly to the *textus receptus*.

Karl Lachmann (1793–1851), the Berlin philologist, was the first to make a decisive break with the *textus receptus*. With the aid of the oldest Greek Majuscules and MSS. of the Vulgate he undertook to reconstruct the text which was in use in the Eastern and Western Churches at the end of the fourth century. His aim was very modest; he did not set out to restore the original or even the oldest possible text, for he considered this impossible; it is precisely in this limitation that the value of his work for its time lies. His first edition appeared in 1831 followed by the great critical Greek-Latin edition in two volumes in 1842–1850. Lachmann's great weakness lay in the fact that he used too few sources.

On the other hand the famous textual critic Konstantin von Tischendorf of Leipzig (1815–1877) is important precisely because he procured abundant textual material. It was he who had the

---

[4] Cf. C. L. Hulbert-Powel, *John James Wettstein*, London 1938.

good fortune to discover the Codex Sinaiticus graecus, and he found a further 21 Majuscules on his numerous journeys; he also used 23 others for the first time, and 18 were republished by him. The most valuable of his numerous editions of the New Testament text is *Editio octava critica maior* (2 vols., Leipzig 1869 to 1872), with its exhaustive *apparatus criticus,* which even to-day is indispensible.[5]

Of greater significance for the establishment of a critical New Testament text was the collaboration over almost 30 years of the two Cambridge scholars, B. F. Westcott († 1901) and F. J. A. Hort († 1892); their work resulted in an edition with the title: *The New Testament in the Original Greek* (London and Cambridge 1881), in two large octavo volumes. Vol. I contains the Greek text with alternative readings on the margin, and at the end of the volume a short apparatus on selected passages. Vol. II (prepared by Hort) gives the principles of their criticism and a detailed commentary on a great number of rejected, but interesting readings.

Westcott and Hort distinguish four textual forms. The latest of them is the Syrian (or Antiochene) form, which is most probably a recension made by Lucian of Antioch towards the end of the 3rd century; it appears in the later Majuscules and the majority of the Minuscules, and was used towards the end of the fourth century by Chrysostom and Theodoret. Chrysostom brought it to Constantinople, and it soon circulated widely in the Byzantine Empire. The *textus receptus* derives from it. This Syrian text is furthest from the originals, and must be considered the poorest of all text forms. The redactor aimed at polishing the style, eliminating obscurities and harmonizing parallel accounts, thereby making the text more acceptable to educated people.

On the other hand, the second text form, the Western Text, is

---

[5] In addition C. R. Gregory published *Prolegomena* (in Latin) as a third volume (Leipzig 1884–1894); an improved and expanded German edition appeared in Leipzig 1900–1909 under the title *Textkritik des NT.*

very ancient. It appears in Codex D and in the Old-Latin version, as well as in the Fathers of the 2nd century; yet it does not give us the original text, for it was created by 2nd century scribes who handled the original freely, introduced interpolations, harmonized, paraphrased, and often also corrected or expunged objectionable peculiarities.

The third textual form (Alexandrian Text) is contained in many older Majuscules (for example, in C and L) and in the Coptic version, but it is not uncontaminated. It was made about 300 A.D. by polished scholars who introduced grammatical and stylistic changes into the original in order to assimilate it more closely to classical forms. Behind this recension lies the Neutral Text, that is, the text which has undergone no significant changes; it has come down to us primarily in the MS. B for the Gospels, Acts, Catholic Epistles (B is not so pure for the Pauline Epistles), and secondarily in the MS. ℵ.

In accordance with this classification and assessment of the textual sources, Westcott and Hort's text depends mainly on the two MSS. B and ℵ.

The text of Westcott and Hort received an eager welcome in some quarters, but elsewhere (particularly in England) it was violently opposed by the supporters of the *textus receptus* (for example, Scrivener, Burgon). There can be no doubt that it represents an important advance, though the idea that B (and ℵ) contain the unrevised original text was an illusion. Their judgment on the so-called Syrian text was quite correct, but they were entirely wrong to reject utterly the Western Text.

The beginning of the 20th century brought a great new edition of the text, the fruit of prolonged investigation of the Greek Minuscules and of intensive study of the History of the Text: Hermann von Soden, *Die Schriften des Neuen Testaments in ihrer aeltesten erreichbaren Textgestalt hergestellt auf Grund ihrer Textgeschichte* (I. Teil: *Untersuchungen,* 1. Bd.: *Textzeugen,* 2. und 3. Bd.: *Text-*

formen, Berlin 1902/07; II. Teil: *Text mit Apparat),* Goettingen 1913.

According to von Soden there were three recensions of the New Testament text in existence about 300 A.D.:

1. Recension K (Κοινή) of Lucian of Antioch (called Syrian Text by Westcott and Hort). It contains numerous families, and with time it became more and more altered. In its most ancient form, however, it is independent of the other two recensions.

2. Recension H of Hesychius, in Egypt. It appears in the old uncials (B ℵ C L etc.), some Minuscules (33, 892, 579, 1241), the Sahidic and Bohairic versions, and in the Alexandrian Fathers Athanasius, Didymus, Cyril and others. It therefore includes what Westcott and Hort called the Neutral and the Alexandrian Text. It is not possible to recognize separate families.

3. Recension I (Ἰερουσαλήμ), from Caesarea in Palestine (Pamphilus) with numerous more or less homogeneous families, which really represent a series of stages in which this recension was affected by the influential K form. The main sources are: D Θ 565, the Ferrar group, the Old-Latin and the Old-Syriac versions.

Von Soden believed that the three recensions go back to one and the same archetype (called HIK), which has not survived, but which may be reconstructed by comparing the recensions either with one another or with the Old-Latin and Old-Syriac versions and the citations of the Fathers; but it must be realized that the original wording was already corrupted in the second century, by Marcion in the case of the Pauline Epistles, and in the case of the Gospels and Acts by Tatian. The discovery and elimination of these corruptions brings us to the original text.

Von Soden's reconstruction has been sharply challenged, and not without reason. The most telling criticisms are directed against the alleged independence of Recension K, the unity of the I text, and the influence of Tatian and Marcion on the development of the text.

134

Competent New Testament scholars do not consider that the time has yet come for a great new recension of the text. First of all the materials must be assembled more extensively, and numerous particular problems must be investigated more thoroughly. In England the preparation of a new edition of the New Testament has begun; on the basis of Westcott and Hort it will present the textual material as faithfully and as fully as possible, thereby preparing the way for a future new recension of the text. Only two volumes have appeared: *NT graece secundum textum Westcotto-Hortianum. Evangelium secundum Marcum,* ed. S. C. E. Legg, Oxford 1935; *Ev. s. Matthaeum,* ed. Legg, Oxford 1940 (cf. the unfavourable reviews by H. v. Soden: Gnomon 1937, 52 sqq., G. D. Kilpatrick: JThSt 43, 1942, 30–34, and T. W. Manson: ibid. 83–92).

Since Legg's work proved unsatisfactory, American and English Protestant scholars under E. C. Colwell of Chicago and R. H. Lightfoot of Oxford are now preparing a new and up to date publication of the entire MS. material for the NT text (Greek MSS. including the lectionaries, citations of the Fathers, and the ancient versions). The undertaking is being financed by the Library of Congress and the Rockefeller Foundation, and the printing and publishing is in the hands of the Oxford University Press. The work on the ancient versions (Syriac, Armenian, Coptic, Sogdian, Nubian, Arabic, Latin and Anglo-Saxon) is under the direction of B. Metzger of Princeton, N. J. For a survey see Parvis-Wikgren (cf. § 11) and M. M. Parvis: Crozer Quarterly 27 (1950) 301–308 (Bb 1952, 305 sq.). The *textus receptus* is the foundation of this "New Tischendorf"; it is drawn up in such a way that all the material is immediately appended to each single verse. The work will run to eight volumes with two volumes of Prolegomena as well. None of the volumes has yet appeared.

The convenient editions in common use in Germany at present are:

1. Eberhard Nestle's edition published (since 1898) by Privilegierte Wuerttembergische Bibelanstalt of Stuttgart; it is not a special edition of the text, but gives the text of Tischendorf, Westcott-Hort, and Bernh. Weiss (which appeared 1894–1900); since the revision by Erwin Nestle (1927) it contains a rich *Apparatus criticus* ([24]1952; Greek-Latin [16]1951);

2. Augustine Merk's edition published by the Pontifical Biblical Institute at Rome ([6]1948), with a very rich *Apparatus criticus* (Greek-Latin);

3. the edition of Heinrich Joseph Vogels ([3]1950, Freiburg i. Br., Herder), with a shorter *Apparatus criticus* which takes note principally of the standard Majuscules and important Minuscules, and also of the Old-Latin material and the Syriac versions.

There is also an edition by A. Souter (Oxford [2]1947) and another by J. M. Bovér S. J. (Madrid [3]1953).

§ 21. THE PRESENT POSITION OF NEW TESTAMENT TEXTUAL CRITICISM

A. Harnack, *Zur ntl Textkritik,* Berlin 1931. F. G. Kenyon, *Recent Developments* (see above § 11) 64–87. Lagrange, *Crit. rat.* passim. W. G. Kuemmel: ThRdsch 11 (1933) 84–107: *Das Problem der Lokaltexte und Rezensionen.* Lagrange and Kuemmel give a fairly full list of the literature up to 1937. Since then K. and S. Lake, *De Westcott et Hort au Père Lagrange et au delà*: RB 48 (1939) 197–506. R. V. G. Tasker, *An Introduction to the MSS. of the NT*: HarvThR 41 (1948) 71–81.—T. Ayuso, EB 6 (1947) 35–90 [the Western and pre-Caesarean texts of the Gospels give us independently the text which lies behind the recensions]. G. Zuntz, *Textual Criticism of the Acts of the Apostles*: CM 3 (1940) 20–46. H. Lietzmann, *Einfuehrung in die Textgeschichte der Paulusbriefe: Commentary on Rom.* ([4]1933). C. S. C. Williams, *Alterations to the Text of the Synoptic Gospels and Acts,* Oxford 1951. G. Zuntz, *Réflexions sur l'histoire du texte paulinien*: RB 59 (1952) 5–22. Idem, *The Text of the Epistles: a Disquisition upon the Corpus Paulinum,* Oxford 1953. L. E. Wright, *Alterations of the Words of Jesus as Quoted in the Literature of the Second Century,* 1952. E. C. Colwell, *Genealogical Method*: JBL 66 (1947) 109–133. E. Fascher, *Textgeschichte als hermeneutisches Problem,* Halle 1953. E. Massaux, *État actuel de la critique textuelle du NT*: NRTh 75 (1953) 703–726 [a survey since 1940; confined to the Gospels]. R. V. G. Tasker, *The Text of the Corpus Paulinum*: NTSt 1 (1955) 180–191 [a report on Zuntz's book].

According to E. Massaux (EphThL 38, 1952, 411–448) Justin Martyr used the Western Text.

According to K. W. Kim (JThSt NS 1, 1950, 74–84) Origen always used for the Gospel of St. John the "Neutral" text, for Mk. first the "Neutral" and then (in Caesarea) the Caesarean (of the type of Θ), for Mt. first the "Neutral" and then (in Caesarea) the text of the type of 1, 1582. In Caesarea the "Neutral" and the Caesarean texts existed side by side.

In the case of the Apc., the Greek tradition has been almost completely covered by H. C. Hoskier (*Concerning the Text of the Apc.,* 2 vols., London 1929) and it has been investigated with additional MS. material by J. Schmid (*Studien zur Geschichte des Apk.-Textes,* 2 vols., Munich 1955/56). According to them the whole Greek textual tradition can be derived from four old lines, which stretch beyond the 4th century, namely 1. AC Oik(umenios), 2. 𝔓⁴⁷ ℵ, 3. Aν (the commentary of Andrew of Cesarea), 4. K. They are not independent of one another. The best source is the AC line, especially A. There are also in existence four forms of later mixed texts which derive from Aν and K. There is no evidence of any trace of the Western Text in the Greek tradition.

K. W. Clark, *The Effect of Recent Textual Criticism upon NT: The Background of the NT,* Studies in Honour of C. H. Dodd, 1956, 27–51.

SINCE Hermann von Soden's monumental work appeared, unexpected finds and intensive study have considerably advanced the investigation of the New Testament text and its history. First place among the finds must go to the Chester Beatty papyri which have shed new light on the various forms of the text in Egypt at the beginning of the 3rd century.

These advances in textual studies are very largely due to English scholars; one need only mention J. Rendel Harris, Burkitt, Kirsopp Lake and F. G. Kenyon. M.-J. Lagrange also rendered good service by his great work of synthesis *Critique rationelle*. Research on Tatian has been substantially advanced by D. Plooij, Anton Baumstark, and Curt Peters.

Von Soden's lasting achievement was to mark out the two text forms H (Hesychius Text) and K (Koine Text). W. Bousset in his *"Textkritische Studien zum Neuen Testament"* (Leipzig 1894) was the first to prove the unity of the H Text and to associate it with Egypt; this association is proved by its agreement with the text of the 4th century Alexandrian Fathers, the Coptic versions, and the papyrus fragments. H. von Soden showed that this H Text is so uniform that no varying types can be discerned among its witnesses. On the other hand he was able to establish a number of groups amongst the sources for the K Text, and subsequent research has in general confirmed his division of them. Yet he did not succeed in solving the main problem of New Testament textual criticism which is posed by the texts which belong neither to H nor to K. These texts are not a unity, as he thought, deriving from a third great recension, the Palestinian (I: Jerusalem; Pamphilus and Eusebius). The most recent scholarship has shown that the sources for I belong to two distinct textual forms, the so-called Western Text and a newly discovered form which is called Caesarean.

1. The Alexandrian (or "Neutral") Text
(von Soden, Merk H; Nestle ℌ)

P. L. Hedly, *The Egyptian Texts* of the Gospels and Acts: ChQR 118 (1934) 23–29, 188–230. E. F. Hills, *A New Approach to the Old Egyptian Text:* JBL 69 (1950) 345–362. P. Benoit, *Le codex paulinien Chester Beatty:* RB 46 (1937) 58–82. F. G. Kenyon, *Hesychius and the Text of the NT:* Mémorial Lagrange (Paris 1940) 245–250.

The existence of this form has been recognized for a long time. H. von Soden includes in it all the material of Westcott and Hort's Neutral and Alexandrian Text. He regards B as its principal witness. Following W. Bousset and others he sees in this form the result of a recension carried out by the Alexandrian scholar Hesychius[1], of whom we know, from St. Jerome's letter to Pope Damasus (cf. § 14, 2), that he undertook an edition of the Septuagint.

This text, which is usually called the "Neutral" Text in English, is short and austere, that is, it is generally shorter than the text of the other forms, the Western being the longest; furthermore it has not undergone grammatical and stylistic polishing like the Koine Text and (to a small extent) the Caesarean Text.

---

[1] According to Eusebius, H. E. VIII 13, there was a Hesychius among the Egyptian bishops who were martyred between 308 and 312 A.D.

The vast majority of important textual critics consider this "Neutral" Text the best of the textual forms which we know, though they have abandoned Hort's optimistic view that B contains the original text unchanged except for slips of the pen.

The Papyrus and MSS. finds of recent years have not substantially increased the material for this text form (if we except $\mathfrak{P}^{46}$), but they have established two facts: 1) that this text form was not the only common one in Egypt, and 2) that either it or its basis or its earlier form goes back to the 2nd century. The papyri prove to us that the Western Text was in circulation in Egypt in the 3rd century, and the pre-Caesarean Text at the beginning of that century ($\mathfrak{P}^{38}$, $\mathfrak{P}^{48}$, $\mathfrak{P}^{45}$). $\mathfrak{P}^{45}$ has a text of Acts which shows close affinity to the "Neutral" Text. For The Gospels $\mathfrak{P}^{45}$ has a text which resembles the Caesarean form, but in reality it is merely a mixture of the Western and "Neutral" Texts; this proves that both go back to the 2nd century. Origen uses the "Neutral" Text in his earlier writings. $\mathfrak{P}^{46}$ also represents an early Egyptian text, which on the whole agrees with the best Egyptian sources.

The question now arises whether the "Neutral" Text as it appears in B is a recension (the result of editing), or whether it represents an unusually pure textual tradition. At the present day it is generally agreed that the "Neutral" Text represents an edition made on the basis of excellent older MSS. which were current in Egypt, but that it is a very careful edition, the work of a skilled scholar whose only aim was to reproduce the original text. The text which he used as his basis must have been already old on all important points. Hort has shown that the MSS. B and ℵ derive through separate and independent ancestors from a common archetype which must be put in the second century, and this is confirmed by the Coptic versions and by the Chester Beatty Papyri. So a new type of text could not have been produced around 300 A.D.; what could have been made was rather a carefully produced representative of an already existing text.

"In the course of the 2nd and 3rd centuries a great diversity of readings arose in the Christian world. In many places a considerable freedom manifested itself in the handing down of the sacred text, while in others more respect was shown for tradition. In Egypt the same variety of texts prevailed as elsewhere; but Egypt (especially Alexandria) was a country with a vigorous tradition of scholarship and experience in textual criticism, with the result that a relatively trustworthy tradition was preserved there. At the beginning of the fourth century a scholar might have sat down to compare the best available representatives of this tradition, and so have produced a text of which B is an earlier derivative.[2] Such a text must have been closely related to the Sahidic and Bohairic versions and to other MSS. of the same type which originated in Egypt, as they have come down to us in ℵ and the T group; and its roots must go far back towards the originals, of which it may well be the best representative now available. We can say nothing about its editor. It may have been Bishop Hesychius, but the only evidence (Jerome's) which we have to connect Hesychius with the New Testament does not support this identification" (Kenyon).

The most important textual sources are:[3]

Gospels: B ℵ W (for Lk. 1, 1 to 8, 12; John 5, 12 to end) C Ψ Z L Δ T (20 leaves Greek-Sahidic) 33, 579, 892, 1241, 𝔓 [1 4 5 22 39 52] bo (sa).

Acts: B ℵ CA 81 𝔓 [45 50].

Pauline Epistles: B ℵ C A H I M P Ψ 33 1739 𝔓[46] (and all the papyrus fragments to date with Pauline text).

Catholic Epistles: B ℵ CA Ψ P 0156, 0157, 6, 33, 89, 104, 326, 1175, 𝔓 [20 23]

Apocalypse: A C 2344 Oik (i. e., the text of Oecumenius, of which 2053 is the standard MS.), less good 𝔓 [47] ℵ.

The "Neutral" or Alexandrian Text is regarded—and rightly —as on the whole the best recension of the text and the nearest to the original. But it has recently been shown by M.-E. Boismard[4]

[2] But Codex B was overvalued not only by Westcott and Hort but also by Lagrange, as recent research proves (e. g. Vaganay: RB 1940, 5–32; Cerfaux: EphThLov 1938, 674–682; Boismard: RB 1950, 400).

[3] It is only with great reservations that Codex ℵ may be included among the material for this text form, for it is a mixed text, and sometimes follows the Western tradition only (RB 1954, 275).—According to Williams, *Alterations* p. 54, the sources for Acts are: B ℵ C Ψ 81, 33, 104, 326, 1175, 𝔓[45], and possibly, 𝔓[8].

[4] *Critique textuelle et citations patristiques:* RB 57 (1950) 388–408. Cf. also 55 (1948) 1–34 (on John 5, 39); 58 (1951) 161–168 *(Lectio brevior, potior)*.

that in addition to the textual tradition of our MSS. there is, or to be more accurate, there was another tradition before it, namely the text tradition of the Fathers; this tradition is found over the whole extent of the ancient Church, but is seldom or never attested by the MSS. or versions. Boismard's explanation of this strange fact is that the Fathers follow an older textual tradition than that of our parchment MSS. of which only two or three belong to the fourth century. It must therefore be assumed that the MS. tradition which the Fathers followed in the second and third centuries was superseded in the fourth and fifth centuries by another tradition of which Codex B is a very good witness. The text of the MSS. is often very verbose in comparison with the older text of the Fathers; the following examples of this are from John: the Fathers read John 14, 2a παρὰ τῷ πατρί (instead of ἐν τῇ οἰκίᾳ τοῦ πατρός μου), 12, 32 without ἐκ τῆς γῆς, 17, 21 ὡς ἐγὼ καὶ σύ ἕν ἐσμεν, ἵνα καὶ αὐτοὶ ἐν ἡμῖν ἕν ὦσιν, 1, 13 οὐκ ἐξ αἵματος οὐδὲ ἐκ σαρκός.

This new thesis is of the greatest importance for the quest after the oldest form of the New Testament text. But the matter cannot be finally settled until the citations of the Fathers have been investigated more thoroughly. The Berlin Academy is preparing a work: *Novum Testamentum apud patres saeculi secundi et tertii repertum.*

2. The Western Text (Merk D)

F. G. Kenyon, *The Western Text in the Gospels and Acts,* Oxford 1939 (cf. RB 49, 1940, 273 sq.). C. C. Tarelli, *The Chester Beatty Papyrus and the Western and Byzantine Texts:* JThSt 41 (1940) 253–260. G. D. Kilpatrick, *Western Text and Original Text in the Gospels and Acts:* JThSt 44 (1943) 24–36. Idem, *Western Text and Original Text in the Epistles:* JThSt 45 (1944) 60–65. A. F. J. Klijn, *A Survey of the Researches into the Western Text of the Gospels and Acts,* 1947 (Diss. theol. Utrecht; additions by B. M. Metzger: ThZ 7, 1951, 230). L. Cerfaux: EphThLov 15 (1938) 674–682. [In second century Alexandria the text of the Gospels was Western.] P. Glaue, *Der aelteste Text der geschichtlichen Buecher des NT:* ZntW 45 (1954) 90–108. [The Western Text is the oldest.]

W. H. P. Hatch, *The "Western" Text of the Gospels,* Evanston 1937.

The existence of a separate text form distinct from the "Neutral" and Koine Text has long been recognized. Griesbach called it the Western Text because it is contained, in the Old-Latin version, the pre-fourth century Latin Fathers, and the Greek-Latin MSS. D^{ev} D^{pl} E F G; the name Western Text was taken over by Hort. The existence of this text form is demonstrable with certainty for Gospels, Acts, and Pauline Epistles, but not for Apc. nor (according to Lagrange) for the Catholic Epistles.

In the past the Old-Syriac version of Gospels and Acts was thought to represent this form, and so the term Western-Syriac was sometimes used. In recent times, however, competent textual critics (Burkitt, Lake, Kenyon, and others) have insisted that the Old-Syriac Gospel text does not belong to the Western form. On the other hand the Old-Latin and Old-Syriac versions and the marginal notes of Harclensis (§ 16, 4) have one and the same text of Acts. Jos. Molitor (cf. § 16, 2) says that Western influence (Marcionite readings especially) can also be detected in the Old-Syriac Pauline text which Ephraem used.

The characteristics of the Western Text are:

1. Obvious additions and omissions, especially in Lk. and Acts.[5] Burkitt has shown that the longer additions are generally to be found in the *Versio Afra* (k, e, Cyprian), which is the oldest form of the *Vetus Latina*, while the shorter additions generally occur in the *Versio Europaea* (a, b, and congeners).

Examples of additions:

a) genuine additions: Mt. 20, 28 + ὑμεῖς δὲ ζητεῖτε ἐκ μικροῦ αὐξῆσαι κτλ (cf. Lk. 14, 8-10) D Φ it sy^c—Mk. 16, 3 + subito autem etc., k—Lk. 6, 5 + Story about the Sabbath D—Lk. 9, 55 + καὶ εἶπεν· οὐκ οἴδατε ποίου πνεύματός ἐστε ὑμεῖς· ὁ γὰρ υἱὸς τ. ἀ. κτλ D al it vg sy^c—Lk. 23, 53 + καὶ θέντος αὐτοῦ ἐπέθηκεν τῷ μνημείῳ λίθου κτλ D (0124, 1071) c sa.—Acts has

---

[5] An extensive list in Westcott and Hort, *The NT* I 571–580; II. Appendix 1–42; cf. also Turner: JThSt 29 (1928) 1 sqq. (on Mk.).

very many additions, e. g., 8, 37; 11, 2; 12, 10; 15, 29; 17, 15; 19, 9; 25, 24 sq.; 27, 5, etc.

b) Expansions from the parallel accounts or harmonizations: Mt. 14, 2 + ὅν ἐγὼ ἀπεκεφάλισα (= Mk. 6, 16) D it—Lk. 5, 14 + ὁ δὲ ἐξελθὼν ἤρξατο κτλ (= Mk. 1, 45) D—Lk. 11, 2 + μὴ βαττολογεῖτε κτλ (like Mt. 6, 7) D.

Examples of omissions:

Lk. 5, 26: καὶ ἔκστασις—θεόν is missing in D Ψ al fam 13 e—Lk. 5, 39 is missing in D it Marcion Eus—Lk. 10, 41: μεριμνᾷς—πολλὰ is missing in it sys (D Aug)—Lk. 22, 19-20 is missing in D it—Lk. 24, 6: οὐκ—ἠγέρθη is missing in D it—Lk. 24, 12: missing in D it—Lk. 24, 40: missing in D it sys+c Marcion—Lk. 24, 51: καὶ ἀνεφέρετο εἰς τὸν οὐρανόν is missing in D it syc.

2. Free shaping of the story compared to the "Neutral" Text: Lk. 5, 13: ἐκαθαρίσθη D e—Lk. 5,5 sq.: οὐ παρακούσομαι· καὶ εὐθὺς χαλάσαντες D e sys.—Cf. also Acts 5, 22 29; 14, 2 5; 15, 2; 16, 35 39 etc.

In the Gospels and Acts somewhat trivial additions and omissions and shaping of the story are very frequent, but these seldom occur in the Pauline Epistles; see Rom. 10, 15 πόδες + τῶν εὐαγγελιζομένων εἰρήνην D G lat (completed from the Septuagint)—2 Cor. 10, 12: οὐ συνιᾶσιν· ἡμεῖς δὲ is missing in D F G it (vg) Ambrst—Gal. 2, 5: οὐδὲ is missing in D* Iren Tert Vict Ambrst Pel.

The Western Text can be traced back to a very early date. It was used by Marcion (and probably Tatian), Irenaeus, Tertullian and Cyprian. Its most important witness is the Old-Latin version which was made about 200 A.D. It circulated not only in North Africa, Italy, and Gaul, but also—as well as other text forms—in Egypt. Clement of Alexandria is a witness to this; though born in Athens, he was also in Rome and could have brought it with him to Egypt. Its presence in Egypt is shown by 𝔓38 (of the third century) and 𝔓48 (early fourth century at latest). W has a text of

Mk. 1, 1 to 5, 30 which is closely related to the Old-Latin version (especially to e). The circulation of the Western Text in Egypt at an early date is also shown by the Sahidic version which has a fair number of Western readings as well as readings from the so-called pre-Caesarean Text (see below).

The problem of the value and origin of the Western Text is still unsolved. Hort treated it as manifestly corrupt, but it has since been recognized that this assessment is too sweeping. The view of Adalbert Merx (cf. § 3, 9a) is equally unacceptable; he says that the Western Text is closest to the original, and that its best representative is syr[sin]. The English scholar A. Clarke (cf. § 29, 6) has recently maintained that for Acts the Western Text is original while the "Neutral" Text is a later abridgement. August Pott († 1926), one of H. von Soden's collaborators, regarded the Western Text as the precanonical text, which is still free from dogmatic and disciplinary influences, unlike the canonical or "Neutral" Text; in general, despite many changes and a certain amount of editing he considered that the Western Text stood closest to the original.[6]

The extreme positions both for or against the Western Text are rejected by the leading textual critics of the present day (Kenyon, Lake, Lagrange etc.). As against Hort they recognize that the Western Text has many good features (original readings) which the "Neutral" Text no longer possesses. So a textual critic at the present day cannot rely on B and its congeners as exclusively and onesidedly as Westcott and Hort did, even though the "Neutral" Text is relatively the best of the four forms.

H. von Soden's suggestion that the Western Text of the Gospels and Acts was made by Marcion (and Tatian) has been fairly generally rejected. Lagrange considered that it was probably made in Alexandria, because from there it could simultaneously spread

---

[6] *Der Text des Neuen Testaments nach seiner geschichtlichen Entwicklung,* Leipzig 1906. The English scholar Turner is also a defender of the Western Text.

both to the West and to the East (Syria). Kenyon on the other hand thinks that the Western Text in the narrower sense (= D, Vetus Latina, Cyprian) was made in North Africa and then became widespread in Italy, but that in principle it remained confined to the Latin speaking churches; the circulation of some copies in Egypt is enough to explain the presence of Western readings in a number of Papyri.

This recension has preserved a number of readings which depend on authentic traditions (especially in Acts); nevertheless, the free expanding of the text which is characteristic of it renders it less dependable than those texts which were made and circulated in Egypt, a country with stricter scholarly traditions.

The most important sources are:

Gospels: D 0171 (Lk. 22, 44–56, 61–63; 4th century, from Egypt); Vetus Latina.

Acts: D 614, 383, $\mathfrak{P}$ [38] [48]; Vetus Latina; Commentary of Ephraem (cf. § 29, 6), the marginal notes of sy[h] (cf. § 16, 4).

Pauline Epistles: the Greek-Latin bilinguals D E G F; Greek Fathers to the end of the 3rd century; Vetus Latina; Syrian Fathers up to about 450 A.D.

3. The Caesarean Text (Merk C)

Th. Ayuso, *Texto cesariense o precesariense*: Bb 16 (1935) 369–415. C. C. Tarelli, *The Chester Beatty Papyrus and the Caesarean Text*: JThSt 40 (1939) 46–55. K. and S. Lake, *Family 13 (The Ferrar Group). The Text According to Mark, with a Collation of Codex 28 of the Gospels*, London 1941 (StD XI). B. M. Metzger, *The Caesarean Text of the Gospels*: JBL 64 (1945) 457–489. E. F. Hills, *Harmonizations in the Caesarean Text of Mark*: JBL 66 (1947) 135–152. Idem, *The Interrelationship of the Caesarean MSS.*: JBL 68 (1949) 148–159. C. C. Tarelli, *Some Further Linguistic Aspects of the Chester Beatty Papyrus of the Gospels*: JThSt 43 (1942) 19–25. According to H. W. Huston (JBL 74, 1955, 262–271) $\mathfrak{P}$[45] does not contain the Caesarean Text, as Kenyon believes, but, together with the other papyrus fragments of the 3rd century, it represents the text which underlies the revisions of the 4th and 5th centuries. D. S. Wallace-Hadrill, *Eusebius and the Gospel Text of Caesarea*: HarvThR 49 (1956) 105–114.

The discovery of this form of the text followed on the publication of the two MSS. W and O. Burkitt (JThSt 1916) noticed that W (in Mk. 6–16) and Θ give a strange text which cannot properly be reckoned among the recognized text forms. Lake and Blake (HarvThR 1923) showed that this text is also to be found in other sources: fam 1, fam 13, Minuscules 28, 565, 700. When the Koine readings which crept in later are eliminated, there remains a mixture of Western and "Neutral" readings.

In his book on the four Gospels, which first appeared in 1924 (cf. § 26), Streeter adduced evidence to show that this text had been used by Origen in Caesarea, and inferred that it must have originated there or have been the local text. He gave it the name Caesarean Text. Lake, Blake and Silva Lake then (HarvThR 1928) carefully collated Mk. 1 6 11, and showed that the witnesses which Streeter put together really contain a common text, and that the Georgian version is to be added as another witness. Tasker furthermore showed (JThSt 1935–1937) that a Caesarean Text exists not only for Mk., but also for Mt. and Lk. Streeter's observations about Origen were checked by these four scholars and were considerably modified. According to them Origen seems to have used the Caesarean Text of Mk. in Books I–V of his commentary on John, which were the only books composed in Alexandria, but in Books VI–X he followed the Alexandrian ("Neutral") Text, while in the following books he used partly the Alexandrian (Mk. 1 to middle of 12) and partly the Caesarean Text (from the middle of Mk. 12 onwards); in the works which he wrote after the commentary on John he used only the Caesarean Text. Tasker has further shown that Eusebius used this text, and that it was used for Mt. and Lk. also by Origen when in Caesarea, and by Eusebius.

New light was shed by $\mathfrak{P}^{45}$ which shows much the same form of text in the Gospels (so does $\mathfrak{P}^{37}$ of the 3rd century, which was published in 1926; Mt. 26, 19–51). It follows that this text form was also in Egypt as early as the first half of the 3rd century.

So far as its special character is concerned, it is a mixture—as has already been shown—of the "Neutral" (B) and the Western (D) Texts. "Evidently its maker knew both and made a kind of compromise; in substance he followed the 'Neutral' Text while retaining any Western readings which did not seem too improbable, for the latter text was widely current, although the former was the better. One may also observe a certain striving after elegance, and so consideration of the needs of the Church" (Lagrange).

Presumably the Caesarean Text originated in Egypt and was brought by Origen to Caesarea where hitherto the best MSS. had been of the Alexandrian type (Kenyon). From Caesarea it went to Jerusalem (Min. 565 goes back to Jerusalem according to the *Colophon*), from there to the Armenians, who had a colony in Jerusalem at a very early date, and thence to the Georgians, whose oldest version of the Gospels is based on the Armenian version (Θ belongs to Georgia). A Caesarean text seems also to be the foundation of the Syro-Palestinian Lectionaries.

According to the most recent investigations of Kirsopp and Silva Lake, it is necessary to distinguish two stages of this "Caesarean" Text (at least for Mk.): 1) $\mathfrak{P}^{45}$ W fam 1 fam 13 28 belong together; they contain the Old Egyptian Text which Origen brought to Caesarea—it may be called the pre-Caesarean Text; 2) through adaptation this took on the form to which we are led back by the common evidence of Θ, 565, 700, the citations of Origen and Eusebius, and the Georgian version (= Caesarean Text properly so called).

In the case of Acts Tasker attempted to show that a similar mixed text is the basis of $\mathfrak{P}^{45}$ and the Minuscules 1739, 614, 431 (JThSt 1937).

In his study of the Pauline Epistles (1952) G. Zuntz believes that he can establish the existence of a similar "Caesarean" text of them, like the text which Lake demonstrated for Mk.; he says that it is attested by 𝔓⁴⁶, 1739, B, sa, bo, Origen and Clement. But as this is really an Alexandrian text, and is older than the text attested by ℵ C 33 etc., he calls it proto-Alexandrian. On the other hand he regards Euthalius' edition of the Pauline Epistles—which depends on the critical work of Pamphilus († 309) (cf. § 11, 2)—as a real Caesarean text.

4. The Koine Text (von Soden, Merk K; Nestle 𝔎)

S. Lake, *Family Π and the Codex Alexandrinus. The Text According to Mark,* London 1936 (StD V); cf. Streeter: JThSt 38 (1937) 225–229. K. and S. Lake, *The Byzantine Text of the Gospels: Mémorial Lagrange* (Paris 1940) 251–258. G. Zuntz, *The Byzantine Text in NT Criticism:* JThSt 43 (1942) 25–30. E. W. Saunders, *Studies in the Doctrinal Influences on the Byzantine Text of the Gospels:* JBL 71 (1952) 85–92. C. C. Tarelli, *The Byzantine Texts and the Lectionaries:* JThSt 43 (1942) 181–183 (contra Zuntz, ibid. 183 sq.).

The more recent Majuscules and the vast majority of the Minuscules show a text of remarkable uniformity. The existence of this textual form was recognized at an early date, but it is still disputed when it was made and by whom. Westcott and Hort called it the Syrian Text because in Chrysostom's time it was used in Antioch in Syria, and they suggested that it was probably made by Lucian of Antioch († 312); for the same reason others called it the Antiochene Text. Others again named it either the Byzantine Text, because in its later form it was the standard text in the Byzantine Empire, or the Ecclesiastical Text, although it was never officially adopted by the Greek Church. H. von Soden called it the Koine Text (K) because in late antiquity it became predominant in the Greek Church.

Its characteristics are the smoothing of harshnesses of language, improvement of the style, small additions to facilitate intelligibility, and widespread harmonizing of parallel passages.

According to von Soden the K Text of the Gospels falls into the groups Kᵃ, Kˡ, Kⁱ (fundamentally merely a witness to Kˡ), Kˣ (MSS. of the 11th and 12th centuries; the finally dominant form), and Kʳ (MSS. of the 13th and following centuries; a revision for liturgical purposes). In his text volume, however, he assigns K^a to the I form (= I^{ka}) and regards K^l as the best form of K. This K^l group includes Ω (on Athos; 8th century), V (in Moscow; 8th or 9th century), S^{ev} (028; in the Vatican; of 949 A.D.), and five Minuscules.

The most recent investigations have substantially modified this picture of von Soden's. According to Silva Lake's detailed examination, the group K^a (= I^{ka})—which contains A K Π and about 20 Minuscules—is to be divided into two families: A and Π K min. The sources Π K (both of the ninth century) min show a uniform text, and are a real textual family, whose archetype is Π. A (only for the Gospels) and fam Π derive from a common ancester X; A is more distant from it than Π; Fam Π may show Lucian's recension (if it was he who made it) in a form which is nearer the original form. The common ancestor X is not later than the fourth century. The X Text itself is a mixed text. On the one hand it resembles the Caesarean, or rather the pre-Caesarean Text (fam 1, fam 13, W, and $\mathfrak{P}^{45}$), on the other hand it shows Alexandrian influence through its contact with C L Δ Ψ 33. So fam Π and A stand half way between the pre-Byzantine Text and the secondary form of the Byzantine Text (represented by Ω V S^{ev}) which later evolved further into the fully developed text of the Majuscules E F G H (= K^i) and the vast majority of minuscules (= K^x).

Therefore the foundation for the Byzantine texts K^l K^x K^r (in H. von Soden's sense) are mixed texts of Alexandrian and Caesarean form. The oldest sources for this text are:

Acts: H L P (9th century), S (8th or 9th century).[7]

Pauline Epistles: K L P (10th century).[8]

Catholic Epistles: K L (9th century).

Apocalypse: Q (9th century).[9]

[7] Cf. Ropes l. c. p. CCLXXVI–CCLXXXIX: *The Antiochian Text.*

[8] Cf. H. Lietzmann, *Roemerbrief* (Text der pl Briefe).

[9] Cf. J. Schmid, *Untersuchungen zur Geschichte des griechischen Apk-Textes. Der K-Text:* Bb 17 (1936).

PART III

THE ORIGIN OF THE NEW TESTAMENT
WRITINGS

Section I. The Gospels and Acts of the Apostles

§ 22. THE GOSPELS IN GENERAL

J. Schniewind, *Euangelion. Ursprung und erste Gestalt des Begriffs Evangelium*, Guetersloh 1927/31 (not completed). G. Friedrich, Art. Εὐαγγελίζομαι, εὐαγγέλιον: ThWB II (1935) 705–735. R. Asting, *Die Verkuendigung des Wortes im Urchristentum*, Stuttgart 1939, 300–457 (the concept of Gospel).

THE most important books of the New Testament are the Gospels, for to them we owe almost all our knowledge of the life and works, the passion and death of Jesus Christ.

We learn little about Christ's life on earth from the other New Testament sources. The most informative of them is St. Paul who often speaks of the birth, passion and resurrection of Jesus. He incorporated into the Epistle to the Philippians a hymn to Christ in which the whole extent of Jesus' work of Redemption is succinctly described from the Incarnation to his Exaltation (2, 5-11; cf. also 1 Tim. 3, 16). In 1 Cor. he gives an account of the institution of the Blessed Eucharist (11, 23-25) and enumerates the appearances after the Resurrection (15, 3-8). Sometimes also St. Paul expressly quotes sayings of Jesus (1 Cor. 7, 10 sq. on indissolubility of marriage; 1 Cor. 9, 14: "they who preach the Gospel should live by the Gospel," cf. Lk. 16, 7; Mt. 10, 9-10; 1 Tim. 5, 18; 1 Thess. 4, 15 sq. on the Resurrection). Acts preserves a saying of Our Lord which is not in the Gospels (20, 35: "It is a more blessed thing to give than to receive"). Rom. 1, 3 (15, 2) speaks of the Davidic descent of Jesus, as does 2 Tim. 2, 8. 1 Tim. 6, 13 tells of his giving testimony under Pontius Pilate. Heb. (5, 7 sq.) stresses his agony in Gethsemani. 2 Pet. 1, 16–18 attests the Transfiguration on the mountain (Thabor?). The missionary discourses in Acts tell of the passion, death and resurrection of Jesus.

That is virtually all that we know from extra-evangelical sources about Jesus.

Of the sayings of Our Lord which are handed down outside the canonical Gospels, only a small part can claim to be genuine.[1] Profane evidence about Jesus is very scanty and to some extent of disputed authenticity.[2]

Since the Gospels are practically speaking our only source of information about Jesus Christ, the Church has always regarded them as particularly sacred. They were the most frequently copied of all the parts of the Sacred Scripture, and the copies were often laid out with great artistry (cf. § 11, 2).

For the early Christians the word εὐαγγέλιον was not the title of a book containing the deeds and words of Jesus; it denoted the good tidings of the Messianic salvation which had already arrived, the message of salvation.

In modern times the history of the concepts εὐάγγελος, εὐαγγελίζεσθαι, εὐαγγέλιον has been clarified by close investigation. Both the verb εὐαγγελίζεσθαι and the adjectival substantive εὐαγγέλιον are derived from εὐάγγελος (bringer of good news). Εὐαγγέλιον originally meant 1) a reward for bringing good news (earliest recorded occurence Homer, *Od.* 14, 152 sq., 166 sq.), 2) the good news itself (Cicero, *Att.* II 3, 1; but cf. εὐαγγέλια θύειν: to celebrate good news by sacrifice, Aristophanes, *Knights* 656). The word then became specialized to mean news

---

[1] Cf. Joachim Jeremias, *Unbekannte Jesusworte,* Zurich 1948 (= BFchrTh 45, 2, 1951); L. Vaganay, Art. *Agrapha:* DB Suppl 1 (1928) 159–198.

[2] Cf. the survey of researches by H. Windisch: ThRdsch N. F. 1 (1929) 266–288 (the problem of the historicity of Jesus: the primitive Christian witnesses); also W. Bienert, *Der aelteste nichtchristliche Jesusbericht: Josephus ueber Jesus,* Halle 1930; Th. Martin, *Le Testimonium Flavianum: Vers. une solution définitive?:* RBPhH 20 (1941) 409–465; H. Fuchs, *Tacitus ueber die Christen:* VCh 4 (1950) 65–93; F. Scheidweiler, *Das Testimonium Flavianum:* ZntW 45 (1954) 230–244; Against him F. Dornzeiff: ibid. 46 (1955) 245–250.

of victory. It got a religious meaning in connection with oracles where it denoted the utterance of the oracle, especially in connection with Emperor Worship. Because the Emperor was regarded as a divine being, the saviour (σωτήρ) of the world and the deliverer of the individual from distress, his birth, his accession to the throne, and his pronouncements are glad tidings. The calendar inscription of Priene in Asia Minor (9 B.C.) says of the birthday of Augustus: "The birthday of the god was for the world the beginning of joyful tidings which have been pronounced on his account" (τῶν δι' αὐτὸν εὐαγγελί[ων]).

But it is in the Old Testament and late Judaism, rather than in the Hellenistic Greek usage, that we must seek the roots of the New Testament concept of "Evangelium". In Hebrew εὐαγγελίζεσθαι and εὐαγγέλιον are *bissar* (Piel) and *besorah* respectively, from the root *bsr*. The profane meaning of both words is the older; they mean respectively to announce good news (especially victory) or the good news itself. Only the verb (and its present participle *mebasser*) had a technical religious significance in the Old Testament.

The use of the word in Deutero-Isaias and the literature which he influenced is of fundamental importance for the creation of the New Testament concept. Its meaning there is to announce the message of the coming salvation, of the dawn of the time of salvation, or briefly, to announce the (beginning of the) time of salvation.

This implies that the announcing of the good tidings introduces the time of salvation. Being a divine message, the announcing of salvation on God's authority is in the proper sense creative; it brings about the new reality.

That is where the Old Testament concept differs from the non-Biblical, Hellenistic idea in Emperor Worship. There the tidings of joy look backwards and are so to speak a reflection of the happy event which has already taken place; in the Bible, on the other hand, the good news looks forward. Indeed the Biblical concept has an eschatological sense; the messenger of joy announces the beginning of the time of salvation and thereby introduces it. The meaning of the word is very nicely expressed in Is. 52, 7–10: "How beautiful upon the mountains are the feet of him that bringeth good tidings (εὐαγγελιζομένου ἀκοὴν εἰρήνης LXX), and that preacheth peace, of him that sheweth good, that preacheth salvation (εὐαγγελιζόμενος ἀγαθά), that saith to Sion: Thy God shall reign!" (v. 7.) Here the prophet sees in spirit how the herald hastening before the people who are returning from Babylon appears on the summit of the mountain, and tells the inhabitants of Jerusalem that Jahweh is coming back to Sion and that His Lordship over the world is beginning. The eschatological time of salvation is introduced by the efficacious word of this messenger of God.

Corresponding to this use in Isaias, Evangelium in the New Testament means the message of salvation, that is 1) the message of salvation which Jesus himself announced ("The Kingdom of God is at hand," Mk. 1, 15); so Mt. 11, 5; Lk. 4, 18; 4, 43; 7, 22 (= Is. 61, 1), Mk. 13, 10; 14, 9 par; 2) the apostolic preaching as the proclaiming of Christ and of the salvation which has come in him, so especially in St. Paul (Rom. 1, 1 sq., 1 Cor. 15, 1 sqq. etc.), or briefly, the proclaiming of Christ (Acts 5, 42; 8, 35; 11, 20). But the word Evangelium always means the living word of preaching, not a writing; and so the itinerant preachers of the message of salvation are also called Evangelists (Acts 21, 8; Eph. 4, 11; 2 Tim. 4, 5).

In the second century the word Evangelium is used to refer to a written account of the life and works of Jesus (so as early as *Didache* 8, 2; 11, 3; 15, 3–4). About the middle of the second century Justin Martyr speaks of the "recollections of the Apostles, which are called εὐαγγέλια" (Apol. I 66). Likewise the description Evangelist is now applied to the authors of Gospel books (Hippolytus, *De Antichristo* 56; Tertullian, *Adv. Prax.* 21, 23).

Since it proclaims the salvation which Christ has brought, the Gospel is naturally one. With time a number of written accounts were made of the deeds and words of Jesus, and finally the four canonical Gospels were accepted everywhere; yet for a long time it was usual to call them "the Gospel", for example (Eusebius, H. E. V 24, 6), or "the four books of the one Gospel" (cf. Muratorian Canon: Tertius evangelii liber secundum Lucam), or, like Irenaeus (*Haer.* III 11, 8; cf. § 6, 1) to speak of "the fourform Gospel" (ἐ. τετράμορφον). To show which of the four books was intended, the name of the author with the preposition κατά (= as presented by) was added to the title of the book. The conviction that the four books of Gospels contain one and the same Gospel retained its living force for a long time (cf. Victorinus of Pettau, *Comment. on Apc.* p. 54 Haussleiter: *(hae) ergo praedicationes, quamvis quattuor sunt, una tamen praedicatio est, quia de uno ore processit, sicut fluvius in paradiso de uno fonte in quattuor partes divisa est).*

This idea inspired the attempt which was made in the second century to fit the four canonical Gospels together into one uniform closed account of the life and work of Jesus, that is, to produce what are called Gospel Harmonies. We still possess Tatian's Gospel Harmony, though not in the original wording. Probably Theophilus bishop of Antioch († c. 186) also made a Gospel Harmony independently of Tatian; but Jerome's evidence on the point is indecisive (Ep. 121, 6 ad Hedibiam et Algasiam: *quattuor evangelistarum in unum opus dicta compingens).*

The order Mt., Mk., Lk., John, which all our editions of the Bible follow, is as old as the Muratorian Canon; it is also attested in B and ℵ, the two oldest parchment MSS., and in the overwhelming majority of Greek MSS. and of versions. On the other hand D and the Old-Latin MSS. have the order Mt., John, Lk., Mk., putting the Apostles first.

The four symbols for the Evangelists (a man for Matthew, a

154

lion for Mark, a bull for Luke, and an eagle for John) derive from the forms of the Cherubim in Ez. 1, 1 (Apc. 4, 7); they are connected with the beginnings of the Gospels; yet their assignment to particular Evangelists is not uniform.[3] Irenaeus (Haer. III 11, 8) is our oldest witness for the use of this symbolism.

§ 23. THE GOSPEL OF ST. MARK

Commentaries: (a) J. Knabenbauer, [2]1907 (CSS). M.-J. Lagrange, *Évangile selon S. Marc*[8], Paris 1947. J. Huby, 1924 (VS II). F. X. Poelzl - G. Stettinger, [3]1935 (see § 3, 9a). J. Dillersberger, *Das Ev des hl. Mk. in theologisch und heilsgeschichtlich vertiefter Schau*[4], Salzburg 1947 ff. J. Schmid, [3]1954 (RegNT 2). C. C. Martindale, 1956. — (b) A. Merx, *Die Evv des Mk. und Lk.*, Berlin 1905. J. Wellhausen, *Das Ev Marci, uebersetzt und erklaert*[2], Berlin 1909. J. Weiss, [3]1917 (Goett NT 1). G. Wohlenberg, [3]1930 (Zahn II). E. Klostermann, [4]1950 (Lietzmann 3). F. Hauck, 1931 (ThHK II). A. Schlatter, *Mk., der Evangelist fuer die Griechen*, Stuttgart 1935. J. Schniewind, [5]1949 (NT Deutsch 1). E. Lohmeyer, 1953 (Meyer I, 2[12], with Supplement). W. C. Allen, *The Gospel According to St. Mark*, London 1915. E. P. Gould, [6]1921 (ICC). H. B. Swete, *The Gospel According to St. Mark*[3], London 1927. A. E. Rawlinson, *The Gospel According to St. Mark*, 1925. B. H. Branscomb, 1937 (Moffatt). V. Taylor, *The Gospel According to St. Mark*, London 1952 (cf. M. Smith: HarvThR 48, 1955, 21–64).

Studies: Joh. Weiss, *Das aelteste Ev*, Goettingen 1903. B. W. Bacon, *The Gospel of Mark, its Composition and Date*, New Haven 1925. M. Werner, *Der Einfluss der pl Theologie im Mk.-Ev*, Giessen 1923. A. Meyer, Die *Entstehung des Mk.-Ev*: Festgabe fuer A. Juelicher, Tuebingen 1927, 35–60. L. Wohleb, *Beobachtungen z. Erzaehlungstil des Mk.-Ev*: RQ 1928 (Sonderdruck). E. v. Dobschuetz, *Die Erzaehlerkunst des Mk.*: ZntW 27 (1928) 193–198. J. Sundwall, *Die Zusammensetzung des Mk.-Ev*, Åbo 1934. M. Zerwick, *Untersuchungen z. Mk.-Stil*, Rome 1937. G. Hartmann, *Der Aufbau des Mk.-Ev*, 1936 (NtA XVII 2–3). T. W. Manson, *The Gospel of Mark*: BJRL 27 (1943) 223–227; 28 (1944) 119–136. R. H. Lightfoot, *The Gospel Message of St. Mark*, 1950. L. Vaganay, *L'absence du Sermon sur la montagne chez Marc*: RB 58 (1951) 5–46. C. H. Bird, Some γάρ-clauses in St. Mark's Gospel: JThSt NS 4 (1953) 171–187. M. Black, *An Aramaic Approach to the Gospels and Acts*[2], Oxford 1954. W. Marxsen, *Der Evangelist Markus. Studien zur Redaktion des Ev*, Goettingen 1956. J. M. Robinson, *Das Geschichtsverstaendnis des Mk.-Ev*, Zurich 1956. R. Schnackenburg, *Mk. 9, 33–50*: Synopt. Studien, Festschrift f. A. Wikenhauser, 1953, 184–206. H. Riesenfeld, *Tradition und Redaktion im* Mk.-*Ev*: Ntl Studien f. R. Bultmann, 1954, 157–164. J. B. Colon, DB Suppl V 835–862. H. A. Guy, *The Origin of the Gospel of Mark*, 1954. H. A. Rigg, *Papias on Mark*: NT 1 (1956) 161–183.

[3] Cf. J. Hoh: BZ 15 (1921) 229–234; J. Sauer: LThK III 890 sq.

The decision of the Biblical Commission of 26th June 1912 declares that external and internal evidence compel us to accept the authenticity of St. Mark's Gospel; the objections of the critics to the authenticity of the conclusion of Mk. (16, 9–20) do not prove their contention; the Gospel was written before 70 A.D. and made use of other sources besides Peter's preaching; it rightly claims full credibility as history (cf. ZkTh 41, 1917, 558 sq.).

1. Content and structure

Preliminaries 1, 1–13

Appearance and preaching of John the Baptist 1, 1–8; Baptism of Jesus 1, 9–11; Temptation of Jesus 1, 12 sq.

First part: The Galilean ministry 1, 14 to 6, 6a

1. The beginning of Jesus' ministry in Capharnaum and the surrounding district 1, 14–45: Jesus' message 1, 14 sq.; call of the first disciples 1, 16–20; a sabbath in Capharnaum (cure in the synagogue of a possessed man, healing of Peter's mother-in-law, cures in the evening) 1, 21–34; preaching of Jesus in Galilee 1, 35–39; healing of a leper 1, 40–45.

2. Jesus in conflict with his Jewish opponents (5 controversial discourses) 2, 1 to 3, 6: The power of Jesus to forgive sins, on the occasion of the curing of the man sick with the palsy 2, 1–12; the call of Levi and justification of his association with publicans and sinners 2, 13–17; the question of fasting 2, 18–22; keeping holy the Sabbath, when the disciples plucked the ears of corn 2, 23–28, and when he cured the man with the withered hand 3, 1–6.

3. Further successes of Jesus and conflicts with his opponents 3, 7 to 35: Concourse of the people and cures 3, 7–12; call of the twelve Apostles 3, 13–19; Jesus and his friends 3, 20 sq.; Jesus' reply to the charge of being in league with the devil 3, 22–30; The true kindred of Jesus 3, 31–35.

4. Jesus discourses in parables 4, 1–34: The parable of the sower 4, 1–9; why he speaks in parables 4, 10–13; explanation of the parable of the sower 4, 14–20; the right hearers 4, 21–25; the parable of the seed which grows by itself 4, 26–29; the parable

of the grain of mustard seed 4, 30–32; conclusion of the parable discourses 4, 34.

5. Further revelation of the power of Jesus by four miracles at the lake of Genesareth 4, 35 to 5, 43: Stilling of the tempest on the lake 4, 35–41; healing of the possessed man of Gerasa 5, 1–20; raising to life of the daughter of Jairus and cure of the woman with the issue of blood 5, 21–43.

6. Conclusion of the Galilean ministry 6, 1–6a: His rejection by his home town Nazareth.

Second part: Jesus continually journeying 6, 6 to 10, 52

1. Sending of the twelve Apostles 6, 6b–13, and their return 6, 30; Herod's opinion about Jesus 6, 14–16; the death of John the Baptist 6, 17–29.

2. First journey of Jesus and his return to Galilee 6, 31 to 7, 23: Feeding of the Five Thousand on the east bank of the lake 6, 31–44; Jesus walks upon the water 6, 45–52; Jesus in the plain of Genesareth 6, 53–56; controversy about clean and unclean 7, 1–23.

3. Second journey and return 7, 24 to 8, 12: Jesus and the Syrophoenician woman (in the territory of Tyre) 7, 24–30; cure of the deaf mute (on the eastern side of the lake) 7, 31–37; feeding of the Four Thousand 8, 1–9; return to the western bank; the Pharisees seek a sign 8, 10–12.

4. Third journey and return 8, 13 to 9, 50: Warning against the leaven of the Pharisees (on the journey to the eastern side) 8, 13 to 21; cure of a blind man in Bethsaida 8, 22–26; Peter's profession at Caesarea Philippi 8, 27–30; first prophecy of the Passion 8, 31–33; the disciples are instructed to imitate the Passion 8, 34 to 9, 1; the Transfiguration 9, 2–13; cure of a possessed boy 9, 14–29; second prophecy of the Passion (in Galilee) 9, 30–32; instructions to the Apostles (vying for honour; the strange exorcist; scandal) 9, 33–50.

5. The journey of Jesus through Perea and Jericho to Jerusalem for the Pasch (of the Passion) 10, 1–52: Controversy about marriage and divorce 10, 1–12; Jesus and the children 10, 13–16; Jesus on riches (the rich young man) 10, 17–27; reward for following him 10, 28–31; third prophecy of the Passion 10, 32–34; the sons of Zebedee seek places of honour; the duty of serving 10, 35–45; cure of Bartimaeus the blind man in Jericho 10, 46–52.

Third part: Ministry of Jesus in Jerusalem, his Passion, Death and Resurrection 11, 1 to 16, 20

a) *The last works of Jesus* 11, 1 to 13, 37:

1. Messianic activity of Jesus 11, 1–26: Solemn entry into Jerusalem 11, 1–11; cursing of the fig tree 11, 12–14; clearing of the Temple 11, 15–19; discourse about the withered fig tree 11, 20–25.

2. Messianic teaching of Jesus 11, 27 to 12, 44: The question of Jesus' authority 11, 27–33; parable of the wicked husbandmen 12, 1–12; the Pharisees ask about the lawfulness of paying tribute 12, 13–17; the Saducees ask about the resurrection 12, 18–27; which is the greatest commandment? 12, 28–34; the Messias as the son of David 12, 35–37 (11, 27–33; 12, 13–37 = 5 controversies in Jerusalem); words of Jesus against the Scribes 12, 38–40; the widow's mite, 12, 41–44.

3. The discourse of Jesus about the end of the world and his Second Coming 13, 1–37: Occasion of the discourse 13, 1–2; the signs before the end of the world (beginning of woes) 13, 3–8; persecutions for the sake of the Gospel 13, 9–13; the acme of tribulation (in Judea) 13, 14–20; the rise of false prophets 13, 21–23; the coming in majesty of the Son of Man 13, 24–27; the time of the end 13, 28–32; exhortation to watchfulness 13, 33–37.

b) *The Passion, Death, and Resurrection of Jesus* 14, 1 to 16, 20:

1. The last activities of Jesus with his Apostles 14, 1–42: Decision of the Sanhedrin to put him to death 14, 1 sq.; the anoint-

ing in Bethany 14, 3–9; betrayal by Judas 14, 10 sq.; preparation for the Last Supper 14, 12–16; the Last Supper 14, 17–25; the journey to Mount Olivet, prophecy of Peter's denials 14, 26–31; Jesus in the Garden of Olives 14, 32–42.

2. Jesus before the Jewish court 14, 43–72: Arrest of Jesus 14, 43–52; trial and condemnation of Jesus 14, 53–65; Peter's denial 14, 66–72.

3. Jesus before the Roman court 15, 1–47: Delivery of Jesus to Pilate, trial and condemnation 15, 1–15; mockery of Jesus by the soldiers 15, 16–20; the way to Golgotha, Crucifixion and Death 15, 21–41; the Burial 15, 42–47.

4. The Risen Christ 16, 1–20: The women go to the tomb and the angel announces the Resurrection of Jesus 16, 1–8; appearances of the Risen Christ (to Mary Magdalen, to the two disciples at Emmaus, and the Eleven) 16, 9-20.

2. *The tradition of the early Church*

The tradition of the early Church held unanimously that the second Gospel was written by Mark, the disciple of the Apostle Peter. The oldest and most important witness to this—on whom later witnesses to some extent depend—is Papias, Bishop of Hierapolis in Phrygia (c. 130 A.D.); in the preface to his *Explanations of the Sayings of the Lord,* he writes: "The Presbyter ('the Elder', i. e., John) said this also: Mark, having been the hermeneut (interpreter) of Peter, wrote down carefully, though not in order, all that he remembered, both words and deeds, of the Lord. For he had neither heard the Lord nor followed him, but only at a later date, as I have already said, followed Peter. Peter arranged his instructions according to the needs (of his audience) and not as making (a continuous and exhaustive) arrangement of the Lord's words. So Mark was not wrong to write down some things as he remembered them, for he took care to omit or falsify nothing which he had heard (from Peter)."[1]

In this fragment of Papias obviously only the first sentence is from "the Elder", who is probably not the Apostle John but a different presbyter of the same name (cf. § 28, 2); what follows is Papias' own comment.

According to the evidence of "the Elder", Mark in his Gospel wrote down carefully from memory—so evidently only after Peter's death—everything which he had learned from Peter's instructions concerning the words and deeds of Jesus. Papias defends the evangelist against the charge of defective arrangement in his Gospel; since Peter had to adapt himself to the needs of his audience when giving instructions, it is unlikely that he could have given a complete and well-ordered presentation of the whole traditional material. Mark found that he was obliged to make for himself an arrangement of the material which he had received from Peter.

It is disputed what is meant by the description of Mark as the "hermeneut" of Peter. The word ἑρμηνευτής means translator or interpreter (cf. 1 Cor. 14, 28); speaking of the Logia of the Lord which Matthew wrote down in Aramaic, Papias says that each one interpreted (ἡρμήνευσεν) them as best he could (cf. § 24, 2). So the simplest assumption is that Peter used Mark as his interpreter when preaching, since he himself was not a fluent Greek speaker.[2] A. Schlatter thinks that Peter's Aramaic sermons

[1] Eusebius, H. E. III 39, 15:

Καὶ τοῦθ' ὁ πρεσβύτερος ἔλεγεν· Μᾶρκος μὲν ἑρμηνευτὴς Πέτρου γενόμενος, ὅσα ἐμνημόνευσεν, ἀκριβῶς ἔγραψεν, οὐ μέντοι τάξει, τὰ ὑπὸ τοῦ κυρίου ἢ λεχθέντα ἢ πραχθέντα. οὔτε γὰρ ἤκουσεν τοῦ κυρίου οὔτε παρηκολούθησεν αὐτῷ, ὕστερον δέ, ὡς ἔφην, Πέτρῳ· ὃς πρὸς τὰς χρείας ἐποιεῖτο τὰς διδασκαλίας, ἀλλ' οὐχ ὥσπερ σύνταξιν τῶν κυριακῶν ποιούμενος λογίων, ὥστε οὐδὲν ἥμαρτεν Μᾶρκος οὕτως ἔνια γράψας ὡς ἀπεμνημόνευσεν. ἑνὸς γὰρ ἐποιήσατο πρόνοιαν, τοῦ μηδὲν ὧν ἤκουσεν παραλιπεῖν ἢ ψεύσασθαί τι ἐν αὐτοῖς.

[2] Cf. D. de Bruyne: RBén 40 (1928) 202; P. Gaechter, Die Dolmetscher der Apostel: ZkTh 60 (1936) 161–187; E. Stauffer: ZKG 62 (1943/44) 42.

to the original community in Jerusalem were translated by Mark for the Hellenistic part of the congregation. Th. Zahn and others maintain that Mark was called Peter's interpreter because he put down in writing the substance of Peter's preaching; they point out that Peter, being a Galilean, would have been bilingual and so would have had no need for an interpreter when preaching in Greek speaking areas. Against this it is urged that Luke is never called Paul's interpreter by the ancients, though it is quite often said that he recorded Paul's preaching.

Papias' evidence is substantially repeated by Irenaeus, who explicitly says that Mark composed his Gospel after Peter's death: "After their (Peter's and Paul's) death, Mark, the disciple and hermeneut of Peter, left us Peter's preaching in writing."[3] Irenaeus is probably drawing on the anti-Marcionite prologue (cf. § 5, 3) which calls Mark *interpres Petri* and says that the Gospel was composed in Italy.[4]

Tertullian also calls Mark *interpres Petri,* and says that his Gospel could be called the Gospel of Peter (*Adv. Marcion.* IV 5). Justin Martyr expresses himself to the same effect when he refers the name "sons of thunder" for the sons of Zebedee—which appears only in Mk. 3, 17—to the "recollections of Peter" (*Dial.* 106; cf. § 5, 2).

The tradition that Peter's preaching was the source of St. Mark's Gospel is also attested by Clement of Alexandria; he says, however, that the Gospel was composed while Peter was living at Rome, although he makes no mention of Mark's activity as an interpreter. In his *Hypotyposes* he gives the following tradition from the old Presbyter: "The following was the occasion of

---

[3] *Haer.* III 1, 1 (= Eusebius, H. E. V 8, 3): Μετὰ δὲ τὴν τούτων ἔξοδον Μᾶρκος, ὁ μαθητὴς καὶ ἑρμηνευτὴς Πέτρου, καὶ αὐτὸς τὰ ὑπὸ Πέτρου κηρυσσόμενα ἐγγράφως ἡμῖν παραδέδωκεν. In III 10, 6 he calls him Peter's *interpres et sector.*

[4] *Iste interpres fuit Petri. Post excessionem ipsius Petri descripsit idem hoc in partibus Italiae evangelium.*

Mark's Gospel: When Peter had publicly preached the word in Rome, and had taught the Gospel in the Spirit, his numerous hearers are supposed to have asked Mark to write down the things which Peter preached; for he had accompanied Peter for a long time and remembered his words. Mark is said to have agreed to their request, and to have given them the Gospel. When Peter learned of it, he neither forbade it nor encouraged it" (apud Euseb., H. E. VI 14). This tradition is repeated by Clement in his comment on 1 Pet. 5, 13, and also in the *Hypotyposes* where he speaks of "imperial knights" as hearers of the Apostle. Origen reports as traditional that the Gospel of Mark was the second to be composed, and that Peter instructed him for it (apud Euseb., H. E. VI 25, 5).—The more recent sources have no independent value.

The Mark in question is the same person as is mentioned in 1 Pet. 5, 13. There is no reasonable doubt that he is none other than the Jewish-Christian John Mark of Jerusalem, who is mentioned a number of times in the New Testament. According to Col. 4, 10 he was a cousin of Barnabas. His mother Mary had a house in Jerusalem which served the original Christian community as a meeting place; this was the house to which Peter went when he was freed from prison (Acts 12, 12). Paul and Barnabas took the young Mark with them to Cyprus on their first missionary journey (Acts 13, 5), but he left them at Perge in Pamphylia and returned to Jerusalem (13, 13), so Paul refused to take him again as companion on his second missionary journey, and this led to the dispute between him and Barnabas. Because of this Barnabas left Paul and went with his cousin to Cyprus (15, 36 sqq.; cf. § 31, 2). Later Mark stayed with Paul during the latter's imprisonment in Rome, and Paul sent him on an important mission to Asia Minor (Col. 4, 10; Philem. 24). Some years afterwards, when Paul was again in prison, he wrote to his disciple Timothy at Ephesus, telling him to bring Mark to Rome, since he would be useful to him (2 Tim. 4, 11). At the time when 1 Pet. was written Mark was in Babylon (= Rome) with Peter, who calls him "his son", evidently because it was Peter who had converted Mark to the Christian faith (5, 13). The tradition that Mark was first bishop of Alexandria is hardly trustworthy; it first appears in Eusebius (H. E. II 16, 1).

It is doubtful whether Mark is identical with the young man who fled from Gethsemani, Mk. 14, 41. A number of exegetes would infer from the Muratorian Fragment that Mark was present as an eyewitness at some of the events which he reports; but it is uncertain how the mutilated sentence *(ali) quibus tamen interfuit et ita posuit* should be completed.

The anti-Marcionite prologue and Hippolytus (*Philos.* VII 30) tell us that Mark had another name κολοβοδάκτυλος (short-fingered).

3. Characteristics and purpose

According to Acts 1, 1 the traditional material about Jesus deals with his words and deeds (cf. Papias also on Mark: ἢ λεχθέντα ἢ πραχθέντα). It is characteristic of St. Mark's Gospel that it mainly contains deeds of Jesus with relatively few sayings.

Mark has only two discourses properly so called, the parable discourse 4, 1–34 and the Parousia discourse 13, 1–37, whereas Matthew has five or six lengthy discourses. The instructions to the Apostles before their mission occupy only four verses in Mark (6, 8–11), while Matthew has 38 (10, 5–42), and Luke has 3+15 (9, 3–5; 10, 2–16). Mark has only a short warning against the Scribes (12, 38–40), while in the corresponding position Matthew has a long denunciation of the Scribes and Pharisees (23, 1–36 = Lk. 11, 37–52; 20, 45–47). Mark has nothing corresponding to the Sermon on the Mount (Mt. 5–7; Lk. 6, 20–49).

Unlike the other Synoptics, Mark has very few parables; besides the three of the parable discourse there is only one long one (The wicked husbandmen 12, 1–12) and two shorter ones (The fig tree 13, 28, and The doorkeeper 13, 35–37). On the other hand this Gospel has numerous independent fragments of discourses referring to the conflict of Jesus with the Jews: 5 conflicts in Galilee and 5 in Jerusalem (2, 1 to 3, 6; 11, 27 to 12, 37), the "Beelzebub" discourse (3, 22–30) and the controversy on clean and unclean (7, 1–23). Often Mark simply says that Jesus taught, without telling us what he said (1, 21 sq. 39; 2, 2 13; 6, 2 6 34; 10, 1; 12, 35). Obviously it was not his intention to repeat in its entirety the tradition which he had received about the words of Jesus.

The Gospel of St. Mark also differs from the others in the form in which the material is presented. Brief and lengthy stories alternate in him. Many events are recounted at great length in comparison with Matthew, and matter of minor importance is amplified. Typical examples of this are: the cure of the man sick of the palsy (2, 1–13), the cure of the possessed man of Gerasa (5, 1–20), the resurrection of Jairus' daughter (5, 21–43), and the cure of the deaf mute (7, 31–37). Obviously when Mark received the individual stories about the deeds of Jesus they had not yet been moulded into a uniform shape.

When Mark really narrates and does not simply state facts, his account is much more concrete, clearer, more lively, and more popular than the accounts of Matthew (and Luke). Only Mark gives the name of the blind man (10, 46), and he alone says that David ate the loaves of proposition "under Abiathar the high priest" (2, 26), and relates that Jesus gave the name "sons of thunder" to the sons of Zebedee (3, 17). It is Mark who tells us that during the storm Jesus was in the hinder part of the ship and was sleeping on a pillow (4, 38), and that the man with the palsy was carried "by four" (2, 3). The popular nature of the narrative appears also in Mark's frequent references to the emotions of the participants (e. g. 10, 24 32), and even of Jesus himself: 1, 41 ("having compassion on him"); 1, 43 ("strictly charged him");

3, 5 ("looking round about on them with anger, being grieved for the blindness of their hearts"); 7, 34 ("looking up to heaven, he groaned and said"); cf. also 8, 12; 10, 14 16 21.

The language and style[5] are much simpler and more popular than in Matthew and Luke. The sentences are very simply constructed. Co-ordination *(parataxis)* prevails throughout the Gospel; the sentences are generally joined by καί, less often by δέ. The narrative is very frequently continued by εὐθύς. Direct speech is preferred within a story, e. g., 3, 11 and 13, 11 (unlike Mt. and Lk.). Prolixity is not uncommon, e. g., 13, 1 ("what manner of stones and what buildings"); 13, 19 ("from the beginning of the creation which God created"); 13, 35 ("at even, or at midnight, or at the cock crowing, or in the morning"); cf. also 2, 4; 4, 2; 9, 2; 11, 1. Mark is particularly fond of the historic present (about 150 times); quite often he changes tense within a sentence (e. g., 11, 6 sq.). His vocabulary is interlarded with colloquialisms, e. g., κράβατος 2, 4 sqq.; πτῶμα 6, 29; κωμόπολις 1, 38; ἐκπερισσῶς 14, 31; he favours diminutives (θυγάτριον, ἰχθύδιον, κυνάριον, κοράσιον, σανδάλιον, ψίχιον, ὠτάριον) and makes frequent use of the verbs δύνασθαι, ἔχειν, θέλειν.

Greek was not Mark's native language as is shown by frequent Semitisms, such as placing the predicate before the subject, and putting a participle of the same meaning before the verb (e. g., 7, 24; 10, 1), repetition of the personal pronoun in a relative clause (οὗ—αὐτοῦ 1, 7; ἧν—αὐτῆς 7, 25), λέγων after a verb meaning "to say" (e. g., 9, 11; 12, 18 26), εἷς for τίς (10, 17), the periphrastic conjugation of verbs (e. g., 2, 18; 4, 38) etc. Aramaic expressions occur in Mark more often than in Matthew and Luke: it is only in Mark that we find βοανηργές 3, 17; ἐφφαθά 7, 34; ταλιθὰ κοῦμι 5, 41; κορβᾶν 7, 11. The strong Semitic colouring does not prove that the Gospel is a version of an

---

[5] Cf. (in addition to Zerwick) Hawkins, *Horae synopticae*[2], Oxford 1909; C. H. Turner, *Marcan usage*: JThSt 25–29 (1924–28).

Aramaic original; but we may infer from it that the author of the Gospel was a native of Palestine whose mother tongue was Aramaic.

There is also a number of Latin words in the Gospel, particularly words connected with the army, the courts, and commerce: λεγιών 5, 9; κῆνσος 12, 14; φραγελλοῦν (flagellare) 15, 15; πραιτώριον 15, 16; μόδιος 4, 21; δηνάριον 12, 15; κοδράντης (quadrans) 12, 42—this word is used by Mark and Luke too; σπεκουλάτωρ (executioner) 6, 27; κεντυρίων 15, 39; ξέστης (sextarius) 7, 4. Latin turns of phrase: ὁδὸν ποιεῖν (iter facere) 2, 23; ἐσχάτως ἔχειν (in extremis esse) 5, 23; τὸ ἱκανὸν ποιεῖν (satisfacere) 15, 15; also 3, 6; 5, 43; 11, 32; 14, 64 65; 15, 19. It is particularly significant that in two passages Greek expressions are explained through Latin: "two mites (lepta), which make a farthing (quadrans)," (12, 42); "ἔσω τῆς αὐλῆς (the palace), ὅ ἐστι πραιτώριον (the praetorium)" 15, 16. These Latinisms are more numerous in Mark than in any other New Testament book; they cannot be taken as proof that the Gospel was written in Rome (or Italy), for Latin words were current in the Greek speaking East; but they do harmonize with the tradition that the book was written at Rome.

According to the tradition of the early Church, the source of St. Mark's Gospel was St. Peter's preaching. In fact it is possible to observe in the Gospel a number of points which show that Peter was the original narrator. It is noticeable that Peter plays an important role in the Gospel. The public life of Jesus begins with his call (1, 16–18). The graphic description of the first entry of Jesus into Capharnaum, with its many details (the teaching and miraculous cure in the synagogue, the healing of Peter's mother-in-law, the curing of the sick in the evening etc.) can hardly derive from anyone other than Peter. In 1, 36 the disciples are called "Simon and they that were with him".

The accounts in 9, 2–13 (Transfiguration) and 14, 32–72 (Gethsemani, trial, denial) are certainly derived from eyewitnesses, which narrows the possible sources to Peter, James and John; and in view of 9, 5 and 14, 37 54 66–72 it is difficult to consider anyone other than Peter. No significance can be attached to the fact that Peter stands first in the list of Apostles (3, 16) and that he always appears at the head of the intimates of Jesus (5, 37; 9, 2; 13, 3; 14, 33); but it is striking that in 11, 21 (the cursing of the fig tree) an expression is put into Peter's mouth which Mt. 21, 20 attributes to the disciples; and again, it is only in Mk. 16, 7 that the women are commissioned to announce to "his disciples and Peter" that the Risen Christ goes before them into Galilee. Mark also recounts matters which were embarrassing to Peter—and at some length (8, 33; 9, 5; 14, 30 sq. 66 sqq.); if the Apostle himself had not told them, Mark would not have mentioned them so openly.

It is beyond doubt that St. Mark's Gospel and the preaching of St. Peter are closely related. Yet it should not be supposed that the theology of the Gospel carries a Petrine stamp. There was no such thing as a Petrine theology in the sense in which we speak of Pauline and Johannine theology; the discourses of Peter in Acts follow the common pattern of primitive Christian preaching (cf. § 29, 4). Furthermore Mark had also accompanied and worked with Paul, and there can be no doubt that he knew others besides Peter who had seen and heard Jesus. So the material in his Gospel cannot be attributed to Peter's sermons exclusively.

However, Pauline thought exercised no strong or clearly defined influence on the Gospel of Mark, as was proved conclusively by M. Werner against the assertions of the Tuebingen school. Throughout his book Mark stands revealed as an individual and independent writer, so much so, that the theological treatment of the traditional material can be due to no one but himself. Furthermore it is certainly Mark himself, and not an eyewitness like Peter, who is responsible for the plan of the public life of Jesus, the geographical and chronological framework in which the individual "deeds and words" of Jesus are arranged. It was for this that the "Presbyter" censured him. Yet we may assume that bye and large Mark's arrangement corresponded to the actual course of events, for neither Matthew nor Luke improved upon it.

Geographically Mark arranges the traditional material into three great sections: Galilee, journeyings, Jerusalem—an arrangement which also provides a chronological sequence. Jesus begins his work in Galilee, and at first is highly successful with the mass of the people, who favour and applaud him. But his opposition to the surveillance of the Scribes and Pharisees drew upon him the enmity of these powerful groups, and they compelled him to withdraw to the pagan territory to the north and east of Galilee; there Peter answered his enquiries by acknowledging him as Messias; he thereupon told the Apostles that he must undergo the Passion, and from that time forward devoted himself to instructing them more deeply. He then travels with them through Perea, and by way of Jericho to the Pasch at Jerusalem. He makes his Messianic entry into the Holy City from Mount Olivet. In a series of controversies he marks himself off from his opponents. The Jewish authorities arrest him and hand him over to the Romans who crucify him. But on the third day he arises glorious from the tomb.

As comparison with St. John's Gospel especially shows, the actual course of events is simplified by this geographical-chronological framework for the history of Jesus. Within this framework the arrangement varies; sometimes the place, sometimes the time, and sometimes the subject matter is the unifying element. Thus, for example, the events of chapter 1 are in chronological order, while it is the subject matter (5 discourses of conflict) which is the unifying factor of chapter 2. Again, although from 6, 17 onwards Jesus withdraws himself from the people, yet the great miracles of feeding the multitudes take place quite openly (6, 30–44; 8, 1–9) and his teaching in Perea (10, 1–27) is done publicly. Mark recounts many episodes in the life of Jesus which we cannot assign to any particular place or time.

Like the other Gospels, St. Mark's Gospel is not an historical treatise or a biography of Jesus. It grew out of the early Christian preaching and was designed to serve it. Biographical interest is entirely lacking in Mark. The name of the (legal) father of Jesus is not mentioned once, nor is there any information about his life before his Baptism. The evangelist's only interest is to proclaim the message that Jesus Christ is Son of God and Messias (cf. 1, 1). The Heavenly Father twice acknowledges Jesus as his Son: at the Baptism (1, 11), where he commissions him for his public life, and at the Transfiguration (9, 7) where the Apostles are ordered to hear him. But this secret, that he is the Son of God, is kept strictly; only the demons know it (1, 24 34; 3, 11; 5, 7), but Jesus forbids them to divulge it. After Peter acknowledged him as Messias at Caesarea Philippi, the secret was gradually revealed to the Apostles, but Jesus ordered them to keep silent about it (8, 30; 9, 9). It is not publicly disclosed until the high priest asks him: "Art thou the Christ, the Son of the Blessed God?" when Jesus admits it, and proclaims that he will come from Heaven for the General Judgment (14, 61 sq.). In consequence of this admission he is condemned by the leaders of the Jewish people, and is handed over to the Romans as a Messianic pretender; the Romans crucify him. But his innocent death brings salvation to men, since God accepts it as the price of Redemption for their sinful guilt (10, 45). And on the third day he raises himself up from the tomb with glorified body (16, 6 sq.).

4. People for whom intended, place and time of composition

The Gospel of St. Mark was intended for Gentile Christians. The Jewish–Christian traits which are a feature of Matthew are not to be found in Mark (permanence of the Law, Mt. 5, 17 sqq.; prohibition of the mission to Samaritans and heathens, Mt. 10, 5). Jewish customs and practices are explained (ablutions before meals and washing of vessels 7, 3 sq.; day of the slaughtering of the Paschal lambs 14, 12; Parasceve, Day of preparation = Day before the Sabbath 15, 42). Aramaic words and sentences are regularly translated (cf. 3, 17; 5, 41; 7, 11 34; 9, 43; 10, 46; 14, 36; 15, 22 34).

The tradition of the early Church (prologue, Clement o Alexandria) placed the composition of St. Mark's Gospel in Rome. According to 1 Pet. 5, 13 Mark was at Rome with Peter in the first half of the sixties of the first century. Peter can hardly have been in Rome when Rom. was written, and so it is assumed by many scholars that both Peter and Mark worked there in the middle of the fifties and left the city shortly afterwards; however, there is no evidence to prove this, and it is not likely (cf. § 49).

The numerous Latinisms in St. Mark's Gospel (see above) support the tradition that it was composed at Rome. In Mk. 15, 21—and only there—Simon of Cyrene is described as the father of Alexander and Rufus; obviously these two sons were known to the readers of the Gospel. In Rom. 16, 13 greetings are sent to a certain Rufus; if he is identical with Simon's son, the tradition about the composition of the Gospel in Rome would be further supported; but Rufus was a very common name, and furthermore it is not entirely certain that chapter 16 was originally part of Rom. (cf. § 37, 6).

If the wording of Mk. 10, 12 (prohibition of divorce), as contrasted with Mt. 19, 9, is due to Mark himself, it indicates that the Gospel was intended for Gentile Christian communities, though it does not prove that Rome was the place of composition; Jewish law confined the right of divorce to the husband, while Graeco-Roman practice gave it to both.

The date of composition cannot be established with certainty.

Tradition is not unanimous on the point. Irenaeus and the ancient Prologue say that Mark did not write until after Peter's death (in 64 A.D.), and it is clear that Papias also presupposes this; Clement of Alexandria, on the other hand, says that Mark wrote while Peter was still alive. The former tradition seems to be better founded (so also D. de Bruyne, J. Huby, and J. Schmid). According to it Mark would have written his Gospel shortly after Peter's death, and certainly before 70 A.D. Many Catholic exegetes date the composition of the Gospel to the middle or second half of the fifties, on the ground that Mark was used by Luke for his Gospel, which was written before 63 A.D. The overwhelming majority of Protestant Scripture commentators date St. Mark's Gospel to the end of the sixties.

5. The Conclusion of Mark, 16, 9–20

There are very serious objections to the authenticity of these verses (i. e., their origin from Mark). They are missing from B ℵ k sy^sin sa arm and some Georgian and Ethiopian MSS. Eusebius (*Quaest. ad Marinum* 1) says that the "accurate" MSS. end with 16, 8 and that 16, 9–20 are missing from "almost all MSS." Jerome is probably following him when he says (*Ep*. 120, 3) that the Ending of Mark is in very few MSS., and is missing from almost all the Greek MSS. Clement of Alexandria, Origen, Tertullian, Cyprian, and Cyril of Jerusalem show no knowledge of it. In a number of MSS. it has been added by a subsequent hand.

On the other hand it is in Tatian—at least in the Arabic version —and Irenaeus cites Mk. 16, 9. So it was certainly in existence around the middle of the second century. Between verses 14 and 15 Codex W (5th century) shows a fairly long addition (the so-called Freer Logion; cf. § 12, 2), whose first half is cited by Jerome, *Adv. Pelag.* II 15.

In addition to these external grounds for impugning its authenticity there are also internal reasons. The ending of Mark interrupts the sequence of thought, for it does not relate the appearance of the Risen Christ in Galilee, which was promised in 16, 7. Instead of continuing the narrative it gives a list of appearances of Our Lord which, in general, are merely short extracts from the accounts of the appearances in the other two Synoptics and in St. John's Gospel (cf. v. 9 sq. with John 20, 11–18; v. 12 sq. with Lk. 24, 13–35; v. 14 sqq. with Lk. 24, 25–49 and John 20, 19–29; v. 15 with Mt. 28, 18–20; v. 19 with Lk. 24, 50–53 etc.).

The vocabulary and style are also unlike Mark (e. g., πρώτη σαββάτου, μετὰ ταῦτα, κτίσις etc.). Mary Magdalen is introduced as the woman "out of whom he had cast seven devils" (= Lk. 8, 2), as if she had not been mentioned previously (16, 1; 15, 40). The title Kyrios instead of the name Jesus is also peculiar.

A few text sources, including L T Ψ k, show a short ending of two sentences, either alone or in addition to the longer ending. Did St. Mark's Gospel originally end with 16, 8? Or was there an original ending which was either lost or deliberately suppressed at an early date? The question is disputed, and no certain answer can be given to it.

Since Luke and Greek Mt. follow Mark till 16, 8, but then diverge completely, it is practically certain that the Gospel of St. Mark circulated without an ending. On the other hand it is improbable[6] that the Evangelist intended the Gospel to end with the words "they said nothing to any man: for they were afraid" (16, 8). So it must be assumed that Mark was prevented by some reason or other from finishing his Gospel, or else that the original

[6] As is agreed by an ever increasing number of (Protestant) exegetes; they are listed by Dibelius, *Formgeschichte des Ev.* (1933) 190, W. Bauer: *Woerterbuch* 1565 sq., and Kuemmel: ThRdsch 1948, 9 note 2, and 1950, 23 note 1. Cf. also W. L. Knox: HarvThR 35 (1942) 13–23; Lightfoot: JThSt 46 (1945) 221–224; P. E. Kahle: JThSt NS 2 (1951) 49–57 (The evidence of the Coptic versions); C. H. Roberts: JThSt 40 (1939) 253–257 (The last leaf of the codex which the Christians used in the first century easily became detached and was lost); O. Cullmann, *Petrus* (cf. § 49) pp. 61–67.

ending was lost at an early date. Even if the longer ending of Mark is not by Mark himself, yet it is an integral part of Holy Scripture (hence the name "canonical ending of Mark", as opposed to the short ending), and it contains dependable ancient tradition.

§ 24. THE GOSPEL OF ST. MATTHEW

Commentaries: (a) J. Dillersberger, *Das Mt-Ev in theologischer und heilsgeschichtlicher Schau*, 6 vols., Salzburg 1952 sq. J. Schmid, [3]1956. J. Knabenbauer, 2 vols. (revised by A. Merk), [3]1922 (CSS). F. X. Poelzel - Th. Innitzer, [4]1932 (cf. § 3, 9a). M.-J. Lagrange, *Évangile selon S. Matthieu*[8], Paris 1947. P. Dausch, [4]1932 (Bonner Bibel 2). J. Schmid, [3]1956 (RegNT 1). A. Durand, [23]1938 (VS 1).—(b)E. Lohmeyer, 1956 (Meyer: Sonderband). J. Wellhausen, *Das Evangelium Matthaei, uebersetzt und erklaert*[2], Berlin 1914. J. Weiss, [3]1917 (GoettNT 1). Th. Zahn, [4]1922 (Zahn I). E. Klostermann, [3]1938 (Lietzmann 4). A. Schlatter, *Der Evangelist Matthaeus, seine Sprache, sein Ziel, seine Selbstaendigkeit*[3], Stuttgart 1948. J. Schniewind, [4]1950 (NTDeutsch 2). W. C. Allen, [3]1912 (ICC). Th. H. Robinson, 1928 (Moffatt). W. Michaelis, *Das Ev nach Mt.*, 3 vols., Zurich 1948 ff. H. Roux, (nouvelle édition) 1956.

Studies: E. v. Dobschuetz, *Mt. als Rabbi und Katechet:* ZntW 27 (1928) 338–348. A. Froevig, *Das Mt.-Ev und die aramaeische Mt.-Schrift des Papias:* NkZ 42 (1931) 344–376. A. Sperber, *NT and Septuagint:* JBL 59 (1940) 193–293. Sh. E. Johnson, *The Biblical Quotations in Mt.:* HarvThR 36 (1943) 135–153. K. Thieme, *Mt., der schriftgelehrte Evangelist:* Judaica V (1949) 130–152; 161–182. E. Massaux (cf. § 5, 2). J. S. Kennard, *The Place of Origin of Mt.'s Gospel:* AThR 31 (1949) 243 ff. [the hinterland of Northern Syria]. B. C. Butler, *The Originality of St. Mt. A Critique of the Two Documents Hypothesis*, Cambridge 1951. K. E. Winter, *Das Ev der jerusalemischen Muttergemeinde:* Judaica 9 (1953) 1–33. G. Bornkamm, *Mt. als Interpret der Herrenworte:* ThLZ 79 (1954) 341–346. L. Vaganay: DB Suppl V 940–956. G. D. Kilpatrick, *The Origins of the Gospel According to St. Mt.*, Oxford 1954 [Mt. was composed for liturgical purposes, and was intended to serve as a revised Gospel Book. It was written about 100 A.D. by an unknown author in Syria, probably in a seaport]. K. Stendahl, *The School of St. Mt. and its Use of the Old Testament*, Uppsala 1954 [Mt. is not the work of an individual, but of a community, a Jewish-Christian "School"; it served for the instruction of subsequent teachers and leaders in the Churches. The OT is used as in the exegesis of the Midrash; the Hebrew, Targum, or Greek Text is used according to need]. N. A. Dahl, *Die Passionsgeschichte bei Mt.:* NTSt 2 (1955) 17–32.

Decision of the Pontifical Biblical Commission of 19th June 1911: According to trustworthy tradition the Apostle Matthew was the first to write a Gospel—not merely a collection of logia—in the native language of Palestine; it was not written after 70 A.D. and the evidence of Irenaeus (*Adv. Haer.* III 1, 1) does not prove that it was written after Paul arrived in Rome. This Aramaic Gospel is *quoad substantiam* identical with the Greek canonical Gospel. Its historical trustworthiness and integrity must be accepted.

1. Content and structure

Preliminaries 1, 1 to 4, 11

1. Nativity and infancy of Jesus 1, 1 to 2, 23: The genealogy 1, 1–17; the miraculous conception of Jesus 1, 18–25; homage of the Magi 2, 1–12; flight into Egypt 2, 13–15; massacre of the Innocents 2, 16–18; return to Nazareth 2, 19–23.

2. Preparation for the ministry of Jesus 3, 1 to 4, 11: Appearance and preaching of John the Baptist 3, 1–12; Baptism of Jesus 3, 13–17; temptation of Jesus 4, 1–11.

First part: The Galilean ministry 4, 12 to 13, 58

1. Beginning of the Galilean ministry of Jesus (Capharnaum) 4, 12–25: Arrival in Galilee 4, 12–17; call of the first disciples 4, 18–22; summary account of the preaching and miraculous work of Jesus 4, 23–25 (cf. 9, 35).

2. The Sermon on the Mount (Jesus as teacher) 5, 1 to 7, 29: The Beatitudes 5, 3–12; the vocation of the disciples 5, 13–16; the attitude of Jesus to the Law 5, 17–20; the old and new justice (six antitheses) 5, 21–48; true and false piety (almsgiving, prayer, and fasting) 6, 1–18; laying up treasure and sollicitude 6, 19–34; judging others 7, 1–5; praying with confidence 7, 6–11; the Golden Rule 7, 12; the two ways 7, 13 sq.; warning against false prophets 7, 15–20; warning against self-deception 7, 21–23; concluding parable 7, 24–29.

3. A cycle of miracles (ten miracles; Jesus as miracle worker) 8, 1 to 9, 34: Three miracles (cure of a leper, of the centurion's servant, and of Peter's mother-in-law) 8, 1–17; two instructions (unconditional following of Christ) 8, 18–22; three miracles

(calming of the storm, possessed men of Gadara, man sick of the palsy) 8, 23 to 9, 8; two instructions (the attitude of Jesus to publicans and sinners, and to fasting) 9, 9–17; four miracles (daughter of Jairus, woman with the issue of blood, two blind men, a dumb man) 9, 18–34.

4. The missionary discourse 9, 36 to 11, 1: Introduction (sheep without a shepherd) 9, 36–38; sending of the twelve Apostles and instructions for the mission 10, 1–16; the persecutions which await the Apostles 10, 17–25; exhortation to confess Christ without fear, and words of consolation 10, 26–39; conclusion (special promises) 11, 1.

5. The disbelief and hostility of the Jews 11, 2 to 12, 50: The Baptist's enquiry and the testimony of Jesus about him 11, 2–19; woes on the impenitent Galilean cities 11, 20–24; Jesus speaks to the Father; invitation to salvation 11, 25–30; two controversies with the Pharisees about the Sabbath (the disciples plucking corn and the man with the withered hand) 12, 1–14; Jesus withdraws and performs cures quietly 12, 15–21; reply to the accusation of being in league with Beelzebub 12, 22–37; rejection of the Pharisees' demand for a sign 12, 38–42; words about relapse 12, 43–45; the true kindred of Jesus 12, 46–50.

6. The parable discourse (seven parables about the Kingdom of Heaven) 13, 1–52: Introduction and parable of the sower 13, 1–9; why he speaks in parables 13, 10–17; explanation of the parable of the sower 13, 18–23; parable of the cockle among the wheat 13, 24–30; double parable of the mustard seed and the leaven 13, 31–33; explanation of the parable of the cockle 13, 34–43; parables of the treasure in the field, the pearl of great price, and the net; conclusion of the discourse 13, 44–52.

7. The rejection of Jesus in Nazareth 13, 53–58.

Second part: Jesus continually journeying 14, 1 to 20, 34

1. Herod's opinion about Jesus; death of the Baptist 14, 1–12.

2. Withdrawal of Jesus to the eastern side of the lake, and his return to Galilee 14, 13 to 15, 20: Feeding of the Five Thousand 14, 13–21; Jesus walks upon the water 14, 22–33; cures by Jesus in the plain of Genesar 14, 34–36; controversy about clean and unclean 15, 1–20.

3. Withdrawal of Jesus to heathen territory and his return to the western side of the lake 15, 21 to 16, 4: Jesus and the Canaanite woman 15, 21–28; numerous cures 15, 29–31; feeding of the Four Thousand 15, 32–39; return to the western bank; the Pharisees and Sadducees seek a sign 16, 1–4.

4. Further withdrawal and return 16, 5 to 17, 27: Words about leaven 16, 5–12; Peter's profession at Caesarea Philippi that he is Messias 16, 13–20; first prophecy of the Passion 16, 21–23; the disciples must imitate the Passion 16, 24–28; Transfiguration of Jesus 17, 1–13; cure of a possessed boy 17, 14–21; second prophecy of the Passion 17, 22–23; the Temple tax 17, 24–27.

5. Instructions to the Apostles 18, 1–35: The disciples dispute about precedence 18, 1–5; warning against scandal giving 18, 6–11; parable of the lost sheep 18, 12–14; treatment of an offending brother 18, 15–18; efficacy of prayer in common 18, 19–20; readiness to forgive; parable of the unmerciful servant 18, 21–35.

6. The journey of Jesus through Perea and Jericho to Jerusalem for the Pasch (of the Passion) 19, 1 to 20, 34: Divorce and celibacy 19, 1–12; Jesus and the children 19, 13-15; Jesus on riches (the rich young man) 19, 16–26; reward for following him 19, 27–30; parable of the labourers in the vineyard 20, 1-16; third prophecy of the Passion 20, 17–19; the sons of Zebedee vie for honour; the duty of service 20, 20–28; cure of two blind men near Jericho 20, 29–34.

Third part: Ministry of Jesus in Jerusalem, his Passion, Death and Resurrection 21, 1 to 28, 20

a) *The last works of Jesus* 21, 1 to 25, 46:

1. Messianic activity of Jesus 21, 1–22: Solemn entry of Jesus into Jerusalem 21, 1–11; clearing of the Temple, cures, homage of the children 21, 12–17; cursing of the fig tree and discourse about the withered fig tree 21, 18–22.

2. Messianic teaching of Jesus 21, 23 to 22, 46: The question of Jesus' authority 21, 23–27; parables of the two sons, the wicked husbandmen, and the marriage feast 21, 28 to 22, 14; questions about the lawfulness of paying tribute, 22, 15–22, about the resurrection 22, 23–33, and the greatest commandment 22, 34–40; the Messias as the Son of David 22, 41–46 (21, 23–27; 22, 15–46: five controversies in Jerusalem).

3. Denunciation of the Pharisees and Scribes 23, 1–36, and prophecy against Jerusalem 23, 37–39.

4. Prophecies of Jesus about the end of the world and his Second Coming (Parousia discourse and parables) 24, 1 to 25, 46: Occasion of the discourse 24, 1–3; signs before the end of the world (beginning of woes) 24, 4–8; persecutions for the sake of the Gospel 24, 9–14; the acme of tribulation (in Judea) 24, 15–22; the rise of false prophets 24, 23–28; the coming of the Son of Man in majesty 24, 29–31; the time of the end of the world 24, 32–41; final exhortations to vigilance (the thief in the night; the faithful and unfaithful servant; the wise and foolish virgins; parable of the talents) 24, 42 to 25, 30; the General Judgment 25, 31–46.

b) *The passion, death, and resurrection of Jesus* 26, 1 to 28, 20:

1. The last activities of Jesus with the Apostles 26, 1–46: Decision of the Sanhedrin to put him to death 26, 1–5; the anointing in Bethany 26, 6–13; betrayal by Judas 26, 14–16; preparation for the Last Supper 26, 17–19; the Last Supper 26, 20–29; journey to Mount Olivet and prophecy of Peter's denials 26, 30–35; Jesus in the Garden of Olives 26, 36–46.

2. Jesus before the Jewish Court 26, 47–75: Arrest of Jesus 26, 47–56; trial and condemnation of Jesus 26, 57–68; Peter's denial 26, 69–75.

3. Jesus before the Roman Court 27, 1–66: Delivery of Jesus to Pilate 27, 1–2; death of Judas 27, 3–10; trial and condemnation of Jesus 27, 11–26; mocking of Jesus by the soldiers 27, 27–31; the way to Golgotha, Crucifixion and Death 27, 32–56; burial of Jesus 27, 57–61; setting of a guard on the tomb 27, 62–66.

4. The Risen Christ 28, 1–20: The women go to the tomb and the angel announces the Resurrection of Jesus 28, 1–8; the Risen Christ appears to the women 28, 9–10; trickery of the Jewish authorities 28, 11–15; appearance of the Risen Christ to the Apostles in Galilee (Command to preach) 28, 16–20.

2. The tradition of the early Church

The tradition of the early Church is unanimous in ascribing the first Gospel to the Apostle Matthew. The four lists of Apostles in the New Testament mention in the seventh (Mk. and Lk.) or eighth (Mt. and John) place an Apostle Matthew; in Matthew, and only there, he is described as ὁ τελώνης (the publican). Mt. 9, 9 sq. tells of Jesus calling a publican named Matthew from the customs house at Capharnaum; undoubtedly the words "the publican" in the list of Apostles (10, 3) refer back to this event, so this Gospel identifies Matthew the Apostle with the former publican. The same story of Jesus calling a publican occurs also in Mark (2, 14 sqq.) and Luke (5, 27 sqq.); but they call him "Levi" (Lk.) or "Levi, Son of Alpheus" (Mk.). So these two Gospels do not connect the publican called by Jesus with the Apostle Matthew. Granted the correctness of the account in Matthew, then this publican must have borne two Semitic names, like Simon Cephas, Joseph Barnabas (Acts 4, 36) and "Joseph, who is also called Caiphas" (’I. ὁ καὶ Καιάφας: Flavius Josephus, Ant. XVIII 2, 7). But in the cases of Cephas and Barnabas the second name was only given later by Jesus or the Apostles; this consideration has suggested to many scholars (for example Th. Zahn) that the publican Levi was not called Matthew

(Aramaic: Mattai for Mattanjah = Gift of God) until he became an Apostle. Others (for example Joachim Jeremias) assume that the publican was a levite, and had the surname "(Ben) Levi" in addition to his own name Matthew.

Protestant scholars generally deny that Levi the publican was the same person as Matthew the Apostle. They say that the author of the Gospel of St. Matthew was not one of the twelve Apostles, nor was he an eyewitness of the events in the Gospel story; they maintain that only when Matthew's authorship of the Gospels had been accepted was the name Matthew substituted for Lev in Mt. 9, 9, and "the publican" added in Mt. 10, 3.

Against this it must be objected that it would be strange if one who was not an Apostle related the call by Jesus, when no other call is related in the Synoptics except that of the two pairs of brothers who played a special role in the college of Apostles (Mk. 16, 16 sqq). It is striking at any rate that Mark and Luke call the same person Levi in the story of the calling and Matthew in the list of Apostles. This difficulty would best be solved by the hypothesis that the publican Levi only got the name Matthew as an Apostle.

Papias of Hierapolis (c. 130 A.D.) is our oldest source of information about St. Matthew's Gospel; he says: "Matthew put together in the Hebrew (i. e. Aramaic) language (cf. Acts 21, 40; 22, 2; 26, 14; John 20, 16) the discourses *(logia)* and each one translated them as best he could."[1] The meaning of Papias' words is disputed. There is no doubt that the word *logia* can and generally does mean 'sayings', that is, it may refer to an arrangement of sayings of Jesus like the "Sayings of the Fathers" *(Mishna)* or the collections of sayings in the Wisdom literature (cf. *The logia or sayings of Zoroaster,* Nicholas of Damascus; Τὰ λόγια τοῦ Κυρίου, Ep. of Polycarp 7, 1; 2 Clem. 13, 3). Papias could therefore have meant that Matthew made a collection of the words of

---

[1] Apud Euseb. H. E. III 39, 16: Ματθαῖος μὲν οὖν Ἑβραΐδι διαλέκτῳ τὰ λόγια συνετάξατο, ἡρμήνευσε δ᾽αὐτὰ ὡς ἦν δυνατὸς ἕκαστος.

Our Lord, and did not compose a Gospel containing both words and deeds of Jesus. But by his time our Gospel of St. Matthew had long been in use in the Church, and it is generally agreed to-day that he was thinking of it and that he means that it was originally composed in Aramaic. This interpretation of the word *logia* is supported particularly by reference to his evidence about the Gospel of St. Mark, where τὰ ὑπὸ τοῦ κυρίου ἢ λεχθέντα ἢ πραχθέντα is immediately described as τὰ κυριακὰ λόγια (cf. also Heb. 5, 12).

The majority of non-Catholic exegetes attack this interpretation of the evidence of Papias on the ground that our Gospel of St. Matthew was originally composed in Greek, and is not the work of an eyewitness. Some of them, however, are prepared to say that Papias was following a tradition which probably related to a collection of Our Lord's sayings made by Matthew; this collection was the main source for the words of Jesus in the Gospels of Matthew and Luke; they would say that Matthew's name was attached to the first Gospel because this collection was incorporated in it, and forms a large part of it (cf. § 26, 5).

The next writer to give information on the matter is Irenaeus, who says[2]: "Matthew (preaching) among the Hebrews also produced in their language a writing of the Gospel, while Peter and Paul were preaching and founding the Church in Rome." Since he explicitly says "a writing of the Gospel" (γραφὴ εὐαγγελίου) he certainly means our Gospel of St. Matthew and not a collection of *logia*. He took the information that it was written in the "Hebrew" language from Papias whose book he had read. It has been asserted that the second clause is not chronological, but it certainly means that the Gospel was written when Peter and Paul were working in Rome in the first half of the sixties.

---

[2] *Haer.* III 1, 1 (apud Euseb., H. E. V 8, 2): Ὁ μὲν δὴ Ματθαῖος ἐν τοῖς Ἑβραίοις τῇ ἰδίᾳ αὐτῶν διαλέκτῳ καὶ γραφὴν ἐξήνεγκεν εὐαγγελίου τοῦ Πέτρου καὶ τοῦ Παύλου ἐν Ῥώμῃ εὐαγγελιζομένων καὶ θεμελιούντων τὴν ἐκκλησίαν.

The anti-Marcionite prologue to Luke which probably was composed before the work of Irenaeus, remarks in passing that Matthew wrote his Gospel in Judea, but it makes no mention of the language or time; this information would have been contained in the lost prologue to Matthew.

Origen († 254) is the next witness; in his commentary on Matthew he says: "With reference to the only Gospels which are accepted ... without controversy in the Church of God, I have learned from tradition: The Gospel according to Matthew, who was first a publican and later the Apostle of Jesus Christ, was the first to be written; it was written in the Hebrew language for the believers from Judaism" (apud Euseb., H. E. VI 25, 4).

The Church historian Eusebius could say: "Matthew, who at first preached among the Hebrews, wrote down in his mother tongue the Gospel which he had proclaimed, when he wished to go to other peoples; for he wished by his writing to replace what those whom he was leaving were losing by his departure" (H. E. III 24, 6). It is not known where Eusebius learned that Matthew wrote his book before departing (when?) from Palestine. He had never seen the Aramaic Matthew himself, as is shown by his story about Pantaenus, the teacher at the Catechetical School at Alexandria (c. 180); the story is that Pantaenus found the Aramaic Gospel in India (probably southern Arabia): "Bartholomew, one of the Apostles, is supposed to have preached to them, and to have left them the writing of Matthew in Hebrew, which was still preserved there" (H. E. V 10). If this report, which Eusebius formulates very carefully, has any historical kernel, there could be confusion with the Gospel of the Hebrews.[3] The more recent sources have no independent value.

[3] The "Gospel of the Hebrews" was in Hebrew, and was in use among the Judaeo-Christian sects from the second, and probably from the first century. For a long time Jerome made the mistake of identifying it with Aramaic Mt.; he maintains that it was in the library at Caesarea in his time, and that he discovered it among the Nazarenes of Beroea (in Syria), and made a copy of it. Only

Summing up we may say: According to the tradition of the early Church, the Apostle Matthew composed in Aramaic a Gospel for his Christian compatriots in Palestine. There is no uniform tradition about the time of composition. We do not know from whom Papias got his information; presumably it was from John the Presbyter to whom he attributes his information about the Gospel of St. Mark (§ 23, 2). There is no tradition about who translated the Aramaic Gospel into Greek. We do not know whether Papias had seen the Aramaic original or whether it was still in existence in his time; but it is unlikely that this was the case. Neither MSS. nor citations preserve remains of the Aramaic text.

3. Literary and theological characteristics

1. This Gospel is composed entirely from a practical point of view. It is intended to convey instruction rather than merely to provide a chronicle. "For him the main thing is not the chronicle but the way in which it is presented." The didactic character of the Gospel is most apparent in the Evangelist's habit of grouping together the sayings of Jesus, as far as possible, into great units, each of which deals with a particular theme; there are six such synthetic discourses which develop the main themes of the preaching of Jesus; most of the recorded sayings of Jesus occur in them. They are: (1) the Sermon on the Mount (ch. 5–7); (2) the discourse giving the Apostles instructions for their mission (ch. 10); (3) the parable discourse (ch. 13); (4) the discourse on the spirit of the apostolate (ch. 18); (5) the woes against the Scribes and Pharisees (ch. 23); (6) the eschatological discourse (ch. 24–25). At the end of these discourses the Evangelist generally makes the transition

fragments of it survive in citations (in Greek); they generally give legendary additions to the text of the Gospels. Cf. Hennecke, *Ntl. Apokryphen,* [2]1929, 48–55; Dodd, *The Gospel according to the Hebrews,* London 1933; H. Waitz: ZntW 36 (1937) 60–71; G. Bardy in: *Mélanges de science religieuse* III, Lille 1946, 5–36 (Jerome and the Gospel of the Hebrews).

to narrative with the formula "and it came to pass when Jesus had fully ended these words" (7, 28; 11, 1; 13, 53; 19, 1; 26, 1; cf. Lk. 7, 1); the only place where this phrase does not appear is at the end of the fifth discourse, for the sixth follows immediately, so that ch. 23–25 comprise a double discourse (judgment discourses). Strictly speaking ch. 18 is not a discourse; it is rather a series of individual sayings strung loosely together and unified by a leading idea; but as the formula at the end (19, 1) shows, Matthew intended it to be read as a unit. Comparison with Luke shows immediately that these discourses are literary syntheses, that is, arrangements according to subject matter of various sayings or groups of sayings of Our Lord; Luke contains most of Matthew's material, but it is scattered through his Gospel except in the case of the Sermon on the Mount ("Sermon on the Plain" Lk. 6, 20–49), and the eschatological discourse.

The Sermon on the Mount of St. Matthew is three times as long as St. Luke's Sermon on the Plain. We cannot assume that Luke found the entire material of the Sermon on the Mount in Matthew and scattered the greater part of it through his Gospel, reporting only one third of it together; the fact is rather that the Sermon on the Mount was originally about the length of Luke's discourse, and that Matthew expanded it with material from other places. Again, comparison with Mark and Luke shows that Matthew considerably lengthened the eschatological discourse by inserting and adding kindred material (eschatological warnings, three parables of the Second Coming, and a description of the Last Judgement). The parable discourse in Mark has three parables; Luke has one parable and an explanation; Matthew on the other hand has seven parables and three explanations. Ch. 10 includes as a unit the selection of the Twelve (Mk. 3, 13–19; Lk. 6, 12–16) and sending them out on the Galilean mission (Mk. 6, 7–13; Lk. 9, 1–6; 10, 1–12), and it also adds as kindred material an instruction to the Apostles (v. 23–39). In ch. 23 also material is brought together which Luke sets in various places (Lk. 20, 45–47; 11, 37–54; 13, 34 sq.).

In the first part of his book Matthew similarly juxtaposes nine accounts of miracles (covering ten miracles) (ch. 8–9), and sets this "miracle cycle", which is threaded by two pairs of sayings (3+2+3+2+3), immediately after the Sermon on the Mount. Thus it was the Evangelist's intention that the Sermon on the Mount and the "miracle cycle" should form a unity; the former shows Jesus as the Messianic teacher, the latter as Messianic miracle worker. The teaching comes first and the deeds follow, for throughout the Gospel of St. Matthew it is the words of Jesus which are stressed. The whole passage of ch. 5–9 is framed by the summary of 4, 23 and 9, 35: "Jesus went about all Galilee, teaching in their synagogues and preaching the Gospel of the Kingdom and healing all manner of sickness and every infirmity among the people."

Matthew endeavours to group homogeneous or related matters, even outside the six great synthetic discourses. Thus in the controversy about the Apostles plucking grain (12, 1–8) he adds a second example of blameless transgression of a ceremonial precept (service of the Temple on the Sabbath), as well as two sayings of Our Lord (which are proper to Mt.); he does the same in the case of the controversy about the cure of the man with the withered hand 12, 9–14 (a sheep which has fallen into a pit; cf. Lk. 13–30). Matthew closes the pericope about the centurion of Capharnaum (8, 5–13) with a promise about the entry of Gentiles into the Kingdom of God—a promise which originated in another context (cf. Lk. 13, 28–30). Words of Our Lord about the Baptist and a denunciation of the three impenitent Galilean cities follow the testimony about the Baptist (11, 7–11); in Mark and Luke these stand in another context (Mk. 9, 13; Lk. 7, 31–35; 16, 16). Cf. also Mt. 9, 13; Mt. 12, 32 (= Lk. 12, 10) 33–35 (= Lk. 6, 43–45) 36–37; 15, 12–14 (cf. Lk. 6, 39) 24; 16, 17–19; 17, 20 (=Lk. 17, 6); 19, 10–12 28 (= Lk. 22, 28–30); 21, 14–16; 26, 52–54.

Since Matthew is interested in teaching and not simply in chronicling, he reports the stories (miracles, controversies, and other narratives) in a very contracted form; comparison with Mark and Luke shows that only the descriptions—and not the discourses—have been curtailed. He simplifies the story of the centurion in Capharnaum (8, 5–13) by having the Gentile approach Jesus directly (unlike Luke), and in the story of the raising of Jairus' daughter he makes the father ask immediately for the raising of the girl who is already dead (9, 18–26); in the cure of the man sick of the palsy he makes no mention of the stripping of the roof (9, 2–8); again the long description of the symptoms of possession is very much curtailed in the stories of the cure of the possessed man of Gadara (8, 28 to 34) and of the possessed boy (17, 14–21); the death of the Baptist is also related very briefly (14, 3–12).

These are the most striking instances, but minor abbreviations are found in most of the stories, and even in some parts of the history of the Passion. Usually it is concrete details and descriptive elements which have been sacrificed (for example, that Jesus was sleeping on a pillow in the boat, Mk. 4, 38; that the woman with the issue of blood had spent all she had on physicians, 5, 26; that Peter and James and John by themselves asked him when the destruction of the temple would take place, 13, 3; that Simon of Cyrene was coming from the country, 15, 21). That is why the narratives in St. Matthew's Gospel are less colourful than those of Mark.

In spite of his endeavours to arrange the material in as systematic a manner as possible, Matthew fundamentally followed the same historic-geographic outline as the other two Synoptics (cf. § 23, 3; 25, 4 5). The author's groupings are neatly fitted into this framework, so that our Gospel contains both a chronological-geographic outline of the work of Jesus and, especially in the discourses, an impressive grouping according to subject matter. This is the reason why it very soon won great popularity and circulated widely in the early Church, and influenced both of the other Synoptics to a greater (Mk.) or lesser (Lk.) degree (see below n. 6).

2. To turn to the theological character of St. Matthew's Gospel, it must be pointed out that the whole work is dominated by the following theme: Jesus is the Messias or Son of David who was promised in the Old Testament and earnestly awaited by the Jews; but through the fault of his people, and particularly of their leaders, he was prevented from fulfilling his mission.

The main thesis of the Gospel is proved by showing that the Messianic prophecies are fulfilled in him; no other Gospel uses and quotes the Old Testament so copiously as Matthew. It is particularly striking how many so-called "reflection citations" there are: statements by the Evangelist that the Scripture has been fulfilled, introduced by a stereotyped formula ("that it might be fulfilled which the Lord spoke by the prophet", 1, 22; 2, 15 23; 4, 14; 8, 17; 12, 17; 13, 35; 21, 4; 26, 56, or "then was fulfilled", 2, 17; 27, 9); there is only one such citation in the other two Synoptics (Mk. 1, 2 = Lk. 3, 4), and it refers to the Baptist (Mk. 15, 28 is spurious, cf. Lk. 22, 37); there are four cases in John (12, 4 38; 19, 36 37). Of the eleven cases in Matthew, six refer to the Infancy and the Passion, which were particularly difficult parts of the Gospel story for Jews to accept.

Two examples will show the great importance which Matthew attached to confirmation from Scripture. Unlike Mark and Luke he says explicitly that Jesus dwelt in Capharnaum on the lake, and in order to use a citation from Isaias (8, 23; 9, 1) in this connection, adopts Old Testament terminology ("in the borders of Zabulon and Nephthalim") to describe where Capharnaum lies. When telling of the entry of Jesus into Jerusalem on an ass, he mentions both an ass and a colt in order to show as clearly as possible that this is the fulfilment of the prophecy of Zacharias who says (9, 9): "riding upon an ass and upon a colt, the foal of an ass" (Hebrew parallelism!).

186

According to Matthew, Jesus himself appeals to Scripture in support of his use of parables 13, 14 ("and the prophecy of Isaias is fulfilled in them, who saith": Is. 6, 9) and to reject the complaint of the Jewish authorities about the Hosannas of the children 21, 16 ("have you never read": Ps. 8, 3). He twice admonishes his opponents (9, 13; 12, 7) with a quotation from Osee 6, 6 ("I will have mercy and not sacrifice").

Jesus is the promised Messias. This is impressed on the reader not only by the scriptural proofs but also by the whole design and plan of the Gospel. It is for this reason that the Gospel begins with the genealogy which makes Jesus "Son of David" (1, 1), and thereby shows that Jesus is the descendant of David who was promised in the Old Testament (cf. 2 Kings 7, 12 sqq.; Is. 11, 1), that is, the Messias (1, 16). Even as an infant he is persecuted by Herod, but miraculously protected by God (2, 13–23), because being Son of David he has the status of "King of the Jews" (2, 2) or Messianic King. He is born in Bethlehem, the city of David (2, 5), in fulfilment of the prophecy of Mich. 5, 1.

In the Sermon on the Mount he appears as the new Lawgiver who fulfils "the law and the prophets", that is, the Old Testament (5, 17–48). His numerous miraculous cures are "works of the Messias" (11, 2). The cure of a possessed man who was blind and dumb, makes the people who had witnessed the miracle ask if he can be "the Son of David" (12, 23). Indeed the two blind men (9, 27) and the Canaanite woman (15, 22) call him "Son of David". In his account of the entry of Jesus into Jerusalem Matthew emphasizes the Messianic elements more than Mark does, by reporting the powerful impression made on the people of the capital (21, 10), the cure of the blind and lame in the temple (21, 14, cf. 11, 5), and the homage of the children (21, 15).

Jesus is the promised King of Israel—but his people refused to acknowledge him and tumultuously demanded that Pilate condemn him, thereby preventing the success of his mission. All the

Gospels tell of the rejection of Jesus by his people, and of the unconcealed hostility of the devout and influential Jews; but in Matthew the rejection of the Messias by his own people is expressed with special clarity in a short episode of the Passion which appears only in him: When Pilate was forced by the Jews to pronounce the death sentence, he washed his hands as a solemn denial of responsibility and cast the blame on the Jews; and "the whole people" accepted responsibility for the condemnation of their Messianic King with the cry: "His blood be upon us and upon our children", thereby invoking the curse upon themselves.

The Gospel of St. Matthew has a strong Jewish-Christian colouring which fits well with the Evangelist's intention of showing that Jesus is the promised Messias. It is no wonder that this Gospel exercises an attraction on those who are expert on late Judaism, especially Rabbinical theology and piety (for example, J. Wellhausen, A. Merx, G. Dalman, A. Schlatter, B. Billerbeck, G. Kittel, J. Jeremias). None of the other Gospels gives as much space as does St. Matthew to the relations between Jesus and the Scribes. The author must have had a certain Rabbinical training to be so familiar with the Old Testament (scriptural proofs) and the Jewish religion, spirituality, and way of life. It is from Matthew alone that we learn many details about Jewish religious and devotional practice: that the pious Jews make a display of their prayer, fasting, and almsgiving in order to win praise from the people (6, 1–6 16–18; 23, 5a); that they make their phylacteries broad and enlarge their fringes (23, 5); that they go round about sea and land to make one proselyte (23, 15); that they pay tithes even on the smallest herbs (23, 23); that the Scribes take the first places and love to be saluted (23, 6). From Matthew we learn to recognize the distinction between greater and lesser commandments (5, 19). In 23, 16–22 we have a sample of Rabbinical casuistry. Only in Matthew do we meet the Rabbinical phrase "to bind and loose" (16, 19) for the authority to declare a thing forbidden or lawful, to impose or lift a ban. Matthew alone uses the rabbinical name Kingdom of Heaven for Kingdom of God; the description of Jerusalem as the Holy City (4, 5; 27, 53) is also rabbinical. It is only in Matthew that we learn of the controversy about divorce between the (strict) school of Shammai and the (lax) school of Hillel (19, 3: "Is it lawful for a man to put away his wife for every cause?").

Mark and Luke also speak of the position of Jesus in regard to the Jewish Law, but since the matter was of little interest to their Gentile readers they quote only a few of his statements about it (cf. Mk. 10, 2 sqq.; Lk. 16, 17 sq.). Matthew, on the other hand, devotes the whole first part of the Sermon on the Mount to the question of the fundamental relation between Jesus and the Law of Moses, and its validity for the new People of God: Jesus has come not to destroy but to fulfil the Law and the Prophets (5, 17), that is, to perfect it by setting forth love, even love of one's enemies, as the totality of the divine will (Gal. 5, 14; Rom. 13, 8–10).[3a] Because of this thought, which is peculiar to him, Matthew begins his account of the work of Jesus with the Sermon on the Mount where Jesus appears as the new Lawgiver, the new Moses who proclaims the Old Testament law, in this new interpretation, as binding on the new People of God. It has been pointed out that Jesus does this from a mountain, just as Moses once climbed Sinai.

The sense in which the "fulfilment" of the Law is to be under-

---

[3a] M. Ljungmann, *Das Gesetz erfuellen. Mt. 5, 17ff. und 3, 5 untersucht,* Lund 1954. Cf. also E. Schweizer (Mt. 5, 17–20: ThLZ 1952, 475–484): Verses 18 and 19 originate from the part of the primitive community which was strictly attached to the Law; they were taken over by Mt., but interpreted by adding the words "till all be fulfilled" (unlike Lk. 16, 17), so that the OT Law finds its continuance and at the same time its fulfilment through the command to love (God and) one's neighbour which Jesus has brought as a new Torah. That is the better "justice" which is called for in v. 20 sqq. For Mt. there is no question of the continuance of the individual precepts of the Torah. Similarly Descamps, *Les Justes et la Justice dans les évangiles,* Louvain 1950, 121.

stood (5, 21–48) is explained in the six so-called antitheses, some of which probably got their form from the Evangelist: not only murder (5th Commandment), but even anger against one's brother is a sin; not only is adultery (6th Commandment) forbidden, but it is sinful even to look lustfully on another's wife; men should not swear at all, they should love even their enemies etc. Three of them (the 3rd, 5th, and 6th) appear substantially in Mark or Luke, but not in the form of antitheses. The antitheses conclude with the sentence "Be you perfect as also your Heavenly Father is perfect" (5, 48). The model for human conduct must be God in his mercy, justice and goodness, which know no limits.

This is not the repeal of the old Law; it rather adds a new dimension to the Law with its numerous individual precepts, as is most clearly apparent when Matthew makes Jesus say that the fulfilment of the Law and the Prophets consists in following the Golden Rule (7, 12) or the precept of loving God and one's neighbour (22, 40). The most important precepts of the Law are not the scrupulous tithing of herbs, but "justice, mercy, and faith" (23, 23 sq.). It is in the light of these statements of Jesus that we must understand the words which Matthew reports, "one jot or one tittle shall not pass of the Law" and that "he that shall break one of these least commandments shall be the least in the Kingdom of Heaven" (5, 18 sq.). In spite of their narrowly Judaistic appearance, Matthew did not understand these sentences as making every single precept of the Mosaic Law perpetual. For him the Law to whose entire fulfilment everything leads was not the Jewish ceremonial Law, but the moral law. "It is only with the interpretation of Jesus that the old Torah is taken quite earnestly, and a call goes out for fulfilling its essence." Furthermore, Matthew takes care to inform us about the attitude of Jesus to the pious practices of the Palestinian Jews (5, 20): for the disciples of Jesus also, almsgiving, prayer and fasting are the three principal exercises of piety (cf. Tob. 12, 8: "Prayer is good with fasting and alms"), but they must not be misused for ostentation, to win human praise (6, 1–6; 16–18).

Matthew alone reports that Jesus forbade the mission to Samaritans and Gentiles (10, 5); on a narrowly Judaeo-Christian interpretation of this prohibition and of the reply of Jesus to the Canaanite woman, attempts have been made to conclude that he was sent only for the lost sheep of the House of Israel (15, 24). But it can be seen from the other Gospels also that his mission was to the House of Israel alone, and that he himself worked only among them. Yet he did not exclude the Gentiles from salvation. In Mk. 7, 27 the answer of Jesus to the Canaanite woman sounds less harsh ("suffer first the children to be filled: for it is not good to take the bread of the children and cast it to the dogs"), and even Matthew tells that he granted her request. The meaning of Mt. 10, 5 is that Israel, as the people of the promise, has a right to hear the message of salvation first, and so the mission should initially be directed to it alone.

Matthew contains clear sayings of Jesus which attest the universality of salvation. In the parable of the wicked husbandmen Jesus says explicitly that the Kingdom of God will be taken from the people of Israel and given to a nation yielding the fruits thereof (21, 43; likewise 8, 11 sq. = Lk. 13, 28–30 and 22, 9 = Lk. 14, 23). And St. Matthew's Gospel ends with the command of the Risen Christ to make all nations disciples (28, 19). So universality and not parochial Judaism is characteristic of the outlook of the first Gospel.

4. The original language

It was the tradition of the early Church that Matthew composed his Gospel in Hebrew, that is, in the Aramaic dialect spoken by the Jews of Syria and Palestine at his time. Neither MSS. (not even fragments) nor citations of this Aramaic Gospel survive. Over the last century and a half there has been increasing agreement among non-Catholic Biblical scholars, both radical and conservative, that the Gospel of St. Matthew never existed in Aramaic. The only modern exegetes of note to uphold the tradition of the ancient Church are Theodor Zahn and Adolf Schlatter. Non-Catholic scholars will admit at most that the Apostle Matthew made a collection of sayings of Our Lord (cf. § 26, 5) which was used by the unknown author of the Gospel; because of this, they say, Matthew's name became attached to the first Gospel. They adduce three arguments:

1. The language of the Gospel of St. Matthew is not what we would expect in a translation from Aramaic. The style and language show a uniformity which no translator could have attained. Not only do subordinate clauses and the genitive absolute occur, but there are plays on words: ἀφανίζουσιν, ὅπως φανῶσιν, 6, 16; κακοὺς κακῶς ἀπολέσει αὐτούς, 21, 41; κόψονται καὶ ὄψονται, 24, 30; Πέτρος—πέτρα 16, 18. It is true that there are Semitisms in Matthew, but they are no more frequent than in Mark and Luke, which certainly were composed in Greek; indeed Semitisms are somewhat more common in Mark. They are due to the fact that the material of the Synoptics was handed down in Aramaic for a considerable time. Only in the case of 1, 21 is it absolutely certain that the original was in a Semitic idiom, for the name ("He will save his people") can be understood only with reference to Hebrew; but this does not prove that the Gospel was not composed in Greek.

To this argument it may be said: it cannot be proved from the linguistic form of our Gospel that it is a translation from Aramaic. If its author was a hellenized Jewish-Christian who also had a certain Rabbinical training, his linguistic and stylistic peculiarities could be satisfactorily explained without necessarily postulating an Aramaic original. Lagrange, who upheld the traditional account, investigated this matter very thoroughly in his commentary; he considered that his observations had a very limited value as proofs.

2. The textual form in which Matthew cites the Old Testament weakens the thesis of an Aramaic original. The Gospel of St. Matthew has 41 Old Testament citations, of which 36 are introduced by a citation formula; of these 20 are peculiar to Matthew[4], and the remaining 21 appear also in Mark, or Luke, or both.[5] An Aramaic work would naturally cite the Old Testament according to the Hebrew text; if such an original underlay our Gospel of St. Matthew, one would expect that the translator would either himself render all the citations into Greek or else insert the LXX form; and so all the citations should consistently show the LXX form or follow the Hebrew text.

But this is not the case. Most of the citations which are common to all three Synoptics follow the wording of the LXX with greater or smaller variations and these variations are often identical in the parallel passages—a fact which points to the literary interdependence of the three Gospels. On the other hand the citations which are peculiar to Matthew—they are generally "reflection" citations—keep close to the Hebrew text, though here and there the influence of the LXX can be traced. In 21, 16 we find Ps. 8, 3 quoted by Jesus according to the LXX reading which alone supports the argument ("praise" instead of "bulwark" of the Hebrew text); cf. also 11, 10; 13, 14 sq. We can only infer from this that the author of Matthew generally quoted the Old Testament according to the Hebrew wording when he was working independently, but when he used the Greek sources (Mk. and Q) he kept to their wording.

K. Stendahl's[6] investigations show that even the citations which are peculiar to Matthew show affinity to the LXX, and that the

[4] Mt. 1, 23; 2, 6 15 18; 4, 15 sq.; 5, 21 27 33 38 43; 8, 17; 9, 13; 12, 7 18-21; 13, 35; 18, 16; 21, 4 sq. 16; 27, 9.

[5] Mt. 3, 3; 4, 4 6 7 10; 11, 10; 13, 14 sq.; 15, 4 8 sq.; 19, 4 sq. 18 sq.; 21, 13 42; 22, 24 32 37 39 44; 24, 15; 26, 31; 27, 46.

[6] *The School of St. Matthew and its Use of the OT*, 1954. A. Baumstark, *Die Zitate des Mt.-Ev aus dem Zwoelfprophetenbuch*: Bb 37 (1956) 269–313.

variations from the LXX text are not approximations to the Hebrew. The peculiar form in the reflection citations is to be explained in the same way as the citations in the *Commentary on Habacuc* which was discovered in 1947. In both works the Old Testament text is presented with a certain freedom in order to make clearer the fulfilment of the words of Scripture concerning the fate of the "Teacher of Righteousness" or of Jesus respectively. The citations in Matthew, therefore, do not provide an argument for an Aramaic original.

3. Comparison of the Synoptics with one another shows that the principal sources of the Gospel of St. Matthew were two Greek works which were already in existence, namely the Gospel of St. Mark and a collection of sayings of Our Lord (Q) which was also used by Luke. In this connection it is particularly significant that Matthew incorporated in his work almost the entire Gospel of St. Mark. Therefore the Gospel of St. Matthew was not composed originally in Aramaic nor was it the oldest Gospel (cf. § 26, 5). This argument is unquestionably much stronger than either of the others, and it deserves serious consideration.

In his work *De consensu evangelistarum* I 2, 4 St. Augustine somewhat derogatorily calls St. Mark *pedisequus et breviator* of Matthew: "There is very little good to be found in him; he has very much in common with Matthew, and his descriptions are almost entirely in the same manner and the same words." This thesis of St. Augustine has found much favour until modern times among Catholic exegetes who maintain that Mark used Aramaic Mt., and was used in turn by Greek Mt. But this view cannot be upheld if we accept the evidence of Papias that Mark recorded Peter's preaching (cf. § 23, 2). For that reason most Catholic scholars to-day deny that Mark used Matthew, but say that whoever produced Greek Mt. made use of Mark; in either case, they say, the author of Greek Mt. was influenced by the style and vocabulary of Mark, while it must furthermore be remembered that he also took over some entire passages, and in parts followed Mark's order of events.

It may be taken as certain that an Aramaic original of the Gospel of St. Matthew can be defended only if we regard Greek Mt. not as a literal translation of the Aramaic, but as a thorough revision made with frequent use of the Gospel of St. Mark. This is consistent with the decision of the Biblical Commission which declares explicitly that the tradition of the early Church is preserved if we uphold the substantial identity of Greek and Aramaic Matthew. Since there are no remains of Aramaic Matthew, and no one knows what it was like, we cannot make any more accurate or more definite statement about the relationship between the two forms of St. Matthew's Gospel.

5. People for whom intended, date and place of composition

In both forms the Gospel of St. Matthew was intended for Jewish-Christians. That is self-evident in the case of the Aramaic original, and the same is true of the Greek revision. This may be seen from the fact that he does not explain Jewish practices and ideas (cf. 9, 20; 14, 1; 15, 2; 23, 5 24 27; 27, 62 in contrast to Mk. 7, 1–4; 14, 12), and sometimes Hebrew words are not translated (ῥακά 5, 22; βεελζεβούλ 10, 25; κορβανᾶς 27, 6); also it is taken for granted (1, 21) that the readers know the meaning of the name Jesus. On the other hand he translates the names Emmanuel (1, 23) and Golgotha (27, 33) and the cry of Jesus on the cross ("My God, my God, why hast thou forsaken me?" Ps. 22, 2) which he also gives in Aramaic.

It is impossible to say with certainty where the readers of the Greek version are to be sought. Palestine is the first place to come to mind, for at that time Greek was fairly widely spoken there; but Syria also deserves consideration. In those territories there were numerous Jewish-Christians, and some Jewish-Christian communities. In spite of being intended for a Jewish-Christian circle of readers, Greek Mt. soon gained currency not only in its homeland, but also in the Gentile Christian Church where it circulated widely and was highly esteemed. Though the Gospel has a strong Jewish colouring, yet it is far removed from Jewish particularism, and displays effectively the universality of the message of salvation, especially in the commission of the Risen Christ with which it ends. There is no record of who made the Greek revision of the Aramaic original (Jerome, *De vir. ill.* 3), but it can only be the work of a Greek-speaking Jewish-Christian of Palestine who also understood Aramaic.

Irenaeus says that the Aramaic original was composed when "Peter and Paul were preaching and founding the Church in Rome" (see n. 2), that is, at the beginning of the sixties. According to the evidence of Eusebius, Matthew wrote his Gospel before leaving Palestine to preach to other peoples (see n. 2). The so-called separation of the Apostles is said to have taken place twelve years after the resurrection of Christ (according to the *Kerygma* of Peter apud Clement of Alexandria, *Stromata* VI 5, 43, and Apollonius the anti-Montanist, c. 197 A.D., apud Euseb. H. E. V 18, 14). If we connect the departure of Matthew with this or with the persecution of the Church by Herod Agrippa I (Acts 12, 1 sq.), the composition of the Gospel of St. Matthew would fall in the year 41–42 A.D. (for example, this is the view of F. X. Poelzl and J. Belser). But this view is not tenable, and is seldom advanced at the present day, for Acts 15 and Gal. 2, 1–10 show that the Apostles were in Jerusalem about the year 49 A.D., and Gal. 2, 7–9 shows that until then no mission had been undertaken by them outside Palestine and there were no immediate plans for one.

If we maintain the substantial identity of Aramaic and Greek Mt., internal evidence will not permit us to date the composition of the Aramaic earlier than the middle of the fifties. The remarks in 27, 8 and 28, 15 ("even to this day") imply that a fairly long time had elapsed since the days of Jesus. Also the Gospel takes for granted that the mission to the Gentiles is in full progress; it was only when the Gentile mission became extensive and caused the breach with Judaism that the hostility of the unconverted Jews to their Christian compatriots became bitter; and it is in the light of such hostility that the vigorously anti-Jewish tone of the Gospel would most easily be understood. The Greek revision was made only after the composition of St. Mark's Gospel, which is probably to be assigned to the period after St. Peter's death (in 64 A.D.) (cf. § 23, 4). The only problem is whether it falls before or after 70 A.D.

We cannot appeal to 24, 15–22 in favour of a date before 70 A.D., for if correctly interpreted this refers not to the destruction of Jerusalem but to the time of Antichrist, which is immediately before the end of the world (cf. J. Schmid on the parallel passage of Mk.). On the other hand we could point to the words of Jesus 10, 23 and 16, 28, according to which the Apostles or some of them would live to see the coming of the Son of Man; we could also refer to the pericope about the temple tax (17, 24–27), for from the year 71 onwards the Jews had to pay this tax to Jupiter Capitolinus in Rome. But these cannot be regarded as decisive arguments, for we are dealing with traditional material which is simply being repeated.

A date later than 70 A.D. would be favoured by 22, 7, if the reference is to the destruction of Jerusalem. Verses 22, 6 sq. are an expansion of the parable which originally embraced 22, 2–5 8–10; they break the connection between vv. 5 and 8, and are missing from the form of the parable which Luke gives (Lk. 14, 16 to 24). Furthermore the punitive expedition against the murderers, who are obviously regarded as living in one city, takes place before the feast, although it had already been prepared; this element does not harmonize with the rest of the parable. The insertion of these two verses gives the parable a somewhat

different meaning. The first group of servants to be sent symbol-
izes the prophets of the Old Testament whose preaching was rejected by their people, and the second group represents the early
Christian messengers of the faith who are maltreated and murdered by their unbelieving kinsfolk, so that God punishes both
them and their city (Jerusalem).

If this is the correct interpretation of the parable, then the form
contained in Matthew may not have been composed until after
70 A.D. This would not in any way discredit as *vaticinium post even-
tum* the prophecy of Jesus about the destruction of Jerusalem, for it
is established by a series of unassailable words of Jesus (Mt. 24, 2;
26, 61 par; John 2, 19–21). In this case the form in which Matthew
reports the parable of the feast would only be a declaration of the
fulfilment of the prophecy of Jesus about the destruction of
Jerusalem.

6. *The Gospel of St. Matthew in the early Church*

In the time of Irenaeus, as E. Massaux has shown, the Church and
Christian literature were more deeply influenced by the Gospel of
St. Matthew than by any other New Testament book. It was the
favourite source for those works of Jesus which were most highly
valued by primitive Christendom. The words by which Our
Lord established the New Law and determined its relation to the
Old Testament economy were taken from the Sermon on the
Mount and from other parts of this Gospel. That explains why
Papias stresses that Matthew had assembled the "words of the
Lord". When Justin Martyr about 150 A.D. wished to collect "the
beautiful oracles of Christ" according to which Christians should
form their lives, he quotes Our Lord's didactic utterances from
Matthew. "Common Christianity rests upon the teachings of
Christ which are drawn from Matthew; in the time of the
Apologists of the late second century Matthew had this normative
character." On the other hand the miracles of Jesus did not

attract any special attention from the early writers. What they looked for in the Gospel was the teaching of Jesus concerning the new religion and the rules of life which it entails. The same is true of the other narratives. The Apocrypha use them, but either embellish or develop them. Word for word citations from Matthew are not very numerous. The writers were more interested in the content than in the exact wording. The nearer we approach the end of the second century the more accurate the citations become. The first to quote Matthew explicitly is Hegesippus the Apologist in the reign of Marcus Aurelius.

Early Christian literature shows no trace of Mark's influence. Luke's influence is clear but unimportant: in Justin's time Matthew's narratives were filled out from Luke. St. John's Gospel also plays a minor role; there are ideas in Ignatius of Antioch which remind us of John, but they are due to a common milieu, not to dependence on John's writings. The use of the Pauline Epistles is common, but it cannot be said that they dominated Christianity in the same way as Matthew; the writers generally confined themselves to the moral exhortations which Paul gave in the paraenetic parts of his Epistles. "No one regards Paul as the essential source of the Christian message." Audet in RB 58 (1951) 600–608 gives important additions to and corrections of Massaux' comprehensive work.

§ 25. THE GOSPEL OF ST. LUKE

Commentaries: (a) J. Knabenbauer, [2]1905 (CSS). M.-J. Lagrange, *Évangile selon S. Luc*[8], Paris 1948. F. X. Poelzl – Th. Innitzer, [3]1922 (see § 3, 9a). P. Dausch, [4]1932 (Bonner NT). J. Dillersberger, *Das Ev des hl. Lukas in theologischer und heilsgeschichtlicher Schau*[3], 6 vols., Salzburg-Leipzig 1947/49. J. Schmid, [3]1955 (RegNT 3). A. Valensin - J. Huby, 1941 (VS III).—(b) J. Wellhausen, *Das Ev Lucae,* Berlin 1904. Th. Zahn, [3]1920 (Zahn III). J. Weiss, [3]1917 (GoettNT 1). A. Plummer, [5]1928 (ICC). E. Klostermann, [2]1929 (Lietzmann 5). J. M. Creed, *The Gospel According to St. Luke,* London 1930. A. Schlatter, *Das Ev des Lk. aus seinen Quellen erklaert,* Stuttgart 1931. H. K. Luce, *The Gospel According to St. Luke,* Cambridge 1933. F. Hauck, 1934 (ThHK III). K. H. Rengstorf, [4]1950 (NTDeutsch 3). W.

Manson, 1930 (Moffat). N. Geldenhuys, London 1950 (New international Commentary on the NT I).

Studies: W. K. Hobart, *The Medical Language of St. Luke,* Dublin 1882 (reprinted 1954). A. Harnack, *Lk. der Arzt,* Leipzig 1906. Idem, *Die Apg.,* ibid. 1908; *Neue Untersuchungen zur Apg und zur Abfassungszeit der syn Evv,* ibid. 1911. H. J. Cadbury, *The Style and Literary Method of Luke. I. The Diction of Luke and Acts,* Cambridge 1919 (HarvThSt VI); *The Making of Luke-Acts,* 1927; *Lexical Notes on Luke-Acts:* JBL 45 (1926) 190 ff. K. Bornhaeuser, *Studien zum Sondergut des Lk.,* Guetersloh 1934. R. Morgenthaler, *Die lk. Geschichtsschreibung als Zeugnis. Gestalt und Gehalt der Kunst des Lk.,* 2 vols., Zurich 1949. H. F. D. Sparks, *The Semitisms of St. Luke's Gospel:* JThSt 44 (1943) 129–138. K. L. Schmidt, *Der geschichtliche Wert des lk. Aufrisses der Geschichte Jesu:* ThStK 91 (1918) 277–292. L. Brun, *Die Kompositionstechnik des Lk.-Ev:* SO 9 (1930) 38–50. S. Antoniadis, *L'évangile de Luc; esquisse de grammaire et de style,* Paris 1930 (Collect. de l'Institut néohellénique 7). N. H. G. Thomas, *Outline Studies in the Gospel of Luke,* 1950. L. Girard, *L'évangile des voyages de Jésus ou la section 9, 51 à 18, 14 de S. Luc,* Paris 1951. H. Conzelmann, *Die geographischen Vorstellungen im Lk.-Ev,* Diss. Tuebingen 1951, unpublished; summary in ThLZ 1953, 690–692. Idem, *Zur Lukasanalyse:* ZThK 49 (1952) 16–33. M. Goguel, *Quelques observations sur l'œuvre de Luc:* RHPhR 33 (1953) 37–51. M.-E. Boismard, *Rapprochements littéraires entre l'év. de Luc et l'Apc.:* Synoptische Studien, Festschr. f. A. Wikenhauser, 1953, 53–63. L. Cerfaux and J. Cambier: DB Suppl V 545–594. H. Conzelmann, *Die Mitte der Zeit. Studien zur Theologie des Lk.,* Tuebingen 1954. E. Lohse, *Lk. als Theologe der Heilsgeschichte:* EvTh 14 (1954) 256–275. P. Winter, *The Treatment of his Sources by the Third Evangelist in Lk. 21–24:* StTh 8 (1954) 138–172. [Since according to P. Winter (NTSt I, 1954/55 111–121) the language of Lk. 1–2 is Hebrew in character, style and spirit, Lk. cannot be the author of these chapters; he is contradicted by N. Turner (ibid. 2, 1955/56, 100–109).] W. L. Knox, *The Sources of the Synoptic Gospels II: Luke,* 1957.

Decision of the Pontifical Biblical Commission of 26th June 1912: External and internal evidence prove that the Gospel (including Lk. 1–2 and 22, 43 sq.) was written by Luke the physician, the companion and helper of Paul. The Magnificat was spoken by Mary. Luke wrote his Gospel third of the Evangelists, not after or shortly before 70 A.D., but before the end of Paul's first Roman imprisonment. He uses other sources, oral or written, in addition to the preaching of Paul, and he is entirely trustworthy in his accounts.

1. Content and structure

Preface 1, 1–4

Preliminaries 1, 5 to 4, 13

1. Promise, birth and childhood of John the Baptist and Jesus 1, 5 to 2, 52: Promise of the birth of John 1, 5–25; promise of the birth of Jesus 1, 26–38; visit of Mary to Elizabeth 1, 39–56; birth of John 1, 57–80; Birth of Jesus 2, 1–20; Circumcision and

Presentation of Jesus in the Temple 2, 21–40; Jesus in the Temple at twelve years of age 2, 41–52.

2. Preparation for the ministry of Jesus 3, 1 to 4, 13: Appearance and preaching of John the Baptist 3, 1–20; Baptism of Jesus 3, 21 sq.; genealogy of Jesus 3, 23–38; temptation of Jesus 4,1 to 13.

First part: The Galilean ministry 4, 14 to 9, 50

1. Beginning of the ministry of Jesus in Nazareth, Capharnaum and district 4, 14 to 5, 16: Return of Jesus to Galilee and preaching in Nazareth 4, 15–30; a Sabbath in Capharnaum (cure of a possessed man in the Synagogue and of Peter's mother-in-law, cures in the evening) 4, 31–41; Jesus preaches throughout Galilee 4, 42–44; miraculous draught of fishes and call of the first Apostles 5, 1–11; cure of a leper 5, 12–16.

2. Jesus in conflict with his Jewish opponents (5 controversial discourses) 5, 17 to 6, 11: The authority of Jesus to forgive sins on the occasion of the cure of the paralytic 5, 17–26; call of Levi and defence of his association with publicans and sinners 5, 27–32; the question of fasting 5, 33–39; keeping holy the Sabbath when the disciples plucked the ears of corn 6, 1–5, and when the man with the withered hand was cured 6, 6–11.

3. Preaching of Jesus 6, 12–49: Choice of the Twelve 6, 12 to 16; concourse of the people 6, 17–19; the Sermon on the Mount ("Sermon on the Plain") 6, 20–49 containing a) beatitudes and woes 6, 20–26; b) foregoing of revenge, and love of enemies 6, 27–36; c) judgment 6, 37–42; d) as the tree, so the fruit 6, 43 to 46; e) concluding parable of the building of a house 6, 47–49.

4. The reception with which the ministry of Jesus meets 7, 1 to 8, 3: The ruler of Capharnaum 7, 1–10; raising of the widow's son of Naim 7, 11–17; the Baptist's enquiry from prison 7, 18–23 and the testimony of Jesus about him 7, 24–35; Jesus and the sinful woman 7, 36–50; women in the service of Jesus 8, 1–3.

5. Jesus discourses in parables 8, 4–21: Parable of the sower 8, 4–8; reason for the parables 8, 9 sq.; explanation of the parable of the sower 8, 11 to 15; "Take heed how you hear" 8, 16–18; the true kindred of Jesus 8, 19–21.

6. Progressive revelation of the power of Jesus by four miracles on and near the Lake of Genesareth 8, 22–56: Stilling of the tempest on the lake 8, 22–25; cure of the possessed man of Gerasa 8, 26–39; raising of the daughter of Jairus and cure of the woman with the issue of blood 8, 40–56.

7. Sending out of the Twelve Apostles and their return; Herod's opinion about Jesus 9,1–9; feeding of the Five Thousand 9, 10–17.

8. The Messianic confession of Peter and instructions to the Apostles 9, 18–50: The Messianic confession and the first prophecy of the Passion 9, 18–22; instruction of the Apostles on their life of suffering 9, 23–27; the Transfiguration 9, 28–36; cure of a possessed boy 9, 37–43a; second prophecy of the Passion 9, 43b–45; instruction of the Apostles (vying for honour, the strange exorcist) 9, 46–50.

Second part: Jesus on the way to Jerusalem 9, 51 to 19, 27 (9, 51 to 18, 54 is Luke's "travel document")

1. The hostile Samaritans 9, 51–56; unconditional following, 9, 57–62; sending out of the seventy disciples 10, 1–16 and their return 10, 17–20; Jesus rejoices in the Holy Ghost and declares the disciples blessed 10, 21–24.

2. True piety 10, 25 to 11, 13: The commandment to love God and one's neighbour (parable of the good Samaritan) 10, 25–37; Martha and Mary (hearing the word of God) 10, 38–42; the Our Father 11, 1–4; parable of the importunate friend 11, 5–8; exhortations to pray with confidence 11, 9–13.

3. Jesus in conflict with his opponents 11, 14–54: Jesus replies to the charge of being in league with the devil 11, 14–23; warning against relapse 11, 24–26; praise of the mother of Jesus 11, 27 sq.;

denunciation of those who seek signs 11, 29–32; the light 11, 33–36; denunciation of the Pharisees and Scribes 11, 37–54.

4. Exhortations to the Apostles 12, 1–53: Warning against the hypocrisy of the Pharisees 12, 1–3; exhortation to profess fearlessly 12, 4–12; parable of the foolish rich man 12, 13–21; solicitude and amassing treasure 12, 22–34; vigilance and faithfulness 12, 35–48; now is the time for decision 12, 49–53.

5. Words to the people about penance 12, 54 to 13, 35: Recognize the signs of the time 12, 54–59; exhortations to penance (the barren fig tree) 13, 1–9; cure of the deformed woman on the Sabbath 13, 10–17; parables of the mustard seed and the leaven 13, 18–21; exclusion of the Jews from the Kingdom of God and entry of the heathens 13, 22–30; Jesus is told of Herod's plot to kill him 13, 31–33; prophecy against Jerusalem 13, 34 sq.

6. Jesus a guest at the house of a Pharisee 14, 1–24: Cure of a man with dropsy 14, 1–6; choice of places when a guest 14, 7–11; who should be invited 14, 12–14; parable of the supper 14, 15–24.

7. Various parables 14, 25 to 16, 31: Magnitude of the decision to follow Jesus (double parable of building a tower and waging war) 14, 25–35; God's love for sinners (parable of the lost sheep, the lost drachma and the prodigal son) 15, 1–32; the right attitude to material goods (parable of the unjust steward and of Dives and Lazarus) 16, 1–31.

8. Instructions and exhortations to the Apostles (parable of the servant) 17, 1–10; gratitude of the Samaritan 17, 11–19; coming of the Kingdom of God and the Day of the Son of Man 17, 20–37; parable of the judge and the widow 18, 1–8; parable of the publican and the Pharisee 18, 9–14.

9. Jesus and the children 18, 15–17; the dangers of riches (the rich young man) 18, 18–30; third prophecy of the Passion 18, 31–34; cure of a blind man near Jericho 18, 35–42; Jesus stays

with Zachaeus, the chief of the publicans 19, 1–10; parable of the servants and the pounds 19, 11–27.

Third part: Ministry of Jesus at Jerusalem, his Passion, Death, Resurrection and Ascension 19, 28 to 24, 53

a) *The last works of Jesus* 19, 28 to 21, 38:

1. Messianic activity of Jesus 19, 28–48: Solemn entry of Jesus 19, 28–40; Jesus weeps over Jerusalem 19, 41–44; cleansing of the Temple 19, 45–48.

2. Messianic teaching of Jesus 20, 1 to 21, 4: The question of Jesus' authority 20, 1–8; parable of the wicked husbandmen 20, 9–19; the Pharisees' question about the lawfulness of paying tribute 20, 20–26; question of the Sadducees about the resurrection 20, 27–40; the Messias as the Son of David 20, 41–44; Jesus speaks against the Scribes 20, 45–47; the widow's mite 21, 1–4.

3. Discourse of Jesus about the destruction of Jerusalem, the end of the world and his Second Coming 21, 4–38: Occasion of the discourse 21, 5–7; signs before the end of the world 21, 8–11; persecution of the disciples 21, 12–19; punishment of the Jewish people and of the city of Jerusalem 21, 20–24; coming of the Son of Man 21, 25–28; the time of the end 21, 29–33; exhortation to vigilance 21, 34–36.—Jesus teaches in the Temple 21, 37–38.

b) *The Passion, Death and Resurrection of Jesus* 22, 1 to 24, 53:

1. The last activities of Jesus with his Apostles 22, 1–46: The Sanhedrin's decision to put him to death, and the betrayal by Judas 22, 1–6; preparation for the Last Supper 22, 7–13; the Last Supper 22, 14–23; dispute among the Apostles about who is greater 22, 24–30; prophecy of Peter's denial 22, 31–34; dark prospect for the future 22, 35–38; Jesus in the Garden of Olives 22, 39–46.

2. Jesus before the Jewish court 22, 47–71: Arrest of Jesus 22, 47–53 and Peter's denial 22, 54–62; trial of Jesus 22, 63–71.

3. Jesus before the Roman court 23, 1–56: Jesus before Pilate 23, 1–5 and Herod 23, 6–12; his condemnation by Pilate 23, 13–25; the way of the Cross 23, 26–32; Crucifixion 23, 33–43, Death 23, 44–49, and Burial of Jesus 23, 50–56.

4. The Risen Christ 24, 1–53: The empty tomb and the angel's message to the women that Jesus has arisen; the disbelief of the Apostles 24, 1–12; appearance of Jesus to the two disciples on the way to Emmaus 24, 13–35; Jesus appears to the Apostles in Jerusalem 24, 36–49; his Ascension 24, 50–53.

2. The tradition of the early Church

No fragment of Papias mentions the Gospel of St. Luke. Irenaeus, after characterizing the Gospels of St. Matthew and St. Mark, writes: "Luke, the companion of Paul, put down in his book the Gospel which Paul preached" (Haer. III 1, 1). The ancient anti-Marcionite prologue is very informative: "There is Luke, an Antiochene Syrian (a native of Antioch in Syria), a physician by profession, a disciple of the Apostles; but afterwards he was a companion of Paul until Paul's martyrdom. After serving the Lord unswervingly he fell asleep at eighty four years of age without wife or children in Boeotia (or "Thebes the capital of Boeotia") full of the Holy Spirit. Gospels had already been written by Matthew in Judea and by Mark in Rome, and Luke, inspired by the Holy Ghost, wrote this whole Gospel in the neighbourhood of Achaea. In the preface he tells us that other (Gospels) had been written previously, and that it was necessary to provide the Gentile converts with an accurate account of the economy of salvation so that they should neither be distracted by the fables of the Jews nor miss the truth being deceived by heretical and vain imaginings . . ." (Translated from Th. Zahn's version.)

Unfortunately the passage of the Muratorian Canon which deals with Luke is so corrupt that some of its content cannot be explained with certainty. It may be reconstructed thus: *Tertium evangelii librum secundum Lucam. Lucas iste medicus post ascensum Christi, cum eum Paulus quasi ut iuris studiosum secum adsumpsisset, nomine suo ex opinione conscripsit; Dominum tamen nec ipse vidit in carne, et ideo, prout assequi potuit, ita et a nativitate Johannis incipit dicere.*

Tertullian tells us that the Church usually connected St. Luke's Gospel with St. Paul (*Adv. Marc.* IV 5). Since the later sources agree with those already mentioned there is no need to quote them (Clement of Alexandria, *Strom.* I 21, 145; Origen apud Euseb., H. E. VI 25, 6; Eusebius, H. E. III 4, 6; Jerome, *De vir. ill.* 7; prologue to his commentary on Mt.).

From the second half of the second century at latest the unanimous tradition of the early Church attributes the third Gospel to Luke the physician who accompanied St. Paul on his journeys. Indeed it can hardly be gainsaid that this tradition is already in evidence in the mid-second century. According to the manuscript tradition the prefixing of the ascriptions (according to Mt., Mk., Lk., and John) to the individual Gospels took place when they were brought together in the Canon of four Gospels about 140–150 (cf. § 5, 2); also Marcion accepted only the third Gospel precisely because it was regarded as the work of Luke, the companion and fellow worker of St. Paul.

When the early sources stress the close relations between Luke and Paul—many of them say that Paul's preaching was the source of Luke's Gospel—their aim is to show that though the author was not an Apostle, yet the Gospel has apostolic authority, just as Mark depends on the authority of Peter. Thus, for example, Origen says that Paul gave his approval to the Gospel of St. Luke, and many of the Fathers maintain that when Paul speaks of "his Gospel" (e.g. Rom. 2, 16; 2 Tim. 2, 8) he is referring to the Gospel of St. Luke. However, St. Paul's preaching cannot be the main source of St. Luke's Gospel, as St. Peter's sermons were for St. Mark, for Paul was not an "eyewitness" (Lk. 1, 2); but undoubtedly in his missionary sermons and instructions he must have repeated stories about the life and works of Jesus (cf. 1 Cor. 7, 10; 11, 23 sq.; 15, 3 sq.), and Luke could have used these when writing his book.

Paul himself (Col. 4, 14) says that his fellow worker Luke was a physician. According to the ancient prologue, Eusebius (H. E. III 4, 6) and Jerome (prologue to the commentary on Matthew), he was from Antioch in Syria. This information cannot be inferred from the writings of Luke, so it must derive from a reliable ancient tradition. No credence can be given to the statement of some writers that Luke was one of the seventy disciples whom Jesus sent out (Lk. 10, 1 sqq.), or the unnamed disciple at Emmaus (Lk. 24, 18). The tradition that he was a painter cannot be traced back beyond the sixth century and does not merit acceptance.

3. The author of the Gospel of St. Luke (and of Acts)

Early Church tradition attributes both the third Gospel and Acts of the Apostles to Luke, the physician and companion of St. Paul. Since his authorship cannot be deduced from the two works— they make no allusions to their author—this must represent a tradition stretching back to the first century. Internal evidence supports it.

1. The Gospel of St. Luke and Acts of the Apostles show such uniformity that they must have one and the same author; this uniformity extends to their vocabulary and style as well as to form and outlook.

In modern times A. Harnack has devoted a number of writings to demonstrating this in detail. There has been no support for the view of the English scholar A. Clark (cf. § 29) who denied that the linguistic arguments prove unity of authorship.

The uniformity which is demonstrated by Harnack extends also to the so-called "We passages" in Acts—the parts where the narrative is in the first person plural (16, 10–17; 20, 5 to 21, 18; 27, 1 to 28, 16). This uniformity rules out the suggestion that the author has merely incorporated a source written in the first person plural without changing it to the third person. He must have taken part in the events which he narrates and the descriptions must be from his own observation. It follows therefore that for a time he was a companion of Paul.

The question now arises whether the author of the "We passages"—and therefore of both books—can be Luke, or is it another companion of Paul. The companions who are mentioned in the third person in these passages may be ruled out; the same applies to those who are mentioned by name elsewhere in the two books, for the first person should have been used in such places. This leaves only a small number, especially when we recall that both books must have been written by an educated Gentile-Christian (see below n. 5). Besides Luke there remain only Demas (Col. 4, 14; Philem. 24; 2 Tim. 4, 10), Crescens (2 Tim. 4, 10), Artemas (Tit. 3, 12), Zenas and Apollo (Tit. 3, 13); Titus is excluded because he was at the Apostolic Council with Paul (Gal. 2, 1 3), and Acts 15 is not a "We passage".

So the opponents of tradition can mention none of the early Christians except Luke who would merit serious consideration as author. They generally admit that Luke was the author of the "We passages"—or of a fairly long "travel document"—and say that this was incorporated by the unknown author without everywhere eliminating the first person.

In view of these facts the scientifically correct course is to accept tradition, particularly since Luke was closely associated with Paul ("Luke, the most dear physician", Col. 4, 14), and he alone stayed with Paul during his last imprisonment (2 Tim. 4, 11).

2. According to Col. 4, 14 and to tradition, Luke the companion of Paul was a physician. Does the double work which tradition ascribes to him show any signs of being written by a

doctor? Seventy years ago the Englishman Hobart made an elaborate attempt to show from the frequency of technical medical terms and from the medical knowledge which these works display that only a doctor could have composed both books. Harnack checked his evidence, and while discarding material which does not prove the point, regarded the conclusion as certain. Now, however, the American scholar Cadbury has shown that almost all the technical terms in question are to be found in LXX, Flavius Josephus, Plutarch, Lucian and others, that is in works which are not by physicians.

So we cannot regard the linguistic argument by itself as proof that only a physician could have composed the two books. Nevertheless the tradition need not be abandoned, and it may still be sustained, for the author displays familiarity with medical terminology (cf. e. g. Lk. 4, 38; 5, 12; 8, 44; Acts 5, 5 10; 9, 40), and he indisputably describes maladies and cures from the point of view of a medical man (e. g. Lk. 4, 35; 13, 11; Acts 3, 7; 9, 18).

4. The sources of St. Luke's Gospel and his treatment of them

Since Luke had neither seen nor heard the words and deeds of Jesus which he wished to record in his book, he had to depend on the reports of others.

In the preface to his Gospel 1, 1–4 he follows the common practice of Hellenistic writers and speaks both of his predecessors and of his own diligence in ascertaining the facts of the life of Jesus from the beginning onwards. Before him "many" had tried to record the things "which have been accomplished among us"; but since these "many" were not immediate disciples of Jesus they depended on the evidence of those who "from the beginning were eyewitnesses (of the events recorded) and (also) ministers of the word". Their authorities were therefore eyewitnesses who had dedicated themselves to spreading the good tidings that the Saviour had appeared. Foremost among these were the immediate disciples of Jesus, particularly the twelve Apostles. Luke does not thereby intend to deny that eye-witnesses (Apostles) had written such books; he means that, though not an eyewitness, he was encouraged to write by the example of many others who had not themselves seen the events and whose writings depended on the testimony of witnesses. So the prologue does not deny that Luke used an Apostle's work; though he does not say so explicitly, yet it may be assumed that in composing his Gospel he made use of earlier accounts in so far as they seemed to him suitable and dependable. However, he did not content himself with these written sources, but also made vigorous efforts to trace and uncover oral traditions which had not yet been recorded, for he assures us that he carefully checked everything from the beginning.

There is almost universal agreement to-day that the Gospel of St. Mark was one of Luke's written sources. Not only did Luke take over more than half of Mark's material—about 350 out of 661 verses—with stylistic improvements and occasional trimming, but he also followed Mark's outline of the work of Jesus. With insignificant exceptions he did not rearrange the material which he took from Mark, and he fitted the material from other sources into Mark's framework.

Of the non-Marcan material, about 325 verses—mainly discourses of Jesus—occur also in Matthew, though generally in a different context from Luke. The vast majority of non-Catholic scholars and a fairly large number of Catholics say that the material which is common to Matthew and Luke comes from one and the same written source (the Discourse Source, Collection of Logia, or briefly Q; cf. § 26, 5).

Almost half of Luke's material is proper to him (548 out of 1149 verses; see the figures in § 26, 1). It is difficult to determine its origin.

210

Many scholars consider that the material which is proper to Luke comes entirely from one written source, which was an independent and complete Gospel. Thus A. Schlatter, for example, followed by Rengstorf, maintains that this (lost) Gospel was a first hand account written for Gentile converts by a disciple of Jesus shortly after the middle of the fifties. But it is much more likely that the proper part of Luke was gathered from a number of sources, probably in the main from oral tradition. A "We passage" in Acts tells that the Evangelist spent about two years in Palestine (cf. § 29, 3), and he may have used this sojourn to collect traditions which were still circulating orally; he must have had access to reliable sources (cf. Acts 21, 8 10 16 sqq.). Yet it is not improbable—indeed it is implied in Lk. 1, 1—that he took parts of his special material from minor written sources.

The greater part of the non-Marcan material was inserted by Luke into Mark's framework in two blocks, namely Lk. 6, 20 to 8, 3 (= "little insertion") between Mk. 3, 19 and 3, 20, and Lk. 9, 51 to 18, 14 (= "greater insertion") between Mk. 9, 50 and 10, 1; in the case of the Infancy and Easter the subject matter determined the position.

The "great insertion" (also called Luke's "travel document") and "great omission" (of Marcan material, Mk. 6, 45 to 8, 26) caused a considerable change in Mark's outline of the public life of Jesus. In Mark Jesus begins continual journeying after the sending out of the Twelve, touching the territory of Tyre and Sidon and the Decapolis but never returning to Galilee, and at 10, 1 he begins the journey (through Perea) to Jerusalem. In Luke he does not leave Galilee until 9, 51, and then he immediately begins to move towards Jerusalem ("When the days of his assumption were accomplishing, he steadfastly set his face to go to Jerusalem"); Peter's confession is not localized in Luke and it is not such an important turning point in the ministry of Jesus as it is in Mark. So all the events recorded by Luke up to 9, 50 seem to take place in Galilee.

Luke therefore divides the public life of Jesus into three great scenes: Galilee, the journey to Jerusalem, and Jerusalem itself. But when examined closely the journey to Jerusalem in Luke is only the frame into which he puts the greater part of the non-Marcan material. Most of the pericopae of Luke's "travel document" are not localized, and many of them belong rather to Galilee. Yet the idea of the journey to Jerusalem is kept before the reader, by the explicit statements of 13, 22 and 17, 11 that Jesus is on his way there.[1]

5. Literary and theological characteristics

1. From a literary point of view the Gospel of St. Luke differs notably from Matthew and Mark. The latter are impersonal community books intended for liturgical use, while the Gospel of St. Luke is rather a literary work intended for Christian readers.

Luke follows the custom of his time and prefixes a preface to his Gospel, which he dedicates to a distinguished person Theophilus by name. Such dedication of literary works was a popular practice among Greek and Roman writers of the Hellenistic age. Thus Flavius Josephus, for example, dedicated his "Antiquities of the Jews" to a rich patron Epaphroditus, and Diogenes Laertius thought it remarkable that Chrysippus the Stoic did not dedicate any of his numerous books to a king.

Luke's preface has not the solemn liturgical sound of the opening of Matthew and Mark; it follows the style of Hellenistic historians. In it Luke speaks in general terms of his predecessors and of his own preliminary work. He claims that his book is a testimony to the truth of the Christian message since it sets out in order the results of thorough and painstaking investigations.

Another difference between Luke and the other Evangelists is

[1] J. Blinzler, *Die literarische Eigenart des sog. Reiseberichtes im Lk.-Ev:* Synoptische Studien 20–52 (against L. Girard, see above). J. Schneider, *Zur Analyse des lukanischen Reiseberichtes:* ibid. 207–229. [His theological position.]

that he does occasionally suggest the place which the story of Jesus occupies in world history. In the course of a sixfold synchronism with the history of the time he gives a definite date (3, 1 sqq.: "the fifteenth year of the reign of Tiberius Caesar") for the public appearance of the Baptist, which was the signal for the ministry of Jesus; again he connects the nativity of Jesus with a census ordered by Augustus during the governorship of Cyrinus (2, 1 sq.); he tells us what age Jesus was (3, 23: "about the age of thirty years") at the beginning of his public life; and he informs us that Johanna, one of the women who followed Jesus, was the wife of Chusa, Herod's steward (8, 3). But Luke's interest in history is proved above all by the fact that he was the first and only man in the primitive Church to have the enterprise to compose a history of the spread of the Christian Church up to the beginning of the sixties (Acts of the Apostles).

Luke has been called the "historian Evangelist", and he deserves the title in view of the abundant material which, as a result of his inquiries, he has incorporated into the Gospel. But it should be remembered that he was unable to improve on the chronology which Mark gives for the ministry of Jesus; instead he adopted Mark's outline and inserted most of the extra material quite extrinsically at two points within this framework. Indeed by the omission of Mk. 6, 48 to 8, 28 he spoiled the order of Mark's plan according to which the rejection in Nazareth led Jesus to continual journeying, during which he visited heathen territory, withdrew more and more from the people and devoted himself to instructing the Apostles until, after Peter's confession, he began the journey to Jerusalem for the Passion.

The third Gospel also differs from the other two Synoptics in language and style. The stylistic excellence of the preface is not maintained throughout the two books, but he nowhere departs from literary Greek. This was already recognized by Jerome when he said: *Lucas igitur, qui inter omnes evangelistas graeci sermonis eruditissimus fuit, quippe et medicus et qui in Graecis evangelium scripserit* (Ep. 20, 4). Unlike the other Evangelists he shuns Hebrew and Aramaic words, and wherever possible replaces them with native Greek expressions. Thus he replaces ῥαββί Mk. 1, 5 by ἐπιστάτης 9, 33, ῥαββοῦνι Mk. 10, 51 by κύριε 18, 41; for ἀββᾶ ὁ πατήρ Mk. 14, 36 he says πάτερ 22, 42; for καναναῖος Mk. 3, 18 he uses ὁ ζηλώτης 6, 15; Acts 1, 13. He does not name Gethsemani nor Golgotha. The only Aramaic words which he uses are: ἀμὴν (infrequent, he usually says ἐπ' ἀληθείας, ἀληθῶς), βεελζεβούλ, μαμωνᾶς, πάσχα, σάββατον, σατανᾶς, σίκερα, γέεννα. There are no Aramaic sentences at all in him. Although Latin loan words had long since been naturalized among Greeks, Jews, and Syrians, he prefers to replace them with native Greek words; thus he says ἑκατοντάρχης Acts 23, 47 instead of κεντυρίων, φόρος 20, 22 instead of κῆνσος, λεπτόν 15, 29 instead of κοδράντης; he does, however, use ἀσσάριον, δηνάριον, λεγίων, μόδιος, σουδάριον. When vernacular expressions occur in his sources he substitutes a more literary vocabulary; e. g. κράββατος Mk. 2, 11 is replaced by κλινίδιον 5, 24; ῥαφίς Mk. 10, 25 by βελόνη 18, 25; κοράσιον Mk. 5, 41 sq. by παῖς 8, 51 54.

In spite of his efforts to attain a certain elegance and to cater for cultured tastes, Luke never forgot that he was writing sacred and not profane history. So in his narratives he modelled himself on the hebraizing style of the LXX, especially in the Gospel and in the first twelve chapters of Acts. That is why the pure Hebraisms of the Synoptics appear almost exclusively in Luke (Dalman); this, for example, is the explanation for the frequent introduction of sentences by "and it came to pass", the phrase "before God" (1, 6 15; 12, 6; 16, 15) etc.

Luke's method of treating his material may be studied most clearly in his handling of passages taken from the Gospel of St. Mark. He made no important change in the wording of Our Lords' utterances, but contented himself with a light revision of the style—with polishing the language. In the narrative passages, however, he revised Mark's wording much more thoroughly, and occasionally made considerable changes; he did the same with the parables, for because of their narrative character they were not equated to the other words of Our Lord, and furthermore many of them were already circulating in widely varied forms. He generally curtails Mark's long narratives (cf. e. g. Mk. 5, 21–43 with Lk. 8, 40–56) and drops a number of Mark's graphic details (e. g. Mk. 1, 33; 4, 36–38; 5, 5). Sometimes he adds an elucidation (e. g. Lk. 4, 43; 18, 36), and substitutes more exact words for Mark's popular descriptions of things (thus, Tetrarch 9, 7 for king Mk. 6, 14; Lake of Galilee 5, 1 sq.; 8, 22 sq. 33 for Sea of Galilee Mk. 1, 16; 5, 13).

2. In spite of the literary merits of Luke's work, it is a Gospel like the works of Matthew and Mark and not simply a biography like the biographies of great men which the classical authors produced. Like the other Evangelists Luke intended his work to awaken faith in Jesus as the God-sent bringer of salvation or to strengthen and deepen the faith of those who already believed (cf. John 20, 31; Lk. 1, 4). In spite of his Hellenism, and even though he dedicates the work to a distinguished Hellenist, he does not consider adapting the Gospel to the Greek outlook; his aim is rather to publish to the Hellenistic world the Gospel, refined in vocabulary and style, but still carrying its original Semitic stamp and with its substance unchanged.

Nevertheless the Gospel of St. Luke has a distinctive stamp when compared to the Gospels of St. Matthew and St. Mark. Matthew proclaimed to the Jewish-Christian Church that Jesus is the Messianic King promised by the Prophets; Mark set him before the Roman Church as the Son of God marked out by mighty miracles; Luke shows him as the Saviour of the world who delivers from all distress and who has appeared for all men, particularly for the poor and sinful.

At the Nativity the angels tell the shepherds: "This day is born to you a Saviour (σωτήρ)" (2, 11). Again matters of purely Jewish concern are relegated to the background in Luke (unlike Mt.), and the centre of interest is universal humanity. The conflicts of Jesus with the Scribes and Pharisees and questions about the observance of the Law occupy much less space in him than in Matthew (or Mark). He does not record at all the great conflict between Jesus and the Pharisees about "clean" and unclean" (Mk. 7, 1–25; Mt. 15, 1–20), nor the passage about divorce (Mk. 10, 1–10; Mt. 19, 1–9). The great section of the Sermon on the Mount (Mt. 5, 17–48) dealing with the relation of Jesus to the Mosaic Law is represented in Luke only by verse 17 (Lk. 16, 18), vv. 39 sq. 42 (Lk. 6, 29 sq.), and the words about loving one's enemies vv. 44–48 (Lk. 6, 27 sq. 32–36); he also (6, 31) contains the "Golden Rule" (Mt. 7, 12), but without the words "this is the law and the prophets" (cf. also Mt. 22, 40).

Luke shows no hostility towards Jews, but rather a high esteem for the Jewish religion, when it appears in its genuine form. This regard is to be seen in the history of the Infancy where he portrays people like Zachary and Elizabeth, Simeon and Anna, models of true Israelite piety; he points out the large part which the Temple played in the life of the parents of Jesus (2, 22 sqq. 41 sqq.); and Luke (22, 30) as well as Matthew (19, 28) records Our Lord's promise that the twelve Apostles shall sit on twelve thrones in his Kingdom and judge the twelve tribes of Israel.

Since Luke was writing for the Gentile-Christian Church it is natural that he should emphasize the universality of the mission of Jesus. This thought appears as early as the hymn of the angels at the Nativity ("Peace to men of good will" 2, 14) and at the Presentation in the Temple Simeon says that the Child will bring to fulfilment the oracles of the Prophets about the conversion of the Gentiles (2, 32). In Matthew the genealogy makes Jesus the descendant of Abraham, the father of Israel; in Luke's genealogy he appears as the son of Adam, the father of all mankind. In his public ministry Jesus does not feel himself bound to national boundaries. Luke does not report the instruction that the Twelve should not enter Gentile or Samaritan territory (Mt. 10, 5 sq.); indeed Jesus seeks lodging in a Samaritan village (9, 52 sqq.); among the ten lepers is a Samaritan who is praised by Jesus for his gratitude (17, 1 sqq.), and the parable of the good Samaritan gives the Jewish Scribe an example of true charity (10, 29 sqq.).[2] The whole work is crowned with the final command of the Risen Christ to preach the remission of sins to all nations (24, 47).

Since Jesus has appeared as the Saviour of all mankind, love of one's neighbour is specially stressed in the reports of his moral preaching. Love of one's enemies is at the core of Luke's Sermon on the Mount (6, 27 sqq.), and the enquiring Scribe is taught through the parable of the good Samaritan that God demands a love of one's neighbour which is ready to undertake any sacrifice to help anyone in need regardless of nationality.

Jesus shows himself the Saviour of men not only by his precepts but also in his actions. He never tires of working to help those in distress and to call sinners to repentance. Luke portrays much more clearly than the other Synoptics the picture of the Saviour of sinners who calls to himself the lost, the despised, and the outcast, and comforts them by the message of forgiveness. "The Son of Man is come to seek and save that which was lost" —words of Jesus which occur only in Lk. 19, 10—stand as the motto of his Ministry. It is only in the third Gospel that we find the parables of the lost drachma and the prodigal son (15, 8 sqq.), and the stories of the sinful woman to whom much was forgiven (7, 36 sqq.) and of Zachaeus the chief of the publicans (19, 1), as well as the consoling promise to the penitent thief: "This day thou shalt be with me in Paradise" (23, 43), and the parable of the publican and the Pharisee (18, 10 sqq.).

[2] Cf. M. S. Enslin, *Luke and the Samaritans*: HarvThR 36 (1943) 277–297.

According to Luke, Jesus as Saviour has a special love not only for sinners, but also for the poor. The Beatitudes are for the poor, the hungry, and those who weep (6, 20 sqq.). After death Lazarus the poor man goes to Abraham's bosom, while the rich spendthrift is buried in Hell (16, 19 sqq.). The parable of the rich farmer is intended to show what happens to a man who stores up material wealth but is not rich in God's sight (12, 16 sqq.). If a rich man gives a banquet he should invite the poor, the maimed, the lame and the blind; he will be rewarded for this in the other world (14, 13 sq.). Men should use material possessions in such a way as to produce a heavenly treasure (16, 1 sqq.; 18, 18 sqq.).

The poor are blessed, wealth is dangerous. Luke contains unusually sharp words of Jesus against the rich, and the quest of profit and pleasure: "Woe to you that are rich" (6, 24); "Take heed and beware of all covetousness: for a man's life doth not consist in the abundance of things which he possesseth" (12, 15, cf. 6, 15). Again and again Jesus demands the renunciation of possessions and the distribution of property as alms: "Sell what you possess and give alms" (12,33); "Every one of you that doth not renounce all that he possesseth cannot be my disciple" (14, 33); "Make unto you friends of the mammon of iniquity" (16, 9); "That which remaineth give alms: and behold all things are clean unto you" (11, 41; contrast Mt. 23, 26). Most of the sayings of Jesus on wealth and property appear only in Luke; those which he shares with Matthew (and Mark) are much more sharply worded in Luke. Some of them go "to the verge of the Ebionite tenet that wealth is in itself reprehensible and that poverty and renunciation of property are good" (J. Behm). But it must be remembered that, when all is said and done, the same condemnation of wealth and of unbridled lust for gain is to be found also in the other two Synoptics, as the story of the rich young man shows: "A rich man shall hardly enter into the Kingdom of Heaven. It is easier for a camel to pass through the eye of a needle than for a rich man to enter into the Kingdom of Heaven" (Mt. 19, 23 sq.; Mk. 10, 23 25). So it would not be true to say that Luke has distorted the attitude of Jesus to material possessions. Yet it may be surmised that in this matter he is using traditions of the poor Palestinian Jews, whose mood is also reflected in Jas. 4, 13 to 5, 6; 1, 9; 2, 7 sqq.

Indeed at that time the problem of material wealth was also a concern of popular ethics (Epictetus, Seneca), and similar tones are adopted in the Stoic-Cynic diatribe. In the Roman-Hellenistic world the masses lived in grinding poverty while a few controlled immense riches which they misused in an unbridled search for pleasure. Luke himself did not like riches and was a lover of poverty, as may be seen from his description of the primitive Christian community where all the believers treated their property as a communal possession (Acts 2, 44; 4, 32).

6. People for whom intended, place and time of composition

Luke dedicated both his works to a certain Theophilus. This name was in use among both Jews and Gentiles; it is not symbolic, but belonged to an actual person about whom nothing else is known. The title κράτιστε ("Excellency") marks him as a man of high social standing, not necessarily the holder of a high political position (cf. 23, 26; 24, 3) nor a member of the aristocracy. He was probably already a Christian or at least a catechumen (1, 4), for whom Luke wrote his Gospel as a proof of the authenticity of the Christian message. It was the custom for a book to become the property of the person to whom it was dedicated and for the recipient to assume responsibility for its publication.

The preface says that the Gospel was written to instruct Theophilus; this does not rule out the possibility that it was also intended originally for general circulation. There can be no doubt that Luke wrote his book for Gentile-Christians; but as it is impossible to determine the date and place of composition, we cannot say whether it was intended in the first instance for a particular Church (Rome) or province (Achaea or Greece).

According to Irenaeus and the ancient prologue, Luke only wrote his Gospel after the death of Paul. Irenaeus mentions the place of composition of Matthew ("among the Hebrews", i. e. in Palestine) and of John (Ephesus), but he does not say where Mark or Luke were written. The ancient prologue, however, gives this information for all four Gospels. It says Luke composed his Gospel in Achaea, and Jerome is following this when he says that it was written *in Achaeae Boeotiaeque partibus* (Prologue to commentary on Mt.). None of the other early Christian sources mentions the time or place of composition.

Since Luke made use of Mark and wrote a second book (Acts) after the Gospel, the dating of the Gospel depends on how we date these two works. Catholic exegetes generally agree in dating the Gospel of St. Luke to 60–62 A.D.; almost all Protestant scholars place it after 70 A.D., the conservatives favouring the decade 70–80 A.D.

They say that Lk. 19, 43 sq.; 21, 20 24 provides a strong argument for dating the Gospel after 70 A.D. In Mt. 24, 15; Mk. 13, 14 Jesus foretells the profanation of the Temple when he speaks of "the abomination of desolation" (the devastating monster) in the holy place (Dan. 9, 27; 11, 31; 12, 11). The parallel passage, Lk. 21, 20, reads: "When you shall see Jerusalem compassed about with an army, then know that the desolation thereof is at hand", and v. 24 adds that some of its inhabitants shall perish by the sword and others shall be led away as captives into all nations, while the Holy City itself shall be trodden down by the Gentiles till the times of the nations be fulfilled (cf. Lk. 19, 43 sq. which contains an almost identical prophecy). The reference here is not to the profanation of the Temple but to the fate of the city of Jerusalem and its inhabitants in 70 A.D. Therefore, they argue, these verses could have been written only after the event; the prophecy of Jesus was fulfilled in 70 A.D., and Luke here expresses it clearly to show his readers that part of the prophecies of Jesus had already been fulfilled. Those who favour an earlier date dispute the strength of this argument on the ground that Luke does not give sufficient details about the fate of Jerusalem and its inhabitants to warrant this conclusion. But this objection does not invalidate the interpretation of 19, 43 sq.; 21, 20 which was outlined above (cf. J. Schmid ad loc.).

So probably the Gospel of St. Luke was not written until after 70 A.D. However, there is no reason for placing it later than about 80 A.D., since in Acts, his later work, Luke shows himself quite independent of the Pauline Epistles.

§ 26. THE SYNOPTIC PROBLEM

Literature (selected, mainly modern): H. J. Holtzmann, *Die syn Evv, ihr Ursprung und ihr geschichtlicher Charakter,* Leipzig 1863. Bernh. Weiss, *Die Quellen der syn Ueberlieferung,* Leipzig 1908 (TU XXXII, 3). P. Wernle, *Die syn Frage,* Freiburg i. Br. 1899. C. Weizsaecker, *Untersuchungen ueber die ev Geschichte*[2], Leipzig und Tuebingen 1901. G. H. Mueller, *Zur Synopse,* Goettingen 1908. J. Wellhausen, *Einleitung in die drei ersten Evv,* Berlin 1905. J. C. Hawkins, *Horae synopticae*[2], Oxford 1909. W. Sanday etc., *Studies in the Syn Problem,* Oxford 1911. F. Spitta, *Die syn Grundschrift in ihrer Ueberlieferung durch Lk.,* Leipzig 1912. Th. Soiron, *Die Logia Jesu. Eine literarkritische und literarhistorische Untersuchung zum syn Problem,* Muenster i. W. 1916 (NtA VI, 4). H. J. Cladder, *Unsere Evv* I, Freiburg i. Br. 1919. M.-J. Lagrange, *Commentaries on Mt., Mk., Lk.* (vide ad loc.). E. Meyer, *Ursprung und Anfaenge des Christentums* I, Berlin 1921. B. H. Streeter, *The Four Gospels. A Study of Origins,* London 1924. W. Bussmann, *Syn Studien,* 3 vols., Halle 1925, 1929, 1931. W. Larfeld, *Die ntl Evv nach ihrer Eigenart und Abhaengigkeit,* Guetersloh 1925, J. M. Vosté, *De synopticorum mutua relatione et dependentia,* Rome 1928. J. Schmid, *Mt. und Lk. Untersuchung des Verhaeltnisses ihrer Evv* (BSt XXIII, 2–4: 1930). K. Grobel, *Formgeschichte und syn Quellenanalyse,* Goettingen 1937. E. Hirsch *Die Fruehgeschichte des Ev,* 2 vols., Tuebingen 1941, I [2]1951 (see E. Haenchen, ThLZ 1942, 5–6; Deutsche Theologie 1942, 10–12). Sickenberger, BZ 21 (1933) 1–9. Schniewind, ThRdsch 1930, 129–189 (survey of research). A. Wikenhauser, RQ 39 (1931) 43–61; Art. *Syn Frage:* LThK IX (1937) 949–954. L. Cerfaux: EphThL 1935, 1–27. E. Schweizer, *Eine hebraisierende Sonderquelle des Lk?:* ThZ 6 (1950) 161–185. T. E. F. Honey, *Did Mark use Q?:* JBL 62 (1943) 319–331. E. Hirsch: ZntW 1942, 101–124. B. C. Butler, *The Originality of St. Matthew. A*

Critique of the Two-document Hypothesis, Cambridge 1951. L. Cerfaux, *La mission en Galilée dans la tradition synoptique:* EphThL 27 (1951) 369–389. B. P. W. St. Hunt, *Primitive Gospel Sources,* London 1951. L. G. da Fonseca, *Quaestio synoptica*[3], Rome 1952. B. H. Trockmorton, *Did Mk. know Q?:* JBL 67 (1948) 319 to 329 [no]. L. Cerfaux: EphThL 28 (1952) 629–649; Synopt. Studien. Festschr. f. A. Wikenhauser, 1953, 64–77. J. Schmid, *Mk. und der aramaeische Mt.:* Synopt. Studien 148–183. H. Helmbold, *Vorsynoptische Evv,* Stuttgart 1953. W. L. Knox, *The Sources of the Synoptic Gospels* I (St. Mark), ed. by H. Chadwick, Cambridge 1953. P. Parker, *The Gospel before Mark,* Chicago 1953. L. Vaganay, *Le problème synoptique. Une hypothèse de travail,* Paris 1954. Idem, *L'absence du sermon sur la montagne chez Marc:* RB 58 (1951) 5–46 (further arguments: NTSt 1, 1955, 192–200). Idem, *Matthieu* (l'év.): DB Suppl V 940–956. Idem, *La question synoptique:* EphThL 28 (1952) 238–256 [comprehensive presentation of his theory]. J. Levie, *L'év. araméen de S. Mt., est-il la source de l'év. de S. Mc.?:* Cahiers de la NRTh 11 (1954) = NRTh 1954, 689–715; 812–843 [no]. X. Léon-Dufour, *Autour de la question synoptique:* RSR 42 (1954) 549–584 [critical report]. Vaganay: EphThL 31 (1955) 343–356, replies to Levie's criticism; Levie answers him: *La complexité du problème synoptique:* EphThL 31 (1955) 619–636. J. Schmidt in his review of recent Synoptic studies (ThR 1956 Nr. 2) examines Vaganay's theory, and produces strong arguments for rejecting it. *La formation des évangiles.* Problème synoptique et Formgeschichte (Recherches bibliques publiées sous le patronage du Colloquium Biblicum Lovaniense II), 1957.

W. L. Knox, *The Sources of the Synoptic Gospels* II: St. Luke and St. Matthew, Cambridge 1957. F. J. McCool, *Revival of Synoptic Source-Criticism:* ThSt 17 (1956) 459–493. R. Bultmann, *Geschichte der synopt. Tradition,* suppl. Goettingen 1957.

The History of Synoptic studies is reviewed by: Th. Zahn, *Einleitung in das NT*[3] II (1907) 187–204; M. Jones, *The NT in the 20th Century,* London 1914, 189–226; Th. Soiron, *Logia,* pp. 1–22; E. Fascher, *Die formgeschichtliche Methode,* Giessen 1924, pp. 1–51; K. Grobel, *loc. cit.* (on German, English and American studies since 1912).

A decision of the Pontifical Biblical Commission of 26th June 1912 leaves open to discussion all those questions which were not answered in the decisions on individual Gospels. But those people would not be in harmony with these decisions who *nullo fulti traditionis testimonio nec historico argumento,* nevertheless adopt the so-called Two Sources Theory. Cf. Sickenberger: BZ 9 (1911) 391–396.

THE first three Gospels agree so extensively in most of their material that for convenience of comparison they can be printed in three parallel columns, so that the common passages stand side by side. Such an arrangement of the text is called a *synopsis (conspectus),* and the Evangelists themselves are called the Synoptics; the name is not derived from the English word Synopsis meaning a summary; it is due to J. J. Griesbach who had such a synopsis printed in 1774 as a text book for lectures on Exegesis. Numerous synopses have been produced since then; the most valuable of them are: A. Huck, *Synopse der drei ersten Evangelien mit Bei-fuegung der Joh.-Parallelen* (in Greek), 9th Edition, Tuebingen 1936; J. Schmid, *Synopse der drei ersten Evv. mit Beifuegung der Joh.-Parallelen,* Regensburg, 2nd edition 1956.

The Synoptic Problem is the problem posed by the unique mixture of widespread agreement and notable divergences *(concordia discors)* within the first three Gospels. It is not therefore a question of harmonizing the three Gospels, but of elucidating the history of their mutual relations.

I. THE PROBLEM

1. The material of the three Synoptics[1]

The Gospel of St. Mark is the shortest of the three Synoptics, containing (without 16, 9–20; cf. § 23, 5) only 661 verses. Almost the whole of its material occurs also in Matthew or Luke or both. It has only about 30 verses of material which is really peculiar to him: Two miracles (cure of a deaf mute 7, 32–37 and of a blind man 8, 22–26), three very short narratives (3, 20 sq.; 11, 11; 14, 51 sq.), the parable of the seed growing by itself 4, 26–29, a few sayings of Our Lord 2, 27; 9, 29 49 50 b; 12, 32–34, and a comment of the Evangelist on ablutions among the Jews. The conclusion of the eschatological discourse is not included in this list in view of the parallels Mt. 24, 45 sqq. and Lk. 12, 40 sqq.; 19, 12 sq.

The Gospel of St. Matthew, with 1068 verses, contains the substance of more than 600 verses of Mark (the narratives are generally curtailed). Only 40 verses of Mark's material are missing from him: Three miracles (cure of a possessed man Mk. 1, 23–28, of a deaf mute 7, 32–37, and of a blind man 8, 22–26), the parable of the seed growing by itself 4, 26–29, the strange exorcist 9, 38

---

[1] There are detailed lists in Streeter, Bussmann and Larfeld.

to 41, the widow's mite 12, 41–44, and also 1, 35–38; 3, 20 sq.; 6, 30 sq.; 14, 51 sq. There is quite a large amount of material peculiar to him (about 330 verses): The early history 1, 1 to 2, 23 (= 48 verses), a number of narratives (cure of two blind men 9, 27–31, of a dumb man 9, 32-34, the Temple tax 17, 24–27, the end of Judas 27, 3–10, guarding of the sepulchre 27, 62–66, appearance of the Risen Christ to the women 28, 9–10, trickery of the high priests 28, 11–15, appearance of the Risen Christ in Galilee 28, 16–20; as well as 14, 28–31; 26, 52–54; 27, 19 24 sq. 51–53; 28, 2–4), eight parables (cockle, treasure in the field, the pearl, the net 13, unmerciful servant 18, 23–35, labourers in the vineyard 20, 1–16, the two sons 21, 28–32, wise and foolish virgins 25, 1–13), and also more than 50 verses of words of Our Lord (including parts of the Sermon on the Mount and some woes in ch. 23).

The Gospel of St. Luke with 1149 verses has taken over rather more than half of Mark's material (about 350 verses), cf. § 25, 4. With the exception of the so-called "great omission" (of 74 verses; 6, 45–8, 26), the omissions of Marcan material occur throughout Luke.[2] They fall into two categories: those for which Luke presents a parallel tradition from another source ("substitute passages"), and those where this is not the case.

1. The following passages of Mark are missing and there is no substitute for them: 1, 5–6 (introduction of the Baptist, his food and clothing); 2, 27 (a logion); 3, 20 sq. (Jesus out of his senses); 4, 26–29 (the seed growing by itself); 4, 33 (conclusion of the parable discourse); 6, 17–29 (end of the Baptist; but cf. Lk. 3, 19 sq.); 6, 45 to 8, 26 (walking on the lake, return to Genesareth and collective report of cures, clean and unclean, the Chanaanite woman, cure of a deaf mute, second multiplication of loaves, the Pharisees seek a sign [parallel Lk. 11, 29 sq.], leaven [cf. Lk.

---

[2] This presupposes that Lk. used Mk. in the form in which we have him; there is not universal agreement about this; see below n. 5

12, 1], blind man of Bethsaida); 8, 32 sq. (Peter rebukes Jesus); 9, 9–13 (words while descending the mountain); 9, 28 sq. (question of the disciples about the possessed boy); 10, 1–10 (words on divorce); 11, 12–14 (cursing of the fig tree); 11, 20–25 (withered fig tree); 13, 10 (logion); 13, 18 (logion); 13, 27 (logion); 13,32 (logion); 14, 3–9 (anointing in Bethany); 14, 38b–42 (Jesus prays the second and third time); 14, 51 sq. (the young man who fled); 14, 55–61 (false witnesses; but cf. Acts 6, 14 sq.); 15, 3–5 (silence of Jesus before the charge of the High Priest); 15, 16–20 (mocking the "king of the Jews"); 15, 34–36 ("last" word on the Cross).

Luke's reason for omitting some of these passages was certainly that he did not wish to swell his book by including two similar passages; thus the anointing in Bethany beside Lk. 7, 36–50; the parable of the seed growing by itself, 4, 26–29, beside the parable of the sower; the cursing of the fig tree beside Lk. 13, 6–9; 17, 6; the mocking of the king of the Jews beside Lk. 22, 63–65; 23, 11. A similar explanation perhaps applies to the "great omission," which is unquestionably very remarkable.

Luke passed over other passages because they were hard to understand or unimportant for his Gentile readers: 7, 1–23 (clean and unclean); 9, 9–13 (words while descending); 10, 1–10 (divorce),—or because they might cause offence: 3, 20 sq. (Jesus out of his senses); 7, 24–30 (Chanaanite woman); 7, 31–37 (cure of the deaf mute); 8, 22–26 (cure of the blind man); 8, 32 sq. (Peter rebukes Jesus); 11, 12–14 20–25 (cursing of the fig tree); 13, 32 (Jesus does not know); 15, 34 ("last" word of Jesus).

2. All the other omissions of Marcan material are replaced by parallel traditions from another source: Mk. 1, 16–20 (calling of the first disciples): Lk. 5, 1–11 (rich haul of fish); Mk. 3, 22–30 ("Beelzebub discourse"): Lk. 11, 14–23; 12, 10; Mk. 4, 30–32 (parable of mustard seed): Lk. 13, 18 sq.; Mk. 6, 1–6 (rejection of Jesus in Nazareth): Lk. 4, 16–30; Mk. 9, 42–48 (on scandal): Lk. 17, 1 sq. (partly); Mk. 9, 49–50 (saying about salt): Lk. 14, 34 sq.;

Mk. 10, 11–12 (unlawfulness of divorce): Lk. 16, 18; Mk. 10, 31: Lk. 13, 30; Mk. 10, 35–45 (Jesus and the sons of Zebedee): Lk. 22, 24–27 (partly); Mk. 12, 28–34 (the greatest commandment): Lk. 10, 25–28; Mk. 13, 15–16: Lk. 17, 31; Mk. 13, 21–23 (false Messiahs): Lk. 17, 23; Mk. 13, 33–37 (concluding parable): Lk. 12, 35–40; 19, 12 sq.; Mk. 14, 27–31 (prophecy of Peter's denial): Lk. 22, 31–34. Probably we must also regard as substitute passages from another tradition Lk. 4, 1–13 (temptation of Jesus) for Mk. 1, 12 sq., and Lk. 23, 32 sq. 39–43 (the two thieves) for Mk. 15, 27 32 b.

Luke treated Mark's history of the Passion with great freedom, making twelve transpositions, omitting Marcan material (e. g., 15, 16–20), and inserting traditions which he found in other (probably oral) sources (cf. Lk. 22, 14–23 31–33 36–38 43 sq.; 23, 6–16 27–31 40–43; 24, 13–53).

There is more peculiar material in Luke than in the others: 548 out of 1149 verses. In addition to an ample history of the Infancy extending to 132 verses (1, 1 to 2, 52), he has a considerable number of narratives and very much discourse material. Among the narratives are five accounts of miracles (the rich haul of fish 5, 1–11; the widow's son of Naim 7, 11–17; the deformed woman 13, 10–17; the dropsical man 14, 1–6; the ten lepers 17, 11–19), also the sending out of the 70 (72) disciples (10, 1 sqq.), the visit of Jesus to Martha and Mary (10, 38–42), Jesus staying with Zachaeus the chief of the publicans (19, 1–10) etc. The story of the Passion has also been enriched with a number of details: Jesus sweats blood in the garden of Olives (22, 43 sq.), Jesus before Herod (23, 6–16), the women on the way of the Cross (23, 27–31), the words to the good thief (23, 40–43). In the history of the Resurrection Luke goes his own way with the appearances of Jesus to the disciples at Emmaus and to the Twelve in Jerusalem (24, 13–53).

In the discourse material which is peculiar to Luke are 16 parables including some of the most beautiful: 1. The two debtors (7, 41 sq.), 2. The good Samaritan (10, 30–37), 3. The importunate friend (11, 5–8), 4. The rich farmer (12, 16–21), 5. The lord returns (13, 35–38), 6. The barren fig tree (13, 6–9), 7. Places at table (14, 7–11), 8. The building of a tower (14, 28–30), 9. Waging war (14, 31 sq.), 10. The lost drachma (15, 8–10), 11. The prodigal son (15, 11–32), 12. The unjust steward (16, 1–12), 13. The rich spendthrift (16, 19–21), 14. Slaves who must always work (17,7 to 10), 15. The unjust judge (18, 1–8), 16. The Pharisee and the publican (18, 9–14). The other words of Our Lord cover about 55 verses.

The content of the parts peculiar to Luke is so rich that it has been suggested that in addition to the Gospel of St. Mark, Luke also used as a source another complete Gospel (cf. § 25, 4).

The Gospels of Matthew and Luke also share a considerable amount of material which does not appear in Mark (about 235 verses). This material may be listed as: (1) three narrative passages (the temptation of Jesus Mt. 4, 1–11 = Lk. 4, 1–13; the ruler of Capharnaum Mt. 8, 5–13 = Lk. 7, 2–9; 13, 28–30; deputation from the Baptist Mt. 11, 2–19 = Lk. 7, 18–35), but in these the stress is laid upon the words of Jesus; (2) seven parables (building a house Mt. 7, 24–27 = Lk. 6, 47–49; leaven Mt. 13, 33 = Lk. 13, 21; the lost sheep Mt. 18, 12–14 = Lk. 15, 4–7; the great supper Mt. 22, 1–14 = Lk. 14, 15–24; the thief in the night Mt. 24, 42–44 = Lk. 12, 39–40; loyal and disloyal servant Mt. 24, 45–51 = Lk. 12, 42–48; the talents Mt. 25, 14–30 = Lk. 19, 11–27) and (3) a large number of sayings of Our Lord. According to the so-called "Two Sources Theory" this material which is shared by Matthew and Luke, comes from a written source.

2. The agreements of the Synoptics

1. A very considerable part of the material occurs in all three or at least in two of the Synoptics ("triple tradition" or "double tradition").

a) The greater part of the narrative material is common to all three Synoptic Evangelists. From this fact some scholars (for example Spitta, Bussmann) have inferred that these passages preserve a tradition which is common to all three Gospels and which was committed to writing at an early date; though this tradition did not yet present a complete life of Jesus, nevertheless the material which belongs to it forms a coherent whole; the work mentioned where and when the incidents happened, and provided the framework for the presentation of the Gospel story (so it is called the Synoptic Foundation Work); it is preserved most faithfully in the Gospel of St. Mark.

b) A considerable part of the discourse material is reproduced in all three Gospels (the substance of the Parable and eschatological discourses, the five conflicts in Galilee and the five in Jerusalem, the "Beelzebub" discourse); there are 235 verses of discourse material common to Matthew and Luke.

2. There is far-reaching agreement also in the arrangement of the material. All three Gospels follow in essentials the same outline for the Gospel story. The preaching and baptism of John is the signal for Jesus to leave the quiet of Nazareth. After the arrest of the Baptist Jesus begins his public ministry in Galilee where he calls his first disciples. This is the principal scene of his work, particularly Capharnaum and its surroundings, and the Sea of Galilee. After some time he sends twelve disciples on a travelling mission in Galilee, and afterwards withdraws to the neighbouring pagan territory of Tyre and Sidon and the Decapolis, though he does not undertake a proper ministry there (this episode in the life of Jesus is missing only from Luke; it is connected with the "great omission"). Peter's confession at Caesarea-Philippi and the first prophecy of the Passion, which take place at this time, mark a turning point in the work of Jesus. He now goes through Galilee and by Perea and Jericho to Jerusalem for the Pasch of the Passion, and in the course of this journey makes

two more prophecies of the Passion (Luke has placed most of the material which is peculiar to him in this journey: "the great insertion" or "the travel document"). The events of Holy Week are described almost identically by the three Evangelists. Matthew and Mark agree entirely in their history of the Passion itself: Luke has made some slight additions to their accounts.

Even within this common outline there are striking agreements. All three Evangelists have the five Galilean disputes in the same order, except that Matthew puts the first three into ch. 9 and the other two into ch. 12. From Mt. 14, 1 onwards Matthew and Mark have their common incidents in the same order.

3. In the same way many passages also show close agreement in wording. In their citation of Is. 40, 3 they agree neither with the Hebrew text nor with the LXX, but they agree among themselves (Mk. 1, 3 par). When reporting the cure of the man sick of the palsy (Mk. 2, 1–12 par), all three use the same parenthesis: "But that you may know that . . .", (he saith to the sick of the palsy) "I say to thee . . ." Rare and unusual words and expressions occur in all three or in two of them: οἱ υἱοὶ τοῦ νυμφῶνος (the sons of the bridegroom = the wedding guests) Mk. 2, 19 par; ἐπίβλημα (piece of cloth) Mk. 2, 21 par; τὸ πτερύγιον (little wing = pinnacle of the temple) Mt. 4, 5 par; ὁ ἄρτος ὁ ἐπιούσιος Mt. 6, 11 par. There are even occasions where whole sentences or groups of sentences correspond almost word for word, e. g., Mt. 3, 7b–10 12 = Lk. 3, 7b–9; Mt. 11, 4–6 = Lk. 7, 22 sq.; Mt. 20, 21–23 = Mk. 10, 37–40; Mt. 15, 32 = Mk. 8, 2–3; Mt. 11, 27–29 = Lk. 10, 21 sq.; Mk. 12, 43 sq. = Lk. 21, 3 sq.; Mt. 23, 37–39 = Lk. 13, 34 sq.; Mt. 24, 32 sq. = Mk. 13, 28 sq.

So among the three Synoptics there is very extensive agreement in content, arrangement, and often even in wording. This agreement is particularly striking when they are compared with the Gospel of John which not only has little material in common with the Synoptics—the correspondences are closest in the history of the Passion—but also follows a different outline from them (cf. § 28, 4).

3. The divergences between the Synoptics

Mention has already been made of the material which is peculiar to individual Evangelists; we must now deal with the divergences within the common material.

a) There are divergences in the arrangement of the material. The 235 verses which Matthew and Luke have in common are mainly grouped by Matthew—together with other material—into the six great synthetic discourses; in Luke on the other hand this material is scattered through ch. 3–17 (19) in a large number of fairly small masses which often have a historical setting. The parable chapter is common to all three (Mt. 13, Mk. 4, Lk. 8), but it contains seven parables in Matthew, while Mark has three and Luke one. Matthew adds to the eschatological discourse other similar material (warning and parables), which is paralleled in Lk. 12 17 19. The rejection of Jesus by Nazareth is placed by Matthew and Mark at the end of the Galilean ministry (Mt. 13, 53–58; Mk. 6, 1–6), while Luke puts it at the beginning (4, 15–30). See also what was said above about the "substitute passages" of Luke.

b) There are also striking divergences within the individual passages. In Matthew the Our Father has seven petitions, but in Luke it has only five, and to some extent the two records differ in wording. Mark and Luke speak of the cure of a possessed man at Gadara (Mk. 5, 1–20; Lk. 6, 28–39), a blind man at Jericho (Mk. 10, 46–52; Lk. 18, 35–43), and of one animal at the entry of Jesus into Jerusalem (Mk. 11, 1–7; Lk. 19, 28–35); in all these cases Matthew speaks of two. Mt. 5, 1–12 has eight Beatitudes, Lk. 6, 20 to 26 has only four—and four woes. Mt. 4, 1–11 and Lk. 4, 1–13 differ in the order of the temptations. Words of Our Lord which occur in both Matthew and Luke are occasionally reported so differently that the meaning is changed, e. g., Mt. 23, 27 sq. ("whited sepulchres") and Lk. 11, 44 ("sepulchres that appear not").

In broad outline that is the situation. How is it to be explained?

II. ATTEMPTED SOLUTIONS

4. *Historical review*

It was only in the mid-eighteenth century that theology met a "synoptic question", and thorough research into it did not begin until the early nineteenth century. It is true that the four Gospels were compared with one another in antiquity and the Middle Ages, but this was done merely in order to harmonize their accounts. In this connection St. Augustine broke new ground with his book *De consensu evangelistarum,* composed in 400 A.D.[3]; he tells us that he wrote it as an apologetic work in reply to the pagans' allegation that the Gospels contain contradictions. Only in passing does he deal with the question of their interdependence; he considered that they wrote in the order Matthew, Mark, Luke and John, and assumed that each used his predecessors. This book by St. Augustine exercised a strong influence on subsequent work. Until the end of the Middle Ages his harmonistic solutions were accepted without discussion.

It is impossible to recount here the history of synoptic studies since they began with the eighteenth century Enlightenment; it must suffice to classify the more important suggested solutions and to outline the situation at the present day. Unquestionably synoptic scholarship has done much work—and on particular points valuable work—but up to the present no real solution has

[3] H. J. Vogels, *Des hl. Augustinus Schrift "De consensu evangelistarum"* (BSt XIII 5, 1908).

been found which explains the highly complex facts of the synoptic problem, nor is it likely that such a solution will be found. Yet it should not be forgotten that the effort expended has been fruitful in a better understanding of the Gospels.

1. The theory of a primitive Gospel (*Urevangeliumshypothese*) suggests that the Synoptics all drew their material from a primitive Aramaic Gospel which has been lost. This theory was due to G. E. Lessing (1778), and was very much developed by J. G. Eichhorn (1794 and 1804). According to him the Synoptics are independent of one another; they all drew upon a comprehensive primitive Gospel which contained the entire life of Christ; this Gospel was composed in Aramaic by a disciple of the Apostles about 35 A.D., and was subsequently translated into Greek and revised a number of times; the Evangelists made use of these revisions when composing their Gospels.

This theory is entirely unsuccessful and has long since been abandoned; the narrations of "many" in Lk. 1, 1 sq. could not be simply editions of such a work. If the theory were true there would be much greater uniformity than there is among the synoptics in content, presentation and language, for example, the primitive Gospel could not have had two genealogies.

A variety of this theory was elaborated in a number of writings between 1923 and 1942 by the Catholic scholar P. Vannutelli; according to him the Hebrew (primitive) Matthew (*Urmatthaeus*), or a Greek version of it, was used by our three Synoptics independently of one another, with Mark and Luke replacing some of its material with matter from other sources.

2. The Diegeses Theory (*Diegesenhypothese*) of Friedrich Schleiermacher (1817) makes our Synoptics draw their material from a large number of pre-existing booklets which were later amplified, and each of which embraced a particular theme (miracles, discourses, parables, etc.). He understands (1832) the words of Papias on Matthew to mean that the Apostle Matthew

made in Hebrew a collection of the discourses of Jesus (logia collection), which was afterwards translated into Greek and revised a number of times; one of these recensions survives as our Gospel of St. Matthew.

Schleiermacher's hypothesis must also be rejected, for it cannot explain the similarity of structure and order of incidents among the Synoptics.

3. The Tradition Theory (*Traditionshypothese*) says that all three Evangelists got their material from oral tradition; none of them depends on the book of the other. The father of this theory was J. G. Herder, the poet and theologian. He attributed (1796 to 1797) the striking resemblances among them to dependence on the Gospel preaching, which, though not committed to writing, had acquired a fixed outline at an early date (c. 35–40 A.D.), as we may infer from the mission sermons of the Apostles in Acts. Herder's idea was taken up and amplified by others.

J. C. L. Gieseler (1818) was the creator of the developed Tradition Theory. Resolutely discarding the hypothesis of a primitive Gospel, he believed like Herder that there was a clearly defined oral Gospel; frequent repetition had automatically produced a stereotyped outline of the Gospel story, within which the most important words and deeds of Jesus would be presented in much the same language by all the narrators and teachers. The transplanting of this Gospel from Palestine to the Greek world naturally wrought changes, for specifically Jewish points were sacrificed to the need for stressing matters of less obscurity and of greater importance for Gentiles. Each of our Synoptic Evangelists presented the material according to his own appreciation and style, Matthew reporting his own preaching, while Mark and Luke recorded the preaching of Peter and Paul respectively. In the past the Tradition Theory was popular even among Catholic exegetes, (for example, Bisping, Kaulen, Knabenbauer, Cornely). At present P. Gaechter is one of its few defenders.

This theory correctly emphasizes that for a fairly long time the Gospel material was transmitted only by words of mouth, so that the stories of particular incidents and even the words of Jesus himself assumed a certain fixed form. This idea, which is quite correct, was the starting point of the modern Form Critics (cf. § 27).

The Tradition Theory explains the divergences among the Synoptics; for variations were inevitable if they drew exclusively upon orally preserved material which with time must have assumed widely varied forms. But it does not satisfactorily account for the striking agreements in wording and arrangement.

The close agreements among the Synoptics can only be explained either by recourse to a primitive Gospel behind them—and this is decisively ruled out—or by literary interdependence.

4. The Use Theory (*Benutzungshypothese*) says that the Synoptic Evangelists depend on one another. It has varied in form according to the view taken of the order of the composition of the Gospels. According to J. L. Hug (1808; cf. § 2) the Gospel of St. Matthew (composed in Greek by the Apostle) is the oldest; Mark had it before him, and Luke used both Matthew and Mark. J. J. Griesbach (1783), on the other hand, held that Luke used Matthew, and that Mark is an excerpt from Matthew and Luke.

This theory explains the common material and the uniform order of a large number of events, but it does not account for the parts which are peculiar to each Gospel. For this reason modern exponents of the theory generally combine it with the Tradition Theory, deriving the peculiar parts of each Gospel from oral tradition. This combined Use and Tradition Theory, which may assume a number of forms, is a special favourite of modern Catholic exegetes (for example, Cladder, Meinertz, Dausch and Innitzer). All agree that Luke depends on Mark, but there is no unanimity about the relation in which Mark and Luke stand to Matthew. In spite of the testimony of Papias the general view is that Mark depends largely on Matthew (Cladder in particular maintains this); the material which Luke shares with Matthew is variously ascribed either to Matthew or to oral tradition.

Recently Léon Vaganay, professor at Lyons, has produced a very complex theory which, in his judgment, does justice both to early Christian tradition and to the textual evidence more satisfactorily than the form of Two Sources Theory which some Catholics profess.

He considers the (pure) Tradition Theory quite inadequate. His Work Theory has attracted widespread attention among Catholics. It may be outlined as follows:

1. The oldest real Gospel was the Aramaic Gospel of St. Matthew which Papias attests (Aramaic primitive Mt.; denoted by M); in its Greek version (Mg) it is the foundation of our canonical Gospels of Matthew, Mark and Luke, that is, of their triple tradition. It was composed not later than 50 A.D., but it is not an independent work of the Apostle Matthew, for it contains in concise form the preaching or catechesis of Peter in Jerusalem; its most prominent traits are universalism and opposition to Pharisaism.

The main arguments to show that Mg is the foundation of our canonical Gospel are:

a) The agreements of Matthew and Luke against Mark (see above p. 227) support the assumption that they used another written source besides Mark. The number of positive agreements between Matthew and Luke is small, but the number of negative correspondences (absence of characteristic Marcan traits) is much greater.

b) This applies also in those cases where the language of Matthew—and occasionally also of Luke—is more archaic than that of Mark. But Vaganay admits that there are few such passages.

He also grants that there are not many passages where Mark is secondary as compared to Matthew and Luke.

This line of argument naturally presupposes that there is no literary dependence between Matthew and Luke. Vaganay proves this at length (and convincingly).

2. Aramaic primitive Matthew was translated into Greek at a very early date (between 50 and 55 A.D.); the extensive (to some degree verbal) agreements of the three Synoptics (see above p. 227) can be explained only by the use of a common Greek original. In this translation certain changes were made (omissions, retouchings, transpositions), since otherwise the Gospel which was made for the Jewish-Christians would have been unsuitable for other communities.

The material of Mg—except the history of the Passion—was divided into five short books, each containing both narrative and discourse; but they all ended with a fixed formula ("When he had ended these words", etc.).

These books may be recognized most clearly in Matthew (see above p. 133), but they may also be seen in Mark and Luke, though Mark omitted the discourse part of the first book (Sermon on the Mount); the absence of the Sermon on the Mount is also a proof that Mark cannot be the foundation of Matthew and Luke. Since the passages of the *traditio triplex* do not always occupy the same position in all three Synoptics, there must have been transpositions, and these are most numerous in Matthew. For example, he transposed the second and third of the five books (putting the mission discourse before the parable discourse), while Mark and Luke follow the original arrangement of Mg.

3. The material which is shared by Matthew and Luke only *(traditio duplex)* derives from a second written source which consisted principally of discourses (logia), and which from the outset was considered a supplement to M (S [source]); originally composed at Jerusalem in Aramaic, probably by Matthew, it was.

soon translated into Greek (Sg). Luke made some changes in its language and inserted it with some omissions between 9, 51 and 18, 14 of his Gospel as a *Livret hors serie* (supernumerary booklet, i. e., additional to the series of five books). Matthew, on the other hand, used it as its author intended, and blended its material with the material of the *traditio triplex*. It also was divided into five books. One hundred and seventy-nine verses which are common to Matthew and Luke are from this source, as is a great part of the proper material of both Matthew and Luke.

Vaganay emphasizes strongly that S has nothing in common with Q of the Two Sources Theory, neither in nature nor in compass. Its vocabulary and style were not uniform, for it consisted of passages which had been shaped and preserved in different places. Its homogeneity lay in the fact of it being a supplement. Mark did not know S.

4. The Gospel of St. Mark derived partly from the preaching of Peter in Jerusalem (Mg), "not, however, from a written account, but through the verbal reminiscences of an original text *(un texte oral)* which always remains more or less clinging in his memory"; it also derived from the Roman preaching of the Prince of the Apostles. The Semitisms and the archaic traits in Mark are derived from the preaching in Jerusalem, the graphic traits (= Pi [Pierre]) from the preaching at Rome.

5. The canonical Gospel of Matthew is the best representative of M (Mg), and for this reason we are justified in calling it St. Matthew's Gospel. Matthew took the *traditio triplex* from Mg (he also knew Mark, and used it as a subsidiary source). That is why he is so colourless. Vaganay admits, however, that he made a number of transpositions of Mg, and often abbreviated his originals, and also that his language and style are less Semitic than those of Mark. But he preserved many archaisms which have disappeared from Mark as well as the Sermon on the Mount.

6. For the *traditio triplex* Luke used Mark as his main source and

Mg. as a subsidiary source; he depends mainly on Sg for the passage 9, 51 to 18, 14. He is quite independent of Matthew.

This hypothesis shows the acumen of its author, but does not give a convincing solution of the synoptic problem. It is examined in detail by Levie, Schmid, Léon-Dufour (see above) and Ph. Vielhauer (ThLZ 1955, 647–652). Only the main points which are urged against it can be outlined here:

1. According to Vaganay the Two Sources Theory respects the evidence of Papias only as far as it fits the theory; but the same objection may be urged against himself. In reality his theory makes Mark—and not Matthew—the best representative of primitive Matthew, for a) the wording of Mg is preserved most accurately in Mark's archaisms; b) Mark retains the arrangement of the material more faithfully than Matthew; c) he omits only two major passages from Mg, while Matthew amplified the material of Mg by incorporating Sg.—Neither Papias nor any other early writer says that M reproduces the preaching of Peter in Jerusalem.

2. Vaganay's theory would make the Gospel of St. Mark a literary enigma. He can give no satisfactory psychological explanation of the typical "mixture of Modern and Archaic which characterizes Mark". Mark is intelligible only as an original unit, not as a conflation of two sources.

3. Vaganay infers from Matthew that M (Mg) was divided into five little books, each containing both narrative and discourse. However, the stereotyped concluding formula (7, 28 sq. etc.) marks not the end of a book, but the transition from discourse to a new narrative. 3—4 do not make a literary or thematic unit; the unity is rather between 5–7 (Jesus as teacher) and 8–9 (Jesus as miracle worker)—and moreover they are enclosed by two sentences (4, 23; 9, 35) of the same meaning, which sum up the theme; we are then shown by the selection and sending out of the Apostles in ch. 10 that in both activities Jesus was gaining helpers

and followers. Vaganay reckons ch. 23 as a narrative—but it is a discourse! It is impossible to trace the five books in Mark where discourse material is not prominent; so it cannot be proved that Mark eliminated the Sermon on the Mount. The grouping of Matthew material is due to the author of the canonical Gospel.

4. Document S is as obscure as Q, the logia source. Vaganay has not proved that it was originally conceived as a supplement to M, nor that it was divided into five books.

A special form of the Use Theory is the Two Sources Theory, which is almost universally accepted by present day non-Catholic scholarship; it is also accepted by many Catholic exegetes with modifications to take account of the tradition of the early Church. In view of its popularity it must be treated at length.

5. The Two Sources Theory; state of the question at present

This theory may be summarized as follows: Mark is the oldest of the four canonical Gospels, and is the foundation of the two more recent ones, Matthew and Luke. These two Evangelists also made use of a second written source; this source, whose existence is conjectured, consisted almost entirely of words of Jesus (sayings, discourses and parables), and so is called "the logia source", the "discourse source", or the "collection of sayings" (Q = Quelle, the German word for source).

The two later Evangelists drew the greater part of their material from these two sources. In addition each of them made use of special sources, either oral or written.

In 1835 the celebrated scholar Karl Lachmann in an article in ThStK inferred from the arrangement of the material which is common to all three Synoptics that Mark must be the source and foundation for Matthew and Luke; as he expressed it: "Mark is the thread of Ariadne for the first three Gospels." Not only do Matthew and Luke reproduce all of Mark's material, "they also follow his arrangement, and if they break it by insertions, they return to it; it is only with reference to Mark that they may be compared" (Wellhausen).

Lachmann, however, did not develop his thesis in detail. A priest in Saxony, Gottlieb Wilke, and Christian Hermann Weisse, a Leipzig philologist, did this in 1838, working independently of each other. At that time, however, the *Life of Jesus* by David Friedrich Strauss, which had appeared in 1835, was at the height of its popularity, and their work attracted little attention. They first obtained recognition through the work of G. H. A. Ewald, an orientalist of Goettingen, in 1849. In the second half of the century the chief exponents of the Two Sources Theory were H. J. Holzmann, C. Weizsaecker, and Bernh. Weiss; they helped to make it widely known, and developed it more thoroughly. In 1889 the results of their work were brought together by P. Wernle.

A. The priority of Mark. Lachmann's thesis is: When Matthew and Luke reproduce the same material, they have the same arrangement of it when they agree with Mark; when they diverge from Mark, they diverge from each other.[4] In the case of Luke, when he reproduces material taken from Mark, he retains Mark's order, with few exceptions. There are only three cases, outside the history of the Passion and Resurrection, where Luke changed Mark's arrangement of the material: (1) In 4, 41 he has conflated Mt. 3, 11 with Mk. 1, 34. (2) The summary of Mk. 3, 7–12 precedes the selection of the Twelve; Lk. 6, 17–19 makes it follow the selection; his purpose is to have an audience for the Sermon on the Mount (Lk. 6, 20 sqq.). (3) In Mk. 3, 31–35 the mother and brethren of Jesus seek for him before the parable discourse; Luke places this incident at the end of the parable discourse, because it forms a good conclusion—the parable of the hearing of

---

[4] Cf. the two lists in RQ 39 (1931) 43 sqq. where the content of Mk. appears in order, and the parallel passages of Mt. and Lk. are noted alongside.

the word (Lk. 8, 4–18) is followed by praise of those "who hear the word of God and do it" (8, 19–21). In all the other cases where he seems to depart from Mark's order, he has omitted the Marcan passage and replaced it elsewhere with similar or parallel material from another source (cf., e. g., Mk. 3, 23–30: Lk. 11, 17–23; the so-called "substitute pericopae," see above n. 1).

So, except for a number of omissions of greater or lesser extent, Luke has incorporated Mk. 1, 2 to 14, 16, and has incorporated it in the same order; there are only three noteworthy exceptions, and they are easy to explain.—On the history of the Passion and Resurrection see above n. 1.

The dependence of Luke on Mark is further proved by the fact that all the non-Marcan material is put into Mark's framework as insertions. This happens in the following places:

1. the "lesser insertion" Lk. 6, 20 to 8, 3 between two passages taken from Mk. 3, 13–19 (selection of the Twelve) and 4, 1 sqq., (parable discourse).

2. the "greater insertion" (the "travel document") Lk. 9, 51 to 18, 14 between the passages of Mk. 9, 42–48 (50) (scandal) and 10, 13–16 (blessing of the children; Mk. 10, 2–12 is omitted). Lk. 9, 51 takes the place of Mk. 10, 1 (departure to Perea). Cf. the second prophecy of the Passion Mk. 9, 32–34; Lk. 9, 43–45: third prophecy of the Passion Mk. 10, 32–34; Lk. 18, 31–34.

3. An insertion Lk. 19, 1–28 between Mk. 10, 46–52 (Bartimaeus) and 11, 1–10 (entry into Jerusalem).

4. An insertion Lk. 19, 39–40 between Mk. 11, 1–10 and 11, 12.

5. In 3, 1 to 5, 11 Luke has skillfully interspersed non-Marcan material with the Marcan original (Mk. 1, 2–44).

So we may conclude that the Gospel of St. Luke contains the greater part of Mark together with non-Marcan material, but its fundamental outline is that of Mark. It is only in the first and last chapters that he has interwoven the Marcan and non-Marcan material more or less thoroughly; elsewhere he put the non-Marcan material at particular points of Mark's text in two major blocks and two smaller insertions.

In the case of Matthew, he has eighty-five passages in common with Mark, of which seventy-eight are the same order in both Gospels. From Mt. 14, 1 = Mk. 6, 14 onwards the arrangement of the common material in the two Gospels is identical. It is possible to explain the seven departures from Mark's order; they are:

1. Four reports of miracles (Mk. 1, 40–45; 4, 35–41; 5, 1–20; 5, 21–43). They all appear in Matthew's miracle cycle (Mt. 8–9), and so have been taken from their Marcan context in order to compose this cycle. After this cycle Matthew reports no other miracles before ch. 14, for the cure in 12, 22 is identical with 9, 32–34.

2. Two passages which concern the twelve Apostles: The selection of the Apostles (Mk. 3, 13–19) and the instruction to them (6, 7–11). Matthew includes these and other words of Our Lord in one of the great synthetic discourses of his Gospel (ch. 10), which follows the miracle cycle.

3. Mk. 1, 22 = Mt. 7, 28 sq. (admiration of the people at the doctrine of Jesus): in both Gospels it follows the first reference to (Mk.) or report of (Mt.) the preaching of Jesus.

Having adopted Mark's material and sequence, Matthew inserts the non-Marcan discourse matter wherever it fits:

1. The Sermon on the Mount (Mt. 5–7) takes the place of the first preaching in the synagogue (Mk. 1, 21), and it ends (Mt. 7,28 sq.) with the same comment (Mk. 1, 22) on the admiration of the hearers. So the cure of the possessed man in the synagogue (Mk. 1, 29–34) and the departure of Jesus from Capharnaum (Mk. 1, 35–38) had to be omitted; the cure of Peter's mother-in-law etc., (Mk. 1, 29–30) was transferred to the miracle cycle (Mt. 8, 14 to 17).

2. The discourse when sending out the Apostles (Mt. 10) corresponds to the discourse when sending out the Twelve in Mk. 6, 6–13. Matthew has here created a great synthetic discourse by

incorporating the material of the discourse to the seventy disciples (Lk. 10, 1–12) and other similar words of Jesus.

3. The parable discourse in Mt. 13 corresponds to Mark's discourse in 4, 1–34: to Mark's material Matthew adds parables from other sources so as to make a large discourse containing seven parables.

4. The instruction to the disciples (Mt. 18) is a collection of individual passages where Jesus teaches his Apostles what their attitude should be. In addition to Mk. 9, 33–37 (= Mt. 18, 1–5: ambition) and Mk. 9, 42–48 (= Mt. 18, 6–9: scandal), Matthew also introduces materials which Mark does not mention at all, and which it is difficult to parallel from Luke.

5. The denunciation of the Pharisees (Mt. 23) is an expansion of Mark's short warning against the Scribes (12, 38–40) into a great synthetic discourse, which brings together all the warnings and woes on the Scribes and Pharisees (cf. E. Haenchen: ZThK 1951, 38–63).

6. The discourse on the Second Coming has been amplified with kindred material (Mt. 24 = Mk. 13), which replaces the short ending of Mk. 13, 33–37.

7. In accordance with the system on which he was grouping the material, Matthew placed the miracle cycle immediately after the Sermon on the Mount (Jesus as teacher and miracle worker!). He included in it three accounts of miracles which are not found in Mark (the ruler of Capharnaum 8, 5–13; cure of two blind men 9, 27–31, and of a dumb man 9, 32–34 [= a doublet of 12, 22–24]).

The miracle discourse is followed immediately by ch. 11 which is entirely composed of non-Marcan material (almost exclusively discourse matter); this material is also reproduced by Luke, but in different contexts. Matthew then records the fourth and fifth Galilean conflicts (12, 1–14 = Mk. 2, 22 to 3, 6), and thereafter faithfully follows Mark's order—with the exception of the selection of the Apostles, which he had already narrated in ch. 10.

Outside the great synthetic discourses Matthew contains other non-Marcan material, which, according to its extent and nature is either interspersed among pericopae from Mark, or is inserted into the passages which are taken from him.[5] As examples of the former we may mention, in addition to ch. 11, 12, 38–42 (the Pharisees seek a sign); 17, 24–27 (Temple tax); 20, 1–16 (labourers in the vineyard); 21, 28–32 (the two sons); 22, 1–14 (the marriage feast); 27, 3–10 (the end of Judas); 27, 62–66 (watch at the sepulchre); 28,9 sq. (appearance of the Risen Christ to the women); 28, 11–15 (bribery of the guards). There are examples of insertion in § 24, 3; cf. also 3, 7–10 12 14 sq.; 4, 1–11; 12, 43–45; 24, 26–28; 27, 19 24 sq. 51 b–53; 28, 2–4.

When both Mark and Q deal with a particular matter—which is not very often—Matthew uses both of them, unlike Luke: in the section on the Baptist Mt. 3, 1–12, he follows Mark for the first six verses, but the preaching of penance and the acknowledgment of the Messias (v. 7–12) are almost word for word from Q. Like Luke Matthew takes his account of the Temptation from Q, but at the end he adds a sentence from Mark's account ("angels came and ministered to him") (Mt. 4, 1–11). The discourse at the sending out of the Apostles (Mt. 10, 1 sqq.) was composed from Mark and Q in the following manner: Mt. 10, 1 = Q (Lk. 9, 1); Mt. 10, 9 sq. = Mk. 6, 8 sq. + Lk. 9, 3; Mt. 10, 11 = Mk. 6, 10; Mt. 10, 12–13 = Q (Lk. 10, 5 sq.); Mt. 10, 14 = Mk. 6, 11; Mt. 10, 15 sq. = Q (Lk. 10, 12 + 3). In this discourse Mark and Q spoke first of entering the house—where they are to abide—and then of the city to which their message is directed; Matthew juxtaposed the two parallel passages, and so was compelled to make changes (v. 11 "city or town" instead of "house" of the original; v. 4 "house or town" instead of "house" of the original; v. 14 "house or city" instead of "city" of the original). In the "Beelzebub discourse", Mt. 12, 22 to 28 is from Q (Lk. 11, 14–20; only v. 25 c is from

[5] J. Schmid p. 25 sq. gives a complete list (covering 38 cases) of Mt.'s additions to pericopae of Mk.

Mk. 3, 25); Mt. 12, 29 = Mk. 3, 27; Mt. 12, 30 = Q (Lk. 11, 23); Mt. 12, 31 = Mk. 3, 28 sq.; Mt. 12, 32 = Q (Lk. 12, 10). The parable of the grain of mustard seed (Mt. 13, 31 sq.) is from Mark 4, 30–32, but it contains some elements from Q (Lk. 13, 18 sq.: a tree; dwell in the branches).

Matthew and Luke quite often abbreviated Mark's material by compressing many sentences and eliminating details which seemed to them superfluous; there is a list of such shortenings in important matters in J. Schmid, 28 sq.; cf. also Bussmann I 85 sqq.; III 8 sqq, and Larfeld 35 sqq.

Was there a smaller proto-Mark *(Urmarkus)* before our Gospel of St. Mark? This question is keenly discussed by the exponents of the Two Sources Theory. A fairly large amount of Mark's material does not occur in Luke; this missing material is largely preserved by Matthew, yet even he has some minor omissions of Marcan material (see above n. 1). Where these passages of Mark deliberately omitted by Matthew and Luke or were they absent from the copy of Mark which these Evangelists used? The answer to this question is not unanimous, but according to Schniewind the theory of a proto-Mark is gaining ground. The various attempts to outline proto-Mark accurately or to reconstruct its wording have not reached any generally accepted conclusion, nor is it likely that they will do so. To take Bussmann as an example, he says that Mark existed in three separate forms: the original form—which he calls the basis of the three Synoptics— was used by Luke; it was followed by a first recension by an unknown hand, which amplified the material, and this was used by Matthew; finally a Roman Christian made a second recension which is identical with our Gospel of St. Mark, so that Mark is the latest of the three synoptic Gospels.[5a]

B. The logia—or discourse—source (Q).

Matthew and Luke share about 235 verses which are missing

[5a] On the Proto-Mark Theory cf. V. Taylor, *Mk.,* 68–72.

from Mark (two-elevenths of Matthew's text, of Luke one-sixth);
they occur almost exclusively in discourses. The Two Sources
Theory explains this fact by saying that Matthew and Luke
used not only Mark but also a second source whose material was
mainly discourse. Theoretically there are two other possibilities;
that either Matthew or Luke used the other, or that they both
drew upon oral material. But both these hypotheses must be discarded. Matthew and Luke diverge so considerably in some of
their common material that one can hardly have used the other;
indeed they differ so much in general—we have only to think of
the history of the Infancy and of the appearances of the Risen
Christ—that they must be independent of each other. Neither
can oral tradition be the source of their common material, for it
would not account for their word for word agreement in much
of this material. This argument is strengthened by the presence of
double traditions or "doublets" in both Gospels, that is, they report sayings of Jesus twice—generally in a somewhat different
form, but identical in substance—once in the part taken over from
Mark and once in the parts which only Matthew and Luke have,
e. g., Mt. 5, 29 sq. (from Q) = Mt. 18, 8 sq. (from Mk. 9, 43 45
47): scandal; Mt. 10, 38 sq. (from Q; Lk. 14, 27; 17, 33) = Mt.
16, 24 sq. (from Mk. 8, 34 sq.); carrying the cross; Mt. 12, 39
(from Q; Lk. 11, 29) = Mt. 16, 2 4 (from Mk. 8, 12): sign of
Jonas; Lk. 8, 16 (from Mk. 4, 21) = Lk. 11, 33 (from Q; Mt. 5,
15): light under the bushel; Lk. 9, 23 (from Mk. 8, 34) = Lk. 14,
27 (from Q; Mt. 10, 38): carrying the cross.

Since this postulated common source of Matthew and Luke
does not survive, attempts have been made to reconstruct it. Such
attempts have been made by P. Wernle, A. Harnack, G. H. Mueller, W. Bussmann and E. Hirsch, but their reconstructions differ
considerably, and none of them has gained general acceptance
among the upholders of the Two Sources Theory. Such reconstruction is extremely difficult and at best is practicable only up

to a point for the following reasons: 1) Since each Evangelist also has material peculiar to himself, it is impossible to define with certainty what exactly is derived from Q. It is unlikely that both copied out the Discourse Source entirely; so it must have contained more than 235 verses. 2) Much of the matter which Matthew and Luke share shows such divergences that one may doubt whether it does come from a common source. For this reason Bussmann splits Q into two discourse sources of fairly equal length, an older source originally composed in Aramaic, and containing only logia, and a later source composed in Greek. He ascribes to the latter the passages where Matthew and Luke agree (almost) word for word; the other passages he attributes to the Aramaic source; he suggests that this source underwent several recensions in Greek, and that Matthew and Luke had differently worded copies.

However, most exponents of the Two Sources Theory still postulate a discourse source composed originally in Aramaic, but they believe that it underwent a number of Greek recensions in different places, and so was changed (especially by additions). They say that Matthew and Luke had different forms of this Greek edition. In modern times a number of exponents of the theory favour not a single written source, but a stratum of tradition which grew differently in different places (for example, Dibelius).

The exponents of the Two Sources Theory all—except E. Hirsch—agree that the common source of Matthew and Luke was a collection of sayings (logia and parables) and not a Gospel properly so called, like Mark. In the history of the Passion and Resurrection and of the Infancy, Matthew and Luke have no common material which does not also appear in Mark. Q contained a few narratives, but only such as served as starting points for Our Lord's words and were adopted for this purpose (cf. Mt. 4, 1 sqq.; 8, 5 sqq.; 11, 2 sqq.; 12, 22 sqq.; 8, 19; 12, 38; 18, 21 and the parallel passages in Lk.).

Yet Q was not a shapeless collection of words and discourses of Our Lord without a connecting thread. Everything indicates that "it contained a certain arrangement of the material, and the foundations of a chronology."[5b] It opened with the preaching of the Baptist followed by (the Baptism of Jesus, the proclamation that he was Messias and) the temptation of Jesus; then came the Sermon on the Mount. It ended with eschatological words of Jesus. The order of the intervening material cannot be established with certainty, but it covered the discourse about the Baptist, instructions to the Apostles for their mission, warnings to the Apostles, woes on the impenitent cities, exultation of Jesus, conflicts with his opponents (Beelzebub discourse, sign of Jonas), woes to the Pharisees and Scribes, and the prophecy of judgment on Jerusalem.

So source Q was not an historical narrative, but a collection of sayings, discourses and parables of Jesus, designed to serve catechetical rather than missionary purposes. "It is not surprising that sayings and discourses of Jesus were collected for their own sake; indeed when one recalls Jewish practice at that time, such a collection is *a priori* probable, and it is confirmed by the language of the Christians, who from the beginning distinguished words and deeds of Jesus; cf. Acts 1, 1; Lk. 24, 19" (Harnack).

In general those who uphold the Two Sources Theory assume that Matthew has remained closer to the wording, Luke to the order of the individual passages of Q.

The question of the relation between Mark and Q has been keenly discussed since Wellhausen (1905). He regards Mark as older, while Harnack favours the priority of Q; at the present day Q is generally taken to be older than Mark. Some critics try to demonstrate that Mark knew and used the Discourse Source, reproducing the sayings of Jesus in abbreviated form (for example, J. Schniewind).

[5b] V. Taylor, *The Order of* Q: JThSt NS 4 (1955) 27–31.

But Matthew and Luke also have each a considerable amount of peculiar material.[6] Does this derive from oral tradition or from other (lost) written sources? Most exponents of the Two Sources Theory assume that a small part of the peculiar material both of Matthew and of Luke comes from Q, for presumably neither of them incorporated all of Q into his book. Beyond this there is no unanimity. They are more inclined to recognize a further written source for Luke than for Matthew. Streeter, for example, considers that the peculiar material of Luke reproduces a real Gospel of about 400 verses without the history of the Infancy. He says that Luke differs so much from the other two Synoptics in the history of the Passion because he conflated this Gospel first with Q (to make Proto-Lk.)[7], and afterwards with Mark to produce our Gospel of St. Luke. Streeter would also refer to a documentary source the material which is peculiar to Matthew. Bussmann and Hirsch[8] say that the peculiar material of both Evangelists is from one documentary source, but they each reconstruct this source quite differently. These and other attempts only serve to show the impossibility of giving a final answer to the question. From Luke's testimony we know that "many" before him had made attempts to narrate "the things which have been accomplished among us", so he was in a position to use quite a number of written sources (Lk. 1, 1 sq.).

6. Synthesis of the results

This sketch of the most important attempts at solution illustrates the difficulty and complexity of the Synoptic Problem. No fully

---

[6] See the lists in Larfeld p. 153–157; 162–178, and Bussmann III p. 89 sqq. 145 sqq.

[7] Streeter's elaboration of the Two Sources Theory into a Four Sources Theory has found support only in English speaking countries. It is explained in Grobel p. 67–121. Cf. also M. Gilmour, JBL 67 (1948) 143–152 (unfavourable to it).

[8] It would be useless to elaborate their Source Theories; they have met with little approval. *Fantastic* is the word to describe Hirsch's theories.

satisfactory solution of the problem has yet emerged, and it is unlikely that such a solution will be reached. Nevertheless there is certainty on some fundamental points about the literary relations among the Synoptic Evangelists.

1. Our Greek Matthew depends on Mark and not vice versa. The tradition of the early Church made Mark the record of the preaching of Peter, and not an extract from Matthew. The brevity of St. Mark's Gospel is principally due to the absence of the history of the Infancy and of much discourse material. Would Mark deliberately have omitted the history of the Infancy and the great discourses of Matthew? Such a supposition is absurd. Furthermore, in the narrative passages which he shares with Matthew, Mark is the more verbose and more primitive. This primitive character may so be recognized in many other places. "Hence Matthew generally incorporated the accounts of Mark into his narrative; in his first half he made many rearrangements, but in his second half he kept to the order of his original. This Marcan material was then enriched by many additions of greater or less extent, of which the longest is the Sermon on the Mount. Matthew frequently makes changes in Mark's text by reproducing him freely, abbreviating him, or improving his style" (J. Sickenberger).

2. Luke also depends on Mark. There is virtual unanimity on this to-day. It is established by arguments which are substantially the same as those used to prove the dependence of Matthew on Mark (especially the order of the common pericopae; cf. § 25, 4). Furthermore, Luke's description of his predecessors (1, 1 sq.) applies perfectly to Mark, the companion and hermeneut of Peter. It is not easy to see why he omitted the material of Mk. 6, 45 to 8, 26. Luke often improved on Mark's style, and made the text easier to understand.

So Mark is the oldest surviving Gospel composed in Greek.

3. There is no direct literary dependence between Matthew and Luke. The non-Marcan material which they share goes back to a

common written source, for much of it shows such striking correspondence of wording and style that it cannot derive from oral tradition.

The independence of the two Evangelists from each other is established by the following considerations:

a) If one Evangelist used the other it is unconceivable that he should have entirely passed over the matter which is peculiar to the earlier Gospel: we need only think of the parables of Our Lord. It would also be difficult to explain the variations in the history of the Infancy and the Resurrection, for they are such as to make harmonizing very difficult. If Luke depended on Matthew it would be impossible to explain why he never adopted within a pericope or a series of pericopae material which Matthew has and Mark lacks. If one Gospel depended on the other the similarity would necessarily be much greater than it actually is.

b) The non-Marcan material which they share cannot have been taken by one Evangelist from the other, for they differ in their arrangement of it and sometimes in their wording. Thus, for example, it is inconceivable that Matthew should have been Luke's source for the non-Marcan material which they both reproduce; if that were the case, Luke would have resolved Matthew's artificial groupings into small units and put them at different points in his Gospel. It may often be demonstrated that Luke has the original context of a discourse while Matthew places it according to his system of grouping. Moreover, in a number of cases Matthew has united the independent accounts of Mark and Luke, so he cannot be a source of Luke. Furthermore, the sharp divergences in part of the common material can be explained only if both Evangelists drew upon a written source which they had in somewhat different forms.

This conclusion is not impaired by the numerous agreements of Matthew and Luke against Mark. These agreements, which in any case are of little real importance, may be satisfactorily explained in a number of ways; we may think of their use both of the common source and of Mark, of the independent adoption by both Evangelists of the same method of treating Mark, of the influence of oral tradition which at that time was still alive, and of subsequent harmonizing by copyists (see especially J. Schmid).

4. The common source of Matthew and Luke consisted principally, but not exclusively, of discourse material (discourse source, collection of sayings). To a small extent its material coincides with the content of Mark (story of the Baptist, temptation, sending out of the Twelve, parable discourse, Beelzebub discourse, etc.). Generally speaking, the wording of the common source is preserved better in Matthew, the order in Luke. Since Matthew and Luke use their common source with freedom, reconstruction of its extent, wording and outline is possible only within modest limits. It is impossible to say whether there is a literary relation between Mark and Q, or which of them is older; there are, however, many indications that Q is older than Mark, but all the indications are that Mark did not know Q.

5. Who was the author of Q? The tradition of the early Church unanimously ascribed the first Gospel to the Apostle Matthew. This unanimity is understandable only if the common source of Matthew and Luke is identical with the logia book which Papias tells us was composed by the Apostle Matthew. At a very early date a number of Greek versions of this book were made (as Papias also attests); for in view of the frequent verbal agreements of Matthew and Luke, the Aramaic work cannot have been their common source. So the book whose existence Papias attests has been absorbed into our canonical Gospel of St. Matthew. Thus the following scheme results:

Aramaic Logia book
of Matthew

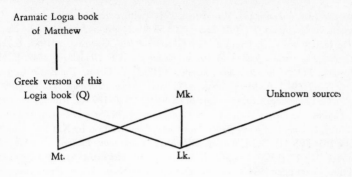

Greek version of this
Logia book (Q)   Mk.   Unknown sources

Mt.   Lk.

§ 27. FORM CRITICISM OF THE SYNOPTIC GOSPELS

M. Dibelius, *Die FG des Ev.*, Tuebingen 1919, ²1933. Idem, *Zur FG der Evv:* ThRdsch NF 1 (1929) 185–216. Idem, *Die Botschaft von Jesus Christus,* Tuebingen 1935. K. L. Schmidt, *Der Rahmen der Geschichte Jesu. Literarkritische Untersuchungen zur aeltesten Jesusueberlieferung,* Berlin 1919. Idem, *Die Stellung der Evv in der allgemeinen Literaturgeschichte:* Eucharisterion, Festschrift H. Gunkel II (1923) 50–134. Idem, *Fondement, but et limites de la méthode dite de la "FG" appliquée aux Évangiles:* RHPhR 18 (1938) 1–26. R. Bultmann, *Geschichte der syn Tradition,* Goettingen 1921, ²1931. Idem, *Die Nachforschung der syn Evv²,* Giessen 1930. M. Albertz, *Die syn Streitgespraeche. Ein Beitrag zur FG des Urchristentums,* Berlin 1921. Idem, *Die Botschaft des NT.* I Die Entstehung der Botschaft, 1. Halbbd.: Die Entstehung des Ev, Zollikon-Zuerich 1947. G. Bertram, *Die Leidensgeschichte Jesu und der Christuskult. Eine feine Untersuchung,* Goettingen 1922. E. Fascher, *Die fg. Methode. Eine Darstellung und Kritik,* Giessen 1924. L. Koehler, *Das fg Problem des NT,* Tuebingen 1927. P. Fiebig, *Der Erzaehlungsstil der Evv,* Leipzig 1925. Idem, *Rabbinische FG und Geschichtlichkeit Jesu,* Leipzig 1931. B. S. Easton, *The Gospel before the Gospel,* New York 1928. J. Schniewind, *Synoptikerexegese und fg.* Forschung: ThRdsch NF 2 (1930) 161–189. V. Taylor, *The Formation of Gospel Tradition,* London 1933. R. H. Lightfoot, *History and Interpretation in the Gospels,* London 1935. O. Perels, *Die Wunderueberlieferung der Syn in ihrem Verhaeltnis zur Wortueberlieferung,* Stuttgart 1934. K. Grobel, *FG und syn Quellenanalyse,* Goettingen 1937. A. Richardson, *The Gospels in the making: an Introduction to the recent Criticism of the Synoptic Gospels,* London 1938. C. H. Dodd, *History and Gospels,* London 1938. F. V. Filson, *Origins of the Gospels,* New York 1938. E. F. Scott, *The Validity of the Gospel Record,* New York 1938. E. J. Redlich, *Form-Criticism: its Value and Limitations,* 1939. D. W. Riddle, *The Gospels: their Origin and Growth,* Chicago 1939. F. Buechsel, *Die Hauptfragen der Synoptikerkritik,* Guetersloh 1939 (BFchTh 40, 6). E. Schick, *FG and Synoptikerexegese,* 1940 (NtA XVIII, 2–3). W. Manson, *Jesus the Messiah. The Synoptic Tradition of the Revelation of God in Christ: with Special reference to Form-Criticism,* London 1943. L. J. McGinley, *Form-Criticism of the*

Synoptic Healing Narratives, Woodstock 1944 (with extensive bibliography). P. Benoit, *Réflexions sur la "fg Methode":* RB 53 (1946) 481–542 (with a fairly complete bibliography). J. Jeremias, *Die Gleichnisse Jesu,* Goettingen ³1954. K. H. Schelkle, *Die Passion Jesu in der Verkuendigung des NT,* Heidelberg 1949. L. H. Marshall, *FC and its Limitations,* London 1942. F. C. Grant, *The Earlist Gospel,* New York 1943. R. Morgenthaler, *FG und Gleichnisauslegung:* ThZ 6 (1950) 1–17. G. Lindeskog, *Logia-Studien:* StTh 4 (1950) 129–189 (on Mt. 13, 12 par). T. Taylor, *The Origin of the Marcan Passion-Sayings* NTSt 1 (1954/55) 159–167. J. Huby, *L'évangile et les évangiles.* New (expanded) edition by X. Léon Dufour, Paris 1954 (VS 11). D. M. Stanley, *Didache as a Constitutive Element of the Gospel-Form* CBQ 17 (1955) 336–348. J. Jeremias, *Die Gleichnisse Jesu,* 3rd (revised) edition, Goettingen 1954. G. Schille, *Das Leiden des Herrn. Die ev Passionstradition und ihr Sitz im Leben:* ZThK 52 (1955) 161–205. W. Marxsen, *Redaktionsgeschichtliche Erklaerung der sog. Parabeltheorie:* ibid. 255–271. H. Riesenfeld, *The Gospel Tradition and its Beginning. A Study in the Limits of "Formgeschichte",* London 1957.

1. The method of Form Criticism

SINCE about 1920 there has been—besides literary criticism—a new approach to the Synoptic Gospels, known as Form Criticism (in German *Formgeschichte,* Form History). The founders and most important exponents of this new method are Martin Dibelius and Rudolf Bultmann. The German name *Formgeschichte* is due to Dibelius, who in 1919 published an outline of this method under the title *Formgeschichte des Evangeliums;* in his choice of a name he was influenced by Eduard Norden, who had added to his book *Agnostos Theos* (1913), the sub-title *Untersuchungen zur Formgeschichte religioeser Rede (Researches into the history of the forms of religious oratory).*

Numerous efforts had been made to develop the literary criticism of the Gospels, starting from the Two Documents Theory which almost all non-Catholics accepted; but these attempts to reconstruct Proto-Mk. or a fundamental Synoptic Book had reached no satisfactory conclusion. It was therefore natural to try to go back behind the written sources and to complement literary criticism by investigating the oral tradition.

The new method has this aim. It investigates the history of the

Gospel material while it was preserved orally, from the first shaping of tradition to its being committed to writing in our Gospels: it also studies the laws which governed this process. By this approach it tries to elucidate the steps of the tradition, that is, to determine whether the individual parts of our Gospel present primary or secondary tradition or editing by the Evangelists.

Form Criticism starts from the principle that among people who are not literate the expression of traditional material falls into a small number of fairly definite categories, which have their own laws of style and form. According to Dibelius it is the function of Form Criticism to put into relief in their original purity the forms which the Gospel material assumed when the shaping of tradition began, to explain the origin of these forms, and to trace their development up to the time when they were committed to writing. Bultmann places the stress on investigating this process of development, and so calls his book "History of the Synoptic Tradition" (*Geschichte der syn Tradition*).

Form Criticism is not an entirely new method. The novelty lies in its thoroughness and in its application to the Synoptic Gospels. Fundamentally it transfers to the New Testament the investigation of categories which Hermann Gunkel († 1932) applied to some parts of the Old Testament (especially Genesis and Psalms). In addition to Gunkel—who in turn was influenced by J. G. Herder (cf. § 26, 4)—the main contributors to the development of this method were the theologian G. Heinrici and the philologists E. Norden and P. Wendland (*Urchristliche Literaturformen,* cf. § 30).

The application of Form Criticism to the Synoptic Gospels rests on two premises:

1. The Gospels are not literary works of a single mould which owe their existence to the personality of a writer; they consist of a considerable number of small units or single passages (single stories and single sayings) which redactors have forged into a

unity with the minimum of change. The Evangelists did not give shape to unformed tradition; they brought together into a unity the Gospel material which had been handed down in fairly set forms. Only the framework into which they set the individual passages is their own work, and this framework is an artificial creation.

At the same time as Dibelius' programme appeared, Karl Ludwig Schmidt produced an extensive work: *Der Rahmen der Geschichte Jesu (The framework of the history of Jesus)*. In this work the connections of the individual passages with one another and the whole framework of the Gospel story were subjected to literary criticism. It really cleared the ground for Form Criticism of the Gospels. Schmidt concludes that only the individual stories and individual sayings are traditional; the framework in which they are set and the joining of the pericopae and sayings into groups are the work of the Evangelists who compiled them. "The most primitive traditions to be handed down about Jesus were pericopae, that is, individual scenes and sayings which in general were preserved within the community without details of their time or place." Broadly speaking the history of the Passion is the only part to which this does not apply. Only fragmentary pieces of the itinerary of Jesus are preserved by Mark where he introduces the pericopae. "The first narrators of the stories about Jesus devoted no or almost no attention to the setting, but were concerned only with the pericopae in isolation, since this isolation is taken for granted in the Liturgy."

2. The Gospels are not biographies, but testimonials to faith. They do not describe the life of Jesus in the sense of following the exterior and interior development of his life and work, depicting his personality and demonstrating his significance in history. They are connected with the primitive Christian proclamation of faith, and in so far as they are a record of Jesus' words and deeds they tell of the works, teaching, and Passion of the God-sent Saviour

of men; they thereby make his work as Saviour live before the eyes of the Christian community. But they lack almost entirely what is indispensable to a biography: the origin and youth of the hero, his spiritual development, the depiction of his character, a theme, and a chronology. In the Gospels we find no description ("pen portrait") either of the person of Jesus or of the people around him. This holds true also of the Twelve Apostles; we know their names, but we have not enough information about them to give their forms flesh and blood. Only Peter is to some extent an exception, yet it is not clear why Jesus made him head of the Twelve in spite of his volatile character. We are not even told what motives induced Judas to betray Jesus; when Luke says (22, 3) that Satan entered into Judas, that is a theological, not a psychological explanation.

Moreover, the Synoptics do not give a chronology of the life of Jesus; from what they say it is quite impossible to ascertain how long the ministry of Jesus lasted—whether less than a year, a full year, or several years. Only Luke, the "historian" among the Evangelists, tells us that Jesus began his public ministry at about (!) 30 years of age, and that his precursor came to the Jordan in the fifteenth year of Tiberius (Lk. 3, 1 23).

Topographical information is also scarce. The place where many incidents happened is indicated, if at all, only in vague terms (house, mountain, desert, strand).

The absence of such details is due to the fact that the Gospels do not aim at satisfying pious curiosity; their purpose is to proclaim in Jesus of Nazareth the Saviour of the world, and to establish, deepen and widen faith in him. Consequently the Gospels are not so much the work of individual Evangelists; to some extent the Christian community from whose life they sprang speaks in them. Their authors write to serve the community and its needs. That is why these books are so impersonal; the prologue to Luke is the only place where an author mentions himself.

As was already explained, Form Criticism aims at reconstructing the origin and history of the traditional passages which are collected in the Gospels. It has first of all to disentangle these passages from the framework in which they are set, and to arrange them according to categories or forms. This task presupposes that these passages of the Gospel tradition have their "living source" in the primitive Christian community, that they grew from expressions of the community's life and needs, and that they had definite and fairly settled forms. The expression *Sitz im Leben* (*living source*) was coined by Gunkel; it does not refer to the life of Jesus, but denotes "the conditions in which the first unconscious shapings of the Gospel material took place" (Dibelius). In the case of the Gospel tradition the "living source" is the religious life of the primitive Christian community with its manifold expressions, or we might say that it is the primitive Christian preaching, understanding preaching in its widest sense to include missionary preaching, sermons (including paraenesis), and catechetical instruction; to some extent it would also cover apologetics, polemics and the discipline of the community.

The entire traditional material of the Gospels falls into two main groups: narrative material (stories about Jesus) and discourse material (words of Jesus); cf. Acts 1, 1 (ποιεῖν τε καὶ διδάσκειν).

It is comparatively easy to classify the discourse material. Bultmann, who uses both formal and material criteria, divides the words of Our Lord into three great groups: 1) Logia or wisdom sayings, proverbs, in which Jesus speaks as teacher of wisdom (e. g., Mt. 6, 19–34; 12, 34; 24, 28). There are parallels to most of them in Jewish wisdom literature (Proverbs, Ecclesiasticus). 2) Prophetic and apocalyptic sayings. In them Jesus proclaims the coming of the Kingdom of God, issues a call to penance, promises salvation to those who are prepared for it, and pronounces his woes on the impenitent (e. g., Mt. 5, 3–9; 11, 5 sq.; 13, 16 sq.; 23 par). 3) Law sayings and rules for the community. The former, like the prophets of old, attack the ostentatious piety of the Jews (e. g., Mt. 5, 21 sq. 27 sq. 33–37; 6, 2–18; Mk. 7, 15), the latter give rules for the conduct of the community and for the mission (e. g., Mt. 10 par; 16, 18 sq.; 18, 15–22). To these three Bultmann adds a fourth group of words where the person of Jesus plays an essential role; he calls them "I sayings", and reckons under this heading those sayings in which Jesus speaks of his coming (e. g., Mk. 2, 17; Mt. 10, 34–36 40; 11, 18 sq. par) or of his person (e. g., Mt. 11, 25–30; 16, 18 sq.; 18, 20; 19, 28–30; 28, 18–20). He enumerates a fifth group of similes of Jesus (metaphors, comparisons, similes properly so called, parables, stories told as examples). He also includes in the discourse material traditional passages which contain a saying of Jesus within a narrative framework; these he calls *apophthegmata* because they resemble in structure the *apophthegmata* of Greek literature. In a considerable number of them he considers that the context in which the words are spoken is a later addition. He divides these *apophthegmata* into controversies and instructions (e. g., Mk. 2, 1 to 12 23–28; 3, 1–6; 7, 1–23; 10, 17–22; 12, 28–34) and biographical apophthegmata (e. g., Mk. 6, 1–6; 10, 13–16; Lk. 9, 57–62).

Dibelius deals with the discourse material under the heading of Paraenesis, "because to his mind the sayings of Jesus were originally collected for paraenetic purposes, in order to give the community advice, watchwords and precepts in the words of the Master." He does not review all the traditional sayings, but generally confines himself to passages which have some sort of imperative content. On purely formal grounds he divides them into six groups: 1) Wisdom sayings *(sententia, gnome)*, 2) Simile,

3) Parable narrative, 4) Prophetic call (beatitudes, woes, eschatological proclamation), 5) Short commandment, 6) Long commandment (joined to a reason like Mt. 5, 44 sqq.; 6, 25 sqq., to a promise like Mt. 6, 2 sqq., or to a threat like Mt. 5, 29 sq.; Mk. 9, 43 sqq.; Mt. 18, 1 sq.). In addition there are sayings which reveal the nature of him who has spoken these paraenetic words (e. g., Mt. 11, 25–30; 23, 34–39). A large part of these "traditional sayings" was collected in Q.

It is more difficult to analyse the narrative material into categories, and the two chief exponents of Form Criticism diverge widely at this point.

Bultmann brings most of the miraculous cures and the miracles of nature under the heading "miracle story", and the remainder of the narrative material under the heading "historical narratives and legends". He, therefore, classifies the material not on grounds of form, but from the point of view of content and historical criticism. The narratives where the chief feature is an authoritative saying of Our Lord rather than the miracle itself (e. g., on healing on the Sabbath or on the forgiveness of sins) are included by him under *apophthegmata*. He applies the name "legend" to those narrative traditional passages which have an edifying character but are unhistorical; but since he maintains that in the Synoptics historical narrative is strictly subordinated to legends, it is impossible in practice to distinguish the two categories.

Dibelius divided the narrative material into the following groups: 1) Paradigm, 2) Novelle, 3) Legend, 4) History of the Passion, 5) Mythus.

By paradigm he means short stories of the anecdote type which lead to a pointed utterance or an exemplary action of Jesus. Preaching was their "living source" and they served as illustrations or examples (hence the name). This type appears clearly defined, for example, in the cure of the lame man (Mk. 2, 1–12), the disciples plucking the ears of corn (Mk. 2, 23–28), the coin for the tribute

(Mk. 12, 13–17) the anointing in Bethany (Mk. 14, 3–9), and less clearly, for example, in the healing in the synagogue (Mk. 1, 23–37), the story of the rich young man (Mk. 10, 17–27), and the cleansing of the Temple (Mk. 11, 15–17). Because of their great antiquity the paradigms are fairly reliable as history.

Novellen are also self-contained single stories; they are distinguished from paradigms by a certain graphic breadth and by the employment of profane topics, the absence of edification as a motive, and the absence of any words of general application spoken by Jesus. They are intended principally to display the divine power of Jesus the miracle worker. Examples are the storm on the lake (Mk. 4, 35–41), the possessed man of Gerasa (Mk. 6, 1–20), and the feeding of the Five Thousand (Mk. 6, 35–44). Their "living source" is not preaching—they were too "worldly" for that—but missionary purposes, "to some extent as a substitute for preaching in a circle of hearers which is already accustomed to miraculous deeds of gods and prophets."[1] These have less historical value than the paradigms.

Legend is used by Dibelius, not as an historical term (= untrue story), but as a term of Form Criticism, meaning an edifying narrative of the life, works, and death of a holy person. He distinguishes two types—the aetiological cult legend which supplied legitimate status to cults or pious practices, and the personal legend whose object is the pious life and death of a holy person. The story of the Last Supper is an aetiological cult legend; so indeed is the whole history of the Passion and Resurrection. The personal legend, so far as the person of Jesus is concerned, is of little importance in the canonical Gospels; for they regard Jesus not as a saint-like man who is under the protection of God because of his piety and virtue, but as the Son of God, the Appear-

---

[1] Dibelius postulates a special class of narrators for the *Novellen,* but the "Teacher"—also—recounted them; cf. H. Greeven, *Propheten, Lehrer, Vorsteher bei Paulus: ZntW* 44 (1952/53) 1–43 (esp. p. 24, note 54).

ance of God in human form, and their aim is to report the divine message which he proclaims. The story of the finding in the Temple (Lk. 2, 41–50) is a personal legend; elsewhere legendary characteristics appear only in a few of the stories about Jesus. On the other hand there are in the Gospels a number of stories which show an interest in the Apostles and followers of Jesus; these must be regarded as personal legends: the haul of fish by Peter (Lk. 5, 1–11), the woman who anoints Our Lord's feet (Lk. 7, 36 to 50), Peter walking on the waves (Mk. 14, 28–31), Peter's profession in Mt. 16, 17–19, the story of Zachaeus, chief of the publicans (Lk. 19, 1–10) etc. Unlike paradigms and novellen, stories which belong to the category of legends cannot be recognized by their form; they are distinguished by the interests or motives which predominate in them.

The history of the Passion does not consist of a number of self-contained passages; it was formed and handed on at a very early date as a continuous account, though shorter than the account in the Gospel of St. Mark. Its "living source" is the preaching of salvation *(kerygma)* which it helped to complete or illustrate.

The Christ mythus, which appears very clearly in the Pauline Epistles (cf. especially Phil. 2, 5–11), enters only very little into the presentation of the life of Jesus. In the Synoptic Gospels there are only three narratives whose content can really be called mythical: 1. The miracle at the Baptism of Jesus; it originally signified the adoption of Jesus as Son of God: "Thou art (i. e., shalt be) my beloved Son" (Mk. 1, 9–11). 2. The temptation of Jesus by Satan, and the devil's controversy with Jesus (Mt. 4, 1–11 par). 3. The Transfiguration in which Jesus appears for a moment in the heavenly nature which makes him Son of God (Epiphany; Mk. 9, 2–8). "Mythical" motifs have also penetrated many *novellen*. Mark accepted them into his Gospel because they proved his Epiphany doctrine that Jesus who walks upon the earth is in reality the divine Son of God who reveals his real nature in his miracles. The "mythical" idea then penetrated the tradition of the words of Jesus, as may be seen especially in Mt. 11, 25–30; 18, 20; 28, 18–20.

As this survey shows, the two chief exponents of Form Criticism agree neither about the names nor about the identity of the categories. This largely reflects their different approaches. Dibelius is deductive and argues from the needs of the primitive Christian community to the categories in which the traditional material was first cast; Bultmann, on the other hand, begins by analysing the traditional material. Except for the *apophthegmata*, Bultmann's division and nomenclature may be accepted in essence as apt.

But the division of the narrative material is difficult. The only point which cannot be challenged is that the substance of the Passion story was from the beginning handed down as a continuous narrative and not in separate pieces. In the remaining narrative material, where the individual elements are very diverse in form and content, it is possible to discern with a certain amount of assurance at least some groups which can be regarded as special categories:

1. Short succinctly related stories which culminate in a significant and sharply pointed saying of Jesus. Bultmann calls them "controversies and instructions", and includes them under the *apophthegmata;* Dibelius calls them "paradigms" (exemplary stories). The use of the name "paradigm" has been attacked as unsuitable, on the ground that it has an established and much wider meaning in Greek literature. Dibelius, on the other hand, objects to the name "controversy", pointing out that the passages in question do not present controversies properly so called, for they usually contain only one statement and are designed to report an authoritative utterance of Jesus. So the category itself is clear, but the difficulty is to give it a name, for its "living source" cannot be established beyond dispute.

2. Graphically reported stories whose content is not a saying but a deed of Jesus, for example, a miracle. Dibelius calls them *Novellen* because, he alleges, their style is worldly and they do not aim at edifying; Bultmann simply calls them "miracle stories" because of their content. Here also a category with special stylistic characteristics can be recognized, but the name *Novellen* is unsatisfactory, for it assumes wrongly that because of their profane style they were not designed for use in preaching, but were formed and handed down by a particular class of narrators.

3. Bultmann has a further category which he calls "biographical apophthegmata"; Fascher suggests the name "anecdotes". They are closely related to the "controversies", and, like them, are a short framework for a saying of universal application by Jesus (e. g., Lk. 13, 31–33; Mk. 14, 3–9; 12, 41–44; Lk. 17, 11–19; 19, 1–10); the difference is that in the "controversies" the saying of Jesus is occasioned by a question, whereas in the biographical apophthegmata the saying arises from the situation. They are called biographical apophthegmata because they give some information about the life of Jesus. Bultmann says that they are best regarded as edifying paradigms used in preaching to give a vivid picture of the Master, and to encourage and console the community. Though these passages have not a strictly proper style, yet they can be brought together in one category. Bultmann considers them—along with the controversies and instructions—as part of the discourse tradition, because he regards most of their frameworks as unhistorical ("ideal scenes"). His assertion must be discarded. But it is correct to say that the biographical apophthegmata stand midway between discourse and narrative traditions.

Dibelius places the remaining narrative material in the categories "legend" and "mythus"; Bultmann speaks of "historical narrative" and "legend". But these categories are not clearly distinct. They each attach a different meaning to the term legend; for one it is a term of Form Criticism, for the other a term of historical criticism; what Bultmann calls legend, Dibelius calls mythus. Since this material is so varied and diverse, and since the form is very much subordinate to it, classification on grounds of form is impracticable; it can be classified only according to content.

The second aim of Form Criticism is to trace the history of the individual pieces of Gospel material from their first formation to the time when they were assembled and committed to writing in our Gospels.

Since these passages were transmitted orally for some decades it cannot be denied that they may have undergone certain changes (amplification and recasting). So we must begin from the latest written form of the tradition passages—in Matthew and Luke— and work back to their oldest original form. There are two useful means of doing this: 1) Certain principles may be observed in the treatment of Marcan and Q material by Matthew and Luke; we may therefore infer that these principles were operative also during the period of oral transmission. 2) There are analogies for this process in the transmission of proverbs, anecdotes and popular narratives.

This task is even more difficult than the separation of the individual passages or categories; there are two reasons for this difficulty: first the original forms are merely conjectural; they seldom appeared quite pure, for the formation of tradition did not take place according to inflexible laws. Furthermore in our Gospels individual pieces (for example, parables, accounts of miracles, conflict discourses) sometimes appear in various forms, and in many cases it can no longer be determined whether they got this form in the course of transmission or if it is due to the Evangelists. The same holds true also of the grouping of similar passages in the Gospels (groups of logia, parables, conflict discourses etc.). Even if the Evangelists were compilers and editors rather than authors, nevertheless, at least to some degree, they worked over the material which they received, and they arranged the pericopae according to a definite plan. One has only to think of Matthew who created great synthetic discourses and a miracle cycle, and who generally shortened the narrative passages (cf. § 24, 3).

Yet there can be no doubt that many traditional passages were notably modified in the period of oral transmission. That may be seen both in the discourse and in the narrative material.

To list first some passages of the discourse material, for changes of form were more frequent there: The saying about light, which is a question in Mk. 4, 21, appears as a statement in Mt. 5, 15; Lk. 11, 33. Of the six antitheses in Mt. 5, 21–48, three (divorce, revenge, love of enemies) have parallels in Lk. 16, 18 (Mk. 10, 11 sq.); 6, 27–35, but these parallels are not in the form of antitheses. In a number of cases the sense of Our Lord's words has been changed by being set in a different context. The advice to be reconciled in time with one's adversary in Mt. 5, 25 sq. has the sense of a rule of prudence, while in Lk. 12, 57–59 it is a graphically expressed call to conversion because of the judgment of God; cf. also Lk. 12, 3 with Mt. 10, 27. The saying "Whosoever shall lose (his life) shall save it" in Lk. 17, 33 (John 12, 25), appears with an explanatory addition "for my sake" in Mt. 10, 39; 16, 25; Lk. 9, 24, and "for my sake and the Gospel" in Mk. 8, 35. The saying of Jesus about giving his life as a redemption for many in Mk. 10, 45; Mt. 20, 28, appears in a very different form in Lk. 22, 27b; Luke's form is not so primitive, and probably comes from another tradition. The same is true of the "sign of Jonas" in Mt. 12, 38–40 compared to Lk. 11, 29 sq. There are important divergences between the two parables of the king's marriage feast in Mt. 22, 1–14 and the great supper in Lk. 14, 15–24; yet there can be no reasonable doubt that these are not two different parables, but one and the same parable in two forms, the divergence in form being due to oral tradition. A similar case is the parable of the entrusting of money; it appears in very different forms in Mt. 25, 14–30 (the talents) and in Lk. 19, 12–27 (ten minae), and the latter has preserved the primitive form more faithfully. It is often clear that the framework of the parables (description of the situation, concluding explanation) represents editing by the Evangelists. It is difficult to say whether particular parables have subsequently received allegorizing additions or allegorical explanations; it cannot be denied entirely (cf. Mt. 22, 6 sq.; 21, 35 sq.; probably also Mt. 13, 36–43 49–50).

In the case of the narrative material also many passages have received different stamps either from oral tradition or from the Evangelists. There are marked divergences between Matthew and Luke in their accounts of the ruler of Capharnaum Mt. 8, 5–13; Lk. 7, 1–10 and of the daughter of Jairus Mk. 5, 21–43; Mt. 9, 18–26; Lk. 8, 40–53. The stories of the feeding of the Five Thousand (Mk. 6, 34–44 par) and of the Four Thousand (Mk. 8, 1–40 par) are probably double accounts of one and the same event (Luke and John have only the first miracle of feeding, and a second is practically ruled out by John 6, 22 sq.). Mt. 9, 32–34 and 12, 22–24 are also parallel accounts (cf. Lk. 11, 14 sq.). In the story of walking upon the water, only Mt. 14, 28–31 has the episode of Peter sinking. In Mt. 21, 18–22 the fig tree withers immediately after the curse, in Mk. 11, 12–14 20 it is noticed only on the following day.

The account of the Temptation in Mt. 4, 1–11; Lk. 4, 1–12 differs from the account in Mk. 1, 12 sq. Only Mt. 16, 18 sq. reports the famous promise of Our Lord to Peter after his profession. In the case of the Transfiguration only Luke tells what was spoken about by Jesus and the two Prophets (9, 31). The account of the Last Supper in Lk. 22, 14–23 (and 1 Cor. 11, 23–25) diverges considerably from the account in Mk. 14, 22–25; Mt. 26, 26–29. In the story of the Passion Matthew, with minor additions, follows Mark's account; Luke on the other hand often goes his own way, making omissions and transpositions and introducing peculiar material which does not appear in the others

(e. g., Jesus before Herod 23, 6–16; the women of Jerusalem 23, 27–32; the penitent thief 23, 39–43). Luke also diverges notably from Mark and Matthew in the story of the happenings after the Resurrection.

Bultmann has examined closely the history of the transmission of the whole Gospel material; however, he is violently sceptical on the question of historicity[2], and this scepticism has led him to conclusions which have been widely rejected, as they deserved (cf. Fascher, Koehler, Taylor, Buechsel, Schick), and which have discredited Form Criticism in many people's eyes. According to him, most of the sayings received their formation on Palestinian territory, as their style and the parallels show, only a small part being formed on Hellenistic territory. Most of the wisdom sayings have corresponding forms in Jewish wisdom literature and in the Rabbinical writings. We must recognize, he says, that the Christian community attributed to Jesus many beautiful sayings which come from the treasury of Jewish wisdom sayings. We may, however, recognize genuine words of Jesus among the prophetic and apocalyptic sayings which proclaim the coming of God's Kingdom and issue a call to penance, though the Christian community (or its Prophets) produced many prophetic sayings and ascribed them to Jesus. The law sayings are exactly paralleled in the preaching of the ancient Prophets against exterior piety; in view of their radical nature they are evidently authentic sayings of Jesus, but "the sayings which contain rules for the conduct of the community and for the mission, are probably all creations of the community." Similarly most of the "I sayings" are creations of the community expressing their faith in Jesus, his work, and his fate. In most cases the parables must be regarded as genuine traditional material, but in the course of transmission many of them were amplified with allegorical elements, or were interpreted and explained as allegories (Mk. 4, 14–20; Mt. 13, 36–43);

. [2] Cf. his book: *Jesus*, Tuebingen 1951.

indeed some of them must be regarded as creations of the community (e. g., Mk. 12, 1–12; Mt. 25, 1–13). It is also highly probable that there are parables from Jewish tradition, which were ascribed to Jesus by the Christian community (thus Lk. 16, 19–31; 14, 7–11 12–14). The explanations which are joined to a number of parables as introduction or conclusion, are often due to oral tradition and do not fit the meaning exactly. The "controversies", instructions, and biographical apophthegmata mostly received their formation in Jewish territory; but in the vast majority of cases they present ideal scenes or community sayings (not reports of historical incidents); in them only the words of Our Lord—and not always they—can be considered authentic; they do, however, reproduce correctly the general character of the life and ministry of Jesus, since they are founded on actual recollections.

It is an axiom with Bultmann that Jesus wrought no miracles in the strict sense of the word, though he admits as a possibility that actual happenings may have provided a foundation for some of the stories of miraculous cures. Most of the miracle stories in the Gospel tradition are popular stories which have been connected with Jesus. The Old Testament may almost be ignored as a source for the Gospel miracle stories—at most 4 Kings 4, 42–44 for the feeding of the multitude. Miracles were ascribed to Jesus even by the Palestinian community, as we may see from certain sayings (Mt. 12, 28) and from those "controversies" which contain a miracle. But most of the miracle stories must be presumed to have a Hellenistic origin, for in Hellenistic territory Jesus was regarded as the Son of God walking on the earth. Some of the miracle stories were probably suggested by sayings of Jesus and were invented by the Christian community (Lk. 5, 1–11 out of the saying about "fishers of men"), or are simply stories of the time after the Resurrection which were put back into the real life of Jesus (Transfiguration, walking on the water).

Even the historical narratives have received a strong legendary colouring. The Baptism of Jesus is to be accepted as an historical fact, but the report of it is a legend telling of the consecration of Jesus as Messias. The confession of Peter, whose original ending is preserved only in Mt. 16, 17–19, is a story from the period after the Resurrection which has been put back into the life of Jesus. Bultmann assumes that the foundation for the story of the Passion was "an old historical account which related very briefly the arrest, condemnation by the Sanhedrin and by Pilate, the way of the Cross, and the Crucifixion (Mk. 14, 43–53a 65; 15, 1–5 15b 20b–24a 27 37). This was gradually amplified, partly by incorporating existing accounts, and partly by newly produced stories" (p. 302).

Dibelius does not deal with the entire traditional material of the Synoptics; in general he confines himself to the narrative material, and does not even deal with all of it; it is only from the point of view of paraenesis that he deals with short extracts from the discourse material. He differs from Bultmann in rejecting the latter's wholesale scepticism on the question of historicity[3]; he also takes a different view of the relevance of Form Criticism to the question of the reliability of the Gospels. Bultmann is dominated by the conviction that literary form is closely related to the life history of the primitive community, and that Form Criticism must therefore lead to factual judgments (on the authenticity of a saying, the historicity of an account etc.); he therefore pays special attention to the question whether a given passage was formulated on Judaeo-Palestinian or Hellenistic territory; he also argues against their historicity from parallels in Comparative Religion. Dibelius, on the other hand, considers that Form Criticism cannot decide whether a tradition is historical but he holds that it can provide a solid foundation for judgment

[3] It is instructive to compare his short book, *Jesus,* Berlin 1935 (Sammlung Goeschen), with Bultmann's book of the same name.

on questions of fact. In historical value he rates the paradigms highest; since they were a necessity even for the simplest preaching, they must have been created while eye-witnesses were still alive. On the other hand the very nature of *Novellen* renders them at best remote from the historical events, for these graphic stories were intended to exalt "the Lord Jesus" as miracle worker, and to display his superiority over heathen gods and heroes; and so when they were being created, there was always the danger of the penetration of foreign motifs, indeed of the adoption of totally unchristian stories. "Yet it would be impossible to explain the emergence of these stories at such an early date, unless Jesus had the reputation of having performed marvellous deeds of this kind." In the case of the legends Dibelius is inclined to grant them an historical kernel, but he stresses that these stories like to report the intervention of supernatural powers, and to transform plain human material with the polish of the miraculous.

2. Assessment of Form Criticism

This new method of treatment has quickly established itself in New Testament studies. It marks a notable advance on the one-sided literary criticism which long dominated non-Catholic Gospel studies, and it may be welcomed as a useful means of illuminating the dark period when the Gospel material was transmitted orally.[4]

On the other hand Form Criticism is still in its infancy, and its

---

[4] There have already been attempts to extend it to the other pieces of the NT writings which contain traditional material, i. e. Acts and the paraenetic parts of the Epistles. Cf. Dibelius, *Stilkritisches zur Apg.*: Eucharisterion, Festschrift fuer H. Gunkel 11 (1923) 27–49, and his survey: *Zur FG des NT* (except the Gospels): ThRdsch NF 3 (1931) 207–242, and also the commentary on Acts by Bauernfeind (cf. § 29) and E. Lichtenstein, *Die aelteste christliche Glaubensformel*: ZKG 63 (1950) 1–74; M. Dibelius, *Jakobusbrief*[2], 1956; D. G. Bradley, *The Topos as a Form in Pauline Paraenesis*: JBL 72 (1953) 238–246. N. A. Dahl, *Fg. Beobachtungen*

founders and chief exponents have come in for justified censure because of the way in which they have applied it. There is need, therefore, for a correct statement of the principles which should govern this method, and for a demonstration of its inherent limitations.

1. The first and most important premiss of Form Criticism is fundamentally correct: the synoptic Gospels are compilations. In them we must distinguish sharply between traditional material and redaction. Only the individual sayings of Jesus and the individual stories are traditional; they must be separated from the framework in which they are embedded, and must be treated by themselves. Only in this way can the original proper significance of a saying or of a narrative be established; exegesis according to the trend of thought, as it was practised in the past, is misleading.

Even if the pericopae are joined by commonly accepted expressions of time, the order in which they stand is not necessarily the chronological order of the incidents recounted in them. The clearest evidence of this is the fact that a number of pericopae have different settings in the individual Gospels; thus, for example, the healing of the leper Mk. 1, 40–45 appears elsewhere in Matthew (8, 1–4) and Luke (5, 12–16). The transition from one pericope to another is generally very indefinite (and, when, then, immediately, in those days, at that time), and to interpret these rigorously would be contrary to the Evangelist's intention; they are generally intended to be understood simply as transition formulae. Even in Mark pericopae are grouped according to content without reference to time or place (for example, the five Galilean conflicts 2, 1 to 3, 6). This applies not only to narratives, but also, indeed even

zur Christusverkuendigung in der Gemeindepredigt: NtlStudien, R. Bultmann, Berlin 1954, 3–9; E. Kaesemann, Das Formular einer ntl Ordinationsparaenese (1 Tim. 6, 11–16), ibid. 261–268; E. Lohse, vide ad § 50 (with literature on Paraenesis); W. Nauck, Freude im Leiden. Zum Problem einer urchristlichen Verfolgungstradition: Zntw 46 (1955) 68–80.

more, to sayings of Our Lord; it may be asserted that all the long discourses of Our Lord in the Synoptics—not excluding the eschatological discourse—are groupings of single sayings according to subject matter. There are, however, some exceptions, of which the most important is the history of the Passion; it may also be assumed that the incidents which Mk. 1, 21–38 reports actually happened on that Sabbath.

Topographical information, when it is given at all, is often as vague as the chronology: 'on the way', 'in a house', 'on the sea', 'on the mountain', 'in one of the cities'. Although Jesus performed many works in Chorozain (Mt. 11, 21; Lk. 10, 13), the New Testament does not locate a single one there. Only a comparatively small number of the pericopae tell where the incident happened (Nazareth, Capharnaum, Naim, Bethsaida, the villages around Caesarea Philippi, Jericho), and it cannot be presumed that these definite indications of place are subsequent additions. So the routes of the journeys of Jesus are not handed down, and it is impossible to reconstruct them.

However, "the framework of the history of Jesus" cannot be dismissed so easily. We must not regard the Evangelists as mere collectors who juxtaposed the words and acts of Jesus quite superficially, and joined them with meaningless connecting words. The outline of the life of Jesus which Mark created and Matthew and Luke adopted, must certainly be considered historical in substance: the imprisonment of the Baptist followed by the Galilean ministry of Jesus which centred around Capharnaum and the north shore of the lake, the lessening of the initial enthusiasm of the people, the withdrawal towards the North (the territory of Tyre, Sidon, and the Decapolis), the gradual revelation to the Apostles that he is Messias and his instructions to them, the journey by Perea to Jerusalem for the Pasch of the Passion.

But while preserving this framework the Evangelists inserted the traditional material with great freedom. We need only think of Matthew's grouping (cf. § 24, 3) and the gathering of most of the non-Marcan material into Luke's so-called "travel document" (cf. § 25, 4); above all the "general accounts" must be regarded as pure redaction (e. g., Mk. 1, 39; 3, 7–12; 6, 7 54–56; Mt. 4, 23–25; 9, 35 sq.; Lk. 4, 15 44).

For these reasons we are not in a position to write a life of Jesus in the sense of a biography which presents the course of its subject's external and interior development. But this does not mean that the entire tradition about Jesus disintegrates into isolated pieces with no inner connection. On the contrary, in all these individual sayings and stories the speaker and actor is he in whom, according to the belief of the primitive Christians, the time of salvation began. They all deal with the great theme of the New Testament: In Jesus of Nazareth the Messias has appeared on earth. And so the traditional passages which seem separate are joined by a strong bond into an inner unity.

2. The classification of the individual pieces of traditional material into categories or forms is a difficult task, as is shown by the divergent arrangements and nomenclature proposed by the various exponents of Form Criticism.

Classification is easiest and most secure in the case of the discourse material, and Bultmann's arrangement may be accepted as adequate. Here we are dealing with forms which for a long time have been fairly firmly set. The various forms which occur in the traditional material of the Gospels may be paralleled exactly in the Old Testament (especially the Prophets and the Sapiential Books) and in Rabbinical literature, and even up to a point among other nations.[5] In view of these parallels it is certain that these forms did not develop on Hellenistic soil, but that they were shaped by the primitive community in Palestine.

[5] For the parables see the exhaustive work of M. Hermaniuk: *La parabole évangélique. Enquête exégétique et critique,* Bruges-Paris 1947.

The classification of the narrative material is more difficult. Here it is not a question of sayings which can be expressed with great freedom, but of deeds and incidents in the life of Jesus which, for the narrators, belonged to the immediate past. Historical events cannot be shaped into clear-cut forms so long as the narrator feels tied to recollection or tradition. It would perhaps be better to regard the "apophthegmata" as discourse material, for their climax is a saying of Jesus; of the remaining material—to prescind from the "apophthegmata"—only the miracle stories can be marked off from the point of view of form as a distinct literary category.

Dibelius' choice of the name *Novellen* is unfortunate. It carries with it the unjustified suggestion that they were shaped and published by a particular class of narrators, and that they were designed to meet the needs of pious instruction, not to aid preaching.

The miracle stories have a superficial resemblance (in theme) to Jewish and heathen miracle stories, but this resemblance must not blind us to the profound differences. The Jewish and heathen miracle stories are intended to exalt the person of the miracle worker; the synoptic miracles on the other hand prove that the mission of Jesus is Messianic, and attest the beginning of the era of salvation in which, according to prophecy, illness, distress, and misery are to cease and liberation from sin is to become a reality (Is. 35, 3–6; Mt. 11, 4–6 par; 12, 28 par). A further difference is that bodily manipulations are almost entirely absent from the Gospel stories (only Mk. 7, 31–37; 8, 22–26), and the miracle is worked simply by the word of command of Jesus.

Here we touch a point which is of great importance for the correct application of Form Criticism. Many of its exponents use Form Criticism as a means of historical criticism; against them it must be strongly emphasized that the form of a traditional passage provides no foundation for a judgment concerning its historicity. The study of content must supplement the study of form; Form Criticism must be complemented by the study of facts.

On the other hand Form Criticism has put out of court the false idea of the narrow literary critics about degrees of reliability; they held that the historical reliability of the synoptic material varies according to the written source from which it has been drawn, for example, that the content of the two oldest sources Mark and Q is more dependable than the peculiar parts of Matthew and Luke. Since all the pieces of the synoptic Gospels derive from oral tradition, each must be treated in the light of the category to which it belongs, and the question whether it comes from this or that source is only of minor importance.

3. The ascription to the primitive Christian community of a really creative power is a serious defect in Form Criticism as it is applied by many of its exponents—notably by Bultmann and Bertram, and, less radically, by Dibelius; they maintain that certain parts of the synoptic Gospels were free creations of the community, or that motifs for their forming—especially for miracle stories or *Novellen*, and legends—were borrowed from Judaism and more particularly from Hellenism. According to them our synoptic tradition was formed outside Palestine (perhaps in Syria: Damascus and Antioch) in Greek by hellenized Jewish Christians who understood both Aramaic and Greek, in other words by believers who to a certain extent were under the influence of Hellenistic ideas.

Against this it must be emphasized vigorously that we may not exclude from the formation of tradition the eyewitnesses of the life and work, passion and death of Jesus. Luke says explicitly that the accounts of his predecessors, which he knows and uses, were guaranteed by those "who from the beginning were eyewitnesses and ministers of the word" (that is, of the proclamation of the Gospel), and he intends his own work to be a proof of all that his readers had learned (1, 1–4). Enough firsthand witnesses were still alive in the few decades during which tradition got its final shaping; we have only to think of Peter, James, and John, the "pillars" of the Church of Jerusalem (Gal. 2, 9) at the time of the Council of Jerusalem (cf. also 1 Cor. 15, 6).

It is false to ascribe the making of tradition to anonymous forces, to say that it was the community and the faith of the community which formed and handed on the tradition about Jesus. Creative power belongs not to a mass but only to individuals who tower over the mass.

In addition to the eyewitnesses an important role was played by missionaries (Evangelists, Acts 21, 8; Eph. 4, 11; 2 Tim. 4, 5) and teachers (1 Cor. 12, 28; Eph. 4, 11; Acts 13, 1; Rom. 12, 7; 1 Pet. 4, 11), that is, by those who had the charismatic offices of testifying to the word. Together with the eyewitnesses they provide a strong guarantee of the truth of the tradition concerning the words and deeds of Jesus.

The popular form of the synoptic narratives may be satisfactorily explained by the fact that they derive from men who belonged not to the world of letters but to the ordinary people.

So the testimony of faith which the Gospel tradition expresses has as its theme history itself (Cullmann).

§ 28. THE GOSPEL OF ST. JOHN

Commentaries: (a) J. Knabenbauer, [2]1906 (CSS). J. E. Belser, *Das Ev des Joh uebersetzt und erklaert,* Freiburg i. Br. 1905. F. X. Poelzl–Th. Innitzer, [4]1928 (cf. § 3, 9a). M.-J. Lagrange, *Év. selon S. Jean*[6], Paris 1936. F. Tillmann, [4]1931 (Bonner NT 3). A. Durand, [24]1938 (VS). A. Wikenhauser, 1949 (RegNT 4). — (b) Th. Zahn, [6]1921 (Zahn IV). A. Merx, 1911. W. Heitmueller, [3]1918 (GoettNT 4). A. Loisy, *Le quatrième év.: les épîtres dites de Jean*[2], 1927. F. A. Bernard, 2 vols., 1929 (ICC). A. Schlatter, *Der Evangelist Joh. Wie er spricht, denkt und glaubt*[2], Stuttgart 1948. W. Bauer, [3]1933 (Lietzmann 6). F. Buechsel, [5]1949 (NTDeutsch 4). E. Hirsch, *Das vierte Ev,* Tuebingen 1936. E. C. Hoskyns-Davey, *The Fourth Gospel*[2], London 1947. R. Bultmann, 1941 (Meyer II[10]; 1953 reprinted with Supplement). G. H. C. Macgregor, 1949 (Moffatt). H. Strathmann, [7]1954 (NTDeutsch

4). G. Spoerri, *Das Ev nach Joh*, 2 vols., 1950. W. Hendriksen, 2 vols., 1952. C. K. Barrett, London 1954 (520 p.). W. H. Rigg, *The Fourth Gospel*, London 1952. R. H. Lightfoot, 1956.

Studies: J. Grill, *Untersuchungen ueber die Entstehung des 4. Ev*, 2 vols., Tuebingen 1902, 1923. W. Wrede, *Charakter und Tendenz des Joh-Ev*, Tuebingen 1903. C. Clemen, *Die Entstehung des Joh-Ev*, Halle 1912. H. Odeberg, *The Fourth Gospel*, Uppsala 1929. G. Hoffmann, *Das Joh-Ev als Alterswerk. Eine psychologische Untersuchung*, Guetersloh 1933. W. von Loewenich, *Joh Denken*: ThBl 15 (1936) 260ff. E. Hirsch, *Studien zum 4. Ev*, Tuebingen 1936. H. Windisch, *Das 4. Ev und Joh*: ThBl 16 (1937) 144ff. Lester-Garland, *The Historic Value of the Fourth Gospel*: the Hibbert Journal 36 (1937/38) 265–277. E. Schweizer, *Ego eimi. Die religionsgeschichtliche Herkunft und theologische Bedeutung der joh Bildreden usw.*, Goettingen 1939. K. Kundsin, *Charakter und Ursprung der joh Reden*, Riga 1939. R. H. Strachan, *The Fourth Gospel: its Significance and Environment*[3], London 1941. J. N. Sanders, *The Fourth Gospel in the Early Church: its Origin and its Influence on Christian Theology up to Irenaeus*, Cambridge 1943. E. B. Allo, *L'év. spirituel de St. Jean*, Paris 1944. R. M. Grant, *The Fourth Gospel and the Church*: HarvThR 35 (1942) 95–116. Idem, *The Origin of the Fourth Gospel*: JBL 69 (1950) 305–322. W. Temple, *Readings in St. John's Gospel*, 1945. W. H. G. Thomas, *The Apostle John. Studies in his Life and Writings*, 1946. H. Fischel, *Jewish Gnosticism in the Fourth Gospel*: JBL 65 (1946) 157–174. A. C. Headlam, *The Fourth Gospel as History*, Oxford 1948. O. Cullmann, *Der joh Gebrauch doppeldeutiger Ausdruecke als Schluessel zum Verstaendnis des 4. Ev*: ThZ 4 (1948) 360–372. E. Ruckstuhl, *Die literarische Einheit des Joh-Ev. Der gegenwaertige Stand der einschlaegigen Forschungen*, Freiburg (Switz.) 1951 (StFriburgensia NF 3). H. Sahlin, *Zur Typologie des Joh-Ev*, Uppsala 1950. E. K. Lee, *The Religious Thought of St. John*, 1950. C. H. Dodd, *Le kerygma apostolique dans le 4me év*: RHPhR 31 (1951) 265–275. E. Kaesemann, *Ketzer u. Zeuge. Zum joh Verfasserprobl.*: ZThK 48 (1951) 292–311. K. Kundzins, *Zur Diskussion ueber die Ego-eimi-Sprueche des Joh*: Eucharisteria J. Koepp, Holmiae 1954, 95–107. S. Mender, *Joh Literarkritik*: ThZ 8 (1952) 418–434. C. H. Dodd, *The Interpretation of the Fourth Gospel*, Cambridge 1953 (478 pp.); see on this R. Bultmann: NTSt 1 (1954) 79–91, and P. Winter: ThLZ 80 (1955) 141–150, C. K. Barrett, *Der Zweck des 4. Ev*: ZsyTh 22 (1953) 259–273. F. Quiévreaux, *La structure symbolique de l'év. de St. Jean*: RHPhR 33 (1953) 123–165. J. Jocz, *Die Juden im Joh-Ev*: Judica 9 (1953) 129–142. E. C. Colwell-E. L. Titus, *The Gospel of the Spirit. A Study of the Fourth Gospel*, NY 1952. H. Blauert, *Die Bedeutung der Zeit in der joh Theologie. Eine Untersuchung an Hand von Joh 1–17 unter bes. Beruecksichtigung des literarkritischen Problems*, Dissertation Tuebingen 1953 (typewritten; summary, ThLZ 1953, 689 sq.). B. Noack, *Zur joh Tradition. Beitraege zur literarkritischen Analyse des 4. Ev*, Copenhagen 1954 (on it R. Bultmann: ThLZ 1955, 521–526). H. C. Snape, *The Fourth Gospel, Ephesus and Alexandria*: HarvThS 42 (1954) 1–14. H. Clavier, *La structure du 4. év.*: RHPhR 35 (1955) 174–195 [on the theology]. H. E. Boismard, *Problèmes de la critique textuelle du 4. év.*: RB 60 (1953) 347–371. H. E. Edwards, *The Disciple who wrote these Things: a New Inquiry into the Origins and Historical Value of the Gospel acc. to St. John*, London 1953. F. W. Howard, *Christianity According to St. John*, London 1943. E. Przywara,

Christentum gemaess Joh, Nuremberg 1954. J. Blinzler, *Eine Bemerkung z. Geschichtsrahmen des 4. Ev:* Bb 36 (1955) 20–35. Joh. Schneider deals with the composition of John 6 (*In memoriam E. Lohmeyer,* 1951, 132–142) and John 7 (ZntW 45, 1954, 108–119). C. H. Dodd, *Some Johannine "Herrenworte" with Parables in the Synoptic Gospels:* NTSt 2 (1955/56) 75–86. W. Grossouw: Studia Catholica 28 (1953) 2–19 (Review of R. Bultmann's commentary). R. A. Edwards, *The Gospel According to St. John. Its Criticism and Interpretation,* London 1954. H. Becker, *Die Reden des Joh-Ev und der Stil der gnostischen Offenbarungsreden,* Goettingen 1956. Surveys of research: R. Bultmann: Chr. Welt 41 (1927) 502–511. W. Bauer: ThRdsch NF 1 (1929) 135–160. J. Behm: ThLZ 73 (1948) 21–30. L. Schmid, *Joh-Ev und Religionsgeschichte,* Theological dissertation, Tuebingen 1933. F. W. Howard, *The Fourth Gospel in Recent Criticism and Interpretation,* ed. C. K. Barrett, London ⁴1955. Ph.-H. Menoud: *L'év. de Jean d'après les recherches récentes,* Neuchâtel 1947. E. Haenchen, *Aus der Literatur zum Joh-Ev 1929–1956:* ThRdsch NF 23 (1955/1957) 195–335.

Decision of the Pontifical Biblical Commission of 29th May 1907: External and internal arguments prove that the Apostle John was author of the fourth Gospel. The deeds of Our Lord which are related in it are not merely allegories or symbols for religious truths; the discourses are not free theological compositions of the author which he attributes to Jesus.

1. Content and structure

The Prologue 1, 1–18

First principal part: The work of Jesus in the world
1, 19 to 12, 50

I. Preparation for the work of Jesus 1, 19–51: The testimony of the Baptist to the emissaries of the Sanhedrin 1, 19–28, and to his own disciples 1, 29–34; the first disciples of Jesus 1, 35–51.

II. The beginnings of the work of Jesus 2, 1 to 4, 54: The marriage at Cana (first miracle) 2, 1–12; Jesus in Jerusalem (first Pasch): purification of the Temple, discourse to Nicodemus 2, 13 to 3, 21; the last testimony of the Baptist about Jesus 3, 32–36; Jesus in Samaria (conversation with the Samaritan woman) 4, 1–42 Jesus in Galilee (second miracle at Cana) 4, 43–54.

III. Jesus at the height of his ministry. He reveals himself during constant controversy with the unbelieving Jews 5, 1 to 10, 39.

1. From the Galilean ministry 6, 1–71[1]: The feeding of the Five Thousand (third miracle) 6, 1–15; Jesus walks upon the water (fourth miracle) 6, 16–21; discourse on the Bread of Life and promise of the Blessed Eucharist 6, 22–59; disbelief of the disciples 6, 60–66; Peter's confession 6, 67–71.

2. Jesus' first revelation about himself in Jerusalem (second Pasch or Pentecost) after the cure of a paralytic at the pool of Bethsaida (fifth miracle) 5, 1–47: Cure of the paralytic on the Sabbath 5, 1–9a; conflict of Jesus with the Jews about the breaking of the Sabbath 5, 9b–18; Jesus reveals that he is the resurrection of the dead and the Judge 5, 19–30; testimony of Jesus for the truth of his claim 5, 31–40; disbelief of the Jews and the reason for it 5, 41–47.

3. Jesus' revelation about himself at the feast of Tabernacles 7, 1–52: Departure of Jesus from Galilee 7, 1–13; at the feast of Tabernacles Jesus gives testimony of his divine mission; the Jewish rulers try in vain to apprehend him 7, 14–52 (Jesus and the woman taken in adultery 7, 53 to 8, 11).

4. Further revelations and conflicts of Jesus with the Jews, 8, 12 to 59: Jesus as the light of the world; the truth of his testimony about himself 8, 12–20; the evil consequences of disbelief 8, 21 to 29; faith in Jesus sets free 8, 30–38; the devil is the father of the unbelieving Jews 9, 39–47; Jesus is greater than Abraham 8, 48–59.

5. The cure of a man born blind (sixth miracle) reveals the blindness of the enemies of Jesus 9, 1–41: Cure of the blind man 9, 1–7; the cured man and his neighbours 9, 8–12; the cured man and the Pharisees 9, 13–34; the cured man and Jesus 9, 35–38; Jesus and the Pharisees 9, 40–41.

6. The discourse about the Good Shepherd 10, 1–21: First parable (the shepherd and the thief and robber) with explanation

---

[1] On the inversion of the order of ch. 5 and 6, see below n. 6.

10, 1–10; second parable (the shepherd and the hireling) with explanation 10, 11–18; the effect of this discourse 10, 19–21.

7. The revelation of Jesus about himself at the feast of the Dedication 10, 22–39: "I and the Father are one" 10, 22–31; answer to the accusation of blasphemy 10, 32–39.

IV. Conclusion of the public ministry of Jesus 10, 40 to 12, 50.

1. The raising of Lazarus (seventh miracle) and its sequel 10, 40 to 11, 54: Return of Jesus to Perea 10, 40–42; the request of the sisters of Lazarus and the departure of Jesus 11, 1–16; Jesus speaks with Martha and Mary 11, 17–32; he goes to the tomb and raises Lazarus 11, 33–44; the council decides to put him to death; Jesus goes to Ephrem 11, 45–54.

2. The last journey of Jesus to Jerusalem (for the third Pasch) 11, 55 to 12, 50: The situation in Jerusalem 11, 55–57; the anointing in Bethany 12, 1–11; messianic entry of Jesus into Jerusalem 12, 12–19; discourse of Jesus on his coming death 12, 30–36; explanation of the disbelief of the Jews; duty of believing in Jesus 12, 37–50.

Second principal part: The return of Jesus to the Father
13, 1 to 21, 25

I. On the eve of his death 13, 1 to 17, 26

1. The Last Supper 13, 1–30: The washing of the feet and its meaning 13, 1–20; prophecy of the betrayal and unmasking of the traitor 13, 21–30.

2. Farewell discourses of Jesus 13, 31 to 16, 33: First farewell discourse 13, 31 to 14, 31 (Jesus will soon leave them; the commandment of charity; he foretells Peter's denial 13, 31–38; he promises to bring the Apostles home 14, 1–4; Jesus is the way to the Father 14, 5–11; promise that the Apostles will continue the work of Jesus 14, 12–14; promise of the Paraclete 14, 15–17; promise of the coming of Jesus, the Father and the Son 14, 18–24; the Paraclete will continue Jesus' work of revelation 14, 25–26;

words of farewell 14, 27–31).—Second farewell discourse 15, 1 to 16, 33 (the Apostles must abide in Jesus 15, 1–8 and the condition for abiding 15, 9–17; the hatred of the world for the Apostles and the reason for this hatred 15, 18 to 16, 4; the Paraclete as accuser of the world and instructor of the Apostles 16, 5–15; the sorrow of parting and the joy of reunion 16, 16–24; promises and words of consolation 16, 25–33).

3. The farewell prayer 17, 1–26; the prayer for the glorification of Jesus 17, 1–5; prayer for the protection and sanctification of the Apostles 17, 6–19; prayer for the unity of the believers 17, 20 to 23; prayer for the eternal salvation of the faithful 17, 24–26.

II. The Passion 18, 1 to 19, 42.

1. Jesus in the hands of the Jewish authorities 18, 1–27: the arrest of Jesus 18, 1–11; Jesus before Annas and Caiphas; Peter's denial 18, 12 27.

2. Jesus before Pilate 18, 28 to 19, 16a: Jesus handed over to Pilate 18, 28–32; the first hearing 18, 33–38a; Barabbas is preferred to Jesus 18, 38b–40; scourging, mocking, and coming forth of Jesus 19, 1–7; the second hearing 19, 8–11; the condemnation 19, 12–16a.

3. Crucifixion, Death and Burial of Jesus 19, 16b–42: Crucifixion and division of the garments 19, 16b–24; his mother and the beloved disciple beneath the Cross 19, 25–27; Death of Jesus 19, 28 to 30; the side of Jesus pierced with a lance 19, 31–37; the Burial of Jesus 19, 38–42.

III. The appearances after the Resurrection. 20, 1 to 21, 25.

The empty tomb 20, 1–18; the Risen Christ appears to his disciples 20, 19–23 and to Thomas 20, 24–29; conclusion of the book 20, 30–31. Postscript 21, 1–25: The Risen Christ appears to his disciples at the lake of Tiberias (heavy draught of fish) 21, 1–14, gives Peter the office of chief shepherd and foretells his martyrdom 21, 15–19; the fate of the beloved disciple 21, 20–23; second conclusion 21, 24–25.

2. The tradition of the early Church

According to early Church tradition the Apostle John, the son of Zebedee and brother of James the Elder, composed the fourth Gospel in his old age at Ephesus in Asia Minor. The principal witness is Irenaeus of Lyons. In his book *Against the Heresies,* which was written about 180 A.D., he writes (III 1, 1): "After them (Mt., Mk. and Lk.) John the disciple (Apostle) of the Lord, who also reclined on his breast (John 13, 23) issued a Gospel while he was living at Ephesus in Asia"; according to him (II 22, 5; III 3, 4), John was still living in Asia Minor or Ephesus in the time of the Emperor Trajan (98–117 A.D.). The evidence of Irenaeus is of great weight because, as he tells us himself, as a youth he had heard Polycarp, the bishop of Smyrna († 155), and Polycarp had known the Apostle John personally (III 3, 4; Eusebius, H. E. V 20, 4).

Further evidence that the Apostle John lived and died in Asia comes from Polycrates, bishop of Ephesus; writing about 190 A.D. to Pope Victor (187–198/99), he mentions among "the great stars who rest in Asia" John "who leaned on the breast of the Lord (John 13, 23), who was a priest and wore the priestly breastplate, and was a witness and teacher; he sleeps in Ephesus" (apud Euseb. H. E. III 31, 3 = V 24, 3).

Clement of Alexandria also knows of John's sojourn in Asia: he tells us that after the death of the tyrant (Domitian) John returned to Ephesus from the island of Patmos (apud Euseb. H. E. III 23, 6). In the *Hypotyposes* he gives a tradition of the old Presbyter about the order of the Gospels; this tradition placed John the Apostle last, for knowing that the exterior-human (in Jesus) had already been treated in the Gospels, he composed a spiritual ("pneumatic") Gospel on the urging of his friends and with the illumination of the Spirit (apud Euseb. H. E. VI 14, 5–7). Eusebius is probably drawing on Clement when he says that

John the Apostle and Evangelist was still alive in Asia under Trajan, and that on his return from exile on the isle of Patmos after Domitian's death, he was leader of the communities there (H. E. III 23, 1).

The ancient anti-Marcionite prologues and the Muratorian Canon (cf. § 6, 2) give us the tradition of the Roman Church. According to the prologue to Luke John the Apostle composed the Apocalypse on the island of Patmos, and wrote the Gospel afterwards. The prologue to John says that "according to Papias, the dear disciple of John, in his five exegetical books, this Gospel was published and sent to the churches of Asia by John himself during his lifetime," so apparently the fourth Gospel was ascribed to the Apostle John as early as the time of Papias (c. 135 A.D.).

The Muratorian Canon tells us that John was persuaded (to compose the Gospel) by his fellow disciples (Apostles) and bishops; he therefore ordered a threeday communal fast to learn God's will, and during that night it was revealed to the Apostle Andrew that John was to write and publish everything under his name but with the approval of all.

This story must be considered legendary, for it contradicts the historical evidence by placing the composition of the fourth Gospel in a period when the twelve Apostles were still alive. A motive for this legend, which the author of the Muratorian fragment adopts, has been suggested recently[2]; it may have been designed to commend the fourth Gospel as the Gospel of Gospels, by giving it the sanction of the twelve Apostles and thereby rendering all the other Gospels superfluous; for according to lines 32–34 of the fragment John in 1 John 1, 1–4 describes himself not only as a first-hand witness but also as the chronicler (in the Gospel) of all Our Lord's miracles.

So in the late second century all the leading personalities of the Church ascribed the fourth Gospel to John the Apostle. It is con-

[2] O. Cullmann: ThZ 1 (1954) 34.

sidered the latest of the canonical Gospels, and Ephesus is named as the place where it was composed. Only the ancient prologue mentions the time of composition; it says that John wrote the Gospel in Asia after composing the Apocalypse on Patmos.

In this period there were only isolated opponents of the Johannine authorship of the Gospel. The evidence concerning them is scanty and not entirely clear; here is A. Bludau's account of them[3]: Irenaeus says (III 11, 9) that defenders of the Church against the Montanists openly rejected the fourth Gospel "where Our Lord promised to send the Paraclete" (14, 16 sqq.); they did this "in order to deny the giving of the Holy Ghost". These people probably belonged to the West (Rome or Gaul). Eusebius (H. E: III 28, 2) and Hippolytus in a fragment of a lost work tell us that Gaius, a learned and orthodox Roman priest, who wrote during the pontificate of Pope Zephyrinus (199–217), rejected both the Apocalypse and also the fourth Gospel which he attributed to the heretic Cerinthus because it apparently contradicted the Synoptic Gospels. The Johannine writings were also rejected for this same reason by a heretical sect whom Epiphanius of Salamis calls the Alogi (*Panarion* 51). Probably these Alogi belonged to Rome and were distinct from the anti-Montanists whom Irenaeus mentions. The author of the Muratorian Canon probably had them in mind when he defended the fourth Gospel by saying that the divergences between the Gospels should not upset the faithful "because everything is entirely explained by the one guiding Spirit: concerning the Nativity, the Passion, the Resurrection etc."

The opposition of the anti-Montanists and Alogi had no effect. The Apostolic origin of the fourth Gospel was accepted universally from the beginning of the third century, and in general that remained the case until 1820. In that year a small book appeared in Leipzig: *Probabilia de evangelii et epistolarum Joannis Apostoli*

[3] *Die ersten Gegner der Johannesschriften* (BSt XXII 1–2, 1925).

indole et origine; in it the author, Karl Theophil Bret-
schneider, General Superintendent of Gotha, argued with great
acumen against the authorship of John the Apostle. The work
was rejected almost everywhere at the time, but the "Johannine
question" which it raised has been disputed ever since.

For about the last hundred years the critics, following Bret-
schneider, have refused to acknowledge the Apostle John as
author of the Gospel (and the three Epistles), and in modern
times a number of more conservative scholars have joined their
ranks. They rely principally on internal evidence (the profound
Christology of the fourth Gospel cannot be the work of an
eyewitness), and also challenge the dependability of tradition on
the following two grounds:

1. The John of whom Polycrates and Irenaeus speak was not
the Apostle but a different person of the same name, a Presbyter, who was also disciple of Jesus and an eyewitness of the
events.

Against the testimony of Irenaeus they urge[4] that he was
evidently mistaken when he identified the John, of whom Polycarp spoke, with the Apostle, for there is no mention of such close
relations with the Apostle John either in the surviving epistle of
Polycarp or in the ancient account of his martyrdom; indeed the
epistle frequently appeals to the authority of Paul, but otherwise
mentions only "the Apostles" as a group. We must therefore
assume, they say, that Irenaeus—no doubt in good faith—attributed to Polycarp his own identification of the John whom Polycarp had mentioned; the reference to Polycarp proves only that
a disciple of Jesus named John made a long sojourn in Asia; since
he is mentioned by name side by side with other firsthand witnesses he must have been an outstanding person, of special authority.

They say that such a mistake would not be surprising, for

---

[4] Cf. F. S. Gutjahr, *Die Glaubwuerdigkeit des irenaeischen Zeugnisses ueber die
Abfassung des vierten kanonischen Ev.*, Graz 1904.

Irenaeus also (*Haer.* V 33, 4) made Papias a disciple of the Apostle John—a point on which Eusebius corrected him. Papias, as Eusebius writes, clearly implies in the prologue to his book that he had not seen or heard the Apostles, for he declares explicitly that he learned the doctrines of the faith from their friends (H. E. III 39, 2). The passage of Papias which Eusebius quotes at this point reads: "I will not hesitate to include for you in my expositions what I learned accurately in the past from the elders (πρεσβύτεροι) and have retained carefully in memory ... If anyone came who had followed the elders I enquired after the words of the elders, what Andrew or Peter had said (τί Ἀνδρέας ἢ τί Πέτρος εἶπεν), or Philip or Thomas or James or John, or some of the other Apostles of the Lord (said), and what Aristion and John the Elder, the disciples of the Lord say (ἅ τε Ἀριστίων καὶ ὁ πρεσβύτερος Ἰωάννης, τοῦ κυρίου μαθηταί, λέγουσι). For I considered that accounts derived from books could not have the same value for me as the words of a fresh living voice" (H. E. III 39, 3–4). Eusebius points out that Papias mentions the name John twice, and places the first John with Peter and the rest of the Apostles, while the second John is listed with others who did not belong to the number of the Apostles. "Thereby it is confirmed that two disciples of the same name lived in Asia and that two tombs were erected in Ephesus each of which even yet bears the name John" (III 39, 6). Eusebius regards the first John as the Evangelist, but is inclined to ascribe the Apocalypse to the second John.

The passage which Eusebius quotes from Papias is a subject of keen controversy up to the present day. If Eusebius understood it correctly, there were two men called John in Asia around 100 A.D. And it can hardly be doubted that he did interpret Papias' words correctly.[5] At any rate we possess no evidence independent

---

[5] Lagrange in his commentary on John, and G. Bardy (DB Suppl IV, 1949, 843–847: Jean le presbytre) agree with this. They reject as an inaccurate gloss the

of Papias and Eusebius that a man named John, distinct from the Apostle, lived in Ephesus around the turn of the century.

But even if two men called John really lived there it does not follow that Eusebius and Polycrates have confused a John, a highly respected disciple of Jesus who lived and died in Ephesus, with the famous Apostle John. Eusebius himself did not draw this conclusion.

2. The Apostle John did not come to Ephesus but suffered martyrdom in Palestine in the sixties.[6] The opponents of Johannine authorship support this with the following evidence:

1) According to Mk. 10, 38 sq. the two sons of Zebedee suffered martyrdom. Mark would not have recorded this Prophecy of Jesus in its present form unless the two brothers had not already died as martyrs when the Gospel of St. Mark was written.

2) Philip of Side in Pamphylia (c. 430 A.D.) says in a later extract from his *Christian History* "Papias in the second book says that John the Theologian and James his brother were killed by Jews."

3) The Syrian Martyrology of the year 411 declares under the 27th December: "John and James the Apostles in Jerusalem" (i. e., died as martyrs).

4) The Syrian Father Aphrahat in his 21st Homily (344 A.D.) says that except for Stephen, Peter and Paul, only two of the Apostles were martyred, James and John. Many of the critics con-

---

description of Aristion and John as "disciples of the Lord"; it does not occur in the Syriac version of Eusebius' *Historia Ecclesiastica*. They point out that both Johns were included among the elders—a vague term which refers to disciples or pupils of Apostles as well as immediate disciples of Our Lord himself; but this title could only have been given to John in order to distinguish him from the Apostle of the same name. There is a different explanation in E. Gutwenger, *Papias. Eine chronologische Studie*: ZkTh 69 (1947) 385–416 (unconvincing).

[6] On this matter see E. Schwartz, *Ueber den Tod der Soehne Zebedaei*, Berlin 1904, and R. H. Charles, *Com. on the Revelation of St. John* I (1920) p. XLV–L. P. Parker, *Two Editions of John*: JBL 75 (1956) 303–314.

clude from this text that the two sons of Zebedee, John and James, suffered martyrdom in Palestine (Jerusalem); they say that John, who was still alive at the time of the Apostolic Council (Gal. 2, 9), was killed either in 62 A.D. at the same time as James, the brother of the Lord, or else in 66 A.D. at the outbreak of the Jewish war. However, this conclusion cannot be considered proven.

Against the correctness of the Papias citation it may be urged that Irenaeus and Eusebius know nothing of it, though they had made an intensive study and use of Papias' book. Presumably there is some confusion. Perhaps Papias spoke of the martyrdom of John the Baptist and the Apostle James the Greater at the hands of Jewish kings, and this account may have been mistakenly referred to the two sons of Zebedee by whoever made the extract from Philip of Side.

The same is probably true of the Syrian Martyrology. Syrian tradition knows nothing of a martyrdom of the Apostle John; so probably the original text spoke of John the Baptist, as the Carthage Martyrology—composed after 505 A.D., but incorporating older material—actually does: "On 27th December: Feast of St. John the Baptist and St. James who were killed by Herod . . ."

Concerning Aphrahat it may be said that he does not speak explicitly of the martyrdom of both Apostles.

The saying of Our Lord Mk. 10, 38 sq. need not necessarily be a prophecy of a violent death; even if that is its meaning, it is not clear why Mark could not have included in his Gospel a prophecy which was still unfulfilled in regard to one of the brothers.

3. Internal evidence concerning the author

Early tradition attests that the author of the fourth Gospel was the Apostle John. The New Testament gives the following information about him: John (= Johanan i. e. God is gracious) and his elder brother James were the second pair of brothers to be called by

Jesus as disciples (Mk. 1, 19 par). Their father was called Zebedee (Mk. 1, 20), their mother Salome (Mk. 15, 40 in conjunction with Mt. 27, 56); the "sons of Zebedee"—as the New Testament frequently calls them (Mk. 10, 35; Mt. 20, 20)—were, like their father, fishermen on the lake of Genesareth.

Because of their impetuous temperament Jesus called them "sons of thunder" (Mk. 3, 17; cf. Lk. 9, 54). With Peter they make up the circle of the three intimate Apostles (Mk. 5, 37; 9, 2; 14, 33 par). They ask Jesus for the places of honour in his kingdom (Mk. 10, 35 sq. par).

John is mentioned alone in Mk. 9, 38; Lk. 9, 49. In Acts he is next to Peter (3, 1 sqq.; 4, 13 19; 8, 14; also 1, 13), and so was evidently a leading personality; this is confirmed by Gal. 2, 9 where he, with Peter and James the brother of the Lord, are described as the "pillars" of the primitive community.

The New Testament gives no further information about his life except for Apc. 1, 1 4 9; 22, 8, if the John mentioned there is identical with the Apostle (cf. § 54, 3). According to Irenaeus, Polycrates, Clement of Alexandria, Tertullian and others, he later worked at Ephesus in Asia Minor, and died there at an advanced age around the turn of the century. There is no tradition about when he emigrated, but presumably it was at the outbreak of the Jewish war.

The fourth Gospel does not mention its author by name, but it provides indirect information about him. In ch. 21—which is not by the author of chs. 1 to 20—the guarantor of the truth of the Gospel and its author is said in v. 24 to be "the disciple whom Jesus loved," who was mentioned in the preceding four verses. Who is this beloved disciple?

He appears in four passages of the Passion and Resurrection story: 1. At the Last Supper he leans on the bosom of Jesus and asks who the traitor is (13, 23); 2. At the foot of the Cross he is entrusted with the mother of Jesus by Jesus (19, 26); 3. On the Sunday morning he reaches the tomb before Peter and comes to believe in the Resurrection of Jesus (20, 3); 4. On the lake of Genesareth he recognizes Jesus before any of the others and receives a mysterious prophecy from him (21, 7 20–23). The disciple who is mentioned in 1, 40 and 18, 15 sq. is probably also the beloved disciple, although we are not told his name and he is not described as "whom Jesus loved".

It is natural to infer from these passages that this mysterious disciple was one of the twelve Apostles. He took part in the Last Supper, where the Synoptics tell us that only Apostles were present. That is evidently the meaning of this Evangelist also, as is shown by a comparison of 13, 18 with 6, 70 ("chosen").

There was a small group of special intimates among the twelve Apostles, namely Peter and the two sons of Zebedee. Peter may be ruled out, for his name is coupled with the beloved disciple several times (13, 23 sq.; 20, 2 sq.; 21, 20 sqq.); James also may be eliminated, for he was executed about 44 A.D. (Acts 12, 2), while the beloved disciple reached an advanced old age (21, 20–23). There remains only John the son of Zebedee, who like his brother is never mentioned by name in the Gospel—an omission which must be intentional. This would also harmonize with the fact that the two sons of Zebedee were present when the Risen Christ appeared at the lake of Genesareth (21, 2). Furthermore tradition has never identified the beloved disciple with anyone except the Apostle John.

So 21, 24 is evidence that the fourth Gospel was written by the Apostle.

4. Literary and theological characteristics

When compared with the Synoptics the fourth Gospel is quite independent in 1. content, 2. form, and 3. theological character.

1. Only a small part of the synoptic material appears in the fourth Gospel, and even in this common material there is not complete agreement.

The agreement is closest in the history of the Passion and Resurrection, but even here there are fairly large divergences; although it deals with the same events the fourth Gospel has not borrowed a single pericope from the Synoptic Gospels.

Elsewhere the parallels are confined to a few pericopae (1, 32 sq.; 2, 13–16; 6, 1–13 16–21 66–71; 12, 1–8 12–19; 13, 1–30). Of the twenty–nine miracles of Jesus which the Synoptics describe, John records only two (multiplication of the loaves and walking on the water 6, 1–21); he contains five additional miracles (changing of water into wine 2, 1–11; cure of the ruler's son 4, 46–54 (possibly identical with Mt. 8, 5–10, as Irenaeus thought); cure of a paralytic 5, 1–9, and of a blind man 9, 1–7; raising of Lazarus 11, 33–44). He reports no cures of possessed persons; the cleansing of the Temple (2, 13–16) and the anointing in Bethany (12, 1–8) appear in a different context from the Synoptics. John gives no account of the conflicts with the Jewish authorities in Jerusalem which occupy the first days of Holy Week in the Synoptics.

The fourth Gospel contains many discourses of Jesus—chs. 3–17 consist almost entirely of discourses or dialogues—yet not one of the discourses reported by the Synoptics appears in John, and the content of the Johannine discourses has little in common with the Synoptics; only a few of the Synoptic sayings of Our Lord reappear in John (2, 19; 4, 44; 12, 25 sq.; 13, 16 20; 15, 20).

There is a fundamental divergence between John and the Synoptics in their outlines of the chronology and geography of the ministry of Jesus.

According to the Synoptics Jesus began his public ministry in Galilee after the arrest of the Baptist, and his work was mainly confined to Galilee; after a considerable time he leaves Galilee and goes to the neighbouring heathen territory though there he does not engage in a ministry properly so called; he then travels by Perea and Jericho to Jerusalem for the Pasch in order to die there. This is the only Pasch mentioned by the Synoptics, and since they give no other chronological information, the ministry of Jesus, as they report it, could have taken place within one year.

In John the outline of Jesus' ministry is much more complicated and covers a wider area. He mentions at least three Paschs (2, 13 23; 6, 4; 12, 1), and four journeys of Jesus to Jerusalem (2, 13; 5, 1; 7, 10; 12, 12); so the public life occupied at least two full years. According to John the ministry of Jesus did not begin with the arrest of the Baptist; for a considerable time they worked simultaneously (cf. John 1, 35 to 4, 54). According to the Synoptics the ministry of Jesus was centered in Galilee and particularly around Capharnaum; John on the other hand says that it was mainly around Jerusalem. The final departure of Jesus from Galilee takes place half a year before his death (John 7, 10), whereas there is no possibility of establishing a chronology from the Synoptics.

The question of John's historicity cannot be treated in detail here. It must suffice to point out that on one important matter the synoptic outline leaves an impression of artificiality. The Synoptics are certainly correct in saying that the first and longest part of the ministry of Jesus was in Galilee after the arrest of the Baptist; but when they speak of only one visit to Jerusalem and one ministry of two to three days immediately before the Passion, their account can hardly correspond entirely to the facts. The catastrophe which broke so suddenly upon Jesus would be scarcely understandable if Jesus had not worked for a fairly long time in Jerusalem and already come into conflict with the ruling circles there. Even in the Synoptics there are indications that he actually had worked there either for a considerable time or on various occasions: 1) The threatening prophecy Mt. 23, 37; Lk. 13, 34 probably presupposes several visits to Jerusalem; 2) Mk. 11, 2 sq.; 14, 3 sqq. show that Jesus had acquaintances in Jerusalem; 3) It would be a legitimate inference from Lk. 10, 38–42 (compared with John 11, 1 sqq.) that he had already spent some time before his death in (the neighbourhood of) Jerusalem; 4) The 120 disciples (Acts 1, 15) can hardly have been all Galileans.

2. The fourth Gospel also shows an individual stamp in the nature and manner of its presentation. Broadly speaking the Synoptic Gospels consist of a large number of small units (pericopae) strung together more or less loosely; passages of similar content are often juxtaposed without regard for chronology, for example, the five Galilean conflicts Mk. 2, 1 to 3, 6, the ten miracles Mt. 8, 1 to 9, 34, the three parables of something lost Lk. 15, 1–32, the three parables of the Second Coming together with the description of the Last Judgment Mt. 24, 45 to 25, 46. The only exception is the story of the Passion which naturally was always a continuous story. The clearest examples of artificiality are the synoptic discourses, which consist of sayings or groups of sayings of Jesus juxtaposed because of their similarity in content or even because of extrinsic similarity (key word arrangement). Up to a point this holds true even of the eschatological discourse, whose kernel is an instruction of Jesus to four intimate Apostles (Mk. 13, 3 sq.). This applies particularly to Matthew who has grouped the traditional sayings of Our Lord into six great discourses (cf. § 24, 3).

The more compact structure of the fourth Gospel stands in contrast to this picture. It does not present narratives, miracle stories, sayings of Jesus, instructions, conflicts and parables loosely strung together into groups; instead we find a small number of graphic narratives which are broadly and dramatically presented and form a coherent unity. The links between them are usually references to place and time. The Evangelist also tries to create unity within the book by referring back to earlier accounts (cf. 4, 45 : 2, 23; 4, 46 : 2, 1–11; 7, 50 and 9, 39 : 3, 1 sq.; 12, 42 : 9, 22; 13, 33 : 7, 33 sq. and 8, 21 sq.; 15, 20 : 13, 16; 18, 14 : 11, 49 sq.). He generally gives the names of the places and also of the feasts to which Jesus went, and because of these details of time and place the reader always knows at what point in the ministry of Jesus he is.

The content of the fourth Gospel consists principally of discourses of Jesus. But these discourses are not individual logia and collections of sayings; they each develop a particular theme, though the trend of thought may not always be strictly logical. Generally they revolve about a particular thought which they illustrate from all angles. It is particularly characteristic of these discourses that the Speaker is often interrupted by questions or objections from the hearers, a thing which never occurs in the Synoptics. Indeed two of them (the Samaritan woman 4, 7–26 and Martha 11, 21–27) would be better described as dialogues. There are such interruptions in all but two of the discourses (5, 19–47 and 10, 1–18). These interjections oblige Jesus to clarify his words and thereby contribute to the development of the thought.

In a number of cases the discourses or conversations are connected with miracles whose deeper symbolism they illustrate (and so the miracles are called "signs"). These cases are the discourse on the Bread of Life (6, 25 sqq.) and the conversations with the man born blind (9, 8 sqq.) and with Martha (11, 20 sqq.). By the multiplication of the loaves Jesus reveals himself as the giver of the true Bread of Life; by the cure of the blind man he shows that he is the bringer of Light, indeed the Light itself in the darkness of the world; the raising of Lazarus reveals him as the giver of Eternal Life. So to some extent these three miracles are illustrations of the words of Jesus, "I am the Bread of Life" (6, 35 48), "I am the Light of the world" (8, 12; 9, 5), "I am the Resurrection and the Life" (11, 25). The long discourse 5, 17–47 (and 7, 15–24) follows a miracle worked by Jesus, the cure on the Sabbath.

In the Synoptics Jesus speaks in a popular, lively, and direct manner; in John his language is abstract, learned, and uniform, seldom using metaphors, comparisons or parables. This phenomenon is said to be due to the fact that in the Synoptics Jesus speaks to the common people while John's discourses are in a different key because there his audience consists of members of the Sanhedrin and Rabbis, that is, learned and cultured men. But this explanation does not entirely fit the facts. John also contains passages of various lengths which are addressed to simple people: the Samaritan woman (4, 7–26), the discourse in the Synagogue at Capharnaum (6, 26 sqq.) and also 7, 37–39 and 12, 23–36. In all these cases the language of Jesus is as elevated as in his discourses with the Jewish priests and legal experts; moreover the farewell discourse and the sacerdotal prayer have the same character as the other discourses (14–17). We must also remember that the Baptist speaks in this same style (1, 29–31; 3, 27–30), as does the Evangelist himself in the prologue and—if they are regarded as his reflections—in 3, 14–21 31–36. But the most significant fact is that the first Epistle of John is cast in the same stylistic and theological mould as the discourses of Jesus in the fourth Gospel.

From these facts we can only infer that in reporting the discourses of Jesus the fourth Evangelist uses his own modes of thought and language, while the Synoptics retain the sayings of Jesus in their original language and form.

3. The theology of the fourth Gospel also bears a distinctive stamp. The dominant theological ideas in John are not those which receive most stress in the Synoptics.

The idea of the Kingdom of God, which in the other Gospels runs throughout the preaching of Jesus, occurs only in the conversation with Nicodemus (3, 3–5) and there it means eternal salvation just as in the Synoptics; Jesus also speaks before Pilate of his kingdom, or rather of his kingship, which is not of this world (18, 36). "Kingdom (Kingship) of God", meaning the salvation which Jesus proclaims, is replaced in John by the expression "eternal life"; but in John this concept denotes something in the present world, while in the Synoptics it means a purely eschatological good.

The idea of the "Son of Man" is closely connected with the Kingdom of God; it is not stressed in the fourth Gospel. The synoptic sayings about the Son of Man fall into two groups: so-called "exaltation sayings" which refer to the coming of Jesus in power and majesty for the judgment (Mk. 8, 38; 14, 62 par and elsewhere), and so-called "humility sayings" dealing with the Passion (Mk. 8, 31; 9, 12 31; 14, 21 41 par). In John the Son of Man is the Emissary of God walking upon earth (1, 51; 6, 27), who is come from Heaven (3, 13; 6, 62), and will be raised again to heavenly lordship (3, 14; 8, 28; 12, 23 34; 13, 31). We are reminded of the "exaltation sayings" of the Synoptics only in the saying that the Father has given the office of judge to the Son because he is the Son of Man (5, 27).

The fourth Gospel is permeated by the ideas of life, light and darkness, above and below, world, faith and confession, truth and glory, all of which are used in a special sense.

The universality of the message of salvation is more strongly stressed in John than in the Synoptics. Salvation is intended for all men, and is accessible to all who become believers (1, 7 9; 3, 16). Jesus is Saviour of the world (4, 22), he takes away the sins of the world (1, 29); to his fold belong also the Gentiles scattered throughout the world, who accept his message with faith (10, 16; 11, 51). The primacy of the Jews is not emphasized as it is in Mk. 7, 26 par, and there is no mention of the lost sheep of the house of Israel.

John does not report the conflicts concerning the Rabbinical interpretation of the Law. The controversies which John records do not deal with levitical cleanliness and the observance of the Sabbath; in the last analysis this is true even of chapters 5 and 9. The Johannine conflicts have as their theme the much more important question of faith or unbelief. In the prologue a contrast is drawn between the Mosaic Law and the grace and truth brought by Jesus (1, 17); yet the Old Testament has permanent significance as testimony to Christ (1, 45; 2, 17; 5, 46 sq.; 7, 38; 8, 56 etc.).

The questions of moral conduct which play so large a part in the Synoptics, for example, the Sermon on the Mount, are almost entirely ignored in John. Just as in the first epistle of John, the whole ethic of Jesus is summed up in the precept of brotherly love which is inculcated with great emphasis (13, 34 sq.; 15, 12 sq. 17; 1 John 2, 7–10; 3, 11 23; 4, 19–21). Time and again Jesus speaks of the observance of the commandments, but he never enters into individual questions such as prayer, fasting, almsgiving, swearing, marriage, and material possessions.

The mystery of the person of Jesus dominates the Gospel of St. John. The fourth Gospel is essentially an account of the self-revelation by the eternal Son of God. The numerous discourses have generally only one theme: the person of Jesus, his pre-existence before the world was, his relation to the Father, his coming into the world, his work in the world, and his return to the Father.

In the older Gospels there are sayings of Jesus which are powerful expressions of his lofty self-consciousness. "There is here a greater than the temple . . . than Solomon" (Mt. 12, 6 42); but this is not stressed in them; on the other hand in the fourth Gospel Jesus continually speaks in the first person: "I am the Light of the world" (8, 12); "the Bread of Life" (6, 35); "the Resurrection and the Life" (11, 25); "I and the Father are one" (10, 30); "Before Abraham was made I am" (8, 58). Fundamentally only one demand is made of the hearers: faith in Jesus as Son of God, revealer of God, bringer of salvation. Whoever fulfills this requirement obtains eternal life here and now, and whoever rejects it falls into eternal ruin. The miracles of Jesus are not so much a demonstration of Jesus' pity for men's distress as a revelation of his divine power and Lordship (2, 11; 9, 3 sq.;

11, 4 40). That is why particularly striking miracles are reported: the cure of a man born blind, of a man paralysed for thirty-eight years, the raising to life of a man who was already four days in the tomb. These miracles are such a clear demonstration of the Lordship of Jesus that no one can refuse to accept them and remain in good faith.

The love for sinners which is stressed in the Synoptic picture of Jesus does not appear at all in John. In the Synoptics Jesus seeks and saves what is lost, and in a special manner takes to himself publicans and sinners; in John he rather appears as shepherd of his own (10, 1-16), who gives his life for his sheep (10, 15) or for the scattered children of God (11, 51 sq.), and takes care that none of those whom the Father has given him may be lost (6, 39; 17, 12; 18, 9). In the fourth Gospel the dichotomy is not between just and sinners, but between faithful and unbelieving, and fundamentally it is the work of Jesus to complete the division between the children of God and the children of this world whose lot is perdition.

Eschatology does not play the same role in John as in the Synoptics. Though he contains such matter, he does not emphasize it; the eschatological discourse of the synoptic Evangelists (Mk. 13 par) is absent from John, and he does not mention when the end shall be nor its signs. In John judgment is something which takes place in the present; whoever believes does not come to judgment, but whoever does not believe is already judged (3, 18); by refusing to believe men automatically pass judgment on themselves, that is, they condemn themselves (3, 19). Eternal life is the possession of salvation here and now by those who believe; whoever believes has eternal life (5, 24); Jesus and the Father come to him and make their abode with him (14, 23).

5. The relation of John to the Synoptics

Even in antiquity the profound divergences between John and

the Synoptic Gospels were appreciated. They caused certain Christian groups to reject the fourth Gospel (Alogi, Caius of Rome, see above n. 2), and they were used by the pagan opponents of Christianity to attack the credibility of the Gospels. The early Christian writers defended the Gospels against these objections by proposing the thesis that the fourth Evangelist intended to supplement the Synoptics both in content and theology (see especially Clement of Alex. apud Euseb. H. E. IV 14, 7; Eusebius himself, ibid. III, 24, 7–13; Epiphanius, *Panarion* 51). These efforts reached their climax in the work of St. Augustine *De consensu evangelistarum*, which exercised a dominant influence throughout the Middle Ages (cf. § 26, 4).

The much more detailed and searching investigations of modern scholarship have produced not one uniform solution, but four different answers to this problem.

The Supplement Theory of the early Church is upheld by most of the scholars who maintain the apostolic authorship of the fourth Gospel, but they no longer say that John merely gleans the material which the Synoptics have passed over. They recognize the independence of the fourth Gospel and the completeness of its structure; but in their view the author assumes that his readers know the older Gospels, and he himself has them in mind throughout his work. So they would say that it is intended to stand beside the Synoptics, and that he acknowledges their reliability, supplements them with valuable new material, and tacitly clarifies possible misunderstandings (e. g., Th. Zahn).

Since it has been realized that the Gospel of St. John is a self-sufficient work, another theory, in addition to the old supplement theory, has found favour with those who defend its apostolic origin (Lagrange, Buechsel, and others); this theory may be called the Independence Theory. Its exponents deny that John intended his work as a supplement to the Synoptics, and if they do not deny outright that he was acquainted with the Synoptic tradition, they insist that he takes account of the older Gospels only to a small extent and at particular points (1, 31; 3, 24; 6, 1 71; 11, 1 sq.; 18, 13; 20, 1); in general, they say, John goes his own way and creates a new form of the Gospel which is independent of the Synoptics.

This theory fits the facts better than the Supplement Theory. It cannot be doubted—and is denied by no one—that the fourth Evangelist knew a rich Gospel tradition which the Synoptics ignore. The only point in dispute is whether he knew our Synoptic Gospels and assumed that his readers were acquainted with them. Some few, such as Bultmann, deny this, but most exegetes assume that he knew Mark, and consider it probable that he also knew Matthew or Luke; at any rate if the Gospel was composed about 90 A.D., it cannot be taken for granted that he was acquainted with all three. Individual contacts in material and particular agreements in certain words and turns of speech do not provide decisive proof that he knew all three Synoptics.

Be that as it may, the fourth Gospel is a self-contained narrative with few allusions to the Synoptic Gospels, and it is possible to understand John without reference to them. Indeed it is very difficult and sometimes quite impossible to be sure where the Synoptic material fits into John's framework; if it was John's intention to supplement the Synoptics, he would certainly have shown clearly how his account was to be harmonized with theirs. He assumes that his readers are acquainted with the synoptic material but is nevertheless self-sufficient and independent of the other Evangelists.

The Synoptic Evangelists were primarily compilers of the traditional material about the words and deeds of Jesus; John is rather a writer who spiritually moulds the raw material and makes it serve his purpose. In particular it was his desire to give theological depth to the picture of Jesus Christ. The Synoptics depict the ministry of Jesus as his disciples experienced it; John gives the picture which a long life of more profound meditation had revealed with ever increasing clearness to the beloved disciple illuminated by the Holy Spirit (cf. John 16, 12 sqq.).

In the course of the nineteenth century critical theologians developed the theory that the fourth Gospel was intended to interpret, correct and improve upon the Synoptic Gospels; it is called the Interpretation or Improvement Theory. They said that the author, occasionally using the synoptic material, created a new and more profound picture of Christ, from which he freely eliminated out-of-date material and instances of narrow Jewish nationalism; in particular he discarded from the synoptic portrait anything which might offend sensitive minds, such as convictions about future events or the presentation of Jesus as the Saviour of sinners, replacing it by an image of Christ acceptable to the Greek mind.

Around the turn of the century this theory was further developed into the Displacement Theory; Hans Windisch[7] in 1926 elaborated the theory fully and thoroughly. According to it the fourth Evangelist's intention was not to supplement but to replace the older Gospels; he rejects them, and aims at driving them out of circulation in the Church, and taking their place himself.

These two theories in the last analysis are derived from the false assumption which negative Gospel criticism makes, namely that only the synoptic portrait of Jesus is true to the facts (for, they allege, he there remains entirely on a human plane), and that John's presentation of Christ as the pre-existing and consubstantial Son of God is incompatible with the synoptic portrait, and so must be rejected.

[7] *Joh. und die Syn. Wollte der vierte Evangelist die aelteren Evv. ergaenzen oder ersetzen?* Leipzig 1926. Idem, *Die Absolutheit des Joh-Ev*: ZsyTh 5 (1928) 3–54. Against him T. Sigge, *Das Joh-Ev und die Syn* (NtA XVI 2-3: 1935), and F. Buechsel: ZsyTh 4 (1926/27) 240–265.

6. Unity and integrity of the Gospel of St. John

Those who deny the Johannine authorship of the fourth Gospel generally also question its integrity. They point to alleged contradictions, duplications, obscurities, breaks, and sharp transitions in composition as well as faults of syntax, and infer that the Gospel has undergone a long process of evolution before reaching its final form.[8] Some of them distinguish an original work and one or more revisions, while others say that it is a conflation of several written sources, and generally maintain that the narrative and discourse material are of different origins.

Following older attempts, a literary approach to the Johannine problem was adopted around the beginning of the present century, particularly by J. Wellhausen[9], E. Schwartz[10], F. Spitta[11], H. H. Wendt[12], and W. Soltau.[13] This approach still has exponents—among them E. Hirsch[14] and R. Bultmann[15]—but it has not been generally adopted even by the critics. Thus E. Schweizer[16], after detailed examination of the language and style, considers that the Gospel of St. John is by and large a single work whose author has stamped the material with his own spirit and style; he concludes from this that it is now practically impossible to make a reliable reconstruction of the, presumably written,

---

[8] On this see Schweizer, *Ego eimi*, p. 82–112; Ruckstuhl, p. 1–19.

[9] *Erweiterungen und Aenderungen im vierten Ev*, Berlin 1907. Idem, *Das Ev Joh*, Berlin 1908.

[10] *Aporien im vierten Ev*: NGGW 1907, 1908.

[11] *Das Joh-Ev als Quelle der Geschichte Jesu*, Goettingen 1910.

[12] *Die Schichten im vierten Ev*, Goettingen 1911.

[13] *Das vierte Ev in seiner Entstehungsgeschichte dargelegt*, SBHeidelberg 1916 N. 6.

[14] *Das vierte Ev in seiner urspruenglichen Gestalt verdeutscht und erklaert*, Tuebingen 1936 (reviewed by Bultmann: EvTh 1937, 115–142).

[15] In his commentary (reviewed by Dibelius: ThLZ 1942, 257–264; E. Kaesemann: *Verkuendigung und Forschung*. Theol. Jahresb. 1942/47, 182–201; Joach. Jeremias: ThBl 1941, 33–46; E. Hirsch: ZntW 43, 1950/51, 129–143).—Another name which may be mentioned here is B. W. Bacon, *The Gospel of the Hellenists*, New York 1932 (discussed by M. Goguel: RHPhR 14, 1934, 415–439).

[16] *Ego eimi*, p. 108.

traditional material upon which the author drew. The unity of the Gospel has been defended by the other school among whom are Bernhard Weiss[17], E. Stange[18], Th. Bromboszcz[19], and E. Ruckstuhl.[20]

If the fourth Gospel was written by the Apostle St. John, then it is superfluous to seek for the sources which he uses, as is done in the case of the Synoptic Gospels. The only question is whether John gave the Gospel its final form, or if there were afterwards additions and appendices.

It is agreed by all that the *pericopa de adultera* 7, 53 to 8, 11 is a later interpolation. In vocabulary, style, and theme, it shows synoptic rather than Johannine traits. The Alexandrian Text form does not contain it; it appears first in Western Text sources (Db c e ff² and the Vulgate) and was also received in the Koine Text; it is unknown to Greek writers before the eleventh century. On the other hand it derives from ancient Tradition, its historicity is unassailable, and there is no doubt that it belongs to the Canonical Text. It has been placed after 7, 52 because of 8, 15: "I judge not any man." Some sources insert it elsewhere (after John 7, 36; 21, 24; Lk. 21, 38; Mk. 12, 17).

Some ancient and important MSS. do not contain 5, 3b–4. These verses were a gloss which later slipped into the text.

The question of the appendix chapter (ch. 21) is more difficult. Most probably it was not written by the Apostle, but was an account heard from him which one of his disciples added to the Gospel shortly after his death—certainly before the publication of the Gospel, for it occurs in all the text sources. The following considerations favour this:

[17] *Das Joh-Ev als ein einheitliches Werk geschichtlich erklaert,* Berlin 1912.

[18] *Die Eigenart der joh Produktion,* 1915.

[19] *Die Einheit des Joh-Ev,* Katowice 1927 (Catholic); pp. 11–19 contain a survey of the work of the literary critics.

[20] See above, and Gaechter: ZkTh 1952, 97–100. Also ThR 1952, 147–150.

1. All Text forms contain the conclusion 20, 30 sq.

2. The appendix presupposes the death of the beloved disciple (v. 20 sqq.).

3. Only here is there mention of the sons of Zebedee (v. 2).

4. The language and style of the appendix show close kinship with the rest of the Gospel; but they also show so many peculiarities which are foreign to the rest of the work that it is very difficult to assume that this chapter is by the same author.[21] Probably 19, 35 also is by the author of the appendix in view of its close relationship with 21, 24; in both verses he attests that the Evangelist is an eyewitness.

The text which has come down to us undeniably falters in places: to explain these difficulties, those who uphold the unity of St. John's Gospel assume that a number of pages have become transposed; these transpositions, they say, took place before the Gospel circulated outside its place of origin, and they impaired the sequence of thought in various places.

Both in Biblical and profane writings there are unquestionable cases where such dislocations have taken place during the transmission of the text from antiquity—for example Ecclus. 33, 13b to 36, 16a has been displaced from its original setting between 30, 24 and 30, 25 by a transposition of pages. Moreover, recent scholarship has shown that from the beginning the Christians used the Codex form (cf. § 12, 1) for their sacred writings. So this theory, which a large number of Catholic exegetes maintain, deserves serious consideration.[22]

The following cases call for examination in the light of this dislocation theory:

1. 3, 31–36 is intelligible neither in the mouth of the Baptist nor as a reflection of the Evangelist. In fact, it fits best after 3, 21.

---

[21] This point is demonstrated at length by Boismard: RB 54 (1947) 473–501.

[22] Cf. also N. Uricchio, *La teoria delle trasposizioni nel vangelo di S. Giovanni*: Bb 31 (1950) 128–163.

2. Chapters 5 and 6 have been interchanged. 6, 1 does not fit well after ch. 5, but it follows naturally after 4, 43–54.

3. 7, 15–24 is the continuation of the discourse of Jesus in 5, 19–47, for it refers to the cure of the lame man.[23]

4. The correct position of the Good Shepherd discourse 10, 1–18 is between 10, 29 and 10, 30; and 10, 19–21 concludes the discussion between Jesus and the Pharisees 9, 40 sq.

5. 12, 44–50 is out of its proper place, for the Evangelist's reflection in 12, 36b–43 closes the first part of the Gospel; the original position of 12, 44–50 was probably between 12, 36a and 12, 36b.

6. 14, 25–31 marks the departure of Jesus from the Apostles. Therefore ch. 15 and 16 are either a subsequent addition by the Apostle or are not in their original position.

7. It is to be presumed that 18, 14 to 23 originally followed immediately after v. 24.

More detailed justification of these transpositions will be found in the commentaries.

Other scholars would explain the numerous difficulties in the text by saying that the aged Apostle did not compose the work in one piece, but formed and composed it part by part over a period of years, dying in the course of the work before he gave it a final revision; after his death his disciples gave it the form in which it has reached us; they inserted into the book particular pieces which they considered valuable (for example, appendixes 4, 31–38; 6, 51c–58; 12, 24–26; 20, 2–10, parallel accounts, ch. 15 and 16 etc.) without fitting them into an organic unity with the rest of the book; they also were the authors of comments such as 4, 2; 4, 44; 11, 2; 19, 35; 21, 24 sq.; this would explain the literary polish of some passages side by side with the unfinished character of others.

Be that as it may, the Gospel, in spite of its literary faults

[23] According to Strathmann (p. 97 sq.), in the original plan ch. 5 stood between 7, 13 and 15, and so refers to the Feast of Tabernacles. 5, 1; 7, 1b; 7, 15 are insertions made by whoever published the Gospel.

and shortcomings, displays such unity in vocabulary, style, theology and presentation that it must have been conceived by one and the same mind.

7. *The purpose of St. John's Gospel*

The first conclusion (20, 30) tells us that it is the Evangelist's intention to confirm and deepen the faith of his readers in Jesus as the Messias and the consubstantial Son of God, and thereby to ensure that by their faith they may obtain Eternal Life. So the Gospel was not written to win over heathens or Jews to the Christian faith; it is intended for believing Christians, to lay a solid foundation for their conviction and faith. However, this didactic-practical aim is common to all four Gospels; the question arises whether the fourth Evangelist had also a special purpose, namely whether he wrote his book in silent controversy with certain opponents of the Christian Church in his day. That is in fact the case.

In this connection the outspoken opposition of the Gospel to Judaism is particularly striking. It is true that the Synoptic Gospels also record conflicts between Jesus and the Pharisees, but the controversies in the fourth Gospel are sharper and more fundamental. The Jews—and only they—are the real opponents of Jesus; they deny that he is the Son of God and of heavenly origin (5, 18; 8, 40–49); not only do they plot against his life (5, 18; 8, 40–59; 10, 31–39; 11, 8–50), but they excommunicate from the synagogue all who acknowledge him (9, 22; 12, 42), and even believe that they do a service to God by killing his disciples (16, 2). So it is easy to understand why the word "Jew" is practically synonymous with "unbelieving Jew" (cf. 2, 18 20 24; 5, 10 16 18; 6, 41–52; 7, 13; 9, 22 etc.).

The whole Gospel is permeated by a quiet but unmistakable polemic against Judaism. The Law was given through Moses, grace and truth come through Jesus Christ (1, 17); he is the end of Jewish ritualism (2, 1–10), and also of the Temple and its worship (2, 13–22; 4, 21–23). Moses could not give the true Bread from Heaven, the Father gives it by sending his Son into the world (6, 32 sq.). In reality the Jews are not (true) sons of Abraham, but sons of the devil (8, 39–44). They have no right to appeal to Moses; he is their accuser (5, 45). They search the scriptures diligently and hope to find life there, but it is to Jesus that the Scriptures bear witness (5, 39). They object that he is from Galilee (7, 52), but they are contradicted by the testimony of Nathaniel (1, 45 sqq.).

The fourth Gospel also impugns the exaggerated esteem in which John the Baptist was held by the sect of John's disciples; Acts 19, 1–8 tells us that this sect was in existence at Ephesus, and it lasted until the third century. The fourth Evangelist entirely ignores the Baptist's preaching of penance and judgment, to which the Synoptics devote much space; he presents the Baptist simply as the witness to the Greater One who comes after him. It is no accident that he delineates only those aspects of the Baptist which demonstrate his inferiority and subordination to Jesus: he is not the light, but is to give testimony of the light (1, 6–8); he is not the Messias nor Elias nor the Prophet (1, 20 sq.), but merely the friend of the bridegroom; Jesus must increase, but the Baptist must decrease (3, 28 to 30). His greatness consists entirely in proclaiming him who, as Lamb of God, takes away the sins of the world (1, 29). This portrayal of John is intelligible only if the Gospel contains a polemic against circles which see and venerate in John the figure of Messianic salvation.

We are told by Irenaeus (III 11, 1), Victorinus of Pettau (Comm. on Apc. 11, 1), Jerome (Prologue to Mt.) and others that on the insistence of the bishops of Asia Minor the Apostle John wrote his Gospel to refute the errors of the Gnostic Cerinthus (and Ebion).[24] Since the Gospel contains no direct polemic against

[24] Cf. H. Cladder, *Cerinth und unsere Evv*: BZ 14 (1917) 317–322.

heresies, it is impossible to infer from it what heresies the Evangelist was opposing. However, 1 John is by the author of the Gospel, and is closely related to it in style and thought, so we may take it that the Evangelist had in mind the same heresies as he attacks directly in the Epistle. As Strathmann says, the Epistle is "an outspoken rebuttal and denunciation of Gnosticism". According to 1 John 2, 22 sq. the heretics deny that Jesus is the Christ. For the early Christians Messiasship and Divine Sonship were indistinguishable, and so this heresy automatically entailed a denial of the Incarnation of the eternal Son of God (the Logos, John 1, 1), as is clear from the profession that Jesus is the Christ (5, 1), or the Son of God (5, 5). Against them the Epistle stresses that Jesus Christ has come in the flesh (4, 2 sq.). This is not a condemnation of Docetism; according to 2, 22 sq. it means that the Son of God has really become flesh, and has not simply dwelt in a transitory manner in the man Jesus. It is evident that the Epistle deals with a form of Gnosticism, and there is much to suggest that it actually was the heresy of Cerinthus, as described by Irenaeus I 26, 1.

Only this Gnostic background explains fully the strong emphasis on the doctrine that "the Word was made flesh" (1, 14), and the vigorous denial of any other Creator of the world besides the Logos (1, 13).

8. The origin of Johannine thought

In the nineteenth century the central problem of Johannine scholarship was the question of authorship; twentieth century efforts to solve the Johannine problem have concentrated on the relationship between Johannine thought and the syncretistic piety of late antiquity.

The critics place great stress not only on the clear distinction between Johannine and synoptic thought, but also on the notable divergence of John from Paul and from the works of Judaeo-

Hellenistic Christianity (Heb., 1 Clem., Epistle of Barnabas, Pastor of Hermas).

In particular those scholars whose approach was based on Comparative Religion asserted that Johannine thought could be regarded as a particular expression of Hellenistic Christianity; they attempted to derive the idea of the Logos (1, 1–14) from Greek speculation, and to explain the Gospel by means of parallels from the Alexandrian philosopher Philo (Grill, Heidmueller). G. P. Wetter, a Swedish scholar, compared the "Son of God" of the fourth Gospel to the Hellenistic "Saviour" (the "divine man"), and regarded John's work as a narrative about a θεῖος ἄνθρωπος.[25] W. Bousset tried to derive the "Christ spirituality" of John from the Hellenistic piety which we find in the mystery religions, and in certain astrological texts and hermetic writings.[26] A. Schweitzer regards Johannine theology as a hellenization of Paul's quite unhellenic spirituality.[27]

All these historical hypotheses have been superseded at the present day by the tendency to treat Johannine theology proper as a derivative from Eastern Gnosis, and to regard Palestine and Syria as its spiritual homeland. It can be shown that from the second century before Christ there were various late Jewish and Oriental Baptism sects in that area, particularly around the Jordan.[28] The best known is the sect of the Mandeans[29], which split off from Judaism in the first century A.D., and built up a Gnosis

---

[25] Der Sohn Gottes. Eine Untersuchung ueber Charakter und Tendenz des Joh-Ev, Goettingen 1916; cf. also L. Bieler, Θεῖος ἀνήρ 1 (1935) 134–140.

[26] Kyrios Christos. Geschichte des Christusglaubens von den Anfaengen des Christentums bis Irenaeus², Goettingen 1921.

[27] Die Mystik des Apostels Paulus, Tuebingen 1930.

[28] They are surveyed by J. Thomas, Le mouvement baptiste en Palestine et Syrie (150 C. to 300 A.D.), Gembloux 1935.

[29] H. Schlier, Zur Mandaeerfrage: ThRdsch NF 5 (1933) 1–34; 69–92. J. Schmid, Der gegenwaertige Stand der Mandaeerfrage: BZ 20 (1932) 121–138; 247–258. W. Baumgartner, Der heutige Stand der Mandaeerfrage: ThZ 6 (1950) 401–410; Idem, Sur la question des Mandéens: Hebrew Union College Annual XXIII 1 (1950/51) 41–71. J. Schmitt, Mandéisme: DB Suppl V, 758–788.

"which to some extent borrowed its principles and its terms from a Syrian Gnosis which, in turn, was under strong Iranian influence; this Gnosis also exercised an influence on the Gospel of St. John and other kindred writings; hence the Mandean writings contain traditions which may be invoked as analogies to clarify primitive Christian language" (Schlier). The Mandeans were located from the first century A.D. on the Upper Jordan, and later, at the end of the fifth century, they migrated to the lower Euphrates (present day Iraq). Their writings have been made accessible by Mark Lidzbarski.[30] His work and the studies of the philologist R. Reitzenstein[31] have aroused interest in early oriental Gnosis, and some exegetes believe that it is the key to understanding Johannine (and to some extent Pauline) thought.

Attempts to demonstrate close agreements between early Gnosis and Johannine thought have been made by W. Bauer (*John*, 3rd edition), and H. Windisch (*Johannine Epistles*, 2nd edition); they produced a rich collection of comparable matter from early Gnostic and Mandean sources as an "Oriental commentary" on John; H. Odeberg, the expert on Judaeo-Gnostic spirituality, has also written in this vein; but its chief exponent has been R. Bultmann in numerous articles[32], in his great commentary on John, and in his *Theology of the New Testament*.[33] His theme is that the fourth Gospel can be understood only against the background of the Gnostic saviour myth.

According to Reitzenstein, with whom Bultmann agrees, a myth of Iranian origin about primitive man and a saviour has recently been discovered, and it can be found not only in the

---

[30] *Das Johannesbuch* (1915); *Mandaeische Liturgien* (1920); *Ginza, der Schatz oder das grosse Buch der Mandaeer* (1925).

[31] *Das iranische Erloesungsmysterium*, Bonn 1921; *Vorchristliche Erloesungslehren*, Uppsala 1922 (separate impression); *Studien zum antiken Synkretismus*, Leipzig 1926; *Die hellenistischen Mysterienreligionen*[3], Leipzig 1927 etc. (Bibliography in Schlier).

[32] Eucharisterion, Festschrift f. H. Gunkel 11 (Goettingen 1923) 1–26; ZntW 24 (1925) 100–146.

[33] 15 and 41–50. Also his *Urchristentum*, Zurich 1949, 181 sqq. 210 sqq.

relatively late Mandean and Gnostic sources, but also in earlier Gnostic and semi-Gnostic writings (Jewish wisdom literature, Ignatius of Antioch, Odes of Solomon, Ascension of Isaias, Acts of Thomas, of James, and of Philip, the preaching of the Naasenes etc.).[34]

This myth, which deals with the fate of the soul ("the self" of man), runs as follows: At the beginning of time a heavenly form of light, primitive man, fell from the heavenly world into matter and was overpowered and divided by the demoniac powers of darkness; they used these pieces of light to construct out of the chaos of darkness the material world, which will last as long as the sparks of light are not withdrawn from it. These elements of light are the souls (the "self" properly so called) of human bodies; the demons try to stupefy them so that they may forget their heavenly origin. That is the cosmological side of the myth, dealing with the origin of souls, which are in need of redemption.

Now the most high Divinity sends down into the world a heavenly form of light, his son, his image (εἰκών), wrapped in a material and human exterior, so that he may escape the notice of the demons; he is sent to reveal to the souls (pieces of light) who are imprisoned in human bodies, their heavenly origin, their true home, and their return to the heavenly world of light. On completing his work this heavenly emissary (the saviour) ascends back into heaven, and so makes a way by which his own people may follow when their "self", their "spark of light", is freed from the body by death. The task of the emissary or saviour is to gather the sparks of light; his work is completed when they have all ascended and been reunited into the original form of light which at the beginning of time descended into matter and was imprisoned and divided. That is the soteriological side of the myth.

[34] Cf. H. Jonas, *Gnosis und spaetantiker Geist* I, *Die mythologische Gnosis*, Goettingen 1934; II 1, *Von der Mythologie zur mystischen Philosophie*, 1954.

In this myth the form of the heavenly emissary (the saviour or revealer) corresponds to the form of the original man. It is of importance that in the myth, saviour and saved stand in a relation to each other of parallelism or identity; the emissary is simply a copy of the soul, which recognizes itself again in him; what happens to the emissary happens to the soul, his salvation is its "saved saviour."

According to Bultmann, the Gospel of St. John presupposes this myth, but only its soteriological side; so we do not find in John the idea that the salvation which the divine emissary brings is the liberation of pre-existing sparks of light which demons hold in captivity in this lower world. Even on the soteriological side we miss the essential part, the parallelism or identity between saviour and saved. Furthermore there is in John a dominant interest, which the myth does not share, in the fate of the soul after death.

Both John (and also Paul) and the Gnosis share a fundamental dualism which is clearly expressed in the antitheses light and darkness, truth and falsehood, above and below, freedom and slavery. But it is only in the Gnosis that we find a metaphysical dualism. In the case of John we can speak only of an ethical or historical dualism; he does not say that man belongs to the heavenly world because his hidden "self" has the nature of light; according to John, man must freely decide for the heavenly world or its opposite (dualism of decision).

Above all, John's presentation of Christ resembles the Gnostic saviour myth. Jesus is the pre-existing Son of God whom the Father has equipped with power and sent into the world. He appears here as a man, and speaks the words which the Father has given him, and does the work which the Father has entrusted to him. In his discourses he reveals himself as the emissary who is in eternal unity with the Father. Since only "his own" understand him, he effects the division between those who hear his word and see, and those who do not hear it and remain in darkness. In the world, from which he calls "his own", he is hated and dishonoured. But he leaves the world again when he has completed his work. By his return to the Father he prepares for "his own" the way to the heavenly mansions into which he will lead them.

Bultmann maintains that it is not his view that the fourth Evangelist simply took over and to some extent christianized the Gnostic saviour myth; he stresses that John is speaking from his own experience of Jesus, though he expresses the story of redemption in and through the ideas of the soteriological myth. He says that John's terminology, which is clearly distinct from that of the Synoptics, originated in Gnostic mythology and not in the ancient Jewish tradition which forms the background to the other Gospels.

This view of Bultmann has met both with acceptance (by Schlier, Kaesemann, and Dibelius), and with various degrees of rejection. It is entirely rejected by Lagrange[35], F. Buechsel[36], Cerfaux[37], and E. Percy.[38]

Percy maintains in his comprehensive book that the Gospel of St. John was not influenced by the Gnosis either in language or in thought; on the contrary, the Gnosis derives from Johannine thought. The idea of a "saved saviour" who is the "self" of the soul is not, he says, of pre-Christian origin, but grew from Gnostic interpretation of Christian soteriology; it first appears in Mani and in the writings of the Christian Gnostics (Acts of John). There has been widespread agreement with this last point of Percy's, but not with his view that Gnosticism originated in Christian thought.

[35] RB 36 and 37 (1927 and 1928).

[36] *Joh und der hellenistische Synkretismus,* Guetersloh 1928.

[37] DB Suppl 3 (1938) 659–701: *Gnose.*

[38] *Untersuchungen ueber den Ursprung der joh Theologie,* Lund 1939 (on this Bultmann: OLZ 1940, 150–175).

Behm, Strathmann and others say that it is impossible to regard John as being influenced by the content of Gnosticism; but they claim that we must take account of Gnosticism and Syncretism if we are to gain a full understanding of the fourth Gospel in the context of its time; in particular, they say, the personified Logos may well originate from pre-Christian Gnosticism: they also maintain that E. Schweizer has demonstrated a connection between the "revelation formulae" of the Gnostics and some at least of John's "I am" sayings ("I am the light of the world, the true vine" etc.). They are therefore inclined to admit that a certain influence was exercised by Gnostic language and ideas.

The question of the source of John's concepts and ideas is discussed by C. H. Dodd in the first chapter of his book on the interpretation of the fourth Gospel (pp. 3–130). He suggests that the Gospel of St. John should be understood principally in the light of late Hellenism which itself had been stamped by Jewish ideas. While many of the concepts, ideas and symbols come directly from the Old Testament, he claims that there are also strong points of contact with Hellenistic and rabbinical Judaism. It is in the hermetic writings that he most often traces a spirit akin to the Gospel of St. John. He absolutely rejects influences from the Mandean writings and Eastern Gnosticism.

G. Quispel, *Het Johannesevangelie en de Gnosis:* Nederlands Theologisch Tijd-schrift 11 (1957) 173-203. H. Becker, *Die Reden des Joh-Ev und der Stil der gnosti-schen Offenbarungsrede,* Goettingen 1956. K. Rudolf, *Die Mandaeer* I. Prolegomena: Das Mandaeerproblem, Diss. Leipzig 1956.

It is quite true that the spiritual forerunner of Johannine writing was the world of Israelite and Jewish thought, and not Gnosticism with its timeless metaphysical dualism of substance, free from any historical setting. But the late Judaism of the time of Christ is a highly complex mass which is by no means satisfactorily known. That has been quite suddenly proved by the well-known MSS. finds which took place near the Dead Sea in 1947. They appear to cast new light on the spiritual antecedents of Johannine theology, for they are closely akin to it in ideas and terminology.

These writings, composed in Hebrew, are the work of a Jewish sect—a kind of "monastic community"—which in all probability is identical with the Essenes, though it probably had not reached the same stage of development as the Essenes whom Philo and Josephus describe. The community centre was at the present day Khirbet Qumran (near the caves) where the ruins of their community house or "monastery" have been discovered and excavated. It is fairly well established that their writings were composed in the years between (the beginning of?) the Macchabean period and the year 68 A.D. when the sect was annihilated or dispersed by the Romans.

These scrolls are closely related to the so-called "Damascus document" (a Zadokite fragment) which was published in 1910 by S. Schechter. This document is the work of a Jewish sect which migrated in the first century A.D. from Jerusalem to Damascus and there set itself up as the "Community of the New Covenant." There is an English version of it in R. H. Charles, *Pseudepigrapha*, Oxford 1913, 785–834.

The most recent writing about it is B. Reicke, *The Jewish "Damascus Documents" and the NT*, 1946 (Symb. Bibl. Ups.); H. H. Rowley, *The Zadokite Fragments and the Dead Sea Scrolls*, Oxford 1952; Chaim Rabin, *The Zadokite Documents*, Oxford 1954. It is impossible to give a survey of the literature about the Dead Sea Scrolls, cf. the reports of W. Baumgartner, *Die palaestinischen Hss-Funde* I (ThRdsch NF 17, 1948/49, 329–346), II (ibid. 19, 1951, 97–154). There are good surveys in G. Molin, *Die Soehne des Lichtes. Zeit und Stellung der Hss vom Toten Meer*, Vienna 1954, G. Vermès, *Les manuscrits du désert de Juda*, Paris ²1954, and H. Bardtke, *Die Hss-Funde am Toten Meer*, ²1953.

These writings have not yet been entirely published, and only initial efforts have been made to estimate how far they elucidate the Johannine writings or explain their religious and philosophical background. Much more research and study will be required before any degree of certainty can be attached to the results. It is possible here to mention only some important studies: K. G. Kuhn, *Die in Palaestina gefundenen hebraeischen Texte und das NT*: ZThK 47 (1950) 192–211; Idem, *Die Sektenschrift und die iranische Religion*, ibid. 49 (1952) 296–316; F.-M. Braun, *L'arrière-fond judaïque du IVme év. et la Communauté d'Alliance*: RB 62 (1955) 5–44; R. E. Brown, *The Qumran Scrolls and the Joh. Gospel and*

Epistles: CBQ 17 (1955) 403–419; 559–574 (with bibliography); W. F. Albright, *Recent Discoveries in Palestine and the Gospel of John: The Background of the NT: Essays in Honour of C. H. Dodd,* 1956, 153–171; L. Mowry, *The Dead Sea Scrolls and the Background to the Gospel of John:* Biblical Archaeologist 17 (1954) 78–97; A. Metzinger, *Die MSS-Funde am Toten Meer und das NT:* Bb 36 (1955) 457–481.

The Gospel and Epistles of John (as well as of Paul) share a striking dualism which is paralleled only in late Jewish apocalyptic writings. Unlike the Iranian dualism it is not absolute, for neither of the principles is uncreated or independent but they are created by God. Evil will be annihilated by him at the end of time. Furthermore it differs from Gnostic dualism, for it is not metaphysical (or cosmological-mythical) but ethical, that is, the opposition is not between matter and spirit, but between good and evil.

In the writings of the sect the antitheses are between light and darkness, truth and evil (wickedness, wrong). Each of the opposing and conflicting worlds is ruled by a prince or angel; one of the rulers is called the prince of lights, the spirit (or angel) of truth, the other is the angel of darkness or of wickedness. Correspondingly men are divided into two mutually hostile camps, sons of light and sons of darkness. The sons of light are the members of the sect. One of their writings which has been discovered bears the title *Book of the Wars of the Sons of Light against the Sons of Darkness;* it is translated by H. Bardtke: ThLZ 1955, 401–420, and by L. Delcor: NRTh 87 (1955) 372–399. The angel of darkness and his supporters try to mislead the sons of light.

Furthermore the spirits of truth and the spirits of wickedness struggle in the hearts of individual men; but in the end God annihilates the spirits of wickedness and gives the sons of light eternal joy in an everlasting life, while eternal ruin, ignominy and distress await the sons of darkness.

In the *Manual of Discipline,* which is the most important book of this sect, an entire section (III, 13 to IV, 26) is devoted to this dualism. K. Schubert discusses its relation to Gnosticism etc. in ThLZ 1953, 495–506. The agreement both in terminology and in thought between John and the writings of the sect is most remarkable. Yet there is a great difference between the two. Because of divine predestination there is a fundamental and irreconcilable cleavage between the members of the sect and the men who live outside their community in union with Belial. In John also we find a fundamental cleavage between the community of Christ and the world which opposes God; but this cleavage is determined by the attitude which each individual adopts to the Person of Christ. So there is no question of John being dependent on the Qumran Sect; cf. G. Baumbach, *Der Dualismus in der Sektenrolle verglichen mit dem Dualismus in den spaetjuedischen Apokalypsen und dem Joh-Ev,* Dissertation, Berlin 1956 (unpublished).

A Gnostic library of forty eight books in Coptic, most of them hitherto unknown, was discovered at the town of Nag-Hammadi (near the ancient Chenoboskion) in Upper Egypt. This find is of great significance for the history of early Christianity, and it will certainly be of considerable value for elucidating the relation between Gnosticism and the Gospel of St. John, which, as the early Fathers tell us, was written to oppose the heresy of the Gnostic Cerinthus (§ 28, 7). Of these writings only one codex is available; it was acquired for the C. G. Jung Institute in Zurich, and is called the "Jung Codex"; cf. H. C. Puech, G. G. Quispel and W. C. van Unnik, *The Jung Codex. A Newly Recovered Papyrus,* 1955. Besides other writings, this codex contains the "Gospel of truth" which was probably composed in Greek by Valentinus himself about 150 A.D.; Irenaeus, Adv. Haer. III 11, 9 tells us that it was used by the followers of Valentinus the Gnostic. The Coptic text has now been published together with versions in French, German, and English: H. Malinine, H.-C. Puech, and G. Quispel: *Evangelium veritatis: Codex Jung,* 1956. According to Quispel the Jung Codex shows no traces of a pre-Christian saviour. "The Gnostic Man (Anthropos) probably comes from the Jewish doctrine about Adam. The origins of this Gnosis are to be sought in the esoteric Judaism of the Middle East and in the syncretistic world of the Near East."

9. Time and place of composition

According to the tradition of the early Church the fourth Gospel was the last of the four canonical Gospels. Since the Apostle John spent the least years of his life in Asia Minor (Ephesus), and died in Ephesus, the Gospel must have been composed there. The ancient prologue to John, Jerome (*De vir.* III 9), and Epiphanius (*Panarion* 51, 12) speak only in general terms of Asia Minor; Irenaeus (III 1, 1) says that it was written at Ephesus.

The only Father to say that it was composed at Antioch in Syria is Ephrem the Syrian in an appendix to his commentary on the *Diatessaron*[39]; it is not clear where he got this information— Tatian himself has been suggested as the source. However, it has found favour with some modern scholars who consider that the Gospel was written in Syria (Antioch); they support their theory by referring to the alleged kinship between the Gospel and the Syrian Gnosis and to its close linguistic and theological contacts with the epistles of Ignatius of Antioch (W. Bauer, E. Hirsch, R. Bultmann and others). But the relationship between the fourth Gospel and Syrian Gnosis is disputed and by no means clear enough[40] to justify such conclusions (see above n. 8).

It is also difficult to determine the time of composition. According to Irenaeus (II 25, 5; III 3, 4) and Clement of Alexandria (apud Euseb. H. E. III 23, 5), John lived into the reign of Trajan (98–117 A.D.), and so must have died about 100 A.D. So the Gospel must have been composed before the turn of the century, presumably in the nineties of the first century, but it is not impossible that some parts had already been committed to writing before 90 A.D.

[39] Printed in ZntW 3 (1902) 193.
[40] Cf. Chr. Maurer, *Ignatius von Antiochien und das Joh-Ev*, Zurich 1949.

This reasoning is supported by the external evidence. It is highly probable that Ignatius of Antioch knows the Gospel[41], and papyrus 52 with fragments of John 18, 31–33 37–38 proves that it was in circulation in Egypt in the early second century (cf. § 12, 3). This has ruled out the attempts which were made in the past to assign the fourth Gospel to the mid–second century.

§ 29. THE ACTS OF THE APOSTLES

Commentaries: (a) J. E. Belser, *Die Apg uebersetzt und erklaert,* Vienna 1905. E. Jacquier, *Les actes des apôtres,* Paris 1926. A. van der Heeren, *Commentarius in Actus apostolorum,* Bruges 1927. A. Boudou, 1933 (VS VII). A. Steinmann, [4]1934 (Bonner NT 4). A. Wikenhauser, [3]1956 (RegNT 5). — (b) H. H. Wendt, 1913 (Meyer III[9]). E. Preuschen, 1912 (Leitzmann 5). R. Knopf, [3]1917 (GoettNT 4). G. Hoennicke, *Die Apg erklaert,* Leipzig 1913. A. Loisy, *Les actes des apôtres,* Paris 1920. Th. Zahn, 2 vols., [3]1922, 1927 (Zahn V). F. J. Foakes-Jackson, 1932 (Moffatt). K. Lake - H. J. Cadbury, *The Acts of the Apostles,* 2 vols., London 1933 (*The Beginnings of Christianity* I 4 and 5). H. W. Beyer, [5]1949 (NT Deutsch 5). O. Bauernfeind, 1939 (ThHK 5). F. F. Bruce, [2]1954 (NIC). E. Haenchen, 1956 (Meyer III[10]; 665 pp.). B. Reicke, *Glauben und Leben der Urgemeinde.* Commentary on Acts 1–7, Basle 1957.

Studies: A. Harnack see § 25. H. Koch, *Die Abfassungszeit des lukanischen Geschichtswerkes,* Leipzig 1911. A. Wikenhauser, *Die Apg und ihr Geschichtswert* (NtA VIII, 3–5: 1921). Idem, *Die altkirchliche Ueberlieferung ueber die Abfassungszeit der Apg:* BZ 23 (1935/36) 365–371. *The Beginnings of Christianity* P. I: *Acts of the Apostles,* ed. F. J. F. Jackson and K. Lake, Vol. 2: *Criticism,* London 1922. M. Dibelius, *Stilkritisches zur Apg:* Eucharisterion (Festschrift fuer H. Gunkel) II (1923) 27–49. E. Meyer, *Ursprung und Anfaenge des Christentums* III, Berlin 1923. H. H. Wendt, *Die Hauptquelle der Apg:* ZntW 24 (1925) 293–305. K. Bornhaeuser, *Studien zur Apg,* Guetersloh 1934. M. Dibelius, *Paulus auf dem Areopag,* 1939 (SBHeidelberg 1938/39 H. 2). Joach. Jeremias, *Untersuchungen zum Quellenproblem der Apg:* ZntW 36 (1937) 205–221. L. Pirot, Art. *Actes des apôtres:* DBSuppl 1 (1928) 42–86. T. W. Manson, *The Work of St. Luke:* BJRL 28 (1944) 382–403. W. L. Knox, *The Acts of the Apostles,* Cambridge 1948. Ph. Vielhauer, *Zum "Paulinismus" der Apg:* EvTh 1950/51, 1–15. M. Dibelius, *Die Reden der Apg und die antike Geschichtsschreibung:* SBHeidelberg 1949 H. 1. Idem., *Studies in the Acts of the Apostles,* S. C. M., 1956 (contains nine previously published and two hitherto unpublished works). A. Voegeli, *Lukas und Euripides:* ThZ 9 (1953) 415–438. H. F. D. Sparks, *The Semitisms of the Acts:* JThSt NS 1 (1950) 16–28.

[41] Cf. Maurer, *op. cit.,* and W. v. Loewenich, *Das Joh-Verstaendnis im 2. Jh.,* Giessen 1932.

J. Dupont, *L'utilisation apologétique du VT dans les discours des Actes:* EphThL 26 (1953) 289-327. Ph.-H. Menoud, *Le plan des Actes des Apôtres:* NTSt I (1954/55) 44-51. Idem, *Remarques sur les textes de l'ascension dans Luc-Actes:* Ntl Studien f. R. Bultmann, 1954, 148-156 [Lk.'s work was originally one book; Lk. 24, 49 was followed immediately by Acts 1, 6]. O. Bauernfeind, *Zur Frage nach der Entscheidung zwischen Paulus und Lukas:* ZsyTh 23 (1954) 337-352 [against Vielhauer]. E. Haenchen, *Tradition und Komposition in der Apg:* ZThK 52 (1955) 205-225 [a documentary account or contemporary picture of the Apostolic Era should not be looked for in Acts: we rather find in it the picture which a later Christian age drew of its own past. Haenchen adopts this approach in his commentary]. H. J. Cadbury, *The Book of Acts in History,* 1955 [the position of Acts in the history of its own time]. J. Dupont, *Notes sur les actes des apôtres:* RB 62 (1955) 45-59. J. N. Sanders, *Peter and Paul in the Acts:* NTSt 2 (1955) 133-143 [on ch. 9-15]. St. Giet, *Les trois premiers voyages de St. Paul à Jérusalem:* RSR 41 (1953) 321-347 (against him J. Dupont: RB 1955, 55-59).

New Editions of the text: J. H. Ropes, *The Text of the Acts,* London 1926 (*The Beginnings of Christianity* I 3). A. C. Clark, *The Acts of the Apostles. A Critical Edition with Introduction and Notes on Selected Passages,* Oxford 1933.

Surveys of Research: C. Clemen, *Die Apg im Lichte der neueren Text-, Quellen- und historisch-kritischen Forschungen,* Giessen 1905. M. Dibelius: ThRdsch NF 3 (1931) 233-242. J. Dupont, *Les problèmes du livre des Actes d'après les travaux récents* (1940-1950), Louvain 1950. See also the surveys on primitive Christianity by H. Windisch (ThRdsch 1933) and W. G. Kuemmel (ThRdsch 1942, 1948, 1950). W. G. Kuemmel *Das Urchristentum:* ThRdsch NF 14 (1942) 81-95; 155-173; 17 (1948) 3-50; 103-142; 18 (1950) 1-52; 22 (1954) 138-170; 191-211.

Decision of the Pontifical Biblical Commission of 12th June 1923; Acts was written by Luke the Evangelist, towards the end of Paul's first Roman imprisonment; it is fully trustworthy.

1. *Content and structure*

Introduction: Prologue 1, 1-2; appearances of the Risen Christ and Ascension 1, 3-14; choosing of an Apostle 1, 15-26.

First part: The Church in its Judaeo-Christian period
2, 1 to 9, 31

I. The original community: Origin and growth, relations with the Jewish authorities, religious-social life 2, 1 to 8, 3.

1. The foundation of the Church through the pouring out of the Holy Ghost at Pentecost; the common life 2, 1-47.

2. First conflict with the Jewish authorities on the occasion of

Peter curing a lame man in the Temple; second description of the common life 3, 1 to 5, 16.

3. Second conflict with the Jewish authorities 5, 17–42.

4. Third conflict with the Jewish authorities 6, 1 to 8, 3: Appointment of seven deacons 6, 1–7; testimony of Stephen before the council, his death 6, 8 to 8, 1a; persecution and dispersal of the original community 8, 1b–3.

II. The Judaeo-Palestinian mission as a preliminary step to the Gentile mission 8, 4 to 9, 31.

1. Philip "the deacon" as missionary: conversion of the Samaritans (Simon Magus) and of the Ethiopian eunuch 8, 4–10.

2. The conversion and vocation of Paul, the leading persecutor of the Church, and afterwards the Apostle of the Gentiles 9, 1–31.

Second part: Foundation and establishment of the Gentile mission 9, 32 to 15, 35

I. The beginnings of the mission to the Gentiles 9, 32 to 12, 25.

1. The baptism of the centurion Cornelius and his household in Caesarea 9, 32 to 11, 18: Peter in Lydda (Aeneas) and Joppe (Tabitha) 9, 32 to 43; Peter and Cornelius 10, 1 to 11, 18.

2. The beginnings of the community in Antioch (foundation); Barnabas and Paul there; collection for relief of the famine 11, 19–30.

3. Persecution of the original community by Herod Agrippa I 12, 1–25: Imprisonment and miraculous liberation of Peter 12, 1 to 19; death of the persecutor 12, 20–25.

II. The establishment of the mission to the Gentiles 13, 1 to 15, 35.

1. First missionary journey of Barnabas and Paul (the first strictly missionary undertaking) 13, 1 to 14, 28: Cyprus (Paphus, the proconsul Sergius Paulus) 13, 1–12; Southern Galatia (Antioch of Pisidia, Iconium, Lystra, Derbe) 13, 13 to 14, 20; return to Antioch 14, 21–28.

2. The decision of the Apostolic Council on the admission of Gentiles to the Church (Apostolic decree) 15, 1–35.

Third part: The mission to the Gentiles and the Apostle of the Gentiles (Paul) 15, 36 to 28, 31

I. Paul at the height of his missionary activity 15, 36 to 21, 14.

1. The second missionary journey (Macedonia and Achaea) 15, 36 to 18, 22: Departure from Antioch 15, 36–41; through Asia Minor (Northern Galatia!) to Troas 16, 1–10; in Macedonia (Philippi, Thessalonica, Beroea) 16, 11 to 17, 15; in Achaea (Athens, Corinth) 17, 16 to 18, 17; return to Antioch by Ephesus and Caesarea 18, 18–22.

2. The third missionary journey (Ephesus) 18, 23 to 20, 4: Apollo the Alexandrian in Ephesus and Corinth 18, 24–28; Paul in Ephesus 19, 1–22; riot of the silversmiths (Demetrius) 19, 23–40; departure of Paul, visit to Macedonia and winter in Achaea (Corinth) 20, 1–4.

3. Last journey to Jerusalem (through Philippi, Troas, Miletus [farewell discourse to the elders of Ephesus], Caesarea); gloomy warnings and prophecies 20, 5 to 21, 14.

II. Paul as the martyr of his missionary work. His testimony as a prisoner for Christ 21, 15 to 28, 31.

1. Arrival in Jerusalem and visit to the original community; attempt to avert the danger threatened by the Jews 21, 15–26.

2. In the Temple and as a prisoner in the Antonia fortress 21, 27 to 23, 35: Attack on Paul by fanatical Jews of the Diaspora, and his rescue by the Roman garrison 21, 27–40; address to the people 22, 1–21; in the fortress 22, 22–29; before the council 22, 30 to 23, 11, Attempt on his life by the Jews 23, 12–33; his transfer to Caesarea 23, 23–35.

3. The trial of Paul before the governor in Caesarea 24, 1 to 26, 32; Trial before Felix 24, 1–23; postponement of the trial 24, 24–27; before Festus; Paul's appeal to Caesar 25, 1–12; Festus

informs King Agrippa II about the trial 25, 13–22; Paul defends himself before Agrippa 25, 23 to 26, 32.

4. Paul is brought to Rome 27, 1 to 28, 14: From Caesarea to Crete by Myra of Lycia 27, 1–8; storm at sea 27, 9–38; shipwreck near Malta with no loss of life 27, 39–44; winter in Malta 28, 1–10; from Malta to Rome 28, 11–16.

5. Two-year imprisonment of Paul in Rome; Paul and the Roman Jews 28, 17–31.

2. Name and purpose

The name Πράξεις (τῶν) ἀποστόλων—*Actus* or *Acta Apostolorum*, Acts of the Apostles—is applied to the book which continues St. Luke's Gospel, and which forms with it a carefully designed historical work. This title is found both in all the ancient MSS. and versions and in all the Fathers without exception; Irenaeus occasionally calls it "true testimony of the acts and teaching of the Apostles" (*Haer.* III 15, 1), or "Discourses and Acts of the Apostles" (III 12, 1), but these names are merely paraphrases of the usual title. The title is not an accurate description of the contents, for generally speaking it records only the acts of the two most important Apostles, Peter and Paul, and its account even of their acts is far from being complete, particularly in the case of Peter. Except for the list of 1, 13 most of the other Apostles are not named at all; only Judas, John and his brother James—and James the brother of the Lord, if he belonged to the Apostolic college (cf. § 47)—are mentioned by name and made the subject of some small happening. On the other hand, men who were not Apostles play a certain role in the book: Barnabas—though he is called an Apostle in 14, 4 13—Stephen, Philip, and Apollo.

Yet it is significant that a list of Apostles is given at the beginning of the book, the filling up of the Apostolic college is reported in 1, 13 sqq., and throughout the first half of the book "the

Apostles" very often appear as a college (2, 14; 5, 18; 6, 2; 8, 14; 9, 27; 11, 1; 15, 2–22), though only their spokesmen and leaders are mentioned by name. In antiquity it was not unusual for a book to get its title from whatever was mentioned in the first pages or columns. Indeed the title "Acts of the Apostles" fits this book fairly well, for it is a continuation of St. Luke's Gospel, whose content can be summed up as "Acts and words of Jesus"—though it is to be noted that the teachings of the Apostles are in no way a counterpart to the teaching of Jesus in the Gospels.

It is impossible to say with certainty whether the title is due to the author himself; very probably it is. The book must have had a title of its own, for it was probably written some time after the Gospel, and separately published; if this was not the case, it is hard to understand why Acts begins by partly repeating and expanding the conclusion of the Gospel, or why it contains a list of the Apostles, since there is a list in Lk. 6, 13–16.

In antiquity the expression πράξεις was very common as a description of the deeds of outstanding individuals such as Hercules or Alexander the Great, and it was occasionally used as a book title. Thus Callisthenes, a nephew of Aristotle, composed a work Πράξεις 'Αλεξάνδρου, and Sosylus, the comrade in arms and language instructor of Hannibal, wrote Πράξεις 'Αννίβα.[1]

Acts is not intended to be a history of the Apostles nor of the primitive Church up to the author's own time; indeed, it is not even an account of the work of the two chief Apostles Peter and Paul, in spite of the fact that it is mainly devoted to their works and vicissitudes. The author is interested not so much in their acts as in the mighty and triumphant progress of the Gospel through the whole known world. The theme of the book is the saying of Our Lord "You shall be witnesses unto me in Jerusalem, and in all Judea and Samaria, and even to the uttermost part of the earth" (1, 8). Hence Luke the Gentile Christian is interested especially

[1] See A. Wikenhauser, *Die Apg und ihr Geschichtswert*, pp. 94—104.

in the turning of the preaching mission from the Jews to the Gentiles, in the rise of the Gentile mission, and in the origin of the Gentile Christian Church. Behind the continuous progress of the message of Christ through all lands he sees the wonderful operation and power of the Holy Ghost, whom the Risen Christ promised and sent to his Apostles (Lk. 24, 49; Acts 1, 4 sqq.; 2, 1 sqq.). So the theme of the book may be summed up thus: Acts depicts the universal spread of the Christian religion which was begun and maintained by the power of the Holy Ghost.

In this connection Luke devoted special attention, as was said already, to the rise of the Gentile mission. That is why he gives such a lengthy account of the Baptism of the Gentile centurion Cornelius and his household, which takes place on the express orders of God, and with the subsequent approval of the mother community in Jerusalem. The conversion of Paul, the great missionary of the Gentiles, and his commission to preach to them is repeated no less than three times (chs. 9, 22, 26). When Paul and Barnabas begin the large scale mission to the Gentiles (ch. 13–14) everything else fades into the background. Peter, the head of the mission to the Jews (Gal. 2, 7), now passes entirely from the centre of the stage; there is no further report of the primitive community at Jerusalem except for the so-called Apostolic Council when they accept the Gentiles into the Church without binding them to the Mosaic Law; the decree of the council is repeated verbatim (15, 23–29).

Luke's account of the rise and development of the Gentile mission is not, of course, even substantially complete—he had not the necessary sources—but he describes it essentially as the work of Paul. He is well aware that Paul was neither the first nor the only missionary to the Gentiles; he tells, though not in detail, how the mission began before Paul and without him. The reason why he confines himself mainly to Paul's missionary work is that this Apostle was indisputably the greatest and most successful missionary to the Gentiles; furthermore, having accompanied Paul for a time, his was the work which Luke appreciated best. Hence the centre of interest in the second part is what Paul does and what happens to him. That is the only way to explain why the imprisonment and trial of Paul occupy so much of the book.

3. The sources

Luke says nothing about the sources which he used in the composition of Acts, but many scholars have applied detailed source criticism in an effort to determine what written accounts or reports he drew upon. Yet up to the present these studies have reached no satisfactory or universally accepted conclusions. Their history up to 1907 has been surveyed by A. Bludau (BZ 5, 1907), and from 1907 to 1920 by Alfred Wikenhauser *(Die Apg und ihr Geschichtswert p. 65 sqq.)*.

The vocabulary and style are so uniform that they are no help in identifying written sources; discrepancies and unevennesses are generally regarded as sure signs that written sources have been used; but these are scattered so regularly throughout the whole of Acts that they do not serve the purpose either. Even the most modern attempts to identify sources have not been widely accepted; among them we may mention Joachim Jeremias (see above), who believes that a source has been incorporated at 6, 1 stretching to 15, 35 or perhaps to the end of the book, from which come 6, 1 to 8, 4; 9, 1–30; 11, 19–30; 12, 25 to 14, 28; 15, 35 sqq.

In the last few decades the view has gradually gained ground that it is quite impossible to prove that written sources were used for the first half of Acts. It is generally assumed that the author of Acts used a number of individual traditions of various lengths, some of which perhaps had already been committed to writing. It is said that the only really tangible written source is an itinerary of Paul's journeys written by one of his companions with short notes on the foundation of the various communities and the result of the mission; the "We passages" are said to derive from this; they say that the author inserted into this itinerary some extra material (particularly the discourses; cf. 13, 15 to 42; 17, 19–33; 20, 17–38) and other traditions, especially self-contained narratives such as the Elymas episode (13, 6–12), the Lystra story (14, 8–18), and the story of Demetrius (19, 23–40). Dibelius proposed this theory in 1923 in his work *"Stilkritisches zur Apg,"* and it was developed in detail by Bauernfeind in his commentary (cf. also Johnson: AThR 21, 1939, 22–31).

If Luke's authorship be granted, there is no serious difficulty in deciding what sources he used for the second half of the book. In the "We passages" he speaks as an eyewitness. These passages also stand out noticeably from the other parts of Acts; their narrative style is very lively and graphic; nowhere else in the work do we find such richness and exactness in the details of time and place; and the persons who appear are generally mentioned by name. Evidently Luke used some written notes—a kind of diary— for these parts, especially for the journeys which he made in Paul's company. He was with or near Paul—probably with interruptions—through the entire period between the departure from Philippi (20, 4) and the arrival in Rome (28, 16); so his account of the imprisonment and trial of the Apostle in Jerusalem and Caesarea is written either at first hand or from the reports of eyewitnesses.

Luke was not with Paul in the period between the first and second "We passages", that is during the greatest part of the second and third missionary journeys. Yet he obtained useful information about this period, for his account is fairly extensive and contains many concrete details—the work in Athens, the name of the proconsul Gallio in Corinth, the length of the Corinthian and Ephesus episodes, the riot of the silversmiths under Demetrius, etc. Nevertheless chapters 17–19 have not the wealth of detail and the exactness which we find in the "We passages";

his account of the work at Corinth and Ephesus omits most of what we learn or can infer from the Epistles to the Corinthians; for example, the information about Apollo and about the disciples of John in Ephesus is very scanty and incomplete.

By spending a year with or near Paul Luke had plenty of opportunities to collect information about the history of primitive Christianity from firsthand witnesses. On Paul's second missionary journey he accompanied Silas from Jerusalem and Timothy from Lystra. In Caesarea he knew important personages of the Palestinian Church, (Philip 21, 8; Agabus 21, 10; Manson 21, 16; James and the presbyters 21, 18 sqq.). So he was in a position to learn the history of the primitive Church by word of mouth. His account of Philip's mission probably goes back to Philip himself, who is probably also the source for the story of the seven deacons and the martyrdom of Stephen. He probably learned in Caesarea about the conversion of the centurion Cornelius and the death of Herod Agrippa. But there can hardly be any doubt that he also used other people's writings in the first third of Acts, though it is impossible to determine with certainty their extent or form.

He did not make use of the Pauline Epistles which are our most important source for Paul's life and theology. They had not been collected when he was writing. He must have known some of them but he did not use them for his account of the Pauline mission.

4. Historical truth

For a long time past the historical truth of the greatest part of Acts, or even of the whole work, has been denied by the critical-liberal scholars.

This movement originated in 1841 with a book by M. Schnekkenburger on the purpose of Acts. He considered that Acts was written to justify Paul in the eyes of the Judaists, and so, he alleged,

Paul is made to resemble Peter as much as possible, and everything is passed over which suggests opposition between him and the Judaists; he is depicted as a loyal keeper of the Law (celebration of Jewish feasts, journeys to Jerusalem with visits to the Temple, circumcision of Timothy), who voluntarily subjects himself to the authorities of the primitive community (Apostolic council, undertaking of the costs for the sacrifice of the Nazarenes). For the same reason Acts makes no mention of his refusal to circumcise Titus (Gal. 2, 3), his confronting of Peter in Antioch (Gal. 2, 11 sqq.), his mission in Galatia, and his struggle against the Judaists. Nevertheless Schneckenburger found no actually false traits in the portrait of Paul in Acts, and he maintained that Luke was its author.

F. Chr. Baur of Tuebingen and his school placed the composition of Acts in the second century and denied that it had any historical value; they regarded it as a tendentious work which assimilated the portraits of the two leading Apostles, Peter and Paul, in the interests of the compromise between Paulinism and Judaeo-Christianity (Peter).

Though the "tendency criticism" of the Tuebingen school (cf. § 2) has long been abandoned, yet even to-day the historical value of Acts is often attacked. It is denied that the author was Luke, the companion of Paul—they attribute only the "We passages" to him—its time of composition is said to be the end of the first century, and it is accused of not giving a true picture of the tensions and divergences which, as the Pauline Epistles show, existed within the primitive Church.

Yet in recent decades there has been a distinct reaction in favour of Acts. Even the critics take its historical character more seriously.

There is no doubt that Acts was intended to be history; it is not a worthless piece of tendentious writing. We do not find in it the entire history of the primitive Church, but it does tell of the origin of the Church and of its spread to the most diverse

lands and provinces of the Roman Empire in spite of all persecutions and hostile opposition. Its historical content is invaluable.
Without this book complete darkness would envelop many
aspects of the growth of primitive Christianity, in spite of the
evidence of the Pauline Epistles.

It is true that Luke cannot be compared with the great ancient
historians like Thucydides, Polybius and Tacitus. Since his aim
was practical and religious he did not attempt to give an extended
and detailed account of the sometimes very sharp and uninteresting
struggles between Paul, the chief standard bearer of universalism,
and reactionary Judaism, nor of the many conflicts and difficulties
which Paul had with his communities (cf. Gal., 1 and 2 Cor.).
In keeping with this practical tendency, Acts concentrates on the
light, though without ignoring the shadows (cf. 5, 1 sqq.; 6, 1 sqq.;
15, 39; 21, 20 sq.).

Naturally Luke, like any historian, depends on his sources. The
more copious and dependable they are, the more valuable is his
account. When he speaks as an eyewitness he is much more
exact, more graphic and more detailed than when he is reporting
at second hand. The nearer he is to the events related, the
greater the value of his account. The first half of the book is
less graphic and exact than the second; in particular it gives
no dates—with the solitary exception of 11, 26—so that it is
difficult to say how much time is covered by the three conflicts
between the Jerusalem community and the Jewish authorities,
and it is hard to make a chronological arrangement of the events
between the death of Stephen and the Apostolic Council. We
can only say that the events reported in the first fifteen chapters
cover about twenty years—and it is the figures in Gal. 1, 18; 2, 1
which enable us to reach this conclusion. The second half, on the
other hand, contains some precise chronological information
(18, 11: a year and a half in Corinth; 19, 8–10: two years and a
quarter in Ephesus; 20, 31: three years in Ephesus; 24, 27: two

years in Caesarea; 28, 30: two years in Rome), which makes possible a much more accurate chronology of the period after the Apostolic Council.

The Pauline Epistles provide a check on much of the content of Acts. If we compare the information about Paul in Acts with the self-revelations in the Epistles, we discover that Acts everywhere stands up to examination. The information in the Epistles is much more copious and more precise, but we learn much from Acts which does not appear in the Epistles about Paul and his work, in particular the routes of his journeys, the places where he preached, and also his trial before the governor's court. There are divergences between the two sources which have not all been completely reconciled, but by far the greatest part of the information about Paul in Acts is confirmed magnificently by the Epistles.[2]

The divergences in question occur particularly in § 11–15. According to Acts, Paul made three journeys to Jerusalem between his conversion and the Apostolic Council: 1) from Damascus soon after his conversion 9, 26–30; 2) from Antioch in company with Barnabas to deliver the famine collection 11, 30; 12, 25; 3) again with Barnabas from Antioch for the Apostolic Council 15, 1 sqq.

On the other hand Paul mentions only two journeys: 1) from Damascus three years after his conversion Gal. 1, 18; 2) from Antioch with Barnabas and Titus fourteen years later Gal. 2, 1.

If we assume that Gal. 2, 1–10 and Acts 15 refer to the same journey, then Gal. makes no mention of the journey with the collection of Acts 11, 30. Is this journey to be regarded as unhistorical? In spite of numerous discussions there is no unanimity on the matter.

However, there is no valid reason to declare Acts 11, 27–30

[2] See the demonstration of this detail in Wikenhauser, *Die Apg und ihr Geschichtswert,* pp. 169–298.

unhistorical in the face of its concreteness and its lack of improba-
bilities, nor to say that there has been confusion with the great
collection in the Pauline missionary territory (1 Cor. 16, 1;
2 Cor. 8–9; Gal. 2, 10). It is questionable whether the list of
journeys in Galatians was intended to be exhaustive, for Paul's
point there is simply that his apostolate was independent of the
authorities in Jerusalem; to prove this he declares that he did not
go to Jerusalem until three years after his conversion, and then he
stayed only fourteen days, returning to Syria and Cilicia without
being known by sight to the Christian communities of Judea.

He is proving a new theme in Gal. 2, 1, namely that the authorities in Jerusalem had approved his Gospel of uncircumcision. If
the delivery of the collection by Barnabas and Paul seems inconsistent with Gal. 1, 18–21 ("I lie not"), the collection in
Antioch need not be discarded as unhistorical; the information
about the bearers can be simply regarded as a distorted tradition.

The critics favour a third possible solution of the divergence
between Acts and Galatians, and it has recently been proposed in
a modified form by a Catholic (J. Dupont, RB 1955, 52–55). The
famine in Palestine took place (Josephus XX 5, 2) under the
procurator Tiberius Alexander (46–48); it probably coincided
with the Sabbatical year 47/48 in which the land was not to be
tilled; so the journey with the collection must be dated to the
year 49 A.D. when the journey to the Apostolic Council (Gal. 2, 1;
Acts 15, 1 sqq.) took place. In other words Acts 11, 30; 12, 25 and
15, 1 sqq. contain two accounts of the same journey which had a
double purpose—the delivery of the collection and the appeal to
the Apostles "about the question" (15, 2). Evidently Luke did
not recognize their identity and placed them at different points
in his book. Since he had no chronological details for the first half
of Acts, he was obliged to use his own judgment in arranging the
facts in their sequence. On this hypothesis the historical truth of
the Antioch collection would not be affected.

There has been much debate[3] about the particularly difficult problem of the relation between Acts 15 and Gal. 2, 1–10. In view of the serious divergences between the two accounts, many exegetes postulate an earlier sojourn of Paul and Barnabas in Jerusalem (generally the one mentioned in Acts 11, 30) for the events of Gal. 2, 1–10. However, it is generally accepted that both accounts refer to the same discussions, and the arguments for their identity are the stronger.

Undoubtedly the two accounts cannot be entirely reconciled; and this need cause no surprise, for Acts is not the entire minutes of the proceedings in Jerusalem, and Gal. 2, 1–10 is a passionate self-justification by the Apostle, where he places special stress and emphasis on certain facts. Presumably Luke's account reflects the common version which was current among the Jewish-Christians, for he represents the old Apostles and the presbyters as the supreme arbiters who settle disputes for the whole Church. Paul on the other hand speaks of agreements between partners of equal standing, and places strong stress on his independence ("to me they that seemed to be something added nothing," . . . "[they] gave to me and Barnabas the right hands of fellowship").

[3] For the most recent discussions see: H. Lietzmann, *Der Sinn des Apostel-dekrets:* Amicitiae corolla (London 1933) 203–211. H. Waitz, *Das Aposteldekret:* ZKG 55 (1936) 226–263. Bauernfeind, Apg. 194–201. L. Cerfaux: Miscell. G. Mercati 1 (1946) 107–126 *(Das Apostelkonzil im Lichte der altchristlichen Literatur).* J. R. Porter: JThSt 47 (1946) 169–174 (the decree and the second journey of Paul). M. Dibelius, *Das sog. Apostelkonzil:* ThLZ 72 (1947) 193–198. O. Linton, *The Third Aspect. A Neglected Point of View. A Study in Gal. 1–2 and Acts 9 and 15:* StTh 3 (1950) 79–95. B. Reicke, *Der geschichtliche Hintergrund des Apostelkonzils und der Antiochia-Episode Gal. 2, 1–14:* Studia Paulina for J. de Zwaan, 1953, 172–187. W. G. Kuemmel, *Die aelteste Form des Aposteldekrets:* Spiritus et Veritas, Festschrift fuer K. Kundzins, 1953, 83–98. [The fourfold form is original: the Gentile Christians are to withdraw themselves from further contamination by pagan gods by avoiding meat offered to idols, blood, flesh which was not killed by Jewish ritual, and unchastity. "Presumably the decree was intended to regulate the difficulties in the way of common life which had arisen in the community at Antioch between the Jewish and Gentile Christians."] H.-M. Féret, *Pierre et Paul à Antiochia et à Jérusalem. Le "conflit" des deux apôtres,* Paris 1955.

The commentaries examine the problem in detail. Here only the following points can be made:

1) Both accounts agree absolutely on the essential point that circumcision is not neccessary for salvation. Converted Gentiles are thus not obliged to have themselves circumcised nor to observe the Mosaic Law. The demand of the Judaists (Acts 15, 1 5) is rejected (15, 10 19 28), and Paul's Gospel of freedom from the Law is recognized—and recognized without conditions (Gal. 2, 3 6–9)—by the authorities in Jerusalem as being perfectly orthodox. 2) The only serious divergence between the two accounts is in the clauses which, at James' suggestion, were added to the Apostolic decree for the Gentiles: "It hath seemed good to the Holy Ghost and to us to lay no further burden on you than these necessary things: that you abstain from things sacrificed to idols and from blood and from things strangled and from fornication." Paul says nothing of these clauses, he merely tells that he was given the injunction to hold a collection for the poor of Jerusalem in his mission territory (Gal. 2, 10).

Many exegetes explain the difference by considering "things strangled" a gloss—which it is in the Western Text—and interpreting the decree merely as an elementary moral direction which condemns the main heathen vices, idolatry, murder and unchastity, and so brings the discussion to a final conclusion. They suggest that Paul did not mention these regulations because time and again he had emphasized these fundamentals of morality in his sermons to the communities. This explanation is not satisfactory, for it could not have happened often that Paul explicitly gave his Gentile communities the self-evident instruction that they should refrain from the three main pagan vices.

The clauses which James proposed must be interpreted, as the overwhelming majority of exegetes does interpret them, as prescriptions of ritual law, and as the minimum conditions for common life—especially at table—between the Gentile Christians and the legally minded Jews. They refer to things which the Jews considered unclean, and which, according to Lev. 17, 18 were to be avoided even by the Gentiles who lived among Israelites, namely: meat offered to idols; meat from animals which had not been ritually slain; meat from animals which were captured and killed with a noose in hunting; marriage within forbidden degrees of kindred and unnatural vice.

Granted this explanation there are two ways to explain the difference without denying their historical truth: 1) Paul knew the decree. It really was passed at the Apostolic Council and he was able to accept it, for the clauses were not declared necessary for salvation, and in such cases he was very accommodating, as we see from 1 Cor. 8, 9–13; 9, 19–23; 10, 23–33; Rom. 14, 1 to 15, 6. But he regarded it as binding only where there were large numbers of Jews, and so did not promulgate it in the communities which he founded on the second and third missionary journeys. 2) Another possible explanation is that Paul did not know the decree at all, for it was not drawn up at the Apostolic Council; had he known it he would not have passed it over in silence. In particular the altercation at Antioch (Gal. 2, 11 sqq.), when Paul rebuked Peter vigorously for ceasing to eat with Gentile Christians, could not have taken place if the question of meats had already been settled by authority. In fact, the decree was passed only after that altercation in order to forestall similar incidents for the time to come. Moreover, as the address shows, it was intended only for Antioch, Syria and Cilicia, where the population was a mixture of Gentiles and Jews. This solution is popular among non-Catholics, and has recently been commended by certain Catholics, who say that Luke has recorded two discussions as if there had been only one, and has added to his account as if it were the same occasion, the regulation which appears in the Apostolic decree (Cerfaux).

The critics object principally to the picture which Acts draws of Paul and his work and thought; they say that it falsely portrays him as being much more Jewish than he really was. According to Acts, they allege, Paul remained a believing Jew and Pharisee even after his conversion; he declares explicitly before the council that he is a Pharisee (23, 6), and before the governor Felix he professes the three basic dogmas of Pharisaic Judaism (24, 14 sq.); he differs from the Pharisees only in believing that Jesus is the Messias who has already come; he maintains the validity of the Law, circumcises Timothy (16, 3), and undertakes Jewish vows (18, 18; 21, 23 sqq.); on his missionary journeys he always begins with the Jews, and turns to the Gentiles only when they reject his preaching (cf. 13, 46; 18, 6; 28, 25 sqq.).

The critics claim that there are essential differences between this and the picture which emerges from the Epistles. The Paul of the Epistles, they say, is not merely a christianized Pharisee; his opposition to the Law was very outspoken (Rom. 7); conversion to Christianity meant for him a radical break with his Jewish past (Phil. 3, 7); the real Paul was a missionary only to Gentiles; he vigorously resisted the demand in Jerusalem that Titus should be circumcised (Gal. 2, 3 sq.). Furthermore, they say, the Paul of the Epistles did not live as a strict Jew; he underwent the purification ceremonies in Jerusalem, but not in order to demonstrate that he was an observer of the Law (Acts 21, 24).

Regarding these arguments, it is unavoidable that a portrait of Paul based on the conflict Epistles should be one-sided. Naturally the Epistles emphasize the struggle of the Apostle against the Mosaic Law, and stress that the Gentiles are free from it. But when there was no principle at stake the Paul of the Epistles could be a Jew to Jews (1 Cor. 9, 20). So there is no objection to the testimony of Acts that he circumcised the half-Jew Timothy. Furthermore when Acts says that Paul usually began his preaching in the synagogue, this is not to be rejected as an unhistorical generalization, for it is sufficiently attested by the Apostle's own declaration that he five times suffered the synagogue penalty of scourging (2 Cor. 11, 24). Neither can his profession of Pharisaism and its main dogmas be described as historically false, for he was then defending himself against the charge of introducing a new religion, and so he placed special stress on what he had in common with Judaism; he could say that the faith which he proclaimed was not a break-away from Judaism but was the fulfilment of the promises given to the Fathers (26, 6–8 22 sq.). Even after his conversion Paul was proud of his origin from Israel, the Chosen People (2 Cor. 11, 18 22; Phil. 3, 4 sq.), and throughout his life he remained bound to it by an inner affection (Rom. 9, 1 sqq.; 11, 13 sqq.).

The reliability of Acts as history may also be verified through extra-Biblical evidence about persons, events, geographical details, organizations, and matters of culture and religion to which it refers. Acts has stood up to such verification.[4] In most cases its facts are brilliantly confirmed by these sources. Only in a few cases are there differences between it and the profane witnesses, but these cannot diminish the value of the book.

There is a widespread view that the discourses in Acts are compositions of the author who here follows the practice of the ancient historians who inserted freely composed speeches into their works. Dibelius in particular has recently given a telling and detailed exposition of this theory (see above), but in this form it cannot be maintained. Of course the discourses of Acts are not word for word reports—they are too short for that—but they do summarize the principal ideas of the actual discourses. Luke himself heard the discourse of Paul at Miletus (20, 18–35), and no part of Acts is closer to the Pauline Epistles in wording and

---

[4] Carried out by A. Wikenhauser, *Die Apg und ihr Geschichtswert*, pp. 298–421. E. Troçmé, *Le "livre des Actes" et l'histoire*, Paris 1957. J. Bihler, *Die Stephanusgeschichte im Rahmen der Apg*, Diss. Muenchen 1957. J. Dupont, *Pierre et Paul à Antioche et à Jérusalem*: RSR 45 (1957) 42–60, 225–239.

thought. Luke could easily have got information from witnesses about the content of Paul's speeches in his own defence (chs. 22–26); the speeches in these chapters are artistic compositions, and they show everywhere the stamp of Luke's style in form and language; they are intended to have a rhetorical effect, but they are not inventions; rather they grow out of the situation, and are a faithful record, in essentials, of what was really said.

The author of Acts intended the celebrated Areopagus discourse 17, 22–31 as a supreme example of a missionary discourse of the Apostle to cultured pagans; it has close contacts with Stoicism, which was widely popular at that time; yet it fits the situation very well, and begins by referring to inscriptions whose existence at Athens is attested with certainty; hence it cannot be described—as Dibelius does[5]—as "totally un-Pauline". The sentences which savour of Stoicism are to be understood in a monotheistic, not a pantheistic, sense. When Paul puts forward such ideas he is only following in the footsteps of Hellenistic Judaism, which held as an axiom that the divine being recognized by the Greek philosophers is the one God of Revelation. Indeed we find the fundamentals of the Areopagus discourse faithfully reflected in 1 Thess. 1, 9 sq. where Paul is summarizing his preaching to the Gentiles.

[5] *Paulus auf dem Aeropag,* SBHeidelberg 1939; he is followed by M. Pohlenz, *Paulus und die Stoa* (ZntW 42, 1949, 64–104), and rejected by W. Schmid, *Die Rede des Apostels Paulus vor den Philosophen und Areopagiten in Athen* (Philologus 95, 1942, 79–120), and G. Schrenk, *Urchristliche Missionspredigt im 1. Jh.*: Festgabe f. Th. Wurm, Stuttgart 1948, 51–66. He is also rejected by B. Gaertner: *The Areopagus Speech and Natural Revelation,* Uppsala 1955 [a detailed examination of the "Stoic interpretation" of the discourse by Dibelius and Pohlenz]. W. Elster, *Gott und die Natur in der Areopagrede:* Ntl Studien f. R. Bultmann, 1954, 202–227. Cf. also P. Dalbert, *Die Theologie der hellenistisch-juedischen Missionsliteratur unter Ausschluss von Philo und Josephus,* Hamburg 1954. H. Hommel, *Neue Forschungen zur Areopagrede:* ZntW 46 (1955) 145–147 (favours Dibelius). W. Hauck, *Tradition und Composition in der Areopagrede:* ZThK 53 (1956) 11–52 (against Dibelius). E. Schweizer, *Zu den Reden der Apg:* ThZ 13 (1957) 1–11. N. B. Stonehouse, *Paul before the Areopagus,* London 1957. M. Delage, *Resonnances grecques dans le discours de S. Paul à Athènes:* Bull. de l'Assoc. G. Budé IV, 3 (1956) 49–69.

Rom. 1, 18–32, which is an example of Paul's missionary sermon to pagans, also shows remarkable resemblances to it.

The discourses of Peter contain an abundance of archaic theological material which suggests that they are not free compositions by the author. The same is true of Stephen's speech in ch. 7, where the sharp attack on the Temple does not harmonize with the tenor of Acts. Paul's discourse in the synagogue at Antioch (13, 16–41) has much in common with the discourses of Peter, but it also contains in 13, 38 sq. the specifically Pauline notion of justification by faith. The missionary discourses to Jewish audiences must have resembled one another closely in content and manner.

The discourses are an integral part of the book. There is no doubt that they are intended to contribute to the literary unity of the work, and in judging them we must take account of this literary function; that they have this function is clear from the fact that the author gives only a selection—no doubt a well-considered selection—of them. Yet this does not justify us in treating them as free compositions by Luke; the inference is rather that he probably exercised great freedom in their actual expression.

Acts has many accounts of miracles and supernatural occurrences. Peter and Paul perform miraculous cures (e. g., 3, 1 sqq.; 9, 32 sqq.; 14, 8 sqq.; 28, 8 sq.), inflict punishments by supernatural power (5, 1 sqq.; 13, 11), and are miraculously rescued from prison (5, 19 sqq.; 12, 4 sqq.; 16, 25 sqq.). Peter raises a dead girl to life (9, 36 sqq.). The Holy Ghost descends on the Apostles at Pentecost and gives them the power of speaking in foreign languages (2, 1 sqq.; cf. also 10, 44–46; 19, 6; 8, 17). Paul has visions and revelations (9, 12; 16, 6–10; 18, 9 sq.; 20, 23; 22, 17 sqq.; 23, 11; 27, 24).

These accounts will not be accepted by those who on principle deny any intervention of supernatural powers in history and human life. That will not be the attitude of those who recognize the possibility of miracles and operations of the Holy Ghost, and who believe that Jesus worked miracles himself and gave this power to the Apostles. The reality of the miracles and supernatural happenings recorded in Acts cannot be confirmed by strict proofs; yet it is obvious that they must be taken seriously, for they differ essentially from the fantastic miracles reported by profane ancient authors and by the apocryphal Gospels and Acts of Apostles.

The New Testament clearly attests that the power of working miracles was part of the Apostles' equipment (Lk. 9, 1 sq. par; 2 Cor. 12, 12; Rom. 15, 18 sq.). As Hebrews says (2, 3 sq.), salvation "having begun to be declared by the Lord was confirmed unto us by them that heard him. God also bearing them witness by signs and wonders and divers miracles and distributions of the Holy Ghost, according to his own will."

5. Time and place of composition

In the early Church there was no uniformity on this point; authorship, rather than the time and place of composition, was the centre of interest in those days.

Irenaeus says nothing on the matter; but his evidence on the composition of the Gospels of Mark and Luke (cf. §§ 23, 2; 25, 2) can only mean that Luke wrote his Gospel—and naturally also Acts—only after the death of Paul.

The ancient prologue to Luke, which was written about 180 A.D. tells us that Luke accompanied Paul until the latter's martyrdom and then composed the Gospel, and afterwards Acts, in Achaea (cf. § 25, 2). Though the prologue does not mention when either work was written, its author clearly thought that Luke did not write until Paul was dead.

The relevant part of the Muratorian fragment (line 34 sqq.) cannot be interpreted with certainty, but it seems to mean that

Luke's silence about Peter's martyrdom and Paul's journey to Spain is due to the fact that he was not an eyewitness of them.

Two of the more recent sources agree with the prologue. In the preface to his commentary on Matthew, which was written in 398 A.D., Jerome says that Luke composed his Gospel *in Achaia Boeotiaeque partibus,* and Achaea is also named as the place of composition of both Gospel and Acts in a short prologue to the four Gospels which is preserved in a Coptic inscription of the sixth or seventh century in a chapel in the Assiut mountain range.

The oldest view throughout the Church—which must be regarded as an ancient tradition—was, therefore, that Luke wrote both books in Achaea, where he evidently worked as a missionary, after Paul's death.

Since the fourth century there has also been another view, namely that Luke composed Acts during the two years of Paul's first imprisonment in Rome, finishing it before the trial came to an end, as may be inferred from the abrupt conclusion of Acts (28, 30 sq.). Eusebius of Caesarea (H. E. II, 22) was perhaps the first to put this forward, and subsequent sources for this dating seem to depend on him. Yet Eusebius does not state explicitly that Luke had finished Acts when the two year imprisonment of Paul came to an end; he says that Luke made Paul's imprisonment the end of his book because he had then separated from the Apostle, an inference from 2 Timothy 4, 16 sq.: "At my first answer no man stood with me", and 4, 11: "Only Luke is with me."

Jerome, *De vir. Ill.* 7, is the first Father to say expressly that Acts was written immediately after the two year imprisonment, and he is obviously drawing on Eusebius. Euthalius also says this, (cf. § 11, 2), and he refers explicitly to Eusebius: Paul was kept imprisoned in Rome for two years; "this fact and the facts leading up to it are reported in Acts by Luke who wrote about that time and knew nothing of what followed; he did not even mention Paul's martyrdom in his book *Prologue to the Pauline Epistles.*"

If the evidence of Irenaeus and the ancient prologue are not accepted as reliable tradition, we are entirely dependent on internal evidence for dating. In this connection the strange ending of Acts is important. Most Catholic exegetes infer from it that Luke completed his work immediately after the two-year imprisonment of Paul, before the trial came to an end. There is nothing inherently improbable in this conclusion, but it raises the question why Luke did not wait for the end of the trial, which must have been near at hand.

The dating of Luke's two works is closely connected with the time of composition of St. Mark's Gospel, which Luke used (cf. § 25, 4). If Mark did not write until after Peter's death in 64 A.D.—and there are strong reasons for thinking that this was the case (cf. § 23, 4)—Luke cannot have written his Gospel earlier than the second half of the sixties. Acts was written after the Gospel.

If Luke wrote Acts in Rome during Paul's imprisonment, he cannot have done so without Paul's knowledge, for he had access to the Apostle at that time (28, 30 sq.). But then we would expect Paul to be his source for those incidents in the Apostle's life of which Luke was not himself an eyewitness. In that case the undeniable divergences between the Pauline Epistles and Acts (chs. 11–15), become an enigma.

So it is more likely that Acts was not written until after Paul's death; this dating is supported by the oldest tradition and by the conclusions about the Gospel of St. Luke (cf. § 25, 6).[6]

The best explanation of the fact that Acts breaks off with the two-year imprisonment is that Luke intended only to record Paul's work before his arrival in Rome. That would not entirely fulfil the programme laid down in Acts 1, 8; but the author describes the mission to the Gentiles as being essentially the work of Paul,

---

[6] The later date is also defended by J. Dupont with detailed arguments in EphThL 26, 1953, 306 n. 32, and by M.-E. Boismard, RB 1954, 275, who thinks that it can hardly be earlier than 80 A.D.

and so he could break off with Paul's entry into Rome, the capital of the world, since this marked a certain high point of achievement.

6. The double Text Form

Acts has come down to us in two widely different text forms. The text in our critical editions of the New Testament derives from the oldest Majuscules (B ℵ A C), and the Alexandrian writers, and is attested as early as the first half of the third century by $\mathfrak{P}^{45}$ (cf. § 12, 3). These sources contain the Alexandrian or Neutral Text. The other form can be traced back to the second century; it appears in the Old-Latin version, the Latin Fathers, Codex D, the Old-Syriac version, and $\mathfrak{P}^{38}$ and $\mathfrak{P}^{48}$. These sources contain the Western Text (cf. § 21, 2). The Alexandrian Text is generally shorter and more polished in style than the somewhat verbose Western Text.

Although the Western Text had been unanimously accepted as the original until his time, the philologist Friedrich Blass in 1894 propounded the startling theory that both textual forms come from Luke himself; he suggested that the Western Text was the first to be written—a rough draft—while the Alexandrian Text was a shorter and stylistically improved fair copy for Theophilus; the former circulated in the West (β, *editio romana*), the latter in the East (α, *editio antiochena*).

This theory of Blass was taken up again in a modified form in 1916 by Theodor Zahn, who supported it with a wide-ranging study of the history of the Text (*Die Urausgabe der Apg des Lk.,* Leipzig 1916). Later the English scholar A. C. Clark proposed the theory that the Alexandrian Text is a methodical abbreviation of the original Western Text (cf. on this ThLZ 57, 1936, 1081 sqq.; JBL 53, 1934, 34 sqq.; JThSt 1943, 129–138; 1950, 16–28).

None of these theories has made a wide appeal, and rightly so.

Yet modern studies have demonstrated that the Western Text deserves serious attention, and that in certain cases its readings are to be preferred to those of the usual critical text. Examples of such cases are: 12, 10 "they descended the seven steps"; 19, 9 "from the fifth to the tenth hour"; 20, 15 "we remained in Trogyllium"; 28, 16 "the centurion handed over the prisoners to the camp commander".

The problem of the origin of the Western Text is still unsolved. Ropes (see above) suggests that it may derive from a recension of the original which was made about 150 A.D., when some parts were rewritten in order to clarify the text and expansions were made from oral tradition. Other scholars suggest that the variants are not the work of one hand, but have arisen because the text was transmitted freely and without ecclesiastical control, for Acts was not used in the Liturgy until the last third of the second century (cf. especially M. Dibelius, *Der Text der Apg*, in *Aufsaetze zur Apg* 76–83).

E. Haenchen, *Zum Text der Apg*: ZThK 54 (1957) 22–55. J. Duplacy, *A propos d'une variante occidentale des Actes des Apôtres* (III, 11): Rev. des Ét. August. (Mémorial Gustave Bardy) 2 (1956) 231–242.

Section II. The Epistles of the New Testament

§ 30. THE EPISTLES OF THE NEW TESTAMENT IN THE LIGHT OF ANCIENT LETTER WRITING

P. Wendland, *Die urchristlichen Literaturformen*[2-3], 1912 (Lietzmann 2). G. A. Deissmann, *Licht von Osten. Das NT und die neuentdeckten Texte der hellenistisch-roemischen Welt*[4], Tuebingen 1923. Sykutris, *Epistolographie*: Pauly-Wissowa, RE, Erg.-Bd. 5 (1931) 186–220. E. von Dobschuetz, *Wir und Ich bei Paulus*: ZsyTh 10 (1932/33) 251–177. O. Roller, *Das Formular der pl Briefe*, Stuttgart 1933 (rejected by Michaelis, *Einl.* pp. 251–254, and Percy, *Die Probleme des Kol. und Eph.* pp. 10–14). J.-A. Eschlimann, *La rédaction des épîtres pauliniennes*, RB 53 (1946) 185–196. E. Lohmeyer, *Briefliche Grussueberschriften*, ZntW 26 (1927) 158–173. P. Schubert, *Form and Function of the Pauline Thanksgivings*, Berlin 1939.

1. *The length of ancient letters*

A great number of letters—about fourteen thousand if we include the letters of the Fathers—have come down to us from antiquity; in addition to copies, many actual original letters have survived.

The private letters which have survived on papyrus[1] average eighty-seven words—the shortest has eighteen words, the longest two hundred and nine. The literary collections of letters have a much greater average length; the 796 genuine letters of Cicero average 295 words each (22-2530), the 124 of Seneca average 995 (149–4134).

As a rule letters were written on papyrus. A page of the better and more expensive papyrus averaged $9^1/_2 \times 10$-12 inches (24 × 25-30 cms.) in size, and contained 150–250 words according to the size of the writing. They usually wrote only on one side of the sheet. For very long letters they used a roll of papyrus made by joining a number of pages together.

---

[1] Cf. St. Witkowski, *Epistulae privatae Graecae quae in papyris aetatis Lagidarum servantur*[2], Leipzig 1911; B. Olsson, *Papyrusbriefe aus der fruehsten Roemerzeit*, Uppsala 1925. A. Wifstrand, *Griechische Privatbriefe aus der Papyrussammlung in Lund*, Lund 1937.

The New Testament Epistles are in general longer than other ancient letters. The thirteen Pauline Epistles average about 1300 words each; Romans has 7101, Titus (the second smallest) 658, Philemon 335. Only 2 and 3 John are shorter than this, with 245 and 185 words respectively.

2. The actual writing of letters

The Epistles were written on papyrus (cf. 2 John 12; 3 John 13). Writing was, however, a slow and tiresome process, for even smooth papyrus was fairly coarse and stringy, so it was usual to dictate letters to a trained professional scribe.

According to O. Roller this was not the only way of using a scribe; there was also a practice of giving him exact instructions about the content of the letter and leaving the expression and choice of wording to him. Sometimes this was done by word of mouth, and sometimes he was given a rough draft or outline. In this case the scribe acted as secretary. Cicero, Atticus, Symmachus and others, inform us about this method of composition. When a letter was written in this way it would be only to a limited extent, if at all, in the style of the person who sent or commissioned it. Yet such a letter must be considered authentic, at least when the sender endorsed it by himself writing the final greeting, ἔρρωσο or *vale,* which took the place of our signature.

When we apply this to the New Testament Epistles the question arises whether the authors wrote them personally or dictated them or left the choice of wording to a secretary. Paul dictated Rom. (or ch. 16) to a certain Tertius (16, 22). In three Epistles he says explicitly that he has written the final greeting with his own hand (1 Cor. 16, 21; Col. 4, 18; 2 Thess. 3, 17). He also refers to his own writing in Gal. 6, 11 and Philem. 19. Most scholars infer from this that Paul wrote the small Epistle to Philemon in his own hand, but dictated the other four except for the final greeting (in the case of Galatians from 6, 11 to the end). The same must also hold true of other Epistles where nothing is said about the point.

A more serious question is whether the New Testament contains Epistles where a secretary had some responsibility for the language and style. It is highly likely that this is how we should understand 1 Pet. 5, 12 ("By Silvanus ... I have written briefly") (cf. § 50, 4). The same is probably true of James. In the cases of Ephesians and the Pastoral Epistles it is disputed.

If a secretary took part in the composition of an epistle, then the vocabulary and style are not decisive criteria for settling its authenticity.

3. The form of epistles

The formal parts of the ancient epistles were: 1) The preliminary greeting or *praescriptio*, which contained in one sentence the name of the sender (in the nominative) and of the recipient (in the dative), together with the introductory greeting. 2) The final greeting: ἔρρωσο or *vale*. In a Greek or Roman letter this was of great importance, for it guaranteed the authenticity of the document. Our practice of personally signing at the end of a letter was unknown in antiquity; the place of the signature was taken by the final greeting written by the sender himself. In many original papyrus letters the final greeting is in a different hand from the rest of the text; that is because the sender has dictated the letter and endorsed it as his own by writing the final greeting himself. Quite often the epistle begins with a formal preamble (wishes for good health, assurance of prayers on behalf of the recipient), and the concluding part of the epistle (good wishes or the like) ends with greetings. Most letters, except for official documents in epistolary form, carried no date.

The form of introduction which was usual in Greek and Roman letters does not occur in the New Testament except for James and the Apostolic Decree and the letter of Lysias (Acts 15, 23; 23, 26).

The introductory part of the Pauline Epistles, of 1 and 2 Pet., 2 John and Jude consists of two sentences. The first sentence names the sender and the recipient, and is usually expanded with titles and attributes, and sometimes also with doctrinal expansions; this is particularly the case with Rom., Gal., and Tit. The second sentence invokes a blessing; only 1 and 2 Pet., 2 John and Jude have a verb. Gal. has in addition a description of Christ as Mediator of Salvation, which grows into a doxology. Paul, and only he, mentions one or more fellow senders besides himself in eight of the Epistles (1 and 2 Cor., Gal., Phil., Col., 1 and 2 Thess., Philem.); this is found very seldom in profane letters. Furthermore Paul does not observe the strict rule of Greek letters that the introduction must be expressed in the third person (e. g., Gal. 1, 1 "Paul ... and all the brethren who are with me"); the same licence occurs also in 2 and 3 John. The division of the *praescriptio* into two sentences, which is characteristic of Paul, had precedents in Middle Eastern (Babylonian and Persian) and Jewish letters.

Paul usually begins the body of the Epistle with an expression of thanks to God (because of the good state of the community: 1 Thess., Col.), and the assurance that he is praying for the recipients (Rom., Phil. etc.). He usually concludes with talk about himself, for example, about his travel plans (Rom. 15, 25 sqq.; 1 Cor.16, 5 sqq.), and greetings. Paul's final greeting is never ἔρρωσο or the like, it takes the form of a final blessing such as ἡ χάρις τοῦ κυρίου ἡμῶν Ἰησοῦ Χριστοῦ. 2 Pet. and Jude end with a doxology.

Two of the Epistles, Heb. and 1 John, have no *praescriptio*. Heb. has the usual Greek conclusion, and the popular theory that the *praescriptio* was lost at an early date is highly unlikely, for the *praescriptio* is missing from none of the numerous original Greek letters which have come down to us. If the first page fell off or was damaged, it would very seldom happen that only the *praescriptio* would be lost; it was so small that more of the beginning would be lost with it. For this reason Roller is inclined to compare both of these Epistles with those which followed the Middle Eastern form in having no *praescriptio*. In fact Hebr. should be treated as a "warning discourse" (13, 22), sent to the recipients with an epistolary ending added (13, 22–25; cf. § 46, 3). The lack of a *praescriptio* in 1 John, is only apparent, for the author clearly imitated it in his introduction, 1, 1–4.

4. Letters and epistles

The letters which have survived from antiquity fall into two clearly distinct categories: there are letters properly so called, that is, written to particular persons or groups on a definite occasion, with information intended for them alone; and documents in letter form—epistles—which were intended for a wide group or even for the world at large (ideal addresses), as, for example, the epistles of Seneca which are moral treatises in epistolary form.

The thirteen Epistles of Paul are all real letters, written because of a particular situation in the life of the Apostle or of those to whom he writes. Except for Philemon, which is addressed to a private person on private business, they are official writings rather than private letters. Most of them are addressed to particular communities or to a small group of communities (Gal. and Eph.); three are primarily to officials and only secondarily to the communities entrusted to them (1 and 2 Tim., Tit.). They all serve the needs of the mission in the widest sense—instruction, edification, and admonition, the removal of misunderstandings in the communities and, not least, the struggle with dangerous heresies.

Many of the other Epistles are more akin to the form of a theological treatise (Heb.; but cf. § 46, 3), of edifying homily (1 Pet., 1 John, 2 Pet.), or of ethical paraenesis (Jas.). However, they were not originally directed to the whole of Christendom, but were intended for particular—even if loosely defined—destinations, and were occasioned by urgent difficulties of the recipients (persecution, heresy, religious or moral laxity).

A. THE PAULINE EPISTLES

(a) F. X. Poelzl, *Der Weltapostel Paulus*, Regensburg 1905. B. Bartmann, *Paulus. Die Grundzuege seiner Lehre und die moderne Religionsgeschichte*, Paderborn 1914. F. Prat, *La théologie de St. Paul*[11], 2 vols., Paris 1925. L. Murillo, *Paulus et Pauli scripta* 1, Rome 1926. K. Pieper, *Paulus, seine missionarische Persoenlichkeit und Wirksamkeit*[2][3] (NtA XII, 1–2: 1929). J. Holzner, *Paulus. Ein Heldenleben im Dienste Christi*, Freiburg i. Br. 1937, [22]1949. F. W. Maier in LThK VIII, 27–43. E.-B. Allo, *Paulus, der Apostel Jesu Christi* (translated from French), Fribourg (Switz.) 1946. G. Ricciotti, *Paolo Apostolo*, Rome 1946 (and often). (b) C. Clemen, *Paulus, sein Leben und sein Wirken*, 2 parts, Giessen 1904. H. Weinel, *Paulus. Der Mensch und sein Werk*[2], Tuebingen 1915. E. Vischer, *Der Apostel Paulus und sein Werk*[2], Leipzig 1921. Joh. Weiss, *Das Urchristentum*, Goettingen 1917, pp. 103–511. A. Deissmann, *Paulus. Eine kultur- und religionsgeschichtliche Skizze*[2], Tuebingen 1925. R. Bultmann, *Paulus:* RGG[2] IV 119–145. W. L. Knox, *St. Paul and the Church of Jerusalem*, Cambridge 1925. Idem, *St. Paul and the Church of the Gentiles*, Cambridge 1939. E. v. Dobschuetz, *Der Apostel Paulus*, Halle 1926-1928. P. Feine, *Der Apostel Paulus. Das Ringen um das geschichtliche Verstaendnis des Paulus*, Guetersloh 1927. A. Schweitzer, *Geschichte der pl Forschung*[2], Tuebingen 1933. H. Lietzmann, *Paulus*[2], Berlin 1934. H. Windisch, *Paulus und das Judentum*, Stuttgart 1935. A. D. Nock, *St. Paul*, London 1938. A. E. Barnett, *Paul Becomes a Literary Influence*, Chicago 1941 (before Irenaeus). K. Lake, *The Earlier Epistles of St. Paul*, London 1919. J. Richter, *Die Briefe des Apostels Paulus als missionarische Sendschreiben*, Guetersloh 1929. E. Seeberg, *Paulus:* ZKG 60 (1941) 1–48. M. Dibelius, *Paul*, Longmans, London 1953. G. Bornkamm, *Das Ende des Gesetzes. Paulusstudien*, Munich 1952. J. Munck, *Paulus und die Heilsgeschichte*, Copenhagen 1954 (cf. P. Benoit: RB 1955, 590–595). A. Brunot, *Le génie littéraire de St. Paul*, Paris 1955. J. Knox, *Chapters in a Life of St. Paul*, 1954. G. Schrenk, *Studien zu Paulus*, Zurich 1954 [a collection of previously published articles; cf. RB 1955, 619 sq.]. Joach. Jeremias, *Zur Gedankenfuehrung in den pl Briefen:* Studia Paulina f. J. de Zwaan, 1953, 146–154. Surveys of research: R. Bultmann: ThRdsch NF 1 (1929) 26–56; 6 (1934) 229–246; 8 (1936) 1–22. St. Lyonnet, *Bulletin d'exégèse paulinienne:* Bb 31 (1951) 104–113; 281–297; 432–439; 569–586.

§ 31. THE LIFE OF ST. PAUL THE APOSTLE

1. To the beginning of the first missionary journey

A. Steinmann, *Zum Werdegang des hl. Paulus. Die Jugendzeit in Tarsus*, Freiburg i. Br. 1928. A. Oepke, *Probleme der vorchristlichen Zeit des Paulus:* ThStKr 105 (1933) 387–424. W. C. van Unnik, *Tarsus of Jerusalem de stad van Paulus' jeugd,* Amsterdam 1952 (Nederlandske Akad., Letterkunde N. R. XV 5, 141–189) [Paul was born in Tarsus, and spent his entire youth in his parents' house in Jerusalem where he learned not Greek but Aramaic. It was as a Christian in Cilicia that he became acquainted for the first time with Greek culture and Syncretism]. A. Omodeo, *Paolo di Tarso, apostolo dei genti,* Naples 1957.

Paul was born of Jewish parents in Tarsus of Cilicia, a centre of Hellenistic culture[1] (2 Cor. 11, 22; Phil. 3, 5; Rom. 11, 1; Gal. 1, 14; 2, 15; Acts 22, 3). From his parents he inherited his membership of the tribe of Benjamin (Rom. 11, 1; Phil. 3, 5) along with both the freedom of Tarsus and Roman citizenship (Acts 16, 37 sqq.; 21, 39; 22, 25 sqq.; 25, 10 sqq.). According to Acts 23, 16 he had a sister.

The name Paul is always used in the Epistles, and appears in Acts from 13, 9 onwards; it was a second name which he was given in addition to the Jewish name Saul; this was a widespread custom in the East. He can hardly have been born before 10 A.D.; at the stoning of Stephen he is called a young man (νεανίας) in Acts 7, 57, while in Philem. he describes himself as old (πρεσβύτης).

His family—which Jerome tells us came from Galilee—belonged to the "Hebrews", that is, to that section of the Jewish people which clung to their mother tongue, Aramaic (2 Cor. 11, 22; Phil. 3, 5), and followed Pharisaism (Phil. 3, 5; Acts 23, 6). So, as well as Greek, which was the language of his mission and of his Epistles, Paul also learned Aramaic and Hebrew from his parents (Acts 21, 40; 26, 14). His parents must have been fairly well-to-do, for, as the Epistles show[2], they were able to give their son a good Greek education. It must have been in Tarsus that Paul learned the trade of tent making (Acts 18, 3); no one was supposed to

---

[1] Cf. H. Boehlig, *Die Geisteskultur von Tarsos im augusteischen Zeitalter mit Beruecksichtigung der paulinischen Briefe,* Goettingen 1913.

[2] Cf. R. Bultmann, *Der Stil der pl Predigt und die kynisch-stoische Diatribe,* Goettingen 1910. A. Marth, *Die Zitate des hl. Paulus aus der Profanliteratur:* ZkTh 37 (1913) 889–895. Andrews, *Paul, Philo and the Intellectuals:* JBL 53 (1934) 150–166. N. W. de Witt, *St. Paul and Epicurus,* 1955 [the Influence of E. on Paul's Epistles].

make money by giving instruction in the Law, so intending lawyers used to learn a trade in order to be able to support themselves.

When about 18 or 20 years old—probably immediately after the death of Jesus on 7th April 30 A.D.—Paul settled in Jerusalem in order to be trained as a Rabbi; his teacher was Rabbi Gamaliel (Acts 22, 3), who was active between 20 and 50 A.D. The Epistles show many traces of Paul's rabbinical education. Most of his expositions of Scripture can be understood only in the light of the Palestinian exegetical tradition.[3] In Jerusalem he became fanatically "zealous for the traditions of the Fathers" (Gal. 1, 14), and a rabid persecutor of the infant Christian Church in which his unerring instinct recognized the mortal enemy of the Jewish legalistic religion (Gal. 1, 13–23; 1 Cor. 15, 9). He set out for Damascus—about 34 A.D.—with a letter of recommendation from the High Priest to the synagogues, in order to extirpate the Christian community there; on the way he was converted near the gates of the city by a vision of Christ in Heaven, and was afterwards baptized by Ananias (Acts 9, 22 26; 1 Cor. 9, 1; 15, 8).

Only the intervention of the Almighty will explain how one who had persecuted Christ in his followers suddenly became transformed into a zealous disciple of Christ. The sources give no reason to think that there was any psychological or theological preparation for it in Paul's soul (cf. Phil. 3, 6 sqq.).[4]

[3] Cf. O. Michel, *Paulus und seine Bibel,* Guetersloh 1929. J. Bonsirven, *Exégèse rabbinique et exégèse paulinienne,* Paris 1939. J. Schmalenbach, *Auslegung und Verwertung des AT in den pl Briefen,* Dissertation, Vienna 1942. W. D. Davies, *Paul and Rabbinic Judaism,* London 1948. S. Amsler, *La typologie de l'AT chez S. Paul:* RThPh 1949, 113–128. P. Blaeser, *Schriftverwertung und Schrifterklaerung im Rabbinentum und bei Paulus:* ThQ 132 (1952) 152–169.

[4] Cf. W. G. Kuemmel, *Roem. 7 und die Bekehrung des Paulus,* Leipzig 1929. O. Kitzig, *Die Bekehrung des Paulus religionsgeschichtlich und religionspsychologisch neu untersucht,* Leipzig 1932. E. Pfaff, *Die Bekehrung des Paulus in der Exegese des 20. Jh.,* Rome 1942. J. Munck, *La Vocation de l'apôtre Paul:* StTh 1 (1947) 131–145. E. Benz, *Paulus als Visionaer,* Wiesbaden 1952. J. Munck, *Paulus und die Heilsgeschichte,* 1954, 1–27. H. G. Wood, *The Conversion of St. Paul:* NTSt 1 (1954/55) 276–282. Ph.-H. Menoud, *Révélation et Tradition:* Verbum Caro 7 (1953) 2–10.

Many scholars say that Paul was an ordained Rabbi before his conversion—forty years was the minimum age for this ordination—and that he was acting as an ordained Rabbi when he condemned the Christians, and that his journey to Damascus was made in an official capacity. But this is untenable. At first he persecuted entirely of his own accord, and though he later had official support, the initiative was always his. Indeed he was unknown to the Christian communities in Palestine, as he tells us explicitly in Gal. 1, 22. This also undermines the modern theory—which in any case is incompatible with his own statement in 1 Cor. 7, 7 sq.—that he had been married in his younger days and then became a widower. The basis of this theory is the fact that for strictly legalistic Jews it was a bounden duty to have a family, and no one could be ordained a Rabbi who avoided this duty.[5]

After his baptism Paul spent a considerable time in the Arabian desert south-east of Damascus (the Nabatean kingdom), where he worked among the Jews; he then returned to Damascus (Gal. 1, 17), and preached in the Synagogue. When the Jews made it impossible for him to work in Damascus any longer (2 Cor. 11, 32 sq.; Acts 9, 33 sqq.), he went up to Jerusalem (Gal. 1, 18 sq.) three years after his conversion. The Christians there naturally avoided their former persecutor until Barnabas succeeded in allaying their distrust. In fourteen days the machinations of the Jews compelled him to leave the city with all speed. He went through Syria to his native city of Tarsus (Gal. 1, 21; Acts 9, 26 sqq.). Some years later—it must have been about 44 A.D.—Barnabas asked him to come and help at Antioch, the capital of Syria, where the predominantly Gentile community was flourishing; he worked there for a year, and his efforts were blessed with great success (Acts 11, 25 sq.).

[5] Thus J. Jeremias: ZntW 25 (1926) 63–76; 28 (1929) 321–323. Against him E. Fascher, ibid. 28 (1929) 62–69, and Oepke loc. cit.

Then the community sent both him and Barnabas to Jerusalem to deliver the proceeds of the collection which had been taken up at Antioch for the relief of the brethren who were threatened by a famine (Acts 11, 27–30, "Famine collection").

2. The three great missionary journeys

Th. H. Campbell, *Paul's "Missionary Journeys" as Reflected in his Letters*: JBL 74 (1955) 80-87 [the details in the Epistles agree well with Acts].

Shortly afterwards the Antioch community commissioned Paul and Barnabas, with John Mark in attendance, to undertake a long journey into lands where the Gospel had not yet been preached. This so-called first missionary journey took place between 45 and 49 A.D. and lasted two or three years (Acts 13–14).

The three of them visited Cyprus, the homeland of Barnabas (Acts 4, 36), where the proconsul Sergius Paulus, who resided at Paphos, was converted. From this time onwards Acts represents Paul as leader of the mission.

Crossing from Cyprus to Asia Minor they separated from Mark in Perge, and preached the Gospel in the cities of Antioch, Iconium, Lystra and Derbe, which were in the Southern part of the Roman province of Galatia. Following Paul's missionary programme (Acts 13, 46) they began with the synagogues, and through "the strangers who served God" they made contact with the Gentiles.[6] In spite of the hostility of the Jews—Paul was stoned in Lystra (cf. 2 Tim. 3, 11)—they were so successful, particularly among the Gentiles, that on the return journey they were able to organize Christian communities and appoint presbyters in those cities.

As a result of the quick spread of Christianity among the Gentiles, a strong Judaistic movement arose in Jerusalem, demanding that the Gentile Christians should receive circumcision and ob-

---

[6] Cf. R. Liechtenhan, *Paulus als Judenmissionar*: Judaica 2 (1946) 56–70.

serve the Mosaic Law. This was a critical situation for the young Church. If the Judaistic movement had prevailed, Christianity would have become a Jewish Messianic sect; on the other hand, there was serious danger of a split into a Judaeo-Christian and a Gentile-Christian Church.

When Judaistic zealots appeared in Syrian Antioch and pressed their demands vigorously, the community sent a deputation under Paul and Barnabas to Jerusalem to have the dispute settled (Acts 15; Gal. 2, 1–10). There the so-called Apostolic Council decided, probably in 49 A.D., that no further burden should be placed upon the Gentiles; they were bidden only to refrain from meat offered to idols, unchastity, blood meat, and things strangled (Apostolic Decree with James' clauses; cf. § 29, 4). This amounted to a solemn declaration that in principle the Gentiles were free of the Law. James' clauses were intended to make it possible for Jewish and Gentile Christians to eat together without depriving the Jews of their legal cleanness. Paul did not promulgate these clauses in communities which were entirely or almost wholly Gentile. At this meeting Paul and Barnabas agreed with the senior Apostles about the division of missionary spheres ("we should go unto Gentiles and they unto the circumcision" Gal. 2, 9), and Paul promised that the Gentile communities would support the poor of Jerusalem.

However, the Judaistic agitation was not quelled by the Apostolic Decree, for it followed Paul throughout his life. Jewish and Gentile Christians used to eat together in Antioch; when Peter was there he also ate with Gentiles, until Judaists from Jerusalem refused to follow the practice; they intimidated Peter into withdrawing, and the other Jewish Christians, including even Barnabas, followed his example. This situation created a very serious danger to the freedom of the Gentiles and to the unity of the Church. Paul immediately recognized the greatness of the danger, and he averted it by sharply rebuking Peter for yielding to the Judaists (Gal. 2, 11 sqq.).

Immediately after this "Antioch incident" Paul began his second missionary journey in (49 or) 50 A.D. (Acts 15, 36 sqq.). Barnabas wished to bring his nephew Mark, and Paul refused to have him, so they separated. Paul took as his companion Silas, a member of the mother community in Jerusalem. He first visited the communities in the south of Galatia province which he had founded on the first missionary journey. In Lystra he won a new companion and loyal associate in Timothy (cf. § 42). He then travelled northwards through Phrygia and Western Galatia, where he was detained for some time by illness; he used this involuntary sojourn to preach the Gospel there to good effect (cf. § 34, 2). He then turned westward, and went to Macedonia in obedience to a call which he received in a vision at Troas. In spite of persecutions, such as scourging and imprisonment at Philippi, he founded vigorous Christian communities in Philippi, Thessalonia and Berea.

Then he went southwards towards Achaea. At the Areopagus in Athens he defended Monotheism in a masterly discourse before the Stoic and Epicurean philosophers, but he got no response to his proclamation of the risen Christ as Judge of the whole world (cf. § 29, 4).

The mission in Athens had scanty results, but in the nearby commercial centre of Corinth he founded a large community. He was assisted there by a married couple, Aquila and Priscilla, who had been exiled from Rome as Jews (Jewish-Christians?) under an edict of the Emperor Claudius. Shortly after his arrival in Corinth Paul wrote the two Epistles to the Thessalonians (cf. § 32, 33). The proconsul Gallio rejected a complaint lodged against him by the Jews. He worked there for a year and a half—probably from autumn 51 to spring 53 A.D.—and then went by sea to Caesarea in Palestine, calling at Ephesus on the way; from Caesarea he travelled—probably by way of Jerusalem—to Antioch.

He did not stay long there. A third missionary journey—which probably began in spring 54 A.D.—brought him first to the North Galatian and Phrygian communities (Acts 18, 23). His next stop was at Ephesus, where he worked "for three years" (Acts 19, 8, 10 22; 20, 31), and met with great success in spite of many difficulties and troubles (Acts 19, 1 sqq.). He probably wrote the Epistle to the Galatians in the early part of his stay at Ephesus (cf. § 34). Some modern scholars argue from 1 Cor. 15, 32; 2 Cor. 11, 23 sq.; Rom. 16, 4 7 that Paul spent some months in prison in Ephesus, and they say that he wrote the Epistle to the Philippians—and some of the other Captivity Epistles—during this imprisonment (cf. § 41, 4). He was certainly at Ephesus when he wrote the first Epistle to the Corinthians (1 Cor. 16, 7 sq.); he probably also paid a brief visit to Corinth, and soon afterwards wrote another Epistle to the Corinthians which is now lost ("the sorrowful Epistle"; cf. § 35). He was obliged to leave Ephesus because of a riot instigated by a silversmith named Demetrius.

Passing through Troas he went to Macedonia, where he stayed for some time and wrote the second (canonical) Epistle to the Corinthians (cf. § 36). He then travelled to Greece (Corinth); and spent the winter there (probably 57–58 A.D.). The Epistle to the Romans was written at the end of this winter sojourn (cf. § 37).

He departed by land for Philippi, where he celebrated the Pasch. Travelling by sea, he bade farewell at Miletus to the presbyters of Ephesus; he then went on to Caesarea on the coast, passing through Tyre; in Caesarea he stayed with Philip "the Evangelist". In spite of a number of warnings he went up to Jerusalem to deliver the proceeds of a generous collection for the poor of the mother community (Rom. 15, 25 sqq.). He reached Jerusalem at Pentecost.

3. From the imprisonment at Jerusalem to the martyrdom in Rome

In Jerusalem the Judaeo-Christians were unfavourably disposed towards Paul, so on James' advice he undertook to pay the expenses of four men taking Nazarene vows. Yet this public declaration of his respect for the Jewish Law did not dispel the hatred of the Jews from Asia Minor. Seeing him in the Temple, they stirred up a riot against him on the ground that he had brought a Gentile—Trophimus, who was a Gentile Christian—into the inner court of the Temple; he would have been killed if the Roman guard had not taken him into custody. To protect him from Jewish attempts on his life, Lysias the Roman commander in Jerusalem, had him taken to Caesarea, where the governor resided. Antonius Felix kept him there in light confinement for two years (58–60 A.D.). Porcius Festus, the successor of Felix, was inclined to accede to the request of the Sanhedrin and send Paul to Jerusalem for trial. Paul then realized that his only remedy was to exercise his right as a Roman citizen and appeal to the Emperor (provocatio ad Caesarem). Festus accepted the appeal and sent Paul to Rome under guard of a detachment of soldiers.

They were shipwrecked on the coast of Malta. Winter came and the journey could not be resumed until the following spring. Paul was kept in custody in Rome for two full years (spring 61 to spring 63); he was allowed to rent a dwelling and to receive visitors and preach the Gospel to them. According to the most popular view it was during this first Roman imprisonment that he wrote the four Captivity Epistles (Eph., Col., Philem., Phil., cf. §§ 38 to 41).

Acts gives Paul's life story up to this point. For his later history we must refer to other sources (cf. § 45, 5). According to these sources the trial ended with the liberation of Paul. Ancient Roman sources tell us that he then carried out the journey to Spain which he had previously planned (Rom. 15, 24). Writing in 95 A.D., Clement of Rome says in his epistle (5, 7) that Paul travelled "to the end of the west" (εἰς τὸ τέρμα τῆς δύσεως), which can only mean Spain.[7] The Muratorian Canon also mentions *profectio Pauli ab urbe ad Spaniam proficiscentis* (lines 38–39).

The Pastoral Epistles show that he also travelled to his mission territory in the East, and left Titus and Timothy there —in Crete and Ephesus respectively—with full authority to combat heresy and organize the Church (Tit. 1, 5; 1 Tim. 1, 3). He was then arrested once more, and again imprisoned in Rome. This imprisonment was much stricter than the first and ended with his martyrdom (2 Tim. 1, 17; 4, 6 sqq.).

It is disputed, and can hardly be settled definitely, whether the Spanish journey or the Eastern journey came first. All the ancient accounts agree that he was martyred in the reign of Nero; he died between the outbreak of Nero's persecution in the summer of 64 A.D. and the death of Nero on 9th June 68 A.D., probably in the second half of this period (perhaps in 67 A.D.).

4. The chronology of St. Paul's life

The two fixed points for dating Paul's life are the proconsulship of Gallio in Achaea, and the assumption by Festus of the procuratorship of Judaea.

Lucius Junius Gallio—a brother of Seneca the philosopher—is named as proconsul of Achaea in an inscription found at Delphi, which was published in 1905[8]; this inscription, which is damaged, contained a letter to the city of Delphi from the Emperor Claudius; the letter was written after Claudius had been saluted as *imperator* for the twenty sixth time, probably therefore between the 25th January and 1st August 52 A.D.

[7] Cf. E. Dubowy, *Klemens von Rom ueber die Reise Pauli nach Spanien* (BSt XXIX 3, 1914).

[8] Cf. particularly A. Deissmann, *Paulus²* p. 203 sqq., and L. Hennequin: DB Suppl 2 (1934) 355–373; Hennequin places Paul's Corinthian mission between the end of November 50 and August or September 52.

The proconsuls of senatorial provinces—of which Achaea was one—held office for a year which ran from spring to spring. So Gallio's proconsulship probably falls in the period spring 52 to spring 53; it was possibly from 51 to 52 A.D., but this is not likely.

From Acts 18, 22 we can infer that Paul was before the proconsul's court in May or June. In that case his eighteen month sojourn in Corinth began in late autumn 51 and ended in the summer of 53 A.D. (Acts 18, 18).

Regarding Porcius Festus, the older and still most common view is that he took up office in the year 59 or 60 A.D.; tradition does not give an exact date. Paul was arrested in Jerusalem around Pentecost 58 A.D. and was taken to Rome between autumn 60 and spring 61 A.D.

By astronomical reckoning F. X. Kugler S. J. and the astronomer Gerhardt have also reached the conclusion that Paul went to Jerusalem for the last time in 58 A.D. Their starting point is the reckoning of Th. Zahn that the fourteenth of Nisan on which Paul celebrated the Pasch at Philippi (Acts 20, 6 sqq.) fell on a Tuesday. However, the astronomical results are not absolutely certain, for the Jews fixed the date of Easter by the actual sight of the new moon.

This is therefore the probable chronology:

Conversion of Paul (3+14 years before the Apostolic Council: Gal. 1, 18; 2, 1):	about 34 A.D.
First missionary journey:	between 46 and 49
Apostolic Council:	49
Second missionary journey:	spring 50 to autumn 53
Third missionary journey:	spring 54 to spring 58
Arrest in Jerusalem:	around Pentecost 58
Imprisonment in Caesarea:	58–60
Taken to Rome:	autumn 60 to spring 61
First Roman imprisonment:	61–63

THE TWO EPISTLES TO THE THESSALONIANS

Commentaries: (a) A. Schaefer, *Erklaerung der zwei Briefe an die Thess und des Briefes an die Gal*, Muenster 1890. J. Knabenbauer, 1913 (CSS). F. S. Gutjahr, *Die zwei Briefe an die Thess und der Brief an die Gal²*, Graz and Vienna 1912. I. M. Vosté, *Commentarius in epistolas ad Thess.*, Rome 1917. A. Steinmann - F. Tillmann, 1935 (Bonner NT). K. Staab, 1950 (Regensburger NT 7). F. Amiot (Gal., 1 2 Thess.), 1946 (VS XIV). B. Rigaux, Paris 1956 (études bibliques). (b) G. Milligan, *St. Paul's Epistles to the Thess.*, London 1908. G. Wohlenberg, ²1909 (Zahn XII). E. v. Dobschuetz, 1909 (Meyer X⁷). J. E. Frame, 1912 (ICC). W. Lueken, ³1917 (GoettNT 2). A. Oepke, ²1935. (NTDeutsch 8). M. Dibelius, ³1937 (Lietzmann 11). W. Neil, 1950 (Moffatt). Ch. Masson, *Les épîtres aux Thessaloniciens*, 1957 (Bonnard 11a).

§ 32. THE FIRST EPISTLE TO THE THESSALONIANS

C. E. Faw, *On the Writing of First Thess.*: JBL 71 (1952) 217–225. T. W. Manson, *St. Paul in Greece. The Letters to the Thessalonians*: BJRL 35 (1953) 428–447 [Composition of the Epistles].

1. *The background*

ON the second missionary journey Paul came with Silas and Timothy (in 50 or 51 A.D.) from Philippi to Thessalonica, now known as Salonica. This city was founded in 297 B.C. by Cassander of Macedon, who named it after his wife, a sister of Alexander the Great; it lay at the north end of the Thermaic Gulf.[1] Through it passed the Via Egnatia, which formed a bridgeway between East and West, for it connected Dyracchium (Durazzo), and ultimately Rome, with Byzantium. Because of its position Thessalonica was a populous commercial centre; every nationality was to be found there. It was capital of the Roman province of Macedonia, and the residence of the pro-consul. After the battle of Philippi in 42 B.C. it became a free city *(civitas libera)* with its own administration and jurisdiction. The administrative and police authority was in the hands of five or six politarchs (Acts 17, 6).

[1] E. Oberhummer, *Thessalonike*: Pauly–Wissowa, RE II. R. 11 (1936) 143 to 163. Ch. Edson, *Cults of Thessalonica*: HarvThR 41 (1948) 153–204.

There was a large Jewish population, and on three consecutive Sabbaths Paul preached in the Synagogue with only scanty results; he had more success, however, among the Gentiles "that served God". This aroused the envy of the Jews, and with the help of an idle mob they stirred up a public demonstration and went to the house of Jason where the missionaries were lodging; they tried to seize them and bring them out to the crowd, but they only succeeded in taking Jason and some Christians whom they brought before the politarchs. In view of this Paul and Silas thought it advisable to leave the city quickly (Acts 17, 1–9).

How long did Paul remain in Thessalonica? A sojourn of four or five weeks would satisfy the account in Acts, but in view of the evidence of the two Epistles it must have been considerably longer than this, extending to two or three months. A few weeks would not be enough for founding the overwhelmingly Gentile community (1 Thess. 1, 9; 2, 14), which was in a flourishing and stable state (1 Thess. 3, 8). A period of some length is required by the description of the devoted and self-sacrificing work of the Apostle among the community (1 Thess. 2, 7–12). Furthermore the Epistles assume that the Thessalonians have a considerable acquaintance with Christian doctrine. Phil. 4, 16 tells us that while Paul was in Thessalonica he twice received assistance from Philippi.

So the report of Paul's foundation of the Thessalonian community is, as usual, highly condensed, and contains only the first and last incidents. After his expulsion from the Synagogue Paul could obviously have remained for a considerable time preaching to the Gentiles.

From Thessalonica they travelled south–west to Berea, now known as Varria. There they had great success in the Synagogue, but this was soon stopped by Jews from Thessalonica. Paul then departed for Athens. Silas and Timothy remained behind for a short time, but were soon instructed to follow him (Acts 17, 10–15). When they joined him, he sent Timothy back to look after and support the community in Thessalonica, for he himself was unable to return (1 Thess. 2, 18 to 3, 5). Paul had little success in Athens and went on to Corinth without waiting for Timothy to come back.

However, Silas and Timothy soon joined him, and then at last he had news from Thessalonica. It was good news; the Thessalonian Christians had remained loyal to the Gospel and its messengers (1 Thess. 3, 6); they stood firm in the Lord (1 Thess. 3, 8); the persecution by their heathen fellow-citizens had not made them waver (1 Thess. 2, 14); their exemplary Christian conduct had contributed to spreading the message of salvation (1 Thess. 1, 8).

Yet there seems to have been a shadow. Paul refers gently to "those things that are wanting to your faith" (1 Thess. 3, 10) which he wants to remedy, and he warns them against the heathen vices of unchastity and dishonesty (1 Thess. 4, 3 sqq.). They are also disturbed about the loss of their dead comrades in the faith (1 Thess. 4, 13 sqq.). The self-justification by Paul in 1 Thess. 2, 3–12 suggests that someone had tried to undermine the loyalty of the community by attributing his missionary work to selfish motives; it is clear that he was concerned lest with time these slanders should have effect; the sharp attack on the anti-Christian Jews (1 Thess. 2, 14–16) shows that they were the source of these rumours.

Delighted at the good news which Timothy had brought back Paul took up his pen and wrote to the community; the result is our 1 Thess., the oldest surviving Pauline Epistle. It was written in the early months of his sojourn at Corinth, probably at the beginning of 52 A.D.

2. Content and structure

Address of greeting 1, 1. Introduction 1, 2–10: Thanksgiving that their faith is so good 1, 2–3; their election by God shows itself a) in the spirit and power of the Apostle's preaching 1, 4–5 and

b) in the exemplary manner in which they accepted the message of salvation 1, 6–10.

I. Survey of the relations between the Apostle and the community 2, 1 to 3, 13.

1. during the foundation of the community 2, 1–16:

a) his unselfish and devoted work in their midst 2, 1–12,

b) they accepted his message with faith and steadfastly endured severe persecutions from their compatriots 2, 13–16;

2. since he left the community 2, 17 to 3, 13:

a) desire and care for them urged Paul to return for another mission and finally to send Timothy 2, 17 to 3, 5;

b) the joy of the Apostle at the good news which Timothy brought back 3, 6–10;

c) his prayer to God to let him return to them and to make them increase 3, 11–13.

II. Warnings and instructions 4, 1 to 5, 24.

1. Exhortation to lead their lives in order to please God, in particular to practise chastity, honesty, and brotherly love, and to work quietly 4, 1–12.

2. Consoling instruction about the Christians who are dead: they shall be awakened at the Parousia, and together with the living they shall be united to Christ 4, 13–18.

3. Recalling of the serious truth of the sudden coming of the day of judgment, and exhortation to sobriety and vigilance 5, 1–11.

4. Various exhortations to the community 5, 12–24.

Conclusion 5, 25–28: prayers and greetings.

3. Authenticity and attestation

F. Chr. Baur accepted only the four principal Epistles (Rom., 1 and 2 Cor., Gal.) as Pauline. He and some of his school denied the authenticity of 1 Thess., alleging that in comparison with the great Epistles it is unoriginal, has no significant dogmatic idea, does not mention the struggle concerning freedom from the Law, and does not cite the Old Testament.

Nevertheless its authenticity is accepted by almost all scholars at the present day. The vocabulary, style and thought are genuinely Pauline. Unlike the Galatians, the Christians of Thessalonica had no trouble with Judaists; their antagonists were unbelieving and bigoted Jews. Paul needed to refer to the Old Testament only when arguing against the justification of the Law.

This Epistle is not devoted to combatting any grave errors; it is a friendly appeal to the still weak Gentile neophytes in Macedonia from the Apostle who had their interests at heart; and it fits the actual situation perfectly. A forger would not have ascribed to Paul the expectation, which was not fulfilled, of living to see the Second Coming of Christ (4, 15).

The Epistle is well attested. Marcion had it in his canon; the Muratorian fragment, Irenaeus (V 1, 6; 30, 2), Tertullian (*De resurr. carnis* 24), and Clement of Alexandria (*Paedagog.* I 5; *Strom.* I 11) know and cite it as an Epistle of Paul. Origen wrote a commentary, which has not come down to us, on 1 and 2 Thess.

§ 33. THE SECOND EPISTLE TO THE THESSALONIANS

Studies: W. Wrede, *Die Echtheit des 2 Thess untersucht* (TU XXIV 2), Leipzig 1903. A. v. Harnack, *Das Problem des 2 Thess* (SB Berlin, phil.-hist. Kl., 1910, 560–578). J. Wrzol, *Die Echtheit des 2 Thess* (BSt XIX 4, 1916). J. Graafen, *Die Echtheit des 2 Thess* (NtA XIV 5, 1930). E. Schweizer, *Der 2 Thess ein Philipperbrief?*: ThZ 1 (1945) 90–105; 286–289; against him W. Michaelis, ibid., 282–286. H. Braun, *Zur nachapostolischen Herkunft des 2 Thess*: ZntW 44 (1952/53) 152–156. [The theological ideas differ so much from those of the authentic Epistles that the composition of this Epistle should be assigned to the generation after Paul.]

1. Occasion

SOME people had come into the Thessalonian community preaching that the Day of the Lord (Day of Judgment) was at hand, and had thereby disturbed and upset the other members of the community; these agitators appealed to sayings of Prophets, and also to a saying or an Epistle of Paul (2, 1 sq.).

It is not quite clear whether the Epistle in question was authentic or not; it might be inferred from 3, 17 that it was not, though Paul would perhaps have spoken more strongly if the Epistle had been spurious. His meaning is probably that such fantasies were quite wrongly being derived from his Epistle (i. e. 1 Thess.).

2 Thess. is devoted primarily to a denial of these fantastic ideas. He had also to turn his attention to idle members who were living off the community (3, 6–16). Though he does not link the excitement about the Parousia with the idleness, it is natural to assume that the two phenomena are connected.

2. Content and structure

Greeting 1, 1–2. Introduction 1, 3–12:

1. Thanksgiving to God that the community is constantly growing in faith and in charity and is enduring persecution steadfastly 1, 3–4.

2. Reference to the just judgment of God at the Second Coming of Christ, where they will be rewarded and their oppressors will be punished 1, 5–10.

3. Prayer of the Apostle for the community that they may be perfected in all good 1, 11–12.

I. Doctrinal Part: Instruction about the time of the Parousia 2, 1–12:

1. The day of the Lord is not yet immediately at hand 2, 1–2.

2. First there must be the apostasy and the appearance of the great evil one (Antichrist), who is still being restrained 2, 3–7.

3. When the Antichrist appears he will by false signs lead astray those men who are to perish, but he will be destroyed by Christ at his Second Coming 2, 8–12.

II. Moral part: Precepts and monitions 2, 13 to 3, 15:

1. Thanksgiving for the election and calling of the recipients 2, 13 to 14, exhortation to hold loyally to the traditions which they have received 2, 15. Prayer for the strengthening of the community 2, 16–17.

2. Appeal for prayers for himself that his work may be fruitful, and that he may be saved from his adversaries 3, 1–3; he has confidence in the obedience of the community, and prays for them 3, 4–5.

3. Correction of the idle members of the community, with reference to his own example and precepts; severe measures should be taken against those who are recalcitrant 3, 6–16.

Final greeting 3, 17–18.

3. The problem of authenticity

In 1801 J. E. Chr. Schmidt asserted that the kernel of the Epistle, the apocalyptic section 2, 1–12, was not Pauline; in 1839 F. X. Kern described its framework as a deliberate imitation of 1 Thess. by a follower of Paul. Even at the present day some scholars impugn the authenticity of the Epistle; the most serious of them was W. Wrede (1903). Yet there are critical exegetes who defend the authenticity of 2 Thess.: Joh. Weiss, E. v. Dobschuetz, Harnack and Dibelius.

Those who dispute its authenticity raise two main objections:

1. The passage about Antichrist 2, 1–12 contains assumptions which are not Pauline, and it is inconsistent with 1 Thess. 4, 13 to 5, 11.

In modern times not even the critics have regarded this argument as very convincing. Wrede practically abandoned it, and now Juelicher admits that the eschatological ideas of 2 Thess. 2, 1–12 do not rule out Pauline authorship even though they do not appear elsewhere in his Epistles.

It is now known that the idea of Antichrist belongs to ancient tradition which can be traced back to Daniel's description of Antiochus IV Epiphanes, the great enemy of God and of his Chosen People; and this idea could have been as familiar to Paul as to a later Christian. It is wrong to assert that Antichrist in 2 Thess. is made to resemble Nero (d. 68 A.D.), for we do not find the traits which were characteristic of Nero—persecutor of Christians, matricide and libertine; a more likely choice would be Caligula, who, to the horror of the Jews, wished his portrait to be set up in the Temple at Jerusalem.

It is also objected that there is an obvious inconsistency in the eschatology of the two Epistles; 2 Thess. 2, 1–12 says that the Parousia shall be preceded by a number of signs (apostasy, appearance and work of Antichrist), while 1 Thess. 5, 1–11 says that the Day of the Lord comes suddenly like a thief in the night. But both elements, suddenness and signs, occur side by side in Jewish and early Christian apocalyptic teaching. Even in the eschatological discourse of Jesus we find harbingers of the Parousia mentioned (Mk. 13, 6 sqq.), alongside the warning to be vigilant because the day is uncertain (Mk. 13, 33 sqq.). There is no inconsistency here, for it is not possible from the signs to determine accurately the Day of Judgment.

2. The second main objection to the Pauline authorship of 2 Thess. is based on the literary relationship of the two Epistles.

It is agreed to-day that the language and style of 2 Thess. are genuinely Pauline and do not provide an argument against authenticity. So there remains fundamentally only one argument which calls for examination, namely the relationship between 2 and 1 Thess.

It is pointed out that there are really remarkable agreements between the two Epistles (e. g. 2 Thess. 1, 3 : 1 Thess. 1, 2 sq.; 2 Thess. 1, 5 : 1 Thess. 2, 12; 2 Thess. 1, 7 : 1 Thess. 3, 13; 2

Thess. 2, 16 sq. : 1 Thess. 3, 11–13; 2 Thess. 3, 8 : 1 Thess. 2, 9; 2 Thess. 3, 16 : 1 Thess. 5, 23; 2 Thess. 3, 18 : 1 Thess. 5, 28); these agreements occur mainly in expressions, turns of phrase, and formulae, each of which is typically Pauline. The strength of the argument lies in the abundance of such resemblances.

This description of the facts is correct. But it is open to question whether we may infer from this that there is a later hand at work. Col. and Eph. stand in a similar relationship to each other. An imitator might have made greater use of 1 Thess.

It is also pointed out that both Epistles deal with eschatology, yet the second Epistle never refers to the first; this is the more surprising since the second Epistle was apparently intended to correct false conclusions which had been drawn from 1 Thess. 5, 1–11 about the suddenness of the Parousia.

This fact is also correct. Does it follow from the silence of 1 Thess. that those who, according to 2 Thess., were excited about the Parousia, were not active when 1 Thess. was written? But how did Paul learn about them? Or if they were disturbing the community even when 1 Thess. was written, why does Paul not denounce them there?

From what has been said it follows that the problem of the authenticity of 2 Thess. may be reduced to two questions: was it written before or after 1 Thess., and what was the occasion of its composition?

The following are the most important solutions proposed: 1. The second Epistle was composed before the first (Joh. Weiss, Hadorn, Michaelis). This is decisively ruled out by the fact that according to 2 Thess. 2, 15 Paul had already written to them, while 1 Thess., according to 2, 17 to 3, 6 is his first Epistle to the community. 2. Both Epistles were written and dispatched at the same time. Harnack suggests that 2 Thess. was intended for the Jewish-Christian minority who had cut themselves off from the Gentile majority. The Old Testament colouring of the Epistle favours this, as does the reading ἀπαρχὴν in 2, 13 which Harnack favours in place of ἀπ' ἀρχῆς; this would describe them as the first to be converted, but if it were the correct reading we should expect a genitive after it. Furthermore it is most unlikely that the apocalyptic excitement affected only the Jewish part of the Christian community.

Dibelius also refers to 1 Thess. 5, 27 and 2 Thess. 3, 17 and questions whether the community was united. He considers it possible that the two Epistles were not intended for the same group; he thinks that 2 Thess. may have been designed for reading in the liturgical assembly of the community; this would explain its cooler and more impersonal tone.

3. The second Epistle was written a few days after the first, and was addressed to the whole community (Graafen). Paul wrote the first Epistle in his initial delight at the good news; but Timothy also informed him about abuses—excitement about the Parousia and idleness—and when he considered the matter more calmly this news worried him; so a few days after the first Epistle he wrote again in a less enthusiastic tone to deal with those faults.

According to this theory only a few days lay between the two Epistles, and this would provide a good explanation of their close agreement in expression, style and thought. But it does not explain why the second Epistle makes no reference to the first. Moreover, 1 Thess. 5, 1 sqq. leaves the impression that when he was writing the first Epistle Paul had no information about the excitement concerning the Parousia.

4. There were two or three months between the two Epistles. Fantastic ideas about the proximity of the Parousia had taken root in part of the community because of the first Epistle, and these ideas were having a bad effect on their whole way of life. Paul learned of this and wrote a second Epistle in which he stressed the other aspect of eschatological expectation, namely that certain events precede the coming of the end, and he then

calmed the excitement and called for energetic measures against those responsible for it. Since there was only a short period between the two Epistles Paul, consciously or not, repeated the wording of 1 Thess., which was still fresh in his memory.

This theory is held by the majority of Catholics and by a large number of others. It has three weak points: first, Paul does not simply refer to 1 Thess. and correct the misunderstanding; secondly, if there was an interval of two or three months, the agreement of the two Epistles is still remarkable; and finally 2, 3 does not make it clear whether the excitement was due to an alleged saying of Paul, to the authentic 1 Thess., or to a spurious epistle.

So if we accept the authenticity of 2 Thess. unsolved difficulties remain, but these cannot rule out Pauline authorship. Since our knowledge of the historical background is so incomplete, a solution to all the problems will perhaps never be found.

Polycarp cites 2 Thess. 1, 4; 3, 15 in his Epistle to the Philippians 11, 3 4. Otherwise the attestation of this Epistle is the same as for 1 Thess.

§ 34. THE EPISTLE TO THE GALATIANS

Commentaries: (a) A. Schaefer, F. S. Gutjahr, cf. § 32. R. Cornely, [2]1909 (CSS). A. Steinmann, [4]1935 (BonnerNT 5). M.-J. Lagrange, *Épîtres aux Galates,* Paris [6]1950. O. Kuss, 1941 (RegNT 6 contains Rom., 1 and 2 Cor., Gal.). F. Amiot. (Gal., 1 and 2 Thess.), 1946 (VS XIV). — (b) W. Bousset, [3]1917 (GoettNT 2). F. Sieffert, 1899 (Meyer VII[9]). E. de Witt Burton, 1921 (ICC). Th. Zahn, [3]1922 (Zahn IX). H. Lietzmann, [3]1932 (HB 10). H. W. Beyer, [5]1949 (NTDeutsch 8). A. Oepke, 1937 (ThHK 9). H. Schlier, 1952 (Meyer VII[11]). G. S. Duncan, 1949 (Moffatt). P. Bonnard (Gal.) and Ch. Masson (Eph.): Commentaire du NT IX, 1953 (cf. § 3, 9) [Gal. is addressed to the Christians of North Galatia; in view of its close kinship with Rom., it was written at the beginning of the winter 56/57 (rather than in 54/55 at Ephesus) either in Corinth or in Macedonia before 2 Cor.; see Benoit: RB 1954, 237–239]. H. N. Ridderbos, 1953 (NIC).
Studies: J. Walter, *Der religioese Gehalt des Gal,* Goettingen 1904. A. Steinmann, *Die Abfassungszeit des Gal,* Muenster i. W. 1906. Idem, *Der Leserkreis des Gal* (NtA I 3/4, 1908). C. H. Watkins, *Der Kampf des Paulus um Galatien,* Tuebingen 1913. W. Luetgert, *Gesetz und Geist. Eine Untersuchung zur Vorge-*

schichte des Gal, 1919 (BFchTh XXVI, 6). V. Weber, *Die antiochenische Kollekte, die uebersehene Hauptorientierung fuer die Paulusforschung*, Wuerzburg 1917. Ph. Haeuser, *Anlass und Zweck des Gal* (NtA XI 3, 1925). J. H. Ropes, *The Singular Problem of the Epistle to the Galatians* (HarvThSt 14, 1929). T. W. Manson, *The Problem of the Epistle to the Galatians*: BJRL 24 (1940) 59–80. K. L. Schmidt, *Ein Gang durch den Gal*, Zollikon 1942. M. C. Tenney, *Galatians. The Character of Christian Liberty*, 1950. O. Linton (cf. § 29, 4). Ch. H. Buck, *The Date of Gal.*: JBL 70 (1951) 113–123. Ch. de Beus, *Paulus Apostel der Vrijheid*, Amsterdam 1955. L. Batelaan, *De strijd van Paulus tegen het Syncretisme*: Arcana revelata, Festschr. f. F. W. Grosheide, Kampen 1951, 9–21 [the antagonists in Gal. are Syncretists who wish to join the ceremonies of heathen cults to the observance of the Jewish Law]. R. M. Grant, *Hellenistic Elements in Gal.*: AThR 34 (1952) 223–226 [in language and style it shows parallels to Hellenistic philosophy and rhetoric]. W. Schmithals, *Die Haeretiker in Galatien*: ZntW 47 (1956) 25–67.

1. *Region and province of Galatia*

THE region of Galatia is in the interior of Asia Minor. It gets its name from the Celtic tribes (Γαλάται = Κέλται) which settled there. In the first half of the third century these tribes were driven from their homeland in Gaul along the Danube to Asia Minor; about 240 B.C. king Attalus of Pergamum defeated them and made them settle in the territory around the cities of Ancyra, Pessinus, and Tavium. In the course of the following century they became largely hellenized. Amyntas, the last king of Galatia, who died in 25 B.C., bequeathed his kingdom to the Romans.

The Romans made it a province, adding on a number of other districts such as Pisidia, Isauria, Phrygia, and parts of Lycaonia. The propraetor of the province resided at Ancyra, now known as Ankara. In the course of time the province expanded, but it had no official name. An inscription of the first century A.D. (CILSuppl 6818) describes its governor as: *leg(atus) Aug(usti) pro pr(aetore) provinc(iae* or *iarum) Gal(atiae) Pisid(iae) Phryg(iae) Lu(caoniae) Isaur(iae) Paphlag(oniae) Ponti Galat(ici) Ponti Polemoniani Arm(eniae)*. Latin writers of the imperial age, such as Tacitus and the elder Pliny, sometimes refer briefly to the province as Galatia. But there is no evidence that the people who belonged to the parts of the province outside the region of Galatia were described or addressed as Galatians.

2. The destination of the Epistle

The Epistle is addressed to the "churches of Galatia", and its recipients are addressed as ὦ Γαλάται (3, 1). In view of the ambiguity of the name Galatia the question arises whether the Epistle was addressed to the people of the Galatia region in the north of the province (North Galatian Theory), or to the people in another part of the province; in the latter case they must have been the communities in the southern part of the province which were founded on the first missionary journey—Antioch, Iconium, Lystra, Derbe (South Galatian Theory). In spite of discussions over the last hundred years there has been no agreement on the matter.

Acts tells us that Paul and Silas at the beginning of the second missionary journey visited the churches which he had founded on the first journey and then "they passed through Phrygia and the country of Galatia" (τὴν Φρυγίαν καὶ Γαλατικὴν χώραν); they then travelled along the border of Mysia to Troas (16, 6–8). At the beginning of the third missionary journey Paul "went through the country of Galatia and Phrygia in order, confirming all the disciples" (18, 23). So on the second missionary journey Paul preached in the region of Galatia, and on the third missionary journey he visited the churches which he had founded on the previous journey. It is remarkable that Acts gives no details about his work there; but as it is not a complete record its silence is not significant. The Epistle itself says little about its recipients, and what it does say is variously interpreted.

Most scholars—including Oepke and Schlier, the most recent commentators—hold the North Galatian Theory. The arguments for it are the stronger; the most important are:

1. It is impossible that Paul should have addressed Pisidians

and Lycaonians—the latter had a language of their own—as "Galatians" (3, 1), just because they happened to belong to a province the centre of which was the region of Galatia; being a native of Cilicia, he must have known that this would offend their national feeling.

2. Gal. 4, 13 says that illness was the occasion of his preaching to the Galatians. Acts makes no mention of illness in its detailed account of Paul's work in southern Galatia, for we cannot identify this illness with the stoning in Lystra, from which he recovered easily (Acts 14, 19 sqq.).

3. Gal. 4, 8; 5, 2 sq.; 6, 12 sq. describes the recipients of the Epistle as former pagans. We cannot infer from 3, 2 sq. 13 sq. 23–29; 4, 2 5; 5, 1 that they were Jewish Christians; these verses merely mean that, in the judgment of the former Jew Paul, the Old Testament Law was valid for all mankind, and even the Gentiles have been freed from the curse of the Law through Christ's death on the Cross. There were Jewish-Christians in the South-Galatian communities.

The South-Galatian Theory has had exponents since 1750 and has been maintained very persuasively in modern times by Sir W. Ramsay, the authority on Asia Minor, as well as by Th. Zahn, a Protestant, and by Val. Weber, a Catholic. They raise various objections to the North-Galatian Theory, of which the following are the most serious:

1. The people of the region of Galatia were not the type whom Paul's mission suited, for the Greek language and Greek culture were not common there, and there is no evidence that there were synagogue communities which would have been natural starting points for his preaching. Against this, Acts 18, 23 shows that there were Christians in the region of Galatia, and it is unlikely that their cities had not been influenced by Greek language and culture.

2. Paul used only the official names of provinces, and so by "Galatia" 1, 2 he must have meant the Roman province and not

the region. This argument does not stand up to examination. In Gal. 1, 21 "Syria and Cilicia" certainly refers to the regions, not the provinces—for Jerusalem also belonged to the province of Syria; and when he mentions Judea (1 Thess. 2, 14; Gal. 1, 21; Rom. 15, 31; 2 Cor. 1, 16) he is thinking of the region, for it was only in Vespasian's time that a separate province of Judea was set up beside Syria; furthermore Arabia in Gal. 1, 17 is the description of a region, not an official name for the Nabatean kingdom.

3. Content and structure

The theme of the Epistle is the defence of the Gospel of freedom from the Law, which Paul has proclaimed.

Introductory greeting 1, 1–5. Introduction 1, 6–9: Paul is surprised at the sudden falling away of the Galatians from the true Gospel, and he takes to task the Judaists who had misled them.

I. Historical part: The Gospel and apostolate of Paul come not from men but from God, and have been entirely accepted by the original Apostles 1, 10 to 2, 21:

1. His Gospel does not derive from the mother community 1, 13–24, for

a) before his conversion he was a zealous Jew 1, 13–14;

b) he had no contact with the rulers of the mother community until three years after his conversion, and then only for fourteen days 1, 15–20;

c) after that he worked as an independent missionary far from Jerusalem in Syria and Cilicia 1, 21–24.

2. His Gospel and his apostolate to the Gentiles were formally recognized by the rulers of the mother community 2, 1–10, and when Peter wavered in Antioch he was corrected by Paul 2, 11–21.

II. Doctrinal part: Faith, and not the Law, brings salvation 3, 1 to 5, 12:

1. The experience of the Galatians themselves teaches them that; they have received the gift of the Holy Ghost because of their faith, and not because of the works of the Law 3, 1–5.

2. Scripture also teaches this; first scriptural proof from the history of Abraham 3, 6 to 4, 7:

a) The blessing promised to Abraham belongs to those who have faith, while those who build upon the Law are under the curse 3, 6–14.

b) The Law, which came later, cannot rescind the promise which carries the inheritance with it; it should be merely our guide to Christ 3, 15–24.

c) Christ has freed us from the slavery of the Law and made us children and heirs 3, 25 to 4, 7.

3. Complaint of the Apostle about their incredible relapse into slavery, and a warm personal appeal referring to their former cordial relations 4, 8–20.

4. Second proof from Scripture 4, 21–31: The story of Agar and Sara shows that the Christians are free from the Law.

5. A vigorous exhortation not to accept circumcision and thereby be deprived of their freedom and lose Christ 5, 1–12.

III. Moral part: Christian freedom is not a licence for the desires of the flesh; it involves moral obligations 5, 13 to 6, 10:

1. Serve one another through charity 5, 13–15.

2. Obey the impulse of the Spirit and not the lust of the flesh 5, 16–26.

3. Correct sinners with meekness and consciousness of your own weakness 6, 1–6.

4. Sow goodness so that you may reap eternal life 6, 7–10.

Conclusion written in his own hand 6, 10–18: a further attack on the Judaizers who are leading them astray, with mention of the Judaizers' ignoble motives.

4. Occasion and purpose

Some time after Paul's second visit to the Galatian communities (4, 13; Acts 18, 23), Judaistic agitators arrived and attacked the Gospel of freedom from the Law which he had preached, at the same time trying to undermine his authority as an Apostle.

They argued that his Gospel was a dangerous heresy; the Law was not repealed by Christ; salvation is available to Gentiles also, but only if they accept circumcision and subject themselves to the Law; if Paul said that they were free from the requirements of the Law, he was only speaking to please men (1, 10). Paul, they said, was not a true Apostle at all; he had not seen Jesus nor been with him; only the Twelve were real Apostles, and they had nothing to say about the repeal of the Law and the abolition by Christ's death of the religious primacy of Israel; Paul received no mission from Jesus, he was merely an agent of the original Apostles, through whose school he had passed and on whose teachings he was dependent. Perhaps the intruders added that in Jerusalem Paul had accepted and preached the necessity of circumcision ("And I, brethren, if I yet preach circumcision, why do I yet suffer persecution?" 5, 11), but had not mentioned it to them in order more easily to convert them (1, 10). Certainly the Judaists represented themselves as the preachers of the only genuine Christianity, which was derived from the mother community, was preached by the original Apostles, and went back to Jesus himself; they claimed to be completing Paul's faulty beginnings (3, 3).

Apparently their agitation was not without effect. Though the Galatians did not fall away from Paul, yet their loyalty to him was shaken (1, 6; 3, 1 sq.). They had already begun to observe the Jewish calendar of feasts (4, 10). Though they had not yet been circumcised, there was a danger that they would be persuaded to undergo circumcision (5, 2; 6, 12). The agitators seem only to have asked them to subject themselves to circumcision and a certain number of indispensible precepts of the Law, but Paul explains to them that by accepting circumcision they bound themselves to observe the entire Law (5, 1–3).

He does not say where the agitators came from, but simply speaks of people who confuse or disturb the Galatians (1, 7; 5, 12). From what he says on one occasion (5, 10) we may infer that an important personage stood behind them, but it is impossible to determine whom he has in mind; in view of 2, 6–9 it was certainly not Peter nor even James. The only certain point is that the agitators were connected with the Judaistic elements who had fought unsuccessfully against Paul in Antioch and Jerusalem (cf. 2, 4).

He does not suggest who had informed him about the Judaistic activity in Galatia. He realized that immediate and energetic action was essential; presumably he was prevented from going to Galatia in person; so he wrote an Epistle in which he unsparingly berates his adversaries and is not very gentle (3, 1) even with his "little children" (4, 19). None of the other Epistles is so permeated with anger and emotion; this is the only one of his Epistles which has no thanksgiving at the beginning or greetings at the end. Nevertheless in the second half the love of his distressed heart for his children triumphs over his displeasure at their fickleness, and he implores them to listen to him (4, 12–20).

We do not know what effect the Epistle had. If Gal. was written before 1 Cor., the Galatians certainly came back to the Pauline Gospel (cf. 16, 1); presumably the preservation of the Epistle is due to the Galatians, and this is a further indication that they did return to him. Paul's silence about the Galatians in 2 Cor. 9, 2 does not disprove this, and neither does the fact that no representative of the Galatians is mentioned in Acts 20, 4 as accompanying Paul on his journey to Jerusalem, for no one from Corinth is mentioned there either (cf. also § 50, 5).

5. Time and place of composition; authenticity

The Epistle was written after Paul's second sojourn in Galatia (4, 13; Acts 18, 23), probably while he was at Ephesus where news from Galatia could most easily reach him. It cannot be determined with certainty whether it was written before or after 1 Cor. (cf. 1 Cor. 16, 1 with Gal. 2, 10). Those who favour the South Galatian Theory say that it was written during the second missionary journey, while he was in Corinth, and some of them regard it as the oldest surviving Pauline Epistle.

No one questions the authenticity of Galatians. Polycarp cites from it three times (3,3 = Gal. 4,26; 5,1 = Gal., 6,7; 5,3 = Gal. 5, 17). Marcion, as might be expected, placed it first in his *Apostolos*.

6. Significance of the Epistle

The background to the Epistle is the conflict between Paul and the Judaistic agitators in Galatia. This conflict revolved around the fundamental and essential problem of the Christian religion. For Paul salvation comes to men from Christ's death on the Cross; for the Judaists it comes from circumcision and the observance of the Mosaic Law; in their eyes only one who was a Jew by birth or by choice could obtain eternal salvation.

Logically the teaching of the Judaists deprived Christ's redemptive death of all value. Perhaps the Judaists did not realize this, but Paul appreciated all that it entailed, and engaged energetically in the struggle against this fundamental error, a struggle which he carried through relentlessly. He prevailed, but at the cost of his freedom (Acts 21, 20 sqq.).

The Epistle to the Galatians is the principal document of this struggle. It was a conflict of great import for the history of the world, for if Paul had been unsuccessful, Christianity would have remained merely a Jewish messianic sect and could never have become a world religion.

THE TWO EPISTLES TO THE CORINTHIANS

Commentaries: (a) A. Schaefer, *Erklaerung der beiden Briefe an die Korinther,* Muenster i. W. 1903. R. Cornely, [2]1909 (CSS). F. S. Gutjahr, *Die zwei Briefe an die Korinther*[2], Graz and Vienna 1916/1922. J. Sickenberger, [4]1932 (Bonner NT 6). O. Kuss cf. § 34.

(b) W. Bousset, [3]1917 (GoettNT 2). H. Lietzmann, [4]1949 (supplement by W.G. Kuemmel; HB 9). H. D. Wendland, [6]1954 (NTDeutsch 7). A. Schlatter, *Paulus, der Bote Jesu. Eine Deutung der Briefe an die Korinther,* Stuttgart 1934. J. Héring, 1949 (Bonnard VII 1 2).

Studies: J. Rohr, *Paulus und die Gemeinde von Korinth* (BSt IV, 4: 1899). W. Luetgert, *Freiheitspredigt und Schwarmgeister in Korinth* (BFchTh XII 3, 1908). T. W. Manson, *The Corinthian Correspondence*: BJRL 25 (1941) 101–120; 26 (1942) 327–341. P. Cleary, *The Epistles to the Corinthians*: CBQ 12 (1950) 10–33.

§ 35. THE FIRST EPISTLE TO THE CORINTHIANS

Commentaries: (a) E.-B. Allo, *Première épître aux Corinthiens,* Paris 1934 (reprinted 1955). J. Huby, 1946 (VS XIII).

(b) A. Robertson-A. Plummer, [2]1914 (ICC). Joh. Weiss, 1925 (Meyer V[10]). Ph. Bachmann, [4]1936 (Zahn VII). K. Barth, *Die Auferstehung der Toten* (particularly about ch. 15), [2]1926. J. Moffatt, 1938 (Moffatt). K. Heim, *Die Gemeinde der Auferstandenen. Vorlesung ueber 1 Kor,* Munich 1949. F. W. Grosheide, 1954 (NIC). Studies: K. Pruemm, *Die pastorale Einheit des 1 Kor:* ZkTh 64 (1940) 202–214. R. Hundstorfer, *Die Adressaten des 1 Kor,* Wels 1948 (91st annual report of Obergymn. Kremsmuenster). P. A. van Stempvoort, *Eenheid en schisma in de gemeente van korinthe volgens 1 Kor.,* 1950 (Theol. Dissertation Amsterdam). H. Schlier, *Ueber das Hauptanliegen des 1 Kor: Die Zeit der Kirche. Exegetische Aufsaetze,* Freiburg i. Br. 1956, 147–159; Idem, *Kerygma and Sophia:* ibid. 206–232. N. A. Dahl: Norsk Teologisk Tidsskrift 54 (1953) 1–23. [On ch. 1—4. There were not factions in Corinth, but anti-Pauline tendencies. Paul is writing in an apologetic vein.] W. Schmithals, *Die Gnosis in Korinth. Eine Untersuchung zu den Korintherbriefen,* Goettingen 1955 [1 Cor. is a conflation of two Pauline Epistles. Paul does not militate against three hostile fronts in Corinth, but against one, and it was Gnostic. The Corinthian Gnostics had their roots in Jewish tradition]. M. R. de Haan, *Studies in 1 Cor.,* 1956.

1. The founding of the Church in Corinth

IN 146 B.C. the Romans under the consul L. Mummius razed to the ground the ancient brilliant city of Corinth. A century later C. Julius Caesar re-established it as a Roman colony *(Colonia laus*

Iulia Corinthus). In 27 B.C., when Greece was cut off from Macedonia and joined to Epirus to form the senatorial province of Achaea, Corinth became the capital of the new province and the residence of the proconsul.

The city lay between two seas—Horace speaks of *bimaris Corinthus*—with a harbour on either side, Cenchreae to the east and Lechaeum to the west; thanks to its geographical position Corinth soon regained its former commercial importance and, like the old city, became "the natural entrepôt between East and West."

The original settlers in New Corinth were of Roman stock; many of Paul's converts had Roman names—Titius Justus, Crispus, Gaius, Quartus, Tertius, Fortunatus and Lucius. It was not long until a strong Greek and oriental element was added to the Roman settlers; the presence of orientals is shown by cult objects of Eastern gods. There was also a large Jewish colony (Philo, *Leg. ad Gaium* 36); the lintel of a synagogue has survived: συν]αγωγη Εβρ[αιων.

Almost every cult of the Mediterranean area was represented among this medley of peoples. There were sacred objects both of Roman and Greek gods, like Jupiter Capitolinus, Aphrodite and Artemis of Ephesus, and of oriental deities like Isis, Serapis, Melkhart, and Cybele.

The new city, like old Corinth, was notorious for its depravity and immorality. Strabo tells us (VIII 6, 20) that the famous temple of Aphrodite in old Corinth had over a thousand *hierodoulae* who sold themselves in honour of the goddess. A lurid light is cast upon the depravity of the city by sayings like οὐ παντὸς ἀνδρὸς εἰς Κόρινθον ἐστ' ὁ πλοῦς (*non cuivis hominum contingit adire Corinthum*, Horace Ep. I 17, 36), and words such as κορινθιάζεσθαι (to be a libertine), κορινθία κόρη (harlot), κορινθιαστής (libertine; the title of a comedy). It was in Corinth that Paul wrote his celebrated description of the moral corruption

382

of the pagan world, Rom. 1, 18–23. Socially there were unparalleled extremes; the most dire poverty stood side by side with immense wealth and extravagant luxury.

On the second missionary journey, about the autumn of 51 A.D., Paul travelled alone from Athens to Corinth where he found employment with the Jewish couple Aquila and Priscilla (Acts 18, 1 sqq.). Here, too, he began to preach in the synagogue. On the arrival of Silas and Timothy with helpers from Macedonia (2 Cor. 11, 7 sqq.), he was able to devote himself entirely to the mission. It was not long until the breach with the synagogue took place. Paul removed to the house of a proselyte, Titius Justus, which was near the synagogue, and encouraged by a nocturnal vision of Our Lord, continued his work. In eighteen months he succeeded in establishing a considerable Christian community which was mainly recruited from the Gentiles (1 Cor. 12, 2; 8, 1–13; 10, 14–33 etc.), though it had a Jewish element also (1 Cor. 7, 18; 10, 32; 12, 13; 16, 19; Acts 18, 8). Most of the members belonged to the lower classes, but there were also converts from the upper classes and well-to-do people (1 Cor. 1, 26–28; 11, 22–32). The Jews tried in vain to have him expelled by the proconsul Gallio. Some time after this he went with Aquila and Priscilla to Ephesus, leaving them there, while he proceeded to Caesarea and to Antioch. After a short stay there he began the third missionary journey which led him through Galatia and Phrygia to Ephesus, where he worked for three years (c. 54–57 A.D.).

Shortly after Paul's departure an Alexandrian Jew named Apollo came to Corinth; he was highly educated (perhaps a trained orator), and was thoroughly versed in the Scriptures; he had been well instructed in Christian doctrine by Aquila and Priscilla at Ephesus. His work at Corinth was very successful (Acts 18, 24–28; 1 Cor. 3, 5–9), and after some time he returned to Ephesus (1 Cor. 16, 12).

2. Content and structure

Introductory greeting 1, 1–3. Introduction 1, 4–9: Thanksgiving for their spiritual riches and reference to their perfection.

First main section 1, 10 to 6, 20: Abuses in the Corinthian community

I. Factions 1, 10 to 4, 21.

1. The division of the community into four "factions" (Paul-, Apollo-, Cephas-, and Christ-party) is absurd, for Christ is not divided 1, 10–17.

2. The wisdom of God, which Paul proclaims—the Cross of Christ—stands in sharp contrast to the wisdom of this world which the Corinthians regret is not in Paul 1, 18 to 2, 16.

3. The various preachers of the Gospel have all the same task, namely to build on Christ, the Foundation which Paul has laid; so they all belong to the whole community 3, 1–23.

4. Application to Paul and Apollo; their work is subject only to the judgment of God; Reprimand of the Corinthians' conceit about them 4, 1–13.

5. A personal message: Paul has sent Timothy to them and will soon come to them himself 4, 14–21.

II. Moral abuses in Corinth 5, 1 to 6, 20.

1. A case of incest 5, 1–13:

a) Censure of the community, punishment of the sinner, exhortation to cleanness of conduct 5, 1–8.

b) Prohibition of contact with profligate members of the community 5, 9–13.

2. Litigation before pagan courts 6, 1–11:

a) This is unworthy of a Christian 6, 1–6;

b) Christians should rather suffer injustice than do wrong, for the unjust shall not possess the Kingdom of God 6, 7–11.

3. Christian freedom does not allow unchastity 6, 12–20.

Second main section 7, 1 to 15, 18: Reply to the problems raised
in an epistle from the Corinthian community

I. Marriage and virginity 7, 1–40.

1. The permissibility of marriage and the fulfilment of the
marriage duties 7, 1–7.

2. The unmarried and the married (divorce) 7, 8–11.

3. "Mixed marriages" *(privilegium paulinum)* 7, 12–16.

4. The general principle is: Let each one remain in the state to
which he is called 7, 17–24.

5. Lengthy commendation of celibacy 7, 25–35.

6. The marriage of virgins 7, 36–38.

7. Widows 7, 39–40.

II. The eating of idols' meat 8, 1 to 11, 1.

1. The Christian is free in principle to eat idols' meat, but out
of charity towards the weak he must be prepared to forego his
freedom 8, 1–13.

2. Paul has given them the example of fulfilling this requirement; he renounced the right which the Apostles have to be
maintained by the community, and made himself the servant of
all 9, 1–27.

3. Lengthy warning against partaking in sacrificial banquets
(history of the Israelites in the desert; partaking in the table
of the Lord is incompatible with assistance at pagan sacrificial
banquets) 10, 1–22.

4. Instructions about eating idols' meat 10, 23 to 11, 1.

III. Abuses in the liturgical assemblies 11, 2–34.

1. The veiling of women at prayers and prophecies 11, 2–16.

2. Sharp censure of the abuses at the Agape and instructions
about the worthy celebration of the Lord's Supper (earliest
account of the Last Supper) 11, 17–34.

IV. Instruction about the gifts of the Spirit (Charisms) 12, 1 to 14, 40.

1. Their multiplicity, their origin from one and the same Spirit, and their purpose 12, 1–31.

2. Charity stands high above all gifts of the Spirit (Encomium on charity) 13, 1–13: its absolute necessity (13, 1–3), its superiority (13, 4–7), its eternal duration (13, 8–13).

3. The superiority of prophecy to the gift of tongues 14, 1–25.

4. Regulations to ensure order in the assemblies of the community 14, 36–40.

V. The resurrection of the dead 15, 1–58.

1. The reality of Christ's resurrection 15, 1–11.

2. The faith in the resurrection of the dead (Christians) rests

a) on the fact that Christ rose from the dead (with an excursus on the Second Coming of Christ and the end of the world 15, 23–28) 15, 12–28.

b) on the conviction that a life full of sacrifice, such as Paul leads, would otherwise be folly 15, 29–34.

3. The risen body; the fate of those Christians who are alive at the Parousia 15, 35–58.

Concluding part 16, 1–23:

1. The collection for Jerusalem 16, 1–4.

2. Paul's plans for travelling; commendation of Timothy whom he is sending to them; concerning Apollo 16, 5–12.

3. Final exhortations; commendation of certain Corinthians; greetings 16, 13–23.

3. Occasion of the Epistle

There was constant traffic between the two seaports of Corinth and Ephesus, and it was not difficult for Paul to maintain regular contact with the Corinthian community. Even before 1 Cor. he had written to them—the Epistle has not come down to us—forbidding any contact with libertines.

The immediate occasion of 1 Cor. was a letter from the community asking for directions about various matters (marriage and virginity; eating of idols' meat; charisms; hope of the resurrection cf. 1 Cor. 7, 1 25; 8, 1; 12, 1; 15, 1 sqq.). This enquiry was evidently delivered by the Corinthians Stephanas, Fortunatus, and Achaicus, who were with Paul when 1 Cor. was written (1 Cor. 16, 15 sqq.). He had learned by word of mouth from "them that are of the house of Chloe"—apparently the slaves of a well-to-do Christian—that the community was divided into four factions or groups: the parties of Paul, Apollo, Cephas, and Christ; he had also been informed about other abuses—a scandalous case of incest which the community had overlooked, ligitation about trivial matters before pagan courts, and neglect of the poor at the Agape.

1 Cor. deals with all these matters, both with the abuses and with the enquiries, and it provides an extraordinarily revealing picture of the lights and shadows in the religious and moral life of a mainly Gentile urban community in the early days of the Church.

We could understand the polemic in 1 Cor. more clearly if we had more accurate information about the differences between the four "factions" or "party groups" of Corinthian Christians which placed themselves under the authority of the four men from whom they received their names. But it is impossible to be quite certain about them, for they are not described closely in the Epistle. In any case they were not organized groups with separate liturgical assemblies (cf. 1, 12; 11, 17; 14, 23: "If therefore the whole Church come together into one place").

It is easiest to describe the parties of Paul and Apollo. The party of Apollo evidently consisted of those Corinthians who felt drawn by the style of Apollo's preaching; Acts describes him as an Alexandrian Jew of great eloquence, and well versed in Scripture. His followers preferred his "wisdom of speech" (1, 17) to

Paul's plain preaching of the Cross. Presumbly this party was the main target of 1, 10 to 4, 21. It is not to be assumed that there was a real opposition between them and the Pauline party, for both missionaries had worked together in Corinth (3, 4 sqq.); furthermore the polemic is never directed against Apollo himself, and when the Epistle was written he and Paul were working together in harmony in Ephesus (16, 12); since there is not a single criticism of Apollo, no fault can attach to him personally. Paul censures both parties for preferring the person of a favourite missionary to the substance of the Gospel. He directs his remarks against the followers of Apollo, for their attitude was the more dangerous; Apollo's style of preaching made great concessions to Greek rhetoric and philosophy, and there was undoubtedly a risk that it might undermine the notion of the "scandal of the cross".

The party of Cephas must have honoured Peter as the authoritative Apostle, and have fostered close relations with the mother church in Palestine. It has been suggested that the existence of the Cephas party was due to missionary work by Peter at Corinth, but there is no proof of this, and it is not probable (cf. § 49). This group may have consisted of Jewish Christians who had immigrated from territory where the Apostles had preached. They probably questioned Paul's apostolate since he was not a personal Apostle of Jesus, and unlike the others had not been called by Jesus himself (9, 1 sqq.; 15, 8 sqq.); they certainly clung to circumcision and to the Mosaic Law, but there is no evidence in the Epistle that at that time the Judaists were a peril in Corinth as they were in Galatia.

It is very difficult to form a correct picture of the Christ party, for 1 Cor. does not give sufficient indications about them. Evidently, unlike the other groups, they rejected human leaders and placed themselves directly under the authority of Christ. Apparently the opponents of Paul in 2 Cor. used the catchphrase "I am Christ's" (10, 7), boasted vigorously of their Jewish origin (11, 23), and represented themselves as the only true Christians (5, 16; 11, 15). In view of this, many exegetes regard the Christ party of 1 Cor. as an extreme Judaistic element like his opponents in Galatia, that is, a Judaeo-Christian movement of greater strictness than the party of Cephas.

But 1 Cor. does not contain any anti-Judaistic polemic, and so other scholars (for example, Allo) more correctly hold that the Christ party consisted of the Corinthian Christians who boasted of a more profound Gnosis—appealing probably to direct revelations from Christ—and who set themselves apart from the community of the Church, at the same time practising moral laxity. Paul's castigation of the abuse of Christian freedom may be directed against them (cf. 6, 12; 8, 1 sqq.; 9, 18 24; 10, 1 9 12; 11, 3); probably they were also responsible for overvaluing the charisms (12–14), and denying the Resurrection (15).

The existence of a separate "Christ party" has often been denied, and the words "And I of Christ" (1, 12), have been regarded as an interpolated gloss from a reader who wrote on the margin of his MS. his own profession of faith. In support of this it is pointed out that in 3, 22 the three names Paul, Apollo and Cephas are mentioned together, while Christ first appears in 3, 23 in a quite different setting. Moreover, 1 Clem. 47, 3 is quoted: Paul "wrote to you concerning himself, and Cephas and Apollo, for even then you had factions"; it is clear that the author of this Epistle did not read that phrase in his text. But these arguments are not compelling.

4. Time and place of composition

Paul wrote the Epistle in Ephesus during the second half of his mission there, for he was able to send greetings from a large number of communities in the province of Asia (16, 19). He intends to remain at Ephesus till Pentecost and then travel by way of Macedonia for a fairly long sojourn at Corinth (16, 5–9). Unless he postponed his departure for a long time (cf. § 36, 1), the Epistle must have been written in the spring of his last year at Ephesus (57 A.D.), around Easter time (5, 6 sqq.). The itinerary which is described in Acts 19, 21 fits in well with this.

§ 36. THE SECOND EPISTLE TO THE CORINTHIANS

Commentaries: (a) J. E. Belser, *Der zweite Brief des Apostels Paulus an die Korinther,* Freiburg i. Br. 1910. E.-B. Allo, *Seconde Épître aux Corinthiens,* Paris 1937 (reprinted 1953). (b) Ph. Bachmann, ⁴1922 (Zahn VIII). A. Plummer, 1915 (ICC). H. Windisch, 1924 (Meyer VI⁹). R. H. Strachan, 1935 (Moffatt).
Studies: E. Kaesemann, *Die Legitimitaet des Apostels:* ZntW 41 (1942) 33–71. R. Bultmann, *Exegetische Probleme des zweiten Korintherbriefes* (SBU 9), Uppsala 1947. P. Ph. Lindsey, *Paul and the Corinthian Church:* JBL 68 (1949) 341–350. E. Golla, *Zwischenreise und Zwischenbrief,* 1922 (BSt XX, 4) [he denies both]. W. C. van Unniek, *Reiseplaene und Amen-Sagen. Zusammenhang und Gedankenfolge in 2 Kor 1, 15–24:* Studia paulina f. J. de Zwaan, 1953, 215–234.

1. Time and place of composition

ON its own evidence the Epistle was written in Macedonia some time after Paul left Ephesus (2, 12 sq.; 7, 5 sq.; 8, 1 sqq.; 9, 2), hence during the journey which is recounted in Acts 20, 1 sq., probably in (late) autumn 57 A.D. When Paul was about to leave Ephesus he sent his fellow worker Titus to Corinth with instructions to proceed to Troas—the port Alexandria-Troas—when he had finished his commission, and to wait for him there. But when Paul reached Troas Titus had not arrived, and when he failed to come the Apostle became worried about the Corinthian situation, and breaking off his mission at Troas he went to Macedonia to meet him. After some time Titus joined him there; the news which he brought was mainly good (7, 6); it was the occasion of 2 Cor.

2. Content and structure

Introductory greeting 1, 1–2. Introduction 1, 3–11: Thanks to God for his comfort in all tribulation, particularly for saving him from danger of death.

First main section 1, 12 to 7, 16: The Apostle defends himself before the Corinthian community, and praises the greatness of the apostolic office

I. Defence against the charge of unreliability, and other matters 1, 12 to 2, 17.

1. The omission of the visit which he had promised and the sending of the last Epistle ("the sorrowful Epistle") were due only to his loving consideration for the community 1, 12 to 2, 4.

2. Paul is pleased to learn of the rebuke of the guilty one, and advises that the penitent be shown forgiveness and charity 2, 5–11.

3. The journey of Paul to Troas and Macedonia; praise of God 2, 12–17.

II. The greatness of the apostolic office 3, 1 to 6, 10.

1. The Corinthian community as a proof of the apostolic office which Paul exercises 3, 1–3.

2. The apostolic office surpasses in greatness the service of Moses 3, 4–18.

3. The Apostle is fearless and outspoken 4, 1–6.

4. Meaning and blessedness of suffering in the exercise of the apostolic office 4, 7–18.

5. Hope of heavenly perfection (glorified body) as a power in suffering 5, 1–10.

6. Paul defends the sincerity of his work 5, 11–13, praises the greatness of his message of regeneration and atonement 5, 14 to 6, 2, and refers to his being tested by all sufferings and tribulations 6, 3–10.

III. The reconciliation of the Apostle with the community 6, 11 to 7, 16.

1. He asks them to restore complete communion, and urges them to turn away from all paganism 6, 11–13 + 7, 2–4 + 6, 14 to 7, 1.

2. Paul is delighted at the good news which Titus brought (repentance of the community) 7, 5–16.

Second main section 8 to 9: The collection for the Church in Jerusalem

1. He requests that they should contribute generously to the collection, and refers to the example of the Macedonian communities 8, 1–15.

2. Recommendation of the three men who are sent to Corinth as his representatives in this matter, and reason for sending them 8, 16 to 9, 5.

3. Generous giving brings the rich blessing of God upon the giver 9, 6–15.

Third main section 10 to 13: In preparation for his forthcoming visit Paul confronts his adversaries and the community which tolerates them

1. Rejection of the charges brought by his opponents and ridicule of their arrogant conduct 10, 1–18.

2. Paul is compelled to praise himself in order to defend the dignity of his apostolate 11, 1 to 12, 13:

a) He asks them to bear with his foolish boasting 11, 1–4 16–21a

b) Paul is equal in birth to "them that are above measure Apostles"; the reason why he renounced his right to be supported by the Corinthians 11, 5–15.

c) Paul's boasting ("I speak foolishly") 11, 21b to 12, 13.

3. Announcement of his forthcoming visit, apprehensions, appeals, threats of severe measures in the case of impenitence 12, 14 to 13, 10.

Conclusion 13, 11–13: Final appeals, greetings, blessing.

3. *The previous events*

The time between the two Epistles to the Corinthians is the most obscure period of Paul's life. We have only oblique references in 2 Cor. to the relations between Paul and the Corinthians during this time, and so any reconstruction of the events must be tentative. It is fairly certain that Paul had made a short visit from Ephesus during this period ("intermediate journey" or "intermediate visit"), and had sent a letter immediately afterwards, "the sorrowful Epistle"—it is lost—which Titus must have delivered.

Presumably this was the course of events: Shortly after he had sent Timothy (and Erastus) through Macedonia to Corinth (1 Cor. 4, 17; 16, 10 sq.; Acts 19, 22), a deputation arrived from the Corinthian community bringing a letter containing a number of enquiries. The Apostle answered these in 1 Cor. However, the Epistle had not the desired effect, and even the sending of Timothy did not improve the situation. Thus Paul decided to go in person to deal with the situation in Corinth; but he was severely disappointed and soon left Corinth, promising that he would return before long. When he finally departed from Ephesus, it was his intention to go to Corinth, then to Macedonia, and then back to Corinth (1, 15 sq.).

It is disputed whether the Apostle had a serious quarrel with a Corinthian Christian on this occasion, or if it was some time afterwards that one of his associates was violently attacked by an enemy of Paul's who had come to Corinth (this is suggested by Allo), and was supported by a section of the community (7, 12; 2, 5 sqq.). The verb ἀδικεῖν "to do wrong" which he uses here would not refer to (personal) injury to Paul.

Paul then changed his plans. Instead of going in person to Corinth he wrote "with many tears" a vigorous Epistle to the community ("the sorrowful Epistle" 2, 4), calling for the punishment of the guilty person. He sent Titus to Corinth with this Epistle, instructing him to travel back through Macedonia to Troas.

4. Purpose

When Titus met Paul in Macedonia he had good news: the majority of the Corinthian community had given a good reception to him and to the Epistle; they acknowledged that Paul's reproach was justified, and had called the guilty party to account; now they were looking forward with pleasure to the Apostle's visit (2, 6; 7, 5–16).

However, Paul, instead of going immediately, sent Titus back with another Epistle, our 2 Cor.; he instructed Titus and two "brethren" who accompanied him to resume the collection which had been interrupted and to complete it (ch. 8–9). But there was another more serious reason for Paul's action. Apparently Titus had informed him that his opponents were continuing their agitation in Corinth and were affecting part of the community; so he decided to settle once and for all the question of his relation to the community, so that when he should arrive he would not have the same distressing experience as during his short visit from Ephesus.

In this Epistle he attacks his adversaries in Corinth, and threatens strong measures unless the community sever all relations with them. The identity of these opponents who are dealt with in 2 Cor. is a matter of dispute. There is no mention in 2 Cor. of the four factions of 1 Cor., except for 10, 7 which probably refers to the Christ party. Many scholars still support the theory which F. Chr. Baur put forward, that the adversaries with whom 2 Cor. deals are Judaists, as is the case in other Epistles; the weakness of this theory is the silence of both 1 and 2 Cor. about Judaistic agitators like those in Galatia.

In 1908 Luetgert suggested that these adversaries were Antinomian Pneumaticists and Gnostics; it would be a case of a Hellenistic-Gnostic-Judaeo-Christianity which was spread by intruding missionaries, and was a serious rival to Paul's Gospel. Luetgert's suggestion has been taken up by many scholars and developed in various forms. Allo, for instance, regards the intruders at Corinth (11, 4 sqq.) as Hellenistic Jews of the Diaspora who taught a kind of Jewish-Gentile-Christian Gnosis, forerunners of those who are described in the Captivity Epistles; they did not preach circumcision nor appeal to the Apostles, but presumably placed themselves, with their speculations and ascetical practices, above every common teaching; these were itinerant preachers who joined with the Antinomians of the Christ party in Corinth, and were not genuinely converted either by 1 Cor. or by Titus.

Perhaps the most acceptable suggestion was made by Kuemmel, who thinks that Paul had to deal with two sets of opponents in Corinth. The intruders were Palestinian Jews, for they are described in 11, 22 as Ἑβραῖοι, and they raised the objection that Paul had not known Jesus personally (5, 16); they claimed the title of Apostles which they refused to Paul—hence he ironically calls them "them that are above measure Apostles" (οἱ ὑπερλίαν ἀπόστολοι) 11, 5; 12, 11—and they lived at the expense of the community. These "false Apostles" and the Pneumatic Gnostics who had been attacked in 1 Cor. joined forces in the struggle against Paul (11, 6; 12, 1 sqq.).

Paul visited Corinth shortly after sending 2 Cor. Acts 20, 3 sq. tells us that he spent three months in Hellas. While in Corinth he wrote Rom., the longest, most serene and clearest of his Epistles; in it he was able to say that the collection in Macedonia and Achaea had fully come up to expectations (15, 26 sqq.). So we may infer from this that Paul had overcome his opponents and firmly restored the bond between the Corinthian community and himself.

395

5. Unity

In general the critics raise no objections to the authenticity of 2 Cor. But even at the present day it is hotly disputed whether all the parts of 2 Cor. belonged to the original Epistle. Many scholars have suggested serious reasons for denying the unity of the Epistle, but in spite of various attempts to divide it into a number of Epistles or fragments, no really convincing case has yet been made out.

1. The passage 6, 14 to 7, 1 interrupts the excellent continuity between 6, 13 and 7, 2; the passage is a warning against paganism, and there is no such warning elsewhere in this Epistle. For these reasons it has been said that the passage is either spurious or an interpolation from another Pauline Epistle—from the "pre-canonical" Epistle to the Corinthians, cf. 1 Cor. 5, 9—or else has been displaced from its original position after 5, 14 to 6, 2. Against these suggestions it must be pointed out that considerations of language and subject matter do not rule out a Pauline origin[1], and there are sharp transitions also in 5, 11; 6, 1; and 6, 11.

2. J. S. Semler (1776; cf. § 2) described ch. 9 as a doublet of ch. 8, and this has often been maintained since. Windisch, followed by E. Osty, regards ch. 9 as a document intended for the churches of all Achaea, distinct from 2 Cor., and written shortly after it. There are three arguments for this theory: first, ch. 9 is a supplement to ch. 8, although the literary form of ch. 8 does not require a supplement; moreover ch. 9 has the appearance of a doublet, for it gives a self-contained treatment of the same theme, and to some extent expresses the same ideas and thoughts as ch. 8; finally there is a certain inconsistency between the two chapters; in 8, 1–5 Paul exhorts the Corinthians to follow the example of the Macedonian communities in their eagerness for the collection, while according

[1] Cf. Schlatter ad loc., and N. A. Dahl, *Das Volk Gottes,* Oslo 1941 p. 221, 324 note 43.

to 9, 1–6 he commends to the Macedonians the generosity of the Achaean communities in the matter; cf. also 8, 7–15 with 9, 6–14. There is no objection on principle to this theory, but the two chapters can be reconciled without undue difficulty, as is pointed out by Lietzmann, Wendland, Allo and others.

3. The most popular theory has been to partition ch. 10–13 as a separate epistle ("the four chapter Epistle"). Hausrath in 1870, and others since, wished to identify it with the "intermediate Epistle", while Krenkel in 1890, followed by Windisch and Osty, thought it a fifth epistle to the Corinthians. The reason for partitioning these chapters is the sharp change of tone between 1–9 and 10–13; this change seems to reflect a different relationship between the author and the recipients; it is pointed out that in 10–13 Paul treats his opponents with the greatest sharpness and with biting irony, while 1–9 is devoted to reconciling his dispute with the community.

Yet both forms of this theory are open to serious objections. These four chapters cannot be identical with the "intermediate Epistle", for there is no reference in these chapters to the "intermediate visit" of 2, 5 sq. and 7, 12; moreover, chapters 1–9 pass over in silence the confronting of his adversaries which is the substance of chapters 10–13.

The second form of this theory presupposes that, when he had already sent off chapters 1–9, Paul learned that since the departure of Titus his opponents in Corinth were using every means to undermine his authority and were not without success in this and in their attack on the legitimacy of his apostolate; a further Epistle—namely chapters 10–13—would be the answer to this.

Against this theory it must be pointed out that the difference in tone should not be exaggerated; chapters 1–9 are addressed to the whole community, while in 10–13 he deals with the intruders and the part of the community which is giving them a hearing; this fact provides a fairly easy explanation of the difference in tone between the two parts. Moreover, the Apostle does defend himself against bigoted attacks in 1–9, and 10–13 is not without expressions of affection and reconciliation (10, 8; 11, 2; 12, 14; 13, 7).

§ 37. THE EPISTLE TO THE ROMANS

Commentaries: (a) *St. Lyonnet*, 1953 (La Sainte Bible de Jérusalem). A. Schaefer, *Erklaerung des Briefes an die Roemer*, Münster i. W. 1891. R. Cornely, [2]1909 (CSS). F. S. Gutjahr, *Der Brief an die Roemer*, Graz and Vienna 1923/27. O. Bardenhewer, *Der Roemerbrief des hl. Paulus*, Freiburg i. Br. 1926. J. Sickenberger, [4]1932 (Bonner NT 6). F. W. Maier, *Israel in der Heilsgeschichte* (BZfr XII 11/12, 1929; Exposition of Rom. 9–11). M.-J. Lagrange, *Épître aux Romains*, [6]1950. O. Kuss, see § 34. J. Huby, 1940 (VS X).—(b) E. Gaugler, I (1945), II (1953), Zurich *(Prophezei)*. O. Michel, 1955 (Meyer IV[11]) [cf. RB 1955, 620 f.]. K. S. Wuest, 1955 (English). B. Weiss, 1899 (Meyer IV[9]). W. Sanday-A. C. Headlam, [5]1905 (ICC). E. Kuehl, *Der Brief des Paulus an die Roemer*, Leipzig 1913. A. Juelicher, [5]1917 (GoettNT 2). Th. Zahn, [3]1925 (Zahn VI). Th. Haering, *Der Roemerbrief des Apostels Paulus*, Stuttgart 1926. K. Barth, *Der Roemerbrief*, 2. edition, 7. impression, Munich 1940. C. H. Dodd, 1932 (Moffatt). H. Lietzmann, [4]1933 (HB 8). P. Althaus, [6]1949 (NTDeutsch 6). A. Schlatter, *Gottes Gerechtigkeit*, Stuttgart [2]1953. A. Nygren, *Der Roemerbrief. Aus dem Schwedischen uebersetzt*, Goettingen 1951.

Studies: P. Feine, *Der Roem. Eine exegetische Studie*, Goettingen 1903. J. Pauels, *Untersuchungen zum Roemerbrief. Der Glaube der Roemischen Kirche vor Paulus*, Bonn 1927. J. H. Ropes. *The Epistle to the R. and Jewish Christianity*, in: Case, *Studies in Early Christianity*, London 1928, 253–268. M. Rauer, *Die Schwachen in Korinth und Rom nach den Paulusbriefen* (BSt XXI, 2/3: 1929). H. Katzenmayer, *Die Entstehung der Kirche Gottes in Rom*: IKZ 1941, 36 ff. T. M. Taylor, *The Place of Origin of Romans*: JBL 67 (1948) 281 to 296. A. Feuillet, *Le plan salvifique de Dieu d'après l'épître aux Romains*: RB 57 (1950) 333–387; 489–529. St. Lyonnet, *Note sur le plan de l'épître aux R.*: RSR 39/40 (1951/52) 301–316. K. Pruemm, *Zur Struktur des Roem; Begriffsreihen als Einheitsband*: ZkTh 72 (1950) 333–349. P. Bonnard, *Où en est l'interprétation de l'épître aux Romains?*: RThPh 1951, 225–243 [since F. Chr. Baur]. E. E. Ortigues, *La Composition de l'épître aux Romains* (I–VII): Verbum Caro 8 (1954) 52–81. J. Dupont, *Le Problème de la structure littéraire de l'épître aux Romains*: RB 62 (1955) 365–397. St. Lyonnet, *Quaestiones in ep. ad Rom.* I, Rome 1955. K. H. Schelkle, *Paulus—Lehrer der Vaeter. Die altkirchliche Auslegung von Roem. 1–11*, Duesseldorf 1956. C. K. Barrett, *A Commentary on the Epistle to the Romans*, London 1957. O. Kuss, *Der Roem*, translated and annotated, Regensburg 1957 (Cath.). J. Munck, *Christus und Israel*. An interpretation of Rom. 9–11, Aarhus 1956.

1. *The beginnings of the Christian community at Rome*

DEEPEST darkness envelops the beginnings of the Christian community at Rome, but it may be regarded as certain that Christianity was introduced at a very early date to the capital of the Roman Empire where men from all countries gathered. It is unlikely that the community there arose as the result of a planned mission; it was due rather to Christian immigrants from Palestine and Syria joining together to form a community.

The Apostle Peter cannot have founded the community, for his arrival in Rome probably took place in the fifties at the earliest. Reports that he worked for twenty or twenty-five years in Rome appear in the Universal Chronology of Eusebius, a Roman Chronograph of 354 A.D., Jerome, *De vir. ill.* 1, and in the Acts of Peter; A. Harnack says that this report was found also in the lost Universal Chronicles of Julius Africanus (completed in 221 A.D.), and of Hippolytus of Rome († 237 A.D.), so that it is attested as early as the beginning of the third century. But the story originated from the legend of Simon Magus, and its foundation is weak. Acts 12, 26 says merely that after his escape from prison Peter left the jurisdiction of Herod Agrippa.

Suetonius in his life of the Emperor Claudius c. 25 says: *Iudaeos impulsore Chresto assidue tumultuantes Roma expulit;* it may be inferred from this that around 49 or 50 A.D. there was a considerable Christian community at Rome, whose members were mainly Jewish.[1] Christus and Chrestus would sound alike, and the Emperor's general regulation was probably due to violent conflicts within the Jewish community at Rome between those who accepted and those who rejected the message that Jesus

---

[1] In the first century A.D. Rome had a large Jewish population, which has been reckoned at 50,000; they were organized into a considerable number of synagogue groups, of which thirteen are still known by name; cf. J. B. Frey, *Corpus Inscriptionum iudaicarum* I (1936) p. LVI sqq. and Bb 12 (1931) 129–156; P. Styger, *Juden und Christen im alten Rom,* Berlin 1934.

of Nazareth was Messias; Suetonius evidently made the mistake of thinking that the instigator of the trouble was a Jew living at Rome whose name was Chrestus, a common name where Latin was spoken. The expulsion of the Jews—including the Jewish-Christians—resulted in a great lessening of the Jewish-Christian element in the Roman community; from this time onwards the Gentile element was probably dominant among the Roman Christians. However, the edict fell into abeyance after the death of Claudius in 54 A.D., and many Jewish-Christians no doubt returned to Rome, while the Jewish elements among the Christians would have increased for other reasons also.

The Epistle to the Romans is our oldest and most reliable evidence about the Roman Christian community. When it was written, Rome had a flourishing community which was celebrated throughout the world (1, 8; 16, 19); it could look back on a fairly long history, for Paul says (15, 22) that he had long intended to visit them and work for some time amongst them (1, 15; cf. also Acts 19, 21).

Aquila and Priscilla were probably his first source of exact information about the Roman community, and it was no doubt during his first sojourn in Corinth that he formed the plan of travelling through Rome to the West to seek a new mission field, when he should complete his work in the Eastern Mediterranean countries. We know from Acts 28, 15 that when Paul landed at Puteoli, Christians came from Rome to meet him.

2. Content and structure

Introductory greeting 1, 1–7; Introduction 1, 8–15: thanksgiving to God for the faith of the community, and an expression of his desire to preach the Gospel among them. Theme of the Epistle 1, 16 sq.: The Gospel is a power of God for salvation to everyone who believes, for in it God's justice reveals itself from faith.

A. Dogmatic part 1, 18 to 11, 36.

I. How justification or the justice of God is obtained 1, 18 to 4, 25 (content summarized in 3, 23 sq.).

1. (negatively) The universal need of men for salvation: Jews and pagans are equally under the wrath of God, and lack the justice of God 1, 18 to 3, 20. This is demonstrated first in the case of the pagans (1, 18-32), and then in regard to the Jews (2, 1 to 3, 20).

2. (positively) Now God's justice is sent to every believer, without merit on his part, in virtue of Christ's death for sin 3, 21 to 4, 25:

a) Through faith Jews and Gentiles receive justification in virtue of the sacrificial death of Christ, so that all boasting is excluded 3, 21-30.

b) Scriptural proof of this from the story of Abraham 3, 31 to 4, 25.

II. The fruits which God's justice produces 5, 1 to 8, 39.

1. It gives the certainty of eternal life 5, 1-21. This is guaranteed

a) by God's incomparable act of love in the pouring out of the Holy Ghost and in giving up his Son for sinners 5, 1-11;

b) by the relation between the life-giving act of obedience of Christ and the disobedience of Adam which brought death 5, 12-21.

2. It frees us from the lordship of sin; so one who is justified is bound to a sinless life 6, 1 to 7, 6.

3. Excursus on the relation between the Law and sin (occasioned by 7, 1-6) 7, 7-25.

4. The redemption in Christ has freed us from the law of sin, and given us the Spirit and sonship of God, and thereby the certainty of eternal perfection 8, 1-17.

5. With complete confidence and patience we await eternal glory 8, 18-39.

III. How the hardening of the Jews in disbelief is to be reconciled with God's promises (Pauline Theodicy) 9 to 11.

Introduction: Paul's distress at Israel's unbelief 9, 1-5.

1. No shadow of blame falls upon God 9, 6–29:

a) God's promise remains in force, for it applies only to children of Abraham in the sense of the promise 9, 6–13.

b) God could have fulfilled this plan, for he is absolutely sovereign in his election to grace 9, 14–29.

2. The entire responsibility for the obduracy falls upon Israel itself 9, 30 to 10, 21:

a) Israel strove for its own justice instead of the justice of God 9, 30 to 10, 3.

b) Scripture attests that true justice is obtained only through faith 10, 4–15.

c) So Israel is inexcusable because it has rejected the salvation which was offered to it 10, 16–21.

3. Nevertheless God has not rejected his people 11, 1–32:

a) At the present time God has allowed a small part to come to faith 11, 1–6.

b) He has hardened the majority of them, not in order to ruin them, but so that salvation may come to the Gentiles 11, 7–12.

c) So the Gentiles have no reason to boast against the unbelieving Israel 11, 13–24.

d) When the fulness of the Gentiles comes in, then all of Israel will also be converted 11, 25–36.

B. Moral part 12, 1 to 15, 13.

I. Particular duties 12, 1 to 13, 14:

1. Sanctification of personal life 12, 1–3;

2. Right use of the gifts of grace 12, 4–8;

3. Brotherly love and love of enemies 12, 9–21;

4. Obedience to the powers ordained by God 13, 1–7;

5. Love is the fulfilment of the Law 13, 8–10;

6. Reference to the Parousia as motive for moral conduct 13, 11–14.

II. The mutual relation of the "strong" and the "weak" 14, 1 to 15, 13:

1. Neither should despise the other nor brand them as heretics 14, 1–12.

2. The "strong" should have charitable consideration for the "weak" 14, 13–23.

3. Both should look to Christ as an example 15, 1–13.

Conclusion 15, 14 to 16, 27: personal information

1. Why he wrote the Epistle 15, 14–21;

2. Plans for travelling 15, 22–33;

3. Recommendation of Phoebe 16, 1–2;

4. List of greetings 16, 3–16;

5. Warning against those who mislead them 16, 17–20;

6. Greetings from Paul's companions 16, 21–23;

7. Final doxology 16, 24–27.

3. The character of the Roman community

F. Chr. Baur considered that the Roman community to which Paul wrote was overwhelmingly Jewish, and had judaizing and particularistic tendencies. In modern times Th. Zahn has maintained strongly that the majority of the Christians there were Jewish, but he acquits them of anti-Pauline Judaistic tendencies in view of Paul's unconditional declaration of the correctness of their beliefs (6, 17). Most present-day scholars, however, hold the view—correctly—that the majority of the Roman Christians were Gentiles.

The problem can be solved only from the evidence of Rom. The following reasons seem to favour the view that the readers were Jewish Christians:

1. In 2, 17 to 3, 8 Paul argues with the self-justified Jews, whom he addresses directly in 2, 17.

2. In 3, 21–31 he defends himself against Jewish charges that by his teaching he is destroying the Law.

3. In 4, 1 he calls Abraham "our father according to the flesh".

4. In 6, 1 to 7, 6 he answers Jewish objections to his doctrine of freedom from the Law.

5. In 9 to 11 the problem of the obduracy of Israel is at the centre of Paul's treatment of history (cf. also 15, 8 sqq.).

6. The "weak" of 14, 1 to 15, 3 are Jewish Christians.

The main argument is that the whole Epistle aims to show that justification is effected by faith without the works of the Law, and not by circumcision and the Law, in other words that the Epistle is a detailed argument against Judaism and the Old Testament, and a vindication of the Pauline Gospel and of Paul's work as missionary to the Gentiles.

There are numerous counter arguments which prove clearly that the Roman community was essentially Gentile.

In the introduction and conclusion Paul mentions his intention of coming to Rome and refers to his office as Apostle of the Gentiles, and explicitly addresses the Romans as Gentiles "among whom are you also" (1, 5 sq.); he has always hitherto been prevented from coming to Rome where he wishes also to gain some fruit, as he has among the other Gentile peoples (1, 13 sq.); he excuses his boldness in writing by appealing to the grace which he has received from Christ of being a servant of Christ among the Gentiles (15, 15 sq.). Even within the dogmatic part he occasionally addresses the recipients as Gentiles: "For I say to you, Gentiles: As long indeed as I am the Apostle of the Gentiles, I will honour my ministry" (11, 13); moreover, in 9, 3 sqq.; 10, 1 sq.; 11, 23 28 31 he speaks to former Gentiles about his own people. In 6, 17 sqq. he reminds his readers of their former sinful lives as pagans.

Yet because of its origins, the Roman community also contained a considerable Jewish minority. The "weak" of 14, 1 sqq. were certainly Jewish Christians or were recruited principally from the Jewish part of the community; this is shown by their observance of particular days (14, 5; probably the Sabbath and

Jewish feast days), the distinction of clean and unclean foods (14, 14 20 sq.), and the grouping of the Christians into former Jews and Gentiles when he commands them to receive one another with brotherly love (15, 7 sqq.).

4. *Time and place of composition*

Romans was written during Paul's last sojourn at Corinth at the beginning of 58 A.D. According to Rom. 15, 19 sqq. the Apostle had finished his work in the Eastern half of the Roman Empire, and he intended to visit Jerusalem in order to deliver the proceeds of the collection which he had organized in the territory of his mission on behalf of the mother community.

We know from Acts 20, 2 sqq. that he spent three months in Greece after his journey through Macedonia, and that he left Greece shortly before Easter, spent Easter at Philippi, and then proceeded to Jerusalem. 1 Cor. 16, 6 tells us that he was considering spending the winter at Corinth; in 2 Cor. 13, 1 he tells the Corinthians of his forthcoming visit, and according to Acts 20, 3 he originally intended to sail from Greece to Palestine; so he probably spent the greater part of the three months in Corinth, and wrote Romans there.

If Rom. 16 is part of the Epistle (cf. sect. 6), Paul evidently sent the letter by the deaconess Phoebe, who was working at Cenchreae, the port of Corinth (16, 1 sq.). If the Gaius, whom Rom. 16, 23 calls his host, is identical with Gaius the Corinthian whom Paul baptized (1 Cor. 1, 14), this would be another indication that the Epistle was written at Corinth.

5. *Occasion and purpose*

According to 1, 10–15; 15, 14–33 the purpose of the Epistle was to announce and prepare for Paul's projected visit to the Roman community. As Apostle of the Gentiles he feels bound to make all nations obedient in the faith to the name of Christ (1, 5).

When he finishes his missionary work in the East he intends to look for a new mission field in Spain, and on his way there he hopes to visit the Roman community as he has long planned. But it is his principle not to build on other men's foundations, so he will preach the Gospel to them only "as I pass", and hopes to be helped on his way to Spain by them. Rome was indispensible as a headquarters for the Spanish mission which he was planning, and so he was obliged to gain the goodwill and support of the Roman community which hitherto had been unknown to him. For this purpose he writes this Epistle to them.

But that is only the immediate occasion of the Epistle. Romans is the most extensive and carefully composed of Paul's writings; it is the most clearly constructed of all his Epistles, and it surpasses the others in theological importance. Calmly and exhaustively, with hardly any polemic, he presents his Gospel, particularly the relation between faith and works, and the contrast of the justification which is a gift from God with that which is wrought by man. Indeed it resembles a theological exposition rather than a letter. How did the Apostle come to write such an Epistle?

This question has been debated since Marcion, and even at the present day it is not entirely solved. Were the theme and content of the Epistle determined by the internal conditions of the Roman community, or were they due to Paul's position at the time?

In spite of what Augustine, Jerome and the ancient prologue say, it is unlikely that Paul intended to heal disputes between the Jewish and Gentile Christians. We may rule out completely the theory, which has supporters even in modern times, that the Epistle is directed against Judaistic agitators who had invaded the community or even against a Judaistic mission of Peter himself.[2] For Romans does not attack the work of Judaistic missionaries

---

[2] Thus Lietzmann: SBBerlin 1930; against him M. Goguel: RHPhR 14 (1934) 461 to 500, and E. Hirsch in ZntW 29 (1930) 65–76.

amongst Christians who are free from the Law; it is in conflict with the doctrine of Judaism concerning the relation between the Law and justification. So far as can be seen, the Epistle makes no reference to actual circumstances within the Roman community, except in 14, 1 to 15, 13 where the "strong" are directed to have consideration for the "weak", and the point at issue there is not fundamental.

So it would seem that the reason why Romans deals with these matters is to be sought in the history of the Apostle and of his work. Paul could have had no better introduction to a community which he did not know than an extensive exposition of his Gospel. The Romans had certainly heard of him and of his work; according to 16, 3 sqq. there were many acquaintances of Paul's in Rome. He might well have wondered whether what the Romans had heard about him was true, for there were no limits to the intrigues of the Judaists against him. Moreover, he now stood at the end of the first great part of his missionary work; it had been stamped by the struggle against Judaists and unbelieving Jews, and it would be natural for him, in view of these past struggles, to deal with the problem of the Law and faith, and of the destiny of the Jewish people who as a body had remained outside the faith. These questions had been of the highest importance throughout his work, and they were highly topical in any Christian community which contained a Jewish-Christian element.

Probably we should also remember that the Christianity of the Roman community was not entirely a Gentile Christianity in Paul's sense of the word; perhaps it had a strongly Jewish-Christian character, without being Judaistic in the sense of being opposed to Paul. Indeed it is not impossible that in the earliest period Gentiles received circumcision and submitted to the Law before Baptism, in communities not founded by Paul. If this was the case, it would shed a new light on those passages which are cited to support the view that the Roman Church was Jewish-Christian (especially 4, 1 sqq.; 5, 20 sqq.; 7, 4 sqq.); this would also make it easier to understand why Paul discusses at such length (9 to 11) the unbelief of the great mass of the Jewish people and their final conversion.

6. Integrity[3]

There were two recensions of Romans one with and one without ch. 15 and 16. In his commentary on Romans Origen tells us that Marcion excised the last two chapters and the doxology; this ¡s possible but not certain. At any rate he used the short recension. These two chapters were missing also from some (lost) Latin MSS. Irenaeus, Tertullian and Cyprian used only the short recension.

F. Chr. Baur and his school regarded these two chapters as a second century addition, but now-a-days no one questions their authenticity.

But it is a matter of dispute whether ch. 16 originally belonged to it. Many exegetes (e. g. Feine, Behm, Michaelis, Gaechter, and A. Feuillet) have adopted the theory of David Schulz (1929) that ch. 16 or 16, 3–20 is an Epistle of Paul (or the conclusion of an Epistle) to the community at Ephesus, which later became attached to Romans. Michaelis says that 16, 3–24 is the conclusion of an Epistle which Paul wrote in Philippi or Troas (cf. Acts 20, 6) instructing the presbyters of Ephesus to come to Miletus (Acts 20, 17). The main arguments for this theory are:

1. Rom. 15, 33 is the concluding blessing written in his own hand.

2. The long list of greetings with 26 names presupposes that Paul had an improbably large number of personal friends and acquain-

---

[3] R. Schuhmacher, *Die beiden letzten Kapitel des Roem* (NtA XIV, 4: 1929). J. Dupont, *Pour l'histoire de la doxologie finale de l'épître aux Romains:* RBén 58 (1948) 3–22. Huby, *Épître aux Romains* 513–520. G. D. Kilpatrick: JThSt 45 (1944) 63 sq.

tances in Rome; his friends are more likely to have been at Ephesus.

3. Epenetus is mentioned in 16, 5 as "the first fruit of Asia"; we would expect him to be in Ephesus rather than in Rome.

4. Acts 18, 18 sq.; 1 Cor. 16, 19 tell us that Aquila and Priscilla went with Paul to Ephesus, and they were there when 2 Tim. was written (2 Tim. 4, 19). It is hardly likely that they removed to Rome and returned again to Ephesus between 1 Cor. and 2 Tim.

5. The enigmatic statement that they both risked their necks to save Paul's life (16, 4), could be understood only in Ephesus where the heroic deed took place.

6. The sharp attack on Judaistic agitators (16, 17–20) is not in harmony with the calm and carefully restrained tone of the Epistle (1, 10 sqq.; 15, 14 sqq.).

7. The oldest MS. of the Pauline Epistles $\mathfrak{P}^{46}$ places the final doxology (16, 25–27) between 15, 33 and 16, 1; from this we may infer that ch. 16 did not originally belong to Romans.

These arguments are certainly strong, but they cannot be considered decisive. If we regard 16, 1–24 as a letter of recommendation for Phoebe to the Christians of Ephesus, then the disproportion between the content of the Epistle and the greetings is too great. If we isolate only 16, 3–20 (or 3–24) and regard them as the remains of an Epistle of Paul to Ephesus, then there is no explanation of how this particular fragment survived and became attached to Romans. So the majority of scholars maintain that this chapter is an original part of Romans.

It has recently been suggested that it is a separate personal covering note which was sent with the main Epistle. When Paul writes to a community which he himself founded, he does not usually send greetings to particular people (1 and 2 Thess.; 1 and 2 Cor.; Gal.; Phil.), nor does he send greetings from his companions (yet cf. 1 Cor. 16, 9; Phil. 4, 22); on the contrary he does both in Col. 4, 10–17. It is quite understandable that the Apostle should prepare for his visit to the Roman community by greeting all whom he knew there, in order to assure himself of a good reception. It is not improbable that he had a large circle of acquaintances in Rome, for there was constant migration from the East to the capital, and many of the Jews and Jewish-Christians whom Claudius had banished probably returned after his death.

The passage v. 17–20 is probably a postscript such as Paul liked to add to his epistles in his own hand; these postcripts also can adopt an energetic tone (Gal. 6, 11–17; 1 Cor. 16, 22). These four verses are not directed against Judaists; the "doctrine", as in 6, 17, is ethical, and the warning is intended to strengthen them against dangers. 16, 20b is written in his own hand, and 16, 21–23 is a postscript.

The authenticity of the doxology 16, 25–27 is disputed; it shows striking resemblances to Eph. (1, 9; 3, 1–12 20 sq.). The reasons for questioning its authenticity are its alleged unpauline character[4] and its various positions in the MSS. It is missing in Marcion, Ephrem, the archetype of G (Boernerianus) and F (Augiensis), and Jerome tells us (in Eph. 3, 5) that many MSS. of his time were without it. The oldest Pauline MS. $\mathfrak{P}^{46}$ places it after 15, 33; in other ancient MSS. it occurs after 14, 23 ($\mathfrak{K}$ L min), or after 16, 23 ($\aleph$ B C D* bo sa vg syP), and in some it appears twice, after 14, 23 and 16, 23 (AP min).

It has the form of a liturgical profession of faith, and its language is paralleled exactly in Eph. 3, 20; 1 Tim. 1, 17; Jude 24 sq.; Mart. Polyc. 20, 2.

Many scholars suggest that it was composed by the Marcionites in order to give Romans, with its truncated ending, a conclusion for reading at community worship; they say that it then found its way into non-Marcionite Bibles, but in various positions.

Yet the doxology is a short summary of the principal ideas of Romans, and its language and style are not so different from Paul

[4] Cf. J. Dupont, Μόνῳ σοφῷ Θεῷ Rom. 16, 27: EphThL 22 (1946) 362–375.

as to compel us to deny Pauline authorship (cf. Rom. 1, 2 3 5; 2, 16; 1 Cor. 2, 6–10; Eph. 3, 3–12; Col. 1, 26 sq.; 2, 2; 1 Tim. 3, 16; 6, 15 sq.; 2 Tim. 1, 1–3). This is the only place in the whole New Testament where the doxology stands at the end of an Epistle, after the greetings and the final blessing. Jude (24 sq.) ends with a doxology, but it has no greetings or final blessing.

THE CAPTIVITY EPISTLES

Commentaries: (a) J. Knabenbauer, 1912 (CSS). M. Meinertz - F. Tillmann, [4]1931 (BonnerNT 7). J. Huby, 1935 (VS VIII). K. Staab, 1950 (RegNT 7).—(b) E. Haupt, 1902 (Meyer VIII IX[7]). P. Ewald, (Eph., Col., Philem.) [2]1910 (Zahn X). A. Lueken,[3]1917 (GoettNT 2). M. Dibelius - H. Greeven (Col., Eph., Philem.)[3]1953 (Lietzmann 12). E. Lohmeyer (Phil., Col., Philem.) 1953 (Meyer IX[9]). E. F. Scott (Col., Philem., Eph.) 1930 (Moffatt). P. Althaus etc.,[5]1949 (NTDeutsch 8). P. Bonnard (Phil.) and Ch. Masson (Col.) 1951 (Bonnard 10).

Studies: J. Schmid, *Zeit und Ort der pl Gefangenschaftsbriefe*, Freiburg i. Br. 1931. W. Michaelis, *Die Gefangenschaft des Paulus in Ephesus*, Gütersloh 1925. G. S. Duncan, *St. Paul's Ephesian Ministry*, London 1929. St. Hanson, *The Unity of the Church in the NT. Col. and Eph.* Lund 1946. O. Perels, *Kirche und Welt nach Eph. und Kol.*: ThLZ 76 (1951) 391–399; cf. also the introduction to these Epistles by P. Benoit: *La Sainte Bible (de Jérusalem)*, Paris 1949. C. H. Dodd, *NT Studies*, Manchester 1953, pp. 83–128 [reprinted from BJRL 1934; Rome and not Ephesus is the place of composition of the Captivity Epistles]. G. S. Duncan (ExpT March 1956) suggests that Paul was twice imprisoned in Ephesus. Phil., which was written before 1 Cor. (cf. Acts 19, 9), was composed during the first, more severe, imprisonment in the winter of 54/55; Col. and Philem. were written after 1 Cor. (cf. 1 Cor. 16, 9), towards the end of his sojourn at Ephesus, during the second, milder imprisonment. G. S. Duncan, *Paul's Ministry in Asia—the Last Phase*: NTSt 3 (1957) 211–217.

THE name "Captivity Epistles" is applied to the four Epistles to the Ephesians, Philippians, Colossians, and to Philemon, because Paul himself tells us that he wrote them in prison (Eph. 3, 1; 4, 1; 6, 20; Col. 1, 24; 3, 3–18; Philem. 19; Phil. 1, 7 12 sq.). 2 Tim. was also written during an imprisonment, but it is included with the Pastoral Epistles.

Three of the Captivity Epistles, Eph., Col., and Philem., were all written at the same period, almost certainly during Paul's first Roman imprisonment (61–63 A.D.). The arguments for this are:

In Col. 4, 7–2 Paul says that he has commissioned his fellow worker Tychicus and the Colossian Onesimus to bring them news of his position. In Philem. he writes to a distinguished Christian in Colossae, named Philemon, to say that he has converted Onesimus, a slave who had run away from him, and that he is sending him back to his master. Col. 4, 17 exhorts a certain Archippus to fulfil his ministry, and this Archippus is mentioned among the recipients of Philem. With one exception the greetings in Col. and Philem. are sent by the same persons: Aristarchus, Mark, Jesus Justus (not in Philem.) Epaphras, Luke, and Demas. In Col. and Eph. Timothy is said to join in sending the Epistle, and both Epistles mention the sending of Tychicus (Col. 4, 7; Eph. 6, 21). It is hotly disputed at the present day whether Phil. was written during this same captivity; it was not composed at the same time as the other three.

G. S. Duncan (ExpT March 1956) thinks that Paul was twice imprisoned at Ephesus; he suggests that Phil., which he places before 1 Cor. (cf. Acts 19, 9) comes from the first, more severe imprisonment in the winter of 54/55 A.D.; Col. and Philem., he says, were written after 1 Cor. (cf. 1 Cor. 16, 9) during the second, milder imprisonment towards the end of Paul's sojourn at Ephesus.

§ 38. THE EPISTLE TO THE COLOSSIANS

Commentaries: (b) T. K. Abbott, 1897 (ICC). C. F. D. Moule, Col. and Philem. 1957.

Studies: F. A. Henle, *Kolossae und der Brief des hl. Apostels Paulus an die Kolosser,* Munich 1887. A. Steinmann, *Gegen welche Irrlehrer richtet sich der Kol?* Strassburg 1906. J. Gewiess, *Christus und das Heil nach dem Kol,* Diss. Breslau 1932 (Excerpt). Idem, *Die Begriffe* πληροῦν *und* πλήρωμα *im Kol und Eph:* Festschrift M. Meinertz pp. 128–141 (NtA, 1. Erg.-Bd. 1951). M. A.Wagenfuehrer, *Die Bedeutung Christi fuer Welt und Kirche. Studien zum Kol- und Eph-Brief,* Leipzig 1941. E. Percy, *Die Probleme der Kol- und Eph-Briefe,* Lund 1946. G. Bornkamm, *Die Haeresie des Kol:* ThLZ 73 (1948) 11–20. E. Kaesemann, *Eine urchristliche Taufliturgie (Kol 1, 13–20):* Festschr. f. R. Bultmann, Stuttgart 1949, 133–148. O. Casel,

Zur Kultsprache des hl. Paulus: Arch. f. Liturgiewissenschaft I (1950) 1–64 (36–59 on Col.). W. Bieder: ThZ 8 (1952) 137–143 (Authenticity). Idem, *Die kolossische Irrlehre und die Kirche von heute,* 1952 (Theologische Studien 33). E. Percy, *Zu den Problemen des Kol und Eph:* ZntW 43 (1950/51) 178–194 (against E. Kaesemann: Gnomon 1949, 342–347).

1. The beginnings of the community at Colossae

THE city of Colossae lay in the valley of the Upper Lycus, a tributary of the Meander, in the southern part of ancient Phrygia. It had a flourishing wool and weaving industry like its larger and more important neighbours, Laodicea and Hierapolis, with which it had close economic ties. When the Epistle was written the city contained a sizeable Christian community; one of its members had a so-called "house church" (Philem. 2). Christianity had also penetrated the nearby cities of Laodicea and Hierapolis (Col. 4, 13–16).

Paul himself tells us that he was not the founder of any of the three communities (Col. 1, 4 sqq.; 2, 1). We may infer from Col. 1, 7; 4, 12 sq. that the community of Colossae—and probably of Laodicea and Hierapolis also—had been founded a few years previously by Epaphras, the Colossian who was with Paul when he wrote the Epistle. Probably Paul had converted him during his mission at Ephesus.

The community at Colossae consisted principally of Gentiles (2, 13; 1, 21 27), but it probably contained a number of Jewish-Christians, for Judaism was widespread in Phrygia.

2. Content and structure

Introductory greeting 1, 1–2. Introduction 1, 3 to 2, 5:

1. Thanksgiving for the fine development of the community since Epaphras founded it 1, 3–8.

2. Prayer for their further progress 1, 9–12 with an instruction about the primacy of the person of Christ, the Mediator of salva-

tion and Reconciler of mankind 1, 13–20, to whom the readers also owe salvation 1, 21–23.

3. Paul has been called as Apostle of the Gentiles, for the Gentiles also are to have a share in Christ according to God's plan of salvation which is now revealed; as Apostle of the Gentiles, he realizes that he has an obligation even to the Phrygian communities whom he does not know 1, 23 to 2, 5.

I. Doctrinal part 2, 6–23: Polemical instruction about the errors which threaten his readers.

1. Hold fast to the faith in Christ which you have received, and do not be misled by a human wisdom which would subject you to angelic powers 2, 6–8.

2. In Christ you possess the true circumcision, he gives you life and frees you from spiritual powers 2, 9–15.

3. So you should not adopt ascetical practices and ritual prescriptions, thereby allowing yourselves to be enslaved by angelic powers 2, 16–23.

II. Moral part 3, 1 to 4, 6: The conduct of their lives should take a new form.

1. In Baptism they put off the old man, and put on the new; this binds them to lead a holy life 3, 1–17.

2. Instructions for particular classes (wives—husbands; children—parents; slaves—masters), the so-called "household lists" 3, 18 to 4, 1.

3. Exhortation to pray, and particularly to pray for the Apostle, and to exercise wisdom in dealing with their non-Christian neighbours 4, 2–6.

Conclusion 4, 7–18: Personal messages:

1. He is sending Tychicus and Onesimus to them 4, 7–9.

2. He sends greetings, commissions them to pass on salutations, and gives instructions 4, 10–17.

3. Greeting written in his own hand 4, 18.

3. Occasion and purpose; the false teachers

Paul wrote this Epistle because of a dangerous error which was threatening the community. Epaphras, who presumably had founded the community, had told him of the riches of their Christian life (1, 8 sq.), and it was probably he who gave Paul more accurate information about the danger. Presumably he visited the Apostle for this purpose, and asked him to instruct and warn the community.

Paul sent the Epistle with Tychicus (4, 7 sq.), and Epaphras remained behind with him, and in Philem. 23 is called "my fellow prisoner" (ὁ συναιχμάλωτός μου); in view of this expression the conjecture has often been made that Epaphras did not visit Paul of his own accord and as a free man, but had been arrested and sent to Rome because of religious disturbances. However, the Apostle uses δέσμιος and not αἰχμάλωτος (prisoner of war) when speaking of his own imprisonment; so apparently he is using a military metaphor (cf. σύνδουλος 1, 7; 4, 7), and means simply that Epaphras is voluntarily sharing his imprisonment.

The nature of the Colossian errors used to be a matter of dispute, but to-day there is widespread agreement about their outline, though there are still obscure details which are a matter of controversy. Evidently it was a syncretist movement of a Jewish-Gnostic character which had followers in Colossae. It is characterized by two traits:

1. A theory about the "elements of the world" (στοιχεῖα τοῦ κόσμου 2, 8 20), i. e., the angelic powers; so Paul speaks of "religion of angels" (θρησκεία τῶν ἀγγέλων 2, 18). These elements of the world are a series of stages of intermediate beings in which the "fullness of the Godhead", the Pleroma, dwells (cf. 1, 19; 2, 9). They were also the cause of creation (cf. 1, 15–17). According to the false teachers they exercise power over men who are subject to them through birth and destiny. To gain reconciliation with

God it is not enough to honour Christ, these beings also must be worshipped. This error is called "philosophy" (2, 8), a name which implies that it is derived from a cosmic theory, that is, a Gnosis.

2. The obligation to observe a number of prescriptions about cleanliness, to celebrate certain days, and to refrain from particular foods and drinks (2, 16 21 sqq.). This asceticism was probably enjoined and practised because of the angelic powers; it was clearly influenced by Jewish legalism (cf. especially Sabbath, new moon 2, 16; circumcision 2, 11); however, neither circumcision nor the observance of the Mosaic Law were actually imposed though both were held in high esteem.

The gravity of the Colossian error lay in its implicit denial of Christ's position as the only Mediator and Redeemer. Hence Paul was obliged to stress the uniqueness of Christ, which he does in two Christological passages 1, 15–20 and 2, 9–15; in these passages he declares that the pre-existing Christ is the Mediator of creation, and the Crucified, Risen and Exalted Christ is the Atoner who brings all to completion; these passages emphasize Christ's position as supreme Lord over all majesty and power.

4. Authenticity

F. Chr. Baur and his school attacked the authenticity of Col. and said that it was the work of anti-Gnostics of the second century. Now-a-days even the critics are almost unanimous in accepting it as authentic. The interpolation theories also have been fairly generally abandoned; H. J. Holtzmann in 1872 was the first to produce such a theory, and it formerly had many supporters.

The objections to the Pauline origin of Col. are twofold: the unusual language and style, and the Christology of the Epistle.

It is true that there are in Col. a number of words which do not occur elsewhere in Paul, including thirty-four words which do not appear elsewhere in the New Testament at all *(hapax legomena)*: e.g., ἐθελοθρησκεία, ἐμβατεύειν, πιθανολογία, φιλοσοφία, χειρόγραφον, as well as unique phrases, such as αἷμα τοῦ σταυροῦ 1, 20; ἀπέκδυσις τοῦ σώματος τῆς σαρκός 2, 11; πλήρωμα τῆς θεότητος 2, 9; ὑστέρημα τῶν θλίψεων 1, 24. Furthermore it is true to say that the style is obscure and overladen, e. g., 1, 3–8; 1, 9–14; 2, 8–15; 1, 12 24 27.

But this is largely explained by the fact that Paul is here combatting new opponents whose vocabulary he uses freely in his polemic. That is why the strange language is most frequent in those parts of the Epistle which attack the false teachers.

The Christology of Col. is more highly developed than that of the major Epistles, but it follows the theme of the earlier writings. When Paul says that not only has Christ created everything, but that in him all things consist (1, 16 sq.), and that everything in heaven and earth has been reconciled by his death, he is merely developing the ideas of 1 Cor. 8, 6; 10, 4; 2 Cor. 5, 19. Col. 2, 15 explains that by the work of redemption Christ has subdued principalities and powers; there are similar expressions in Gal. 4, 3 9; Rom. 8, 38 sq.; Phil. 2, 10 sq.

5. Time and place of composition of Col. (Eph. and Philem.)

Paul had been imprisoned a number of times before he wrote 2 Cor. (2 Cor. 6, 5; 11, 23); except for the imprisonment at Philippi (Acts 16, 23 sqq.), we know nothing about the place, date or duration of those spells in prison. After the time of 2 Cor. Acts tells us that he spent two and a half years in prison in Jerusalem and Caesarea (58–60 A.D.), and two years in Rome (61–63 A.D.).

Tradition placed the composition of all four Captivity Epistles in the period of his first Roman imprisonment, and many exegetes still maintain this. David Schulz in 1829 made the suggestion that Col., Eph., and Philem. were written while he was a prisoner at Caesarea, and even in recent times this theory has had supporters, such as E. Lohmeyer. In 1900 H. Lisco produced the theory that all four Captivity Epistles were written at Ephesus during an imprisonment which Acts does not mention, at the time of his three-year sojourn there; A. Deissmann in 1923 was the first to develop this theory thoroughly, and it has become increasingly popular in recent decades, though some would assign only Phil. to this time.

Col., with Eph. and Philem., was not written in the same circumstances as Phil., so the question of date must be examined separately for the two cases. It cannot in any case be simply asserted that all four Epistles were written during the same imprisonment.

The vast majority of Catholic exegetes, and some others, such as Juelicher, Behm, and Percy, say that Col., Eph., and Philem. were written in Rome, and this may be considered the best supported theory. As early as the Marcionite prologue Ephesus was mentioned as the place of composition. It would have been the most convenient place for Epaphras to visit Paul. But, to prescind from the question of whether Paul was imprisoned there for any length of time (cf. § 41, 4), Col. and Eph. contain greetings from Mark and Luke; there is no evidence that they worked with Paul at Ephesus, and it is not likely that they did.

So the choice lies between Rome and Caesarea. There are no absolutely unequivocal and decisive arguments for either city. If we leave Phil. out of account, the only really firm argument in favour of Rome rather than Caesarea is drawn from Acts 24, 23 sq., according to which Felix did Paul a special favour by allowing his friends to serve him during his imprisonment; it follows that he certainly did not preach in Caesarea, as according to Acts 28, 30 sq. he did in Rome. But Col. 4, 3 11; Philem. 24 tell us that in spite of his imprisonment Paul was able to carry on the work of the Gospel.

There is one argument against Rome—though it is equally valid against Caesarea: According to Philem. 22 Paul was planning to visit the Lycus valley after his release—which he thought was imminent—and he instructs Philemon to prepare lodgings for him; Rom. 15, 24 sqq. on the other hand tells us that he intended to travel westwards from Rome. However, he says nothing of this in Col., so it can hardly have been a definite plan; or perhaps bad news from the East may have made an immediate journey there seem necessary.

The theology of Col. and Eph. provides a strong argument for a late date (Rome). Compared to the major Epistles (Gal., 1 and 2 Cor., Rom.), they show a development of his theological thought, and can hardly have been written before those Epistles. In particular Eph. clearly presupposes Rom., and cannot have been written before it.

§ 39. THE EPISTLE TO PHILEMON

Commentaries: (a) E. Eisentraut, *Des hl. Apostels Brief an Philemon*, Wuerzburg 1928. (b) M. R. Vincent, 1897 (ICC).
Studies: M. Roberti, *La lettera di S. Paolo al Filemone e la condizione giuridica dello schiavo fuggitivo*, Milan 1933. J. Knox, *Philemon among the Letters of Paul*, Chicago 1935. Th. Preiss, *Vie en Christ et éthique sociale dans l'épître à Philem.*: Festschrift f. M. Goguel 1950, 171–179. P. R. Coleman-Norton, *The Apostle Paul and the Roman Law of Slavery*: Studies in hon. of A. S. Johnson (Princeton 1951) 155 to 177.

1. *Content and structure*

Introductory greeting 1–3. Introduction 4–7: Thanksgiving for Philemon's faith and love for the brethren.

Principal section 8–21: A request to Philemon to receive his runaway slave Onesimus as a beloved brother, and to put to Paul's account whatever harm he has done; Paul has won Onesimus for Christ and would be very eager to retain him in his service.

Conclusion: 22–25: Request for lodgings; greetings.

2. Occasion and purpose

Philemon was a well-to-do Christian who had a "house church" (v. 2); he had evidently been converted by Paul, presumably in Ephesus (v. 19). His slave Onesimus is called a Colossian (Col. 4, 9), and Archippus, who belonged to his community, was from Colossae (Col. 4, 17), so he must have lived in that city.

A slave called Onesimus had run away from Philemon and had found refuge with Paul, who converted him; the details of the story are not known; Onesimus had previously damaged his master's property (v. 11 and 18).

The Apostle had been able to make good use of his services, but he did not wish to keep Onesimus on his own authority; so he now sent him back to his master with a letter earnestly appealing to Philemon to receive the runaway well, not as a slave but as a beloved brother. He promises humorously to make good any damage which Onesimus has caused.

3. Authenticity and significance

Philemon formed part of the Pauline collection from the beginning. In the early Church certain groups questioned its inspiration and authenticity either because it was not devoted to edification, or because it seemed unfitting—as in the case of the Pastoral Epistles —that private letters should have a place in a Canon which was intended for the whole Church (cf. Muratorian Canon l. 59—63). In the last century some critics said that Philem. was the work of a second century forger who wished to provide a Pauline ruling on the problem of slavery; but in that case Philem. would be a very clumsy forgery, for Paul does not clearly direct that Onesimus be set free.

At the present day its authenticity is universally recognized, and in spite of its shortness it is treasured as a precious jewel; it gives us a deep insight into Paul's kindness, and displays clearly·

those qualities of nobility and humaneness which were wonderfully proclaimed by the Christian faith.

The theological significance of this Epistle lies in its clear demonstration of the fundamental attitude of the early Church to slavery, which at that time was a burning social problem: Paul does not call for freedom, but wishes the master to treat his slave as a brother in Christ (cf. Col. 3, 22; 4, 1).

§ 40. THE EPISTLE TO THE EPHESIANS

Commentaries: (a) H. Schlier, Duesseldorf 1956. F. A. Henle, *Der Eph des hl. Apostels Paulus*[2], Augsburg 1908. J. Vosté, *Commentarius in Epistulam ad Ephesios*[2], Paris 1932. J. Dillersberger, *Der neue Gott*, Salzburg 1935.—(b) Ch. Masson, 1953 (Bonnard IX) [Written towards the end of the first century by a disciple of Paul's; in the praescriptum Laodicea (Marcion!) was named as destination, but the Epistle was intended for the whole Church.] Cf. ThZ 9 (1953) 377 ff. and RB 1954, 239–242 (Benoit). T. K. Abbott, 1897 (ICC). J. A. Robinson, *St. Paul's Epistle to the Ephesians*, London 1903. Fr. Rienecker, *Praktischer Handkommentar zum Eph.*, Neumuenster 1934.

Studies: J. Schmid, *Der Eph des Apostels Paulus. Seine Adresse, Sprache und literarischen Beziehungen untersucht* (BSt XXII, 3/4: 1928). H. Schlier, *Christus und die Kirche im Eph*, Tuebingen 1933. E. J. Goodspeed, *The Meaning of Eph.*, 1933. W. Ochel, *Die Annahme einer Bearbeitung des Kol im Eph*, Diss. phil., Marburg 1934. M. Goguel, *Esquisse d'une solution nouvelle du problème de l'épître aux Éphésiens:* RHR 111 (1935) 254–284; 112 (1935) 73–99. P. Benoit: RB 46 (1937) 342–361; 506–525. Wagenfuehrer and Percy (cf. § 38). H. Schlier und V. Warnach, *Die Kirche im Eph*, Muenster i. W. 1949. N. A. Dahl, *Adresse und Prooemium des Eph:* ThZ 7 (1951) 241–264. Chr. Maurer, *Der Hymnus von Eph 1 als Schluessel zum ganzen Brief:* EvTh 11 (1951/52) 151–172. C. L. Mitton, *The Epistle to the Ephesians. Its Authorship, Origin and Purpose*, 1951. W. Rieder, *Das Geheimnis des Christus nach dem Eph:* ThZ 11 (1955) 329–343. E. F. Goodspeed, *The Key to Eph.*, 1956 [The author of Eph. and collector of Paul's letters was the slave Onesimus]. G. Schille, *Liturgisches Gut im Eph,* Dissertation Goettingen 1953 (typewritten; summary ThLZ 1955, 183). According to W. Nauck 2, 11–18 is based on the terminology of the Christian Baptism Liturgy, and 2, 19–22 is a Baptism Hymn (EvTh 13, 1953, 362–371); according to B. Noack the citation in 5, 14 is from an eschatological hymn which probably belonged to the Baptism Liturgy (StTh 5, 1951, 52–64). F. Mussner, *Christus, das All und die Kirche*, 1955 (Trierer Theolog. Studien 5).

J. Couts, *Ephesians I, 3–14 and I Peter I, 3–12:* NTSt 3 (1957) 115–127. G. Schille, *Der Autor des Eph:* ThLZ 82 (1957) 321–334.

1. Content and structure

Introductory greeting 1, 1–2.

I. Doctrinal part 1, 3 to 3, 21: Jews and Gentiles are equally marked out for salvation in Christ.

1. Thanksgiving to God who has called and redeemed in Christ both Jewish and Gentile-Christians that they may be children of God 1, 3–14.

2. Thanksgiving for the faith of his readers, and a prayer that God may let them have an ever deeper grasp of the greatness and preciousness of the salvation which has been given to them, salvation which consists of awakening from the death of sin and the gift of eternal life 1, 15 to 2, 10.

3. Hitherto the Gentiles have been far from God, but through God's mercy they have obtained access to salvation, and being justified equally with the Jews they belong to the one new man, the one divine structure of the Church whose corner stone is Jesus Christ 2, 11–22.

4. The mystery of the admission of the Gentiles has now been revealed for the first time to the Apostles and prophets; Paul is charged to proclaim it, so he prays for the readers that God may let them grow in faith, love, and understanding 3, 1–21.

II. Moral part 4, 1 to 6, 20: Exhortations to a way of life worthy of their calling.

1. Preserve the unity of the Spirit in the community, amongst all the diversity of the gifts of grace which are intended to build up the Body of Christ 4, 1–16.

2. Put off the old man of your former sinful way of life and put on the new man of justice and holiness 4, 17–24.

3. Particular injunctions for them all, that they should lead a faultless moral life 4, 25 to 5, 21.

4. Exhortations to particular members of the household (wives

—husbands, children—parents, slaves—masters), so-called "household lists" 5, 22 to 6, 9.

5. Final exhortation: Wearing the armour of the spirit, fight against the devil and evil spirits, and pray for me that I may rightly discharge my office of preaching 6, 10–20.

Conclusion 6, 21–24: Tychicus will tell them the news about Paul; Blessings.

2. Destination

In the MSS. this Epistle is described as πρός ᾽Εφεσίους, and according to most witnesses to the text, it was addressed to "the saints who are at Ephesus and to the faithful in Christ Jesus" (τοῖς ἁγίοις τοῖς οὖσιν ἐν ᾽Εφέσῳ καὶ πιστοῖς ἐν Χριστῷ ᾽Ιησοῦ). However, both the character of the Epistle and considerations of textual criticism provide serious reasons for doubting the correctness of this address.

a) The tone of the Epistle is so impersonal that Paul cannot have written it to a community which he had founded and taken care of for three years. The questions with which he deals have no particular relevance to this community, and the Epistle makes no reference to the author's experiences at Ephesus. According to 1, 15; 3, 2 sqq.; 4, 21 the author and recipients were quite unknown to each other. How could Paul himself have written "If yet you have heard of the dispensation of the grace of God which is given me towards you: how that, according to revelation, the mystery has been made known to me, as I have written above in a few words" (3, 2 sq.)?

It is quite clear that the recipients of the Epistle were exclusively Gentile-Christians; they are addressed as such (2, 1 sqq. 11 sqq.; 3, 1), and the injunctions are intended for former pagans who are exhorted to lay aside entirely the vices of their pagan past (4, 17 sqq. 25 sqq.; 3, 5 sqq.). Acts tells us that there was a strong Jewish-Christian element in Ephesus (18, 19 sq.; 19, 8 13–17 34; 20, 21).

· In direct contrast to Col. and Philem., there are in Eph. no greetings from Paul's companions, though both Timothy and Aristarchus were personally known to the Ephesians (Acts 19, 22 29; 1 Cor. 4, 17).

Cumulatively all these peculiarities drive us to the conclusion that the epistle cannot have been written to the community which Paul founded in the metropolis of Asia.

b) This conclusion is corroborated by the history of the text.

With the solitary exception of Marcion, Christian antiquity was unanimous that the Epistle was addressed to the Ephesians. The first to question the correctness of the traditional address was Theodore Beza, the Geneva reformer, in 1598.

It is demonstrable, and is fairly generally agreed to-day, that the two words ἐν Ἐφέσῳ in the initial greeting are not original. They are missing from 𝔓⁴⁶, the oldest MS. of the Pauline Epistles (beginning of the third century), B, where the words have first been added in the margin by a later hand, ℵ, where they have been added by the corrector, and 1739; in 424 they have been erased by the corrector. Origen did not read these words in his text; Basil (Contra Eunomium 11, 19) tells us that they are missing from old texts, and Jerome (In Eph. 1, 1) knows texts which read "in Ephesus", as well as others without these words; Tertullian (Adv. Marc. V 11 17) informs us that Marcion did not read "in Ephesus" in his text of 1, 1.

The history of the text shows that: (1) originally no place was mentioned in the introductory greeting—the oldest text in the Corpus Paulinum reads: Παῦλος . . . τοῖς ἁγίοις τοῖς οὖσιν καὶ πιστοῖς ἐν Χριστῷ Ἰησοῦ: B ℵ Orig etc.); (2) but since the second half of the second century the Epistle has been regarded and cited within the Church as the Epistle to the Ephesians—except for Marcion, who called it the Epistle to the Laodiceans; (3) the oldest sources for the words "in Ephesus" in 1, 1 are the Latin commentary of Victorinus Afer in the second half of the fourth century, and the late MSS. which Basil and Jerome know.

What was the original destination of the Epistle? Two different answers are given to this question:

1. The encyclical or circular epistle theory: The Epistle is a circular letter to a group of communities which were near one another, but were not personally known to Paul. Eph. and Col. are closely related in content, and both must have been delivered by Tychicus; so it must have been addressed to communities near Colossae, that is in Asia Minor or Phrygia, in the hinterland of Ephesus. Colossae and Hierapolis belonged to this area (Col. 4, 13), and Eph. is most probably the Epistle which according to Col. 4, 16 was to come to the Colossians from Laodicea. Most of the supporters of this theory would not include Ephesus among the communities in question.

Goguel, Schmid, and others suggest that the original reading was: τοῖς ἁγίοις καὶ πιστοῖς ἐν Χριστῷ Ἰησοῦ; the Epistle, they say, was distributed from Ephesus, and so was headed πρὸς Ἐφεσίους, which slipped into the introductory greeting as τοῖς οὖσιν ἐν Ἐφέσῳ; when it was realized that Paul would hardly have sent such an Epistle to Ephesus, the words ἐν Ἐφέσῳ (only) were eliminated.

2. The Laodicea theory says that Eph. is the letter to Laodicea alone which is mentioned in Col. 4, 16, and that Laodicea was mentioned in the address; Marcion either preserved the correct address, or else he had access to reliable tradition which enabled him to restore the place name correctly, if it was not in his copy. Harnack put forward the theory—which is ingenious rather than convincing—that the name of Laodicea was eliminated because of the condemnation in Apoc. 3, 14; he suggested that the name of Ephesus was substituted because of the close relations between Paul and the community there, and in view of the fact that Ephesus had no Epistle from the Apostle.

It is objected that if the Laodicea theory were correct, Paul would not have mentioned the Laodiceans in Col. 4, 15 sq., for he could have sent the message in this Epistle; but this objection has no weight, for the message in question merely contains greetings, and the instruction to send for the letter "of the Laodiceans" would be superfluous in a circular Epistle. The praise in Eph. 1, 15 and the mention of why he is sending Tychicus would be more fitting in an Epistle to a single community than in a circular letter.

The following form of the encyclical theory is preferable: At the same time as he wrote Col. and Philem. Paul also sent with Tychicus a circular letter, couched in general terms, to a fairly small group of communities in the hinterland of Ephesus, including Laodicea and Hierapolis (cf. Col. 2, 1–3; Eph. 6, 21 sq.; 1, 13–15; 2, 21 sq.). Some copies bore the name of the community for which the copy was intended. This Epistle was copied in Ephesus, and because it was a circular letter the space for the name of the recipients was left blank. The Epistle was sent out from Ephesus without any place being named, and so it was regarded as an Epistle to the Ephesians, and when it was taken into the *Corpus Paulinum* it was headed πρὸς Ἐφεσίους; at a later date this slipped into the blank space in the introductory greeting in the form ἐν Ἐφέσῳ.

3. *Authenticity*

The controversy about the authenticity of Eph. has been much stronger than in the case of any other Pauline Epistle, except the Pastoral Epistles. The Pauline origin of the Epistle was first challenged in Germany by de Wette in 1829 and 1843, and no substantial objection has since been raised which he did not anticipate. In contrast to its companion Epistle Col., which is the subject of favourable judgments at the present day, Eph. is accepted as genuine by only a few of the critics such as A. Harnack and A. Deissmann, while A. Juelicher and Rudolf Knopf are undecided. M. Goguel thinks that it is a genuine Epistle of Paul, written at the same time as Col., but that it underwent interpolation ten to twenty years afterwards; W. Ochel considers it a later recension of Col. which was intended to supersede that Epistle, although Col. survived because circumstances favoured it. According to Wagenfuehrer, it was written about Paul's time, probably by one of his disciples who wrote either around the time of the Apostle's death—which would make it the free composition of a secretary— or in the eighth decade of the first century—in which case it is the work of a pseudepigrapher.

Three main arguments are urged against the authenticity of this epistle:

1. Language and style. There is a fairly marked difference between the vocabulary of Eph. and that of the other Pauline Epistles. It contains 39 words which do not occur elsewhere in the New Testament *(hapax legomena)*, 83 words which do not occur in the other Pauline Epistles, except the Pastoral Epistles, and 36 words which are found in New Testament Greek, but not in Paul. It is particularly striking that only Eph. and the Pastoral Epistles use διάβολος instead of ὁ σατανᾶς which is Paul's usual word, and τὰ ἐπουράνια is not found outside Eph., at least beside οἱ οὐρανοί.

It is almost universally agreed to-day that this undoubtedly peculiar vocabulary cannot by itself prove that the Epistle is spurious, for in the undeniably genuine Pauline Epistles the situation is similar; Gal., for instance, has 36 *hapax legomena*. Moreover, Eph. has 22 words which are in no New Testament author except Paul.

The ponderousness of the style and its overloaded pleonasm provide a stronger argument. For example, there are numerous collocations of nouns joined sometimes by the genitive and sometimes by prepositions (e. g., 1, 11 19; 2, 14 15; 4, 13); there is also a large number of long periods with numerous relative clauses and participles (1, 3–14; 1, 15–23; 2, 1–10; 3, 1 sqq.; 4, 11–16 etc.).

However, there are similar stylistic peculiarities, though not in such numbers, in Pauline Epistles of unquestioned authenticity, for example, in Rom. 3, 21–26; 2 Cor. 9, 8–14, and above all in Col. (cf. 1, 3–8 9–20). The strangeness of the style may well be due to the author's lofty and elevated emotion.

2. Doctrinal content. In this respect also Eph. shows marked peculiarities when compared with the older Epistles. The problem is to decide whether these are incompatible with the doctrine of the older Epistles, or if they can be regarded as a development of Pauline ideas by the Apostle himself.

The central doctrine of the Epistle is the Church, and particularly 1) its universality and 2) its mysterious union with the exalted Christ. According to 2, 13 sqq. and 3, 5 sq., the purpose of Christ's redeeming work was to join into a new man and into the one divine structure of the Church the two sections of mankind: Israel the people of the Promise, and the Gentile world which was far from God. This idea of one universal Church, embracing both Jews and Gentiles, is not new; it appears clearly, though not so explicitly, in the major Epistles (Gal. 3, 27–29; 1 Cor. 12, 12 sqq.; Rom. 3, 21 sqq.; 11, 11 sqq.). This universal church is composed of Jews and Gentiles as members with equal rights.

In Eph. 1, 23; 4, 12 16; 5, 30 we are told that the Church forms the Body of Christ, and according to 1, 22; 4, 15; 5, 23 it has as its head the exalted Christ. The older Epistles describe the Christians as forming one body in Christ (Rom. 12, 5), or the Body of Christ (1 Cor. 12, 27); this is the same picture as in Eph., except that there is not a clear distinction between Christ and the Church. Moreover, in Col. 1, 18; 2, 19 Christ appears as the Head of his Body, the Church.

So Eph. develops an idea and a picture which must be ascribed to Paul himself. The universal Church is prominent in Eph., so the redeeming work of Christ is connected immediately with it: Christ is the saviour of his Body 5, 23; he loved it and delivered himself up for it 5, 25 sqq.

The expectation of Christ's Second Coming does not receive the emphasis which it had in the older Epistles; yet—as in Col. also—there are clear references to it: 1, 14 ("the pledge of our inheritance"); 4, 30 ("unto the day of redemption"); 5, 6; 6, 8.

Those who deny authenticity take exception unjustifiably to the passages (4, 11; 2, 20; 3, 5) where he speaks of offices in the Church: apostles, prophets, Evangelists, pastors and doctors[1]. The charismatic offices of apostles, prophets and doctors were listed in 1 Cor. 12, 27, and pastors form one group with doctors; evangelists do not appear in Paul—though they are mentioned in Acts 21, 8, a "We passage"—but there is no difficulty in applying this title to men who preached the Gospel alongside or after the Apostles. The silence of Eph. about those charisms which are listed in 1 Cor. 12–14 is simply due to the theme of the Epistle which requires mention of just those charisms which are of importance for the building up of the Church.

3. The relationship between Eph. and Col. These two Epistles show closer contacts in content, language and style than any other Epistles. So, as Dibelius has pointed out, it is in the light of this closeness that the problem of authenticity must be decided.

Broadly speaking Col. has peculiar material only in 1, 15–20 (the supreme majesty of Christ); 2, 1–9 16–23 (combatting of false teachers); 3, 1–4 (seek what is above); 4, 9–18 (greetings and injunctions). In the case of Eph. the peculiar passages are: 1, 3–14 (Hymn in praise of God); 2, 1–10 (the new life); 3, 14–21 (prayer that the readers may comprehend the mystery of Christ); 4, 1–16 (exhortation to unity); 5, 8–14 (walk in the light); 5, 23–32 (the mystical marriage of Christ); 6, 10–17 (spiritual armour). Wagenfuehrer has made an accurate reckoning of the peculiar matter of both Epistles, and has discovered that thirty percent of the entire matter of Col. has no parallel in Eph., while half of Eph. is independent and without parallel in Col.

[1] F. Brosch, *Charismen und Aemter in der Urkirche,* Bonn 1951.

The agreements and contacts are clear and striking; they are found both in terminology (e. g. σῶμα, κεφαλή, πλήρωμα, μυστή-ριον), and in the thought: the Church as the Body of Christ and Christ its head, the spiritual powers, the making of peace through the Blood of Christ, the old and new man etc.; they are most frequent in the moral part, for example in the household lists. The main themes of the doctrinal parts are related: Col. proclaims the unique significance of Christ in creation and salvation, and Eph. depicts the corresponding relation between Christ in Heaven and the universal Church which is his Body.

From a literary point of view Col. is unquestionably the earlier, but Eph. has a number of primitive traits and cannot be considered a later revision of Col. by an unknown hand.

Recently an attempt has been made to justify denying Pauline authorship on the ground that although the two Epistles share a common terminology, the terms do not carry the same meaning in both Epistles. Thus σῶμα in Col. 2, 19 is supposed to refer to the universe, while in Eph. 4, 16 it means the Church; but in Col. 2, 19 Paul does not mean that growth "into the increase of God" can be predicated only of the Church. They also refer to μυστήριον; but this is not defensible either, for the word is found in Col. 1, 26 sq. ("among the Gentiles") with the meaning which it bears in Eph. 3, 39 (salvation is available to the Gentiles also).

The most natural and best founded theory is that Paul is the author of both Epistles. He wrote Col. with the concrete purpose of combatting errors, and at the same time composed Eph., which was more general and was sent to the communities near Colossae. The language, style, and theology of the two Epistles show many divergences, so we cannot rule out the possibility that he commissioned a disciple to write Eph. according to his instructions and ideas. This would be the best explanation of his use of the phrase "his holy Apostles" (3, 5).

§ 41. THE EPISTLE TO THE PHILIPPIANS

Commentaries: (a) K. J. Mueller, *Des Apostels Paulus Brief an die Philipper*, Freiburg i. Br. 1899. E. Peterson, *Apostel und Zeuge Christi*, Freiburg i. Br. 1941.
(b) J. B. Lightfoot, *St. Paul's Epistle to the Philippians*, London 1888. M. R. Vincent, [3]1922 (ICC). P. Ewald, [4]1923 (Zahn XI). A. Plummer, *The Epistle to the Philippians*, London 1919. J. H. Michael, 1929 (Moffatt). M. Dibelius, [2]1927 (Lietzmann 11). K. Barth, *Erklaerung des Phil*[2], Munich 1933. W. Michaelis, 1935 (ThHK XI). Studies: P. Feine, *Die Abfassung des Phil in Ephesus* (BFchTh XX, 14: 1916). W. Michaelis, *Die Datierung des Phil*, Guetersloh 1933. T. W. Manson, *The Date of Phil:* BJRL 23 (1939) 182–200.

1. The community at Philippi

THE city of Philippi[1] was founded by Alexander the Great's father, Philip II of Macedon, on the site of the ancient town of Crenides ("Spring town"). Augustus made it a Roman military colony and granted it the *jus italicum*. In Paul's time most of the Philippians were descended from Roman settlers (cf. Acts 16, 21: "us . . . being Romans"). Inscriptions show that at least half the population was of Roman origin. There was also a small Jewish community with a meeting place on the Eastern bank of the Gangites.

On the second missionary journey Paul came to Philippi with Silas and Timothy (and Luke) in 50 or 51 A.D. He founded a Christian community which evidently met in the house of a well-to-do convert, Lydia, a seller of purple, from Thyatira. The community consisted mainly of Gentiles, as we may infer from Acts 16, 12–40 and Phil. 2, 15 sq.; 3, 3 sq.; 4, 8 sq.

Philippi was Paul's favourite community, with which he maintained steady and very cordial relations. He received fairly regular assistance from it (Phil. 4, 15 sq.; 2 Cor. 11, 8 sq.). On the

---

[1] Cf. Joh. Schmidt, Art. Philippi: Pauly-Wissowa, RE 1. R. 38 (1938) 2006 to 2044. P. Lemerle, *Philippes et la Macédoine orientale à l'époque chrétienne et byzantine*, 2 vols, Paris 1945 (RB 1947, 132 sqq.).

third missionary journey he paid two visits to it (in late autumn 57 and around Easter 58). It was probably the place where he wrote 2 Cor.

2. Content and structure

Introductory greeting 1, 1–2. Introduction 1, 3–11: Thanksgiving and prayer for the community.

I. Paul's situation, and the state of Gospel preaching in the place of his imprisonment 1, 12–26.

1. His imprisonment is furthering the spread of the Gospel 1, 12–18.

2. Whether the trial results in life or death, it will be a blessing for him 1, 19–22.

3. He desires to be united with Christ, yet for the sake of the Philippians he wishes and hopes to remain alive 1, 23–26.

II. Instructions to the community 1, 27 to 2, 18.

1. Exhortation to struggle unanimously for the faith against external adversaries, to practise humility and unselfishness on the model of Jesus Christ (Christ hymn 2, 5–11) 1, 27 to 2, 11.

2. Exhortation to work out their salvation in fear and trembling, and to lead exemplary lives in a perverse world, so that on the Day of Judgment the community may be a credit to the Apostle 2, 12–18.

III. Personal messages 2, 19 to 3, 1.

1. As soon as he is sure about the outcome of his trial he will send to them Timothy, his loyal fellow worker, and he hopes afterwards to visit them himself 2, 19–24.

2. Meanwhile he is sending back Epaphroditus who had brought him their gift; he tells about Epaphroditus' illness and recovery 2, 25 to 3, 1.

IV. Warnings and injunctions; the example of the Apostle 3, 2 to 21.

1. Warning against Jewish (or Judaistic) agitators, who preach

circumcision 3, 2–3; all external merits are worthless beside the knowledge of Christ and of the justification which comes from God 3, 4–16.

2. Warning against wicked Christians (?) who strive for the things of earth and not the things of heaven 3, 17–21.

V. Final exhortations both to the community and to individuals 4, 1–9.

VI. Thanks for the gift which they had sent him 4, 10–20.
Conclusion 4, 21–23: Greetings and blessings.

3. Occasion and purpose

When the Philippians heard of Paul's imprisonment they sent Epaphroditus, a member of the community, to bring him money. Epaphroditus fell critically ill while he was with Paul, and when the Philippians learned of this they were concerned about him; on his recovery Epaphroditus heard of their solicitude and wanted to return home in order to prevent them from worrying needlessly. So Paul sent him back sooner than he had intended, and apparently sent the Epistle with him.

In the Epistle Paul explains why Epaphroditus is returning to them, expresses his satisfaction with the services which he had rendered him (2, 25–30), and thanks them for the gift which they had sent (4, 10–20). He also speaks of himself; his trial has unexpectedly taken a turn for the better, and he hopes confidently to be released in the near future (1, 12 sqq.). He also refers to the state of the community at the moment; he has no serious fault to find with them, but he must warn them to preserve unity (1, 27 sqq.), and he rebukes two women, Evodia and Syntyche (4, 2 sq.), for quarrelling.

It is disputed, and can hardly be decided with certainty, who the people are against whom he warns the Philippians in a vigorous polemic. In 3, 2–3 he probably has in mind not Judaizing

Christians but Jewish agitators (thus Dibelius and Benoit), who had opposed him throughout his missionary journeys (cf. 1 Thess. 2, 15); though they had not yet come to cause trouble in Philippi, yet the Philippians should be on guard against them. In 3, 18–19 he mentions "enemies of the Cross of Christ"; these are either the same people as he mentioned in 3, 2–4—this is the view of most exegetes—or they are wicked (apostate) Christians, Antinomians, as Dibelius and Michaelis suggest. But they are not to be sought in Philippi. A much more likely danger to the community at Philippi was internal disunity which Paul combats very vigorously.

4. Time and place of composition

It was the universal view in antiquity that the Epistle to the Philippians was written during Paul's first Roman imprisonment (61–63 A.D.). The oldest evidence for this is in Marcion's prologue, but it cannot be shown that the tradition on which this view rests was ancient or reliable. It was only in modern times that the traditional view was challenged when some scholars suggested that Philippians was written during the imprisonment at Caesarea (58–60 A.D.); it has recently been ascribed to a—merely conjectured—imprisonment during his mission at Ephesus (54–57 A.D.).

The view that Rome was the place of composition is an inference from 1, 13 and 4, 22. In the former passage Paul says that his bands are made manifest in Christ ἐν ὅλῳ τῷ πραιτωρίῳ καὶ τοῖς λοιποῖς πᾶσιν, where the reference is to the Praetorian Guard. A comparison of this verse with Acts 28, 30 sq. shows that Paul was now imprisoned in a different place; so it is inferred that the Epistle was not written during the two years which he spent in the hired lodging, but that he had been transferred to more strict custody, probably in the barracks of the Praetorian Guard on the Palatine, because the trial was in progress. Another

434

argument in favour of Rome is 4, 22 where οἱ ἐκ τῆς καίσαρος οἰκίας send greetings; these were the servants of the Emperor's court, who were entirely freedmen or slaves.

In recent times many scholars have defended the Roman origin of the Epistle; most of them are Catholics, but there are also others like Th. Zahn and Juelicher; Dibelius is undecided between Rome and Ephesus.

The arguments in favour of Caesarea as the place of composition are very weak. This theory was first proposed by Pfleiderer, Spitta and others, and has recently been supported by Lohmeyer. They say that there was a πραιτώριον in Caesarea, Herod's palace, which served the procurator as a residence (Acts 23, 25). But if Phil. 1, 13 refers to the Praetorian Guard, the argument fails, for there is no evidence that there were Praetorians at Caesarea. Imperial slaves (4, 13), were scattered throughout the Empire, and there are inscriptions which prove that there were such slaves at Ephesus, where the Emperor had large estates; but there is no such evidence for Caesarea.

The Ephesus theory is the only one which deserves serious consideration alongside the traditional view. It is growing increasingly popular among non-Catholic scholars, and has also some Catholic support (P. Gaechter, P. Benoit), for there are strong arguments in its favour. This theory can appeal to the fact that there was also a Praetorium (= Governor's palace) at Ephesus, and there were imperial slaves—or freedmen—there. It is supported mainly by the following considerations:

1. Phil. 1, 26 30; 4, 15 sq. make it highly probable that Paul had not revisited the community since he founded it; in that case the Epistle would have been written before Acts 20, 1 sq. and 2 Cor.

2. According to Phil., Paul was arrested because he preached the Gospel (1, 7 12–13; 1, 30 cf. with Acts 12, 20 sq.); on the other hand Acts 21, 28; 24, 6; 25, 8 tell us that the Roman imprisonment was due to alleged defilement of the Temple.

3. The place of Paul's imprisonment was not far from Philippi, for the journey between the two was made four times in the period before the Epistle was written (2, 25 sq.). The journey from Rome to Philippi took 5–7 weeks, so Rome is quite unlikely as the place of composition.

4. We are told in 1, 26; 2, 24 that Paul intended to visit Philippi when he regained his freedom; Rom. 15 says that he plans to travel from Rome to the West. If the imprisonment at Ephesus took place during the last year of Paul's sojourn there, then the mission of Timothy to Philippi (Phil. 2, 19–22) and Paul's own visit are the same journeys as are recorded in Acts 19, 21 sq.; 20, 1; 1 Cor. 4, 17; 16, 5 10; 2 Cor. 2, 12 sq.; 7, 5.

5. The controversy with the Judaists suits the period when he wrote Gal. and 2 Cor. better than the time around 63 A.D.

The principal argument against the Ephesus theory is the silence of Acts about an imprisonment of Paul in Ephesus. The defenders of the theory attempt to adduce as evidence 1 Cor. 15, 32; 2 Cor. 11, 23; Rom. 16, 4 7, and Clement of Rome 5, 6 (ἑπτάκις δεσμὰ φορέσας). These passages establish a possibility, but are not a certain proof of the fact. However, Acts is so incomplete that its silence does not rule out such an imprisonment.

So it is not possible to decide with certainty between Rome and Ephesus.

5. Authenticity and unity

The authenticity of Phil. was denied by the Tendency Critics of the Tuebingen school (cf. § 2), but this attack has been entirely abandoned at the present day.

The attestation is old. Ignatius, Philad. 10, 1 probably contains an allusion to Phil. 1, 8. Polycarp in his epistle (3, 2) reminds the Philippians that Paul taught them the words of truth with thoroughness and certainty when he was with them, and when absent he wrote them epistles (ἐπιστολαί), by which they could be built up in the faith which had been given to them, if they would study these deeply.

Scholarship is not so sure about the unity of the Epistle as it is about authenticity. In particular it is striking that the structure is fairly loose, and deviates from the practice in the Epistles to the Churches where a fairly short moral section is added to a rather long doctrinal part. The composition breaks abruptly at 2, 19; 3, 2; 4, 2 10. It is possible—but cannot be proved—that Phil. is a conflation of several writings which Paul composed and sent to Philippi at various times.

At any rate, the entire Epistle bears the stamp of Paul's language and style. It is uncertain whether Polycarp actually knew several Epistles of Paul to the Philippians, or if he merely made a conjecture, perhaps from 3, 1. Marcion had only one Epistle to the Philippians in his canon (cf. § 5, 3).

THE PASTORAL EPISTLES

Commentaries: (a) J. E. Belser, *Die Briefe des Apostels Paulus an Timotheus und Titus,* Freiburg i. Br. 1907. J. Knabenbauer, 1913 (CSS). M. Meinertz, [4]1931 (BonnerNT 8). C. Spicq, *Les épîtres pastorales,* Paris 1947. J. Freundorfer, 1949 (RegNT 7). A. Boudou, 1950 (VS XV). P. de Ambroggi, 1953 (La Sacra Bibbia).

(b) H. J. Holtzmann, *Die Past,* Leipzig 1880. B. Weiss, 1902 (Meyer XI[7]). F. Koehler, [3]1917 (GoettNT 2). G. Wohlenberg, [3]1923 (Zahn XIII). W. Lock, 1924 (ICC). M. Dibelius - H. Conzelmann, [3]1955 (Lietzmann 13). Joach. Jeremias, [5]1949 (NTDeutsch 9). A. Schlatter, *Die Kirche der Griechen im Urteil des Paulus,* Stuttgart 1936. R. Falconer, *The Pastoral Epistles,* Oxford 1937. B. E. Easton, *The Pastoral Epistles,* New York 1947. E. F. Scott, [2]1949 (Moffatt).

Studies: F. W. Maier, *Die Hauptprobleme der Past*[3] (BZfr III, 12: 1920). P. N. Harrison, *The Problem of the Pastoral Epistles,* Oxford 1921. W. Michaelis, *Past und Gefangenschaftsbriefe,* Guetersloh 1930. G. Thoernell, *Pastoralbrevens Aekthet,* Goteborg 1931. E. Fascher, Art. *"Timotheus"* and *"Titus":* Pauly-Wissowa, R. E. II 12 (1937) 1342–1354; 1579–1586. O. Michel, *Grundfragen der Past: Festschr. Th. Wurm,* Stuttgart 1948, 83–99. H. Schlier, *Die Ordnung der Kirche nach den Past: Die Zeit der Kirche,* Freiburg i. Br. 1956, 129–147. W. Nauck, *Herkunft des Verfassers der Past,* Theological dissertation, Goettingen 1950. H. von Campenhausen, *Polykarp von Smyrna und die Past,* SBHeidelberg 1951, 2. J. Gewiess, *Die ntl Grundlagen der kirchlichen Hierarchie:* Hist. Jahrbuch d. Goerres-Ges. 72 (1953) 1–24.

W. Nauck, *Die Theologie der Pastoralbriefe, 1. Die philos. u. theol. Voraussetzungen.* Dissertation Goettingen 1950 (typewritten).

Decision of the Pontifical Biblical Commission of 12th June 1913: Tradition proves the authenticity of the Pastoral Epistles. Tradition cannot be weakened by Fragment Theories nor by objections concerning style, the Gnosticism of the false teachers or their picture of Church organisation etc. They were written between the end of the first Roman imprisonment and Paul's death.

SINCE the second half of the eighteenth century, the two Epistles to Timothy and the Epistle to Titus have been known as the Pastoral Epistles. Timothy and Titus had been associated very closely with Paul in his mission work, and he left them in Ephesus and Crete respectively in the course of the Eastern journey which he made after his release from imprisonment in Rome.

The three Epistles are closely related in both matter and form. Being devoted principally to advice about the exercise of the pastoral office, they are not private letters but official documents with comprehensive instructions about combatting heresy, organization of the Church, and the pastoral care of particular classes. 2 Tim., the testament of Paul on his way to face martyrdom, is the only one of them which in form and matter (like Philem. and 3 John) resembles a private letter.

Being official documents they—at least 1 Tim. and Tit.—are intended for the communities of Asia Minor and Crete as much as for their rulers. In them the instructions which Paul had given orally to his fellow workers are brought together, completed and expanded: at the same time the Epistles are intended to give endorsement to Timothy and Titus in the eyes of their communities.

The regulations which these epistles contain are the beginnings of Canon Law, as the author of the Muratorian Canon realized: "(Being written) through love and affection, yet they have been held sacred through the esteem of the universal Church for the ordering of ecclesiastical discipline" (lines 60–63). There is also much dogmatic material in these Epistles, particularly Christology

(e. g., the Hymn to Christ 1 Tim. 3, 16; also 1 Tim. 6, 15 sq.; 2 Tim. 1, 8–10; 2, 8–13; Tit. 3, 4–7).

The principal problem of the Pastoral Epistles is the question of their authenticity.

§ 42. THE FIRST EPISTLE TO TIMOTHY

1. Content and structure

THE Epistle is loosely constructed; it contains instructions about the combatting of false teachers and about problems of Church organization and community life.

Introductory greeting 1, 1–2.

I. The combatting of false teachers is the special task of Timothy in Ephesus 1, 3–20.

1. These false teachers spread (Jewish) fables and speculations and desire to be teachers of the Law 1, 3–7.

2. The Law is made only for gross sinners, as the Gospel teaches 1, 8–11.

3. With incomprehensible mercy Christ has called Paul to preach the Gospel 1, 12–17.

4. Timothy must struggle against the falsification of the Gospel by the false teachers 1, 18–20.

II. Problems of Church discipline 2, 1 to 3, 16.

1. Public worship 2, 1–15:

a) Prayer for all men especially for those in authority 2, 1–7.

b) The position of men and women at public worship 2, 8–15.

2. The ministers 3, 1–13:

a) Requirements for bishops (Mirror of bishops) 3, 1–7;

b) Requirements for deacons (Mirror of deacons) 3, 8–13.

3. The underlying reason for these prescriptions is the greatness of the divine mystery which is entrusted to the Church ("Christ hymn") 3, 14–16.

III. The false teachers and their demands 4, 1–11.

1. They forbid marriage and order abstinence from certain foods 4, 1–5.

2. Timothy should explain to the faithful the absurdity of these demands, and should himself grow in piety and inculcate its practice 4, 6–11.

IV. Advice to Timothy on the discharge of his office 4, 12 to 6, 2.

1. General exhortation to lead an exemplary life and to work zealously 4, 12–16.

2. Attitude to people of different ages 5, 1–2.

3. Widows 5, 3–16.

4. Presbyters (elders) 5, 17–25.

5. Slaves 6, 1–2.

V. Further dispute with the false teachers 6, 3–19.

1. Pride and covetousness of the false teachers 6, 3–10.

2. Exhortation to Timothy to fight the good fight of the faith; doxology 6, 11–16.

3. The rich should make good use of their wealth 6, 17–19.

Conclusion: Further warning against the false Gnosis of the false teachers 6, 20–21.

2. The recipient and the circumstances of composition

Timothy was a native of Lystra in Lycaonia; his father was a Gentile, his mother a Jewess (Jewish-Christian) called Eunice (2 Tim. 1, 5). While still a young man (1 Tim. 4, 12) he joined Paul at the beginning of the second missionary journey and was circumcised by him (Acts 16, 1–3), and thereafter he was seldom out of the Apostle's company. During the second missionary journey Paul sent him on important business from Athens to Thessalonica (1 Thess. 3, 2 sqq.), and during the third missionary journey he performed a similar commission, travelling from

Ephesus through Macedonia to Corinth (1 Cor. 4, 17; 16, 10; Acts 19, 22). He is named as joint sender in six of Paul's Epistles (1 and 2 Thess., 2 Cor., Col., Philem., Phil.). According to Col. 1, 1; Philem. 1; Phil. 1, 1 he shared Paul's first imprisonment at Rome.

According to 1 Tim. 1, 3 sqq. Paul left him in Ephesus to counteract the false teachers who were a peril to the Church in Asia Minor, and to govern the community. This appointment cannot have taken place during the third missionary journey (54–57 A.D.), for Timothy remained with Paul throughout it, except when he was away on a mission; moreover, the errors which are attacked in 1 Tim. had not appeared in Ephesus during the third missionary journey (Acts 20, 29); and furthermore the organization of community life which 1 Tim. calls for shows that the community at Ephesus had already passed the first years of its existence.

So there is no point before Paul's first imprisonment to which the Epistle can be assigned. Therefore, unless we regard it as a pseudonymous work, we must date it between 63 and 65 A.D., and assume that Paul wrote it while staying in Macedonia (1 Tim. 1, 3), shortly after a further visit to Ephesus which he made on his release from prison.

§ 43. THE EPISTLE TO TITUS

1. Content and structure

Introductory greeting 1, 1–4.

I. Duties of Titus in Crete 1, 5–16.

1. Appointment of bishops in each city; requirements for the office of bishop (Mirror of bishops) 1, 5–9.

2. Combatting the false teachers there who cling to Jewish fables and commandments of men (regulations about cleanliness) 1, 10–16.

II. Questions of Church discipline 2, 1 to 3, 11.

1. The duties of different classes: old and young men and women, slaves 2, 1–10.

2. Foundation of these duties is the grace of God which they have received 2, 11–15.

3. Duties to those in authority and fellow men 3, 1–2.

4. The foundation of this is the rebirth which they have experienced 3, 3–8.

5. Attitude to errors and false teachers 3, 9–11.

Conclusion: Instructions, greetings 3, 12–15.

2. Recipient and circumstances of composition of the Epistle

Titus was a Gentile Christian, a member of the Antioch community, who travelled to Jerusalem with Paul and Barnabas for the Apostolic Council (Gal. 2, 1–5). He is never mentioned in Acts. Towards the end of the third missionary journey he was sent from Ephesus to Corinth with the "sorrowful Epistle" (2 Cor. 2, 13; 7, 6 sqq.), and he handled this difficult assignment so neatly that he restored this community which had almost been lost to Paul. Shortly afterwards Paul sent him back to Corinth from Macedonia in order to complete the collection, and on this occasion he delivered 2 Cor. (2 Cor. 8, 6; 12, 18).

The Epistle to Titus is closely related to 1 Tim. in content and form, and both Epistles must have been written about the same time. There is no point in Paul's life before 63 A.D. at which he could have written it. According to Tit. 1, 5 Paul had worked with Titus in Crete for some time, but the Christian communities there were still in need of organization, and he left Titus behind to carry out this work. As soon as Artemas or Tychicus relieve him, he is to come to Nicopolis in Epirus, where Paul intends to spend the winter (3, 12).

Acts records only one visit of Paul to Crete, and that was when he was being taken as a prisoner to Rome (autumn 60 A.D.). This was a short period and the work with Titus cannot have taken place then. It is quite improbable that they had worked together there at an earlier date. So Paul must have spent some time there after his release from imprisonment at Rome, and the Epistle must have been sent to Titus shortly afterwards; like 1 Tim., it was probably written in Macedonia.

§ 44. THE SECOND EPISTLE TO TIMOTHY

1. Content and structure

Introductory greeting 1, 1–2. Introduction 1, 3–5: Thanksgiving for Timothy's loyalty to the faith; Paul desires to see him again.

I. Exhortations to Timothy to sacrifice himself loyally in the service of the Gospel 1, 6 to 2, 13.

1. Exhortation to profess the faith fearlessly and to bear sufferings cheerfully like Paul himself 1, 6–14.

2. Reference to Paul's painful experiences in Ephesus, and praise of the loyalty of Onesiphorus 1, 15–18.

3. He instructs Timothy to disseminate the traditional teaching of the Apostles, and again exhorts him, with reference to his own example, to be willing to suffer 2, 1–13.

II. Instructions about the attitude to adopt to false teachers 2, 14 to 4, 8.

1. A warning against useless argument and empty babbling; this leads only to falling away from the faith, but the Church, the sure foundation of God, stands firm 2, 14–21.

2. Charitable instruction, and not wrangling, converts those who have gone astray 2, 22–26.

3. The moral confusion, which has been foretold for the last days, is already appearing in the work of the false teachers 3, 1–9.

4. In the face of this, Timothy, the loyal imitator of Paul in everything, must hold fast to the doctrine which he has received and to the testimony of Scripture 3, 10–17.

5. In view of the forthcoming departure of Paul he must preach the message of salvation with zeal and force 4, 1–8.

Conclusion 4, 9–22: Paul's position; requests, instructions, greetings.

2. The circumstances of composition of the Epistle

This Epistle was written at Rome (1, 17), where Paul was in prison, fettered like a criminal (1, 8 16 sq.; 2, 9); he expects to be executed soon (4, 6). He feels lonely, and asks Timothy to hurry to him before winter, when navigation ceases (4, 9 21).

This Epistle was not written during the first imprisonment which was very much milder (cf. Acts 28, 30 sq. with 2 Tim. 2, 9); if it was composed then, it would be necessary to assume that Paul's treatment grew very much worse after the two-year period in the hired lodging. 4, 13 also shows that the Epistle was not written at that time; the sojourn which Acts 20, 5 sqq. reports was his last visit to Troas before the first imprisonment at Rome: so if 2 Tim. was written during the first Roman imprisonment, the cloak and books must have been in Carpus' house for about five years! Moreover, 4, 20 tells us that Paul left Trophimus sick in Miletus, and this could not be reconciled with Acts 21, 29 where we are told that he accompanied the Apostle to Jerusalem.

So if 2 Tim. is authentic it must have been written during a second, far more severe imprisonment at Rome, which ended with Paul's martyrdom; this imprisonment was preceded by a journey to Asia Minor (Troas and Miletus; 4, 13 20). It is the last of the surviving Pauline Epistles, and may be considered the testament of the Apostle to "his dearly beloved son" (2 Tim. 1, 2; 2, 1; Phil. 2, 22).

§ 45. THE AUTHENTICITY OF THE PASTORAL EPISTLES

THE oldest evidence for the existence of the Pastoral Epistles is to be found in the Apostolic Fathers. Polycarp's epistle to the Philippians—see § 5, 2 for the date of its composition—repeats three passages from them (4, 1: 1 Tim. 6, 10 7; 9, 2: 2 Tim 4, 10; 12, 3: 1 Tim. 2, 1 sq.). The epistles of Ignatius contain so many reminiscences of the Pastoral Epistle that it is probable that he knew them. Jerome in the prologue to his commentary on Titus tells us that Tatian acknowledged the Pauline origin of Tit., but rejected 2 Tim. Marcion had not the Pastoral Epistles in his canon at all; Harnack thinks that he did not know them at all, but others hold that he rejected them. Since the second half of the second century they have certainly been known in the whole Church and accepted as Pauline and canonical just like the other ten Epistles of Paul.

That was the situation until the beginning of the nineteenth century. The attack on authenticity began in 1807 when Schleiermacher rejected 1 Tim., and in 1812 Eichhorn rejected all three as spurious. F. Chr. Baur (1835) and his school also denied the authenticity of all three Epistles, and the present day critics consider their spuriousness an established fact of scholarship. H. J. Holtzmann in 1880 produced the standard work of modern criticism; the most recent critical commentary in German is by M. Dibelius (2nd edition 1931; revised by H. Conzelmann 1955).

H. von Campenhausen suggests that Polycarp of Smyrna († 155/56) brought them into general use in the Church, and that they were written either by Polycarp himself or on his instructions

445

by one of his clergy who shared his ideas. These scholars say that they were composed in the first half of the second century.

Other critics regard them as containing genuine Pauline material (particularly the personal comments Tit. 3, 12–15; 2 Tim. 4, 9 sqq. etc.), in spite of being pseudo–Pauline writings ("Fragment theory"; e. g., Harnack, Harrison, Falconer), or consider that they are works by Paul which have undergone interpolation. On the other hand the authenticity of all three is firmly upheld by conservative Protestants (B. Weiss, Th. Zahn, G. Wohlenberg, A. Schlatter, F. Torm, W. Michaelis, J. Behm, Joach. Jeremias).

The objections to authenticity may be summarized under five headings:

1. In language and style the Pastoral Epistles show such marked differences from the other ten Pauline Epistles that they cannot possibly be works of the same author.

Their total vocabulary[1] embraces 848 words (plus 54 proper names), of which 306 do not occur in the other ten Pauline Epistles. The following is the distribution of these 306 *hapax legomena*: 1) 1 Tim. 127; 2 Tim. 81; Tit. 45; — 2) 1 and 2 Tim. 17; 1 Tim. and Tit. 20; 2 Tim. and Tit. 7; — 3) all three Past 9.

The great majority of these *hapax legomena* occur in only one epistle, so the Pastoral Epistles cannot be the work of a forger, otherwise the non–Pauline words would be more evenly distributed. So the uneven distribution must be due to a difference in the circumstances. Moreover, Rom. has practically the same proportion of *hapax legomena* (261 out of a total vocabulary of 993 words, excluding proper names). Hence it is agreed at the present day that the attack on authenticity cannot be supported by the statistical method.

The following observations are of greater importance: Certain

---

[1] Cf. F. Torm, *Ueber die Sprache in den Past:* ZntW 18 (1917/18) 225–243; W. Michaelis, *Past und Wortstatistik:* ibid. 28 (1929) 69–76.

words and expressions which are characteristic of Paul do not appear in the Pastoral Epistles, e. g. ἀκροβυστία, ἀποκάλυψις, δια-θήκη, δικαιοσύνη θεοῦ, σῶμα Χριστοῦ, the God and Father of Our Lord Jesus Christ, words cognate with ἐλευθεροῦν, ἐνεργεῖν, καυ-χᾶσθαι, περισσεύειν etc., the particles ἄρα, διό, ἔπειτα, ἔτι, μήπ ως, ὅπως, πάλιν, a number of prepositions (e. g. ἀντί, ἔμπροσθεν, σύν), and above all οὖν.

On the other hand, words and turns of speech which are charac-teristic of the Pastoral Epistles do not appear elsewhere in Paul, e.g., σώφρων — σωφρονίζειν — σωφροσύνη — σωφρονισμός, εὐσεβεῖν — εὐσεβῶς—εὐσέβεια, συνείδησις ἀγαθή (and καθαρά), πιστὸς ὁ λόγος (five times), many compounds with ὑγιαίνειν, ἐπιφάνεια (for παρουσία). As Joach. Jeremias says, "When compared to Paul's general usage, the vocabulary of the Pastoral Epistles as a whole shows closer contacts with the educated everyday language of the Hellenistic world, and with the language of Hellenistic-Jewish wisdom teaching, of popular philosophy, and of court style."

There is also a striking difference between the style of these and other Pauline Epistles. Elsewhere the fulness of thought striving for expression breaks through the literary form and leads to numerous anacoloutha and parentheses; but in the Pasto-ral Epistles the diction flows smoothly like a river between its banks. There is hardly anything which can strictly be called deduc-tion or demonstration; in place of logical argument there is simply assertion and instruction. Another remarkable feature is the rarity of the small particles μέν, δέ, τε, καί etc., which are an essential element of personal style. So, although the average number of letters to a word in the other ten Epistles varies from 4.66 in Philem. to 5.02 in 1 Thess., the figures for the Pastoral Epistle are 5.26 (2 Tim.), 5.58 (1 Tim.) and 5.66 (Tit.). "These figures provide a clear demonstration of the difference in style between the Pastoral and the other Epistles" (Roller).

Their peculiar vocabulary and style are undeniable, but

they do not disprove authenticity. Many of the peculiarities can be explained by the special nature and purpose of these Epistles, which are directions to the leaders of the communities.

Recently many scholars have adopted the suggestion that Paul made use of some intimate assistant, such as Luke, as amanuensis for the writing of these Epistles. This was quite a normal practice in antiquity (cf. § 30, 2). They point to the severe conditions which prevailed in prisons in antiquity, and argue that Paul could not have written or dictated word by word a lengthy Epistle like 2 Tim. while he was fettered in prison; but the three Epistles stand or fall together, so, they say, we must assume that he used the same close friend to write all three. Nevertheless many of those who uphold the authenticity of the Pastoral Epistles, such as Michaelis, reject the "amanuensis theory" as undemonstrable and unnecessary.

2. The Christianity of the Pastoral Epistles differs essentially from that of the genuine Pauline Epistles; it is a "Christianity of orthodoxy and good works" (Dibelius).

It is true that the idea of orthodoxy plays a great part in them. They alone contain the expression "sound doctrine" (ἡ ὑγιαίνουσα διδασκαλία) and other phrases with ὑγιής and ὑγιαίνειν. (1 Tim. 1, 10; 2 Tim. 4, 3; Tit. 1, 9; 2, 1—1 Tim. 6, 3; 2 Tim. 1, 13; Tit. 2, 8—Tit. 1, 13; 2, 2). In some passages (1 Tim. 4, 1 6; 6, 21) the word πίστις approaches the meaning "the doctrine of the faith." They also stress the preservation of tradition (1 Tim. 6, 20; 2 Tim. 1, 12 14; 2, 2); but this thought appears elsewhere in Paul (1 Cor. 11, 2 23; 15, 3; 2 Thess. 2, 15; 3, 6), and Rom. 6, 17 speaks of τύπος τῆς διδαχῆς, "form of doctrine".

When assessing these facts we must bear in mind that the Pastoral Epistles are combatting heretical movements within Christianity, and to counter them the stress had to be placed on traditional orthodoxy. Sound doctrine is an apt name for orthodoxy, for heresy is a malady which destroys the healthy body of the Church. It was as a part of the struggle against heresy that he introduced the older professions of faith and hymns which bear the stamp of a less developed Christology than the other Pauline Epistles (Tit. 2, 5 sq. 8; 1 Tim. 6, 13–16).[2]

A further remarkable feature is the stress which they lay on good works (1 Tim. 2, 10; 5, 10; 6, 18; 2 Tim. 2, 21; 3, 17; Tit. 2, 14), but that should not be considered a sign that they are of post-apostolic origin. Good works are mentioned in the older Pauline Epistles (2 Thess. 2, 17; 2 Cor. 9, 8; Rom. 2, 7; 13, 3; Col. 1, 10; Eph. 2, 10), and the practical nature of the Pastoral Epistles explains their stronger emphasis on the matter. Exactly like the other Epistles the Pastoral Epistles regard good works as a revelation of the powers of the new life which has been given to Christians (2 Tim. 3, 17). When Tit. 3, 5 says "not by the works of justice which we have done, but according to his mercy", it presents an authentically Pauline antithesis between works and grace (similarly 2 Tim. 1, 9); Tit. 2, 14 says that Christ redeemed us that we might become a "pursuer of good works", a thought which is similar to the "fruit of the Spirit" in Gal. 5, 22 sqq. The meritoriousness of good works (1 Tim. 6, 18 sq.; 2 Tim. 1, 18; 4, 1 7 sq.), appears in Gal. 6, 9 sq. and Rom. 2, 6 sq., where eternal happiness is presented simultaneously as grace and merit.

3. They reflect an organization of the Church which is so highly developed that these Epistles cannot be from Paul's time.

They mention the offices of episcopi (who are also called πρεσβύτεροι, cf. Tit. 1, 5; 1, 7), of deacons and widows, and perhaps also of deaconesses (1 Tim. 3, 11; though this may refer to deacons' wives).

The duty of episcopi is to govern (1 Tim. 5, 17: οἱ καλῶς προεστῶτες πρεσβύτεροι; 3, 5: ἐπιμελεῖσθαι ἐκκλησίας θεοῦ), that is, to lead the community, but this did not necessarily involve preaching and instruction (1 Tim. 5, 17). They formed a college

[2] H. Windisch, *Zur Christologie der Past:* ZntW 34 (1935) 213–238.

(τὸ πρεσβυτέριον 1 Tim. 4, 14), but there is no evidence that there was one man at the head of the college. We cannot infer that it was monarchical from the use of the singular in 1 Tim. 3, 2 sqq., for this must be read in conjunction with 3, 1, and there is a similar confusion of singular and plural in ch. 5, where verse 3 speaks of widows in the plural, while 4–10 use the singular.

The offices of episcopi and deacons are mentioned side by side in Phil. 1, 1, and Acts 20, 17 tells us that Paul called the presbyters of Ephesus to Miletus and reminded them in his farewell discourse that the Holy Ghost had placed them as ἐπίσκοποι to rule the Church of God (Acts 20, 28; "We passage"). There are other passages also in the older Epistles of Paul which show that in his communities there were office holders (leaders of territorial communities), e.g., 1 Thess. 5, 12; 1 Cor. 16, 16 sq.; Rom. 12, 8. The first evidence of an ecclesiastical institution of widows occurs in 1 Tim. 5, 3–16, but women hold prominent positions also in Rom. 16, 1 (Phoebe), 16, 3 (Prisca), 16, 12 sq. (Tryphaena and Tryphosa; Persis), and in Phil. 4, 2–3 (Evodia and Syntyche). We can recognize that compared with the older epistles the Pastoral Epistles show a development of ecclesiastical organization in this respect, but the very explicitness of Paul's instructions shows that the institution is not old at Ephesus.

The Pastoral Epistles make no reference to charismatics, but this does not imply that when they were written, the charismatics had been supplanted by ecclesiastical office holders. There is indirect evidence of the existence of charismatics in the prohibition against women speaking in the assembly of the community (1 Tim. 2, 12), for this presupposes that other men besides the episcopi (1 Tim. 5, 17) may speak. It must be remembered that the Pastoral Epistles aim at regulating the organization of the community, and even in Corinth the charismatics did not perform the duties which they assign to episcopi and deacons. Furthermore, charisms followed their own laws, so the charismatics as a group could not be bound by fixed rules, though they also must observe order at divine worship (1 Cor. 14, 26 sqq.).

4. The heresies which the Pastoral Epistles combat belong to a post-Pauline age.

F. Chr. Baur put forward the theory that the false teachers referred to in the Pastoral Epistles show all the marks of developed second century Gnosticism, particularly of the Marcionites whose antitheses are meant by ἀντιθέσεις τῆς ψευδονύμου γνώσεως in 1 Tim. 6, 20. The critics have long since abandoned this theory. It is also admitted to-day that the Epistles cannot be dated with certainty from the concrete details which the attacks on false teachers contain—prohibition of marriage and certain foods 1 Tim. 4, 3; preoccupation with fables and genealogies 1 Tim. 1, 3 sq.; Tit. 1, 14 sq.; spiritualizing of the resurrection hope 2 Tim. 2, 18. And therefore this point cannot be urged as a proof of spuriousness (Dibelius).

The following passages deal with the false teachers: 1 Tim. 1, 3 to 11; 4, 1–10; 6, 3–5 20 sq.; 2 Tim. 2, 14 23; 3, 1–9 13; 4, 3 sq. Tit. 1, 10–16; 3, 9–11. In spite of occasional obscurities there can be no doubt that these false teachers were Jewish members of the Christian Church. The Epistle to Titus speaks explicitly of "Jewish fables and commandments of men" (1, 14 sq.)— the commandments of men are prescriptions about cleanliness—, issues a warning against "foolish questions and genealogies and contentions and strivings about the Law" (3, 9), and condemns specially "they who are of the circumcision" (1, 10). The "fables and genealogies" of 1 Tim. 1, 4 are probably speculative explanations of the primitive history in the Bible, myths probably referring to the account of creation and genealogies to the history of the Patriarchs.[3]

The Dualist ideas which are referred to in 1 Tim. 4, 3 and 2 Tim. 2, 18 are foreign to genuine Judaism, so it is natural to conclude

[3] G. Kittel, Die γενεαλογίαι der Past: ZntW 20 (1921) 49–69.

that the false teachers proclaimed an early form of Gnosis which had developed in Jewish-Hellenistic territory. The error which the Pastoral Epistles fight against can therefore be described as a gnosticizing Judaism (G. Kittel). As early as Col. 2, 16 there is evidence of a similar Gnosis in Asia Minor.

5. The situations which they presuppose cannot be fitted into the life of Paul as we know it from Acts and the other Pauline Epistles.

If the Pastoral Epistles are authentic, they can only have been written, as was said already, after the two-year imprisonment in Rome, Acts 28, 30 sq.

Those who deny their authenticity say that this imprisonment ended with Paul's execution, but there is no proof of this. If he had suffered martyrdom then Acts would certainly have recorded it, for there could hardly have been a more striking ending. In the light of his trial before the Roman governor (Acts 23, 29; 25, 18 25; 26, 31 sqq.), it would be surprising if the imperial court condemned him to death, for his legal position was very favourable. The nature of his imprisonment at Rome— *custodia libera* in his own hired lodging with considerable freedom of movement—does not suggest a crime which Roman Law would have considered worthy of the death penalty.

Paul's release from imprisonment at Rome and his subsequent journey to the East are not disproved by the gloomy prophecy at Miletus that the presbyters of Ephesus would not see his face again (Acts 20, 25), for this was not a formal prophecy but a personal presentiment of Paul, who was full of sinister forebodings (cf. Rom. 15, 31; Acts 20, 22 24; 21, 13).

Moreover, the Tradition of the early Church presupposes that Paul was set free. Clement of Rome tells us (5, 5–7) that he went to the boundary of the West: that he actually carried out the missionary journey to Spain which he had planned. This is also attested by the Muratorian Fragment (lines 37/38), and by the apocryphal Acts of Peter (ch. 1 and 3); cf. § 31, 3.

§ 46. THE EPISTLE TO THE HEBREWS

Commentaries: (a) A. Schaefer, *Erklaerung des Heb,* Muenster i. W. 1893. J. Graf, *Der Heb, wissenschaftlich-praktische Erklaerung,* Freiburg i. Br. 1918. J. Rohr, ⁴1932 (Bonner NT). J. Bonsirven, 1943 (VS XII). O. Kuss 1953 (Reg NT 8). C. Spicq, I (Introduction), Paris 1952; II (Commentaire), 1953 (pp. 445 + 457). [The Epistle was probably written by Apollo in Italy about 67 A.D.—so during the serious troubles in Palestine between 66 and 68—and was addressed to Jewish priests who had become Christians and who were living in exile in a city on the coast of Palestine (Caesarea) or in Syria (Antioch); it was intended to prepare them for the forthcoming disasters. Paul did not commission the author to write it, nor did he read and approve it before it was sent. The author was merely a spiritual disciple of Paul's, who made use of the Apostle's writings in his work. The originality of his thought is undeniable. Heb. is perhaps more deeply marked by Judaism than any other NT Epistle.] Cf. P. Benoit (RB 1954, 242–247) and O. Michel (ThLZ 1955, 321–324). Teodorico da Castel S. Pietro, 1952 (*La Sacra Bibbia,* see § 3, 9).

(b) J. Héring, 1954 (Bonnard XII). [Probably written by Apollo about 70 A.D. Ch. 1–12 are a homily, 13, 1–21 an epistle which the author added when he sent a copy of the homily to a particular community; 13, 22–25 are a postscript by another hand, probably by Paul who intended them as a commendation of his friend's work.] F. Bleek, *Der Brief an die Hebraeer,* 3 vols., Berlin 1828/40. A. Seeberg, *Der Brief an die Hebraeer,* Leipzig 1912. G. Hollmann, ³1917 (GoettNT 3). E. Riggenbach²⁻³ 1922 (Zahn XIV). J. Moffatt, 1924 (ICC). Th. Haering, *Der Brief an die Hebraeer,* Stuttgart 1925. H. Windisch, ²1931 (Lietzmann 14). Th. H. Robinson, 1933 (Moffatt). H. Strathmann, ⁶1953 (NTDeutsch 9). O. Michel, 1955 (Meyer XIII⁹).

Studies: B. Heigl, *Verfasser und Adresse des Heb,* Freiburg i. Br. 1905. J. Nikel, *Der Heb* (BZfr VII, 6), 1914. L. Pirot, *Hébr. et la Commission biblique:* DB Suppl III (1938) 1409–1440. K. Pieper, *Verfasser und Empfaenger des Heb* (Ntl Untersuchungen, Paderborn 1939). W. Leonard, *The Authorship of the Epistle to the Hebrews,* London 1939. J. Ungeheuer, *Der grosse Priester ueber dem Hause Gottes. Die Christologie des Heb.* Diss. Freiburg i. Br. 1939. A. M. Dubarle, *Rédacteur et destinataires de l'épître aux Hébr.:* RB 48 (1939) 505–529. J. van den Ploeg, *L'exégèse de l'AT dans l'ép. aux Hébr.:* RB 45 (1947) 187 to 228. C. Spicq, *L'authenticité du ch. XIII de l'ép. aux Hébr.:* CNT XI (1948) 226 to 238. Idem, *Le philonisme de l'ép. aux Hébr.:* RB 56 and 57 (1949 and 1950). J. Cambier, *Eschatologie ou Hellénisme dans l'ép. aux Hébr.:* Anal. Lovanensia biblica et orientalia II, 12, 1949. T. da Castel S. Pietro, *La chiesa nella lettera agli Ebrei,* Rome 1945. H. M. Esteve, *De caelesti mediatione sacerdotali Christi iuxta Hebr.,* 8, 3–4, Madrid 1949. W. Wrede, *Das literarische Raetsel des Heb,* Goettingen 1906. J. Behm, *Der gegenwaertige Stand der Frage nach dem Verfasser des Heb,* Parchim 1919. K. Bornhaeuser, *Empfaenger und Verfasser des Heb,* Guetersloh 1932. E. Kaesemann, *Das wandernde Gottesvolk. Eine Untersuchung zum Heb,* Goettingen 1939. M. Dibelius, *Der himmlische Kultus nach dem Heb:* ThBl 21 (1942) 1–11. F. Graber, *Der Glaubensweg des Gottesvolkes. Eine Erklaerung von Heb 11 als Beitrag zum Verstaendnis des AT*, Zurich 1943. A.-C. Purdy, *The Purpose of the Ep. to the Heb. in the Light of Recent Studies in Judaism*: Amicitiae Corolla 1933, 253–264. T. W. Manson, *The Problem of the Ep. to the Heb.*: BJRL 32 (1949) 1–17. A. Oepke, *Das neue Gottesvolk*, Guetersloh 1950, 11–24; 57–74. W. Manson, *The Epistle to the Hebrews: An Historical and Theological Reconsideration*, London ²1953. F. J. Schierse, *Verheissung und Heilsvollendung. Zur theologischen Grundfrage des Heb*, Munich 1955. G. Schille, *Erwaegungen zur Hohenpriesterlehre des Heb*: ZntW 46 (1955) 81–109. [From the frequent variation between the titles "Priest" and "High Priest" it may be inferred that the author of the Epistle was influenced by a tradition in which the idea of "Priest" was important (cf. 7, 1–25; 8, 4 to 9, 10; 10, 2–10) while he himself preferred the title "High Priest"; cf. 2, 17; 3, 1; 4, 14f.; 5, 5 10.] G. Vos, *The Teaching of Heb.*, 1956. C. K. Barrett, *The Eschatology of Heb.*: The background of the NT, St. in hon. C. H. Dodd, 1956, 363–393. O. Kuss, *Der theologische Grundgedanke des Heb.* The interpretation of the death of Jesus in the NT: MThZ (1956) 233–271.

Surveys of research: A. Vitti, *Ultimi studi sulla lettera agli Ebrei*: Bb 22 (1941) 412–432. St. Lyonnet, Ibid., 33 (1952) 240–257. O. Kuss, *Ueber einige neuere Beitraege zur Exegese des Heb*: Theol. u. Glaube 42 (1952) 186–204.

Decision of the Pontifical Biblical Commission of 24th June 1914: The doubts about the canonicity of the Epistle which were entertained in the West cannot be used as an argument to disprove its Pauline origin. Criteria of language and content prove that Paul was the author. Yet it is not necessary to assume that Paul gave the Epistle its form.

1. Content and Structure

The theme of the Epistle is that Jesus is the true High Priest.

I. The superiority of the new divine revelation, 1, 1 to 4, 13.

1. The Son, the bearer of the new and final revelation, is superior to the angels 1, 1–14; hence the greatness of our responsibility 2, 1–4.

2. The temporary condescension of the Son (Incarnation, Passion and Death) was the prerequisite for the exercise of his office as High Priest 2, 5–18.

3. The Son is superior to Moses 3, 1–6.

4. Warning against losing the promised rest of God through apostasy, as the generation in the desert did (exposition of Ps. 95) 3, 7 to 4, 13.

II. Jesus the true High Priest 4, 14 to 10, 18.

1. Jesus possesses the requirements of a genuine High Priest (capacity for compassion and call from God); so we must turn to him with confidence 4, 14 to 5, 10.

2. Exhortation of the readers as a preliminary to the immediately following discussion of the difficult main theme 5, 11 to 6, 20.

a) In spite of the spiritual dullness of the readers, the author will not deal with the elements of doctrine, for they have not fallen away from the Christian faith, and if they had fallen away, further conversion would be impossible 5, 11 to 6, 10.

b) He encourages them to hold loyally to their hope, and confirms it by the reliability of the promise sworn to Abraham 6, 11–20.

3. Christ is the perfect High Priest for ever according to the order of Melchisedech, and as such is superior to the levitical priesthood 7, 1–28:

a) Melchisedech's priesthood is superior to the levitical priesthood 7, 1–10.

b) The imperfect levitical priesthood has been eliminated by the establishment of Jesus as High Priest according to the order of Melchisedech 7, 11–18.

c) In Jesus we have received the entirely perfect High Priest whom we need 7, 19–28.

4. Jesus is High Priest in the heavenly Holy Place and Mediator of a New Testament which revokes the Old Testament 8, 1–13.

5. The sacrificial work of the Old Testament and the sacrificial work of Christ 9, 1–28:

a) The Blood of animals which the High Priest of the Old Testament offered once a year was not capable of making a real atonement 9, 1–10.

b) Christ by his own blood has entered once for all into the Holies and has wrought a perfect reconciliation 9, 11–14.

c) By his death he has become the founder of a New Testament and has made an eternal propitiation for sins 9, 15–28.

6. The insufficiency of the sacrifices of the Old Testament and the efficacy of the sacrifice of Christ 10, 1–18:

a) The inefficacy of the Old Testament propitiatory sacrifices is clear from their annual repetition and from the incapacity of animal sacrifices to take away sins 10, 1–4.

b) So the Old Testament system of sacrifices is superseded by Christ's sacrifice of his life 10, 5–10.

c) His sacrifice took place once only because it was efficacious 10, 11–18.

III. Exhortation to be loyal to the faith 10, 19 to 13, 17.

1. Stirring exhortation to hold fast to the hope of eternal salvation and to remain loyal to the Christian community (10, 19 to 25), with reference to the fearful consequences of apostasy (10, 26–31), to their exemplary perseverance during a previous persecution (10, 32–34) and to the future reward for perseverance in the faith (10, 35–39).

2. It was through such faith that the saints of the time before Christ distinguished themselves (examples in the faith), without experiencing the fulfilment of their hopes, for they were not to attain the fulfilment without us 11, 1–40.

3. Looking back upon them and looking at Christ, let us not be led astray from the faith by suffering; a further warning against apostasy and its irremediable consequences 12, 1–29.

4. Injunctions to practise brotherly love, purity, contentment, grateful remembrance of dead pastors, loyalty to Christ, obedience to their present pastors 13, 1–17.

Conclusion of the Epistle 13, 18–25: Personal message, blessing, greetings.

2. The Tradition of the early Church

The Epistle tells us nothing about its author or destination, and it has no introductory greeting. The title πρὸς Ἑβραίους is found as early as 200 A.D. both in the East (Pantaenus, Clement of

Alexandria, $\mathfrak{P}^{46}$), and in the West (Tertullian). The title means that
the Epistle was intended for born Jews, but presumably it is nothing
more than an inference drawn from the content of the Epistle. There
were, of course, Christian Jews outside Palestine, but the Fathers
generally considered that the Epistle was addressed to Palestinians.

As far as can be seen, the Eastern churches always included
Heb. among the canonical scriptures, and regarded it as a work
of Paul's; yet they were, nevertheless, aware that the Pauline
authorship was not everywhere accepted.

The Alexandrian Church attributed Heb. to Paul, at least from
the time of Pantaenus (c. 180 A.D.); Eusebius (H. E. VI 14, 4)
tells us that Pantaenus explained the absence of Paul's name by
the fact that Christ himself had been sent as Apostle to the Hebrews, whereas Paul was appointed Apostle to the Gentiles, and
had written to the Hebrews about his vocation. Pantaenus was
succeeded by Clement; his explanation of the divergence in style
between Heb. and the Pauline Epistles is that Paul wrote to the
Hebrews in their own language, and the Epistle was translated
into Greek by Luke and circulated among the Greeks; he says
that Paul omitted his name because of the prejudice against him
among the Jews (Eusebius H. E. VI 14, 23). Origen also maintained that the Epistle was a work of Paul's, but considered him
only the indirect author; the thoughts alone are his, the expression
and style belonged to someone who remembered what he had
said and who noted down his teaching; no one knows who actually wrote it, but tradition mentions Clement, the Bishop of
Rome, and also Luke (Eusebius H. E. VI 25, 11–14). In the
thirty-ninth Easter letter of 367 A.D. Athanasius includes Heb.
among the fourteen Epistles of Paul, and places it after the Epistles to the Churches. It occupies this position also in the ancient
Majuscules B ℵ A C H P; it is placed after Rom. in $\mathfrak{P}^{46}$.[1] Egypt's

---

[1] Cf. Hatch, *The Position of Heb. in the Canon of the NT:* HarvThR 1936,
133–151 (see also § 5, 1: Buck).

neighbour Palestine considered that Paul was the author, as we see from Eusebius of Caesarea (H. E. III 3, 5; 38, 2) and Cyril of Jerusalem; so did Asia Minor, as is shown by Methodius of Olympus and Amphilochius of Iconium; in the case of the Syro-Antiochene Church, we have the evidence of Titus of Bostra, Apollinaris of Laodicea, Severianus of Gabala, Theodore of Mopsuestia and others. The national Syrian Church also regarded Heb. as canonical and Pauline, indeed it was a favourite book of the Syrians.

In the Western Church Heb. was known at a very early date, but in spite of being esteemed and used, it was not considered Pauline and canonical until about 350 A.D. Clement of Rome made great use of it in ch. 12 and 36 of his Epistle, and he imitated it in ch. 17. It was also used by the Pastor of Hermas, by Justin in his Dialogus, and by Ptolemy the Valentinian in his Epistle to Flora. There is no certain citation in Irenaeus, but Hippolytus uses it, though he explicitly denies that it is Pauline. It was translated into Latin at an early date (see § 14, 2). Tertullian knows it as an epistle of Barnabas, and though he does not consider it canonical, yet he allows it a certain authority when he says that it is more widely accepted *(receptior)* in the Church than the Pastor of Hermas (*De Pudic.* 20). Cyprian never cites Heb.

Between 350 and 400 A.D., under Eastern influence the Western Church accepted it into the Canon as a work of Paul's. Yet there were wide fluctuations of opinion up to 400 A.D. It is not cited by the African Optatus of Mileve; Zeno of Verona, a native of Africa, says that Paul wrote only thirteen Epistles, and it is not named in the Canon Mommsenianus of 360 A.D. Ambrosiaster comments on only thirteen Pauline Epistles—he makes only sparing and cautious use of Heb.; as late as about 405 A.D. Pelagius in Rome admitted only thirteen Pauline Epistles.

On the other hand, the Pauline origin and the canonicity of Heb. were defended under the influence of Greek tradition by

Hilary of Poitiers, who was exiled to Asia Minor from 356 to 360 A.D., by Lucifer of Cagliari, who spent from 355 to 361/3 in the East, and also by Faustinus of Rome, Pacianus, Priscillian, and Philaster of Brescia; Ambrose cites it copiously, but only occasionally refers to it as a work of Paul's. Jerome is quite definite about its Pauline origin. Because of the authority of the Eastern Church Augustine accepts it as canonical; at first he cites it unhesitatingly as Pauline, but after 409 he never mentions the author's name. The synod of Rome in 382 A.D. and the council of Carthage in 419 speak of fourteen Epistles of Paul, but the two African councils of 393 and 397 speak of 13 + 1 Epistles of Paul.

3. Literary character

Hebrews and 1 John are the only Epistles in the New Testament which have no introductory greeting with the name of the author and the recipients; but, unlike 1 John, Heb. has a conclusion (13, 18–25), like the Epistles of Paul.

We can safely rule out any suggestion that Heb. originally had an introduction which was lost or suppressed at an early date. In the history of ancient epistles there is no case where damage to the papyrus roll caused only the introduction to perish by accident (cf. § 30, 3). There is not the slightest objection—and that is also the case with 1 John—to the beginning which we have (1, 1–4), and this was undoubtedly the original beginning of Heb. Moreover, there is no question of deliberate suppression of the praescriptum because it contained the name of a non-Apostle; if there had been such a praescriptum, the obvious course would have been to substitute the name of some Apostle such as Paul.

To turn to the question of the literary character of Heb., it has long ago been observed that Heb. has more resemblance to a theological treatise than to an Epistle; instead of dealing with a large number of more or less related matters it develops a single theme—the High Priesthood of Christ; and it develops the theme in a logical and careful manner which is not paralleled even by Rom., the best constructed of the Pauline Epistles.

So it has been suggested that Heb. is not an epistle, but a theological tractate constructed according to the rules of rhetoric or an artificial letter: in other words, it is described as a literary work intended not for a single community or a small group of communities, but for general circulation. Deissmann wished to see in it the earliest artistic work of Christian literature. Those who uphold this view would consider the personal conclusion (13, 18 sqq.) as either a later addition or a deliberate literary fiction intended to provide the work with the conventional epistolary conclusion on the model of the Pauline Epistles (hence the mention of Timothy 13, 23).

This suggestion must be rejected. Heb. is not a theological treatise for expounding theological doctrine. It has one great purpose: to call upon the readers to hold loyally to the profession of Jesus as the one Mediator of salvation. The doctrinal passages which make up the greater part of the Epistle serve this practical purpose of giving pastoral exhortation. So the author quite aptly concludes by calling his epistle "words of warning" (λόγος παρακλήσεως 13, 22 [Knox version]).

A peculiarity of Heb., which marks it off from Paul's Epistles, is that it does not separate doctrine and exhortation as is the case in Rom., Gal., Eph., Col., 1 and 2 Tim.; doctrinal and paraenetic passages are intermingled. Thus, the first chapters, which are a preparation for the development of the theme in 7, 1 to 10, 18, are interspersed with paraenetic passages (2, 1–4; 4, 14–16; 5, 11 to 6, 20). The longest doctrinal section 7, 1 to 10, 18, is followed by a long moral section—the great final exhortation 10, 19 to 13, 17—but this in turn is interrupted by two doctrinal sections, one of which is quite long (11, 1–40; 12, 18–24).

This peculiar feature of Heb. has led some modern scholars to view it as a written-down sermon, which is mainly general in tone, but is intended for a particular community and so occasionally deals with concrete matters (Windisch, O. Michel, Strathmann). Since the preacher is away from the community but hopes to see them soon (13, 23), he sends them the sermon with an epistolary conclusion, and asks them to give it a sympathetic hearing. The author calls it a "word of warning", a term which Acts 13, 15 applies to the edifying synagogue discourse. This is the correct description of it. The nearest parallel to Heb. is the Hellenistic address to the synagogue, of which 4 Macch. etc., provides a specimen.

Undoubtedly this way of describing Heb. is nearer the truth. It is undeniable that 1, 1 to 13, 17 does not so much resemble an epistle as an exposition such as a sermon (cf. especially 2, 6; 6,1; 8, 1; 9, 5). When regarded in that light the absence of an introductory greeting presents no difficulty. But the conclusion cannot be considered a later addition or a literary fiction, and its personal tone shows that this work was composed for a particular occasion and for a quite definite purpose (cf. 13, 19 23 sq.). The allusions to the circumstances of the recipients are few and fairly indefinite, but they are sufficient to show that the author was not simply writing to the Church—as Dibelius, for example, wishes to make out—but has in mind a particular community or a small group of communities which he knows well and has under his charge (cf. especially 10, 24 sq. 32–34; 12, 4; 6, 10).

4. The destination of the Epistle

Until the nineteenth century Heb. was universally regarded as being addressed to Jewish Christians, and this is still the view of almost all Catholic exegetes and of a small number of others—Th. Zahn, Riggenbach, Buechsel, Bornhaeuser, and Strathmann. This view is supported by the following considerations: The author presupposes in his readers an intimate knowledge of the Old Testament and particularly of Old Testament Ceremonial (sacrifices); he gives a lengthy demonstration from Scripture and a large number of Old Testament citations.[2] Moreover the entire theological antithesis of Christ above Moses, Christ and Melchisedech, Christ's High Priesthood and the levitical priesthood, seems designed for former Jews.

Yet the Epistle is not addressed to all Jewish Christians, but to some particular community or communities, for the author intends to visit them soon (13, 23). Where were these readers? Jerusalem or Palestinian communities in general are usually suggested.

Bornhaeuser—and K. Pieper—thinks that it was written for Jewish priests in Jerusalem who had become Christians (cf. Acts 6, 7). Spicq agrees with this, but assumes that when the persecution of Christians broke out after the death of Stephen (Acts 8, 1; 11, 9), these priests were obliged to flee and settled either in a maritime city of Palestine (Caesarea) or in Syria (Antioch), where they formed a closed self-contained group. Th. Zahn and Strathmann suggest that the Epistle was addressed to the Jewish-Christian group in the Roman community; Riggenbach proposes Cyprus, and others suggest various places outside Palestine.

It is impossible to reach any certainty, but the mother community in Jerusalem is most unlikely, for it was poor and had to be supported by other communities (cf. Gal. 2, 10; Acts 24, 17), whereas Heb. 6, 10 tells us that the readers often assist poor Christians. According to 2, 3 they had not heard Jesus preaching. The rulers of the mother community would not have been called ἡγούμενοι (13, 7). Certainly what 10, 32 sqq. says about the readers being persecuted shortly after their conversion does not fit the description which Acts gives of the original community.

---

[2] Cf. G. Harder, *Die LXX-Zitate des Heb* (in: Theologia viatorum, ed. by M. Albertz 1939, 33–52); L. Vénard, *L'utilisation des Psaumes dans l'épître Hébreux* (Mélanges Podechard, Lyon 1945, 253–264).

Moreover, if Paul was the author, the Epistle cannot have been addressed to Jerusalem nor to any other community in Palestine, for by returning there Paul would have faced very serious danger, while according to 13, 23 the author intended to visit the recipients. So only a Jewish-Christian community outside Palestine can be seriously considered.

E. M. Roeth in 1836 first put forward the theory that the people to whom Heb. was addressed were mainly Gentiles, or were simply Christians without reference to whether they were Jews or Gentiles. This view was developed in detail in 1884 by H. von Soden, and in modern times it has been adopted by the majority of non-Catholics, for example, by Juelicher, Harnack, Wrede, F. Barth, A. Seeberg, Windisch, Michaelis, Oepke, Moffatt, and E. F. Scott; among Catholics it has been adopted by Dubarle, and has recently been defended very effectively by Schierse.

The defenders of this view point particularly to passages like 3, 12 ("to depart from the living God"); 6, 1 sq. ("Turn away from dead works and be converted to faith towards God"); 9, 14 ("How much more shall the Blood of Christ cleanse our conscience from dead works to serve the living God?"), which can apply only to former pagans. They also adduce the Epistles to the Romans and Galatians to show that Gentile Christians were quite as capable as converted Jews of appreciating arguments drawn from the Old Testament. It is urged against them that the Epistle is addressed to readers who had been demoralized by a persecution and in their discouragement were tempted by the attractiveness of Jewish worship to relapse into Judaism; to this they reply that, as far as we know, the Palestinian Jewish Christians had never abandoned the observance of the Law and participation in Jewish worship (Acts 21, 20 sqq.).

The emphasis of Heb. on the superiority of Christ's sacrifice over the Old Testament sacrifices is intended to remind the readers of the greatness of the punishment for unbelief. The exhortations which are scattered throughout the Epistle are not warnings against relapsing into Judaism; they are general exhortations to lead a life conspicuous for religion and morality.

When dealing with Jewish prescriptions about food the author speaks of "various and strange doctrines" (13, 9), an expression which suggests a syncretism of Jewish and pagan tendencies rather than official Judaism. In view of this, Dubarle has recently suggested that the Epistle was addressed to Asia Minor, to Galatia where, as we see from Gal., the attraction of the Mosaic Law was felt very strongly (cf. especially 4, 9; 5, 1); he says that in spite of having only a minority of Jews these communities had a lively interest in the Old Testament (cf. Gal. 4, 21–31 with Heb. 3, 7 to 4, 11; 7, 1–10). Heb., he maintains, is addressed to much the same readers as Jude and 1 and 2 Pet.

T. W. Manson considers that Heb. was written by Apollo to the communities of the Lycus valley (particularly Colossae and Laodicea) and is earlier than Col., for Paul had a copy of Heb. when writing the latter Epistle. But these are merely conjectures which can hardly be substantiated.

Schierse also produces strong arguments for denying that Heb. was addressed to Jewish Christians, but he does not enter into the question of what particular communities it was intended for; he says that the emphasis on the excellence of the High Priest of the New Testament and on the superiority of his unique sacrifice for sin over the Old Testament worship was not intended to restrain Jewish Christians from relapsing into Judaism with its brilliant liturgy; the theme is rather purely internal to Christian theology: The way of the New Testament People of God with their High Priest Christ into the heavenly Holy Place to win there the "immovable kingdom" (12, 28). "The proper purpose of the Epistle—which is really a written (liturgical) sermon—is practical and religious: to counteract the momentary state of weakness" of the community, which "is in danger of growing faint on the way to the heavenly fatherland, not so much because of extrinsic difficulties as through interior loss of strength."

Among Protestants it is generally assumed that the Epistle was sent to Rome, either to the whole community, or to some particular smaller group or to a house church. In support of this they point to the fact that the earliest attestation of the Epistle comes from Rome (1 Clem. and *Pastor* of Hermas); they say that the natural inference from 13, 24 ("The brethren from Italy salute you") is that the author is writing outside Italy and Christians of Italian origin send the greetings; they also remind us that the Roman community was well known for works of charity (cf. Dionysius of Corinth apud Euseb. H. E. IV 23 with Heb. 6, 10; 10, 32–34), that the description of the superiors as ἡγούμενοι 13, 7 24 occurs also in 1 Clem. 1, 3, and *Pastor* Hermae Vis. II 2, 6; III 9, 7 and that Timothy, who is mentioned in 13, 23, was well known to the Roman Christians (Col. 1, 1; Philem. 1).

To sum up, the question of the destination of Heb. is still hotly disputed, but it must be admitted that the balance of evidence favours denying that it was written to Jewish Christians.

5. *The author of the epistle*

In the Eastern Church, whether Greek or Syriac speaking, all the important theologians since the third century have regarded Heb. as an Epistle of Paul. The earliest evidence comes from the Egyptian Church through Pantaenus (c. 180 A.D.), for whom this was evidently a trustworthy tradition (apud Euseb. H. E. VI 14, 4). Yet Origen, who was aware of the dispute about its origin, ascribed the Epistle to an unknown writer who remembered Paul's words and described his doctrine, but he does not say that this unknown author was commissioned by Paul (apud Euseb. H. E. VI 25).

In the Western Church, on the other hand, no one attributed

Heb. to Paul before the mid-fourth century. Barnabas is mentioned as its author by Tertullian (*De pudicitia* c. 20), and in the *Tractatus Origenis* (X p. 108) which is probably the work of Gregory of Elvira († after 392).

Catholic scholars at the present day are almost all agreed that Paul is only the indirect author. In modern times some have again defended Paul's direct authorship—e. g., Heigl in 1905—but they have found little support.

The following internal arguments can be adduced in favour of the view that Paul himself wrote Heb.:

1. The conclusion 13, 16 sqq. (Personal messages, greetings, warnings) shows extraordinarily close contacts with the Epistles of Paul; thus 13, 18 sq. with 2 Cor. 1, 11 sq.; 13, 19 23 with Philem. 22 and Phil. 2, 19 23 sq.; 13, 16 with Phil. 4, 18; 13, 24 with Phil. 4, 21 sq.

2. Timothy, who for many years was Paul's most loyal assistant, is an associate of the author of the Epistle (13, 23).

3. There are close correspondences between the theological ideas contained in Heb. and Pauline theology. Thus Heb. also teaches that before the Incarnation Christ possessed divine majesty, was the Mediator of creation, and keeps everything in being through his power (Heb. 1, 2 3 6 compared with Col. 1, 15–17; 1 Cor. 8, 6; 2 Cor. 4, 4; Phil. 2, 5 sq.), that he humbled himself and became man (2, 14–17 compared with Rom. 8, 3; Gal. 4, 4; Phil. 2, 7), that as a reward for his obedience God exalted him, and that he is far superior to the angels, and sits on the right hand of God (1, 3 sq. 5–14 compared with Eph. 1, 20 sq.; Col. 2, 10; 3, 1; Rom. 8, 34; Phil. 2, 9). Heb. also regards his Passion and Death as the essential redeeming act (2, 18; 5, 7 sq.; 9, 14–18; 10, 14). Moreover, Heb. also teaches that through Christ's atoning death the Old Testament Law was repealed and the Old Covenant was superseded by the establishment of a New Testament (7, 19; 8, 6 sqq. compared with 2 Cor. 3, 9 sqq.).

There are many other such correspondences of various degrees of clearness between Heb. and Paul. But the divergences are so numerous and so sharp that the Epistle cannot have been written by Paul. The religious ideas, the style, and the mode of expression point to someone other than Paul as author. Yet the agreements show that the author was a spiritual alumnus of Paul's, though he was an entirely original thinker, and the Epistle was neither commissioned nor written by Paul (Spicq).

This explanation fully satisfies the tradition of the Eastern and Egyptian Church.

The following are the most important grounds for denying that Paul is the author:

1. In regard to language (vocabulary) and style, the divergences from Paul outweigh the agreements. 168 words in Heb. do not occur elsewhere in the New Testament, and a further 124 do not appear in Paul. The Greek of Heb. is much more cultured than is the case with Paul; the Epistle uses words and figures of speech which were found at that time only in literary Greek, such as αἴτιος, ἀποβλέπειν, ἔπος, νέφος, πηγνύναι. Some expressions come from contemporary philosophy, such as αἰσθητήριον, δημιουργός, μετριοπαθεῖν. The author shows knowledge and mastery of rhetoric in his use of alliteration (πολυμερῶς, πολυτρόπως, πάλαι, πατράσιν, προφήταις 1, 1 sq.), of paronomasia—play upon words— (ἔμαθεν ἀφ' ὧν ἔπαθεν 5, 8; also 3, 12; 4, 12; 5, 14; 10, 38 sq.; 13, 14), and chiasmus (2, 5; 4, 16; 7, 3; 11, 17). Rhetorical constructions appear also in sentences such as 7, 9; 9, 5; 11, 32.

The style of Heb. is far superior to that of the Pauline Epistles. Paul's style is sometimes terse to the point of being enigmatic, and it is not unusual for it to reflect his serious agitation and contain numerous anacoloutha. Heb. on the other hand is written in a uniformly unruffled style, carefully ·polished and rhythmically constructed, and contains a number of artistic periods, e. g., 1, 1–4; 2, 2–4; 7, 20–22 23–25; 12, 18–24.

2. Heb. also differs from the Pauline Epistles in structure. In them a (usually rather long) doctrinal section is followed by a moral part, while in Heb. doctrine (theology) and paraenesis are continually interlaced (see the analysis).

3. The Old Testament citations in Heb. are not introduced in the same way as is customary in the Pauline Epistles. None of Paul's favourite phrases occur (γέγραπται, ἡ γραφὴ λέγει etc.); instead Heb. prefaces the citations with: God, His Son, the Holy Spirit or someone says. Heb. differs from Paul in always citing from the LXX and never quoting from memory.

4. According to 2, 3 the author includes himself among those who had been instructed by the hearers of Our Lord, that is, the disciples of Our Lord; Paul cannot be speaking here, for he stresses most vigorously his independence from the Apostles in Gal. 1, 1 11 sqq.

5. The central idea of the Christology of Heb.—the High Priesthood of Christ—never appears in Paul. The saving efficacy of Christ's death is assured according to Heb., not by the Resurrection—which is never mentioned expressly—but by the Ascension through which he has become our High Priest. There is no mention of the mystical union of Christians with the Glorified Christ.

6. Like the Pauline Epistles, Heb. teaches that the Old Testament Law was given by angels (2, 2: Gal. 3, 19), was strictly binding on the Jewish people (2, 2; 10, 28: Gal. 3, 10; Rom. 3, 19 sq.), was incapable of leading those who were subject to it to their end (by giving them the perfect blessing; 7, 18 : Rom. 8, 3), and was repealed by Christ (7, 12 : Rom. 10, 4 and elsewhere). But Heb. regards the Law only as a ceremonial law, an institution for wiping out sins of weakness, while for Paul it contains the moral law for men, and has a deadly effect because it cannot be fulfilled (Rom. 7, 9). So for Heb. the repeal of the Law means the end of levitical worship, while for Paul it is the liberation of mankind from the slavery which the Law imposed on each individual man.

7. Heb. makes no reference to the important Pauline doctrine of justification not by the works of the Law but by faith.

In view of these and other divergences between Heb. and the Pauline Epistles, Paul cannot be the immediate author. It is now impossible to establish who the real author of the Epistle was.

In antiquity Barnabas, Luke, and Clement of Rome were mentioned in certain circles as authors; in modern times Apollo, Silvanus, Philip the deacon, Aquila and Priscilla, Jude "the brother of the Lord", and Aristion have also been put forward. Of these only Barnabas and Apollo deserve serious consideration.

Riggenbach, Bornhaeuser, Strathmann, Prat, Aug. Merk, K. Pieper and others favour Barnabas. His levitical origin (Acts 4, 36) and his close relations with Paul (Acts 11, 25 sqq.) are the main points in his favour; a levite would be interested in Old Testament ceremonial, and his closeness to Paul would explain how he saw no difficulty in the superseding of the Old Testament Law by Christ's work of redemption (cf., e. g., Gal. 2, 13). On the other hand, Barnabas later broke with Paul (Acts 15, 37 sqq.), and we do not know whether they were ever associated afterwards. Moreover, the inaccuracy in 9, 4—where the golden censer is said to stand in the Holy of Holies; but cf. 7, 27—can hardly be due to a levite who had spent a considerable time in Jerusalem. It is also open to question whether the Cypriot Barnabas had the rhetorical training which the author of Heb. possessed.

The Epistle may well have been written by the Alexandrian Apollo, who has been suggested by M. Luther, Bleek, Th. Zahn, Appel, Belser, Rohr, Vogels, Spicq, and Héring; he was well versed in Scripture and according to Acts 18, 24 sqq. had received a rhetorical training; moreover, he was on terms of friendship with Paul (1 Cor. 1, 12; 3, 4 sqq.; 16, 12; Tit. 3, 13). But this cannot be called more than a probability, and it is not supported by Heb. 2, 3 compared with Acts 18, 26.

So the only certain statement we can make is that Heb. was

the work of a theologian deeply versed in Scripture who had received an Alexandrian education, a Jewish Christian who had been influenced by philosophical writings. Spicq and Schierse in particular have demonstrated this.

6. *Time of composition*

If Heb. is even indirectly Paul's work, it was written before the year 67, and probably in Rome—or Italy—after his release from the first Roman imprisonment in 63 or 64 A.D. (cf. 13, 24). Spicq would date it to the year 67, but his theory about its destination and purpose is not convincing.

Only a few non-Catholic scholars—Riggenbach, Bornhaeuser, and Héring, for example—say that it was written before 70 A.D., between Paul's death and the destruction of the Temple; the overwhelming majority—and also the Catholics Kuss and Schierse —date it after 80 A.D. but before 90 A.D., for it was used in 95 A.D. in the first epistle of Clement.

When Heb. refers to the Temple the allusion is to the Tabernacle of the Pentateuch, not to Herod's Temple; so its silence about the destruction of the Temple and the discontinuance of sacrificial worship cannot prove that it was written before 70 A.D.

B. THE CATHOLIC EPISTLES

Commentaries: (a) Th. Calmes, *Épîtres catholiques, Apocalypse,* Paris 1907. A. Camerlynck, *Commentarius in epistolas catholicas,* [5]Bruges 1909. M. Meinertz and W. Vrede, [4]1932 (Bonner NT 9). J. Chaine, *Les épîtres catholiques* (2 Pet., Jude, 1–3 John) Paris 1939. P. de Ambroggi, [2]1949 (S. Garofalo, La Sacra Bibbia XIV, 1). J. Michl, 1952 (RegNT 8).

(b) H. Windisch, [3]1951 (Lietzmann 15; with additions by H. Preisker). F. Hauck, [5]1949 (NTDeutsch 10). P. Eaton, *The Catholic Epistles,* London 1937. F. Moffatt, *The General Epistles (James, Peter and Jude),* 1928 (Moffatt). R. C. H. Lenski, *Interpretation of the Epistles of St. Peter, St. John, St. Jude,* 1938.

In Addition to the collection of St. Paul's Epistles, the New Testament Canon also contains a further group of Epistles, the so-called Catholic Epistles: Jas., 1 and 2 Pet., 1–3 John, and Jude. As the history of the Canon shows, it was a long time before all seven were universally acknowledged as sacred and inspired Scriptures. Eusebius (H. E. II 23, 24 sq.) is the first to speak of seven Catholic Epistles.

They are called Catholic because they are intended for general circulation or at least for a fairly wide circle of readers, unlike the Pauline Epistles which are addressed to particular communities. The title "Catholic" is not entirely apt, for 2 and 3 John are addressed to a particular community and an individual person respectively. But 1 John makes no mention at all of its destination, while Jas., 2 Pet. and Jude use such general expressions that they leave the impression of being addressed to the whole Church; though 1 Pet. is addressed to a definite geographical area, this area contained a large number of communities.

So far as our evidence goes, the title καθολικὴ ἐπιστολή was first used by Apollonius the anti–Montanist about 197 A.D. (apud Euseb. H. E. V 18, 5). Apparently the name was first attached to 1 John because, unlike the other two Epistles of John, it gives no information about the recipients; the name was later transferred to the whole group. In the West the name *epistolae canonicae* was preferred, that is, Epistles which, unlike other writings such as the epistle of Barnabas, belong to the Church's Canon and possess authority.

The Epistles occupied different positions within the Canon in East and West. The Pauline Epistles, as being the oldest and most important collection of Epistles, were placed immediately after Acts in the West, while in the East this position was occupied by the Catholic Epistles, which were the testimony of the original Apostles and of members of the mother community.

Being Catholic, these Epistles tend to stress matters of universal importance at the expense of personal, concrete and merely transient affairs. They deal with the problems which occupied Christendom, or at least large parts of it, at the time when they were written, for example, certain false doctrines (a form of Gnosis in Asia Minor: 1 John; Gnostic-antinomian tendencies: Jude, 2 Pet.), the non-appearance of the Parousia (2 Pet.), severe sufferings and persecutions of the Christian communities (1 Pet.).

Only 1 Pet. and 2 and 3 John conclude with personal messages and greetings; only 1 Pet. has a final blessing; 2 Pet. and Jude conclude with a doxology; the conclusion of 1 John is 5, 13 (cf. Philem. 21; Heb. 13, 22; 1 Pet. 5, 12), and this is followed by an appendix, 5, 14–21. Jas. has no epistolary conclusion.

§ 47. THE EPISTLE OF ST. JAMES

Commentaries: (a) J. E. Belser, *Die Epistel des hl. Jakobus*, Freiburg i. Br. 1909. J. Chaine, *L'épître de St. Jacques*, Paris 1927. O. Bardenhewer, *Der Erief des hl. Jakobus*, Freiburg i. Br. 1928.—(b) A. Ross, *The Epistles of James and John*, 1954 (NIC). F. Spitta, *Der Brief des Jakobus*, Goettingen 1896. J. B. Mayor, *The Epistle of St. James*[3], London 1913. J. H. Ropes, 1916 (ICC). G. Hollmann - W. Bousset, [3]1917 (GoettNT 3). M. Dibelius (with Supplementary volume), 1956 (Meyer XV[8]). F. Hauck, 1926 (Zahn XVI). S. Schlatter, *Der Brief des Jakobus ausgelegt*, Stuttgart 1932. J. Marty, *L'épître de Jacques*, 1935.

Studies: H. F. Cladder, *Die Anlage des Jak:* ZkTh 28 (1904) 37–57. Idem, *Der formale Aufbau des Jak:* Ibid. 295–330. M. Meinertz, *Der Jak und sein Verfasser* (BSt X, 1–3: 1905). A. Gaugusch, *Der Lehrgang der Jakobusepistel*, Freiburg i. Br. 1914. G. Hartmann, *Der Aufbau des Jak:* ZkTh 66 (1942) 63–70 J. Bonsirven: DB Suppl. IV (1949) 783–795.—E. Grafe, *Die Stellung und Bedeutung des Jak in der Entwicklung des Urchristentums*, Tuebingen and Leipzig 1904. A. Meyer, *Das Raetsel des Jak*, Giessen 1930. G. Kittel, *Die Stellung des Jakobus zu Judentum und*

Heidenchristentum: ZntW 30 (1931) 145–156. Idem, *Der geschichtliche Ort des Jak*: Ibid. 41 (1942) 71–105. K. Aland, *Der Herrenbruder Jakobus und der Jakobusbrief*: ThLZ 69 (1944) 97–103. H. Schammberger, *Die Einheitlichkeit des Jak im anti-gnostischen Kampf*, Gotha 1936. A. T. Cadoux, *The Thought of St. James*, London 1944. W. Bieder, *Christliche Existenz nach dem Zeugnis des Jak*: ThZ 5 (1949) 93–113. W. L. Knox, *The Epistle of St. James*: JThSt 46 (1945) 10–17. M. Lack-mann, *Sola fide, Eine Exegetische Studie ueber Jak 2*, Guetersloh 1949. G. Kittel, *Der Jak und die apostolischen Vaeter*: ZntW 43 (1950/51) 54–112. E. Stauffer, *Zum Kalifat des Jak*: Zeitschr. f. Religions- und Geistesgeschichte 4 (1952) 193–214. P. Gaechter, *Jakobus von Jerusalem*: ZkTh 76 (1954) 129–169. G. Eichholz, *Jakobus und Paulus: Ein Beitrag zum Problem des Kanons*, 1953. M. H. Shepherd, *The Epistle of James and the Gospel of Matthew*: JBL 75 (1956) 40–51. E. Lose, *Glaube und Werke*. The theology of James: ZntW 48 (1957) 1–22.

1. Content

The Epistle consists of exhortations, warnings and instructions which are fairly loosely juxtaposed; they deal with moral and religious life. The Epistle may be analysed as follows:

1. Tribulations and temptations 1, 2–18: The blessing of tribu-lations 2–4; confident prayer for wisdom is heard 5–8; high and low 9–11; endurance under temptation earns eternal life 12; temptation comes from men, not from God, who sends only good gifts 13–18.

2. Hearing and doing 1, 19–27: Be doers of the word of God and not merely hearers 19–25; the true service of God is care for widows and orphans and moral self control 26–27.

3. Against slighting the poor and favouring the rich 2, 1–13: There should be no favouritism at the liturgical assemblies 1–7; this runs counter to the precept of charity and provokes the judgment of God 8–13.

4. Faith and works 2, 14–26: Faith without works is dead (practical charity) 14–20; this is proved by the example of Abra-ham and Rahab 21–26.

5. The tongue 3, 1–12: Do not make yourselves teachers 1; the sinister power and danger of the tongue 2–10a; warning against misusing it 10b–12.

6. False (quarrelsome) and true (meek) wisdom 3, 13–18.

7. Avarice and concupiscence 4, 1–12: The contentions among the readers are due to their love of this world 1–3; this world and God are irreconcilable opposites 4–6; injunction to be penitent and to turn humbly to God 7–10; warning against detraction and judging one's brother 11–12.

8. Against foolhardy plans of business people for the future 4, 13–17.

9. Woe to the godless rich who have heaped up treasures, revelled, and kept back the wages of their labourers 5, 1–6.

10. Injunction to persevere patiently, looking to the forthcoming Parousia, following the example of the Old Testament prophets and of Job; warning against swearing 5, 7–12.

11. The power of prayer 5, 13—18: The priests of the Church should pray over the sick and anoint them with oil 14–15; confess your sins to one another and pray for one another 16; the example of Elias shows the power of the just man's prayer 17–18.

12. The blessing of converting a brother who has gone astray 5, 19 and 20.

2. The Epistle of St. James in the early Church

It was only at a late date and with difficulty that Jas. became firmly established in the Canon. The oldest author to mention it by name is Origen, for example in his commentary on John 8, 24; he is aware that the canonicity of Jas. is not universally acknowledged, though personally he considers it one of the canonical Scriptures and cites it fairly often; he occasionally names James the Apostle as author. The copious writings of Clement of Alexandria do not contain a single citation from Jas. (or 2 Pet. or 3 John), so despite the evidence of Eusebius (H. E. VI 14, 1; see § 7, 1), it is doubtful whether Clement accepted this Epistle as canonical. Jas. 3, 1 sq. is cited as Sacred Scripture in pseudo-Clement *Ad virgines*

(11, 4), which was probably written in Palestine in the first half of the third century. Eusebius H. E. II 23, 25 lists Jas. among the *Antilegomena,* but says that it is read in most churches. Cyril of Jerusalem (348 A.D.) accepts all seven Catholic Epistles as canonical, and considers that Jas. was written by the bishop of Jerusalem, James the brother of the Lord. At the time of John Chrysostom, and probably under his influence, the three larger Catholic Epistles—Jas., 1 Pet., 1 John—were accepted as Sacred Scripture. About 400 A.D. the National Syrian Church took over the canon of the Church of Antioch, which contained Jas. (Peshitta).

The West did not accept Jas. into the Canon until about 370 to 380. The Muratorian Fragment, Tertullian and Cyprian do not know it, and it does not appear in the chief witnesses to the Old-Latin version of the New Testament. Irenaeus and Hippolytus of Rome probably knew it. Under the influence of Jerome and Augustine it was quickly accepted in the West.

There is a number of striking echoes of Jas. in 1 Pet., the first epistle of Clement and the *Pastor* of Hermas, from which many scholars infer that Jas. was known and esteemed in Rome at an early date, but was later forgotten.[1]

3. *Literary character*

James cannot be considered an epistle in the sense in which we speak of St. Paul's Epistles to the Churches. Except for the introductory greeting—which cannot be regarded as a later addition, for χαράν in v. 2 echoes χαίρειν of v. 1—it has none of the other formal parts which were usual in ancient letters: introduction of the subject, commissions, greetings, and final blessing. Moreover, Jas. was not written for a particular concrete occasion. There is not the slightest trace of any personal relationship between the

[1] Cf. A. Meyer, *Das Raetsel des Jak,* pp. 8–108.

author and the recipients. It gives no inkling of the reasons for composing it. The personal side of the author is overshadowed by the content of the work.

The closest analogies to Jas. are the Sapiential Books of the Old Testament (Proverbs, Ecclesiasticus, Wisdom), the moral parts of Tobias, the Testaments of the Twelve Patriarchs, the Ethiopian Book of Enoch, the Sayings of the Fathers (Mishna), and the epistle of Aristeas etc., and in the New Testament, the Sermon on the Mount and the moral parts of the Pauline Epistles (1 Thess. 4, 1–12; 5, 1 sqq.; Gal. 5, 13 sqq.; 6, 13 sqq.; Rom. 12 and 13; Col. 3 and 4; Heb. 13, 1–21).

The author gives his readers instructions, injunctions and warnings, all of which concern the religious and moral conduct of everyday life. Christology and Soteriology are almost entirely absent. The topics which he deals with are only loosely connected with one another.

So Jas. is to be assigned to the literary category of Paraenesis; it is a kind of Book of Proverbs. It can be described as a paraenetic work of instruction.

4. Destination

The Epistle is addressed to "the twelve Tribes which are scattered abroad". This somewhat equivocal expression can mean: 1. The Jews of the Diaspora in general, who were living scattered in pagan countries outside Palestine. But since a Christian is speaking to Christians in the Epistle (cf. 1, 18 25; 2, 1 12; 5, 7–9), this meaning is impossible. 2. The Jewish Christians of the Diaspora. 3. The whole of Christendom as the new people of God dwelling far from their true (heavenly) homeland.

There is no evidence that anyone except the Jews regarded themselves as the people of the twelve tribes (Acts 26, 7; 1 Clem. 55, 6: τὸ δωδεκάφυλον τοῦ Ἰσραήλ). Nevertheless early Christianity regarded itself as the true Israel (Gal. 6, 16: "The Israel of

God"), the true circumcision (Phil. 3, 3: "we are the circumcision"), and the seed of Abraham (Gal. 3, 29; Rom. 4, 16); so
it would not be surprising if it also called itself "the twelve tribes",
and by the expression "scattered abroad" meant that they have
their true home in Heaven (Phil. 3, 20), and on earth are in a
foreign land (1 Pet. 1, 1; 2, 11; Heb. 11, 13).

Nevertheless there can be no doubt that the Epistle is intended
for Jewish Christians, though its message is worthy of consideration by all Christians. If it is the work of James the brother of the
Lord, who was the ruler of the mother community, it may be
taken for granted that it is addressed not to Gentile Christians
or to Christians in general, but to Jewish Christians who were
within his reach, somewhere in Syria or Cilicia. The following
observations support this: The description of the readers as "hearers of the word" in 1, 22 means that hearing the word (the
Law) is one of the duties which they practise. The places where
they assemble for worship are called synagogues in 2, 2. It is
presupposed in 5, 4 that the rich are bound by the prescription
of Lev. 19, 13; Deut. 24, 14. The faults which the Epistle attacks
were characteristic of Jews: uncharitable judgments on one's
neighbour (3, 14; 4, 11), and in general all kinds of sins of the
tongue (3, 2–12; 4, 2 11), rash oaths (5, 12), the fondness for
instructing others by word rather than by exemplary conduct
(3, 1 13) etc. On the other hand there is no mention of idolatry,
drunkenness, and impurity, the specifically pagan vices against
which Paul has continually to warn the Gentile Christians (cf.
1 Cor. 6, 9–11; Gal. 5, 19–21).

The people to whom the Epistle was written were mainly
uninfluential people in country districts (4, 13; 5, 4 7), who have
to suffer financial pressure from wealthy landlords (2, 5 sqq.;
5, 1–6). The goods of this world often stir up eager desires in
them (4, 2); if a rich man comes to their liturgical assemblies they
show him special honour and precedence over the poor (2, 2–3).

5. *Its Christian origin*

In 1896 F. Spitta suggested that this Epistle was written by a Palestinian Jew for the Jews of the Diaspora, probably in pre-Christian times; he said that it was transformed into a Christian work by various minor changes including the interpolation in two places (1, 1; 2, 1) of the name Jesus Christ. Spitta based his theory on the close spiritual relationship between Jas. and Jewish Paraenesis, and on the absence of Christological passages. Others have also maintained such a theory.

In 1930 Arnold Meyer put forward another form of this theory. According to him Jas. is based on a Hellenistic Jewish pseudepigraphon of the first half of the first century A.D., in which the Patriarch Jacob writes to the twelve tribes in the Diaspora (Jas. 1, 1); the clue to the arrangement of ideas is to be found in the allegorical meanings which tradition attached to the names Jacob and Rebecca, Lia and Rachel, and the twelve sons; he points out that such ethical allegory in the interpretation of names was not new to the Jews; Philo and the Testaments of the Twelve Patriarchs provide exact parallels to Jas., and there is something similar even in the explanation of the names in Gen. 49. Meyer claims that this discovery has introduced order into the apparently haphazard series of warnings and instructions in Jas. He says that between 80 and 90 A.D. an unknown Christian—probably in Caesarea—christianized this Jewish work without entering deeply into its content.[2]

The theory that Jas. is a work of Jewish origin must be rejected. It is true that the author's spiritual roots are deeply imbedded

[2] In place of Meyer's theory G. Hartmann suggests the following: James the brother of the Lord wrote a letter of exhortation to the Christians in which he speaks to them as a father to his sons; he connected this with the interpretations of the names of the twelve sons in Gen. 29, 32 to 35, 18—which were certainly familiar to every Jew—following the order of the Patriarchs' names and their meanings; he uses each of the interpretations as a key-word on which he develops what he has to say.

in Israel and Judaism, and that the Old Testament and late Jewish literature provide almost exact parallels to his exhortations. But this Epistle contains more echoes of Our Lord's words than any other book of the New Testament; see, for example, 5, 12 (Mt. 5, 34–37); 2, 5 (Mt. 5, 3–5); 2, 8–11 (Mt. 22, 39 sq.; Rom. 13, 8–10); 2, 13 (Mt. 5, 7); 2, 15 (Mt. 6, 25); 3, 12 (Mt. 7, 16). Even if the name Jesus Christ is eliminated from 1, 1; 2, 1 as an interpolation— for the style is simpler without it—this does not achieve anything; for there are passages of an unmistakeably Christian character where no theory of interpolation can be upheld: 1, 18 (ἀπαρχή); 2, 7 ("the good name that is invoked upon you"); 2, 14 sqq. (contrast of faith and works).

And what is of still greater weight than these echoes of particular sayings of Our Lord is the fact that the whole spirit and outlook of the Epistle is very close to the spirit and outlook of Jesus. In contrast to the Jewish approach to ethics, James ignores the motive of a material reward. In spite of his harsh attitude to the rich and the threats of divine judgment (5, 1–6), he is far from the (authentically) Jewish idea that at the end the poor will be able to avenge themselves on their rich oppressors. While large parts of the Sapiental Books are devoted to rules of prudence and etiquette rather than to moral instructions, James concentrates much more strongly and more directly on ethics. Much the same applies to the eschatological thought; it is not emphasized in Wisdom literature, but in Jas., as in primitive Christianity, it is vigorously stressed.

6. The author

The Epistle is described as the work of "James, the servant of God and of Our Lord Jesus Christ" (1, 1). This can only be James "the brother of the Lord" (Gal. 1, 19), who from a very early date occupied a leading position in the community at Jerusalem.

James the son of Zebedee was martyred about 42 A.D. (Acts 12,2), so he cannot possibly be the author.

It has been disputed since patristic times whether James the brother of the Lord is identical with James the son of Alpheus, who was one of the twelve Apostles. Most Catholic exegetes say that he is. According to Gal. 1, 19 James the brother of the Lord was one of the Apostles, and Gal. 2, 9 calls him one of the pillars of the Church at Jerusalem; so he is identical with the James who is mentioned in Acts 15, 13 (12, 17; 21, 18). Only two of the Apostles were named James, and the son of Zebedee is ruled out, so the brother of the Lord is the son of Alpheus.

The Protestants and a growing minority among modern Catholics—for example, Bardenhewer, Pieper, Gaechter, Batiffol, Durand, Chaine, Cerfaux, Bonsirven, and Dupont—distinguish the brother of the Lord from the son of Alpheus; their reasons are: In the introductory greeting of Jas.—as in Jude—the title of Apostle is not used. According to John 7, 5 (and Mk. 3, 21 sq. 31 sqq. par) the "brethren" of Jesus (James, Joses or Joseph, Jude, Simon) did not believe in him; John could not have written that if two of them (James and Jude) were Apostles. The brethren of the Lord are always distinguished from the Twelve in the New Testament (Acts 1, 13 sq.; 1 Cor. 9, 5; 15, 5–8). Gal. 1, 19 is no exception, for εἰ μὴ can also have an adversative meaning ("but only"; cf. Mt. 12, 4; Lk. 24, 26; Rom. 14, 14; Acts 9, 4; H. Koch: ZntW 33, 1934, 204–209). This view is preferable.

James the brother of the Lord, who was favoured with a special appearance of the Risen Christ (1 Cor. 15, 7), must have held a leading position within the mother community at an early date (Gal. 1, 19; Acts 12, 17). Paul makes him one of the three "pillars" and places him first of the three (Gal. 2, 9). At the discussion in the Apostolic council it was his opinion which proved decisive (Acts 15, 13 sqq.). Apparently he spent most of his time in Jerusalem, but in view of 1 Cor. 9, 5 we cannot rule out the possibility that he also undertook a mission (among the Jews). In Acts 21, 18 sqq. he appears as the recognized head of the mother community.

Personally he was a firm observer of the Jewish Law, but he was not a narrow-minded Judaist, as we see from Gal. 2, 2 sqq; Acts 15, 13 sqq.; 21, 18 sq. It would not be justifiable to infer from Gal. 2, 12 that he approved of the attitude of the Judaists who came to Antioch. As a loyal follower of the Law he was highly esteemed by the unbelieving Jews.

Flavius Josephus (Ant. XX 9, 1) tells us that Ananus II the High Priest had him stoned in the interregnum between the death of Festus and the arrival of his successor Albinus in 62 A.D. The Jewish-Christian Hegesippus (about 180 A.D.) wrote an account—which is strongly tainted with legend—of the life and death of James; according to him (apud Euseb. H. E. II 23), shortly before the outbreak of the Jewish war—about 66 A.D.—James was thrown down from the battlement of the Temple, stoned, and beaten to death by a fuller.[3]

7. Authenticity

Tradition ascribes the Epistle to James the brother of the Lord. Can this ascription be accepted? It is supported by the following considerations:

1. Both content and form show clearly that this Epistle is the work of a Jewish Christian. There are various indications that it was written in Palestine, for example, the figure of three and a half years for the duration of the drought in 5, 17, as against the three years of 3 Kings 18, 1; three and a half was a colloquial round number which was frequently used in Palestine (= half of seven). The

---

[3] Nicklin and Taylor, *James, the Lord's Brother:* Church Quarterly Review 147 (1948) 46–63.

pictures of the storm-tossed wave (1, 6), of the ship which obeys the rudder (3, 4), of the fig tree and the vine (3, 12), and of the early and latter rain (5, 7) fit Palestine well, with its population of peasants and fishermen.

2. The author speaks with authority without feeling obliged to justify or defend his position. He utters sharp censure (4, 1–10), threats (5, 1–6), encouragement (1, 2–12; 5, 7–11), warnings (3, 1 sq.), and injunctions—in short he has the tone of a teacher and pastor of high authority who takes obedience for granted. This suits the picture which we must draw of the head of the mother community (Gal. 2, 9 12; Acts 15, 13 sqq.; 21, 18 sqq.). No one had a better right than he to issue such a warning to the Jewish Christians.

3. Dibelius, Windisch, Hauck and others hold the theory that Jas. is a pseudonymous work. It is difficult to reconcile this theory with the unpretentious way in which the author introduces himself: "James, the servant of God and of our Lord Jesus Christ"; nowhere can we detect anxiety to establish the work as an epistle written by the famous head of the mother community. If an unknown Christian had published the Epistle under the name of the brother of the Lord, he would certainly have added a full title ("brother of the Lord", "Apostle") to the name James.

The following serious objections are raised to the authorship of James the brother of the Lord:

1. James the brother of the Lord cannot be the author in view of the language and style of the Epistle, the constant use of the LXX, a strong influence of Greek Rhetoric, and the adoption of the Diatribe form.

The facts are as follows (see especially Chaine):

James is written in good Greek; indeed the language is purer and more cultured than in any other New Testament book, including Heb. It employs a rich vocabulary and shows a fondness for sophisticated language, e. g. δελεάζω 1, 14; ἀποκυέω 1, 15 18; τὰ ἐπιτήδεια τοῦ σώματος 2, 16; κατήφεια 4, 9. It contains the relatively high number of 63 *hapax legomena,* of which 45 occur in the LXX, and 18 are not found elsewhere in the Bible. Regarding the syntax, participles are widely used, though the genitive absolute construction does not occur. There are few periods (cf. 2, 2–4; 2, 15–16; 4, 13–15), but rhetorical elements are frequent: plays upon words (χαίρειν—χαρά 1, 1 sq.; ἀδιάκριτος — ἀνυπόκριτος 3, 17; φαινομένη—ἀφανιζομένη 4, 14, etc.), alliteration (πειρασμοῖς περιπέσητε ποικίλοις 1, 2 etc.), rime (ἐξελκόμενος καὶ δελεαζόμενος 1, 14; 1, 6). The Diatribe form is used particularly in 2, 1 to 3, 12, and is also found elsewhere: rhetorical questions (2, 14 20; 3, 11 12; 4, 4 12; 5, 13 sq.), rhetorical address (4, 13; 5, 1), invective (2, 20; 4, 4), objection of the interlocutor (2, 18), personifications (1, 15; 2, 13; 3, 5; 4, 1; 5, 3 4).

Yet the language and syntax of Jas. cannot conceal the Semitic foundation of his thought. Particles, which are a constant feature of Greek, are used sparingly in the Epistle—μέν appears only in 3, 17; it is not uncommon to find a number of statements strung together with καί (1, 11; 1, 24; 4, 7–11; 5, 2–3 14–15 17 to 18), or juxtaposed without any conjunction at all (1, 19 27; 2, 13; 3, 8–9; 5, 6). Metataxis instead of parataxis is a Semitic characteristic (1, 11 24; 4, 2 sq.; 5, 17 sq.); so is parallelism (2, 6 10 11 12; 3, 6 9; 4, 7 sqq.; 5, 2 4) and the substitution of an abstract noun in the genitive case for an adjective (ἀκροατὴς ἐπιλησμονῆς 1, 25; εὐχὴ τῆς πίστεως 5, 15; also 1, 21 23; 2, 1; 3, 6 13). Certain phrases are modelled on Old Testament language, such as ποιεῖν ἔλεος 2, 13; προσευχῇ προσεύχεσθαι 5, 17; cf. also 1, 8; 2, 1 5 8; 4, 10; 5, 4 7 10 17 18. Another Semitic trait is the use of the proverb form as contrasted with the Diatribe which likes to present its thoughts in speech and counter speech, question and answer.

These facts do not rule out the authorship of James, the brother of the Lord. Greek had been fairly widespread in Jerusalem from the time of the Macchabees, and from an early date the mother community contained a considerable number of Greek speaking Jews (Acts 6, 1 sqq.). So there can be no doubt that the head of the Christian community must have had a full command of the Greek language. Moreover, being a Galilean, James was almost certainly bilingual from childhood.

Yet it must remain an open question whether James could have written unaided an Epistle in such good Greek, showing the influence of Greek rhetoric. The ancients occasionally employed a secretary for writing letters, so there is good reason for thinking that James was assisted by a Hellenist member of the mother community who had received a rhetorical education; this would also provide an easy explanation of the practically exclusive use of the LXX (cf. 1 Pet. 5, 12—thus, e. g., Chaine, Bonsirven, Kittel, Michaelis, and Behm).

2. James the brother of the Lord was a loyal adherent of the entire Jewish Law including ceremonial law, which was considered an essential part of the worship of God; the author of Jas., on the other hand, acknowledges only a law which can be reduced to the religious and moral precepts (1, 27; 2, 8 sqq. etc.).

Against this, the history of James, the brother of the Lord, shows that he was not an extreme ritualist. Though he still obeyed the ceremonial law as a Christian, he did not consider that its observance was necessary for Gentile Christians; Acts 15, 13 sqq. distinguishes him from the fanatical legalists who were converted Pharisees, and according to Gal. 2, 9 he acknowledged the orthodoxy of St. Paul's Gospel of freedom from the Law. The Epistle was a moral exhortation to Jewish Christians, and so there was no occasion to touch upon the ceremonial prescriptions of the Law. As the Mishna tract *Sayings of the Fathers* shows, it is quite possible to find thoroughly Jewish works of that period which entirely follow the style of the wisdom sayings in the books of Wisdom and Ecclesiasticus; nothing is further from the truth than the idea that pious Judaism of the first century A.D. confined itself to the ceremonial laid down by the Thora and its forms (G. Kittel).

Even the expression "Law of liberty" in 1, 25 and 2, 12 could perfectly well come from James, for it means the word of God as a norm for human action, whose observance liberates from the slavery of sin.

3. One would expect a work by a brother of the Lord to speak at length about Jesus, his Messiahship, his exemplary life, the saving effect of his Death, his Resurrection and Ascension into majesty in Heaven. There is not a word about this in Jas.

It is true that the personal side of Jesus plays no part in Jas. It is not he, but Old Testament figures (Job, Elias and the prophets), who are held up as examples to the readers. This is in sharp contrast to 1 Pet., which resembles Jas. in many other respects; in it the Passion of Christ is held up both as a model and as the cause of our salvation (1 Pet. 2, 21–25).

But it should not be forgotten that the whole of Jas. is permeated with clear echoes of the words of Jesus (see above n. 5 and Schlatter pp. 9–19). In moral elevation Jas. is far superior to Old Testament wisdom literature. This superiority can be explained only if the author was deeply influenced by Christ's moral teaching. The author's purpose was to instruct and exhort his readers, and this end was attained by presenting Christ's moral teaching without entering into Christology. Moreover, it should be noted that the Epistle speaks of the proximate Second Coming of the Lord (Christ) and of his judgment (4, 7 sqq.). The readers are reminded in 2, 7 of their intimate union with Christ which is brought about by Baptism. According to 5, 14 anointing of the sick is done in the name of the Lord (Jesus Christ), who thereby becomes present.

So the balance of evidence favours the view that the author of the Epistle was the brother of the Lord.

8. Date

The scholars who consider this Epistle the work of James the brother of the Lord are not agreed on the date of its composition. Some place it shortly before the death of James, that is in the early sixties, while others consider it the earliest surviving book of the primitive Church, and date it to the middle forties, before the Apostolic Council or St. Paul's first missionary journey.

The early date is favoured by many Catholic exegetes including Belser, Bardenhewer and Meinertz, and this is also the view of some conservative Protestants such as Th. Zahn, G. Kittel, and W. Michaelis. Among their arguments are the following: Christianity is portrayed as Judaism which has reached maturity (1, 1). The author does not seem to know of Gentile-Christian communities. The Epistle makes no allusion to the problem of the validity of Mosaic ceremonial law; it was only after St. Paul's first missionary journey that this problem became acute—but if the Epistle had been written after that time it could hardly have passed over the matter in silence. Moreover, it is inconceivable that after the Apostolic Council James the brother of the Lord could have produced a polemic like 2, 14–26 (faith and works), which does not refer to Paul or affect the real Paul; for at the time of the council James had learned Paul's true doctrine on the relation between faith and Law, and had approved its orthodoxy. But before the council he might possibly have written such a polemic, and he might even have thought it advisable to impugn a view which had some connection with Paul even though it was not the real Paul (G. Kittel).

Other scholars prefer the later date. They have various reasons for their preference. F. W. Maier thinks that the urge to write had not been aroused as early as the forties; Chaine, Bonsirven and Behm think that the polemic in 2, 14–26 is directed against a misinterpretation of the Pauline doctrine on faith and works (cf. 1, 22 23 25 with Rom. 2, 13; 3, 14 with Rom. 11, 18; 2, 9 11 with Gal. 2, 18, Rom. 2, 25 27); Gutbrod (ThWB IV, 1073 to 1075) considers that in view of its attitude to the Law Jas. must belong to a period after the controversy about the validity of the Old Testament Law.

Those who deny that James is author place the composition of the Epistle at various points between 70 and 150 A.D. (Hauck: not long after Paul's death; Arnold Meyer: 80–90; Windisch: 70–100; Dibelius: 80–130; K. Aland: beginning of the second century).

§ 48. THE EPISTLE OF ST. JUDE

Commentaries: (a) Felten, Chaine, Vrede, see before §§ 47 and 49.

(b) F. Spitta, *Der 2 Petr und der Brief des Jud,* Halle 1885. J. B. Mayor, *The Epistle of St. Jude and the Second Epistle of St. Peter,* London 1907. Knopf, Bigg, Wohlenberg, see before § 49. Hollmann-Busset, *Jud und 2 Petr* (GoettNT 3). Studies: F. W. Maier, *Der Judasbrief. Seine Echtheit, Abfassungszeit und Leser* (BSt XI 1–2: 1906). K. Pieper, *Zur Frage nach den Irrlehrern des Jud:* Ntl Untersuchungen, Paderborn 1939, 66–71. R. Leconte: DB Suppl IV (1949) 1285–1298.

1. *Content and structure*

THE epistle is an energetic call to fight against false teachers of Gnosticism and Antinomianism.

Introductory greeting 1–2.

1. Occasion of writing: the intrusion of false teachers who preach dissoluteness and deny Christ 3–4.

2. Wrongness and punishment of the false teachers 5–19: (a) he reminds them of the judgments which have fallen upon similar evildoers (Israel in the desert, the sinful angels, Sodom and Gomorrha) 5–7. (b) In a polemical tone he gives a description of the vicious activity of the false teachers 9–13 16 19; (c) Enoch prophesied the punishment which awaits them, and the Apostles foretold their coming in the last time 14–15 and 17–18.

3. He exhorts the readers to remain loyal to the faith 20–21, and

instructs them about the treatment of (heretics and [?]) erring people 22–23.

4. Final doxology 24–25.

2. Purpose

The author intends to warn his readers against a small group (τινές, v. 4) who have recently come among them and are a serious peril to them because of their false teaching and sinful lives.

These intruders are Christians, for they take part in the Agape (v. 12). It is quite clear from the description of them that they are Antinomians. They are led only by their sensual appetites (v. 10), they walk according to their own desires (v. 16 18), defile their flesh by foul sins of impurity (v. 8 23)—perhaps by unnatural sin (v. 7)—lead a voluptuous life of pleasure (v. 4 12), disseminate their teaching for gain (v. 11), and court the favour of the wealthy (v. 16). They justify their immoral conduct by appealing to the grace which God has given them (v. 4).

It is difficult to form a clear picture of their doctrine, for the references to it in the Epistle are obscure. Probably v. 4 should be translated "the only sovereign Lord and Ruler, Jesus Christ", and v. 8 "these men despise the dominion (of Jesus Christ)" (Chaine and others); in that case they are accused of denying the eminence of Christ. The Epistle does not make it quite clear whether this means a practical denial by disobeying his commandments, or a doctrinal denial by not acknowledging his position of eminence and power in heaven.

They are also accused of blaspheming majesties (δόξαι v. 8), that is, of depreciating majesties by denying them the acknowledgment which is their due. These "majesties" are probably to be understood as good angels which late Judaism regarded as custodians of the world order. According to Acts 7, 38 53; Gal. 3, 19; Heb. 2, 2 the Old Testament Law was given by angels.

Probably the explanation is that the intruders consider themselves spiritual men (pneumatics) who are not bound by the eternal laws and ordinances which control the world and are under no obligation to their custodians. They even resist God's ordinance (v. 11), speak insolently against God (v. 15), and speak proud things (v. 16). The fundamental reason for their disavowal of Christ and blasphemy of the majesty of the angels is that they have not the Spirit (v. 19), and so do not know the heavenly powers, but only things which lie in the natural sphere (v. 10). The author appears to mean that the intruders engage in erroneous speculations which attack the honour of Christ and permit the intruders to lead a licentious life.

So their doctrine was probably an Antinomian Gnosis. Yet there is no justification for connecting it with the developed Gnosticism of the second century. Probably the meaning of v. 19 is simply that the false teachers claim for themselves and deny to the other Christians the possession of the Spirit and consequent freedom from the moral law. The intruders whom Jude describes are rather to be compared to the exponents of an embryonic Gnosis who are mentioned in 1 Cor., Col., the Pastoral Epistles and the Apc. There is a striking resemblance between these false teachers and the Nicolaites of Apc. 2, 6 14 sq. 20 sq. who are also accused of sins of unchastity. So the essence of their error lay not in the doctrinal field, but in the sphere of morals.

3. Destination

The introductory greeting is expressed in very general terms: "to them that are beloved in God the Father and preserved in Jesus Christ and called", and the ending is not like the conclusion of a letter; yet it would be unjustifiable to say that the Epistle is addressed to the whole Church.

The content and purpose of the Epistle show that it was

addressed to a quite determinate group of readers; since the Epistle does not contain any greetings, it was probably intended for a group of communities rather than for one single community.

It is disputed whether the Epistle was addressed to Jewish or Gentile Christians. Most Protestant commentators and almost all Catholics consider that it was intended for Jewish Christians; they point out that throughout the Epistle the proofs are drawn from the Old Testament and from Jewish Apocalyptic literature (v. 9–14) and legends (v. 9 11), and that such a line of argument would be presented only to Jewish Christians and only they would understand it.

Yet, as Chaine, Leconte, and U. Holzmeister point out, the intruders were Gnostic Antinomians, so it is more likely that both they and the readers were Gentile Christians. As the Pauline Epistles show, such Antinomianism, especially in sexual matters, appeared among Gentile rather than Jewish Christians (cf. Gal. 5, 13; 1 Cor. 6, 12 sqq.), and it was a more serious danger to Gentile Christians than to former Jews. On the other hand it is not impossible that the Epistle was addressed to Hellenistic-Jewish Christians, for pagan ideas and practices could more easily affect the somewhat heterodox Judaism of the Diaspora than the Judaism of Palestine (cf. the false teachers in Col.).

It is impossible to be certain where the readers lived. Perhaps they were smallish communities in Syria.

4. Author and authenticity

The author of the Epistle calls himself "brother of James". This James can only be the "brother of the Lord" (Gal. 1, 19; 2, 9; 1 Cor. 15, 7; Jas. 1, 1), who was highly respected both in the mother community and throughout the primitive Church.

So Jude is the "brother" of Jesus who is mentioned in the third or fourth place in Mk. 6, 3 par. Like his celebrated brother he probably did not belong to the college of Apostles, for in v. 1 he does not call himself an Apostle, and in v. 17 he seems to distinguish himself from "the Apostles of Our Lord Jesus Christ" (cf. § 47, 6).

This is all we know about him. We have no knowledge of whether he always remained in Palestine or undertook missionary journeys (1 Cor. 9, 5). Hegesippus (apud Euseb. H. E. III 20, 1 sqq.) says that towards the end of Domitian's reign (81–96) two of Jude's grandsons were tried by the Emperor on suspicion of Davidism, but were acquitted as harmless; he says that they were rulers of Christian communities (apparently in Palestine), and lived into the reign of Trajan (98–117).

The critics impugn the authenticity of the Epistle on the ground that it combats later Gnostic errors, and so cannot have been written before the end of the first century. This cannot be upheld (cf. n. 2).

In favour of the authorship of Jude the brother of the Lord is the unpretentious description which he gives of himself, "servant of Jesus Christ and brother of James." A later pseudepigrapher would hardly have written under the name of Jude the undistinguished and almost unknown brother of the Lord.

5. Date

The Epistle was not written before the middle of the sixties. Expressions like "your most holy faith" (v. 20), and "the faith once delivered to the saints" (v. 3), show that the date is rather late.

Jude is used by 2 Pet.; so if the latter is Peter's work (cf. § 51, 5), Jude must have been written shortly before Peter's death in 64 or 67 A.D. (cf. § 49); if 2 Pet. is pseudonymous (§ 51, 5), then Jude could have been written between 70 and 80 A.D. (Chaine), for Jude could still have been alive in that decade.

There is no necessity to place its date later than that. On the other hand, we are not obliged to date it before 70 A.D. because the destruction of Jerusalem is not mentioned among the punishments in v. 5–7, for the author draws his proofs from punishments which took place in antiquity, and is following a Jewish tradition about sins and punishments (cf. Ecclus. 16, 6–10; Wis. 10, 4–6; 3 Macch. 2, 4 sqq.: the giants, the generation of the deluge, the men of Sodom, the generation in the desert; Lk. 17, 26 sqq.).

6. Attestation

By about 200 A.D. Jude was firmly established in the Canon in Rome (Muratorian fragment), Carthage (Tertullian), and Alexandria (Clement, Origen). Cyril of Jerusalem, and probably Eusebius of Caesarea also, like the Latin Fathers, include it among the canonical Scriptures. Origen, Eusebius, Jerome and Didymus of Alexandria are aware that a number of Churches do not accept it; evidently they have in mind the ecclesiastical province of Antioch where the four smaller Catholic Epistles were placed among the *Antilegomena* until about 400 A.D.

The authorship of Jude the brother of the Lord was sometimes denied on internal evidence, according to Didymus because of v. 9 (Michael's struggle with the devil), and according to Jerome because of v. 14 sq. (the citation from the Book of Enoch). There is a full account in Leconte.

THE EPISTLES OF ST. PETER

Commentaries: (a) L. J. Hundhausen, *Das erste (bzw. zweite) Pontifikalschreiben des Apostelfuersten Petrus,* Mainz 1873 (bzw. 1878). J. Felten, *Die zwei Briefe des hl. Petrus und der Judasbrief,* Regensburg 1929. W. Vrede, [4]1932 (Bonner NT 9). (b) Ch. Bigg (1 and 2 Peter, Jude), [2]1910 (ICC). R. Knopf (1 and 2 Peter and Jude), 1912 (Meyer XII[7]). G. Wohlenberg (1 and 2 Peter and Jude), [3]1923 (Zahn XV). J. W. C. Wand (1 and 2 Peter and Jude), London 1934.

§ 49. THE LIFE OF ST. PETER THE APOSTLE

M. Meinertz, LThK VIII (1936) 131–135. U. Holzmeister, *Vita S. Petri,* Paris 1937 (Separately printed from his Com. on 1 Peter). E. Fascher, Art. *Petrus,* Pauly-Wissowa, R.-E. XIX, 2 (1938) 1337 ff. H. Katzenmayer, IKZ 1938–1941; 1944 and 1945. H. Strathmann, *Die Stellung des Petrus in der Urkirche:* ZsyTh 20 (1943) 223–283. E. Stauffer, *Zur Vor- und Fruehgeschichte des Primatus Petri:* ZKG 62 (1943/44) 1–34. O. Cullmann, *Petrus. Juenger—Apostel—Maertyrer. Das historische und das theologische Petrusproblem,* Zurich 1952. See also footnote 1, § 49. B. Haesler, *Sprachlich-grammatische Bemerkungen zu Gal 2, 6:* ThLZ 82 (1957) 393 sq. Th. Klauser, *Die römische Petrustradition im Lichte der neuen Ausgrabungen unter der Peterskirche,* Köln-Opladen 1957.

PETER'S proper name was Simon in Greek—in Semitic this was Symeon, which appears only in Acts 15, 14; 2 Pet. 1, 1. He was a native of Bethsaida on the Lake of Genesareth (John 1, 44), the son of a certain John (John 1, 42; 21, 17), about whom nothing further is known. In Mt. 16, 17 his father is called Jona (βαριωνά), which is probably not a contraction but an erroneous reading of the contracted spelling of Johanan. Peter had a brother Andrew (John 1, 40), and according to 1 Cor. 9, 5; Mk. 1, 29 sqq. he was married. At the time of the public ministry of Jesus he lived in the nearby town of Capharnaum where he had a house (Mk. 1, 29), and worked with his brother Andrew as fisherman (Mk. 1, 16 sq.). Like other men of the same outlook, he was attracted by the movement of John the Baptist.

Andrew introduced Peter to Jesus (John 1, 40 sqq.); it was on this occasion that Jesus told him, as a sign of his later dignity, that he would be called Cepha (Aramaic for rock; Greek Πέτρος). It was probably only at the call of the Apostles that he was actually given the new name (Mk. 3, 16), and its meaning was revealed at Caesarea Philippi (Mt. 16, 18). The Aramaic form Cephas never appears in the Gospels, though Paul uses it; the Evangelists use only the Greek equivalent Πέτρος with masculine ending.

When Jesus began his Galilean ministry on the arrest of the Baptist (Mk. 1, 14 par), he called Peter and his brother Andrew to leave their fishing and follow him (Mk. 1, 16 sqq.; Lk. 5, 1 sqq.). Peter was energetic and decisive in action, but impetuous; among the twelve Apostles whom Jesus chose from a larger group of disciples (Mk. 3, 14 sqq.), he was undisputed leader, and his name always stands first in the lists of Apostles. He was one of the three Apostles who were special intimates of Jesus, and who alone witnessed the raising of Jairus' daughter, the Transfiguration, and the Agony in the Garden; even amongst these three Peter is always named first, being placed before James and John, the sons of Zebedee (Mk. 5, 37; 9, 2; 14, 33).

As spokesman of the Apostles at Caesarea Philippi he acknowledged Jesus as the Messias sent by God (Mk. 8, 29; John 6, 68 sq.), and received the promise that Jesus would build the Church on him as upon a rock, and would give him the power of the keys in the kingdom of God and the authority to bind and loose (Mt. 16, 18 sq.).

Peter's deep respect and burning love for his Master is proved by his conduct at the washing of the feet (John 13, 6 sqq.), at the news of Judas' treachery and the flight of the other Apostles (John 13, 23 sqq.), and at the arrest of Jesus in the Garden of Gethsemani (John 18, 10 sq.). But he had reason to regret bitterly his rashness in declaring his readiness to die with Jesus (Mk. 14, 29 sqq.); he denied his Master three times through fear of men (Mk. 14, 66 sqq.), but atoned for his sin by immediate repentance (Mk. 14, 72). The Risen Christ distinguished Peter by appearing to him alone before showing himself to any of the other Apostles or disciples (1 Cor. 15, 5; Lk. 24, 34). At the appearance at the Lake of Genesareth he fulfilled the promise recorded in Mt. 16, 18 sq., by solemnly appointing Peter supreme ruler of his Church (John 21, 15 sqq.).

Acts shows that Peter was head and leader of the primitive Church. He initiated the election of a successor to Judas the traitor (1, 15 sqq.), and was the first to preach at Pentecost (2, 1 sqq.), in the Temple after the cure of the lame man (3, 1 sqq.), and before the council (4, 8 sqq.; 5, 29 sqq.). It was he who received Cornelius and his household, the first Gentiles to enter the Christian Church (10, 1 sqq.). And after his conversion Paul thought it necessary to visit Peter in Jerusalem (Gal. 1, 18).

He was imprisoned about 42 A.D. by Herod Agrippa I, who intended to execute him publicly after the Pasch, but he was miraculously freed, and went "unto another place" (Acts 12, 1 sqq.; cf. § 37, 1). At the time of the Apostolic Council in 49 A.D. he was back in Jerusalem, where he with James the brother of the Lord and John the son of Zebedee formed the "pillars" of the Church (Gal. 2, 1–9; Acts 15, 1 sqq.). Soon afterwards he stayed in Antioch where he was sharply rebuked by Paul for allowing Jewish Christians from Jerusalem to make him cease eating with the Gentile Christians (Gal. 2, 11 sqq.; cf. § 37, 1).

We are poorly informed about Peter's subsequent life, and his missionary journeys outside Palestine (cf. 1 Cor. 9, 5 and Gal. 2, 7). From the destination mentioned in 1 Pet. 1, 1 Eusebius H. E. III 1, 2; 4, 2 infers that he had preached to the Jews of the Diaspora in Pontus, Galatia, Cappadocia, Asia and Bithynia, but this conclusion is not inescapable (cf. § 50). There is equally little certainty that Peter worked in Corinth, where according to 1 Cor. 1, 12 there was a Cephas party, though Dionysius, bishop of Corinth about 170 A.D. says in his Epistle to the Roman community that Peter and Paul had planted the Corinthian Church (apud Euseb. H. E. II 25, 8).

On the other hand it must be accepted as historical fact that Peter spent the last years of his life at Rome and suffered martyrdom there; even non-Catholic scholars in modern times generally agree about this.[1] It is implied in 1 Pet. 5, 13 (Babylon =

[1] Cf. H. Lietzmann, *Petrus und Paulus in Rom²*, Berlin 1927; Idem, *Petrus roemischer Maertyrer:* SB Berlin 1936 XXIX; against the most recent denials H. Dannebauer (HistZ 146, 1932, 239–262; 159, 1939, 81–88), J. Haller (*Das*

Rome)[2], the first epistle of Clement (5, 4) and Ignatius of Antioch (Rom. 4, 3: "I do not order you as Peter and Paul did"). It is said explicitly by Dionysius Bishop of Corinth (apud Euseb. H. E. II 25, 8: Peter and Paul worked in Rome and suffered martyrdom there together), Irenaeus (*Haer.* III 1, 1: " . . . when Peter and Paul were preaching the Gospel and founding the Church in Rome"), Tertullian (*De praescript.* 36: Peter was crucified in Rome; *Adv. Marcion.* IV, 5: Peter and Paul left to the Romans the Gospel sealed in their blood), Clement of Alexandria (apud Euseb. H. E. IV 14, 6: "When Peter had publicly preached the word and announced the Gospel in Rome . . ."), and Gaius the Roman priest, who about 200 A.D. in his *Dialogue with Proclus* speaks of the trophies (τρόπαια) of Peter on the Vatican and of Paul on the road to Ostia (apud Euseb. H. E. II 25, 7).

Papsttum I, [2]1950, 1–17; 472–485) and H. Heussi (*War Petrus in Rom?* Gotha 1936; *War Petrus wirklich Maertyrer?* Leipzig 1937; *Neues zur Petrusfrage,* Jena 1939). See on this E. Molland: ThLZ 1937, 439–444. Cf. also G. Krueger, ZntW 31 (1932), 301–306; H. Katzenmayer, IKZ 1938, 129 sqq.; P. Meinhold, ZKG 58 (1939) 82–129; M. Dibelius, *Rom und die Christen im ersten Jh.,* 1942 (SB Heidelberg 1941/42: 2); O. Perler, Div. Thomas (Fr.) 22 (1944) 433–441; W. G. Kuemmel, ThRdsch 1948, 34–40; B. Altaner, HistJb 62/69 (1949) 25–30; E. Schaefer, EvTh 1950/51, 459–479; and especially Cullmann, *Petrus* p. 63–169. St. Giet, *Le témoignage de Clément de Rome sur la venue à Rome de S. Pierre:* RevSR 29 (1955) 123–136. K. Heussi, *Die roemische Petrustradition in kritischer Sicht,* Tuebingen 1955 [Peter was not in Rome; it follows from Gal. 2, 6 (ἦσαν) that he was already dead when this Epistle was written.] H. Katzenmayer impugns Heussi's interpretation of Gal. 2, 6: IKZ 42 (1952) 178–181. On O. Cullmann's *Petrus* cf. Benoit (RB 1953, 565–579), M. Goguel (RHPhR 35, 1955, 196–209), and A. Gilg (ThZ 11, 1955, 185–206); the whole international literature is critically surveyed by R. Beaupère: Istina 1, 1955, 347–372. St. Lyonnet, *De ministerio Romano S. Petri ante adventum S. Pauli:* Verbum Domini 33 (1955) 143–154 [negative]. G. Schulze-Kadelbach, *Die Stellung des Petrus in der Urchristenheit:* ThLZ 81 (1956) 1–14. K. Aland, *Wann starb Petrus? Eine Bemerkung zu Gal 2, 6:* NTSt II (1956) 267–275.

[2] According to Boismard (see § 54) "the two witnesses" Apc. 11 to 13 symbolize the two Apostles Peter and Paul who were killed by Nero in Rome (v. 8 "the great city" is Rome, and the clause "where their Lord also was crucified" is a gloss, inspired probably by Mt. 23, 37); Munck (see ibid.) also holds the same view though for other reasons.

The only uncertain points are the time of his arrival in Rome, the duration of his ministry there, and the year of his death. The tradition that he came to Rome in the second year of the Emperor Claudius (= 42 A.D.), and occupied the see of Rome for twenty five years on end, goes back to about 200 A.D., but it is not well founded (cf. § 37, 1).[3] Some present day scholars infer from 1 Cor. 1, 12 that Peter arrived in Corinth shortly after Paul's departure and worked there for some time[4]; from there, they say, he went on to Rome, but he left the capital before Paul wrote Rom. (spring 58), and travelled probably to the communities of Asia Minor which are addressed in 1 Pet.; Mark was with him during this sojourn in Rome, that is, between 53 A.D. and the end of 57 (cf. § 23). Peter, according to them, did not return to Rome until Paul had been released and had begun his missionary journeys (in 63 A.D.).

Peter's death—tradition says that he was crucified—took place in the later years of Nero's reign (d. 68 A.D.). The majority view now-a-days is that he suffered in Nero's persecution of 64 A.D., though others consider 67 A.D. a more probable date.

§ 50. THE FIRST EPISTLE OF ST. PETER

Commentaries: See before §§ 47 and 49; also (a) U. Holzmeister, 1937 (CSS).—
(b) H. Gunkel, [3]1917 (GoettNT 3). A. Schlatter, *Petrus und Paulus nach dem ersten Petrusbrief,* Stuttgart 1937. E. G. Selwyn, *The First Epistle of St. Peter*[2], London 1947. F. Beare, *The First Epistle of Peter,* Oxford 1948. C. E. Carnfield, *The First Epistle of Peter,* London 1950.
Studies: Th. Spoerri, *Der Gemeindegedanke in 1 Petr* (Ntl Forschungen II 2: 1925). B. Reicke, *The Disobedient Spirits and Christian Baptism. A Study of 1 Pet.* 3,

[3] Cf. C. Schmidt, *Studien zu den Pseudo-Clementinen,* 1929, 357 sqq. (TU 46/1).

[4] But Lietzmann's suggestion (SB Berlin 1930, 153 sqq.: *Die Reisen des Petrus*) cannot be upheld; according to it, Peter was the guiding spirit of the anti-Pauline (judaistic) propaganda in Paul's missionary territory, and as such he came to Galatia, Corinth, and (before 58 A.D.) to Rome; cf. M. Goguel, RHPh 14 (1934) 461–500.

19 and its Context (Acta Sem. Neotest. Upsal. XIII: 1946). R. Bultmann, *Be-kenntnis- und Liedfragmente in 1 Petr:* CNT XI (1947) 1–14. N. A. Dahl, *Dopet* (Baptism) *i Efesierbrevet:* Svensk Th. Kvartalskrift 1945, 85–103. F. L. Cross, *1 Peter. A Paschal Liturgy,* 1954. W. G. van Unnik, *The Teaching of Good Works in 1 Pet.:* NT Studies 1 (1954) 92–110. [The epistle is the work of Peter, who used the services of Silvanus when writing it. The agreement with the Pauline Epistles is not due to dependence; it is parallelism.] E. Lohse, *Paraenese und Kerygma in 1 Petr:* ZntW 45 (1954) 68–90 [1Peter is not a Baptism sermon (Perdelwitz, Preisker). In spite of a certain undeniable closeness to Pauline theology, there is no literary dependence on Paul. Its relationship to 1 Clement justifies us assuming that this is an Epistle to the suffering communities of Asia Minor written by the Roman Church under the authority of Peter.] W. Nauck, see footnote 4, § 27. C. F. D. Moule, *The Nature and Purpose of 1 Peter:* NTSt 3 (1956) 1–11. M.-E. Boismard, *Une liturgie baptismale dans la Prima Petri* (son influence sur Tit., 1 Jn., Col., Jac.): RB 63 (1956) 182–208; 64 (1957) 161–183.

1. Content and structure

THE theme of the first Epistle of St. Peter is the preservation of the Christian faith in sufferings and persecutions.

Introductory greeting 1, 1–2. The introduction 1, 3–12 (praise of God for the greatness of the salvation which He has sent to the Christians) is followed by exhortations which are often interrupted by doctrinal passages. The Epistle is loosely con-structed, but the following three parts may be distinguished:

First part: Exhortations of a general nature 1, 13 to 2, 10:

1. Lead a blameless life looking to God who is holy and the strict Judge, and think of the high price which was paid for your Redemption (the Blood of Christ) 1, 13–21.

2. Practise sincere brotherly love corresponding to the new life into which you have been reborn, so that you may become ever more perfectly incorporated into the new spiritual temple whose corner stone is Christ 1, 22 to 2, 10.

Second part: Special injunctions for particular states of life 2, 11 to 4, 6:

1. Give the lie to heathen slanders by honourable conduct 2, 11–12.

2. Obey the (pagan) authorities because of your position as Christians 2, 13–17.

3. Slaves, obey your masters, even unjust masters, looking to the sufferings of the innocent Christ 2, 18–25.

4. Wives, be subject to your husbands, and seek to win them (to the Christian faith) by a virtuous life, which is the true adornment of a God-fearing woman 3, 1–6.

5. Husbands, treat your wives with consideration and honour, as being companions in the faith 3, 7.

6. Let all be full of love and consideration for your fellow men so that you may attain eternal life 3, 8–12.

7. Answer the slanders of the pagans by candid and prudent explanation and by faultless conduct 3, 13–17.

8. The example of Christ shows you the blessing of innocent suffering; He, the Just, died for the unjust (Descent of Christ into Hell and the power of Baptism) 3, 18–22.

9. Give up entirely your former pagan life of sin, even though the pagans revile you for doing so 4, 1–6.

Third part: Exhortations in view of the time of suffering which has befallen them and of the coming judgment 4, 7 to 5, 11:

1. The proximity of the end of all things calls for caution, brotherly love, hospitality and a right use of the gifts of grace for the honour of God 4, 7–11.

2. The present sufferings should not lead you astray, for they are inseparable from being a Christian, and they bring a reward from the Lord 4, 12–19.

3. The elders (presbyters) should fulfil their duty as shepherds with wisdom, the young men should be subject to the elders, and all members of the community should display humility, vigilance and perseverance in the persecution which has now broken out 5, 1–11.

Conclusion 5, 12–14: Silvanus wrote (composed) the Epistle; greetings and blessing.

2. Destination

The Epistle is addressed to "the strangers dispersed through Pontus, Galatia, Cappadocia, Asia, and Bithynia, elect" (1, 1). These names must refer to ancient districts and not to Roman provinces, for Pontus and Bithynia were not two separate Roman provinces, there was only one *Provincia Bithynia-Pontus*.

From the description which the Epistle gives of the recipients (1, 14–18; 2, 9 sq.; 4, 3 sq.), it is obvious that they were Gentile Christians; however, in the districts of Pisidia and Lycaonia, in the south of the Province of Galatia, the Christian communities contained a considerable number of Jewish Christians (Acts 13–14). So this epistle must have been intended for the communities in the northern and western part of Asia Minor.

Diaspora is not used in its proper sense; the word refers here to the Christians as the true new People of God, who live scattered among pagan communities, and who regard themselves as strangers on earth, because they have their true home in Heaven (cf. Phil. 3, 20; Heb. 13, 14; 1 Clem. Inscr.; *Pastor Hermae*, Sim. 1; *Ep. ad Diogn.* 5, 5; 6, 8). So the author speaks of the time of their "sojourning here" (παροικία 1, 17), and calls them "strangers and pilgrims" (2, 11).

3. Occasion and purpose

The author says explicitly that the work is intended to strengthen the recipients in their faith (5, 12). So this Epistle is designed as a word of exhortation, though it also contains a number of rather short doctrinal passages which are intended to justify the injunctions: 1, 3 23 (rebirth); 1, 3–9 (the heavenly inheritance); 1, 10–12 (the Old Testament prophets foretold salvation); 1, 18–21 (summary of the primitive Christian message); 2, 4–10 (the Church); 3, 18–22 (death, descent into hell, preaching in hell, resurrection and ascension of Christ; effect of Baptism.) All the exhortations aim at calling the readers to endure steadfastly, indeed cheerfully, the sufferings and trials which will soon come upon them, or have already begun.

The immediate occasion of the Epistle is unknown, but we may infer from it that there was a danger of recent sufferings causing the readers to waver in their faith. The Epistle speaks of "divers temptations" by which they have been "made sorrowful" (1, 6; cf. 4, 12 sqq.), mentions that the pagans slanderously accuse them of being "evil doers" (2, 12; 3, 16), but also says that they must suffer for the sake of their Christian name or faith (4, 16). According to 4, 15 they are also accused of crimes ("murderer, thief, railer"), and probably also of being a political danger (ἀλλοτριεπίσκοπος = interfering in other people's affairs). They are exhorted to refute these malicious charges by leading a blameless life (2, 12 15; 3, 2 13 sqq.). Evidently judicial proceedings had already been taken against them and penalties had been inflicted (cf. 3, 13–17; 4, 15–19). "If they succeeded in clearing themselves from such charges, apparently they were occasionally punished as adherents of the Christian sect (4, 16); but the conclusion was never drawn in the first instance that the state should proceed against this sect as such."[5]

So the civil authority had not yet begun its violent persecutions of Christians. This view is supported by the hypothetical form of 1, 6; 3, 14; 4, 16, and by the fact that the same kind of tribulations are falling on the Christians of the whole world (5, 9), as well as by the emphasis on the duty of honouring the Emperor and obeying him and his officials (2, 13–17).

4. Author and authenticity

In the introductory greeting the author calls himself "Peter, an apostle of Jesus Christ", and in 5, 1 he claims to have been an

[5] M. Dibelius, *Rom.* etc. (see above n. 1) p. 18.

"(eye-)witness of the sufferings of Christ". In 5, 13 he calls Mark his (spiritual) son, which immediately reminds us of how Peter went to the house of John Mark's mother when he was miraculously freed from prison (Acts 12, 12); it also calls to mind the ancient tradition that Mark served Peter as interpreter (cf. § 23, 2). Moreover, this Epistle contains clear echoes of synoptic sayings of Our Lord: cf. 3, 9 14 17; 2, 20; 4, 14 with Mt. 5, 10 sq.; Lk. 6, 22;—1, 13 with Lk. 12, 35;—2, 12 with Mt. 5, 16;—4, 10 with Lk. 12, 42. Yet this epistle does not emphasize the Jesus of the Sermon on the Mount, as Jas. does; here, as in Paul, the stress is on Christ who achieves his work of Redemption by his death and resurrection (Hauck). Nevertheless we may infer that this is the work of a personal disciple of Jesus from his fairly frequent references to the example of Christ's patient suffering, in 3, 18; 4, 1 and particularly 2, 21–24 where verse 23 refers to Our Lord's bearing before his Jewish and pagan judges, although Peter was probably not an eyewitness at the actual trial.

The authenticity of this Epistle has been impugned by the critics since F. Chr. Baur. The following is a summary of their principal objections to Petrine authorship:

1. Language, style and consistent use of the LXX. The author writes good Hellenistic Greek. The Semitic colouring of his language and style is less noticeable than is the case with Paul. His diction has not the grace and perfection of Jas. and Heb., but it does not fall far short of them. Moreover, he occasionally uses the rhetorical devices of good Greek writers, for example, sharp verbal antitheses (2, 14 23; 3, 18; 4, 6; 5, 2), cumulation of synonyms (1, 8 10; 2, 35; 3, 4), juxtaposition of a number of (negative) adjectives for the sake of assonance (1, 4 19), denoting of the same matter by a double expression, first negatively and then positively (1, 14 sq. 18 sq. 23; 2, 16; 5, 2 sq.); cf. also 4, 11; 2, 22 sqq. He also displays a keen ear for rhythmic arrangement of his text (for example, in the introductory "hymn" 1, 3–12). The Old Testa-

ment citations are always from the LXX; indeed the author is so familiar with it that his vocabulary is saturated with it; of his 61 *hapax legomena,* 34 or 35 occur in the LXX. Only someone very familiar with the LXX could have written 2, 1–10.

2. The close kinship with Pauline Theology and the numerous contacts with passages in the Pauline Epistles (especially Rom. and Eph.). The theological ideas of 1 Pet. are strongly reminiscent of Paul. The Epistle fundamentally presents in the same way as Paul the themes of Christ, the saving power of his death and the new life which is sent through Christ. He even uses Pauline expressions and formulae (ἐν Χριστῷ 3, 16; 5, 10 14; ζωοποιεῖν 3, 18; ἀναστροφή 1, 15 18; 2, 12; 3, 1 2 16 etc.).

The contacts with Rom. and Eph. are particularly striking, for example, 1, 14 with Rom. 12, 2; 2, 4–8 with Rom. 9, 32 sq. (the linguistic form of the citation from Isaias); 4, 1 with Rom. 6, 7; 4, 10 sq. with Rom. 12, 6; 3, 9 with Rom. 12, 17; 2, 13–17 with Rom. 13, 1–7; 3, 22 with Eph. 1, 20 sq.; 3, 18 with Rom. 5, 2, Eph. 2, 18 and 3, 12; 5, 8 with Eph. 6, 10 sqq. We may not conclude from these that the author of 1 Pet. knew and used both these Pauline Epistles. Form Criticism has shown that the New Testament Epistles made much more use than was formerly suspected of traditional, particularly liturgical and paraenetic, material. So the suggestion of literary dependence has been received with scepticism.

There are also contacts between 1 Pet. and Heb. (see Holzmeister particularly), but these do not rest upon literary dependence. The undeniable resemblances between this Epistle and Jas. (cf. especially Arn. Meyer), are to be attributed either to dependence on the same primitive traditional material or more probably, as Chaine suggests, to literary use of Jas. by 1 Peter.[6]

---

[6] Selwyn pp. 363–466 makes a very detailed examination of the relations between 1 Pet. and the other NT Epistles, but denies that there is any literary dependence. In regard to the relation of 1 Pet. to Eph. this is also the view of Percy: *Die Probleme der Kolosser- und Epheserbriefe,* 1946, 433–440.

3. The conditions which 1 Pet. presupposes do not fit the sixties, but point to the last years of Domitian's reign (d. 96 A.D.). The faith of the Christian communities has to be tried by fire (1, 7; 4, 12) throughout the world (5, 9), so that the end can no longer be distant (4, 7 17). So the readers must have been living in a period of systematic persecution when Christians as such were persecuted (4, 16)—a state of affairs which began towards the end of Domitian's reign at earliest.

With some critics the theory that 1 Pet. consists of two heterogeneous parts enjoys great popularity. This theory, which is brilliant rather than well-founded, proposes to divide the Epistle into (1) a "Baptism address", 1, 3 to 4, 11, i.e., a discourse to newly converted people (inferred from 1, 3 23; 2, 2; 3, 21), and (2) a work of exhortation which was intended especially to guide their conduct in the universal persecution of Christians which had just broken out.

They point to the fact that the first part contains only very general references to the sufferings which can befall the readers (1, 6 sq.; 3, 13 sq.), while in the second part the references are to trials which have already come upon the recipients (4, 12 because of their membership of the Christian Church (4, 14 sqq.); they claim that the unknown author of 1 Pet. composed an encyclical letter by joining words of warning and consolation to a sermon which he had once delivered (together with elements of community paraenesis 2, 18 to 3, 7; 4, 7–11), and that this was published under the name of the Apostle Peter.

There is no unanimity about the place of composition. Some (Juelicher, Windisch and Arn. Meyer) think that it was composed, probably on the instructions of the Roman community, in the last years of Domitian's reign for the Christian communities of Asia Minor; the author was a priest who had probably witnessed Nero's persecution (5, 1); they say that it is a counterpart of the first epistle of Clement; in view of the.

dangerous situation the author must have used a literary fiction to date the Epistle to the time before Nero's persecution. Knopf, Lietzmann and others think that the Epistle was composed in Asia Minor, for the earliest reference to it (Polycarp and Papias) is to be found there.

H. Preisker (in Windisch[3] p. 156–162) has recently put forward the following form of the "Baptism address" theory: he considers that the whole work 1, 3 to 5, 11 is a report of a liturgical assembly of the Roman community (about 80 A.D.), which consisted of a Baptism ceremony (1, 3 to 4, 11), followed by a service for the whole community (4, 12 to 5, 11); this would provide a simple explanation of the striking contrast between the references to Christians in the two parts: in the first part sufferings are merely a possibility—the newly baptized have hitherto had no experience of persecution, but now that they are members of the community they must realize the necessity of undergoing such trials; in the second part, on the other hand, actual persecutions are mentioned—the community as a body has already undergone persecution because of their profession of Christ. Preisker suggests that the report of this meeting was drawn up by Silvanus and was sent in the form of an epistle to the communities of Asia Minor which Peter had probably once visited.

Of the three objections mentioned above, the last mentioned is not valid (see above n. 3), but the other two deserve serious notice. They certainly demonstrate that the Apostle cannot have composed this Epistle without outside assistance. Even if Peter was bilingual from childhood, being—like James the brother of the Lord—a Galilean, he would yet not have had the capacity to write Greek of as good quality as in 1 Pet.

The author declares expressly at the end of the Epistle that he has written briefly "by Silvanus", whom he considers a faithful (reliable) brother (5, 12). In view of this characterization of Silvanus we cannot assume that he merely wrote to dictation or simply delivered the Epistle. Everything points rather to Peter having used him as a helper (amanuensis) for the composition of the work. Peter probably merely gave him an outline of the content and left him free to work out the wording; then, when the work was finished, Peter added a conclusion in his own hand 5, 12 sqq.

This Silvanus is identical with the Silas[7] mentioned in Acts, as a leading person in the mother community at Jerusalem with prophetic gifts (15, 22 32), who for many years was a fellow worker of Paul's (Acts 15, 40 sqq.; 18, 5; 1 Thess. 1, 1; 2 Cor. 1, 19). This fact explains the features which are strange in an epistle written by Peter: the good Greek, familiarity with the LXX, the close relationship to Pauline theology and the stress on the essential achievement of Jesus rather than on personal recollections, as well as the entire absence of allusions to the words of Our Lord. This was fundamentally the view expressed by Jerome, who was familiar with the practice of that time in composing epistles, when he wrote Ep. 120 (ad Hedibiam) quaest. 11: *Duae epistolae, quae feruntur Petri, stilo inter se et charactere discrepant structuraque verborum, ex quo intelligimus pro necessitate rerum diversis eum usum interpretibus.* Interpres here means an independent amanuensis as distinct from a secretary who wrote to dictation.

5. Place and time of composition

On its own evidence the Epistle was composed at Rome. In the conclusion Peter sends greetings from "the church that is in Babylon, elected together with you" (5, 13), and it is fairly generally accepted to-day that Babylon was a pseudonym for Rome in first century Apocalyptic among both Jews and Christians.

There was an army station in the Nile Delta called Babylon

---

[7] Cf. A. Stegmann, *Silvanus als Missionar und "Hagiograph"*, Rottenburg 1917; L. Radermacher, *Der erste Petrusbrief und Silvanus*: ZntW 25 (1926) 287–299.

(Strabo XVIII, 30; Flavius Josephus, Antiq. II 15, 1 ch. 315), but it cannot be the place in question. Neither can the city of Babylon on the Euphrates, which was still inhabited at this time, but had long lost its ancient greatness and importance; Flavius Josephus (Antiq. XVIII 9, 8) tells us that the Babylonian Jews migrated to Seleucia about the middle of the first century A.D. So there is no reason for thinking that Peter's missionary journeys (1 Cor. 9, 5) took him to this city of Babylon.

So Babylon can only be a symbolic name for Rome, the capital of the Roman Empire which was the enemy of God; this was also the view of the early Church (Eusebius H. E. II 15, 2: Peter figuratively (τροπικώτερον) calls the city of Rome Babylon in 1 Pet. 5, 13; Jerome, *Vir. ill.* 8).

This symbolism was also quite familiar to Jewish apocalyptic writers at that time, as is shown by 4 Esd. 3, 1 sq. 28 31 (Babylon a symbolic name for Rome), Orac. Sibyll. 5, 139 143 159 sqq. (Nero flees from Babylon to the Parthians v. 143), and Apc. Baruch 67, 7 ("the king of Babylon [Titus], who has now destroyed Sion"). In the Old Testament prophets the world power hostile to God is identified with Babylon more often than with any other pagan city such as Tyre; the prophets associated the fall of Babylon closely with the time of salvation (e. g., Is. 21, 9; Jer. 28, 4). So in late Judaism Babylon became a symbol for the civil power which rules the world and is God's enemy. The word came into use as a secret-symbolic name for Rome after the Roman general, Pompey, reduced the independent Hasmonean kingdom and incorporated it into the province of Syria in 63 B.C.

Primitive Christianity adopted this symbolic name from Judaism as we see from Apc. 14, 8; 16, 19; 17, 5; 18, 2 10 21; at latest it was taken over when the Roman administration began to persecute Christians because of their faith. But, so far as we know, this did not happen before the middle of the sixties.

1 Pet. displays none of the hostility to Rome which we find

in the Apc., but exhorts the recipients to obey the Emperor and his representatives (2, 13 sq.); moreover, it shows no knowledge of violent martyrdoms such as are attested by Apc. 6, 10; 17, 6; 18, 24; 19, 2. Therefore it must have been written before Nero began his violent persecution of the Roman Church in the late summer of 64 A.D. Yet in view of the strong eschatological tone which runs through the Epistle, it cannot have been written long before that time; according to 4, 7 "The end of all is at hand"; the sufferings and distress which have befallen the recipients are harbingers of the coming judgment which according to God's plan begins with "the house of God" i. e., God's community (4, 17; cf. Jer. 25, 29; Ez. 9, 6).

This dating is also supported by the fact that, as we see from the address of the epistle, Christianity had already spread beyond the territory of Paul's mission (Bithynia, Pontus and Cappadocia).

It is remarkable that Peter wrote to communities which lay in Paul's missionary territory. The explanation is probably that Paul had then left Rome again on a missionary journey (Spain?), so that Peter thought it his duty to encourage and console these Gentile Christian communities in their distress, although he had not converted them. We do not know who told him of their plight; Silvanus is usually mentioned, for he was well-known to the communities of Asia Minor, having accompanied and worked with Paul on the second missionary journey. It is assumed that when he parted from Paul—probably at the end of the second missionary journey, cf. Acts 18, 5; 2 Cor. 1, 19—he returned to the mission field in Asia Minor.

O. Roller and P. Gaechter are among the few who uphold the not very likely theory that the communities of Galatia turned away from Paul but remained loyal to Silvanus their second missionary, and with him later became attached to the Apostle Peter; they point out that this would explain how Peter comes to write through Silvanus to these communities of Asia Minor.

6. Attestation

Papias of Hierapolis, according to Eusebius "used testimonies from the first epistle of John and also from that of Peter" (H. E. III 39, 17), and Polycarp in his epistle to the Philippians refers several times to "the first Epistle of Peter" (IV 14, 9); cf. Phil. 1, 3 (=1 Pet. 1, 8); 2, 1 (=1, 13 21); 2, 2 (=3, 9); 5, 3 (=2, 11); 7, 2 (=4, 7); 8, 1 (=2, 22 24); 8, 2 (=3, 14; 4, 14); 10, 2 (=2, 11 sq.). It is impossible to determine whether the first epistle of Clement used it (cf. 16, 17; 36, 2; 49, 5).

It has been an undisputed part of the New Testament Canon since the end of the second century. Origen and Eusebius list it among the *Homologoumena* (H. E. III 3, 1 4; 25, 2; VI 25, 8). Irenaeus, Tertullian, Cyprian and Clement of Alexandria cite sentences from it as sayings of the Apostle Peter. It does not appear in the Muratorian Canon, almost certainly because of textual corruption (cf. § 6, 2).

§ 51. THE SECOND EPISTLE OF ST. PETER

Commentaries: (a) See before §§ 47 and 49, and at § 48. (b) G. Hollmann und W. Bousset, ³1917 (Goett NT 3).

Studies: K. Henkel, *Der zweite Brief des Apostelfuersten Petrus geprueft auf seine Echtheit* (BSt IX, 5: 1904). H. Grosch, *Die Echtheit des zweiten Briefes Petri²*, Berlin 1914. E. J. Robson, *Studies in the Second Epistle of St. Peter*, Cambridge 1915. U. Holzmeister: Bb 30 (1949) 339–355 (Vocabulary). E. Kaesemann, *Eine Apologie der urchristlichen Eschatologie*: ZThK 49 (1952) 272–296. [This Epistle is directed against Gnostic sectaries, and defends the eschatology of primitive Christianity. Contains arguments for dating it to the middle of the second century.]

1. Content and structure

Introductory greeting 1, 1–2.

I. Preliminary injunctions and their justification 1, 3–21.

1. The high cost of the saving gifts which we have received demands on our part an energetic struggle to confirm and in-

crease our possession of them in view of the completion of salvation which has yet to come 1, 3–11.

2. So Peter wishes before his approaching death to confirm the reliability of the prophecies about the Second Coming of Christ in power; he is able to do this, having been an eyewitness of the Transfiguration 1, 12–21.

II. Warning against Antinomian teachers 2, 1–22.

1. He announces their appearance and the judgment which threatens them 2, 1–3.

2. The certainty of this judgment is based on three examples of punishment from Sacred History (fall of the angels, deluge, Sodom and Gomorrha) 2, 4–9.

3. Description of the sinful conduct of the false teachers (denying the Lord, sensual pleasure, debauchery, avarice); the danger for the newly converted 2, 10–22.

III. Reflections on the reasons why the Parousia has not yet taken place and on the certainty that it will come 3, 1–13.

1. In the Epistle Peter wishes to remind the readers of what the Prophets foretold and of the command of Christ which the Apostles gave them, since in the last days scoffers with Antinomian notions will come and deny the Parousia because of its long deferment 3, 1–4.

2. Attack on those who deny the Parousia 3, 5–13: a) The world catastrophe which Christ foretold and which is closely connected with his Second Coming will certainly take place as a judgment of fire—as the deluge, its counterpart, shows 3, 5–7; b) It has been delayed hitherto because God has different measures of time from us, and he waits full of patience for the conversion of all men 3, 8–9; c) the day of the Lord comes suddenly like a thief, and brings a world conflagration, which will be followed by a renewal of the world 3, 10–13.

Final exhortations 3, 14–18: So they must prepare themselves for the day of judgment by a faultless life, as Paul has written in his Epistles also, and protect themselves from being misled.

2. Destination

According to the introductory greeting the Epistle is intended for all Christendom (cf. also Jude 1). But the author had already written to the recipients (3, 1); if this refers to 1 Peter, as most exegetes rightly think—for example Camerlynck, Vrede, Felten, Chaine, Knopf, Windisch, and Hauck—then 2 Pet. was really addressed to the Gentile Christian communities of northern and western Galatia.

We can also infer from the content that it was addressed to Gentile Christians; the attack on Antinomianism as well as the reference to Paul's Epistles and to his authority (3, 16), fit only Gentile Christian communities. The newly converted (2, 81) and the apostates (2, 20–27) are clearly described as former pagans.

3. The relation between 2 Peter and Jude

The relationship between 2 Pet. and Jude is so close that there can be no doubt about literary dependence on one side or the other. Of the twenty five verses of Jude, nineteen appear wholly or partly in 2 Pet. The description of the efforts of the Antinomian teachers and the polemic against them which we find in 2 Pet. 2, 1–22 show a close kinship with the corresponding passages of Jude in content, order of ideas, and wording: 1) Signs of the false teachers 2 Pet. 2, 1–3 = Jude 4 (denial of the Lord). 2) Examples of punishments from the Old Testament 2 Pet. 2, 4–9 = Jude 5–7 (fall of the angels, Sodom and Gomorrha). 3) Defilement of the flesh and blasphemy of the angels by the false teachers 2 Pet. 2, 10–12 = Jude 8–10. 4) Their debauchery and corruption 2 Pet. 2, 13 sq. = Jude 12. 5) They follow the way of Balaam 2 Pet. 2, 15 sq. = Jude 11. 6) Characterization of the false teachers by comparisons drawn from nature 2 Pet. 2, 17 = Jude 12 sq. 7) Their arrogant talk 2 Pet. 2, 18 = Jude 16.

There are also various remarkable parallels between Jude and the other two chapters of 2 Pet.: 2 Pet. 1, 5 with Jude 3; 2 Pet. 1, 12 with Jude 5; 2 Pet. 3, 2 sq. with Jude 17 sq.; 2 Pet. 3, 14 with Jude 24; 2 Pet. 3, 18 with Jude 25. There is a weighty argument in the fact that some of the words used in the parallel passages do not occur elsewhere in the New Testament (ἐμπαίκτης, ὑπέρογκα), or even in the whole Greek Bible (συνευωχέομαι), or seldom appear elsewhere (ζόφος, σπίλοι — σπιλάδες).

It is universally conceded to-day that there is literary dependence, the only matter in dispute is on which side the dependence lies. The prevailing view rightly favours the priority of Jude; only a small minority of modern exegetes, including Spitta, Zahn, Wohlenberg, and Felten, uphold the other view.

The principal arguments for the priority of Jude are these:

1. Either the essence of Jude's content was elaborated into a main section of 2 Pet., or else Jude borrowed only the anti-libertine polemic from 2 Pet. and published it as an independent work, passing over the remainder of the Epistle—particularly the attack on those who deny the Parousia. In view of the relative sizes of the two Epistles, it is much more natural and more easily understandable that Peter should have borrowed from Jude, rather than vice versa.

2. The principal theme of 2 Pet. is the defence of the Christian hope of the Parousia; 1, 12–21 and 3, 1–18 are devoted to this. The second chapter, which deals with the Antinomians, appears to break the sequence. Yet its language and style agree with that of the other chapters, and there are allusions to Jude in 1, 5 12; 3, 2 3 14 18. So ch. 2 cannot be considered a later interpolation, as Kuehl and others have suggested.

3. 2 Pet. does not contain the following matters which appear in Jude: the reference to the nature of the angels' sin (Jude 6 sq.: 2 Pet. 2, 6 10), the dispute of Michael with the devil (Jude 9: 2 Pet. 2, 11), the "wandering stars to whom the storm of darkness is reserved for ever" (Jude 13: 2 Pet. 2, 17), and the citation from the Book of Enoch (Jude 14). These passages had already appeared strange, and it is easier to explain their omission or recasting by the author of 2 Pet. than to understand how Jude came to fill out the obscure allusions of 2 Pet. with apocryphal material.

2 Pet. 2, 11 can be understood only in the light of Jude 9. The picture of "clouds without water which are carried about by winds" Jude 12 is damaged by the addition "fountains (without water) and (clouds)" 2 Pet. 2, 17, and the relative clause "to whom the mist of darkness is reserved" applies only to the "wandering stars" Jude 13, which are not mentioned in 2 Pet.

4. It is highly unlikely that Jude 5–7 upset the historical order of the instances of punishments in 2 Pet. 2, 4–7 (angels, deluge, Sodom), whereas it would be perfectly natural if 2 Pet. gives the chronological order, and substitutes the deluge for the generation which wandered in the desert, for he used the latter in his polemic against those who denied the Parousia.

4. Attestation

In the first two centuries little use was made of this Epistle. There are traces of its use in the Acts of Peter (Actus Vercellenses) c. 20 and 21, which was probably written about 200 A.D. (2 Pet. 1, 17 sq.), and it was probably used also in the Apocalypse of Peter, which belongs to the first half of the second century.

The first Father to make explicit mention of 2 Pet. is Origen; he considers it canonical, but observes that the matter is disputed (apud Euseb. H. E. VI 25, 8). The Alexandrian Church had 2 Pet. in its Canon probably from about 200 A.D. It is likely that Clement of Alexandria wrote a commentary on it (cf. § 7, 1), but it is not cited in his surviving works. Apparently it did not appear in Codex B or its ancestor.

Eusebius of Caesarea lists it among the *Antilegomena,* and personally considers it spurious (H. E. III 3, 1 4). On the other hand Cyril of Jerusalem († 386 A.D.) regarded it as canonical (*Catech.* IV, 36).

In Antioch, Asia Minor, and Constantinople the four small Catholic Epistles, of which 2 Pet. is one, were an object of dispute until about 400 A.D. (cf. § 7, 2). In Asia Minor the Epistle was accepted as canonical in the third century by Firmilian of Caesarea in Cappadocia, a pupil and friend of Origen (ep. 75, 6 to Cyprian), and by Methodius of Olympus in Lycia (fragment from *De resurrectione*).

To turn to the West, Hippolytus of Rome probably knew and made use of the Epistle. On the other hand Irenaeus, Tertullian, Cyprian and the Muratorian Canon are silent about it. It has been considered authentic and canonical throughout the Latin Church since about 370–380 A.D. (cf. § 8). When Jerome, who accepted the authenticity of 2 Pet., says that Peter's authorship is denied by many *propter stili cum priore dissonantiam* (*Vir. ill.* 1), he has in mind the Greek writers of the third and fourth centuries and third century Latin writers.

5. *The problem of authenticity*

In the introductory greeting the Epistle names the Apostle Peter as its author ("Simon Peter, servant and Apostle of Jesus Christ"); it also makes this claim in other passages: in 1, 16 where the author describes himself as an eyewitness of the Transfiguration; in 3, 1 he alludes to an earlier Epistle which he had sent these people, which almost certainly refers to 1 Pet.; and in 3, 15 sq. he claims equal apostolic authority to "our most dear brother Paul", whose Epistles he defends against misinterpretation by "the unlearned and unstable".

Despite these definite statements, almost all modern Protestant scholars consider the Epistle spurious. Very few even of the conservative Protestants (Th. Zahn, Wohlenberg, H. Grosch) uphold its authenticity; the majority regard its spuriousness as proven (for example, Barth, Feine, Appel, Behm, Torm, F. Hauck, Michaelis). Among Catholics, Cajetan held this view in the sixteenth century, but almost all modern Catholic exegetes defend authenticity, with the exception of Calmes, Vogels, K. Th. Schaefer, and especially Chaine and J. Michl, who favour spuriousness (pseudonymity).

It cannot be denied that serious arguments are raised against Peter's authorship; they are principally these:

1. The poor attestation of 2 Pet. in contrast with the very good authority for 1 Pet. and the reasonably good attestation of the small Epistle of Jude: Didymus of Alexandria († 398 A.D.), in a fragment which has survived in Latin, says that 2 Pet. is a forgery and not part of the Canon (Migne PG 39, 1773 sq.). But this does not agree with his attitude elsewhere to 2 Pet., so it should probably be considered evidence for a view which he himself did not share, particularly as Jerome tells us that many people regarded the Epistle as spurious. This is remarkable in view of the fact that the Epistle explicitly describes the Apostle Peter as its author.

2. The use of Jude by the author of 2 Pet.: Since Jude was not written until after 70 A.D., 2 Pet. cannot be the work of the Apostle. Moreover, it is highly unlikely that the Apostle Peter would have incorporated into his work almost the whole Epistle of Jude the brother of the Lord. 2 Pet. is demonstrably a forgery, for it foretells for tne future the coming of those who deny the Parousia (2, 1 sqq.; 3, 3 17), whom Jude represents as in the present, yet 2 Pet. also speaks of them in the present tense (2, 10 12 sqq. 20) and even in the praeterite (2, 15 22). So the peril which 2 Pet. deals with is present and not simply future; the future

tense is used in 2, 1 sqq.; 3, 3 17 in order to support the fiction that Peter had written the Epistle, in spite of the fact that the scoffers at the Parousia first appeared in post-apostolic times.

3. The polemic against the denial of the Parousia: The principal purpose of 2 Pet. is to combat those who deny the expectation of the Parousia, and who ask mockingly: "Where is his promise or his coming? For since the time that the fathers slept, all things continue as they were from the beginning of the creation" (3, 4).

There is no other evidence in the New Testament of doubts or denials of the Second Coming of Christ, and it is unlikely that they were raised before the destruction of Jerusalem, whereas the deferment of the Parousia after 70 A.D. could well have occasioned them. The earliest evidence of such doubt is in the first epistle of Clement (23, 3 sq.), which rejects the doubts; quoting from an unknown book which was evidently familiar to the Christians he gives a saying of the scoffers which resembles the question in 2 Pet.: "We heard this even in the days of our fathers, and behold, we have grown old and none of it has befallen us."

The fathers who have fallen asleep in 2 Pet. 3, 4 probably are the first Christian generation. But a certain length of time has elapsed since their death, and the first disciples were certainly not called fathers until they belonged to the past; so the situation reflected by verse 4 is no longer the first generation. In 1 Pet. 4, 7 17; 5, 4 the Parousia is awaited as being close at hand, and no doubts are raised about its coming. It is quite unlikely that such a change should have taken place between the writing of 1 Pet. (63 or 64 A.D.) and Peter's death.

4. The sharp differences between 1 and 2 Pet. in vocabulary, use of the Old Testament, and thought (see especially Chaine):

1 Pet. with a total of 469 words and 2 Pet. with 330, have in common 100 words, that is, one seventh of the total vocabulary of both Epistles. It is not uncommon to find the same or similar

ideas expressed by different words (e. g., ἄθεσμος : ἀθέμιτος, ἐπόπτης : μάρτυς, ὑπόδειγμα : ὑπόγραμμος). On the other hand there is no characteristic difference in the style of the two Epistles.

2 Pet. uses the Old Testament only in five places (2, 2 22; 3, 8 12 13) apart from the three Old Testament examples (2, 4 6 15) which are borrowed from Jude. In contrast to this, 1 Pet. uses the Old Testament at least 31 times, sometimes citing at length (1, 24 sq.; 2, 6; 3, 10–12; 5, 5), and occasionally employing the usual introductory formula (1, 16; 2, 6). Both Epistles make reference to the deluge, but in different senses; for 2 Pet. it means the destruction of the old world by water (2, 5; 3, 5–7), whereas for 1 Pet. it is a figure of Baptism (3, 20 sq.).

1 Pet. has greater theological depth than the other Epistle, particularly in Christology. In 2 Pet. Christ is simply the object of Christian profession rather than the model for Christians. In 1 Pet. Christological thought dominates and permeates the whole content, and makes the Epistle a unified work which reflects an intense spiritual life centered entirely on the person of Christ.

Marked differences may also be observed in the passages dealing with the Parousia. Instead of παρουσία (2 Pet. 1, 16; 3, 4 12), 1 Pet. always uses ἀποκάλυψις 1, 7 13; 4, 13. The Second Coming of Christ is expected soon in 1 Pet. (4, 7 17; 5, 4), while 2 Pet. attacks those who deny the Parousia, and attributes its deferment to the long-suffering of God (3, 8–9). In the first Epistle the Parousia is understood as the coming of Christ in judgment (4, 5 17), and the author rejoices that eternal joy will begin with it (1, 7–9; 4, 13; 5, 4 10), whereas 2 Pet. speaks of the cosmic catastrophe which is connected with the Parousia (3, 7 10–13), and this is not a specifically Christian idea.

These divergences were observed even in antiquity and were regarded as decisive arguments against the authenticity of 2 Pet. as Jerome tells us (see above § 50, 4); Jerome himself offers in explanation the theory of different secretaries.

5. The Hellenistic colouring of 2 Pet.: The language and thought of this Epistle show such strong influence of Hellenism that only a Jewish Christian with a good Greek education can have written it. The following are examples of words and expressions from Hellenistic piety: θεία δύναμις 1, 3; ἐπίγνωσις 1, 2 sq. 6 8; 2, 20; 3, 18; εὐσέβεια 1, 3; δόξα καὶ ἀρετή 1, 3; θείας φύσεως κοινωνός 1, 4; ἀποφυγεῖν τῆς ἐν τῷ κόσμῳ ἐν ἐπιθυμίᾳ φθορᾶς 1, 4; ἐπόπτης 1, 16 (an expression from the Mysteries). As Windisch says, "Hellenistic piety is summed up in the flight from transitoriness, the share in the divine nature given us by God's power, and the perception of God and of imperishable being."

6. The allusion to a collection of Pauline Epistles: To give greater emphasis to his commendation of a holy life as a preparation for the Parousia the author appeals to Paul: "As also our most dear brother Paul according to the wisdom given him, hath written to you: as also in all his Epistles, speaking in them of these things; in which are certain things hard to be understood, which the unlearned and unstable wrest, as they do also the other scriptures (γραφαί), to their own destruction" (3, 15 sq.).

So when 2 Pet. was written, there existed a collection of Pauline Epistles—of what extent we do not know—which was in general circulation and enjoyed canonical standing. Yet this does not oblige us to date the Epistle to the second century, as is generally done. We are in the second Christian generation, and Paul has been dead for some time (Chaine).

These objections to authenticity are certainly serious, but the majority of modern Catholic exegetes do not think that they justify considering the Epistle to be pseudonymous. In particular the differences between 1 and 2 Pet. can be explained satisfactorily by Jerome's theory that the Apostle used two different secretaries.

Others consider that this solution cannot be accepted, for the principal difficulty is to fit 2 Pet. into the period before the Apostle's death. They point out that when the Council of Trent described it as an Epistle of Peter, it had no intention of deciding the problem of authorship as a matter of faith; they also instance Ecclesiastes and Wisdom which claim to be the work of Solomon, and were accepted as such by the Church for a long time, yet to-day it is universally recognized that they are pseudonymous. Pseudonymity was a literary convention in the ancient world, so, they say, there is no obstacle to assuming that God should have inspired a writer who followed this practice; if the author of 2 Pet. speaks as though he were the Apostle Peter, this is not a false claim but a literary fiction; he borrowed the name of the great Apostle in order to give his work greater authority, which was quite legitimate in literary practice at that time.

If 2 Pet. is pseudonymous, it was probably written about 90–95 A.D. by an unknown author.

On the problem of pseudonymity see: Arnold Meyer, *Religioese Pseudepigraphie als ethisch-psychologisches Problem:* ZntW 35 (1936) 262–279. F. Torm, *Die Psychologie der Pseudonymitaet im Hinblick auf die Literatur des Urchristéntums,* Guetersloh 1932 (on this work see A. Meyer: ThLZ 1933, 354–357). J. C. Fenton, *Pseudonymity in the NT:* Theology, London, 58 (1955) 51–56.

6. Place and time of composition

If Peter was the author of this Epistle, it was written in Rome shortly before his death (cf. 1, 14), that is in the middle of the sixties.

If the work is pseudonymous, it is hardly possible to determine the time and place of composition. Chaine dates it about 80 A.D., for it is highly likely that doubts about the Parousia arose in the decade after the destruction of Jerusalem and of the Temple.

Protestant scholars date its composition to the second century, between 120 and 180 A.D., on the grounds that the author assumes the existence of a collection of Pauline Epistles (3, 15 sq.), and the construction of the New Testament Canon, and also because he combats a movement which, they allege, has the essential marks of second century Gnosis (cf. 1, 16).

THE THREE EPISTLES OF ST. JOHN

Commentaries: (a) J. E. Belser, *Die Briefe des hl. Johannes,* Freiburg i. Br. 1906. W. Vrede, [4]1932 (Bonner NT 9). J. Bonsirven, 1954 (VS IX). R. Schnackenburg, 1953 (HThK XIII, 3).—(b) B. Weiss, 1900 (Meyer XIV[6]). A. E. Brooke, 1912 (ICC). O. Baumgarten [3]1918 (Goett NT 4). Th. Haering, *Die Johannesbriefe,* Stuttgart 1927. F. Buechsel, 1933 (ThHK XVII). C. H. Dodd, 1946 (Moffatt). Studies: H. H. Wendt, *Die Johannesbriefe und das joh. Christentum,* Halle 1925. R. Leconte: DB Suppl. 4 (1949) 797–815. W. F. Howard, *The Common Authorship of the Johannine Gospel and Epistles:* JThSt 48 (1947) 12–25.

§ 52. THE FIRST EPISTLE OF ST. JOHN

Studies: A. Wurm, *Die Irrlehrer im 1 Joh* (BSt VIII, 1: 1903). R. Bultmann, *Analyse des ersten Joh:* Festgabe fuer A. Juelicher, Tuebingen 1927, 138–158; against him F. Buechsel, ZntW 28 (1929) 235–241. E. Lohmeyer, *Ueber Aufbau und Gliederung des 1 Joh:* ZntW 27 (1928) 225–267. R. Schwertschlager, *Der 1 Joh. in seinem Grundgedanken und Aufbau.* Diss. Univ. Gregoriana, Coburg 1935. C. H. Dodd, *The First Epistle of John and the Fourth Gospel:* BJRL XXI (1937) 129–156. O. A. Piper, *1 John and the Didache of the Primitive Church:* JBL 66 (1947) 437–451. W. G. Wilson: JThSt 49 (1948) 147–156. R. Bultmann, *Die kirchliche Redaktion des 1 Joh:* In memoriam Ernst Lohmeyer, Stuttgart 1951, 189–201. H. Braun, *Literar-Analyse und theologische Schichtung in 1 Joh:* ZThK 48 (1951) 262–292. E. Kaesemann: ZThK 48 (1951) 306–308 (A. 2). A. P. Salom, *Some Aspects of the Grammatical Style of 1 John:* JBL 74 (1955) 96–102 [Identity of authorship with the Fourth Gospel is supported by the style]. W. Nauck, *Die Tradition und der Charakter des 1 Joh,* Tübingen 1957.

1. *Content and structure*

THE thought of the Epistle does not follow any logical arrangement. The individual observations, exhortations and warnings are fairly loosely strung together without apparent order. Fundamentally the same ideas are repeated in more or less varied form. In modern times attempts have been repeatedly made, though without success, to show that there is an artistic arrangement.

Introduction 1, 1–4: Having himself been an eyewitness, the author tells his readers of the Life which was manifested on earth so that they also may have a share in his fellowship with the Father and Son.

I. The fellowship of God 1, 5 to 2, 27.

1. God is light; so we can have fellowship with him only if we walk in the light, confess our sins, and have them washed away by the Blood of Christ 1, 5 to 2, 2.

2. There can be knowledge of God and fellowship with him only if we keep his commandments 2, 3–6.

3. Only he walks in the light who keeps the old-new commandment of brotherly love 2, 7–11.

4. Since the readers are in possession of salvation they must not love the world and its concupiscence 2, 12–17.

5. The false teachers who deny that Jesus is the Christ are the Antichrist whose coming at the last hour was foretold; hold fast to the faith in Christ which you have received (cf. 4, 1–6) 2, 18–27.

II. Being children of God 2, 28 to 4, 6.

1. The children of God should look forward with joy to the coming of the Lord, for they shall then be made like him 2, 28 to 3, 3.

2. The children of God avoid sin and practise justice, but the children of the devil commit sin 3, 4–10.

3. Those who are of God practise active brotherly love 3, 11–18.

4. The consciousness of fulfilling the commandments gives us confidence before God 3, 19–22.

5. Faith in Jesus Christ and brotherly love, which sum up the content of his commandments, assure us of eternal union with God 3, 23–24.

6. Further warning against the false teachers: the spirits who confess that Jesus Christ has come in the flesh are of God, those who deny this are of Antichrist; you are of God and have overcome those who are of the world 4, 1–6.

III. Love and faith 4, 7 to 5, 12.

1. God is love; he proved his love for us by first sending his Son; this obliges us to love our brothers 4, 7–11.

2. Brotherly love and confession that Jesus is the Son of God are the foundation and proof of our union with God 4, 12–16.

3. Perfect love drives out fear of judgment 4, 17–19.

4. Love for God and love for our fellowmen are inseparable 4, 20–21.

5. Faith in Jesus as the Christ and the Son of God is the mark of one who is born of God; such a person can observe God's commandments and overcome the world 5, 1–5.

6. Water, blood and spirit give testimony of Jesus as the Giver of eternal life who was sent by God 5, 6–12.

Conclusion of the epistle 5, 13 (cf. John 20, 31).

Appendix 5, 14–21.

1. As believers we may be certain that our requests will be heard as well as our prayers for a brother who has sinned, unless it be a sin "to death" 5, 14–17.

2. There are three fundamental truths: whoever is born of God does not sin—we are of God—the Son of God has brought us true knowledge of God 5, 18–21.

2. Literary character

1 John has no introductory greeting, sending of good wishes, or final greeting, all of which were features of the ancient Graeco-Roman epistle. There is not a single name mentioned throughout the whole work, and there is no sign of personal contact between the author and readers, such as we find in the Pauline Epistles. Furthermore it does not deal with individual problems of a community's life.

These facts create the impression that 1 John is a theological or religious treatise intended for the whole Church, rather than an epistle to a particular, more or less defined destination. This is the view of the critics, but it is not a correct description of the work, which does presuppose a concrete historical situation.

False teachers are carrying on their agitation among the readers to whom the work is addressed, and the author takes issue with them (2, 18–27; 4, 1–6). Although there is no serious danger of the readers apostatizing—they know the orthodox Christian doctrine (2, 21 27 sq.), and have already resisted the false teachers (4, 4)—yet the author considers it necessary to recall to them and to inculcate in their souls the essential and decisive points of the Christian faith.

So it can be seen that he has in mind a definite group of readers—perhaps a fairly large number of communities—for whom he writes his instructions, exhortations and warnings. In the Epistle he adopts such a familiar tone to them, calling them "little children" (2, 1 18 28; 3, 7 18; 4, 4; 5, 21) and "dearly beloved" (2, 7; 3, 2 21; 4, 1 7 11), and shows such a feeling of responsibility for them, that we must assume that he considers himself their spiritual father and leader.

Thus the work is not entirely without epistolary character.

3. Purpose

The epistle is intended to warn the readers against false teachers who are a serious danger to them, and to exhort them to hold loyally to the Christian faith which they have received and to fulfil conscientiously the duties, particularly brotherly love, which flow from it.

He does not give an exact description of the false doctrines which he attacks, but confines himself to hints. This makes it difficult to determine the exact nature of the errors.

Yet at the present day there is hardly any further doubt that it was a Gnostic error. The false teachers claim to be bearers of the spirit (4, 1–3 6), but are really false prophets (4, 1). They are three times called Antichrists (2, 18 22; 4, 3; cf. 2 John 7), because Antichrist, whose coming in the last days was foretold, is incarnate in them. They are not intruders from outside, but emerged from within the community, although in spirit they had never belonged to it (2, 19). Even though they are now cut off from the community (2, 19; 4, 4), they are still a danger, for they wish to mislead the faithful into their errors (2, 27; 3, 7; 2 John 7).

The Epistle gives the following information about these "Antichrists":

1. They claim a knowledge of God (2, 4; 4, 8), love for God (4, 20), and fellowship with God (1, 6; 2, 6 9), which is far superior to that of ordinary Christians, but, according to 1 John, these are false claims.

2. They deny that Jesus is the Christ (2, 22), the Son of God (4, 15; 5, 5)—in early Christian faith these expressions both meant the consubstantial Son of God. They also deny that Jesus Christ has come in the flesh (4, 2; 2 John 7).

So the false teachers assert that the Logos-Christ (or Son of God) whom God sent into the world, did not become man nor receive Baptism nor die on the Cross (5, 6), in other words that the man Jesus was not the Son of God; they say rather that Christ the spiritual Being came upon the man Jesus at his Baptism at the Jordan and dwelt in him as a guest, but before his death on the Cross left him to return to the Father. This seems to be the meaning of what the Epistle says. The denial of the Incarnation of the Son of God simultaneously entails denying the redemptive value of the death of Jesus (1, 7).

3. The false teachers also impugn the fundamental moral teachings of the Christian Church. One of the principal aims of the Epistle is to demonstrate the intrinsic, inseparable union between knowledge, fellowship, love and sonship of God on the one hand, and the breach with sin and observance of the commandments on the other (2, 3 sq. 9 11; 3, 10 sqq.; 4, 20 sq.). So we may infer that the false teachers had declared in the authentic

Gnostic manner that sin is of no account in those who possess the perfect knowledge of God. Yet, unlike the false teachers in Jude and 2 Pet., they are not accused of Antinomianism.

The Christological error of the Antichrists should not be identified with Docetism, which held that Christ who came from heaven had only an apparent body; it is related rather to the teaching of Cerinthus, according to whom the heavenly Christ dwelt as a guest in the man Jesus for some time, namely from his Baptism to his Passion (Irenaeus, *Haer.* I 26, 1); this is the opinion of Zahn, Lagrange, Vrede, Chaine, Strathmann, etc. But it is impossible to be entirely clear about the false teachers (cf. also § 28, 7).

4. *Authorship and relation to the fourth Gospel*

The early Church attributed this Epistle to the Apostle John, the author of the fourth Gospel. And in fact there is such a close kinship between it and the Gospel that there is no room for doubting that both are by the same author, as Dionysius of Alexandria realized (apud Euseb. H. E. VII 25, 18 sqq.), and as most modern scholars agree—though there are exceptions such as F. Chr. Baur, E. Schwarz, M. Dibelius, and C. H. Dodd. The agreements between the Epistle and Gospel appear not only in language and style, but also in theological ideas.

A whole series of particularly characteristic expressions, formulae and turns of phrase appear only in 1 (2 and 3) John and in the fourth Gospel: e. g. αἴρειν τὴν ἁμαρτίαν, ἔχειν ἁμαρτίαν, ποιεῖν τὰ ἀρεστά, ποιεῖν τὴν ἀλήθειαν, τιθέναι τὴν ψυχὴν ὑπέρ, to be of God, to be of the world, to have life, to abide in God, to abide in love, to walk in light (in darkness); the only begotten Son, the Saviour of the world, the Paraclete.

Peculiarities of style: Sentences joined by καὶ or without any conjunction, sparing use of particles, synonymous and antithetical parallelism.

There is far-reaching identity in the theological ideas of both works: The Father and Son can only be possessed together (1, 3; 2, 22–24: John 5, 23; 15, 23; 14, 9; 12, 45); God sent his only begotten Son into the world (4, 9 14: John 3, 16); the eternal Son of God has been made flesh (4, 2: John 1, 14); he takes away the sins of the world (3, 5: John 1, 29). Both works are permeated by the great contrasts of God and world (2, 15–17; 4, 5–6; 5, 4 19), God and devil (3, 8–10), light and darkness (1, 5–7; 2, 9–11), life and death (3, 14), truth and falsehood (1, 6; 2, 4 9; 4, 20). True charity is shown by observing the commandments (2, 5; 5, 3: John 14, 15 21). The world hates the disciples of Jesus (3, 13: John 15, 18 sq.; 17, 14). He who believes has eternal life already (3, 14: John 5, 14).

Yet when compared to the Gospel the Epistle also shows peculiarities of its own. Certain expressions which are characteristic of the Gospel do not appear in it, such as δόξα, δοξάζειν, τὸ πνεῦμα τὸ ἅγιον, κρίνειν, while only the Epistle uses χρῖσμα, σπέρμα θεοῦ, κοινωνία, ἱλασμός, παρουσία, ψευδοπροφήτης. The name Paraclete is used of Christ (2, 1), and not of the Holy Ghost (but cf. John 14, 16: "another Paraclete"). The λόγος John 1, 1 14 appears in the Epistle only as λόγος τῆς ζωῆς 1, 1. Matters peculiar to the Epistle are the close connection between love for God and brotherly love (4, 20 sq.; 3, 17), the vigorous struggle against sin (1, 8 to 2, 3; 3, 6 9; 5, 18), the frequent reference to the atoning power of the death of Jesus (1, 7; 2, 2; 3, 5; 4, 10; 5, 6), the inculcation of brotherly love (2, 9–11; 3, 10 sq. 15–17; 4, 11 sq. 20 sq.; 5, 1 sq.), and the reference to the Parousia (2, 18 28; 3, 2).

These and other peculiarities of the Epistle are simply explained by the fact that he is combatting the Gnostic heresy. In order to protect his readers against it, the author had to make it clear what a peril the false teachers were (false prophets), and stigmatize their false Christology as deepest heresy (ἀντίχριστοι 2, 18 22; 4, 3); he had also to emphasize that there can be no genuine

Christianity without struggling against sin, observing the commandments and practising charity, and that love for God must be proved in that way.

5. Unity

In modern times R. Bultmann in particular has impugned the unity of this Epistle. According to him the author has done the same as in the fourth Gospel: he has used pagan-Gnostic revelation discourses as the basis for his work, and has written a homiletic gloss or commentary on them. Thirty-two verses of the epistle wholly or in part belong to this original document, namely 1, 5–10; 2, 4 5 9–11 29; 3, 4 6–10 14 15 24; 4, 7 8 12 16; 5, 1 4; 4, 5 6(?); 2, 23; 5, 10 12. The original is recognizable by its characteristic style: Parallel clauses are joined into pairs, and sometimes a pair is antithetic to the preceding or following pair, being a simple conversion of the thesis. The expression is sententious and apodeictic; no reasons are given. Its content is a description of the nature of man under revelation; the stress falls throughout on the need for unity between the possession of salvation and moral conduct.

The author's style is homiletic-paraenetic. Like the Gospel of John, Bultmann says, the Epistle was re-edited by the Church to bring its theology into line with the traditional eschatology and the Church's belief in sacraments; three verses were interpolated in support of the traditional eschatology of Judaism and primitive Christianity: 2, 28 (ἐὰν φανερωθῇ, ἐν τῇ παρουσία αὐτοῦ); 3, 2 (ἐὰν φανερωθῇ); 4, 17 (ἐν τῇ ἡμέρᾳ τῆς κρίσεως), and three others in the interests of an article of the Church's dogma, which is closely related to the belief in sacraments, namely atonement through the Blood of Christ: 1, 7b; 2, 2; 4, 10b. The passage 5, 14–21 is to be regarded as an appendix added—like John 21, when the Church edited the work, where a new theme (intercession for sin v. 16 sq.) is introduced, and at the same time ideas already put forward are recapitulated (v. 14 sq. 18–21).

H. Braun agress in principle with Bultmann's method and with many of his results, but he questions whether unity of content can be found in the passages of the original which are discovered by stylistic comparison. In his view the original contained both Christian—that is, only mediately Gnostic—and purely Dualist-Gnostic tradition; thus, for example, in 1, 5–10 and 2, 9–11 the original contained Christian elements, while in 3, 7–10 the author took over Gnostic-dualist ideas (born of God).

On the other hand, E. Kaesemann vigorously rejects the distinction between original and redaction both in the Gospel of John and in the Epistle; since the alleged original was of a Christian and not of a pagan character, as Bultmann's own study shows, it derives not from pagan but from Christian Gnosis; it therefore follows necessarily that the variations in style are not decisive criteria for splitting the original unity of both works; they only show "that the author could and did draw upon double tradition, namely the Gnostic discourse and Christian homiletic."

Of the conservative scholars, F. Buechsel in 1929 combatted Bultmann searchingly. He draws a comparison between the antitheses of John and remarkable parallels in Jewish traditional literature (Mishna, Midrash), and shows that there is no real incompatibility between the antitheses and the homiletic-paraenetic passages.

6. Attestation

Of the Catholic Epistles 1 John and 1 Pet. are the best attested (cf. § 6, 2). Polycarp cites 1 John 4, 2–3 in his Epistle to the Philippians 7, 1. Eusebius H. E. III 39, 17 says that Papias also made use of it. It is probable that Justin knew it (cf. Dialogus 123, 9 with 1 John 3, 1).

The authorship of John the Apostle is attested by Irenaeus (*Haer.* III 16, 5), Clement of Alexandria (*Strom.* II 15), Tertullian (*Adv. Prax.* 15; *Adv. Marc.* V 16), Origen (apud Euseb. H. E. VI 25, 10),

Dionysius of Alexandria (apud Euseb. H. E. VII 25, 7–8) etc. Clement commented on it in his *Hypotyposes* (cf. § 7, 1). The Muratorian Canon quotes 1, 1–4 and ascribes it to John the Evangelist.

Origen (apud Euseb. H. E. VI 25, 10), Eusebius (H. E. III 25, 2) and Jerome (*Vir. ill.* 9) include it among the scriptures whose canonicity is universally accepted *(Homologoumena)*. It appears in all the ancient lists of the Canon. As with Jas. and 1 Pet. it was not until the Peshitta that the Syrians got it (cf. § 16, 3).

7. *The so-called Johannine Comma*

In the official Vulgate 1 John 5, 7 sq. reads: "Quoniam tres sunt qui testimonium dant *in caelo: Pater, Verbum et Spiritus Sanctus, et hi tres unum sunt. Et tres sunt qui testimonium dant in terra:* Spiritus et aqua et sanguis, et hi tres unum sunt." The words in italics—the so-called Johannine Comma—occur neither in the Greek MSS. nor in the ancient oriental versions and Old-Latin MSS. Moreover, no Greek Father cites them, and Priscillian († 380 A.D.) is the first Latin writer to quote them; when we recall the great trinitarian controversies, this is a cogent argument against their authenticity. The oldest known citation of the Comma is in Liber Apologeticus 4 of the Spaniard Instantius.

Probably it began as an allegorical exegesis of the three witnesses, and was first written as a marginal gloss in a Latin MS. of 1 John; it then slipped into the text of the Bible in the fifth century in Spain or Africa, for it occurs predominantly in Spanish and African sources. It does not appear in MSS. of the Vulgate before 800 A.D.

Literature: K. Kuenstle, *Das Comma Iohanneum,* Freiburg i. Br. 1905. E. Riggenbach, *Das Comma Johanneum,* Guetersloh 1928. A. Lemonnyer, Art. C. J.: DB Suppl 2 (1943) 67–73. T. Ayuso Marazuela: Bb 28 (1947) 83–112 216–235; 29 (1948) 52–76.

§ 53. THE SECOND AND THIRD EPISTLES OF ST. JOHN

Studies: H. Poggel, *Der zweite und dritte Brief des Apostels Johannes,* Paderborn 1896. B. Bresky, *Das Verhaeltnis des zweiten Joh zum dritten,* Muenster 1906. H. H. Wendt, *Zum zweiten und dritten Joh:* ZntW 23 (1924) 18–27. E. Kaesèmann, *Ketzer und Zeuge* [see above § 28]. R. Schnackenburg, *Der Streit zwischen dem Verfasser von 3 Joh und Diotrephes und seine verfassungsgeschichtliche Bedeutung:* MThZ 4 (1953) 18–26 (against Kaesemann).

1. Content of 2 John

Introductory greeting v. 1–3.

Principal section v. 4–11: (1) Exhortation to hold fast to the commandments which they have received, especially brotherly love v. 4–6. (2) Warning against false teachers (Antichrists) who deny the Incarnation of Jesus Christ, and a prohibition against receiving them v. 7–11.

Conclusion v. 12–13: He will soon visit them; greetings.

2. Content of 3 John

Introductory greeting v. 1.

Principal section v. 2–12: (1) Eulogy of the recipient because he "walks in the truth", is hospitable to missionaries who are passing by, and a request that he should fit them out for the continuation of their journey v. 3–8. (2) Censure of the domineering Diotrephes, who did not accept an epistle which the author had sent to the community, and who expelled the brethren who came v. 9–10. (3) Favourable testimony for a certain Demetrius v. 11–12.

Conclusion: He will soon visit the recipient; greetings.

3. Destination of both Epistles

2 John is addressed to "the lady Elect and her children" (v. 1). This does not refer to a Christian matron who provided lodging for the wandering missionaries (v. 10), but to some particular

Christian community—we do not know which. This is shown by the fact that "the lady" has many children, who are loved by all Christians (v. 1 4), and that she is greeted by "the children of (her) sister Elect" (v. 13).

3 John is addressed to a distinguished and well-to-do Christian called Gaius, who was probably converted by the writer of the Epistle (v. 4), and who, with his friends, remains loyal to the author (v. 15). The Christian community to which he belongs is governed tyranically by a certain Diotrephes, who refuses to receive an epistle sent to the community by the author and the brethren (who brought it?) (v. 9 sq.). This epistle is hardly 2 John, for its content does not fit the situation which 3 John implies.

4. Occasion and purpose

The purpose of 2 John is to exhort the community to persevere in truth and love, particularly in the true faith in Christ which they have received. The exhortation is due to the coming of false teachers who deny the Incarnation of Jesus Christ and proclaim their new doctrine as developed Christianity. The community must protect itself against this false doctrine and show no hospitality to its exponents.

The main purpose of 3 John is to acknowledge the cordial hospitality of Gaius to passing preachers of the Gospel, and to ask him to help them on their way—they are evidently travelling back again. He then adds a complaint about the domineering and uncharitable conduct of Diotrephes, and says that on his next visit he himself will reprimand him publicly.

5. Attestation

According to Eusebius H. E. VI 14, 1 Clement of Alexandria commented on all three Johannine Epistles in his *Hypotyposes*, though only fragments of his comments on 1 and 2 John have survived (cf. § 7, 1). Origen (apud Euseb. H. E. VI 25, 10) and Dionysius of Alexandria (ibid. VII 25, 11) attribute 2 and 3 John to John the Apostle; so does Eusebius in *Dem. ev.* III 5, 88, though in H. E. III 25, 3 he says that they "are to be ascribed either to the Evangelist or to another John"; Origen and Eusebius list them among the *Antilegomena* because they are not accepted in every church.

In the West, Irenaeus cites 2 John, but not 3 John (*Haer.* I 16, 3; III 16, 8), while Hippolytus cites neither of them. The Muratorian Canon speaks of two Epistles of John (line 68 sq.), and cites 1 John 1, 1–4 (lines 29–31), so its author knew at least one of the other two besides 1 John. In Africa Tertullian (*De carne Christi* c. 24) probably cites 2 John 7 and not 1 John 4, 2 sq. At the Council of Carthage in 256 A.D. Bishop Aurelius quoted 2 John 10 sq. as a saying of the Apostle John.

In the second half of the fourth century both Epistles were accepted as canonical throughout the whole Latin and Greek Church, except by the followers of the Antiochene school.

6. Author

The author of 2 and 3 John does not mention his name, but describes himself as ὁ πρεσβύτερος. This is an unusual way to describe oneself. πρεσβύτεροι appear a number of times in the New Testament as office holders in particular communities (Jerusalem: Acts 11, 30; 15, 2; 21, 18; Antioch, Iconium, Lystra: Acts 14, 23; Ephesus: Acts 10, 17; also in the Pastorals), but they always form a college (cf. πρεσβυτέριον 1 Tim. 4, 14); so ὁ πρεσβύτερος here is not an official title; it describes its bearer as a person of authority, and is also a substitute for his name, so it should be rendered "the Ancient".

This "Ancient" has a high authority which extends over a

fairly wide area, for he gives praise and censure, encouragement and warning to strange communities. Diotrephes—who has evidently usurped the leadership in the *Presbyterium* of some community—does not recognize his authority, but the Ancient will come in person and call him to account.

Who is this Ancient who does not give his name? The early Church—though not unanimously[1]—thought that he was the Apostle John, the author of the fourth Gospel and of 1 John. The critics usually ascribe both Epistles—as well as 1 John—to the John the Presbyter whom Papias mentions along with Aristion (cf. § 28, 2); they infer from his use of the title ὁ πρεσβύτερος that he could not call himself an Apostle, and point out that Diotrephes' contrariness would be inconceivable towards one of the original Apostles. But neither of these arguments is cogent. Paul encountered similar difficulties from the Corinthians, and it is quite likely that the Apostle John was known by this name in Asia Minor in his old age (cf. Peter describing himself as συμπρεσβύτερος 1 Pet. 5, 1).

Even the critics fairly generally admit that 2 and 3 John were written by the same author as 1 John. The three Epistles are very closely interrelated in language, style and ideas; thus, for example, the expression "the Antichrist" occurs only in 1 and 2 John; "not a new commandment" appears only in 1 John 2, 7 and 2 John 5, and only 1 John 3, 6 and 3 John 11 say that the evil-doer has not known God, etc.

So anyone who ascribes 1 John (and the fourth Gospel) to John the Apostle, must also attribute 2 and 3 John to him.

---

[1] Jerome (*De vir. ill.* 9 and 18) ascribes 2 and 3 John to the John the Presbyter whom Papias mentions after Aristion (cf. § 28, 2), and whose tomb was pointed out in Ephesus; so does the decree of the synod of Rome under Pope Damasus in 383 A.D. (cf. § 8). Eusebius was aware that both Epistles were ascribed by many to a John different from the Apostle (H. E. III 25, 3), and Ambrose introdces a citation from 2 John with the words: *alius vir Sancto locutus Spiritu* (Ep. 11, 4).

Section III. The Prophetic book of the New Testament

§ 54. THE APOCALYPSE OF ST. JOHN

Commentaries: (a) L. Cerfaux and J. Cambier, 1955 (Lectio divina 17). J. Rohr, [4]1932 (BonnerNT 10). E. B. Allo, *St. Jean, L'Apocalypse*[3], Paris 1933. J. Sickenberger, *Erklaerung der Joh-Apk*[2], Bonn 1942. A. Wikenhauser, 1947 (RegNT 9). M.-E. Boismard, *Apc.*, 1950 *(La Ste. Bible de Jérusalem)*. J. Bonsirven, 1951 (VS XVI).—(b) W. Bousset, 1906 (Meyer XVI[6]). H. B. Swete, *The Apocalypse of St. John*[3], London 1909. J. Weiss - W. Heitmueller, [3]1918 (GoettNT 4). R. H. Charles, 2 vols., 1920 (ICC). A. Loisy, *L'Apocalypse de Jean*, Paris 1923. Th. Zahn, 2 vols., 1924, 1926 (Zahn XVIII). E. Lohmeyer, [2]1953 (Lietzmann 16). W. Hadorn, 1928 (ThHK XVIII). J. Behm, [4]1949 (NTDeutsch 11). M. Kiddle, 1940 (Moffatt). E. F. Scott, *The Book of Revelation*, New York 1940. H. Mosbech, Copenhagen 1943. K. L. Schmidt, *Aus der Johannesapokalypse. Sechs Radiovortraege*, Basle 1944. Ch. Bruetsch, [4]1955.

Studies: M. Kohlhofer, *Die Einheit der Apk* (BSt VII 4: 1902). A. Schlatter, *Das AT in der Joh-Apk* (BFChTh XVI, 6: 1912). F. Boll, *Aus der Offb Johannis*, Leipzig 1914 (Stoicheia I). J. Freundorfer, *Die Apk des Apostels Johannes und die hellenistische Kosmologie und Astrologie* (BSt XXIII 1: 1929). W. Foerster, *Die Bilder in Offb 12 f. und 17 f.*: ThStK 104 (1932) 279–311. R. Schuetz, *Die Offb des Joh und Kaiser Domitian*, Goettingen 1933. P. Touilleux, *L'Apc. et les Cultes de Domitien et de Cybèle*, Paris 1935. H. Schlier, *Vom Antichrist* (on Apc. 13): Theol. Aufsaetze f. Karl Barth, Munich 1936, 110–123 (reprinted: *Die Zeit der Kirche*, 1956, 16–29). D. Haugg, *Die zwei Zeugen* (Apk 11, 1–13) (NtA XVII 1: 1936). G. Bornkamm, *Die Komposition der apokalyptischen Visionen in der Offb Joh*: ZntW 36 (1937) 132–149. C. Clemen, *Dunkle Stellen in der Offb Joh*, Bonn 1937. J. Sickenberger, *Die Messiasmutter im 12. Kap. der Apk*: ThQ 126 (1946) 357–427. A. Wikenhauser, *Das Problem des 1000jaehrigen Reiches in der Joh-Apk*: RQ 40 (1932) 13–25. Idem, *Die Herkunft der Idee des 1000jaehrigen Reiches in der Joh-Apk*: ibid. 45 (1937) 1–25. Idem, *Weltwoche und 1000jaehriges Reich*: ThQ 127 (1947) 390–417. R. Loennertz, *Plan et division de l'Apc.*: Angelicum 18 (1941) 336–356. H. Bietenhard, *Das 1000jaehrige Reich. Eine biblisch-theologische Studie*, Zurich [2]1955. K. Holzinger, *Erklaerungen zu einigen der dunkelsten Stellen der Offb Joh*, 1936 (SBWien 216/3). P. Gaechter, *Semitic Literary Forms in the Apc. and their Import*: ThSt 8 (1947) 547–573; *The Role of the Memory in the Making of the Apc.*: 9 (1948) 419–452; *The Original Sequence of Apc. 20–22*: 10 (1949) 485–521. M.-E. Boismard, "*L'Apc.*" ou "*les Apcs.*" *de S. Jean*: RB 56 (1949) 507–541. K. L. Schmidt, *Die Bildersprache in der Apk*: ThZ 3 (1947) 161–177. B. J. Le Frois, *Eschatological interpretation of the Apc.*: CBQ 13 (1951) 17–20. J. Munck, *Petrus und Paulus in der Offb Joh*, Copenhagen 1950. M.-E. Boismard, *Notes sur l'Apc.*: RB 59 (1952) 161–181. S. Giet, "*La guerre des Juifs*" *de Flavius Josèphe et quelques énigmes de l'Apc.*: RevSR 26 (1952) 1–29. M. Rissi, *Zeit und Geschichte in der Offb des Joh*, Zuerich 1952. M.-E. Boismard: Lumière et vie 1951, 107–128; 1952, 111–128. L. Goppelt, *Heilsoffenbarung und Geschichte nach der Offenbarung des Joh*: ThLZ 77

(1952) 513–523. St. Giet, *Les épisodes de la guerre juive et l'Apc.*: RevSr 26 (1952) 325–362. J. Cambier, *Les images de l'AT dans l'Apc. de St. Jean*: NRTh 87 (1955) 113–122. B. J. Le Frois, *The Woman Clothed with the Sun (Apc. 12), Individual or Collective?*, Rome 1954. [In the literal sense the woman is Mary, and only secondly the Church: denied by Boismard: RB 1955, 292–296.] J. Bloch, *On the Apocalyptic in Judaism* (The Jewish Quarterly Review Monogr. Ser. II), Philadelphia 1952 (see CBR 1954, 98–100). H. H. Rowley, *The Relevance of Apocalyptic*, London ²1947. J. W. Bowman, *The Drama of the Book of Revelation*, Philad. Westm. 1955. Surveys of research: E. Lohmeyer, *Die Offb des Joh*, 1920–1934: ThRdsch 6 (1934) 269–314; 7 (1935) 28–62; cf. also Bb 1940, 64–78.

1. *Content and structure*

TITLE with information about the origin and purpose of the book 1, 1–3: The work is in the form of a circular letter to seven churches of Asia Minor and begins with an epistolary introduction and blessing 1, 4–8.

In the introductory vision John is commissioned by the glorified Son of Man to commit to writing his visions ("the things which are and which must be done hereafter"), and to send the account to seven churches of the province of Asia which are mentioned by name 1, 9–20.

First or admonitory part: Seven Epistles containing praise and blame, promise of reward and threat of punishment, to churches of Asia Minor 2, 1 to 3, 22, namely to Ephesus 2, 1–7, Smyrna 2, 8–11, Pergamon 2, 12–17, Thyatira 2, 18–29, Sardis 3, 1–6, Philadelphia 3, 7–13, Laodicea 3, 14–22.

Second or prophetic part: The drama of the end of the present epoch and the coming of the future world era 4, 1 to 22, 5.

Introductory vision: The visionary sees how God sits on his throne in his court and accepts the acts of homage which are offered to him 4, 1–11.

First Act of the eschatological drama: The events which introduce the decisive struggle between God and Satan 5, 1–11, 14.

1. The vision of the seven seals with the announcement of terrible calamities for men 5, 1 to 8, 1: The Lamb which was slain

(Christ) receives from the hand of God the book sealed with seven seals (= the decrees of God concerning the completion of salvation) in order to open it 5, 1–14. As each seal is opened terrible events follow: the opening of the first four seals brings war, civil war, famine, and death (= the horsemen of the Apocalypse) 6, 1–8; when the fifth seal is opened, the souls of the martyrs under the heavenly altar cry for vengeance 6, 9–11; the opening of the sixth seal is followed by a violent convulsion of the fabric of the world 6, 12–17.

There is a pause in the course of the eschatological action; the seer sees a twofold vision which refers to the vicissitudes of the Church as the eschatological events progress: 1. The sealing of one hundred and forty four thousand servants of God as a symbol of their preservation in the coming time of tribulation 7, 1–8; 2. An innumerable multitude of those who were preserved in the time of tribulation standing before the throne of God 7, 9–17 (anticipatory scene).

When the seventh seal is opened there is silence in heaven for half an hour 8, 1.

2. The vision of the seven trumpets with the announcement of even more fearful calamities 8, 2 to 11, 14.

Introductory scene: An angel brings the prayers of the saints before God and casts fire upon the earth 8, 2–6.

The first four trumpets cause severe destruction in the sphere of nature (land, sea, rivers and fountains of waters, heavenly bodies), whereby many men also are killed 8, 7–12.,

The last three blasts of the trumpet (announced by threefold "woe" 8, 13) set demoniac forces in motion: the fifth trumpet releases swarms of locusts which torment men 9, 1–12, the sixth sets loose a demoniac army of horsemen who kill a third of mankind 9, 13–21, but men remain impenitent.

The course of the eschatological events is again broken by a double interlude: 1. An angel announces that God's secret design shall be accomplished at the sounding of the seventh trumpet, and he gives the seer an open book to eat so that he can foretell other events 10, 1–11; 2. The seer must measure the Temple of God and the altar and those that adore in it, but not the outer court (of the Gentiles), as a sign that both the court and the city will be given over to the Gentiles to be sacked; during this time two preachers of penance ("witnesses") appear there; they are murdered, but are miraculously raised and taken into heaven 11, 1–14.

Second Act of the eschatological drama: The decisive struggle between God and Satan for the possession of "the kingdom of this world"(11, 15) 11, 15 to 20, 15.

Introductory scene: At the seventh blast of the trumpet songs of victory sound in heaven, which celebrate beforehand, as already achieved, the coming establishment of the kingship of God over this world 11, 15–19.

1. The attack on the Church by the powers hostile to God (=the great time of tribulation) 12, 1 to 14, 5: The dragon (Satan) tries in vain to devour the infant Messias at birth; he is cast from heaven to the earth by Michael and now pursues the mother of the Messias, but she finds protection in the desert; so he now directs his attacks against "the rest of her seed" (the Christians) 12, 1–18. To help him in his struggle he sends two beasts, one from the sea—the Antichrist—and one from the land—the false prophet; the first beast, a monster with seven heads and ten horns, blasphemes God and makes war on the saints, the second beast performs all sorts of amazing miracles and leads men to adore the first beast; whoever opposes him is lost 13, 1–18. But the hundred and forty-four thousand who were sealed remain under God's protection 14, 1–5.

2. God's judgment of annihilation on the powers hostile to him (God's counter-stroke) 14, 6 to 20, 15:

Announcement and anticipatory presentation of the judgment under the form of harvest and vintage 14, 6–20.

The vision of the seven vials with the announcement of terrible calamities and disasters, a last fruitless attempt to bring godless and sinful mankind to conversion and repentance by means of chastisement 15, 1 to 16, 21:

Seven angels appear in heaven with seven vials filled with the wrath of God; the seer sees before God's throne those who triumphed over the first beast and he hears their song of victory 15, 1–8.

The first four vials poured out over the land, sea, rivers and fountains of waters, and the sun, produce dreadful torments for men 16, 1–9.

The fifth vial, poured out over the throne of the beast, darkens his kingdom 16, 10–11.

When the sixth vial is poured out on the Euphrates, three unclean spirits gather the kings of the earth for the decisive battle at Armagedon 16, 12–16.

The seventh vial, poured out upon the air, causes a violent earthquake which produces widespread devastation and a great hailstorm 16, 17–21.

The judgment on Babylon, the capital and representative of the world kingdom which is hostile to God 17, 1 to 19, 10:

The seer sees Babylon under the form of a sumptuously clad harlot who sits upon the beast with the seven heads and ten horns, bears upon her forehead the mystery name "Babylon the great", and is drunk with the blood of the martyrs of Christ 17, 1–6.

An angel explains to him the beast (the seven heads mean seven kings of the kingdom hostile to God, of whom five have already fallen, the sixth now reigns, and the seventh will have only a short reign—and the ten horns are allied kings) and the harlot (the great city of Babylon) 17, 7–18.

He then witnesses in a number of scenes the total annihilation of the city and hears the laments of the kings, merchants, and sea-captains for its downfall 18, 1–24.

He then hears the heavenly glorification of God for fulfilling the judgment on Babylon and for the forthcoming nuptials of the Lamb 19, 1–10.

The judgment on the beast and the false prophet and their army by the Rider on the white horse (Christ), the so-called Messianic Battle 19, 11–21:

The appearance of the heavenly king with his celestial warriors 19, 11–16.

The struggle between the heavenly and earthly armies. The beast and the false prophet are defeated and cast alive into the pool of fire, and their army is annihilated 19, 17–21.

Judgment on Satan 20, 1–10:

Binding of Satan for a thousand years 20, 1–3;

Resurrection of the martyrs and their thousand-year reign with Christ 20, 4–6;

When Satan is released again he leads the nations of Gog and Magog against the city of the saints; fire falls from heaven and devours the attackers; Satan is cast into the pool of fire 20, 7–10.

The conquest of all the powers hostile to God is followed by the general resurrection of the dead and the last judgment 20, 11–15.

Third Act of the eschatological drama: The eternal kingdom of God with the heavenly Jerusalem as its centre upon a new earth 21, 1 to 22, 5:

The new creation as the abode of the presence of God, perfect happiness and eternal life 21, 1–8;

The new Jerusalem in its grandeur and magnificence (form, size, precious things; river of water of life, trees of life) 21, 9–22, 5.

Conclusion of the book 22, 6–21: The reliability of the visions 22, 6–9; Jesus will soon come in judgment 22, 10–17; severe penalties for anyone who tampers with the book 22, 18–21.

This literary analysis of the Apocalypse presupposes that it must be considered a strictly unified work by one individual author. If this premise does not prove correct (see on this matter n. 4), then it can only be regarded as an attempt to understand the intention of the redactor who produced the form of the book which has been handed down to us.

2. Character

The Apocalypse of John is the only prophetic book of the New Testament. The word ἀποκάλυψις in the title is the name of the book, but in 1, 1 it describes the revelation or disclosure of future or rather eschatological events which Christ granted to John. As far as is known, this is the first place where the word is used in that sense. The verb ἀποκαλύπτειν and the noun ἀποκάλυψις first got a religious meaning in the LXX. In the New Testament they are used in a different sense and always mean the disclosure of hidden things which are known only to God: The Son reveals the Father to the "little ones" (Mt. 11, 27; Lk. 10, 22), and God reveals his Son to Paul (Gal. 1, 16). At the end of this world the Son of Man shall be revealed (Lk. 17, 30); but first the man of sin (Antichrist) shall reveal himself (2 Thess. 2, 3 6 8). At the Parousia of Christ the glory of the saved which is still hidden shall be revealed (Rom. 8, 18).

Late Judaism produced a large number of books of the type of the Ápc. of John, though—with the exception of the Apocalypse of Baruch—they are never called Apocalypse; most of these works survive only in versions, and a large number have perished entirely. The oldest apocalyptic work is the Book of Daniel (chs. 7–12), which the Hebrew Bible places among the "Writings" (see the prologue to Ecclesiasticus about this), while LXX has it among the Prophets. The Apc. of John also describes itself as "prophecy" (1,3). But even in the older prophetic books of the Old Testament there are parts with an apocalyptic character, such as Is. 24–27, Zach. 9–12, and large passages of Ezechiel (37, 1 to 14: vision of the dry bones; 40, 1 sqq.: the new temple).

The one great theme of these apocalypses—to use a convenient name for them—is the conclusion of history, the end of this world era and the future world (or the other world), described in virtue of (real or alleged) revelations or disclosures by God. Thus the author of the Book of Daniel in a series of visions foresees the course of historical events which reach their climax in the severe affliction of the Jewish people in Macchabean times, particularly under Antiochus IV Epiphanes; he foretells the happy ending of these tribulations, and the grant of lordship over all peoples and kingdoms to the nation of the holy ones of the most High, and the establishment of the eternal kingdom of God. A feature common to all these books is that their prophecies of the future are not in clear language but in a concealed form, namely in pictures, symbols and allegories, where numbers, colours, stars, and beasts each have a particular more profound significance.

For the understanding of the Apc. of John it is important to know not only Old Testament prophecy, including the Book of Daniel, but also the apocryphal Jewish apocalyptic writings which appeared in large numbers between the first century B.C. and the second century A.D. These are all pseudonymous works; the authors do not give their true names but represent their books as the work of some distinguished person of the past. Thus there are three books of Enoch, of which the first—the so-called Ethiopian Enoch—is the most important, the Testament of the Twelve Patriarchs, the Assumption of Moses, an Apocalypse of Esdras (4 Esd.) and of Baruch. These books are pseudonymous because late Judaism considered that prophecy was exhausted; cf. Apc. Baruch 85, 3 "The just have been gathered (to the fathers) and the prophets have laid themselves to sleep . . . and now we have nothing except the Almighty and the Law." That was why no one ventured to publish a prophetic book under his own name.

The apocalyptic writings vary greatly in content, but they are all primarily concerned with the end of time and the coming of the era of salvation. Many of them begin with an outline of the history of Israel from the time of the alleged author to the end of time, in the form of prophecy; the historical, events up to the real author's time are presented in a fairly concrete form, and then the "prophecy" grows very indefinite and general, and soon passes to a description of the judgment and of the commencement of the era of salvation. Thus the first book of Enoch contains in chs. 85–90 a sketch of world history from Adam to the establishment of the Messianic kingdom in the form of a symbolic dream which Enoch had. The accuracy with which the course of history is presented up to the time of the first readers and of the real author is designed to guarantee the reliability of the prophecies concerning the future.

Naturally descriptions of the end of time occupy a great deal of space in the apocalyptic writings. According to the Apc. of Esdras 10, 59 God intends to show in the fifth and sixth judgment "what he intends to do to the inhabitants of the earth in the last days". Many of these works contain detailed descriptions in darkest colours of the terrible tribulations which immediately precede the end, and this sombre background increases the brightness with which the era of salvation appears.

Yet these apocalyptic writings with their confused fantasies are not idle triflings designed for entertainment. They had an eminently practical purpose, for, being written in times of severe affliction and distress, they were designed to encourage and console the readers and to fill them with confidence in God, the arbiter of human destiny, who will finally bring everything to a good conclusion.

From the formal point of view there is a sharp distinction between Old Testament prophecy and the apocalyptic writings. The prophets receive divine revelations and commissions mainly through the inner word; visions have a merely subordinate role in them. On the other hand the author of an apocalypse receives the revelations of divine mysteries—which form the content of his book—mainly through visions, whether ecstasies (when awake) or dreams (asleep). In the apocryphal apocalyptic writings the visions are not as a rule genuine divine revelations, but are merely the literary form in which the author clothes his own aspirations and fears, instructions and exhortations. Yet it is not impossible that an inner experience, whether of hearing or of sight, may underlie certain particular cases such as the Apocalypse of Esdras, the most beautiful of these books. As examples of visions in dreams we have Daniel's vision of the four beasts 7, 1–17, Esdras' visions of the eagle 11, 60 to 12, 3 and of the Son of Man-Saviour 13, 1–13. Ecstatic visions are Daniel's vision of the struggles of the protecting angel of the nations 10, 1 sqq., and various visions of Enoch (1 Henoch 1, 2 sqq.; 39, 4 sqq.), of Esdras (9, 38 to 10, 37) and of Baruch (13, 1 sqq.; 22, 1 sqq.). In their visions the apocalyptic writers are often taken to a distant place on earth or in heaven; such withdrawals occur as early as Ezechiel (8, 3 sqq. 40, 2 sqq. to Jerusalem).

The apocalyptic writers present the course of history in pictures, symbols and allegories. In Daniel (1, 1 sqq.) four beasts represent the godless world kingdoms which succeed one another, in Esdras the eagle is an allegory of the Roman Empire and its three horns and numerous wings represent the individual rulers (11, 1 sq.). In Baruch the dark and clear waters which in turn fall from a cloud upon the earth represent the corresponding number of events in world history from Adam to the Babylonian captivity (53 sqq.). Like all allegories, these visions call for an explanation which is given by an angel at the request of the visionary. Yet even these explanations do not entirely elucidate the mystery.

The Apocalypse of St. John belongs to this literary category of Apocalypsis.

Eschatological and apocalyptic ideas and notions were alive also in other places in primitive Christianity, but not in the fantastic forms which they assumed in late Judaism. In the New Testament writings there are eschatological passages of fairly small extent—in the Synoptic Gospels (Mk. 13 par; Lk. 17, 20–37), in Paul (1 Thess. 4, 15–17; 2 Thess. 2, 1–12; 1 Cor. 15, 20–28) and in 2 Pet. 3, 10–13; but in extent and significance they are surpassed by the Apc. of John, which is universally considered the most beautiful and valuable of all apocalyptic writings. After John's Apc. a whole Christian apocalyptic literature arose which christianized and expanded Jewish apocalyptic writings or created new works (Apc. of Peter, Apc. of Paul, Pastor of Hermas etc.).

Both in form and content the Apc. of John shows close kinship with Jewish apocalyptic writings. It presents a continuous series of symbolico-allegorical visions which the author experienced while in a state of ecstasy during which he was several times transported (4, 1; 17, 3; 21, 10). According to 1, 1 and 22, 8 an angel shows him the visions. Yet unlike the other apocalyptic writings, the Apc. of John does not contain an orderly explanation of the events by an angel or by God himself; only the scarlet woman and the beast on which she rides are explained by an angel (17, 1 sqq.).

The principal theme here, as in most apocalyptic writings, is the view of the last events (the terrible period of tribulation under the lordship of Antichrist, and the divine punishment of the godless powers), and of their outcome—the Second Coming of Christ, the general judgment and the happiness of the elect in the new world era. There is no lack of religious and moral exhortation, for, like all apocalyptic literature, the Apc. of John has a practical religious purpose. Its essential aim is to strengthen the readers in loyalty to God and Christ, to encourage them to persevere patiently in the severe persecutions which threaten them, and to inspire them to bear martyrdom cheerfully. The admonitions appear principally in the seven letters to the Churches of Asia Minor, though the strictly apocalyptic part has also a number of short sentences of the same kind (13, 9 sq.; 14, 13; 16, 15; 19, 9; 20, 6).

In spite of the kinship between the Apc. of John and Jewish apocalyptic writing we should not overlook its clearly marked individuality. It is not a product of the study or of intensive meditation on the signs of the times; the Apc. was born from the ecstatic experiences of a prophet.

The author is a genuine prophet. Like the great Old Testament prophets in the past who were called to the office of prophet in a real vision (Is. 6, 1–13; Jer. 1, 4 sqq.; Ez. 2, 1 sqq.), John also received a call when the glorified Christ appeared to him on the Lord's day in Patmos, and commissioned him to write down and send to the Churches of Asia Minor the vision which he was about to receive (1, 9 sqq.). The prophetic consciousness of the, author is attested by the whole book, above all by the seven letters with which it begins. In them John shows true prophetic insight in penetrating to the depths of the heart, and in his words of praise and censure, exhortation and condemnation he demonstrates the prophetic power which is his. Perhaps the strongest proof of the genuinely prophetic character of the book is the fact that the author writes under his own name to definite Christian churches of his own time and castigates them unsparingly. There is nothing similar in the apocryphal apocalyptic writings of Judaism.

It is not a valid objection to the prophetic character of the Apc. of John to say that much of the material which it presents is not original, for the apocalyptic does not see in his visions the forms and happenings which he describes in the book. When he experiences the vision, God communicates to him ideas and truths concerning the vicissitudes of the Church and of unbelieving mankind, the enemy of God and Christ; he clothes these in pictures, forms, and happenings, that is, he translates into visible symbols what God has revealed to him, and in doing so makes use of the material which tradition has preserved, particularly the parts of the Old Testament prophetic writings which are akin to his book, though he uses this material with great freedom and independence (for example, the vision of the chariot of the throne Ez. 1, and the four beasts Dan. 7).

Yet he attaches no importance to describing carefully-formed pictorial visions. It would therefore be idle to form a picture of the Lamb with seven horns and seven eyes (5, 6) and of the beast with seven heads and ten horns (13, 1), and to enquire how the ten horns and seven heads are distributed. We must be content with grasping the symbol intellectually, without stopping at the not uncommon incongruities. Seven is the number for perfection, so the seven horns and seven eyes mean that the Lamb has the fullness of power (horns) and knowledge (eyes), and the beast represents the Roman Empire with seven emperors and ten vassal kings; in the same way a special meaning attaches to the colours (white, scarlet), numbers ($3\frac{1}{2}$, 4, 7, 10, 12, 42, 666, 1000) and other things such as the sword coming from the mouth (2, 12; 19, 15), and the long garment (1, 13). It is only if we grasp this relation between vision and literary formulation that we can appreciate also the artistry which has gone into the composition of the book where, for example, groups of seven (sometimes divided 4 + 3) play a dominant role.

The Apc. of John is a Christian book. No less than the other New Testament books it proclaims Jesus Christ the Crucified, the eternal Son of God and Saviour of men, who now sits on the right hand of God and will appear on earth as Judge at the end of time.

Like the Jewish apocalyptic writings it deals with the last events, but in John's eyes the end is only the consolidation and completion of what happened with the appearance of Christ (12, 1 sqq.). So the Messias has quite a different role here from his role in Jewish apocalyptic literature. In the latter the era of salvation is brought about not by the Messias, but by God; indeed the Messias hardly has an active part, and he does not appear at all in some of these writings. On the other hand, in the Apc. of John it is Jesus Christ who sets the last events in motion by opening the seals of the book which contains the universal plan for mankind. By his sacrifice on the Cross he has redeemed men from sin (1, 5; 5, 9; 7, 14; 12, 11; 22, 14), and so he alone is worthy to open the sealed book (5, 69; 13, 8). He now shares God's throne in Heaven (3, 21; 7, 17; 22, 1 3), and is the glorified Lord of the faithful to whom he gives praise, encouragement, consolation, and, if they deserve it, threats of punishment. At the end of time he will appear in judgment (19, 11 sqq.) and reveal himself as the Lord of the world who was foretold in Ps. 2 (2, 26 sqq.; 12, 5; 19, 15). In the new Jerusalem he with God is the source of everlasting life and eternal happiness to the elect (21, 22 sq.; 22, 1 sqq.).

3. Author

The author gives his name as John in four places of the Apc. (1, 1 4 9; 22, 8), and in 1, 9 he describes himself as the brother of the readers and a partner in their tribulation. He nowhere makes an explicit claim to be one of the College of Twelve Apostles; but he does wish to be accepted and listened to as a prophet (1, 1–3; 22, 6). Yet there is no suggestion in the book that he had previously been a prophet or is respected as such by the readers. He probably did not hold this office until he received the call to write his book; the call came to him on the island of Patmos which lies opposite Miletus on the west coast of Asia Minor (1, 9 sqq.); he had come there—evidently not long before—"for the word of God and for the testimony of Jesus".

The letters to the Churches of Asia Minor show an accurate knowledge of conditions prevailing there, so it must be assumed that he had lived and worked for a considerable time in those churches. Moreover, he had undisputed authority over them, as we see from the fact that he does not hesitate to reveal unsparingly and castigate remorselessly the faults and shortcomings of those churches. Who is this John, the mention of whose name was sufficient to identify him to the readers?

The tradition of the early Church was almost unanimous in identifying him with John the Apostle, son of Zebedee and brother of James the Elder (§ 28, 2). The earliest witness to this identification is Justin Martyr, who says in his *Dialogue with Trypho the Jew,* composed 151–155 A.D.: "A man of ours, by name John, one of the Apostles of the Christ, prophesied in a revelation vouchsafed to him, that those who become believers in our Christ will dwell for a thousand years in Jerusalem (cf. Apc. 20, 4–6), and that afterwards the universal—and in brief— eternal resurrection of all men and the judgment will take place together" (81, 4). Around the turn of the second century the author of the Apc. is identified with John by the anti-Marcionite prologue to Luke (about 160–180 A.D.; cf. § 5, 3), Irenaeus of Lyons (*Haer*. IV 30, 4; V 26, 1), Tertullian (*Adv. Marc.* III 14; IV 5), Clement of Alexandria (*Paed.* II 119, 1), and Hippolytus of Rome (*De Antichristo* 36, 50). In one passage (*Commentary on John* II 5 ch. 45; about 225 A.D.), Origen says explicitly that John the Apostle wrote both the Apc. and the fourth Gospel.

Nevertheless there were dissentient voices in antiquity. At the beginning of the third century the Apc. was ascribed to Cerinthus the Gnostic by the Roman priest Gaius because of its alleged Chiliasm, and also by the Alogi (anti-Montanists) in view of apparent contradictions between it and the other New Testament writings (Eusebius H. E. III 28, 2; Epiphanius, *Haer.* 51); on this matter see the articles by Bludau mentioned in § 28, 2 above. The most important opponent of its apostolic origin was Dionysius, the great bishop of Alexandria († 264 A.D.); he considered the Apc. the work of a saintly and divinely inspired man, but thought that John the Apostle could not be its author in view of the divergence of language, style, and ideas between it and the works which he did ascribe to the Apostle, namely the fourth Gospel and 1 John. He preferred to attribute it to a presbyter of Ephesus called John, a distinct person from the Apostle (Eusebius, H. E. IV 39; VII 25, 16). His influence made Eusebius doubt to which of the two he should ascribe the Apc. (H. E. III 25).

But these denials or hesitations were entirely based on dogmatic or exegetical arguments. Wherever the Apc. was accepted as canonical, the Apostle John was considered its author.

Does internal evidence support this tradition of apostolic authorship? There is no need to prove that Cerinthus cannot have written it; such an idea could be entertained only by those who found a gross Chiliasm taught in the Apc. Dionysius himself explicitly rejected this view.

How is Dionysius' own view to be assessed? It is a fact that the majority of modern exegetes who reject the tradition of Johannine authorship, attribute the Apc. with various degrees of confidence to John the Presbyter of Ephesus; both Bousset and Lohmeyer do so in their commentaries, while Swete does not commit himself; Charles, on the other hand, ascribes the composition of the fourth Gospel and the three Johannine Epistles to John the Presbyter, and thinks that the Apc. is the work of a "seer" named John, who in advanced old age migrated from Galilee to Ephesus. Unlike Dionysius these scholars do not regard the Apostle as the author of the fourth Gospel and the Johannine Epistles.

So the problem is crystallized in the question which was first clearly recognized and posed by Dionysius of Alexandria: Can one and the same author be responsible for all five Johannine writings, on the one hand the fourth Gospel and the Epistles, and on the other the Apc.? We no longer have the work *On the promises* where he dealt with the problem, but Eusebius incorporated a lengthy summary of it in his History (VII 25, 1–26). In the light of this summary we must admit that Dionysius reached his conclusions only after a painstaking comparison of the Apc. with the fourth Gospel and 1 John. Indeed it may be said that modern scholarship has not added a single substantially new point.

His first point, which is the weakest, is that the author of the Apc. gives his name at the very beginning, while the fourth Evangelist does not mention his name either in the fourth Gospel or in the first Epistle. If the Apostle John had written the Apc., he would have described himself as the disciple whom the Lord loved—as he does in the Gospel—or who leaned on his breast, or as the brother of James, or as the disciple who had seen the Lord with his own eyes and heard him with his own ears (1 John 1, 1).

The second point is more serious. In the fourth Gospel and in 1 John "the same fundamental ideas and expressions occur everywhere; anyone who reads them attentively will frequently find in both writings the words: life, light, turning away from darkness; also truth, grace, joy, the flesh and blood of the Lord, judgment, remission of sins, the love of God for us, the commandment that we love one another, that we should observe all the commandments, the conviction of the world, of the devil, and of the Antichrist, the promise of the Holy Ghost, our adoption as sons of God, the faith which is required of us, the Father and the Son. Compared to these writings the Apc. is entirely different and singular; there is no connection or relationship. Indeed it has hardly a syllable in common with them."

The third point is equally strong: "the divergence in style between the Apc. and both the fourth Gospel and the Epistle. The latter are not only written in faultless Greek, but are most felicitous in their manner of expression, development of thought, and connection of sentences; one can hardly discover in them a barbarous touch, a solecism or even a vulgarism." On the other hand the language and mode of expression of the Apc. are not pure Greek; it uses barbarous expressions, and occasionally even solecisms.

These observations of Dionysius are correct, and it would be perverse to underestimate their significance.[1] The language and style of the Apc. differ remarkably from that of the other Johannine writings, so much so that Gaechter, Sickenberger, and other exegetes who defend tradition feel themselves driven time and again to assume that the good Greek of the Gospel and Epistles is the work of a disciple who translated and wrote down the Aramaic expositions of the Apostle, his master.

In style the Apc. is quite unique. The author writes in Greek, but thinks in Hebrew; he often translates Hebrew expressions literally into Greek. Grammatical and stylistic irregularity is the rule with him, though it is not deliberate but unconscious. As examples we may mention 1, 4 ἀπὸ ὁ ὢν καὶ ὁ ἦν ... καὶ ἀπὸ ʼI. Χριστοῦ ὁ μάρτυς ὁ πιστός; 11, 4 αἱ δύο λυχνίαι αἱ ... ἑστῶτες; 2, 26; 3, 21 ὁ νικῶν, δώσω αὐτῷ; 11, 1 καὶ ἐδόθη μοι κάλαμος ... λέγων. Very often a superfluous demonstrative appears in relative clauses: 3, 8 ἣν οὐδεὶς δύναται κλεῖσαι αὐτήν (also 7, 2 9; 13, 8 12; 20, 8); 12, 6 ὅπου ἔχει ἐκεῖ (12, 14; 17, 9; 16, 19); Hebraisms occur also in 10, 7 καὶ ἐτελέσθη (for τελεσθήσεται) and in 14, 9 sq.

Attempts have been made to explain away the strong divergences between the Apc. and the other Johannine writings by dating the Apc. twenty or twenty five years earlier. But even if such an early date were acceptable, this would not solve the problem, for the remarkable difference in thought and ideas is even more serious. As Dionysius rightly perceived, the Apc. lacks a large number of ideas which are peculiar to Johannine theology. Moreover, the

---

[1] The language of the Apc. is examined at length in the commentaries of Bousset p. 159–179; Charles I p. XIX–XXXVII; CXVII - CLIX; Allo p. CXXIX to CLIV.

thought of the Apc. is dominated entirely by eschatology; in the other Johannine writings the possession of eternal life here and now through grace outshines eschatology so much that a number of critics like Bultmann eliminate their few allusions to eschatology as later interpolations by an ecclesiastical editor. Furthermore the presentation of Antichrist in the two sets of works is entirely different. So the question arises whether one man in the same period of his life could have composed two works which show such fundamental differences as there are between the Apc. and the other Johannine writings.

The exegetes who defend tradition emphasize that as well as differing the two sets of writings have remarkable elements in common.[2] In both places Christ is described as a lamb (ἀρνίον is very frequent in Apc., it occurs only in John 21, 15; elsewhere ἀμνός is used John 1, 29 36); "waters of life" in Apc. 7, 17; 21, 6; 22, 17 is reminiscent of the living water John 4, 10 sq.; 7, 37 sq. and the invitation in Apc. 22, 17: "he that thirsteth, let him come. And he that will, let him take the water of life freely" suggests John 7, 37; both use Zach. 12, 10 with the same variation from the LXX Apc. 1, 7; John 19, 37. On the other hand the description of Christ as "the word of God" in Apc. 19, 13 has a different meaning from "the word" in John 1, 1 sqq., and is to be explained from Wis. 18, 15. But the same meanings attach to ζωή, θάνατος, μαρτυρία, μαρτυρεῖν, νικᾶν, τηρεῖν τὸν λόγον and τὰς ἐντολάς, δεικνύναι (reveal). The silence of Apc. 21, 22 about the Temple in the new Jerusalem is paralleled in John 4, 21.

In view of these and other agreements those who reject John's authorship, concede at least that there is a relationship between the two authors.

To sum up: There are strong divergences in language and matter between the Apc. and the other Johannine writings; if

[2] These are enumerated in Bousset p. 177–179, Charles I, p. XXXII - XXXIV, and Lohmeyer p. 134 sq.

552

both are the work of the same author there is no really satisfactory explanation of these divergences. Yet in spite of belonging to quite distinct literary categories, the two groups show remarkable agreements, and so almost all Catholic exegetes feel bound to uphold the authorship of John the Apostle, particularly as John the Presbyter—or seer—of Ephesus is a very elusive figure, even if we admit his existence as established.

Yet some Catholic exegetes, such as Boismard, emphasize that the authorship of the Apc. is not a matter of faith. If a disciple of John's was author of the work, then we have the same situation as with Heb., which was not written by Paul himself (cf. § 46, 5) and yet is included in the Canon. This ascription of the Apc. to a disciple of John the Apostle would fit in well with the report in Eusebius (cf. § 28, 2) and of the Apostolic Constitutions VII 46, 7; according to them, a Christian named John, who lived in Asia Minor, was made bishop of Ephesus, the religious capital of all Asia Minor, by John the Apostle. The exponents of this theory draw attention particularly to the important point that the author of Apc. is aware of the distinction between Apostles and Prophets (18, 20), yet he places himself in the category of prophet (22, 9) without making the slightest claim to the title of Apostle (cf. also 21, 14).

4. Place and time of composition

According to the tradition of the early Church, John wrote the Apc.—which he had seen on the island of Patmos (1, 9 sqq.)—towards the end of Domitian's reign; Domitian was Emperor from 81 to 96 A.D., so around 94 or 95 A.D. would be the traditional date of composition.

The first witness to this tradition is Irenaeus, according to whom the Apc. "was seen not long ago, but almost in our own time, namely at the end of the Emperor Domitian's reign" (*Haer.* V 30, 3; cf. II 22, 5; III 3, 4). Irenaeus wrote ninety years after Domitian's death, so this report was probably taken from Papias' book, written about 130 A.D., which Irenaeus used elsewhere, for the expression "almost in our own time" does not fit Irenaeus well.

Victorinus of Pettau († about 305 A.D.), the oldest Latin commentator on the Apc., says that John the Apostle was relegated by Domitian to the island of Patmos and there saw the Apc. (*Comm. in Apc.* 11, 11; 17, 10). Eusebius (H. E. III 18, 1) appeals to Irenaeus when he says that towards the end of Domitian's reign "the Apostle and Evangelist was relegated to Patmos because of his defence of the word of God". In his chronicle he places the relegation in the fourteenth year of Domitian. Jerome (*De vir. ill.* 9) adopted the account of Eusebius, and almost all subsequent writers followed these two sources.

There are isolated voices in antiquity which place the writing of the book earlier (under Claudius or Nero) or later (under Trajan), but they are mostly fairly late and somewhat unreliable; they cannot prevail against the other evidence.

The only other historically conceivable time for the composition of the Apc. would be under Nero or shortly after his death in 68 A.D. He was the first Emperor to persecute the Christians (in 64 A.D.), so John could have been banished in his reign; attempts have been made to show that Tertullian had this in mind in his reference to John's martyrdom in oil (*Praescr. haer.* 36), but he is so vague that no reliable inference can be drawn. The Muratorian Canon also seems to mean that the Apc. was written in Nero's reign when it says (lines 48–50) that Paul wrote to only seven churches "following the rule of his predecessor".

In the last century many Protestant exegetes dated the Apc. to the interregnum between Nero's death on 8th June 68 A.D. and Vespasian's accession on the 1st July of the following year, or to the beginning of the latter's reign (69–79). They argued from internal evidence; from the prophecy about the preservation of the Temple and of Jerusalem they concluded that the book was written before 70 A.D. when the city and the Temple were destroyed; they reckoned the seven Emperors (Apc. 17, 9–11) from Augustus onwards, which brought them to Galba, or, ignoring the three Emperors of the interregnum, to Vespasian, as the sixth Emperor under whom, according to 17, 10, John had his visions. This dating is occasionally put forward even to-day, for example, by Hadorn.

The following arguments support 94–95 A.D. as the time when the Apc. was written:

1. The Epistles to the Churches of Asia Minor presuppose that Christianity had spread fairly widely in those areas, more widely than was the case before 70 A.D. Moreover, the internal conditions of these churches show that they already had a fairly long history behind them, for the first fervour of some of them had grown cold (Ephesus, Sardis, Laodicea).

2. John has an intimate knowledge of religious and moral conditions in those churches, and he has a superior authority over them. This presupposes a fairly long sojourn in the province and a protracted period of activity. But he did not go to Asia Minor till the outbreak of the Jewish war in 67 A.D.

3. The author of the Apc. foresees the coming of great tribulation on the whole world (3, 10). In ch. 13 we are told the character of this persecution, which will affect all Christians: The (Roman) civil power which deifies itself will engage in a life or death struggle with the Christian Church; the persecution which they have already experienced (6, 9–11; 17, 6) will flare up again and assume even worse forms, and this time it will not spare the Church in the province of Asia.

This description applies not to conditions under Nero, but to the time of Domitian. Towards the end of his reign Domitian took the unprecedented step of demanding personal divine worship; this demand applied to all subjects of the Empire, and as the cult of Caesar was at its most flourishing in Asia Minor, it was impossible for the Church there to escape very severe conflicts. This is the only background to explain sentences like 13, 14 to 17; 14, 9–11.

If the Apc. is a coherent work written at one time by one and the same author, it can hardly have been produced earlier than the end of Domitian's reign. On the other hand, if the author did not write it all at once, but incorporated a greater or lesser number of written sources of various dates—sources are suggested from the time of Caligula, Nero, Galba and Vespasian—then we must say that the Apc., in the form in which we have it, was composed towards the end of Domitian's reign.

The original form of the Apc. is a matter of dispute among non-Catholic scholars. Swete, Hadorn, Lohmeyer, Behm and others vigorously defend the strict unity of the book, while others, like Bousset and Charles, hold the theory that the author of our Apc. has incorporated into his work various written sources[3], though he has given such uniformity to the language and style that it is difficult, if not impossible, to detach with certainty the borrowed material.

Catholics up to the present day are strong defenders of unity. Yet they have realized that some passages—particularly ch. 11 and 13—present almost insuperable difficulties to the exegete who defends unity, and they have a number of times referred to the strict parallelism between chs. 4–9 and 12–16 which is not easy to explain.

To meet these difficulties Fr. Boismard O.P. has recently (1949) put forward a theory: Our Apc. is a conflation of two similar works, both written by the Apostle John, but at different times. The older of these two apocalyptic works was written during the reign of Nero, but before the deaths of the Apostles Peter and Paul; it embraces chs. 12–16 and some verses of ch. 10 (2a

[3] There is a survey in Bousset p. 108 sqq. and Allo p. CLV 189.

3 sq. 8–10 11) and chs. 17–22 (17, 10 12–14; 18, 4–8 14 20 22 sq.;
19, 11–20; 20, 11 sq.; 21, 1–4; 22, 3–5, 21, 5–8). The beast of 17,
10 is the Roman Empire; the seven heads are seven Emperors; the
death wound of the beast is the assassination of Julius Caesar,
which was a mortal wound to the Roman state, though it lived
on more vigorously under Augustus; in the person of Nero, the
reigning Emperor, it unleashes the violent persecution of Christians which is described in ch. 11 and 13; the two witnesses of
11, 3 sqq. are Peter and Paul who have been put to death (cf. § 49)
in Rome, the great city of 11, 8. The appendix 11, 1–13 19 was
added shortly afterwards to this older Apocalypse.

The more recent Apocalypse, which was written after 70 A.D.
under Vespasian or at the beginning of Domitian's reign, consists
of chs. 4–9; 10, 1 2b 5–7; 11, 14–18 and the remainder of chs. 17–22.
The beast of 17, 8 which "was and is not and shall come up" is
the emperor Nero; he has now disappeared, but popular legend
had it that, as *Nero redivivus,* he would return at the head of the
Parthians—the coalition with the ten kings, 17, 16 sq. refers to
this—to take vengeance on Rome.

The letters to the seven churches are later than either Apocalypse, for they make use of both these works. The situation
which they describe fits the condition of the churches of Asia
Minor during Domitian's reign, before the persecution broke
out in 95 A.D. It was at this time or somewhat later that the
Apc. was published in its final form, almost certainly by another hand, who united the pieces into one work.

The author has not yet worked out his theory in detail and
it cannot be discussed here. The same applies to Gaechter's
theory, which adopts a different approach; he ascribes the
numerous "discrepancies" and "inconsistencies" which he recognizes to the faulty memory of the disciples of the Apostle who
used their master's discourses as the material for the book (cf.
on this ThR 1952, 57–60).

5. Interpretation

Throughout the ages the Apc. has been subjected to the most varied and contradictory interpretations. The Fathers were deeply interested in it, but even they had no uniform interpretation. The interpretations which have been placed on the Apc. provide an instructive historical study, but it is impossible to enter upon them here.[4] It must be sufficent to deal briefly with the interpretation which saw in the Apc. the history of the world or of the Church; this was very popular from the Middle Ages until well into the nineteenth century.

This historical interpretation is due to the Franciscan Alexander of Bremen (about 1250), and it appears in a more developed form in the *Postille* of Nicholas of Lyra (1321). According to it, the Apc. foretells the whole course of history to the end of the world, so far as the relation between the Church and worldly powers is concerned. Its visions mysteriously depict the great epochs and most important events, the most influential figures and the most significant situations in the history of the world and of the Church. All exponents of this interpretation share the belief that the end of the world is not far away; they like to make a reckoning of the events which are still to come. Usually they divide the course of history into seven periods and a few of them even find these seven periods of Church history reflected in the seven letters. There is no doubt that this interpretation of the Apc. was a great and unfortunate error. The most

---

[4] They are treated at length by Bousset p. 49–119. Cf. also W. Kamlah, *Apk und Geschichtstheologie. Die mittelalterliche Auslegung der Apk vor Joachim von Fiore*, Berlin 1935 (Histor. Studien 235); A. Wachtel: Franzisk. Studien 24 (1937) 201 to 259 305–363 (on Alexander of Bremen); *Der Apk-Kommentar des Minoriten Alexander von Bremen*, hg. von A. Wachtel, Weimar 1955 (Mon. Germ. Hist.). K. Benz, *Joachim-Studien*: ZKG 50 (1931) 32—111; 51 (1932) 415—4551; 53 (1934) 52—116; Id., *Die Geschichtstheologie der Franziskanerspiritualen des 13. und 14. Jh.*: ZKG 52 (1933) 90—121; Idem, *Ecclesia spiritualis*, 1935.

striking proof of its ineptitude is provided by the fact that the interpretation had to be changed from century to century when the expected end of the world did not take place.

Present day scientific exegesis accepts only three forms of interpretation: eschatological, historical, and traditional. None of these by itself fits the book, and only a combination of all three makes it possible to give an explanation which fits the facts, in so far as such an explanation is possible at all. Despite long and devoted study not all the riddles of this book have been solved and they probably never will be. Present day exegetes are not unanimous even on the questions of who are represented by the beasts in ch. 15 and by Babylon in ch. 17, although the whole understanding of the Apc. depends essentially on this.

The Apc. is not a prophetic sketch of world history or of Church history; it is a prophecy dealing with the end of time and the arrival of the era of the next world, and so it must be understood eschatologically. In ch. 13 the seer views the pernicious activity of Antichrist, who, according to 2 Thess. 2, 3–12; 1 John 2, 18, appears immediately before the Second Coming of Christ; from 14, 6 onwards he describes the consummation of the last judgment in its various phases, and then he deals with the regeneration of the earth and the kingdom of God in it. According to this method of interpretation the Apc. presents in chronological order and in first causes the sufferings, tribulations, and judgments, which shall befall both Christendom and the unbelieving world at the end of the present era of the world.

Yet the purely eschatological interpretation does not fit the book.[5] To begin with, it robs the Apc. of its topicality. The Apc. was written for its own time, and its encouragement, consolation,

---

[5] Sickenberger and Ketter, among others, hold it. Cf. Sickenberger, *Die Joh-Apk und Rom*: BZ 17 (1926) 270–282; Ketter, *Der roemische Staat und die Apk*: Trierer Theol. Studien 1 (1941) 70–93. The most recent scholar to attack the purely eschatological interpretation is D. Cullmann, *Der Staat im NT*, Tuebingen 1956, 51–61.

and confirmation were intended not for distant generations but for contemporary Christians. Primitive Christianity did not believe that the end of the world was in the remote distance; they hoped and desired that it would come soon. Hence the Apc. foretells events which are to take place soon (1, 1 3; 22, 6 10).

Secondly, the book makes clear allusions to historical events and to political and religious conditions of the author's time. As most exegetes, including Catholics, recognize, the beast which emerges from the sea (13, 1) is to be understood as the Roman Empire, the false prophet (13, 11 sqq.; 16, 13; 19, 20) is Emperor worship which deifies the ruler, and Babylon (17, 1 sqq.), the capital of the godless kingdom, is pagan Rome.

So the historical and eschatological interpretations must be combined, for the seer does not view the end as something in the distant future, he rather sees its approach clearly foreshadowed in certain circumstances and events of his own time. This is the only sense in which the historical interpretation can be justified. It cannot be defended in the sense that the seer "prophesies" only past or present matters and not future events, that his visions, under the guise of foretelling the future, contain only the past or the present, as is the case in many Jewish apocalyptic writings. It is only in ch. 12 that the seer views events of the past (birth and exaltation of the Messias, persecution of the woman by the dragon), but these visions could not be omitted, for they form the premiss for the vision of the coming of the two beasts in ch. 13. In any case, ch. 12 does not claim to be a vision of the future.

The historical interpretation, which arose as a reaction to the fantastic method of interpreting the Apc. as history of the Church, is to-day confined mainly to ch. 13 and 17 (and 11). It regards these chapters as a prophecy of the forthcoming life and death struggle between the Christian Church and the Roman state with its totalitarian claims; but behind these two historical entities stand super-historical powers, heavenly and infernal powers. In the struggle between the Church and the Roman state John sees the decisive struggle between God and Satan which ends with the victory of God and the final annihilation of all powers hostile to God; this struggle ushers in the end of this world-period and the beginning of the everlasting kingdom of God.

So the visions of the Apc. contain one unified picture of the last events which the seer knows from the Old Testament, the religious tradition of the Jewish people and the primitive Christian faith, together with the severe persecutions which will come in the near future. That is the imperfection of all genuine prophecy which lacks perspective. So the historical interpretation of ch. 13 —which in any case does not exhaust its content—is not open to the objection that it takes insufficient account of the prophetic character of the book. In the book of Daniel also, which is the oldest Biblical apocalypse and the model for all the others, the prophecy of the subjugation of God's people by Antiochus IV, the type of Antichrist, is juxtaposed with the prophecy of the Messianic kingdom, even though the two events are separated in time (cf. Dan. 7, 21: 7, 22; 7, 24–26: 7, 27). Again Dan. 12, 1–3 interweaves an "historical" prophecy (the saving of Israel from Antiochus IV) with an "eschatological" prophecy (the salvation of God's people at the end of time), just as in the Apocalypse of John.

The most recent form of interpretation is the traditional or mythological. It was first put forward in 1895 by Hermann Gunkel and was developed by Bousset, Charles, Lohmeyer, and Boll. It is a wholesome reaction to the narrowly historical interpretation which everywhere suspected allusions to events or conditions of the seer's own time or of the recent past. It is in sharp contrast to that interpretation, for it maintains that very ancient mythological or other traditions are the foundation of many pictures, forms, and happenings in the visions of the Apocalypse. Gunkel refers to Babylonian myths, Bousset to Iranian traditions, Lohmeyer to the writings of the Mandeans, a Gnostic sect, while Boll tries to explain a large number of passages in the light of Hellenistic astrology and astral mythology. The pictures and images which often appear so strange to us cannot all be understood from the Old Testament and late Jewish tradition. The justification and significance of this method is that it clarifies their meaning and origin. But that is also its limitation. At best it can make clear the use and origins of these forms, but it does not tell us what the author of the Apc. intended to convey through them.

6. Canonicity[6]

Around the year 200 A.D. the Apc. was accepted as canonical in the whole Church with the exception of the Syrian national Church which was just arising at that time in and around Edessa. In the West it has remained an undisputed part of the Canon ever since it was first known. Irenaeus of Lyons and Hippolytus of Rome valued it highly; the latter, according to Jerome, composed a commentary on it which is now lost. The first commentary on the Apc. to be written in Latin was the work of Victorinus of Pettau in Styria († 304), and it was followed by the commentaries of the Donatist Tychonius in Africa (370–380 A.D.), Primasius bishop of Hadrumetum in Africa (about 540 A.D.), Apringius of Pace in Portugal in the sixth century, the Venerable Bede (672 to 735), and the priest Beatus of Liébana in Asturia (about 786)—clear indications of the standing which the book enjoyed in the Western Church.

In the early Egyptian Church the canonical nature of the Apc. is attested by Clement of Alexandria († 215 A.D.) and Origen († 255 A.D.). In Asia Minor, where it was written, the witnesses are older and more numerous. According to Eusebius, Melito bishop of Sardis wrote a—now lost—book about it (H. E. IV 26, 2), and about 197 A.D. Apollonius the anti-Montanist (bishop of Ephesus?) adduced arguments drawn from the Apc. (H. E. V 18, 14). We

[6] Cf. N. B. Stonehouse, *The Apc. in the Ancient Church*, Goes 1929.

562

should also include among the witnesses from Asia Minor Irenaeus, who was born there, and Justin Martyr, who lived in Ephesus from about 130 to 135 A.D. Andrew of Caesarea says explicitly (see above § 5, 2) that Papias knew and esteemed the book. The Apc. was also in the Canon of the Church of Antioch towards the end of the second century, as we see from the fact that Theophilus bishop of Antioch (169–177 A.D.) drew upon it for arguments in a controversy with Hermogenes (Eusebius, H. E. IV 24).

In the mid third century Dionysius bishop of Alexandria (248 to 264 A.D.) raised a serious challenge to it during his controversy with Nepos bishop of Arsinoe in the Fayum; he denied that the Apc. was the work of the Apostle John and so caused its canonicity to be queried (see above n. 3). This opinion of the Patriarch of Alexandria and the appeal of the Chiliasts to the Apc. caused an eclipse of the Apc. in the Greek Church, though strangely the Egyptian Church was not affected by these factors, for it maintained the apostolical and canonical nature of the book. Athanasius (367 A.D.), Didymus († about 398 A.D.) and Cyril of Alexandria († 444 A.D.) accepted it.

But outside Egypt it was seriously challenged until about 500 A.D. Eusebius of Caesarea († 340 A.D.) is doubtful whether to list it among the universally accepted books or among the works which are to be rejected as spurious. Cyril of Jerusalem (*Cat.* IV 36) does not have it in his Canon. Even the Antiochene exegetical school does not recognize it. The fourth century writers of Asia Minor are not agreed on the point.

It is only at the beginning of the sixth century that the Apc. reappears in the Canon of the Greek Church outside Egypt; but it did not succeed in gaining the same high standing as it had in the West. The Syrians have never accepted it into their Canon, and it was only towards the end of the twelfth century, under Nerses, archbishop of Lampron, that the Armenians recognized it as canonical (see §§ 7, 2; 18).

INDEX OF PERSONS

INDEX OF PERSONS

INDEX OF SUBJECTS

See also the list of contents

INDEX OF SUBJECTS